A History
of American
Psychology in
Notes and News
1883–1945

An Index to Journal Sources

Bibliographies
in the
History of Psychology and Psychiatry
A Series

Robert H. Wozniak, General Editor

A History
of American
Psychology in
Notes and News

1883–1945

An Index to Journal Sources

Ludy T. Benjamin, Jr.

Randall Pratt   Suzanne Fitzgerald
Deborah Watlington   Monica Franklin
Lana Aaron   Brian Jimenez
Thomas Bonar   Regan Lester

KRAUS INTERNATIONAL PUBLICATIONS
A Division of The Kraus Organization Limited
Millwood, New York

First Printing 1989

Printed in the United States of America

This book is printed on acid-free paper. It is Smyth sewn
and casebound in F-grade Library Buckram, which contains
no synthetic fibers. The paper and binding of this book
meet the guidelines for permanence and durability of the
Committee on Production Guidelines for Book Longevity
of the Council on Library Resources.

Library of Congress Cataloging in Publication Data

A history of American psychology in notes and news, 1883–1945 : an
  index to journal sources / compiled by Ludy T. Benjamin, Jr. ... [et
  al.].
        p. cm. — (Bibliographies in the history of psychology and
psychiatry : 5)
    ISBN 0-527-06626-5
    1. Psychology—United States—History—Sources—Periodicals—
Indexes.   I. Benjamin, Ludy T., 1945– . II. Series.
Z7201.H52   1989
[BF108.U5]   89-15251
016.15'0973'05—dc20   CIP

Contents

Introduction

When G. Stanley Hall opened his psychological laboratory at Johns Hopkins University in 1883, it marked the beginning of a new scientific era in American psychology. Among the laboratory sciences, psychology was a little late in transforming itself into a scientific discipline, missing by about a decade what Robert Bruce (1987) has called the "launching of modern American science" during the years 1846 to 1876. Nevertheless, the "new psychology" advanced rapidly. By the end of the 1880s there were seven American laboratories, with another 27 founded in the following decade. Initially, American psychologists took their graduate training in the universities of Europe, but by 1903, only 20 years after the founding of Hall's laboratory, there were more than 100 American psychologists who had received their doctorates at home (Napoli, 1981). A 1921 survey of the 377 members of the American Psychological Association who possessed doctoral degrees showed that only 36 had been earned at foreign universities (Fernberger, 1921).

Shortly after the founding of Hall's laboratory, the standard trappings were added to create the discipline. Organizations were begun to further the interests of the new science and its practitioners, and journals were founded to publish the new research. Characteristically, Hall did not leave this initial work in other hands. In 1887, he inaugurated the *American Journal of Psychology* and, in 1892, he organized the American Psychological Association. Within a few years, other journals in the new psychology followed, the most important of which was the *Psychological Review*, begun by James Mark Baldwin and James McKeen Cattell in 1894. As a means of keeping psychologists abreast of the field and as a vehicle for the publication of their work, these new journals were of great importance. In addition, however, they also served another central function; they provided a mechanism by which psychologists could communicate with one another in an informal, albeit published, manner. This communication was accomplished through special sections of the journals devoted to "notes and news."

The notes and news sections of the early journals constitute an important source of information about the history of psychology. Typically these sections, which occupied from one to three pages in each issue, announced such things as the founding of new laboratories, new societies, new journals, travels of psychologists, deaths, new appointments, changes in journal editorships, promotions, lectures, fellowships, elections, leaves of absence, grants, meetings, and awards. In many cases these announcements are the only generally available record of the events they describe.

Although notes and news items form an important body of historical information, retrieving any particular item can prove to be a difficult and time-consuming task. The early journals characteristically failed to include notes and news in any indexing system they may have used, and no simple means exists to effect a search for a particular psychologist, organization, institution, or subject. Unless a search involves an occurrence on a known date, it is often necessary to examine every single issue of a given journal, a task that is laborious and too often ends in failure. The object of this index, therefore, is to provide a finding aid to this vast fund of information that will serve to expedite the research task.

In compiling this index, information was gathered from the six journals that were most important as sources of notes and news in American psychology, with some coverage of the related fields of philosophy, education, and psychiatry between 1883 and 1945. The initial date marks the beginning of the journal *Science*, which even in its first notes and news section published information about psychology, and also represents the beginning of laboratory psychology in America. The ending date marks the beginning of a new era in psychology and was selected for three reasons: (a) it marked the end of World War II which represented the beginnings of an exponential growth in American psychology after 60 years of slow, steady growth; (b) it marked the reorganization of the American Psychological Association and the founding of the journal, *American Psychologist*, which would become the principal published source of notes and news items in psychology; and (c) some cut-off date was needed to make the indexing task manageable.

The six journals are:

Science (1883-1945)

This index covers 125 volumes of *Science*. Although there are many citations to psychology and related areas in the early volumes, such citations increased dramatically once the journal was purchased by James McKeen Cattell in 1894. He served as its owner/editor until his death in 1944. In indexing *Science* two news sections were surveyed, one entitled "Scientific Notes and News" and the other labeled "University and Educational News."

American Journal of Psychology (1887-1945)

As America's first psychology journal, the *American Journal of Psychology* is the most comprehensive chronicle of psychology's news during the time frame covered by this index. In addition to the usual news items, brief research notes, often in a kind of letter-to-the-editor format, were carried as part of its "notes and news" section. These notes have been included in this index because they are an integral part of the notes and news section of the journal and because they are not included in the journal's own index of its articles and reports.

Psychological Review (1894-1903)

Founded by James Mark Baldwin and James McKeen Cattell, the *Psychological Review* published notes and news items until the appearance of the *Psychological Bulletin* in 1904 when this function was taken over by the *Bulletin*.

Psychological Bulletin (1904-1945)

Also founded by Baldwin and Cattell, the *Psychological Bulletin* became, with the *American Journal of Psychology*, the standard source of news material in psychology from its inauguration until the advent of the *American Psychologist* in 1946.

Journal of Philosophy, Psychology, and Scientific Method (1904-1945)

The *Journal of Philosophy, Psychology, and Scientific Method* reflected ties between psychology and philosophy that existed for some years after the growth of the laboratory movement in psychology and the growing division between philosophy and experimental psychology that eventually resulted in philosophers leaving the American Psychological Association. For this reason it serves as a unique and important source of news, particularly before 1921 when the journal shortened its name to the *Journal of Philosophy* and began to carry fewer news items relevant to psychology.

Journal of Applied Psychology (1917-1945)

Begun in response to the considerable growth of psychology in applied research as a result of World War I, the *Journal of Applied Psychology* contained news items concerning psychology's applied activities. As such, it is frequently the only source of news items relating to the work of psychologists who had taken jobs outside the university framework.

All the notes and news items from the *American Journal of Psychology*, *Psychological Review*, *Psychological Bulletin*, and the *Journal of Applied Psychology*, appear in this index. For *Science* and the *Journal of Philosophy, Psychology, and Scientific Method*, items were selected that, in the judgment of the compilers, had even a slight relevance for psychology. In summary, the journals and entries selected represent all of the principal notes and news sources for American psychology during the time period 1883 to 1945. And, in addition, they provide wide coverage of psychology as science, as philosophy, and as an applied field.

The citations from these journals have been combined in one completely cross-referenced, alphabetized index comprising approximately 5,000 main entries and 20,000 secondary entries. Most of the secondary entries have multiple citations, making the total citations approximately 40,000. Main entry headings include the names of individuals, organizations, educational institutions, clinics, hospitals, agencies, awards, granting agencies, congresses, expositions, psychological tests, journals, books, apparatus, and a number of psychological subject areas.

This index is intended for use by historians of psychology, social science, philosophy, psychiatry, and education. Because the journals indexed will be found in most college and university libraries, it should be equally useful to college students researching the history of a particular topic in psychology, or to any scholars looking for the historical beginnings of their psychological subfields. With this index, for example, the researcher can quickly locate the many references to Edward Bradford Titchener, eugenics, faculty appointments at Vassar College, gifted children, announcements of meetings of the New York Branch of the American Psychological Association, or changes in editors for the *Journal of Nervous and Mental Disease*. Supplementing the *Psychological Index* (1894-1935) and *Psychological Abstracts* (1927 to date) which provide access to the articles published in psychology's journals, this volume, for the first time, allows ready access to published non-article material in these same journals that has heretofore been inaccessible except through exhaustive search.

A project of this kind represents an enormous amount of clerical work. Three individuals deserve much credit for their work on this book and to them we express special thanks. Therese Marcellin typed the original manuscript from thousands of index cards. She worked at it for months, through her pregnancy, and through moving her family to another state. It was an onerous task which she pursued with care and good humor. Priscilla Benjamin proofread the manuscript in several drafts, checking every item in the typed manuscript against the original index cards. She too worked with good cheer; however, she has cautioned her husband that he should never again become involved in such a project. Robert Wozniak, historian of psychology and editor of the reference series of which this volume is a part, used his vast library to check many of the ambiguous citations turned up in our search. His diligent work filled in much missing information and prevented many errors from appearing in this volume.

Finally, we gratefully acknowledge the work of Barry Katzen, Director of Kraus International Publications, and his publications staff for their important work on the production of this book.

Ludy T. Benjamin, Jr.
Randall Pratt
Deborah Watlington

References

Bruce, R. V. (1987), *The Launching of Modern American Science, 1846-1876*. Ithaca: Cornell University Press.

Fernberger, S. W. (1921). Further statistics of the American Psychological Association. *Psychological Bulletin, 18,* 569-572.

Napoli, D. S. (1981). *Architects of Adjustment: The History of the Psychological Profession in the United States*. Port Washington, NY: Kennikat Press.

How To Use This Book

This book consists of a single, continuous, alphabetized index. All subject entries are fully integrated within the one index. Thus under the letter B the user will find such entries as Babinski, Joseph; Baboon boy of South Africa; Barnard College of Columbia University; Binet Simon tests, Binocular fusion; and the Bonnie Brae Farm for Boys in New Jersey. Cross-referencing is also extensive. Thus the user would find the baboon boy mentioned under headings for South Africa and feral children, Barnard College listed under a heading for Columbia University, the Binet-Simon tests cross-referenced under intelligence, the Bonnie Brae Farm listed under New Jersey, and binocular fusion listed in the section on vision.

Although we have tried to provide those cross-references that will be most helpful to the user, the index does not include every possible cross-reference. The user is therefore encouraged to check all headings that may seem relevant. For example, information on evolution can be found under the heading Evolution but also under Congress of Evolutionists and under Darwinian theory. Entries also exist for Darwin, Lamarck, Huxley, and Lyell, to mention only some of the principal figures.

Entries have been placed in the index according to a principle of common usage. Thus the New Jersey Training School for Feeble-minded Girls and Boys is listed as the Vineland Training School. Johns Hopkins University will, of course, be found under the letter J, yet the Henry Phipps Psychiatric Clinic will be found under Phipps (cross-referenced to Johns Hopkins University) because it was commonly known as the Phipps Clinic. Although this principle should guide the user in the initial search, we encourage searches under other forms of a given name as well.

Some of the information in the notes and news sections of the journals is ambiguous. For example, a "Professor Robinson" may be cited as having "lectured last month at the State Normal College." Although the reader in 1910 may have known to which Professor Robinson and to which State Normal College the item referred, this information may no longer be available. Whereas in every case we have made a serious attempt to uncover and verify such information, in a few instances this has been impossible. When this has been the case, this material has been indexed with a question mark [?] placed where identifying information is missing.

Other ambiguities abound. For example, many entries refer to appointments. It is not always clear if the appointment was permanent or temporary, as in summer work or short visiting assignments. Papers sometimes referred to addresses delivered and at other times to published works. Degrees were sometimes earned, and other times honorary, yet distinctions were not always made. Departures might be dismissals, leaves of absence, retirements, or "calls" to another university. If one of these labels was employed in the journal note, it was included in the index. If not, ambiguities were dealt with as follows. If the reason for a departure was not specified, it was labeled *departure*. All addresses, of whatever variety, were labeled *lecture*, published works were labeled *publication*, and if it was not possible to tell whether a cited work was a lecture or publication, the label *lecture* was used.

In main entries, the most complete known form of the names of persons has been used. However, in secondary entries initials of first and middle names have been used to save space.

To facilitate ease of reading and minimize errors of interpretation, abbreviations have been employed for only the most frequently used terms. Those appear in the table of abbreviations on pages xvii and xviii.

The citations for *Science* sometimes have an asterisk (e.g. SCI°). The asterisk (°) is used to mark Volumes 1-23 of the Old Series (1883-1894). When Cattell purchased the journal, he began numbering again with Volume 1 in 1895 for what is called the New Series of *Science*.

In each entry the journal citation or citations appear in parentheses. The abbreviated name of the journal is printed in large and small capital letters and is followed by the volume number (in italics) and the page number(s). Multiple citations will appear within the same parentheses. Consider the following sample entries:

Clark University (Worcester, Massachusetts)
Anniversary celebration: 20th (JoP, *6*, 419, 503, 559; BULL, *6*, 327)
Appointment: Burt, B. C. (SCI°, *14*, 215, 437)

These entries indicate that references to the 20th anniversary celebration of Clark University exist in both *Psychological Bulletin* and the *Journal of Philosophy, Psychology, and Scientific Method*. The entries are located in Volume 6 of both journals. Further, there are three separate notes in Volume 6 of JoP which can be found on pages 419, 503, and 559. The appointment of B. C. Burt appears in Volume

14 of the Old Series of *Science* in two separate notes in that volume. By looking up the main entry for Burt, you can find that his full name was Benjamin Chapman Burt.

Because the year of publication will not typically be needed to locate the journal source in the library, that information was excluded from the index citations as a space-saving measure. To assist users who wish to determine the date of a particular entry, however, tables matching years and volume numbers for each of the six journals appear following the table of abbreviations.

Every attempt has been made to ensure the accuracy of the citations in this book. Despite considerable effort, errors no doubt exist. Some will be errors created by the fact that nine different individuals researched the journals in compiling this index, using slightly different selection and coding criteria. Others will occur because of transcription errors when the original information was recorded on the more than 40,000 index cards generated for this index. When users find errors, they are encouraged to contact the first author in order that the citations can be corrected in future printings.

Abbreviations Used in This Index

Abbreviations for Journals used in the Citations

AJP	American Journal of Psychology (1887-1945)
BULL	Psychological Bulletin (1904-1945)
J APP	Journal of Applied Psychology (1917-1945)
JoP	Journal of Philosophy, Psychology, and Scientific Method (1904-1945)
REV	Psychological Review (1894-1903)
SCI°	Science, old series (1883-1894)
SCI	Science, new series (1895-1945)

Other Abbreviations

AAAP	Association for the Advancement of Applied Psychology
AAAS	American Association for the Advancement of Science
AAP	Association of Applied Psychologists
Acad.	Academy
Admin.	Administration
Amer.	American
Anthro.	Anthropology
APA	American Psychological Association
Assoc.	Association
Corp.	Corporation
Dept.	Department
Div.	Division

Other Abbreviations (continued)

EPA	Eastern Psychological Association
MPA	Midwestern Psychological Association
NAS	National Academy of Sciences
NRC	National Research Council
NYAS	New York Academy of Sciences
Psych.	Psychology
RMPA	Rocky Mountain Psychological Association
Sec/Treas.	Secretary/Treasurer
SEP	Society of Experimental Psychologists
SPSSI	Society for the Psychological Study of Social Issues
SSPP	Southern Society for Philosophy and Psychology
Univ.	University
U.S.	United States
USDA	United States Department of Agriculture
Wash.-Balt.	Washington-Baltimore (Branch of the American Psychological Association)
WPA	Western Psychological Association

Journal Year and Volume Tables

Science* (Old Series)

Year	Volume
1883	1
1883	2
1884	3
1884	4
1885	5
1885	6
1886	7
1886	8
1887	9
1887	10
1888	11
1888	12
1889	13
1889	14
1890	15
1890	16
1891	17
1891	18
1892	19
1892	20
1893	21
1893	22
1894	23

* Note: these volumes are marked with an asterisk (*) in the citations.

Science (New Series)

Year	Volume	Year	Volume	Year	Volume
1895	1	1912	35	1929	69
1895	2	1912	36	1929	70
1896	3	1913	37	1930	71
1896	4	1913	38	1930	72
1897	5	1914	39	1931	73
1897	6	1914	40	1931	74
1898	7	1915	41	1932	75
1898	8	1915	42	1932	76
1899	9	1916	43	1933	77
1899	10	1916	44	1933	78
1900	11	1917	45	1934	79
1900	12	1917	46	1934	80
1901	13	1918	47	1935	81
1901	14	1918	48	1935	82
1902	15	1919	49	1936	83
1902	16	1919	50	1936	84
1903	17	1920	51	1937	85
1903	18	1920	52	1937	86
1904	19	1921	53	1938	87
1904	20	1921	54	1938	88
1905	21	1922	55	1939	89
1905	22	1922	56	1939	90
1906	23	1923	57	1940	91
1906	24	1923	58	1940	92
1907	25	1924	59	1941	93
1907	26	1924	60	1941	94
1908	27	1925	61	1942	95
1908	28	1925	62	1942	96
1909	29	1926	63	1943	97
1909	30	1926	64	1943	98
1910	31	1927	65	1944	99
1910	32	1927	66	1944	100
1911	33	1928	67	1945	101
1911	34	1928	68	1945	102

American Journal of Psychology

Year	Volume	Year	Volume	Year	Volume
1887-1888	1	1910	21	1928	40
1888-1889	2	1911	22	1929	41
1890-1891	3	1912	23	1930	42
1891-1892	4	1913	24	1931	43
1892-1893	5	1914	25	1932	44
1893-1895	6	1915	26	1933	45
1895-1896	7	1916	27	1934	46
1896-1897	8	1917	28	1935	47
1897-1898	9	1918	29	1936	48
1898-1899	10	1919	30	1937	49
1899-1900	11	1920	31	1937	50
1900-1901	12	1921	32	1938	51
1902	13	1922	33	1939	52
1903	14	1923	34	1940	53
1904	15	1924	35	1941	54
1905	16	1925	36	1942	55
1906	17	1926	37	1943	56
1907	18	1927	38	1944	57
1908	19	1927	39	1945	58
1909	20				

Psychological Review

Year	Volume
1894	1
1895	2
1896	3
1897	4
1898	5
1899	6
1900	7
1901	8
1902	9
1903	10

Psychological Bulletin

Year	Volume	Year	Volume
1904	1	1925	22
1905	2	1926	23
1906	3	1927	24
1907	4	1928	25
1908	5	1929	26
1909	6	1930	27
1910	7	1931	28
1911	8	1932	29
1912	9	1933	30
1913	10	1934	31
1914	11	1935	32
1915	12	1936	33
1916	13	1937	34
1917	14	1938	35
1918	15	1939	36
1919	16	1940	37
1920	17	1941	38
1921	18	1942	39
1922	19	1943	40
1923	20	1944	41
1924	21	1945	42

Journal of Philosophy, Psychology, and Scientific Method

Year	Volume	Year	Volume
1904	1	1925	22
1905	2	1926	23
1906	3	1927	24
1907	4	1928	25
1908	5	1929	26
1909	6	1930	27
1910	7	1931	28
1911	8	1932	29
1912	9	1933	30
1913	10	1934	31
1914	11	1935	32
1915	12	1936	33
1916	13	1937	34
1917	14	1938	35
1918	15	1939	36
1919	16	1940	37
1920	17	1941	38
1921°	18°	1942	39
1922	19	1943	40
1923	20	1944	41
1924	21	1945	42

°Name of journal shortened to Journal of Philosophy

Journal of Applied Psychology

Year	Volume	Year	Volume
1917	1	1932	16
1918	2	1933	17
1919	3	1934	18
1920	4	1935	19
1921	5	1936	20
1922	6	1937	21
1923	7	1938	22
1924	8	1939	23
1925	9	1940	24
1926	10	1941	25
1927	11	1942	26
1928	12	1943	27
1929	13	1944	28
1930	14	1945	29
1931	15		

A History
of American
Psychology in
Notes and News
1883–1945

An Index to Journal Sources

A

Aaron, Sadie
Appointment: U.S. Naval Hospital (BULL, 42, 485)
Leave of absence Houston, TX Public Schools (BULL, 42, 485)

Abbott, Alexander Crever
Appointment: Hygienic Institute of Philadelphia (SCI°, 17, 339)
Appointment: Johns Hopkins Univ. (SCI°, 14, 351)
Resignation: Johns Hopkins Univ. (SCI°, 17, 339)

Abderhalden, Emil
Editor of *Pfluger's Archives* (BULL, 17, 200)

Abel, Theodora Mead
Appointment: Director of Clinical Psychology Internships (BULL, 39, 809-810)
Leave of absence Letchworth Village (BULL, 41, 267)

Aberdeen, University of (Scotland)
Anniversary, 400th (JoP, 3, 616)
Appointment: Sorley, W. R. (REV, 2, 104)
Appointment: Stout, G. F. (AJP, 8, 430; REV, 3, 588; SCI, 4, 199)
Degree (honorary) for Burt, C. L. (SCI, 90, 79)
Degree (honorary) for Stout, G. F. (SCI, 92, 460)
Departure: Lord, A. R. (JoP, 2, 392)
Departure: Sorley, W. R. (SCI, 12, 120)
Establishment: psychology lectureship (SCI, 4, 76)
Gifford Lecturer, Seth Pringle-Pattison, A. (JoP, 9, 448)
Münsterberg, H., delegate at 400th anniversary celebration (SCI, 24, 477)

Ability tests, national
Presented in a book by Cody, S. (J APP, 3, 194)

3

Abney, William de Wiveleslie
Honors conferred by Great Britain (REV, 7, 216)

Abnormal psychology
Assoc. for Research in Nervous and Mental Diseases, Officers elected (SCI, 79, 9)

British Medical Research Council Committee on Mental Disorders (SCI, 79, 383)

Conference on Clinical Adjustment of Behavior: Problems of School Children, U. S. Office of Education (J APP, 22, 317)

Eugenics grant for surgical procedures (SCI, 69, 668)

Eugenics Research Assoc. Contest on genetics of mental disorders (SCI, 81, 483)

International Congress of Arts & Sciences, St. Louis, Meyer, A. elected Section secretary (JOP, 1, 532)

Lecture: Brill, A. A., New York Univ. (BULL, 12, 128)

Lecture: Campbell, C. M., Univ. of Illinois (SCI, 75, 262)

Lecture: Prince, M., Clark Univ. (SCI, 60, 587)

Lecture: Prince, M., Univ. of California (BULL, 7, 75; JOP, 7, 28; SCI, 30, 914)

Lecture: White, W. A. on social significance of mental disease, Georgetown Univ. (SCI, 69, 376)

Meeting: Assoc. for Research in Nervous and Mental Diseases (SCI, 81, 42; SCI, 84, 551)

Meeting: International Congress of Arts & Sciences, Section D (JOP, 1, 420)

Meeting: 60th of American Assoc. on Mental Deficiency (BULL, 33, 303-304)

Meeting: 63rd of American Assoc. on Mental Deficiency (J APP, 23, 312)

Michigan State Psychopathic Hospital, Waggoner, R. W., Director (SCI, 85, 14)

Nephritis research grant (SCI, 69, 137)

Paper: Maier, N. R. F., Experimentally produced neurotic behavior in the rat (BULL, 36, 220)

Paper: Squires, P. C., Psychological loss in paretics and schizophrenics (AJP, 48, 169)

Paper: Turner, W. D. & Carl, G. P., Sympathomimetic drugs (BULL, 34, 636)

Publication: *Psychosomatic Medicine*, quarterly journal announced (BULL, 36, 219; J APP, 22, 663)

Reading improvement in retarded students (J APP, 21, 244)

Research: Bentley, I. M. (SCI, 75, 189)

Syphilis research grant, Mehrtens, H. G. (SCI, 69, 37)

Abramowski, Edward
Death notice (JOP, 16, 84)

Absolute objectivity
Lehman, H. C. & Witty, P. A. paper (AJP, 41, 492)

Academic status of psychologists & philosophers
Department distinctions made (BULL, 12, 127)

Académie Française
Award: Grand Prix Broquette Gonin to Grasset, J. (JoP, *10*, 420)

Academy of Medicine (Washington, D. C.)
Lecture: Treadway, W. L., Mental hygiene: Interaction between man and his environment (Sci, *84*, 530)

Academy of Moral and Political Science
Paper competition announced (JoP, *3*, 280)
Prizes awarded, listing of (Rev, *6*, 120)

Academy of Natural Sciences
Election: committee and officers (Sci, *9*, 158-159)

Academy of Sciences (Berlin)
Election: James, W. (Sci, *11*, 556)
Election: Rowland, H. A. (Sci, *11*, 556)
Election: Stokes, G. (Sci, *10*, 91)
Helmholtz Medal to Virchow, R. L. C. (Sci, *9*, 300)

Academy of Sciences (California)
Election: officers (Sci, *9*, 661)

Academy of Sciences (Washington)
Election: officers (Sci, *9*, 268)

Ach, Narziss
Appointment: Chair of Philosophy, Marburg Univ. (JoP, *1*, 308; Bull, *4*, 338; Sci, *25*, 760)

Achilles, Paul Strong
Appointment: Assistant Director Personnel Research Federation (Bull, *22*, 260)
Election: Psychological Corporation; Secretary/Treasurer (J App, *11*, 81; Bull, *24*, 80)
Election: Psychological Corporation; Vice-president (J App, *25*, 600)
Lecture: American Assoc. for the Advancement of Science (J App, *16*, 334)

Acoustical Society of America
Luncheon in honor of Seashore, C. E. (Sci, *90*, 510)

Acoustics and sound localization (*see also* Audition, Hearing, Sound)
Robnett, J. C., fellowship (Bull, *39*, 682)

Acta Psychologica
Founded editorial board (AJP, *48*, 174)

Activity
Lecture: James, W. (JoP, 2, 28)

Adams, Clifford Rose
Personal Audit (J App, 25, 360)

Adams, Donald Keith
Appointment: Research Assistant, Yale Univ. (Bull, 22, 444)
Guggenheim Fellowship (Bull, 34, 499)

Adams, Elizabeth Kemper
Appointment: Smith College (Bull, 2, 427)
Esthetic experience: Its meaning in a functional psychology (JoP, 3, 721)
Promotion: Smith College (JoP, 9, 168)

Adams, Elmer C.
Appointment: Univ. of Michigan (Bull, 5, 379)

Adams, Ernest Kempton Research Appointment
Appointment: Dodge, R. (JoP, 14, 392)

Adams, George Plimpton
Leave of absence: Univ. of California (JoP, 8, 392)

Adams, Grace K.
Appointment: Goucher College; Instructor (Bull, 21, 240)

Adams, Henry Foster
Appointment: Univ. of Kansas (JoP, 7, 280; Bull, 7, 148)
Appointment: Univ. of Michigan (JoP, 8, 364; Bull, 8, 333; Sci, 33, 892)
Promotion: Univ. of Michigan (JoP, 15, 504)

Adams, John
Appointment: Univ. of California summer school (JoP, 4, 336)

Adams, Messrs. R. G. & Company
Publication: *The Field of Philosophy* (JoP, 15, 308)

Adamson, Robert
Departure: Owens College Victoria Univ., Manchester to Aberdeen (Rev, 1, 112)

Adelbert College
Appointment: Huntley, C. W. (Sci, 93, 615)
Appointment: Ladd, G. T. (JoP, 3, 140)

Adelphi College (Garden City, New York)
Appointment: Fehlman, C. (Bull, 42, 255)

Appointment: Ray, W. S. (BULL, *41*, 409, 498)
Transfer: Henderson, E. N. (JoP, *6*, 644; BULL, *6*, 427)

Adjustment
Lecture: Starbuck, E. D. (JoP, *7*, 223)
Research on problems of high school students, Abel, T.M. (BULL, *41*, 267)

Adkins, Dorothy Christina
Editor (associate) of *Educational and Psychological Measurement* (J APP, *25*, 266)
Paper: Washington-Baltimore Branch of APA (BULL, *39*, 683)

Adler, Alfred
Appointment: American Peoples College in Europe (J APP, *19*, 223)
Editorial Board of *Character and Personality* (J APP, *16*, 439)
Editor of *International Journal of Individual Psychology* (J APP, *19*, 353)
Editor of *Zeitschrift für Individual-Psychologie* (BULL, *11*, 232)
Lecture: International Congress for Individual Psychology-4th (SCI, *72*, 167)
Lecture: International Congress of Individual Psychology (SCI, *66*, 57)
Lecture: series in New York City (SCI, *65*, 12)

Adler, Felix
Appointment: Columbia Univ., Chair in Social and Political Ethics (SCI, *21*, 600)
Appointment: Univ. of Berlin (JoP, *4*, 252)
Death notice (JoP, *30*, 280)
Lecture: centenary of death of Kant (JoP, *1*, 140)

Adler, Herman Morris
Appointment: Chicago Psychopathic Institute, Director (BULL, *14*, 115)
Appointment: Univ. of Illinois (BULL, *16*, 392)
Research: Facilities for dealing with mental diseases (SCI, *44*, 745)

Adolescence
Publication: Slaughter, J. W. (JoP, *7*, 644)

Adolescents, social hygiene of
Prize for paper, American Social Hygiene Assoc. (BULL, *12*, 204)

Adrian, Edgar Douglas
Chairman, British Medical Research Council Mental Disorder Committee (SCI, *79*, 383)

Adult learning
Lecture: Thorndike, E. L. (J APP, *10*, 129)

Advancement of Science and Art Teaching
Formation of a new association (SCI°, *2*, 210)

Advertising
Research: Sentiment toward wartime advertising (J App, 27, 208)

Advisory Board on Clinical Psychology of the Office of the Adjutant General (see also United States Army)
Appointment: Seidenfeld, M. A. (Sci, 100, 166)

Aesthesiometer
Binet-Buzenet version (JoP, 7, 28)
Invention by Jastrow, J. (AJP, 1, 552)

Aesthetics (see also American Society for)
Election: Meyer, M., International Congress of Arts and Science, St. Louis (JoP, 1, 532)
Lecture: Kulpe, O., German Society of Experimental Psychology (Sci, 22, 727)
Lecture: Münsterberg, H. (Bull, 3, 379)
Meeting: Modern psychology and the aesthetic experience, Ohio College Assoc., Philosophy Section (JoP, 35, 140)
Paper: Gilman, B. I. (Sci°, 19, 33)
Publication: Bosanquet, B., history of (JoP, 7, 644)

Affiliated Science Societies
Election: Cattell, J. McK. as president (Sci°, 15, 77-78)

Age
Compendium of the tenth census in Nature (Sci°, 2, 209)

Aggression
Bibliography by Huntington, T. W. & Stagner, R. (Bull, 38, 248)

Aging (see also Gerontology)
National Institute of Health, Organization of research by (Bull, 38, 67)
National Research Council reactivates committee to study (Bull, 42, 332)
Report from Germany (Sci°, 8, 56)
Research: Stieglitz, E. J. (AJP, 54, 133)
Survey on problems of aging, Nuffield Foundation Trustees (Sci, 99, 363-364)

Agnes Scott College (Decatur, Georgia)
Meeting: 31st annual Southern Society for Philosophy and Psychology (JoP, 33, 223)

Aikins, Hebert Austin
Lecture: Carnegie Institute of Technology, Psychotherapy Problems (Sci, 49, 118)
Lecture: Third Annual Educational Conference (J App, 7, 188)

Air-age education research
Purpose of (J App, 28, 80)

Air Force, United States (*see also* United States Strategic Air Forces)
Strecker, E. A. appointed consultant to Secretary of War (SCI, *97*, 551)

Akron, University of (Ohio)
Appointment: Painter, W. J. (BULL, *42*, 792)

Alabama, University of (Tuscaloosa)
Appointment: Dresslar, F. B. (BULL, *5*, 348)
Commemorative, centenary of death of Kant (JoP, *1*, 140)
Lab opened, 1939 (BULL, *36*, 500)

Alberta, Earl D.
Appointment: Univ. of Toronto (SCI, *60*, 475)

Alberta, University of (Edmonton)
Appointment: Klemm, O. (BULL, *11*, 192; JoP, *11*, 224; SCI, *39*, 423)
Appointment: Lodge, R. C. (JoP, *12*, 336)

Albuquerque, Jesuino de
Visiting the United States from Brazil (SCI, *101*, 61)

Alcan, Felix
Philosophical works translated (SCI°, *8*, 510)

Alcohol (*see also* Research Council on Problems of)
Lecture: Dodge, R. (BULL, *12*, 160; JoP, *12*, 196; SCI, *43*, 710)
Research award by Research Council on Problems of Alcohol (J APP, *27*, 208; BULL, *40*, 311-312)
School of Alcohol Studies established, Yale Univ. (SCI, *97*, 441)

Alcoholism
Quarterly Journal of Studies on Alcohol (BULL, *37*, 755)
Washingtonian Hospital in Boston, reorganized with a psychiatric staff (SCI, *93*, 254)
Research Council on Problems of Alcohol; program announced (BULL, *37*, 61)
Research: Crothers, T. D. (AJP, *1*, 362)
Treatment of (AJP, *2*, 674)

Aldrich, Virgil Charles
Appointment: Wells College (JoP, *41*, 532)
Departure: Rice Institute (JoP, *41*, 532)

Aleck, Adolph William
Appointment: Huntingdon College (BULL, *42*, 791)

Alexander, Archibald Browning Drysdale
Publication, *History of Philosophy* (JoP, *4*, 364)

Alexander, Franz
Harvey Society Lecture, 4th; "Psychoanalysis and Medicine" (Sci, 73, 64)
Psychosomatic Medicine; Editor, Psychoanalysis (J App, 22, 663)

Alexander, Hartley Burr
Appointment: Univ. of Nebraska (Bull, 5, 244)
Lecture: on truth (JoP, 7, 223)
Paper: Wolfe, H. K. remembrance sketch (JoP, 15, 532)
Programs of the Amer. Phil. Assoc. (JoP, 14, 643-644)

Alexander, Samuel
Accepts chair at Owens College, Manchester (Rev, 1, 112)
Gifford lectures at Glasgow Univ. (JoP, 14, 224)

Allan, William
Appointment: Department of Eugenics, Bowman Gray School of Medicine of
    Wake Forest College, N.C. (Sci, 94, 111)

Allee, Wayne Leighton
Appointment: Stephens College (Bull, 42, 485)
Departure: Univ. of Colorado (Bull, 42, 485)

Allen, Frederick Harold
Appointment: Univ. of Pennsylvania, Medical School (Sci, 62, 371)
Research: Preston School of Industry-California (J App, 3, 196)

Allen, Fredrick W.
Election: Mental Hygeine, National Comm. for; Treasurer (Sci, 72, 557)

Allen, Grant
Death notice (Sci, 10, 662)

Allen, Henry J.
Lecture: 10th anniversary Wichita Child Guidance Center (Bull, 38, 126)

Allin, Arthur
Appointment: Ohio Univ. at Athens (Rev, 3, 468; Sci, 3, 900)
Appointment: Univ. of Colorado (Rev, 5, 109; AJP, 9, 250; Sci, 6, 702)
Death Notice, Nov 17, 1903 (Sci, 18, 703; JoP, 1, 28)

Allport, Floyd Henry
Appointment: Harvard Univ. (Bull, 16, 391-392; Sci, 50, 345)
Appointment: Syracuse Univ. (Sci, 60, 200; Bull, 21, 660; JoP, 21, 532)
Appointment: Univ. of N. Carolina (Sci, 55, 617; JoP, 19, 532; Bull, 19, 410)
Election: APA Council of Directors (Bull, 25, 123)
Election: APA representative Social Science Research Council (Bull, 26, 56;
    Sci, 69, 36)
Grant: Social Science Research Council (Bull, 34, 409)

Lecture: Methods in the study of collective action phenomena at Society for the Psychological Study of Social Issues (SCI, *94*, 230)
Lecture: Science (JoP, *41*, 280)
Resignation: Harvard Univ. (SCI, *55*, 617)

Allport, Gordon Willard

Appointment: Dartmouth College (J APP, *10*, 393)
Appointment: Harvard Univ. Assistant Professor (BULL, *27*, 496; JoP, *27*, 560)
Appointment: National Research Council (BULL, *37*, 755)
Editor: *Journal of Abnormal and Social Psychology* (BULL, *34*, 179, 272)
Election: APA, president (SCI°, *88*, 373)
Election: APA, representative to Social Science Research Council (SCI, *82*, 247)
Election: EPA president (SCI, *95*, 452; BULL, *39*, 423)
International seminar in psychology (BULL, *38*, 191)
Lecture: APA 47th annual meeting (JoP, *36*, 476)
Lecture: EPA 1943 (SCI, *97*, 374)
Lecture: Leipzig congress for psychology (AJP, *34*, 612)
Lecture: Psychological supper club (BULL, *37*, 656)
Meeting: psychological factors on national morale (BULL, *37*, 829)
Obituary for Stern, W. (AJP, *51*, 770-773)
Promotion: Harvard Univ. (SCI, *83*, 518)
Publication: announced of *German psychological warfare,* (J APP, *25*, 359)

Alpha Omega Alpha

Meeting: Detroit, 1941 "Mental attitudes for national defense" (SCI, *93*, 372)

Alster, Benjamin

Publication: announced of *Aspects of personality* (J APP, *22*, 318)

Alternating current

Research on physiological effects of, Thomson, Elihu (SCI°, *17*, 201)

Alvarenga Prize

Conner, G. J. for study in Functional localization in the cerebellum (SCI, *100*, 47)

Alzheimer, Alois

Death announcement (BULL, *13*, 148; SCI, *43*, 236)

American Academy for Arts and Sciences

Award for research on diseases of genital organs (SCI, *89*, 386)
Election: fellows (BULL, *34*, 409)
Election: Heaviside, O. (SCI, *9*, 118)
Election: officers May 10, 1899 (SCI, *9*, 724)
Election: officers 1884 (SCI°, *1*, 558)
Election: Pratt, C. C.; Fellow (SCI, *77*, 506)
Election: Walcott, C. D. (SCI, *9*, 118)
Lecture: Thorndike, E. L. (SCI, *92*, 451; SCI, *87*, 232)

Paper: Feb 14, 1883 (SCI°, *1*, 85)
Paper: Feb. 24, 1883 (SCI°, *1*, 156)
Research: DeSilva, H. R.; grant recipient for body voltage (SCI, *80*, 425)

American Academy of Arts and Letters
Lecture: Bergson, H. (JOP, *14*, 252)

American Academy of Political and Social Science
Publication: first handbook (SCI°, *17*, 286)

American Airlines, Inc.
Purpose of air-age education research (J APP, *28*, 80)

American Anthropological Association
Joint meeting with APA, Harvard Dec. 1919 (JOP, *17*, 56)
Members, Division of Anthropology and Psychology (JOP, *17*, 83)

American Anthropologist, The
Report: status of sciences after war, Division of Anthropology and Psychology of the Committee on International Cooperation in Anthropology (SCI, *102*, 643)

American Association for Applied Psychology
Announcement: "Applied psychology monographs" (J APP, *27*, 115)
Announcement: plans to merge with APA (BULL, *41*, 602)
Clarification of clinical section (J APP, *26*, 108)
Committee on Psychology in Junior Colleges; instruction investigated (J APP, *25*, 361)
Convention dates, 1939 (J APP, *23*, 634)
Directory of Applied Psychologists (J APP, *25*, 268)
Election: Bingham, W. V.; President, 1942 (J APP, *26*, 107)
Election: Bryan, A. I.; Executive secretary at meeting, (SCI, *96*, 292)
Election: Fryer, D. H. (J APP, *21*, 603, 713; BULL, *34*, 865)
Election: Louttit, C. M.; President (SCI, *96*, 292)
Employment report: *Psychology as an Occupation* (J APP, *22*, 311)
Established section of military psychology (BULL, *41*, 267-268; SCI, *99*, 34; J APP, *28*, 79)
Founded: officers and membership criteria (J APP, *21*, 603, 713)
Lecture: Doll, E. A. "Scientific freedom," 1941 (SCI, *94*, 230)
Meeting: affiliation with AAAS and APA approved (BULL, *36*, 218)
Meeting: canceled (J APP, *26*, 572)
Meetings: committees, chairs, members listed by name, 1938 (J APP, *22*, 442)
Meeting: 5th annual; program chairmen (J APP, *25*, 265)
Meeting: 1938; Ohio State Univ. (JOP, *35*, 280)
Meeting: 1939 (AJP, *52*, 476-477; J APP, *23*, 421; BULL, *36*, 712)
Meeting: 1942 (BULL, *39*, 684; J APP, *26*, 857)
Meeting: 1943 (J APP, *28*, 79)
Meeting: 1944 (J APP, *28*, 530-531)

Meeting: with APA (Sci, *94*, 230)
Newsletter: 1943 about postwar planning (J App, *27*, 114- 115)
Organization of and officers elected (Sci, *86*, 284)
Publication: *Directory of Applied Psychologists* (Bull, *38*, 304)
Succeeds Assoc. of Consulting Psychologists (Bull, *34*, 864)
Voted: Bylaws of APA, 5 sections will become charter divisions of APA (J App, *28*, 530-531)

American Association for Labor Legislation

Lecture: Münsterberg, H. on industrial efficiency psychology (Sci, *35*, 924; JoP, *9*, 364)

American Association for the Advancement of Science

Abstracts sent to Carmichael, L., 1940 (Sci, *92*, 351-352)
Appointment: Cattell, J. McK.; Delegate to American Scientific Congress (Sci, *82*, 299)
Appointment: Cattell, J. Mck.; Delegate to British Assoc. centenary meeting (Sci, *74*, 240, 409)
Appointment: Dodge, R.; Vice-president and chairman of psychology section (Bull, *19*, 63)
Appointment: Ogden, R. M. (Bull, *10*, 424)
Award: Maier, N. R. F. (Sci, *89*, 7, 313; Bull, *36*, 220)
Carmichael, L.; Secretary Section I; 1937 meeting (J App, *21*, 604)
Celebration Darwin centennial (JoP, *6*, 112)
Conjunction with medical sessions discuss biochemistry and physiology relating to mental disease, 1940 (Sci, *92*, 552)
Dallenbach, K. M.; "The psychology of magic" (Sci, *82*, 591)
Election: (Bull, *33*, 223)
Election: Bentley, M.; Vice-president (Sci, *72*, 499)
Election: Bessey, C. E.; President (JoP, *8*, 56)
Election: Boring, E. G.; Vice-president, Section I (Bull, *27*, 240)
Election: Burtt, H. E. (Bull, *40*, 458)
Election: Dixon, R. B.; Vice-president (Bull, *7*, 75)
Election: Dunlap, K.; Vice-president, Section I (Bull, *29*, 80)
Election: executive committee 1899 (Sci, *10*, 660-661)
Election: Haggerty, M. E.; Vice-president (Bull, *23*, 112)
Election: held (Bull, *26*, 56)
Election: Kelly, T.; Vice-president (Bull, *25*, 123)
Election: McGeoch, J. A.; Secretary (Sci, *79*, 406)
Election: officers (JoP, *6*, 84)
Election: officers (Sci°, *8*, 184)
Election: officers, 1883 (Sci°, *2*, 253)
Election: officers, 1885 (Sci°, *4*, 298)
Election: officers, 1886 (Sci°, *6*, 238)
Election: officers, 1889 (Sci°, *12*, 95-96)
Election: officers, Section I (Bull, *38*, 191)
Election: Poffenberger, A. T. (Bull, *34*, 179)

Election: Terman, L. M., President of Pacific Division (SCI, *91*, 591)
Election: Thorndike, E. L.; President (SCI, *80*, 583)
Election: Warren, H. C.; Vice-president, Section I (BULL, *25*, 123)
Election: Washburn, M. F.; Vice-president, Section I (BULL, *23*, 112)
Election: Woodrow, H. (BULL, *40*, 458)
Evaluation of speeches and papers (SCI°, *2*, 340)
Granted $400.00 Dodge, R. (BULL, *19*, 141)
Granted $200.00 Pressey, S. L. (BULL, *20*, 664)
Granted $300.00 Smith, F. (BULL, *19*, 141)
Grant teletactor (BULL, *33*, 223)
Invitation to British Assoc. (SCI°, *2*, 549)
Lecture: Cattell, J. McK. (REV, *5*, 677)
Lecture: Jastrow, J., Lancaster Branch (SCI, *88*, 449)
Lecture: Judd, C. H., Lancaster Branch (SCI, *88*, 449)
Lecture: Langley, S. P. (SCI°, *10*, 80-81)
Lecture: Thorndike, E. L. (SCI, *75*, 632)
Letter from British Assoc. for the Advancement of Science (SCI, *3*, 396-397)
List of delegates of foreign scientific societies to attend Philadelphia meeting, 1884 (SCI°, *4*, 140, 156)
Meeting: (SCI°, *2*, 384)
Meeting: agenda, 1883 (SCI°, *2*, 116-117)
Meeting: announced Aug 1885 at Michigan (SCI°, *5*, 283, 509)
Meeting: announced 1889, Ontario (SCI°, *13*, 479)
Meeting: announced, 1896 (REV, *3*, 468)
Meeting: announced, 1906 (BULL, *3*, 421)
Meeting: announced, 1907 (BULL, *4*, 369)
Meeting: announced, 1930 (SCI, *72*, 499)
Meeting: announced of Section I (SCI, *86*, 306)
Meeting: April 1899, Washington (SCI, *9*, 557, 629)
Meeting: April 1900, Washington (SCI, *11*, 676)
Meeting: Aug 1888, Cleveland (SCI°, *11*, 312)
Meeting: Aug 1890, Indianapolis (SCI°, *16*, 21, 90)
Meeting: Dec 27-29, 1938 symposium "Recent advances in the psychology and physiology of audition" (SCI, *88*, 399)
Meeting: delayed to allow cooperation with the British Assoc. (SCI°, *3*, 797-798)
Meeting: 48th annual 1899, Columbus, Ohio (SCI, *10*, 259)
Meeting: 50th annual Aug 24-31, 1901, Denver, CO (SCI, *14*, 118, 301)
Meeting: Johns Hopkins Univ. (SCI, *12*, 933)
Meeting: 1934 (BULL, *32*, 112)
Meeting: 1939, Columbus, Ohio (SCI, *90*, 392)
Meeting: Panama-Pacific International Exposition (JoP, *11*, 720)
Meeting: program (SCI°, *8*, 121-122)
Meeting: program for Aug. 1885 (SCI°, *6*, 116)
Meeting: program *Science* (JoP, *15*, 700)
Meeting: report of 1908 (JoP, *6*, 28)
Meeting: Section I (Psych), 1936 (SCI, *84*, 371)
Meeting: Section I, 1937 (BULL, *34*, 634)

Meeting: Section I, 1939 (J App, *23*, 630)
Meeting: Section I, 1941 (J App, *25*, 727; Bull, *38*, 908)
Meeting: Section I with WPA (Sci, *79*, 406)
Meeting: Sept. 1883, Philadelphia (Sci°, *2*, 253)
Meeting: with APA (JoP, *8*, 28, 55, 699-700)
Meeting: with APA (JoP, *12*, 532)
Meeting: with APA in San Francisco (Bull, *12*, 204)
Meeting: with APA/SSPP (Bull, *11*, 443)
Meeting: with Section Q (Education), 1939 (Sci, *90*, 392)
Meeting: with WPA (Bull, *31*, 380)
Membership invitation to APA members (Rev, *4*, 339)
Paper: Mead, G. H. (JoP, *7*, 308)
Proposal to change (Bull, *16*, 392)
Re-election: Cattell, J. McK. (Sci, *57*, 48)
Report: McGeoch, J. A. on Section I, Psychology (J App, *26*, 107-108)
Report: membership increase (Sci°, *2*, 179)
Represented by Franz, S. I. at Cardiff meeting of the British Assoc. (Bull, *17*, 351)
Request: Cattell, J. McK. continuation in organization (Sci, *46*, 381)
Research Council on Problems of Alcohol (Bull, *37*, 61)
Research: list of grants (Bull, *17*, 239)
Retirement: Cattell, J. McK. (Sci, *46*, 336)
Summer session and special representatives (J App, *16*, 695)
Symposium: "The internal environment and behavior" (Sci, *90*, 392)

American Association for the Study of the Feeble-minded

Meeting: Columbus, Ohio (Bull, *11*, 268)

American Association of Clinical Psychologists

Announcement: joint meeting with APA, 1919, Harvard (JoP, *16*, 700; JoP, *17*, 56)
Announcement: new organization (Sci, *47*, 534)
Meeting: annual canceled (Bull, *15*, 360)
Officers announced (Bull, *15*, 360)
Organization of (J App, *2*, 194)

American Association of Scientific Workers

Election: officer Tolman, E. C. (Sci, *93*, 590)
Program on science and war, 1942 (Sci, *96*, 250)

American Association of University Professors

Election: Calkins, M. W.; Vice-president (Sci, *59*, 482)
Investigation at Univ. of Utah (Bull, *12*, 244)

American Association on Mental Deficiency

Meeting: 1936 (Bull, *33*, 303)
Meeting: 62nd, 1938; officers (J App, *22*, 109)

Meeting: 63rd (J App, *23*, 312)
Whitten, B. O.; President, 61st annual convention (J App, *21*, 241)

American Board of Psychiatry and Neurology
Founded, officers elected (Sci, *80*, 476)

American Branch of the Society for Psychical Research (*see* American Society for Psychical Research)

American British Association
List of names signing to consider an international congress (Sci°, *4*, 329)

American Catholic Philosophical Association
Meeting: 11th annual announced (JoP, *33*, 27)
Meeting: 13th annual; program (JoP, *34*, 722)
Meeting: 15th annual; program (JoP, *37*, 27)

American College Personnel Association
Meeting: 1938; constitution (J App, *22*, 106)
Meeting: 1941 (Bull, *38*, 126)
Purpose (Bull, *38*, 126)

American Council of Guidance and Personnel Associations
Convention, 7th annual; program (J App, *24*, 97)

American Council on Education
Discussion of educational credits for military personnel (AJP, *56*, 450)
Distributing child study films (Bull, *38*, 248)
Paper: Teacher education in a democracy at war (J App, *26*, 714)
Publication: "Selected educational motion pictures: A descriptive encyclopedia"
   (J App, *26*, 570)

American Division of the Club for Research on Aging
Election: officers, 1945 (Sci, *101*, 219)

American Documentation Institute
Operating a technical translation clearing house for foreign psychological
   journals (Bull, *41*, 411)

American Educational Research Association
Award: merit to Swift, F. (Sci, *93*, 346)
Freeman, F. N. received citation for book on twin studies, 1940 (Sci, *91*, 287)

American Ethnological Society
Meeting: with Section of Anthropology and Psychology concerning the growth
   of children (JoP, *14*, 644)

American Eugenics Society
Dinner honoring Holmes, S. J. (Sci, *88*, 494)

Editor: Bentley, M. (BULL, *39*, 807)
Editor change E. B. Titchener from G. S. Hall (BULL, *18*, 110)
Editor change in (REV, *2*, 641)
Editor: Scripture, E. W. (SCI°, *19*, 130)
History of experimental psychology in Italy (JOP, *2*, 448)
Index of first 30 volumes (AJP, *38*, 156)
Paper: Univ. of Toronto new curriculum (SCI°, *16*, 258-259)
Removed from Cornell Univ. to California Inst. of Tech (SCI, *102*, 221)
Resignation: Titchener, E. B. editor (BULL, *23*, 112)

American Journal of Religious Psychology and Education, The
Name change (Jan-Mar, 1912) to *Journal of Religious Psychology* (BULL, *8*, 438)
Publication announced (BULL, *1*, 414)

American Journal of Sociology
"The relation between the individual and the group" (BULL, *36*, 711)

American Magazine, The
Publication: Culver, S. W. Educating the Negroes of the South (SCI°, *9*, 584)

American Management Association
Korhauser, A. W.; "The techniques of market research from the standpoint of
a psychologist" (SCI, *81*, 589)
Lazarsfeld, P.; "The techniques of market research from the standpoint of a
psychologist" (SCI, *81*, 589)
Meeting: 1942 (J APP, *26*, 713)
Uhrbrock, R. S.: "A psychologist looks at wage incentives" (SCI, *81*, 589)

American Medical Association
Celebrates 75th birthday of Pavlov (SCI, *60*, 264)
Grant: American Institute for the Deaf-blind (BULL, *32*, 862)

American Medico-Psychological Association
Election: officers, Niagara Falls meeting (SCI, *37*, 936)
Election: Wagner, C.; President (SCI, *43*, 598)
Lecture: Riley, I. W. (SCI, *29*, 931; JOP, *6*, 364)
Meeting: Baltimore announcement (SCI, *39*, 783)

American Men of Science (*see also* Biographical Dictionary of)
Distribution of psychologists in 6 editions (AJP, *52*, 278-292)
Listing of psychologists included (BULL, *41*, 604)
Supplemental data on psychology by Visher, S. S. (AJP, *57*, 573-574)

American Naturalist, The
Meeting topic: "The inheritance of acquired characteristics" (SCI°, *16*, 314)
Paper: evolution by Baldwin, J. M. (SCI, *4*, 139)

American Neurological Association
Election: Halstead, W. C. (BULL, *40*, 619)
Election: Pollock, L. J.; President, 1941 (SCI, *93*, 614-615)

American Optical Company
Grant: Yale Univ. (SCI, *101*, 87)

American Ortho-Psychiatric Association
Election: results (SCI, *60*, 82)
Meeting: 12th annual (BULL, *32*, 112)
Meeting: 13th (BULL, *33*, 148)
Meeting: 14th (BULL, *34*, 58)
Meeting: 15th (BULL, *35*, 125)
Meeting: 16th (BULL, *36*, 140)
Meeting: 17th (BULL, *37*, 123)
Meeting: 18th, 1941 (BULL, *38*, 126; BULL, *39*, 72)
Meeting: 19th, 1942 (SCI, *94*, 386)

American Otological Society
Meeting: 1929 (SCI, *69*, 618)

American Peoples College in Europe
Appointment: Adler, A. (J APP, *19*, 223)

American Philological Association
Meeting: July 1886, New York (SCI°, *6*, 200)

American Philosophical Association
Call for papers: Dec. 26-28, 1912, Columbia Univ (JOP, *9*, 615 616)
Committee: discuss ethics and international relations (JOP, *14*, 616)
Dewey, J.; 36th meeting (JOP, *33*, 700)
Election: Dewey, J.; President (SCI, *21*, 37)
Election: James, W.; President (SCI, *23*, 38)
Election: Montague, W. P.; Vice-president (SCI, *27*, 76)
Election: Münsterberg, H.; President (SCI, *27*, 76)
Election: officers (JOP, *8*, 27-28)
Election: officers, 1912 (SCI, *69*, 11)
Grant: Rockefeller Foundation for a Commission on the Function of Philosophy
    in Liberal Education (JOP, *40*, 587-589)
Invitation for meeting to eastern APA members (BULL, *7*, 426)
Lecture: Dewey, J. (SCI, *56*, 416, 683)
Meeting: announcement (JOP, *8*, 699)
Meeting: announcement and call for papers (JOP, *7*, 672)
Meeting: announcement and call for papers (JOP, *8*, 503-504)
Meeting: announcement, 1919, New York (JOP, *16*, 615-616)
Meeting: cancelled, 1942 (JOP, *40*, 28)
Meeting: 1st and list of papers (REV, *9*, 327)
Meeting: 1917 program (JOP, *14*, 472-476)

Meeting: 1918 program (JoP, *15*, 721-722)
Meeting: 19th at Cornell, 1919 (JoP, *17*, 56)
Meeting: Princeton Univ. (JoP, *8*, 27-28)
Meeting: report of 7th annual, 1907 (JoP, *5*, 28)
Meeting: report of 11th (JoP, *9*, 28)
Meeting: special session honor Dewey, J. 80th birthday (JoP, *36*, 336)
Officers: list of (BULL, *10*, 40; JoP, *7*, 28; JoP, *10*, 28)
Schneider, H. W.; 36th meeting (JoP, *33*, 700)

American Philosophical Association, Eastern Division

Election: officers, 1936 (JoP, *34*, 28)
Election: officers, 1937 (JoP, *33*, 56)
Election: officers, 1938 (JoP, *35*, 28)
Election: officers, 1942 (BULL, *39*, 423; SCI, *95*, 452)
James', W. 100th anniversary (JoP, *38*, 308)
Lecture: Fitch, F. B. (JoP, *35*, 699)
Lecture: Schutz, A. (JoP, *37*, 699)
Meeting: 1920 (JoP, *17*, 279-280, 672)
Meeting: announced, 1940 (JoP, *37*, 420)
Meeting: announced, 1942 (JoP, *39*, 643-644, 698-699)
Meeting: announcement, 1936 (JoP, *33*, 280, 699)
Meeting: canceled, 1942 (JoP, *39*, 722)
Meeting: canceled, 1945 (JoP, *42*, 84)
Meeting: 38th annual; program (JoP, *35*, 699)
Meeting: 40th annual; program (JoP, *37*, 698)
Meeting: 41st annual (JoP, *38*, 700)
Meeting: program, 1937 (JoP, *34*, 392, 699)

American Philosophical Association, Western Division (also called Pacific Division)

Election: officers, 1936 (JoP, *33*, 56, 280)
Election: officers, 1937 (JoP, *34*, 168, 308)
Election: officers, 1938 (JoP, *35*, 28)
Meeting (JoP, *34*, 27)
Meeting (JoP, *36*, 722)
Meeting (JoP, *37*, 223)
Meeting (JoP, *38*, 196)
Meeting (JoP, *39*, 55-56)

American Philosophical Society (Philadelphia, Pennsylvania)

Angell, J. R. delivered Penrose Memorial Lecture (SCI, *95*, 219, 428)
Appointment: delegates (SCI, *35*, 772)
Delegate list (JoP, *9*, 251-252)
Election (SCI, *49*, 445)
Election: announcement (SCI, *45*, 427)
Election: announcement (SCI, *47*, 91)
Election: Eastern division officers, 1931 (JoP, *28*, 56)

Election: Keen, W. W.; President (Sci, 27, 117)
Election: Lashley, K. S. (Bull, 35, 408)
Election: officers (Sci°, 15, 276)
Election: officers (Sci°, 17, 118)
Election: officers (Sci, 49, 41)
Election: officers (Sci, 51, 112)
Honors longtime member Hoover, H. (Sci, 69, 66)
Meeting: announcement (Sci°, 15, 236; 397)
Meeting: announcement (Sci, 17, 477)
Meeting: announcement (Sci, 45, 332)
Meeting: announcement (Sci, 49, 21)
Meeting: honoring Dewey, J. 80th birthday (Sci, 91, 14)
Meeting: joint with APA (JoP, 10, 167-168, 335, 699; Bull, 10, 490)
Meeting: May, 1888 (Sci°, 11, 252)
Meeting: Memorial for Brinton, D. G. (Sci°, 11, 38, 78)
Meeting: Philadelphia, 1905 (Sci, 21, 358, 599)
Meeting: Program (Bull, 17, 240)
Officers: list of (Bull, 11, 28)
Paper: Ferree, C. E. (JoP, 10, 336; Bull, 10, 252)
Paper: Stowell, T. B. on the nerves of a cat (Sci°, 8, 453)
Publication: Barker, G. F., on constant battery (Sci°, 2, 150)
Publication: *Proceedings and Transactions* index to 1883 (Sci°, 5, 119)
Symposium: Advances in Psychology, speakers announced (Sci, 93, 348)
Symposium: Psychology in War and Education (Bull, 17, 240)
Symposium: "Recent Advances in Psychology" (Bull, 38, 778)
Wistar, I. J., trip to Mediterranean and Orient (Sci, 19, 275)

American Photofile of Psychology

Microfilm or photoprints; Journals, abstracts, manuscript (Bull, 37, 407)

American Physiological Association

Meeting: Dec, 1887, organizational (Sci°, 11, 8)
Meeting: Dec, 1888 (Sci°, 13, 6)
Symposium: "Special senses in relation to war problems" (Sci, 97, 114)

American Psychiatric Association

Election: Campbell, C. M.; President (Sci, 83, 517)
Election: Chapman, R. M.; President; Cheney, C. O. steps down (Sci, 83, 517)
Election: Hall, R. W.; President (Sci, 91, 520)
Election: Meyer, R.; President (Sci, 65, 612)
Election: officers, 1941 (Sci, 93, 614)
Election: Wells, D. F.; Vice-president (Sci, 91, 520)
Meeting: 84th annual (Sci, 67, 553)
Meeting, 1944 (Sci, 99, 382-383)

American Psychological Association (*see also* Eastern Branch, New York Branch, North Central Branch, Northwestern Branch, Terminology Committee, Washington-Baltimore Branch)

AAAP, 5 sections become charter divisions (J App, *28*, 530-531)

Accreditation of clinical psychologists (Sci, *55*, 47)

Allport, G.; presidental address 47th annual meeting (JoP, *36*, 476)

Animal research legislation; precautions in animal experimentation (Sci, *77*, 189)

Announcement: "Abstracts References of the Psychological Index" (Bull, *37*, 187)

Appointment: Committee on Publications in Applied Psychology (J App, *2*, 196)

Appointment: Langfeld, H. S., editor of *Psychological Bulletin* (Sci, *79*, 247)

Appointment: Louttit, C. M. (Sci, *98*, 321)

Appointment: Marquis, D. (Sci, *98*, 321)

Appointment: Martin, Chair of San Francisco program (Sci, *41*, 605; JoP, *12*, 280)

Appointment: officers (Bull, *14*, 32)

Appointment: Peterson, editor *Psychological Monographs* (Sci, *79*, 247)

Appropriation: to National Research Council for support of Office of Personnel, 1944 (Sci, *98*, 470)

Appropriation: work on mental tests (Rev, *5*, 344)

Baldwin, J. M., presidential address (AJP, *9*, 250)

Bliss, C. B. comments on proposed philosophical section formation (Rev, *6*, 237-238)

By-laws, adoption of new (J App, *28*, 530)

Carmichael, L., chair of panel discussion, 1942 (Sci, *95*, 405)

Cattell, J. McK., delegate to 7th American Scientific Congress (Sci, *82*, 298)

Cattell, J. McK., testimonial by Poffenberger, A. T. at 1935 meeting (Sci, *82*, 298)

Committee formed for curriculum in psychology for war preparation, 1942 (Bull, *39*, 895)

Committee on Displaced Foreign Psychologists organizes international seminar in psychology (Bull, *38*, 191)

Committee on Examination Questions in Psychology preparing pool of exam questions (Bull, *39*, 326)

Committee on Relations with Medical Education, list of members (JoP, *9*, 28)

Committee on Standardizing of Procedure in Experimental Tests; report by Yerkes, R. M. & Watson, J. B. (JoP, *8*, 559-560)

Committee on Terminology: call for assistance from psychologists on psychological terms (AJP, *31*, 220)

Committee to formulate *Standards for Certification of University Psychological Programs* (Sci, *51*, 137)

Constitutional amendment (Bull, *39*, 196)

Contest on music research (JoP, *17*, 671-672; Bull, *17*, 352)

Correction on report read at Pennsylvania State College (Bull, *38*, 192)

Council of Directors, special meeting (Bull, *14*, 143)

Dallenbach, K. M. Director of panel discussion, 1942 (Sci, *95*, 405)

Division on Adulthood and Old Age is proposed (Bull, *42*, 793)

Divisions, comment by Bentley, M. (AJP, *58*, 394-397)

Dodge, R., presidential address (Sci, *44*, 673)

Election: Allport, F.; Director (Bull, *25*, 123)

Election: Allport, G. W.; President (Sci, *88*, 373)

Election: Allport, G. W.; Representative to Social Science Research Council
  (Sci, *82*, 247)

Election: Anderson, J. E. (Sci, *80*, 242)

Election: Angell, J. R.; President (Sci, *23*, 38)

Election: Angier, R. P.; Director (JoP, *12*, 112)

Election: Bingham, W. V. D.; Secretary-treasurer (Bull, *8*, 32; Sci, *33*, 22)

Election: Boring, E. G.; President (Sci, *67*, 12)

Election: Bott, E. A.; Director (Sci, *76*, 251)

Election: Bryan, W. L.; President (Sci, *17*, 158)

Election: Calkins, M. W.; President (Sci, *21*, 37)

Election: Carmichael, L.; President (Sci, *90*, 249)

Election: Carr, H.; President (Sci, *63*, 41)

Election: Dallenbach, K. M.; Director (Bull, *25*, 123)

Election: Dashiell, J. F.; Director (Sci, *71*, 64)

Election: Davis, W. H.; Secretary (Sci, *21*, 37)

Election: Dewey, J.; President (Sci, *9*, 38)

Election: Dodge, R.; President (Sci, *43*, 17)

Election: Franz, S. I.; President (Sci, *51*, 41)

Election: Garrett, H. E.; Director (Sci, *76*, 251)

Election: Gesell, A.; Director (Sci, *71*, 69)

Election: Hall, G. S.; President (Sci, *59*, 13)

Election: Hollingworth, H. L.; President (Bull, *24*, 80)

Election: Hull, C. L.; President (Sci, *82*, 247)

Election: Jones, H. E.; Director (Sci, *82*, 247)

Election: Judd, C. M.; President (Bull, *6*, 32)

Election: Langfeld, H. S.; President (Sci, *71*, 64; Sci, *72*, 599)

Election: Lashley, K. S.; President (Sci, *69*, 11)

Election: Marshall, H. R.; President (Sci, *25*, 37; Bull, *4*, 32)

Election: May, A. (Sci, *82*, 247)

Election: Miles, W. S.; Director (Bull, *24*, 80)

Election: officers (Sci, *15*, 78)

Election: officers, 1898 (AJP, *11*, 280)

Election: officers, 1900 (Sci, *11*, 39)

Election: officers, 1904 (JoP, *1*, 28)

Election: officers, 1905 (JoP, *2*, 28)

Election: officers, 1907 (Bull, *5*, 32)

Election: officers, 1910 (JoP, *7*, 56)

Election: officers, 1911 (JoP, *8*, 55)

Election: officers, 1912 (JoP, *10*, 56)

Election: officers, 1913 (Sci, *39*, 94)

Election: officers, 1916 (Bull, *13*, 40)

Election: officers, 1919 (AJP, *32*, 157; BULL, *16*, 32)
Election: officers, 1920 (JoP, *17*, 56)
Election: officers, 1928 (BULL, *25*, 123)
Election: officers, 1929 (SCI, *69*, 363; BULL, *26*, 56)
Election: officers, 1941 (SCI, *94*, 253)
Election: officers, 1942 (SCI, *96*, 292; BULL, *39*, 684)
Election: officers, 1944 (J APP, *28*, 530; BULL, *41*, 602)
Election: Paterson, D. G.; Secretary (SCI, *86*, 439)
Election: Peterson, J.; Director (BULL, *24*, 80)
Election: Pillsbury, W. B.; President (SCI, *31*, 22; BULL, *7*, 36)
Election: Poffenberger, A. T.; President (SCI, *80*, 242)
Election: Robinson, E. S. (SCI, *80*, 242)
Election: Scott, W. D.; President (SCI, *49*, 19; JoP, *12*, 112)
Election: Seashore, C. E.; President (SCI, *33*, 22; BULL, *8*, 32)
Election: Thorndike, E. L.; President (SCI, *35*, 23; BULL, *9*, 140)
Election: Thurstone, L. L.; President (SCI, *76*, 251)
Election: Tolman, E. C.; President (SCI, *84*, 307)
Election: Warren, H. C.; President (SCI, *37*, 55; BULL, *10*, 40; JoP, *10*, 699-700)
Election: Washburn, M. F.; President (SCI, *53*, 18)
Election: Watson, J. B.; President (JoP, *12*, 112)
Election: Woodrow, H.; President (J APP, *24*, 855)
Election: Woodworth, R. S.; President (BULL, *11*, 28)
Establishment of Office of Psychological Personnel (SCI, *95*, 527-528; BULL, *39*, 270)
Establishment of Section of Consulting Psychologists (SCI, *56*, 277)
Honors: Jastrow, J. on long tenure at Univ. of Wisconsin (SCI, *59*, 25)
Hunter, W. S.; presidential address (SCI, *74*, 171)
Lecture: Hartmann, G. W.; 47th annual meeting (JoP, *36*, 476)
Lecture: Herrick, C. J. (JoP, *8*, 699-700)
Lecture: Judd, H., 1911 (SCI, *34*, 680)
Lecture: Marshall, H. R. (JoP, *8*, 699-700)
Lecture: Yerkes, R. M., 1911 (SCI, *34*, 680)
Meeting: 1893 report (REV, *1*, 214)
Meeting: 1894 announcement (SCI, *2*, 803)
Meeting: 1894 report (AJP, *7*, 145)
Meeting: 1895 report (AJP, *7*, 306)
Meeting: 1896 announcement (REV, *3*, 705)
Meeting: 1896 report (AJP, *7*, 448; REV, *4*, 230)
Meeting: 1897 announcement (REV, *4*, 339; SCI, *8*, 73)
Meeting: 1897 report (AJP, *9*, 135)
Meeting: 1898 announcement (REV, *5*, 677; REV, *5*, 554, 677; AJP, *9*, 423)
Meeting: 1899 (REV, *7*, 104; AJP, *11*, 280; SCI, *10*, 741)
Meeting: 1900 (SCI, *12*, 893)
Meeting: 1901 (SCI, *14*, 781)
Meeting: 1904 announcement (JoP, *1*, 28)
Meeting: 1904 joint with AAAS (JoP, *1*, 721)

Meeting: 1905 joint with AAAS (AJP, *17*, 144; BULL, *2*, 36, 427; BULL, *3*, 36; JoP, *2*, 28, 699; JoP, *3*, 27)

Meeting: 1906 announcement (BULL, *3*, 421; JoP, *3*, 700)

Meeting: 1906 report (BULL, *5*, 32; JoP, *4*, 27; AJP, *18*, 156)

Meeting: 1907 announcement (BULL *4*, 369)

Meeting: 1907 report (BULL, *5*, 379; JoP, *5*, 83)

Meeting: 1908 announcement (JoP, *5*, 672)

Meeting: 1908 report (JoP, *6*, 28; BULL, *6*, 32)

Meeting: 1909 announcement (JoP, *6*, 308, 644, BULL, *6*, 184, 400)

Meeting: 1910, announcement and call for papers (JoP, *7*, 644)

Meeting: 1910, joint with AAAS (JoP, *8*, 55)

Meeting: 1911 announcement and agenda (JoP, *8*, 28, 699-700; BULL, *8*, 406)

Meeting: 1911 report (SCI, *34*, 680)

Meeting: 1912 (BULL, *9*, 486; JoP, *9*, 28)

Meeting: 1913 joint with American Philosophical Society (JoP, *10*, 335, 699-700; BULL, *10*, 490)

Meeting: 1914 announcement (SCI, *40*, 739; SCI, *41*, 606)

Meeting: 1914 joint with AAAS and SSPP (BULL, *11*, 443; JoP, *11*, 700)

Meeting: 1914 joint with Amer. Philosophical Assoc. (JoP, *11*, 56)

Meeting: 1914 joint with New York Academy of Sciences (JoP, *11*, 721)

Meeting: 1915 joint with AAAS (BULL, *12*, 128, 204, 243, 440; JoP, *12*, 532, 672, 721)

Meeting: 1916, 25th anniversary celebration (JoP, *13*, 644, 700; BULL, *13*, 408; SCI, *44*, 673)

Meeting: 1917 announcement (BULL, *14*, 366)

Meeting: 1918 announcement (J APP, *2*, 386-387; BULL, *15*, 360)

Meeting: 1918 rescheduled (JoP, *15*, 672, 700)

Meeting: 1919 joint with Amer. Assoc. of Clinical Psych. (JoP, *16*, 700; JoP, *17*, 56)

Meeting: 1919 joint with the Amer. Anthropological Assoc. (JoP, *17*, 56)

Meeting: 1920 (AJP, *32*, 157)

Meeting: 1922 announcement (AJP, *35*, 310)

Meeting: 1924 announcement (AJP, *37*, 310)

Meeting: 1926 announcement and elections (BULL, *23*, 112; JoP, *23*, 616)

Meeting: 1927 announcement (JoP, *24*, 722)

Meeting: 1928 announcement (JoP, *25*, 672)

Meeting: 1929 joint with Ninth International Congress of Psychology (BULL, *26*, 56; SCI, *69*, 11)

Meeting: 1930 announcement and description of program (JoP, *27*, 616; BULL, *27*, 76, 660; SCI, *72*, 499, 599; AJP, *54*, 134-136)

Meeting: 1931 announcement (SCI, *74*, 170)

Meeting: 1932 (AJP, *45*, 174)

Meeting: 1933 (AJP, *46*, 150)

Meeting: 1934 (AJP, *47*, 166)

Meeting: 1935 (AJP, *48*, 172; AJP, *49*, 140; SCI, *81*, 513)

Meeting: 1937 (AJP, *51*, 172; J APP, *21*, 243)

Meeting: 1938 (SCI, *87*, 297; AJP, *52*, 127-130; JoP, *35*, 280; J APP, *22*, 443)

Meeting: 1939 (JoP, *36*, 476)

Meeting: 1940 joint with Amer. Speech Correction Assoc., Assoc. for Applied Psych., Society for the Psychological Study of Social Issues, and the Psychometric Society (SCI, *91*, 500)

Meeting: 1941 (AJP, *55*, 130-132; BULL, *39*, 196; SCI, *94*, 230)

Meeting: 1942 announcement (SCI, *95*, 405)

Meeting: 1942, 50th anniversary cancelled; "Skeleton" meeting held in New York City (SCI, *96*, 178, 294)

Meeting: 1943 (SCI, *98*, 172, 321)

Meeting: 1945 postponed (BULL, *42*, 256)

Members in national service (J APP, *2*, 294-295, 386)

Merger: APA and AAAP (BULL, *41*, 602)

Miles, W. R. retires as president (SCI, *76*, 251)

National Committee on Education and Defense (BULL, *37*, 828)

National Research Council (JoP, *14*, 504)

Office of Psychological Personnel (SCI, *96*, 294)

Officers: list of (BULL, *11*, 28)

Officers: list of (BULL, *12*, 44)

Publication: copies available of Edgerton-Paterson "Tables of Standard Errors..." (BULL, *40*, 724)

Publication: Proceedings of first and second meetings (REV, *1*, 335)

Reorganization of psychology from Intersociety Constitutional Convention (SCI, *98*, 321)

Washburn, M. F. dinner in her honor (SCI, *67*, 101)

World's Fair Connection (J APP, *16*, 695)

American Public Health Association

Meeting: 1884, Missouri (SCI°, *3*, 802)

Meeting: 1885 program, Washington (SCI°, *6*, 449- 450)

Meeting: 1886, Canada (SCI°, *8*, 229)

Meeting: 1886 program, Ontario (SCI°, *7*, 324)

Meeting: 1889 announcement, Brooklyn (SCI°, *14*, 196)

Meeting: 1889 program (SCI°, *14*, 217)

Meeting: 1899, Minneapolis (SCI, *10*, 542)

Meeting: 27th annual (SCI, *9*, 599-600)

American Red Cross

Appointment: Witmer, L. (BULL, *14*, 420)

Services to armed forces: social welfare workers and educators needed (J APP, *26*, 711)

Work by Morse, J. (BULL, *14*, 420)

American School Hygiene Association

Election: Terman, L. M., Council of Thirty (JoP, *10*, 616)

Prize for best paper on social hygiene for adolescents (BULL, *12*, 204)

American Scientific Congress (7th)
Cattell, J. McK. ; Delegate for 4 agencies (SCI, *82*, 298)

American Scientist
Paper: *The times and the United States strategic forces in Europe* (SCI, *101*, 61)

American Social Science Association
Paper: Walker, F. A. on industrial education (SCI°, *4*, 536)

American Society for Aesthetics
Meeting: 1942 (JoP, *39*, 699)
Meeting: 1942 cancelled (JoP, *39*, 722)
Meeting: 1944 (JoP, *41*, 586-587)
Organizing (JoP, *39*, 280; BULL, *39*, 423; JoP, *40*, 364)
Receives ownership of *Journal of Aesthetic and Art Criticism* (JoP, *42*, 252)

American Society for Psychical Research
Account of formation in the *Journal of the Society of Psychical Research* (SCI°, 5, 62)
Awarded Hyslop-Prince fellowship; Taves, E., 1942-43 (BULL, 39, 423)
Committee on Thought Transference requests interested individuals (SCI°, 5, 204)
Committee on Thought-Transference, report (SCI, 5, 491)
Death: Hodgson, R. (SCI, 22, 886)
Established fellowship in memory of Hyslop, J. H. and Prince W. F. (BULL, 39, 71)
James, W., presiding (SCI°, 15, 144)
Meeting: 1885 program, Boston (SCI°, 5, 491)
Meeting: 1887 program for Boston (SCI°, 10, 287)
Meeting: 1890, Boston (SCI°, 15, 144)
Proceedings, issues (SCI°, 8, 629)
Sale with Cupples, Upham and Co. (SCI°, 7, 140)
Termination of corporate existence (SCI°, 15, 57)

American Society for the Hard of Hearing
Listing of available publications (BULL, 42, 192)

American Society for the Study of Speech Disorders
Cooperative stammering study (BULL, 28, 255)

American Society of Naturalists
Election: Jennings, H. S.; President (SCI, 33, 22)
Election: officers (SCI, 21, 37)
Lecture: Jennings, H. S., Heredity and personality, Dec 28, 1911 (SCI, 34, 709, 870)
Nominations and qualifications for membership, 1941 (SCI, 94, 537)

American Speech Correction Association
Meeting: with APA (SCI, *91*, 500)

American University (Washington, D.C.)
Appointment: Marston, W. M. (SCI, *56*, 195)
Appointment: Strong, E. (BULL, *42*, 793)
Promotion: Marston, W. M., Professor (BULL, *20*, 60)

American Youth Commission
Bell, H. M.; *Matching youth and jobs*, (J APP, *24*, 854)
Post-war youth employment, published, 1943 (J APP, *27*, 114)
Report, "Youth in the CCC" by Holland, K. and Hill, F. E. (J APP, *26*, 570)

Amerika-Institut (Berlin)
Appointment: Münsterberg, H., Director (BULL, *7*, 396)

Ames, Edward Scribner
Courses in psychology of religion, Univ. of Chicago (JoP, *1*, 336)

Ames, W. R.
Appointment: Univ. of Montana (BULL, *17*, 116)

Amherst College (Massachusetts)
Appointment: Newlin, W. J. (JoP, *4*, 363; BULL, *4*, 337)
Appointment: Woodbridge, F. J. E. (BULL, *4*, 128)
Degree to Tufts, J. H. (BULL, *1*, 334)
Election: Meiklegjon, A.; President (JoP, *9*, 336)
Paper: Tyler, J. M. on the relations of animal to human psychology (SCI°, *6*, 100)
Paper: Upton, I. H. on the relation of the mind to the body (SCI°, *6*, 100)
Research: Dept. physical education researches eyesight (SCI°, *7*, 414)

Amnesia
Discussion: Jones, F. N. and Ghiselli, E. E.; "Organic amnesia and relearning" (AJP, *51*, 169-170)

Amory, Francis
Prize money for research in cure of diseases of human genital organs (SCI, *89*, 386)

Amsden, George S.
Appointment: N. Y. Hospital-Cornell Med. College assoc; psychiatry (SCI, *74*, 169)

Amsterdam (Holland)
Meeting: international congress proposed (JoP, *4*, 252)

Analysis
Paper: Pace, E. A. (JoP, *2*, 56)

Anastasi, Anne
Appointment: Queens College, NYC (SCI, *90*, 439)
Appointment: Queens College, NYC, Chair of dept. (BULL, *37*, 122)
Discussion on Trait relationship; "Some ambiguous concepts in the field of mental organization" (AJP, *47*, 511)
N.Y.A.S.; Secretary (J APP, *21*, 717)

Anderson, Amos Carey
Head of committee to honor Porter, J. P. (SCI, *98*, 382)

Anderson, David Allen
Appointment: Dept. Head at Pennsylvania State College (SCI, *46*, 385; BULL, *14*, 366, 420)

Anderson, Edward Eric
Promotion: Wilson College (Penn.) (BULL, *41*, 343)

Anderson, Gordon Vladimir
Appointment: Northwestern Univ. (BULL, *42*, 791)

Anderson, Harold Homer
Awarded James McKeen Cattell grant-in-aid, 1942-43 (BULL, *39*, 683)
Brewer, J. E.; post-doctoral work, Univ. of Illinois (BULL, *37*, 827)

Anderson, John Edward
Appointment: Director Institute of Child Welfare Univ. of Minnesota (BULL, *22*, 444; SCI, *62*, 347)
Appointment: Minnesota committee of the White House Conference on Children in a Democracy (BULL, *39*, 267)
Appointment: *Psychological Bulletin* cooperating editor (BULL, *25*, 444)
Appointment: *Psychological Bulletin* editorship (J APP, *26*, 392)
Election: APA council (BULL, *23*, 112; SCI, *80*, 242)
Election: APA representative Social Science Research Council (BULL, *27*, 76)
Honorary degree from Univ. of Wyoming (BULL, *39*, 682)
Lecture: 12th annual Ohio State Educational Conference (J APP, *16*, 97)
Promotion: Yale Univ. (SCI, *53*, 456; BULL, *18*, 296)
Writes obituary for Downey, J. E. (AJP, *45*, 362-363)

Anderson, L.
Appointment: Univ. of Illinois (SCI, *30*, 709; BULL, *6*, 427)

Anderson, Oscar Daniel
Transferred to psych. dept., Cornell Univ. (BULL, *36*, 804)

Anderson, Rose Gustava
Mental testing article (J APP, *22*, 215)
Psychological Corporation meeting with APA and AAAP, 1941 (J APP, *25*, 600)

Anderson, Victor Vance
Appointment: Boston Police Court, head of psychological laboratory (SCI, *44*, 129; JoP, *13*, 560; BULL, *13*, 408)

Andrew, Maria
Appointment: Buena Vista, Iowa (BULL, *14*, 366)

Andrews and Company
Publication: "Philosophical papers of the University of Michigan" (SCI°, *11*, 265)

Andrews, Thomas Gaylord
Appointment: Univ. of Chicago (BULL, *41*, 603)
Departure: Columbia Univ. (BULL, *41*, 603)

Androp, Serge
Eugenics research contest winner (SCI, *82*, 513)

Anesthesic, effects of
Paper: Babinski, J. F. F. (AJP, *1*, 201)

Angell, Frank
Belgian relief work (JoP, *13*, 84)
Death notice (AJP, *53*, 138-141; BULL, *37*, 122)
Leave of absence, war relief work (SCI, *43*, 18; BULL, *12*, 481)
Retirement announced (J APP, *6*, 301)

Angell, James Rowland
Appointment: director of Hall of Fame for Great Americans (BULL, *41*, 199)
Appointment: Hall of Fame of New York Univ. (SCI, *99*, 34)
Appointment: National Broadcasting Co. (SCI, *86*, 9)
Appointment: National Committee for Mental Hygiene, 25th anniversary (SCI, *80*, 446)
Appointment: National Research Council (SCI, *46*, 407; JoP, *14*, 700; BULL, *16*, 222; BULL, *14*, 366)
Appointment: National Research Council; Chairman (SCI, *49*, 467)
Appointment: president of Yale Univ. (BULL, *18*, 236)
Appointment: Sorbonne (SCI, *40*, 23)
Appointment: Univ. of Chicago (SCI, *1*, 81; SCI, *33*, 770; BULL, *1*, 291; REV, *1*, 440, 552)
Appointment: Univ. of Chicago, Dean of Faculties of Arts, Literature and Science (SCI, *33*, 770; BULL, *8*, 222)
Appointment: Univ. of Minnesota (REV, *1*, 112)
Appointment: U.S. Bureau of Education (BULL, *12*, 481)
Attendance at commemorative to Zeller, E. (SCI°, *8*, 452)
Awarded degree from Dartmouth College (SCI, *83*, 180)
Awarded degree from Rutgers Univ. (SCI, *85*, 601)
Awarded degree from Univ. of the State of New York (SCI, *88*, 372-373)
Awarded degree from Univ. of Vermont (BULL, *12*, 280)

Awarded degree Stanford Univ. (SCI, *79*, 337)

Awarded Doctor of Laws degree from Columbia (SCI, *53*, 531)

Awarded Doctor of Laws degree from Princeton, Yale, Harvard and Columbia (SCI, *54*, 11; BULL, *18*, 438)

Awarded Doctor of Laws degree from Wesleyan Univ. (SCI, *57*, 737; BULL, *21*, 240)

Awarded Doctor of Laws degree from Univ. of Pennsylvania (SCI, *87*, 572)

Awarded Doctor of Letters from Univ. of Liverpool (SCI, *74*, 146)

Awarded French Legion of Honor (SCI, *74*, 408)

Awarded honorary degree from Illinois College (SCI, *70*, 375)

Awarded National Institute of Social Science gold medal (SCI, *85*, 479)

Awarded Ph.D. from Univ. of Michigan (SCI, *73*, 490)

Celebration, 70th birthday (SCI, *67*, 155)

Committee for APA/International Congress for Psychology (JoP, *8*, 196)

Committee on Education and Special Training (BULL, *15*, 97-98)

Conference: National Research Council, "Psychological factors on national morale" (BULL, *37*, 829)

Declines the presidency of Dartmouth College (SCI, *28*, 558)

Declines the presidency of Univ. of Washington (SCI, *40*, 813)

Departure to go abroad (BULL, *7*, 147)

Editor for *Psychological Monographs* (BULL, *6*, 296)

Election: APA president (SCI, *23*, 38)

Election: Carnegie Corp.-New York president (JoP, *17*, 308; SCI, *51* 411; BULL, *17*, 200)

Election: member, American Museum of Natural History (SCI, *85*, 476)

Election: member of NAS (BULL, *17*, 200; SCI, *51*, 459)

Invitation to accept presidency at Univ. of Michigan (SCI, *49*, 283)

Invitation to accept presidency at Univ. of Washington (SCI, *40*, 743)

Leave from Yale to convalesce (SCI, *72*, 336)

Lecture: American Association of Physical Anthropologists, annual dinner toastmaster (SCI, *83*, 460)

Lecture: Carnegie Institute of Technology (SCI, *50*, 480)

Lecture: Carnegie Institution of Washington (SCI, *81*, 250)

Lecture: Columbia Univ., "Imageless thought" (SCI, *33*, 214; JoP, *8*, 112)

Lecture: commencement Univ. of Buffalo, 1939 (SCI, *89*, 579)

Lecture: 100th anniversary of College of Literature, Science, and the Arts of Univ. of Michigan (BULL, *39*, 72)

Lecture: Penrose Memorial address for American Philosophical Society (SCI, *95*, 219, 428)

Lecture: postponed at Sorbonne due to war (JoP, *11*, 721)

Lecture: series at Union College (JoP, *8*, 28; SCI, *32*, 551; BULL, *8*, 32)

Lecture: series at Union College, "Makers of psychology" (SCI, *45*, 85)

Lecture: series completed at Columbia Univ. (JoP, *12*, 280)

Lecture: series with Institute of Philosophy, Bowdoin College (JoP, *34*, 168)

Lecture: Swarthmore College (SCI, *86*, 371)

Lecture: 25th anniversary, Mental Hygiene Movement (SCI, *70*, 536)

Lecture: Union College, "Modern psychology" (JoP, *14*, 168; BULL, *14*, 80)

Lecture: Univ. Lecture Assoc. (Chicago) (BULL, *11*, 116)
Lecture: Univ. of California (REV, *10*, 464)
Lecture: Univ. of California summer school (SCI, *17*, 992)
Lecture: Univ. of Chicago, "Psychology in Army" (SCI, *48*, 89)
Lecture: Yale, "Evolution" (SCI, *54*, 546)
Lecturer, nominated at the Sorbonne, 1915 (BULL, *11*, 268; JoP, *11*, 448)
Mental hygiene anniversary dinner (SCI, *70*, 536)
Mental hygiene, National Committee for; Vice President (SCI, *72*, 557)
National Academy of Sciences welcomed at Yale, 1931 (SCI, *74*, 481)
National Advisory Council on Radio in Education: Weekly broadcast (SCI, *74*, 411)
Portrait painted (SCI, *52*, 578; SCI, *58*, 104, 328)
Portrait to be painted (BULL, *18*, 111)
Promotion: Univ. of Chicago (JoP, *1*, 336)
Psychology republished in England (JoP, *2*, 308)
Relieved of duties at Univ. of Chicago (SCI, *46*, 407)
Resignation: editorship of *Psychological Monographs* (SCI, *59*, 60; JoP, *21*, 56)
Resignation: Univ. of Chicago (SCI, *52*, 153)
Retirement: Yale Univ. (SCI, *85*, 195; SCI, *86*, 9)
Returned from survey of educational broadcasts in Eurpoe (SCI, *86*, 262, 516)
Society of Experimental Psychologists dinner honoring Angell (AJP, *47*, 344)
Trip to Great Britain (SCI, *31*, 663)

Angier, Roswell Parker

Appointment: Assoc. Dean, Yale Univ. (BULL, *35*, 61; SCI, *86*, 438)
Appointment: Director at Yale Institute of Psychology (J APP, *8*, 450)
Appointment: Univ. of Chicago (SCI, *59*, 422; BULL, *21*, 360)
Appointment: Yale Univ. (BULL, *17*, 116)
Appointment: Yale Univ.; Chairman Institute of Psychology (BULL, *22*, 612)
Appointment: Yale Univ.; Dean, freshman (SCI, *50*, 590)
Appointment: Yale Univ., fills position left by Münsterberg, H. (SCI, *45*, 63; JoP, *14*, 84)
Appointment: Yale Univ.; Instructor (JoP, *3*, 196; BULL, *3*, 147)
Commissioned, Captain in the Sanitary Corps (JoP, *15*,700)
Commissioned, U.S. Army (SCI, *48*, 415)
Editorial direction of *The Psychological Bulletin*, (BULL, *15*, 324)
Editorial supervisor, *Psychological Bulletin* (BULL, *13*, 187)
Editorial supervisor, *Psychological Bulletin* (BULL, *14*, 142)
Editor: Issue on the Physiology of the Central Nervous System of *Psychological Bulletin* (BULL, *8*, 146; BULL, *10*, 164; BULL, *11*, 152; BULL, *12*, 160)
Election: APA council (JoP, *12*, 112)
Lecture: Univ. of California (JoP, *4*, 168; BULL, *4*, 95)
Lecture: Yale Univ., "History of psychology" (SCI, *52*, 384)
Portrait at Yale Univ. (BULL, *38*, 907)
Portrait presented to Yale Univ. (SCI, *94*, 61)
Promotion: Yale Univ. (JoP, *5*, 168; BULL, *5*, 96)
Promotion: Yale Univ. (BULL, *14*, 191)

Resignation: Dean of freshman (BULL, *22*, 612)
Retirement: Yale Univ. (BULL, *38*, 777, 907; SCI, *93*, 276; SCI, *94*, 61)

Anglo-American libraries
Central Europe loaned books (JoP, *17*, 307-308)

Anglo-Polish Committee
Meeting, commemorating 400th anniversary of death of Copernicus (SCI, *97*, 577)

Animal behavior (*see also* Comparative psychology)
Establishment: Institute for the Study of Animal Behavior (BULL, *33*, 580)
Lecture: Craig, W. at Harvard (SCI, *56*, 686)
Lecture: Mendal, L. B. on animal intelligence (SCI°, *15*, 117)
Lecture: Tyler, J. M., on relation to human psychology (SCI°, *6*, 100)
Lecture: Watson, J. B. at Columbia Univ. (SCI, *37*, 367)
Lecture: Watson, J. B. at Columbia (JoP, *10*, 196)
Publication: Wundt, W. on *Animal and Human Psychology* (SCI°, *23*, 96)

Animal experimentation guidelines (*see also* Vivisection)
California state proposition on prohibition of animal use (SCI, *88*, 473)
Chicago court decision on animal use (SCI, *86*, 78)
Publication: British Parliament (SCI, *12*, 199-200)
Report by British Home Office (SCI, *92*, 10)

Animal Industrial Conference
Meeting, 10th annual at Pennsylvania State College (SCI, *69*, 492)

Animal intelligence
Lecture: Thorndike, E. L., Middletown scientific association (SCI, *31*, 65)

Animal Mind, The
Letter, Washburn, M. F. (JoP, *5*, 587)

Animal morale
Facts in *Revue scientifique* (SCI°, *14*, 181)

Ankara, University of (Turkey)
Appointment: Pratt, C. C. (SCI, *102*, 374; JoP, *42*, 616)
Leave of absence of Sherif, M., fellowship in U.S. (JoP, *42*, 616)

Annales de l'Institut Superieur de Philosophie
Fire at the Univ. of Louvain (JoP, *17*, 420)

Année psychologique
Appointment: Pieron, H.; Editor (BULL, *10*,40; BULL, *9*, 359)
Papers: list of, 1895 (REV, *3*, 243)
Publication announcement (REV, *2*, 216)

Publisher, change of (BULL, *1*, 333)
Purchase of (REV, *4*, 339)

Ansbacher, Heinz Ludwig
"Military psychology" in *Psychological Bulletin* (J APP, *25*, 359)

Anschutz, Georg
Appointment: Univ. of Constantinople (BULL, *12*, 404)

Anthropoid Station at Orange Park, Florida
Money given for lab by Rockefeller Foundation (SCI, *89*, 266)

Anthropology and Psychology, Division of (*see also* National Research Council)
List of members (JoP, *17*, 83)
Report on science status after the war in *The American Anthropologist* (SCI, *102*, 643)

Anthropology, psychological
Creation of Board of Anthropological Studies at Cambridge (JoP, *1*, 364)

Anticonvulsants
Study by Goodman, L. S. (SCI, *101*, 197)

Antioch College (Yellow Springs, Ohio)
Appointment: English, H.; Professor (BULL, *24*, 312)
Appointment: Leuba, C.; Associate professor (BULL, *27*, 564; SCI, *71*, 556)
English, H. returns to former position, (J APP, *11*, 165)
Leave of absence: Leuba, C. (BULL, *38*, 248)

Antiquity of humans
Discussion by Dawkins, B. (SCI°, *2*, 779)

Anti-vivisection (*see also* Animal experimentation guidelines)
Exhibit in Paris (SCI, *10*, 93)

Apes (Intelligence of)
Lecture: Köhler, W. (BULL, *22*, 444)

"Apotheosis of Science"
Paintings of 50 scientific men (SCI, *93*, 324)

Apparatus
Aesthesiometer invented by Jastrow, J. (AJP, *1*, 552)
Appunn wire forks (JoP, *1*, 196)
Binet-Buzenet Aesthesiometer (JoP, *7*, 28)
Discussion by Kreezer, G., "Electro-physiological methods and their use in the investigation of growth and development" (AJP, *49*, 479)
Electro-encephalogram; extensive discussion, diagrams (AJP, *51*, 737)

Exhibition by Sommer, K. R. (JoP, *1*, 335)
Hathaway psychogalvanic apparatus (AJP, *45*, 522)
Lecture: Bishop, H. G., Stern variator (AJP, *34*, 150)
Lecture: Fernberger, S. W., improvement of Sanford chronoscope (AJP, *37*, 154)
Lecture: Pattie, F. A., Galton whistle (AJP, *35*, 308)
Lecture: Scott, W. D., pendulum (JoP, *2*, 280)
Ordering of Hering tissue papers (JoP, *2*, 56)
Presentation by Cattell, J. McK. (JoP, *1*, 224)
Research: Wissler, C., ergograph (SCI, *15*, 547)
Ruckmick, C. H., employed by Stoelting Company of Chicago (J APP, *23*, 530)
Scientific Apparatus Makers of America (SCI, *69*, 376)
Symposium on learning at Indiana Univ., 1937 (BULL, *37*, 61)

Apperception
Paper: Pillsbury, W. B. (AJP, *9*, 421)

Appetite
Effects of benzedrine sulfate on satiation (AJP, *52*, 297-299)
Grant: Univ. of Illinois, food preference in rats (SCI, *95*, 600)
Publication: NRC, food habits (J APP, *26*, 858)
Research: drug effects on taste (SCI°, *8*, 54)

Appleton, D. and Co.
Announcement: publication (JoP, *7*, 196)
Announcement: publication of letters by Darwin, C. R. (SCI°, *16*, 158)

Applied Design, School of
Instruction: Gordon, K. (JoP, *13*, 112)

Applied psychology
AAAP succeeds Assoc. of Consulting Psychologists (BULL, *34*, 864)
Announcement: Forest Service, USDA; civil service employment for psychologists (SCI, *85*, 382)
Cattell, J. McK. grants-in-aid research offered (J APP, *26*, 389)
Committee on Publications (J APP, *2*, 196)
Committee on Selection and Training of Air Craft Pilots, National Research Council (BULL, *37*, 827)
Consiglio Nazionale Delle Ricerche of Italy (BULL, *37*, 329)
Directory of Applied Psychologists (J APP, *25*, 268)
Election: N.Y. State Assoc. for Applied Psychologists, 1940 (BULL, *37*, 405)
Institute established (BULL, *3*, 392)
Lecture: Münsterberg, H. at Union College (JoP, *9*, 168)
National Board of Researches, permanent commission for the application of psychology (BULL, *36*, 713)
Paper: Darley, J. G., "The fields of applied psychology" (J APP, *24*, 370)
Psychological Corporation grants for research, 1943-44 (J APP, *28*, 79)

Applied Psychology Monographs
Editor: Conrad, H. S. (J App, 27, 115)
Publication begun (Bull, 40, 311)

Archives de Psychologie de la Suisse Romande
Publication begun (Rev, 8, 657)

Archives of Philosophy, Psychology and Scientific Methods
Changes to two publications (JoP, 3, 644)

Archives of Psychology
Editor: Woodworth, R. S. (Bull, 3, 421; JoP, 3, 644)
Name changed (Bull, 3, 422)
Publication announced (JoP, 3, 644)

Archiv für die gesammte Psychologie
Philosophische Studien renamed (Rev, 10, 103-104)
Publication index (Sci°, 5, 432)

Archiv für Frauen-kunde und Eugenik
Publication begun (Bull, 11, 232)

Archiv für Geschichte der Philosophie
Editor: Stein, L. (Sci°, 9, 583)
Publication: Berlin (Sci°, 9, 583)

Archiv für Religionspsychologie
Publication begun (JoP, 11, 448, 700)

Archivio italiano di psicologia
New journal for psychology (Bull, 17, 280; JoP, 17, 616)

Ardigo, Roberto
Introspective psych. sectional president 5th International Congress of
Psychology (JoP, 2, 56)

Aristotelian Society
Lecture: Waismann, F. (JoP, 35, 252)
Lecture: Wolf, A., repression (JoP, 11, 532)
Meeting: joint session with British Psychological Society/Mind Assoc, July 3-5,
1915 (JoP, 12, 448)
Meeting: joint session with Mind Assoc and Scots Philosophical Club (JoP, 33,
252)
Meeting: joint session with Mind Assoc, 1937 (JoP, 34, 252)
Meeting: joint session with Mind Assoc, 1938 (JoP, 35, 252)
Paper: Bosanquet, B. (JoP, 8, 55)
Paper: Carr, H. W. on psychophysical parallelism in psychology (JoP, 8, 280)
Paper: Edgell, B. on memory (JoP, 9, 363-364)

Paper: Hicks, G. D. (JoP, 7, 251)
Paper: Hoernle, R. F. A. on volition (JoP, 10, 196)
Paper: Jacks, L. P. on consciousness (JoP, 10, 224)
Paper: Moore, G. E. (JoP, 7, 55)
Program: winter 1887 (Sci°, 10, 272)
Report on joint meeting with British Psychological Society and the Mind Assoc
   (JoP, 7, 420)

Aristotle
Paintings, "Apotheosis of science" (Sci, 93, 324)
Publication on metaphysics (JoP, 9, 447-448)

Arizona State Teachers College, (Tempe)
Departure: Fenton, N. (J App, 10, 287)
Departure: Smith, H. P. (Bull, 11, 603)

Arizona, University of (Tucson)
Appointment: Walker, J. F.; Dean of graduate school (Bull, 41, 603)
Appointment: Weaver, H.; Assistant professor (J App, 13, 415)
Awarded doctorate of science to Cattell, J. McK. (Sci, 59, 506)
Lecture: commencement by Cattell, J. McK. (Sci, 59, 457)

Arkansas, University of (Fayetteville)
Appointment: Crosland, H. R. (Sci, 46, 111; JoP, 14, 504; Bull, 14, 333, 420)
Appointment: DeBoer, C. (Bull, 25, 700)
Appointment: Ericksen, S. C. (Bull, 35, 796)
Appointment: Fracker, G. C. (Sci, 60, 13, 40; Bull, 21, 660)
Appointment: Jordan, A. M. (JoP, 16, 504)
Appointment: McGeoch, J.; Director of lab (Bull, 25, 700)
Apppointment: Waters, R. H. (Bull, 25, 700)
Promotion: Waters, R. H. (Sci, 84, 58)
Psychology lab enlarged (Bull, 25, 700)
Return of Jordan, A. M. (Sci, 50, 136)

Arleth, Emil
Death at Univ. of Innsbruck (JoP, 7, 84)

Arlitt, Ada Hart
Appointment: Univ. of Cincinnati, Head, Dept. of Child Care and Training
   (J App, 9, 204)

Armstrong, Andrew Campbell, Jr.
Appointment: Oxford Univ. (Rev, 6, 673)
Eulogy (JoP, 32, 307)
Leave of absence: Wesleyan Univ. (Rev, 6, 571; AJP, 11, 130)
Travels abroad, 1900 (Sci, 10, 341)

Armstrong, Harry G.
Received John Jeffries award of the Institute of the Aeronautical Sciences (SCI, 95, 93)

Army Air Corps (see United States Army Air Corps)

Army Alpha Test
Revision, Brimhall, D. R. (J APP, 10, 287)

Army ant behavior
Schneirla, T. C. investigating for John Simon Guggenheim Foundation in southern Mexico (SCI, 100, 517)

Army Committee on Classification of Personnel
Members listed (J APP, 1, 395-396)
Merges with other committees (J APP, 2, 385)
Organization of and appointments (BULL, 14, 334)
Publication: Personnel (J APP, 2, 384-385)
Summary of work (J APP, 3, 195)

Army hospitals
Reconstructive work of psychologists (BULL, 15, 324)

Army Medical Department-Washington
Appointment: Cobb, M. (JoP, 15, 560)
Appointment: Fernald, M. (JoP, 15, 560)

Army Mental Test
National Research Council plans for public schools (JoP, 16, 672)
Special committee puts them to use in schools (J APP, 3, 393)

Army, U.S. (see United States Army)
Psychological examining (J APP, 1, 394)

Army War College
Training in personnel by Yerkes, R. M. (SCI, 57, 145)

Arnold, F.
Lecture: Baltimore (BULL, 3, 392)

Arnold, Henry J.
Election: president, Hartwick College, Oneonta, N.Y. (BULL, 36, 712)

Arps, George Frederick
Anniversary dinner at Ohio State Univ. (SCI, 72, 165)
Appointment: Ohio State Univ. (BULL, 9, 407; JoP, 9, 560)
Death: (AJP, 53, 141-142; SCI, 91, 499)
Departure: Univ. of Illinois (BULL, 9, 407; JoP, 9, 560)
Election: APA council member (AJP, 32, 157)

Arsenian, Seth
Leave of absence from Springfield College, Mass (BULL, *41*, 343)

Arthur, Mary Grace
Grant renewed for standardization of point performance scale (J APP, *11*, 320)

Artley, A. Sterl
Appointment: Stephens College, Columbia, MO (BULL, *39*, 896)
Departure: Reading Clinic, Pennsylvania State College (BULL, *39*, 896)

Arts and Sciences, Society of
Gold Medal Award to Cattell, J. McK., 1930 (SCI, *71*, 310)

Asch, Solomon Elliott
Awarded: Guggenheim Fellowship (BULL, *40*, 540)
Conference for New School for Social Research: methods in philosophy and the sciences (JoP, *34*, 560)

Ashbaugh, Ernest James
Paper: AAAS, 1941-42 (J APP, *26*, 108)

Asher, Eston Jackson
Appointment: Purdue Univ. (BULL, *42*, 332)

Ashton, Philip Frederick
Promotion: Houghton College, NJ (BULL, *41*, 267)
Returns to Seattle Pacific College (BULL, *42*, 63)

Aspiration, level of
Use of coefficient of correlation in study of D-score (AJP, *55*, 442-446)

Assagioli, Roberto
Editor: *Psiche* (JoP, *9*, 56)

Association
Lecture: Association of ideas, Titchener, E. B. (SCI, *45*, 360; JoP, *14*, 364)
Lecture: Wells, F. L., free association (JoP, *7*, 700)

Association for Applied Psychology of New York City
Election: officers (SCI, *100*, 27)

Association for Research in Nervous and Mental Disease
Election: officers (SCI, *61*, 831)
Election: officers, 1934 (SCI, *79*, 9)
Election: officers (SCI, *85*, 42)
Election: officers for 1945 (SCI, *101*, 35, 85)
Meeting: 1936; speakers announced (SCI, *84*, 551)
Meeting: officers installed (SCI, *81*, 42)
Meeting: postponment (SCI, *102*, 325)

Association for Symbolic Logic
Election: Langford, C. H., president (JoP, *40*, 196)
Election: officers, 1942 (JoP, *39*, 84; Sci, *95*, 118)
Election: officers, 1943 (JoP, *40*, 196)
Election: officers, 1944 (JoP, *41*, 252)
Election: officers, 1945 (JoP, *42*, 476)
Meeting: 1942 announcement (JoP, *39*, 560)
Meeting: 1942, canceled (JoP, *39*, 722)

Association for the Advancement of Psychoanalysis
Founded, May 1941 (Bull, *38*, 779)

Association for the Advancement of Science in Marketing
Founded, officers (Sci, *74*, 336)

Association for the Education of Women (Oxford, England)
Lecture series on scientific education (Sci°, *10*, 250)

Association of Applied Psychologists
Election: English, H. B., president (Sci, *90*, 613)
Meeting: with APA (Sci, *91*, 500)

Association of Consulting Psychologists
Lecture: Fryer, D. H. (J App, *21*, 241)
Meeting: 8th annual, Brubacher, A. R., President (J App, *21*, 241)
Meeting: spring 1933 (Sci, *77*, 424)
Succeeded by American Assoc. of Applied Psychologists (Bull, *34*, 864)

Association of German Scientific Men and Physicians
Presentation by Külpe, O. (JoP, *7*, 504)

Association of Teachers of Psychology in the Colleges and Normal Schools of the North Central States
Meeting: report (JoP, *6*, 224; Bull, *6*, 152)

Astor, Frank
Lecture: Child research clinic of the Woods School, exceptional child (J App, *21*, 131)
Lecture: 5th annual Conference on Education and the Exceptional Child (J App, *23*, 312)

Asylums Committee/Technical Education Board (London)
Offers scholarships at Claybury Asylum (Sci, *9*, 790)

Atchley, Dana W.
Psychosomatic medicine; Associate Editor (J App, *22*, 663)

Athenaeum
Announcement: release of C. Darwin's biography by his son (Scɪ°, *8*, 411-412)

Athenaeum Club
Election: Rivers, W.H.R. (Bull, *19*, 171)

Athens, University of (Greece)
Awarded: honorary degree, Murchison, C. (Scɪ, *86*, 239)
Awarded: honorary degree, Thorndike, E. L. (Scɪ, *86*, 369)
Centenary (Bull, *34*, 635)
Centenary honorariums (Bull, *34*, 864)

Atlantic Monthly
Articles on modern psychology (Rev, *5*, 110)

Atlantic University (Virginia Beach, Virginia)
Appointment: Wallin, J.E.W. (Scɪ, *71*, 582)

Atreya, Bhikhan Lal
Election: president of Psychology and Education section of Indian Science Congress, 1943 (Scɪ, *96*, 12)

Attention
Lecture: Hicks, G. D. (JoP, *7*, 420)
Lecture: Starch, D. (JoP, *7*, 223)
Lecture: Titchener, E. B. at Univ. of Minnesota (Scɪ, *33*, 367)
Paper: Chapman, D. W.; "Attensity, clearness, and attention" (AJP, *45*, 156)
Paper: Jenkins, J. G.; "The effects of distraction" (AJP, *45*, 173)
Seminar: Dallenbach, K. M. (Scɪ, *91*, 311; AJP, *40*, 337)

Attitudes
Conscription produced; S.P.S.S.I. study (Bull, *37*, 829)
Lecture: Lehman, H. and Witty, P. A. (AJP, *43*, 664)
Paper: Bolton, T. L. (JoP, *1*, 224)
Paper: Fernberger, S. W. (AJP, *42*, 317)

Attribute and sensation
Discussion: Boring, E. G. (AJP, *35*, 301)

Atwood, Wallace Walter
Lecture: Clark Univ., Founders day exercises (J App, *9*, 87)

Audition *(see also* Acoustics, Hearing, Sound)
Appunn wire forks (JoP, *1*, 196)
Baconian lecture by Gault, R. H. (Scɪ, *73*, 123)
Bentley, M., American Otological Society (Scɪ, *69*, 618)
Discussion: Davis, H. and Saul L. J.; "Auditory action currents" (AJP, *45*, 358)

Discussion: Newman, Volkmann and Stevens on Loudness; "On the method of bisection and its relation to a loudness scale" (AJP, *49*, 134)
Discussion: Rich, G. J.; on auditory analysis (AJP, *35*, 467)
Howard Crosby Warren Medal to Wever, E. G. and Bray, C. (BULL, *33*, 476; SCI, *83*, 367)
Paper: Bruner, F. G. (JOP, *2*, 224, 280)
Stevens, S. S.; "Are tones spatial?" (AJP, *46*, 145)
Symposium at A.A.A.S., 1938 (SCI, *88*, 399)
Trimble, O. C.; National Research Council grant (SCI, *80*, 585)
Wever, E. G. and Bray, C.; National Research Council grant (BULL, *33*, 579)

Austin College (Sherman, Texas)
Appointment: Wade, B. (BULL, *42*, 793)

Australasian Association for the Advancement of Science
Meeting: first Aug, 1888 (SCI°, *12*, 226)

Australasian Association of Psychology and Philosophy
Meeting: 9th annual (JOP, *28*, 364)
Meeting: 10th annual (JOP, *29*, 532)
Meeting: 15th annual general announced, 1938; Univ. of Sydney (JOP, *35*, 448)
Meeting: 20th annual 1943 at Sydney Univ. (JOP, *41*, 56)
Meeting: 21st annual (JOP, *42*, 56)
Public lecture (JOP, *30*, 420)

Australian and New Zealand Association for the Advancement of Science
Meeting: 1939 (SCI, *88*, 495)

Australian tribes, organization of
Howitt, A. W. in the transactions of the Royal Society of Victoria (SCI°, *16*, 91)

Austrian Army
Urban, F. M., said to be with (JOP, *11*, 588)

Authoritarianism
Conference on methods in philosophy and the sciences (SCI, *87*, 277)

Authority in the modern state-Laski
Publication: Yale Univ. Press (JOP, *15*, 532)

Automobile
Desilva, H. R. heads auto-driver research, Yale (BULL, *36*, 140; SCI, *88*, 471)

Avebury, Lord (*see* Lubbock, John)

Aveling, Francis Arthur Powell
British army (London) University College (BULL, *12*, 364)
Death (AJP, *54*, 608-610; BULL, *38*, 777)

Election: British Assoc., Sect. J president (SCI, *77,* 17)
Lecture: with 5 other psychologists; "Points of view in psychology" (SCI, *69,* 450)
Psychic Research Council, Univ. of London (SCI, *80,* 183)

Avery, George True
Member: Rocky Mountain Branch of the APA (BULL, *36,* 500)
Death: (BULL, *42,* 127)

Aviation psychology (*see also* Flying)
Lecture for society of Sigma Xi by Miles, W. R. at Vanderbilt Univ. (SCI, *99,* 446)
Organization of Institute of Aviation Psychology, Univ. of Tennessee (J APP, *28,* 351-352)

Aviation Psychology Section of the Bureau of Medicine and Surgery
Appointment: Dunlap, J. W. (SCI, *97,* 327)

B

Babb, W. W. Martin
Publication: psychophysics (AJP, *44*, 367)

Babinski, Joseph François Felix
Article: effects of anesthesia (AJP, *1*, 20)

Baboon Boy of South Africa (*see also* Feral children)
Discussion: case (AJP, *53*, 455-462)
Discussion: Foley, J. P. (AJP, *53*, 128-133)

Babyhood
Paper: Chapin, H. D., "The summer care of children" (Sci°, *13*, 441)
Paper: list, June, 1889 issue (Sci°, *13*, 441)

Bach, George Robert
Appointment: Kent State Univ. (Bull, *42*, 581)
Appointment: Western Reserve Univ. (Bull, *42*, 127)

Bacon, Francis
Statue of (JoP, *5*, 672)

Bagby, English
Appointment: government service (Bull, *14*, 366)
Appointment: Univ. of North Carolina (Bull, *22*, 504; Sci, *61*, 588)
Appointment: Yale Univ. (Sci, *52*, 223)

Bagley, William Chandler
Editor *Journal of Educational Psychology* (JoP, *6*, 700; Bull, *6*, 427)

Bailey, E.H.S.
Research on sense of smell in different sexes (Sci°, *9*, 294)

Bailey, Pearce
Death notice (SCI, 55, 176)

Baillie, James Black
Publication announcement for "Phenomenology of mind" (JOP, 7, 644)

Bailor, Edwin Maurice
Appointment: Dartmouth College, Assistant professor (BULL, 22, 672)

Bain, Alexander
Death notice (REV, 10, 690; SCI, 18, 414)

Bair, Joseph Hershey
Appointment: Columbia Univ. (REV, 9, 536)
Appointment: Univ. of Colorado (BULL, 1, 94; SCI, 19, 160; JOP, 1, 56)

Baird, John Wallace
Appointment: Clark Univ. (SCI, 31, 108; JOP, 7, 84)
Appointment: Johns Hopkins Univ. (BULL, 1, 413)
Appointment: National Research Council (J APP, 2, 196)
Appointment: research assistant to Titchener, E. B. (SCI, 17, 677)
Appointment: *The Psychological Review* (JOP, 2, 672)
Appointment: Univ. of Illinois (SCI, 23, 864; BULL, 3, 184)
Death notice (SCI, 49, 213; AJP, 30, 120)
Departure: Univ. of Illinois to Clark Univ. (SCI, 31, 108)
Editor: *Journal of Applied Psychology* (JOP, 14, 252; BULL, 13, 482)
Editor: *Psychological Bulletin* (BULL, 5, 316; BULL, 6, 356; BULL, 7, 251)
Paper: Introspection (JOP, 2, 56)
Promotion: Univ. of Illinois (JOP, 4, 448; BULL, 4, 236)

Baker, Harry Jay
Announcement: publication of Detroit General Aptitude Exam (J APP, 23, 419-421)

Baker, Judge Harvey Foundation (Boston)
Appointment: Healy, W. (BULL, 14, 32; J APP, 1, 98)

Baker, Lawrence Manning
Director: Kentucky Psychological Assoc. (J APP, 25, 725)

Baker University (Baldwin City, Kansas)
Appointment: Cowling, D. J. (BULL, 3, 288; JOP, 3, 504)

Bakewell, Charles Montague
Appointment: Bryn Mawr College (REV, 5, 449)
Appointment: Harvard Univ. (REV, 3, 356)
Appointment: Univ. of California (REV, 7, 428)
Departure: Bryn Mawr College (REV, 7, 428)

Election: president of American Philosophical Assoc. (JoP, 7, 28)
Presentation: American Philosophical Assoc. (JoP, 8, 27-28)
Presentation: empiricism (JoP, 2, 700)

Baldwin, Bird Thomas

Appointment: APA committee on certification (Sci, 51, 137)
Appointment: Johns Hopkins Univ. (JoP, 13, 700; Bull, 13, 407)
Appointment: Swarthmore College (Bull, 9, 128; JoP, 9, 168; JoP, 3, 336; Sci, 35, 303)
Appointment: Univ. of Chicago (Bull, 6, 184)
Appointment: Univ. of Iowa (Bull, 14, 365)
Appointment: Univ. of Texas (Sci, 32, 342, 464; Bull, 7, 364)
Chair: committee on child development National Research Council (Bull, 22, 672)
Collaboration with Terman on gifted children study (Sci, 57, 380)
Commissioned in the Sanitary Corps (Bull, 15, 98)
Course: Johns Hopkins Univ. (Bull, 12, 403)
Death notice (Bull, 25, 376)
Departure: Univ. of Chicago (Bull, 7, 364)
Departure: Univ. of Texas (Bull, 9, 128)
Editor: *The Psychological Bulletin* (Bull, 14, 365; Bull, 15, 324; Bull, 12, 403; Bull, 16, 391)
Election: APA office (Bull, 16, 32)
Leave of absence: Swarthmore College (Bull, 6, 184)
Leave of absence: West Chester State Normal School (Bull, 6, 184)
Publication: correction (AJP, 33, 449)

Baldwin, James Mark

Address on selective thinking at APA (AJP, 9, 250)
Appointment: French Academy of Moral and Political Sciences (JoP, 7, 420)
Appointment: Johns Hopkins Univ. (Rev, 10, 690; Sci, 18, 352)
Appointment: National Univ. of Mexico (JoP, 7, 672)
Appointment: Oxford Univ., Herbert Spencer Lecturer for 1915 (Bull, 12, 204; JoP, 12, 336)
Appointment: Paris (Bull, 14, 420)
Appointment: Princeton Univ. (Sci°, 21, 187)
Award: Danish Royal Academy of Arts and Sciences (Rev, 4, 340)
Collaboration: Richet, C. on a book (Sci, 2, 187)
Comments on edition of *Dictionary of Philosophy and Psychology* (JoP, 8, 504)
Course: Mexican Department of Public Instruction on university organization (Sci, 29, 788)
Course: psychosociology, National Univ. of Mexico (Bull, 7, 396)
Criticism of article on instinct by Mills (Sci, 3, 669)
Death notice (JoP, 31, 671)
Degree: College of South Carolina (Bull, 2, 88)
Degree: Oxford Univ. (Rev, 7, 427)
Degree: Univ. of Geneva (JoP, 6, 560; Bull, 6, 328)

Degree: Univ. of Glasgow (REV, 8, 552; SCI, 14, 37)

Editor: *Dictionary of Philosophy and Psychology* (REV, 3, 467; AJP, 7, 452; REV, 5, 345)

Editor: *Psychological Bulletin* (JoP, 1, 84)

Editor: *The Library of Historical Psychology* (BULL, 1, 29; REV, 10, 344)

Election: French Acad. of Moral and Political Sciences, corresponding member (SCI, 32, 108; BULL, 7, 251)

Election: 6th International Congress of Psychology, President (SCI, 30, 202)

Endorses International Society of the Psychical Institute (SCI, 12, 238)

Grant: Univ. of Toronto (AJP, 3, 593)

History of psychology volumes listed (REV, 10, 592)

International committee, 5th International Congress of Psychology (JoP, 2, 56)

International Congress of Arts and Sciences, St. Louis (JoP, 1, 419)

Leave of absence: Princeton Univ. (SCI, 10, 341; AJP, 11, 130)

Leaves for England to finish *Dictionary of Philosophy and Psychology* (REV, 6, 572; SCI, 13, 598)

Leaves for Europe (SCI, 17, 597)

Leaves for Paris (JoP, 10, 112)

Lecture: Columbia College for Women (BULL, 10, 123)

Lecture: Glenmore Summer School of the Culture Sciences (BULL, 1, 334)

Lecture: Johns Hopkins Univ. (BULL, 3, 36)

Lecture: Mexico City Board of Education (JoP, 6, 308)

Lecture: National Univ. of Mexico, psychosociology (BULL, 9, 208; JoP, 9, 335)

Lecture: Paris (BULL, 10, 123)

Lecture: series announced on social psychology (JoP, 1, 280)

Lecture: Univ. of California (BULL, 2, 159; REV, 9, 328; SCI, 22, 32; JoP, 2, 420; SCI°, 15, 400)

Lecture: Univ. of Chicago (BULL, 3, 83; REV, 10, 224; JoP, 3, 168)

Lecture: Univ. of South Carolina (BULL, 10, 123)

Lecture: Univ. of Tennessee (BULL, 1, 173; JoP, 1, 280)

Letter contradicting Hall, G. S. (SCI, 2, 627)

Notice of publication of *Dictionary of Philosophy and Psychology* (SCI, 3, 702)

Obituary by Washburn, M. F. (AJP, 47, 168)

President of Southern Society for Philosphy and Psychology (JoP, 1, 168)

Protests placing psychology under physiology (AJP, 11, 281)

Publication: announcements on thought and Darwinism (JoP, 7, 644)

Publication: evolution in *The American Naturalist* (SCI, 4, 139)

Publication: in press (BULL, 3, 392)

Publication: *Library of Historical Psychology* (SCI, 17, 679)

Publication: *Mental Development in the Child and the Race* (SCI°, 23, 95)

Publication: translated into German (BULL, 4, 200)

Publication: translated into German and French (REV, 5, 677)

Publication: translated into German and French, *Mental Development of the Child and the Race* (REV, 3, 356)

Publication: translated into Spanish (BULL, 1, 93; BULL, 4, 200)

Research: abroad for summer to work on *Dictionary of Philosophy and Psychology* (REV, 8, 335)

Research: Mexican universities (BULL, *3*, 36)
Resignation: International Congress for Psychology, 7th (BULL, *7*, 108)
Resignation: Johns Hopkins Univ. (JoP, *6*, 448) (BULL, *6*, 256; SCI, *30*, 81)
Resignation: Princeton Univ. (BULL, *1*, 134)
Resignation: *Psychological Review* (JoP, *7*, 140)
Returns to U.S. from Oxford (SCI, *12*, 157; REV, *7*, 532)
Revising *Dictionary of Philosophy and Psychology* at Oxford (REV, *6*, 673)
Withdraws name from Committee of Patrons of the International Psychical
   Institute of Paris (REV, *8*, 112)

Baldwin, Joseph
Death notice (SCI, *9*, 118)

Baldwin Lectureship
Appointment: Wenley, R. M. (BULL, *4*, 401)

Balfour, Arthur James
Appointment: Gifford Lecturer (JoP, *9*, 336)

Ball, Josephine
APA, Wash-Balt Branch, 1940 (BULL, *37*, 657)

Ball, Rachel Stutsman
Appointment: Goucher College (BULL, *42*, 791)

Ball, Richard Stuart
Indiana Univ. Psych lab 50th anniversary commemoration; "The Bryan
   Symposium" (J APP, *23*, 631)

Baller, Warren Robert
Address at MPA; "Dull" people experiment (J APP, *24*, 369)

Ballet, Gilbert
Death notice (BULL, *13*, 188)

Balliol College (Oxford, England)
Endowment: memory of Spencer, H. (JoP, *1*, 252)
John Locke scholarship (JoP, *1*, 56)
Meeting: International Medical Society of Psychotherapy (BULL, *35*, 408)
Resignation: Caird, E. (JoP, *4*, 336)

Baltimore, Maryland
Tribute Gilman, D. C. (SCI, *11*, 38-39)

Baly Medal of the Royal College of Physicians
Award: Bartlett, F. C. (SCI, *98*, 238; BULL, *40*, 723)

Balz, Albert George Adam
 Election: Executive Committee of Eastern Division of the American
   Philosophical Assoc. (JoP, *34*, 28)
 Lecture: SSPP 35th meeting (JoP, *37*, 196)
 President: SSPP 31st meeting (JoP, *33*, 223)

Banay, Ralph
 Appointment: Yale University Clinic for Inebriates (Sci, *99*, 99)

Barber, Alda
 Resignation: Univ. of Texas (Bull, *14*, 263)

Barber, Frank Louis
 Appointment: Univ. of Toronto (Bull, *3*, 36; Bull, *4*, 32)

Barker Foundation of Chicago
 Touch and language research grant to Gault, R. (Sci, *74*, 264; Bull, *28*, 645)

Barker, Lewellys Franklin
 Election: Vice-President of Assoc. for Research in Nervous and Mental Diseases
   (Sci, *79*, 9)

Barker, Roger Garlock
 Appointment: Harvard Psychological Clinic (Bull, *34*, 635)
 Award: Social Science Research Council (Bull, *39*, 683)

Barmack, Joseph Ephraim
 Discussion: boredom (AJP, *52*, 467-471)

Barnard College, Columbia University (New York, New York)
 Appointment: Henmon, V. A. C. (Bull, *3*, 248)
 Appointment: McMurray; Simpson; Spragg, S.; Youtz, R. (Bull, *34*, 635)
 Appointment: Woodrow, H. H. (Sci, *29*, 455; JoP, *6*, 252; Bull, *6*, 152; Bull,
   4, 336)
 Departure: Andrews, T. G. (Bull, *41*, 603)
 Departure: Crawford, M. P. (Sci, *92*, 31)
 Promotion: Hollingworth, H. L. (Bull, *11*, 232; Bull, *19*, 350; Sci, *43*, 641; JoP,
   11, 336; JoP, *13*, 280)

Barnes, Earl
 Appointment: Cornell Univ. (Rev, *5*, 344)
 Lecture: Univ. of Chicago (Rev, *3*, 356)
 Vineland lab 25th anniversary (Sci, *74*, 286)

Barnes, Jasper Converse
 Appointment: Wyoming, summer (Sci, *67*, 13)
 Death notice (Bull, *29*, 91)

Election: SSPP office (BULL, *13*, 40; JoP, *13*, 112)
Lecture: SSPP, "Voluntary Isolation of Control in a Group" (JoP, 7, 28)

Barnes, Julius H.

Public Service New York City (J APP, *3*, 290)

Barrett, Albert Moore

Death notice (SCI, *85*, 14)

Barrett, F. W.

Account of trip to America in *The Journal of the Society for Psychical Research*
and formation of American Society (SCI°, 5, 62)
Presidency of Society for Psychical Research (JoP, *1*, 112)

Barrett, Laura

Social Science Research Council; Secretary for fellowships and grants-in-aid
(BULL, *37*, 829)

Barrows, Samuel J.

Appointment: National Library (SCI, 9, 267-268)
Librarian of Congress confirmation failed (SCI, 9, 380)

Barry, Herbert, Jr.

Finkelstein, S.; "The visual imagery of a lightning calculator" (AJP, 45, 353)

Bartlett, Frederic Charles

Appointment: British Medical Research Council (SCI, *94*, 605; BULL, *39*, 196)
Appointment: Cambridge (SCI, *56*, 43)
Award: Baly Medal of the Royal College of Physicians, London (BULL, *40*, 723;
SCI, *98*, 238)
Departure: Univ. of Cambridge (BULL, *39*, 196)
Election: Fellow of Royal Society (BULL, *29*, 460)
Election: psychology president of British Association for the Advancement of
Science (SCI, *88*, 612)
Lecture. (Huxley) at Royal Anthropological Institute (BULL, *41*, 136; SCI, *98*,
512)
Lecture: Thomas Young oration on visual perception (SCI, *97*, 577)
Panel for censorship of scientific papers in journals to assist Press and
Censorship Bureau (SCI, *91*, 288)

Barton, Joseph Wesley

Appointment: Univ. of Idaho (BULL, *19*, 171)
Appointment: Univ. of Wyoming (SCI, *52*, 537; BULL, *18*, 111)
Promotion: Univ. of Idaho (SCI, *55*, 262)

Baskett, Edgar D.

Promotion: Univ. of Missouri (SCI, *74*, 146)

Basoglu, Muzaffer Serif (*see also* Sherif, Muzafer)
Fellowship granted at Princeton Univ. (SCI, *100*, 516)

Basset, Gardner Cheney
Appointment: Eugenics Record Office of the Station for Experimental
Evolution at Cold Spring Harbor (BULL, *10*, 291; SCI, *37*, 903; JOP, *10*,
503-504)
Appointment: Gettysburg College (SCI, *72*, 315)
Appointment: Univ. of Kentucky (SCI, *64*, 448; J APP, *10*, 522)
Appointment: Univ. of Pittsburgh (BULL, *11*, 443)
Appointment: Univ. of Wisconsin (BULL, *24*, 136)
Departure: Carnegie Lab of Evolution at Cold Spring Harbor (BULL, *11*, 443)
Promotion: Univ. of Pittsburgh (BULL, *12*, 404)

Bassi, G.
Research on mental distress (SCI°, *18*, 88)

Bates, Marjory
Promotion (BULL, *20*, 172)

**Battle Creek Chamber of Commerce and County Medical
Society (Michigan)**
Kellogg, J. H., guest of honor at dinner (SCI, *95*, 298)

Battle Creek Sanitarium (Michigan)
Changed to government managed, name changed to Percy L. Jones General
Hospital (SCI, *96*, 133)
War department took over as hospital, 1942 (SCI, *95*, 551)

Bavarian Maximillian Order
Award: Mach, E. (JOP, *3*, 476; SCI, *24*, 60)

Bawden, Henry Heath
Moved to California (BULL, *13*, 407)
Publication: announcement (BULL, *5*, 243)
Publication: pragmatism (JOP, *5*, 447)

Bayley, Nancy
Appointment: Univ. of Wyoming (J APP, *10*, 523)

Bayton, James Arthur
Appointment: Southern Univ. (BULL, *42*, 791)

Beach, Frank Ambrose
Lecture: Indiana Univ. "The neural and hormonal factors involved in
reproductive behavior" (SCI, *99*, 168)

Beals, A. H.
Appointment: Georgia Normal and Industrial College, Milledgeville (Sci°, *18*, 297)

Beals, Clyde
Editor *Propaganda Analysis Bulletin* (J App, *25*, 597)

Bean, Robert Bennett
Publication: "The negro brain century" (JoP, *3*, 615)

Beard, George Miller
Sounds alarm over worries regarding civilization (Sci°, *3*, 56)

Beard, John
Paper: heredity (JoP, *1*, 420)

Beatty, A. J.
Appointment: Carnegie Insitute of Technology (Bull, *14*, 263; JoP, *14*, 616)
Resignation: Carnegie Insitute of Technology (JoP, *15*, 336)

Beaumont, Commodore Louis D.
Donation for hypertension research at Western Reserve Univ. (Sci, *93*, 37)

Beaumont, Henry
Appointment: Kentucky (Sci, *72*, 315)
Psychological residential study tour (J App, *17*, 97)

Beaunis, Henri Etienne
Death notice (Bull, *18*, 568)

Becher, Erich
Appointment: Univ. of Munich (JoP, *14*, 56)
Appointment: Univ. of Munster (JoP, *7*, 84)
Death notice (Sci, *69*, 68)
Succeeds Külpe, O. at Univ. of Munich (Bull, *13*, 448)

Beck, Lester Fred
Appointment: Brown Univ. (Bull, *28*, 412)
Appointment: Ohio Univ. (J App, *20*, 421)
Election: Oregon Psychological Assoc., Secretary (Sci, *85*, 518)

Beck, Roland Lycurgus
Leave of absence from Central State College, Oklahoma (Bull, *41*, 409)

Beck, Samuel Jacob
Appointment: Harvard Medical School (Bull, *29*, 603; Sci, *76*, 97)
Appointment: Michael Reese Hospital (Bull, *34*, 58)
Course on Rorschach test, 1941 (Bull, *38*, 305)
Course on Rorschach test, 1942 (Bull, *39*, 325-326; J App, *26*, 248)

Course on Rorschach test, 1943 (J App, 27, 207)
Course on Rorschach test (Bull, 36, 219; Bull, 37, 406; Bull, 40, 384; Bull, 41, 343; Bull, 42, 256; J App, 23, 207; J App, 24, 245)
Resignation: Boston Psychopathic Hospital (Bull, 29, 603)
Resignation: editorial board of *Journal of Clinical Psychology* (Bull, 42, 485)

Beckham, Albert Sidney
Degree awarded from Lincoln Univ. (Bull, 42, 791)

Bedford College (London)
Appointment: Harding, D. W. (Sci, 102, 219-220)
Lecture: series on ethical and psychological aspects of war (JoP, 12, 140)

Beebe-Center, John Gilbert
German Psychological Warfare (J App, 25, 359)

Beebe, Ruth White
Appointment: Child Study Center of Maryland (Bull, 41, 409)

Beenham, Ethel
Psychic research (Sci, 80, 183)

Beers, Clifford Whittingham
Lecture: 20th anniversary Massachusetts Society for Mental Hygiene (Sci, 77, 423)
Mental Hygiene anniversary dinner (Sci, 70, 536)
National Committee for Mental Hygiene (Sci, 80, 446)
National Committee for Mental Hygiene, secretary (Sci, 72, 557)
National Inst. of Social Sciences; gold medal for mental hygiene achievements (Sci, 77, 423)

Behavioral research
Fund established (Sci, 64, 648)
Harvard tercentenary conference (Bull, 33, 476)
Hunt, W. A., awarded grant for research by National Research Council (Bull, 33, 578)

Behaviorism
Course: Watson, J. B. (Bull, 20, 172)
Discussion: 10th conference of Experimental Psychologists (Bull, 10, 211-212)
Ogden, R. M.; "Gestalt psychology and behaviorism" (AJP, 45, 151)
Paper: Pickworth, F. E. (AJP, 38, 660)

Behavior Monographs
Publication: announcement by Henry Holt and Co. (JoP, 8, 559-560)

Beier, Delton Clifford
Appointment: Indiana Univ. (Bull, 42, 791)

Award: James McKeen Cattell grants-in-aid, 1942-43 (BULL, *39*, 683)
Departure: Univ. of Wisconsin (BULL, *42*, 791)

Beiträge zur Psychologie der Aussage

Name changed to Zeitschrift fur Angewandte Psychologie und Psychologische
  Sammelforschung (AJP, *18*, 529)
New publication (REV, *10*, 464)

Beiträge zur Psychologie und Philosphie

New German journal edited by Gatz Martius (SCI, *3*, 354)
Publication announced (REV, *3*, 355)

Bekhterev, Vladimir Mikhailovich

Anniversary: 40th as professor (SCI, *62*, 453; SCI, *63*, 160)
Appointment: New Psycho-Neurological Institute, St. Petersburg, Director
  (SCI, *27*, 320; JOP, *5*, 224: BULL, *5*, 168)
Death notice (BULL, *25*, 568)

Belgian Academy of Sciences

Election: Koch, R. (SCI, *9*, 420)

Belgian relief work

Angell, F. takes part (JOP, *13*, 84)

Belgium

Psychology exhibition, 1888 (SCI°, *12*, 9)

Belgium Neurological Society (*see* Neurological Society of)

Belhomme Prize

Competition announced (AJP, *1*, 197)

Bell, Alexander Graham

Appearance before the British Royal Commission (SCI°, *11*, 252)
Lecture: Fallacies concerning the deaf (SCI°, *2*, 635)
Paper: Teaching a deaf boy to read and write (SCI°, *2*, 780)

Bell, Alexander Melville

Publication: Teaching methods of visible speech (SCI°, *2*, 30)
Visible-speech letters criticized by Fernald, F. A. (SCI°, *2*, 452)

Bell, Elizabeth

Appointment: Park College (MO) (BULL, *40*, 723)

Bell, Hugh McKee

Adjustment inventory (J APP, *23*, 420)

Bell, James Carleton
Appointment: Brooklyn Training School for Teachers (Sci, *26*, 32; Bull, *4*, 236; JoP, *4*, 392)
Appointment: Univ. of Texas (JoP, *9*, 364; Bull, *9*, 280)
Appointment: Wellesley College (JoP, *2*, 336; Bull, *2*, 426; Sci, *21*, 800; JoP, *3*, 28)
Course: Univ. of Tennessee (Bull, *12*, 403)
Editor: *Journal of Educational Psychology* (JoP, *6*, 700; Bull, *6*, 427)
Lecture: NYAS meeting, Binet-Simon and Squire tests comparison (JoP, *13*, 700)
Resignation: editor, *Journal of Educational Psychology* (JoP, *9*, 364)
Retirement: City College of New York (Bull, *40*, 310)

Bell, John Elderkin
Appointment: Clark Univ. (Bull, *42*, 191)

Bell, Sanford
Appointment: Mount Holyoke College (Sci, *13*, 1000)

Bellevue Hospital (New York, New York)
Appointment: Bowman, K. M.; Director of Psychiatry (Sci, *83*, 181)
Appointment: Hollingworth, L. S. (JoP, *13*, 476)
Appointment: Wortis, S. B. (Sci, *96*, 293)
New psychiatric hospital (Sci, *70*, 306)
Psychological lab established (JoP, *13*, 476; Bull, *13*, 376)

Bellingham State Normal College (Washington)
Kilpatrick, E. A., exchange professor (JoP, *14*, 224)

Bellows, Roger Marion
Instructor for course on personnel psychology at New York Univ. (Sci, *98*, 299)
Lecture: APA, Wash-Balt Branch, 1939 (Bull, *36*, 712)

Beloit College (Wisconsin)
Appointment: DeWeerdt, O. (Sci, *58*, 465)
Appointment: McGinnis, J. M. (Bull, *41*, 72)
Appointment: Tawney, G. A. (Rev, *4*, 106)
Appointment: Waugh, K. T. (Bull, *6*, 427)
Promotion: Tawney, G. A. (Rev, *6*, 239)

Benjamin, John
Psychoanalytic case studies of suicides (J App, *22*, 108)

Bennett, Alexander Hughes
Death notice (Sci, *14*, 821; Rev, *9*, 104)

Bennett, Charles J. C.
Appointment: Louisiana State Univ. (Sci, *22*, 648; Bull, *2*, 427)
Degree: Columbia Univ. (Sci, *22*, 648)

Bennett, Charles Wesley
Publication: Pedagogics (Sci°, 22, 254)

Bennett, Chester Clarke
Rochester Guidance Clinic, NY; Mental hygiene (BULL, 36, 841)

Bennett Foundation, George Slogum
Lecture: Wesleyan Univ., Thorndike, E. L. (Sci, 71, 283)

Bennett, George Kettner
Editor: *Test Service Bulletin* (J App, 23, 421)
Psychological Corporation meeting with APA and AAAP, 1941,
  Assistant-secretary (J App, 25, 600)

Bennington College (Vermont)
Appointment: Hanks, L. M. (BULL, 39, 808)

Bensley, Mary L.
Appointment: Univ. of Buffalo (BULL, 42, 791)

Benson, Charles Emile
Leave of absence: New York Univ, 1942-43 (BULL, 39, 682)
Lecture: Conference on Education and the Exceptional Child, 5th (J App, 23,
  312)
Retirement: New York Univ. (BULL, 42, 331)

Bentham, George
Eulogy: at Linnaean Society (Sci°, 11, 277)
Implications of his will (Sci°, 5, 122)

Bentley, Arthur Fisher
Paper at conference on methods in philosophy and the sciences (Sci, 87, 277)

Bentley, Issac Madison
American Journal of Psychology, cover page change (AJP, 48, 177)
Appointment: Cornell Univ. (Sci, 96, 249; Sci, 67, 215; BULL, 39, 807; AJP, 9,
  135; AJP, 10, 166; Sci, 15, 880)
Appointment: Cornell Univ., Sage professor (BULL, 25, 307; JoP, 25, 504)
Appointment: Library of Congress (Sci, 88, 31)
Appointment: managing editor of AJP (temporary) (AJP, 55, 583)
Appointment: Univ. of Illinois (JoP, 9, 588; BULL, 9, 407; Sci, 36, 401)
Attendance at summer station in psychology, Cornell Univ. (Sci, 91, 430)
Award: doctor of laws degree (BULL, 32, 862)
Award: honorary degree from Univ. of Nebraska (Sci, 82, 34)
Chair: Div of Anthro. and Psych. at National Research Council (Sci, 72, 11)
Departure: Cornell Univ. (BULL, 9, 407; JoP, 9, 588)
Discussion: by Dallenbach, K. M. "Professor Bentley retires from teaching"
  (AJP, 51, 579)

Discussion: "Conjunctive research in the sciences of life" (AJP, *48*, 519)
Discussion: individual psychology (AJP, *52*, 300-301)
Discussion: "Psychological background of the doctoral candidate" (AJP, *51*, 171)
Editor: *American Journal of Psychology* (BULL, *39*, 807; SCI, *96*, 249; SCI, *63*, 88)
Editor: Psychological Index (BULL, *12*, 403)
Election: AAAS Section I; Vice-president (BULL, *26*, 56)
Election: AAAS; Vice-president, 1930 (SCI, *72*, 499)
Election: editorial board Psychological Review Publications (BULL, *12*, 403; JoP, *12*, 644)
Experimental psychology in the Orient (AJP, *37*, 154)
Guest of American Otological Society (SCI, *69*, 618)
Leave of absence: Cornell Univ. (BULL, *32*, 322)
Leave of absence: Indian research, Cornell Univ. (SCI, *80*, 378)
Leave of absence: mental disorder studies, Cornell Univ. (SCI, *75*, 189)
Lecture: APA, Wash-Balt branch, 3rd meeting, 1939 (BULL, *36*, 500)
Lecture: Clark Univ. (SCI, *63*, 65)
Lecture: Goucher College (SCI, *94*, 38)
Lecture: Library of Congress (SCI, *94*, 38)
Lecture: Mayo Foundation (SCI, *76*, 270)
Lecture: Sigma Xi of Missouri and Kansas (SCI, *59*, 14, 160)
Lecture: Rochester Psychology Society, 1941 (SCI, *94*, 38)
Lecture: Univ. of California (SCI, *57*, 689)
Lecture: Univ. of California, summer school (BULL, *18*, 438; BULL, *19*, 236)
Paper: on tones (JoP, *2*, 223)
Portrait at Cornell (BULL, *35*, 577; SCI, *88*, 31)
Promotion: Cornell Univ. (REV, *9*, 432)
Rebuttal to paper by Dashiell, J. (AJP, *42*, 320)
Rebuttal to paper by Williamson, E. G. (AJP, *42*, 320)
Retirement: Cornell Univ. (SCI, *88*, 31; SCI, *87*, 482)

Bentley, Rufus C.
Promotion: Clark Univ. (SCI, *16*, 80, 200)

Benton, Arthur Lester
Appointment: Personnel Bureau of City College, New York (SCI, *89*, 217)
Treasurer N.Y. State Assoc. for Applied Psych (BULL, *37*, 405)

Benussi, Vittorio
Death notice (BULL, *25*, 568)

Bergman, L. V.
"Portraits useful to the psychologist" (AJP, *45*, 165)

Bergson, Henri
Announcement: guide to Bergson philosophy by Lindsay, A. D. (JoP, *9*, 84)
Appointment: Columbia Univ. visiting professor (JoP, *9*, 112; JoP, *10*, 112)
Lecture: American Academy of Arts and Letters (JoP, *14*, 252)
Lecture: French Academy acceptance (JoP, *15*, 196)

Lecture: Gifford lecture at Univ. of Edinburgh (JoP, 9, 56)
Publication: announcement of "Matter and memory" (JoP, 7, 644)

Bergström, John A.
Appointment: Indiana Univ. (REV, 2, 432)
Death notice (BULL, 7, 147; JoP, 7, 224)
Leave of absence: Indiana Univ. (SCI, 13, 598)

Beringer, Kurt
Succeeds Bostroem, A., Psychiatry chair, Munich (SCI, 77, 20)

Berkeley, Henry J.
Donation of books to Johns Hopkins Univ. (SCI, 45, 185)

Berkey, Charles P.
Councillor to NYAS (JoP, 9, 28)

Berlin Academy of Sciences
Celebration of 200 years (SCI, 11, 518)
Election: Heinze, M. (REV, 7, 323)
Election: James, W. (REV, 7, 323)
Election: Wundt, W. (REV, 7, 323)

Berlin Anthropological Society
Award: Rudolf-Virchow Medal to Pearson, K. (SCI, 77, 16)

Berlin Museum of Hygiene
Opening (SCI°, 8, 513)

Berlin Physiological Society
Speech by Rosenthal, I. on calorimetric experiments (SCI°, 13, 379-380)

Berlin Psychiatric and Neurologic Clinic
Resignation: Ziehen, T. (JoP, 9, 140)

Berlin, University of (Germany)
Announcement: exchange with Harvard Univ. (JoP, 2, 140)
Appointment: Adler, F. (JoP, 4, 252)
Appointment: Dessoir, M. (SCI°, 6, 736)
Appointment: Erdmann, B. (JoP, 6, 560, 700; BULL, 6, 368)
Appointment: Hess, H. (SCI, 35, 215)
Appointment: Köhler, W. (SCI, 55, 313)
Appointment: Münsterberg, H. (SCI, 33, 212)
Appointment: Piper, H. (BULL, 6, 120)
Appointment: Riehl, A. (JoP, 2, 644)
Appointment: Schumann, F. (AJP, 7, 152)
Appointment: Stumpf, C. W. (BULL, 4, 338; JoP, 4, 560)
Appointment: Woodbridge, F. J. E. (JoP, 28, 308)

Appointment: Ziehen, T. (BULL, 1, 174)
Celebration of 89th birthday of Zeller, E. (SCI, 17, 398)
Chair of hygiene (SCI°, 5, 204)
Chair of psychiatry filled by Ziehen, T. (JOP, 1, 196)
Death: Helmholtz, H. (SCI, 1, 55)
Death: Lazarus, M. (SCI, 17, 718)
Departure: Dilthey, W. (JOP, 2, 644)
Departure: Ebbinghaus, H. (REV, 1, 440)
Election: Stumpf, C. Rector (SCI, 26, 325)
Helmholtz statue (SCI, 9, 917)
Hygienic laboratory to be instituted (SCI°, 5, 204)
Institute of Hygiene building progress (SCI°, 6, 360)
Köhler,W., visiting lecturer at Harvard (JOP, 22, 252)
Köhler,W. visiting professor at Clark Univ. (JOP, 22, 56)
Laboratory forming (AJP, 7, 152)
Promotion: Dessoir, M. (REV, 5, 109)
Return: Köhler,W. (SCI, 63, 161)
Stumpf, C. accepts chair (REV, 1, 112, 336)

Berliner, Sarah, Research Fellowship for Women

Announcement and application information (JOP, 8, 420; BULL, 8, 302)
Award: Rand, M. G., for work on psychology of vision (JOP, 9, 168)
Request for workers in psych. (AJP, 22, 475)

Berman, Arthur

Discussion: boredom (AJP, 52, 471-473)
Discussion: satiation (AJP, 52, 297-299)

Bernhardt, Martin

Death notice (BULL, 12, 204)

Bernreuter, Robert Gibbon

Appointment: Univ. of Hawaii (J APP, 11, 404)
Appointment: U.S. Army (BULL, 39, 807)
Appointment: Washington Univ. (J APP, 13, 415)
Leave of absence: Pennsylvania State College (SCI, 96, 250; BULL, 39, 807)
Major's commission in U.S. Army Specialists Corps (SCI, 96, 250)

Berrien, Frederick Kenneth

Appointment: Harvard Univ. (temporary) (BULL, 42, 791)
Leave of absence: Colgate Univ. (BULL, 42, 791)

Berry, Charles Scott

Appointment: State Dept. of Education of Ohio, mentally handicapped (SCI, 72, 316)
Election: sec/treas Clinical Psychology Section, APA (BULL, 23, 112)

Berry, Richard James Arthur
Lecture: Univ. of Melbourne (SCI, 55, 125)

Berry, William
Appointment: Univ. of Rochester (BULL, 19, 586)

Bertheau, Rudolph
American Eugenics Society, in charge of new offices (SCI, 83, 573)

Bertheldt, M.
On "Introduction à l'étude de la chimie des anciens et du moyen age" at the
Academy of Sciences, Paris (SCI°, 13, 238)

Bertillon, Alphonse
Identification of criminals (AJP, 1, 205)

Bertocci, Peter Anthony
Appointment: Boston Univ (BULL, 42, 191)

Bethe, Albrecht
Editor: *Pflüger's Archiv* (BULL, 17, 200)

Betz, Wilhelm
Death notice (AJP, 43, 145)

Bianchi, Leonardo
Director of university clinic for nervous and mental diseases (JoP, 13, 448)
Hygienic and social problems arising out of war (JoP, 13, 448)
Member of new Italian Ministry (JoP, 13, 448)
Paper: hysteria (AJP, 1, 202)

Biel, William Collins
Appointment: Miami Univ (BULL, 37, 827)
Appointment: Ohio State Univ. (J APP, 21, 474; BULL, 34, 499)

Bigelow, Newton J. T.
Appointment: New York State, Assistant Commissioner of Mental Hygiene (SCI,
98, 447)

Bigham, John
Appointment: DePauw Univ. (REV, 2, 642)
Appointment: Univ. of Michigan (REV, 2, 104)
Retirement: DePauw Univ. (REV, 5, 449)

Billings, John Shaw
Lecture: science of hygiene in a liberal education, Johns Hopkins Univ., 1885
(SCI°, 5, 101)

Bills, Arthur Gilbert
Appointment: Univ. of Cincinnati (BULL, *34*, 325)
Appointment: Univ. of Cincinnati, Dept head (SCI, *85*, 424)
Appointment: Univ. of Minnesota (BULL, *23*, 455)
Discussion: 11th annual meeting Midwestern Psychological Assoc. (AJP, *48*, 526)
Discussion: 12th annual meeting Midwestern Psychological Assoc. (AJP, *49*, 486)
Election: president MPA (J APP, *22*, 106; J APP, *21*, 716)
President MPA meeting, 1938 (BULL, *35*, 188; SCI, *87*, 84)

Bills, Marion Almira
Election: AAAP, treasurer (J APP, *28*, 79)

Binet, Alfred
Comment on his work (JoP, *8*, 672)
Death notice (SCI, *34*, 558; BULL, *8*, 406; JoP, *8*, 644)
Editor: *Intermédiaire des Biologistes* (AJP, *9*, 250)
Publication: *Année Psychologique* (REV, *1*, 336)
Publication: "Sensation and the outer world" in *The Open Court* (SCI°, *13*, 217)
Publication: *The Mind and the Brain* (JoP, *4*, 504)

Binet-Buzenet aesthesiometer
Presentation by Hill, D. S. (JoP, *7*, 28)

Binet-Simon tests
Conference (SCI, *38*, 329)
Conference: Terman, L. M. (BULL, *10*, 424; JoP, *10*, 560)
Paper: Decroly, O. J. (BULL, *11*, 191)
Work at George Washington Univ. (BULL, *12*, 244)

Bingham, Harold Clyde
Appointment: Yale Univ. (SCI, *61*, 388; BULL, *22*, 444)

Bingham, Walter Van Dyke
Appointment: Carnegie Institute of Technology (BULL, *12*, 160; JoP, *12*, 196)
Appointment: Dartmouth College (SCI, *31*, 950; BULL, *7*, 220; JoP, *7*, 448)
Appointment: Dartmouth Summer School (JoP, *9*, 224)
Appointment: National Council of Research, Div of Anthropology and Psychology; Chair (SCI, *50*, 522)
Appointment: National Research Council (JoP, *17*, 83; J APP, *3*, 394)
Appointment: Personnel Research Federation; Director (BULL, *22*, 140)
Appointment: Stevens Institute of Technology (BULL, *27*, 674)
Attendance: 4th International Congress of Techno-psychology (SCI, *66*, 298; BULL, *25*, 198)
Award: emblem for exceptional civilian service from Secretary of War (SCI, *100*, 400-401)
Bureau of Salesmanship Research (JoP, *13*, 140)

Biophysikalisches Centralbaltt
Publication announced (JoP, 2, 721)

Bird, Charles
Publication: "Higher education in Germany and England" (Sci°, 4, 502)

Bird, Grace Electa
Appointment: Rhode Island State College (Bull, 16, 392)
Retirement: Rhode Island State College (Bull, 40, 79)

Bird temperament
Research: Torrey, B. (Sci°, 2, 386)

Birkbeck College (University of London)
Appointment: Mace, C. A. (Bull, 42, 63)

Birmingham, University of
Annual conference of British Child-study Assoc. (JoP, 2, 280)
Course: McDougall, W. (Bull, 17, 200)

Bisch, Louis E.
Appointment: New York City Police Dept. (Bull, 13, 188)

Bishop, Homer Guy
Appointment: Smith College (Sci, 61, 117; Bull, 22, 140, 260)
Appointment: Wittenberg College (Bull, 23, 456; J App, 10, 522)
Discussion: Demonstrational color series (AJP, 34, 469)
Discussion: Stern variater (AJP, 34, 150)

Bishop, Margaret Kincaid
Appointment: Wittenberg College (Bull, 23, 456; J App, 10, 522)

Bitterman, Morton Edward
Discussion: electromyographic technique in recording eyelid movement (AJP, 58, 112-113)
Discussion: fatigue (AJP, 57, 569-573)

Blacker, Charles Paton
Essay on "Eugenics and social progress" (JoP, 34, 644)

Blackett, M.
Grant from Laura Spelman Rockefeller Fund for industrial psych research (Sci, 66, 374)

Blakeslee, Albert Francis
Lecture: Phi Beta Kappa at College of Wooster "Personality in relation to science and society" (Sci, 95, 220)

Blanchard, Phyllis
Appointment: Univ. of Pennsylvania Medical School (SCI, *62*, 311; BULL, *23*, 60)

Blanford, G. F.
Death notice (SCI, *34*, 376; SCI, *34*, 376)

Blanton, Smiley
Appointment: Vassar College (SCI, *64*, 649)

Blatz, William Emet
Appointment: Iowa State College of Agriculture and Mechanical Arts; visiting (BULL, *41*, 498)
Appointment: Univ. of Chicago (SCI, *56*, 660)
Lecture: 6th Institute on the Exceptional Child (J APP, *23*, 744)

Blayney, Ed Forest
Lecture: psychology instruction in Iowa (JoP, *7*, 222)

Bleckwenn, William J.
Appointment: consultant to Sixth Service Command (SCI, *100*, 145)

Bliss, Charles Bemis
Comments on proposed change in APA for a separate section for philosophical papers (REV, *6*, 237-238)
Summering abroad (REV, *6*, 456)

Bloch, E.
Research: sensations (AJP, *1*, 550)

Block Designs Test (*see* Kohs Block Designs Test)

Blood pressure
Discussion: Landis, C. (AJP, *34*, 470)
Research: Robbins, S. D. (BULL, *17*, 239)

Bloomingdale Hospital (New York)
Centenary celebration (SCI, *53*, 532)

Bloomington Asylum (White Plains, New York)
Appointment: Hoch, A. (BULL, *2*, 260)

Blum, Milton L.
Leave of absence: College of the City of New York (BULL, *41*, 267)

Board of National Research Fellowships in the Biological Sciences
Fellowships awarded in psychology (SCI, *81*, 482; BULL, *23*, 292)

Boas, Franz
Publication announcement (JoP, *8*, 560)
Retirement: president of NYAS (JoP, *9*, 27-28)

Boas, George
Leave of absence: Johns Hopkins Univ. (SCI, *98*, 469)

Bobba, Romualdo
Death notice (JoP, *3*, 112)

Bock, Carl
Appointment: Univ. of Missouri (BULL, *9*, 408; JoP, *9*, 616)

Boder, David Pablo
Consultant to U.S. Army Signal Corps Training Program (BULL, *40*, 723-724)
Counselor with Illinois Institute of Technology (BULL, *42*, 793)
Demonstration of apparatus, Psychological Museum (BULL, *41*, 410)
Election: Vice-president chapter of the Society of the Sigma Xi at Illinois
 Institute of Technology, 1942 (SCI, *95*, 551)

Bohn, Georges
Paper: comparative psychology (JoP, *6*, 559)
Paper: correction (BULL, *5*, 379)

Bois, J. S. Anselme
Appointment: Stevenson and Kellogg (BULL, *42*, 581)

Bolton, H. Carrington
Requests data on words and expressions used in addressing domestic animals
 (SCI°, *11*, 70-71)

Bolton, Thaddeus Lincoln
Appointment: Normal School, San Jose, CA (SCI, *4*, 142)
Appointment: Professor emeritus (SCI, *86*, 152)
Appointment: Temple Univ. (BULL, *14*, 420)
Appointment: Univ. of Nebraska (REV, *7*, 323-324; BULL, *1*, 334; SCI, *17*, 400)
Leave of absence: Univ. of Montana (BULL, *12*, 481)
Obituary: Kirkpatrick, E. A. (AJP, *49*, 489)
Paper: attitudes (JoP, *1*, 224)
Position announced (JoP, *1*, 364)
Promotion: Univ. of Nebraska (SCI, *17*, 760)
Resignation: State Normal School at Worcester, MA (SCI, *4*, 142)
Retirement: Temple Univ. (SCI, *86*, 152)

Bolton's Catalogue of Scientific and Technical Periodicals
Publication: Smithsonian Institution (SCI°, *2*, 91-92)

Bond, Earl Danford
Resignation: Institute for Mental Hygiene and Pennsylvania Hospital (SCI, *88*, 591)

Bonn, University of
Appointment: Bühler, K. (BULL, *6*, 368)
Appointment: Külpe, O. (JoP, *7*, 84; JoP, *6*, 560; BULL, *6*, 368)
Appointment: Marbe, K. (AJP, *7*, 152)
Death notice: Verworn, M. (BULL, *19*, 63)
Degree: Martin, L. J. (BULL, *10*, 424; AJP, *25*, 147; SCI, *38*, 400; JoP, *10*, 616)

Bonnie Brae Farm for Boys (New Jersey)
Appointment: Doll, E. A. (BULL, *40*, 539; SCI, *97*, 420)

Boodin, John Elof
Lecture: truth (JoP, *7*, 223)
Publication announcement (JoP, *8*, 392, 560)

Boody, Bertha May
Death notice (BULL, *41*, 72)

Book, William Frederick
Appointment: Indiana Univ. (BULL, *9*, 407-408; JoP, *9*, 588)
Death notice (AJP, *53*, 617; BULL, *37*, 407; J APP, *24*, 517)
Departure: Leland Stanford Univ. (JoP, *9*, 588, 644)
Departure: State Univ. of Montana (BULL, *9*, 407-408; JoP, *9*, 644)
Lecture: genetic psychology at Clark Univ. (J APP, *9*, 88; SCI, *63*, 162)
Lecture: Indiana Univ. psych lab 50th anniversary commemoration (J APP, *23*, 631)
Lecture: learning (JoP, *2*, 223)
Purchases *Journal of Applied Psychology* (J APP, *6*, 301)
Retirement: Indiana Univ. (SCI, *80*, 475)
Return: from world tour (SCI, *67*, 578)
Return: Indiana Univ. (BULL, *13*, 296; SCI, *67*, 578)

Books
"Book reviews in psychological periodicals"; discussion by Schultz, R. S. and Pallister, H. (AJP, *46*, 508)

Books for prisoners of war
Request for (BULL, *40*, 232, 311)

Books of Science, The
Publication: Lane W. C. (SCI°, *2*, 342)

Boraas, Harold Orlando
Appointment: St. Olaf College (BULL, *42*, 191)

Boredom
Discussion: Barmack, J. E. (AJP, 52, 467-471)
Discussion: Berman, A. (AJP, 52, 471-473)

Boring, Edwin Garrigues
Acta Psychologica board (AJP, 48, 174)
American Journal of Psychology cover page change (AJP, 48, 177)
Appointment: Clark Univ. (JoP, 16, 672; Sci, 50, 251; Bull, 16, 257)
Appointment: Harvard Univ. (JoP, 19, 420; AJP, 33, 450; Bull, 19, 350; Sci, 55, 538)
Appointment: Harvard Univ., Director of psych lab (Sci, 60, 428; Bull, 21, 660)
Appointment: Univ. of California (Bull, 21, 360)
Chair: SEP (AJP, 46, 511; AJP, 45, 539)
Discussion: attribute and sensation (AJP, 35, 301)
Discussion: consciousness in siamese twins (AJP, 32, 448)
Discussion: differential limen for pitch (AJP, 53, 450-455)
Discussion: "Isochromatic contours" (AJP, 49, 134)
Discussion: lag of publication in psychology journals (AJP, 49, 137)
Discussion: optical geometry of Emmert's Law (AJP, 53, 293-295)
Discussion: temporal perception and operationism (AJP, 48, 522)
Election: AAAS, section I, vice-president (Bull, 27, 240)
Election: APA office, 1920 (JoP, 17, 56)
Election: APA President (Sci, 67, 12; Bull, 25, 123)
Grant: $150.00 from AAAS (Bull, 18, 111)
Honored at dinner by faculty of Clark Univ. (Sci, 55, 638)
Lecture: Brown Univ. (Bull, 32, 323)
Lecture: 5th Institute of National Science (Bull, 28, 324)
Lecture: Stanford Univ. summer school (Bull, 18, 438)
Lecture: Wellesley (Sci, 55, 451)
Meeting: Inter-Society Color Council, 1939 (Bull, 36, 142)
Obituary: on Müller, G. E. (AJP, 47, 348)
Organized text, *Psychology for the Fighting Man* (J App, 27, 475)
Paper: psychology of perception and war (AJP, 55, 423-435)
Publication: announcement *German Psychological Warfare* (J App, 25, 359)

Bornhausen, Karl
Library proposed with psychology of religion collection included (JoP, 10, 84)

Bosanquet, Bernard
Comments on paper by Sorley, W. R. (JoP, 7, 27)
Election: British Academy of Science (Sci, 17, 635)
Paper: inductive reasoning (JoP, 8, 55)
Publication: announcement on esthetics (JoP, 7, 644)
Requested to become Gifford lecturer at Edinburgh Univ. (JoP, 7, 140)

Boston College of Physicians and Surgeons
Lecture: Hall, G. S. (Sci, 27, 1000)

Boston Evening Transcript
"Listener" dream account (Sci°, *16*, 272-273)
Retirement: Calkins, M. W. (JoP, *26*, 531)

Boston Juvenile Court
Appointment: Healy, W. (J App, *1*, 98)

Boston Normal School
Departure: Scott, C. A. (Bull, *12*, 280)

Boston Police Court
Establishment: psychological lab (Bull, *13*, 296, 408; JoP, *13*, 560)

Boston Psychoanalytic Institute
Sigmund Freud Memorial Fellowships for psychoanalytic training (Bull, 37, 827)

Boston psychologists
2nd meeting (Sci, 55, 347)

Boston Psychopathic Hospital
Appointment: Campbell, C. M. (Sci, *52*, 290; Bull, *17*, 351)
Appointment: Solomon, H. C. (Sci, *98*, 321)
Appointment: Wells, F. L. (AJP, *32*, 160)
Construction begins (Sci, *33*, 60)
Departure: Guthrie, R. H. (Sci, *89*, 125)
Departure: Wells, F. L. (Sci, *88*, 278)
Grant: Rockefeller Foundation (Sci, *79*, 291)
Memorial of Southard, E. E. (Sci, *60*, 564)
Paper: Swift, W. B. (Bull, *13*, 407)
Resignation: Beck, S. J. (Bull, *29*, 603)
Summer Training School of Psychiatric Social Work (Bull, *15*, 36; JoP, *15*, 671-672; J App, *2*, 384)

Boston University (Massachusetts)
Appointment: Bertocci, P. A. (Bull, *42*, 191)
Appointment: DeWolf, L. H. (JoP, *34*, 83)
Appointment: Overholser, W. (Sci, *62*, 371)
Appointment: Rejall, A. E. (JoP, *14*, 224)
Appointment: Seward, J. P. (Bull, *42*, 582)
Appointment: Van Riper, B. W. (JoP, *9*, 168)
Award: honorary degree, Carmichael, L. (Sci, *87*, 276; Bull *35*, 333)
Award: honorary degree Overholsger, W. (Sci, *92*, 8)
Lecture series sponsored (Bull, *42*, 794)

Boswell, Foster Partridge
Appointment: Harvard Univ. (JoP, *1*, 644)
Appointment: Hobart College (Sci, *28*, 922; Bull, *6*, 32)

Appointment: Univ. of Wisconsin (Sci, *20*, 616; Bull, *1*, 488)
Paper: light (JoP, *2*, 280)

Botkin, Frances
Appointment: Smith College (Bull, *19*, 236)

Bott, Edward Alexander
Election: APA (Sci, 76, 251)

Boulogne-sur-seine
Statue of Marey, E. (Bull, *11*, 268)

Bouman, Harry D.
Appointment: Univ. of Rochester (Sci, *94*, 276)

Bourdon, Benjamin
Retirement: Univ. of Rennes (Bull, *28*, 254)

Bousfield, Weston Ashmore
Appointment: Connecticut State College (Bull, *36*, 406)
Discussion: calculating abilities of Finkelstein, S. (AJP, *45*, 353-358)

Boutroux, Emile
Appointment: Herbert Spencer lecturer at Oxford Univ. (JoP, *14*, 588; JoP, *15*, 28)
Election: Gifford Lecturer, Univ. of Glasgow (Rev, *9*, 328)
Honorary degree (JoP, *7*, 224)
Lecture: Harvard and Cambridge on religion and contemporaneous philosophy (JoP, *7*, 140)
Paper: preface to *Egotism in German Philosophy* (JoP, *15*, 112)

Bowditch, Henry Pickering
Letters from G. Stanley Hall (AJP, *41*, 326)

Bowdoin College (Brunswick, Maine)
Angell, J. R., "Philosophy and the layman" (JoP, *34*, 168)
Institute of philosophy lecture series (JoP, *34*, 168)

Bowers, Paul E.
Appointment: Loyola Univ., professor of abnormal psychology (Sci, *69*, 14)

Bowman, Ethel
Appointment: Goucher College (JoP, *14*, 644; Bull, *17*, 279)
Promotion: (Bull, *20*, 172)

Bowman Gray School of Medicine (*see also* Wake Forest College)
Appointment: Allan, W., Dept of Eugenics (Sci, *94*, 111)

Bowman, Isaiah
Appointment: Secretary of State advisor (SCI, *101*, 85)

Bowman, Karl Murdock
Appointment: Bellevue Hospital, Director of psychiatry (SCI, *83*, 181)
Appointment: Langley Porter Clinic, State Department of Institutions, Medical School of the Univ. of California (SCI, *94*, 323)
Election: American Psychiatric Association, president, 1944 (SCI, *99*, 382-383)
Member of National Committee Concerned with Men Rejected by Induction Boards for Neuropsychiatric Reasons (SCI, *98*, 298)
Research Council on Problems of Alcohol (BULL, *37*, 61)
Resignation: New York College of Medicine (SCI, *96*, 293)

Bown, Max Duane
Promotion: Whitman College (BULL, *40*, 723)

Bowne, Borden Parker
Death notice (BULL, *7*, 180; JoP, *7*, 224)

Boyd, Jr., David A.
Appointment: School of Medicine, Indiana Univ. (SCI, *90*, 369)
Departure: Neuropsychiatric Institute, Univ. of Michigan (SCI, *90*, 369)

Boynton, Paul Lewis
Appointment: George Peabody College for Teachers (SCI, *72*, 315)
Departure: George Peabody College for Teachers (BULL, *39*, 681)
Election: Stephen F. Austin State Teachers College, president (BULL, *39*, 681)

Braceland, Francis James
Appointment: School of Medicine, Loyola Univ., Chicago (SCI, *93*, 325)

Bradley Memorial Hospital (Providence, Rhode Island)
Allows Brown Univ. use of psych labs (BULL, *28*, 412)
Appointment: Pollock, M. (BULL, *29*, 411)

Brain (*see also* Cerebellar, Cerebral, Cerebrum)
Discussion: Diven, K. "Dandy's radical extirpations of brain tissue in man" (AJP, *46*, 500)
Guttmann, E. investigation of injury (SCI, *94*, 111)
Lecture: Luriia, A., brain pathology (SCI, *89*, 433)
Lecture: Münsterberg, H. (JoP, *1*, 168)
Paper: Freeman, E., brain localization (AJP, *43*, 503)
Paper: Hrdlicka, A. preservation of brains (JoP, *3*, 476)
Paper: Stratton, G. M., brain localization (AJP, *43*, 128)
Publication: Ferrier, D., functions of (SCI°, *8*, 480)

Braithwaite, Richard Bevan
Paper: Mind Assoc. and Aristotelian Society meeting (JoP, *35*, 252)

Brandt, Francis Burke
Paper (JoP, *1*, 84)

Brandt, Frithiof
Appointment: Univ. of Copenhagen (BULL, *20*, 416)

Branham, Vernon Carnegie
Journal of Criminal Psychopathology (BULL, *36*, 842)

Bray, Charles William
Appointment: Princeton Univ. (SCI, *87*, 411)
Award: Warren medal, SEP (SCI, *83*, 367; BULL, *33*, 476)
National Research Council grant (BULL, *33*, 579)
Promotion: Princeton Univ. (BULL, *42*, 581; BULL, *28*, 503)

Brazilian Psychiatrical, Neurological, and Medical Society
Meeting: organizational, Moreira, J. elected president (SCI, *27*, 903)

Breed, Frederic Stephen
Appointment: Univ. of Michigan (BULL, *7*, 220; JoP, *7*, 560)
Appointment: Yale Univ. (BULL, *7*, 148; JoP, *7*, 196, 252)
Departure: Yale Univ. (JoP, *7*, 560)
Monograph on work done at Harvard Psychological Lab (JoP, *8*, 559-560)

Breese, Burtis Burr
Appointment: Univ. of Cincinnati (SCI, *20*, 192; BULL, *1*, 372; JoP, *1*, 476)
Appointment: Teachers College, Columbia (REV, *5*, 677)

Bregman, Elsie Oschrin
Election: Psychological Corporation, Asst secretary (BULL, *24*, 80; J APP, *11*, 81)
Research on women secretaries (J APP, *10*, 393)

Breitweiser, Joseph Valentine
Appointment: Univ. of California (BULL, *16*, 221)

Bremner, Marjorie
Appointment: Bureau of Naval Personnel (BULL, *40*, 231)
Completed WAVES training (BULL, *40*, 231)

Brennan, Robert Edward
Appointment: Univ. of Montreal (BULL, *40*, 310)

Brentano Society
Founding of (JoP, *29*, 672)

Breslau, University of
Appointment: Ebbinghaus, H. (REV, *1*, 440)
Departure: Ebbinghaus, H. (JoP, *2*, 644)
Laboratory, formation of (AJP, *7*, 152)

Brett, George Sidney
Death notice (BULL, *41*, 807)

Brewer, Joseph Everett
General Education Board Fellowship, Univ. of Illinois (BULL, *37*, 827)

Briarcliff Junior College (New York)
Appointment: Clapp, H. S. (BULL, *41*, 267; BULL, *40*, 794)

Bridges, James Winfred
Appointment: Clark Univ. (SCI, *64*, 39)
Appointment: Univ. of California School of Medicine (BULL, *29*, 460)

Bridgman, Laura
Hall, G. S. writes introductory note for manuscripts of (SCI°, *9*, 435)
Publication: manuscripts of, Sanford, E. C. (SCI°, *9*, 435)
Death notice (SCI°, *13*, 421)

Brigham, Carl Campbell
Appointment: Princeton Univ. (BULL, *17*, 239)
Death notice (BULL, *40*, 230; AJP, *56*, 305-306)
Election: APA secretary (BULL, *26*, 56; SCI, *69*, 36)
Resignation: Princeton Univ. (BULL, *14*, 115)

Brigham Young University (Provo, Utah)
Dusenberry, I. S., sabbatical (BULL, *28*, 410)
Promotion: Gibb, T. R. (BULL, *39*, 681)

Brightman, Edgar Sheffield
President, American Philosophical Assoc., Eastern Division (JoP, *33*, 56)

Brill, Abraham Arden
Laity Lecture "The Freudian epoch", 1942 (SCI, *94*, 484)
Lecture: psychoanalysis and abnormal psychology, New York Univ. (BULL, *12*, 128)
Salmon Thomas William lectures, 1943 (SCI, *98*, 383)

Brill, Moshe
Death notice (BULL, *41*, 199)

Brimhall, Dean R.
APA, Wash.-Balt. Branch, 1940 (BULL, *37*, 405)
Paper: families of science men at NYAS/NY Branch of APA (JoP, *15*, 140)
Supervised a revision of the Army Alpha Test (J APP, *10*, 287)

Brinton, Daniel Garrison
Appointment: Univ. of Pennsylvania (SCI°, *8*, 452)
Award: medal of the Société americaine de France (SCI°, *6*, 558)

Lecture: Languages of the American Aborigines, Lowell Institute, Boston (SCI°, 4, 522)
Memorial meeting: American Philosophical Society (SCI, 11, 38, 78)
Publication: "The Lenâpé and their legends..." (SCI°, 5, 159-160)

Bristol, University of (England)
Appointment: Morgan, C. L. (BULL, 17, 280)
Presentation honoring Morgan, C. L. (JOP, 7, 336)
Presentation: Morgan, C. L. (JOP, 7, 252)
Resignation: Morgan, C. L. (JOP, 6, 504; BULL, 17, 280)

British Academy of Science
Announcement: Volume 1 of its proceedings (JOP, 2, 672)
Bicentenary of death of Locke, J. commemorated (JOP, 1, 672)
Election: Bosanquet, B. and Stout G. F. (SCI, 17, 635)
Election: James, W., corresponding member (SCI, 26, 94; JOP, 4, 448; BULL, 4, 338)
Meeting: commemorating Kant (JOP, 1, 139)
Reception for exiled scholars and scientists (SCI, 89, 174)

British and American Associations for the Advancement of Science
List of names signing to consider an international congress (SCI°, 4, 329)

British and French Philosophical Societies
Meeting: Oxford, England, 1920 (JOP, 17, 280)

British Army
List of teaching and scientific staffs (JOP, 12, 560)

British Association for Preservation at Down House
Received Darwin's manuscripts, 1942 (SCI, 96, 493)

British Association for the Advancement of Science
Cattell, J. Mck., AAAS delegate to centenary meeting (SCI, 74, 240, 409)
Discussion: color vision (SCI, 8, 30)
Election: Aveling, F., president, Section J (SCI, 77, 17)
Election: Bartlett, R. J., sectional president (SCI, 88, 612)
Election: Collins, M. J., president, Section J (SCI, 85, 13)
Election: Dawson, S., president, Section J (SCI, 78, 599)
Election: Jones, L. W., president, Psychology Section (SCI, 80, 583)
Election: Myers, C. S., centenary psychology, Section J, president (SCI, 73, 62)
Election: officers, Sept. 1885, Aberdeen (SCI°, 5, 432)
Election: Valentine, C. W., Psychology Section, president (SCI, 71, 212)
Election: Wolters, A. W.P., president, Section J, psychology (SCI, 83, 29)
Establishment: Psychological Society (BULL, 1, 452; JOP, 1, 616)
Establishment: separate section for psychology (BULL, 18, 111; SCI, 52, 536)
Franz, S. I. represents AAAS at the Cardiff meeting (BULL, 17, 351)

Inaugural meeting, Aug 6, 1924 (J App, *8*, 258)
Inclusion of psychology for Birmingham meeting (Sci, *38*, 301)
Lecture: McDougall, W. (Sci, *60*, 130)
Letter to American Association (Sci°, *3*, 396-397)
List of members to be presented at the Montreal meeting, 1884 (Sci°, *4*, 186-187)
Meeting: attended by Cattell, J. McK (Bull, *28*, 646)
Meeting: Aug 6-13, 1924, Toronto, Canada (Bull, *21*, 188)
Meeting: Aug 27, 1883, Montreal (Sci°, *2*, 452)
Meeting: Edinburg discussion of (AJP, *33*, 159)
Meeting: Sept. 1889 (Sci°, *14*, 129)
Meeting: Sept., 1883, Southport (Sci°, *2*, 29)
Meeting: Univ. of Cambridge, 1938 (Sci, *87*, 61-62)
Membership invitation to APA members (Rev, *4*, 339)
Paper: call for Toronto meeting (AJP, *8*, 584)
Paper: Psychology as independent subject area (JoP, *10*, 532)
Paper: Spiller, J. on "An experiment of color-blindness" (Sci°, *14*, 267)
Psychology subsection formed (JoP, *11*, 140)
Wheeler, R. H., U.S. representative, psychology, Section J (Sci, *76*, 252)

British Child-Study Association
Annual conference announced (JoP, *2*, 280)

British Colonial Office
Announces colonial research fellowships in natural or social sciences (Sci, *100*, 216)

British Columbia, University of (Canada)
Appointment: Davis, F. C. (J App, *22*, 106)
Resignation: Irving, J. A. (Bull, *42*, 485; JoP, *42*, 364)

British Home Office
Report on experiments on living animals (Sci, *92*, 10)

British Honorary Fellows
Election: Royal Society of Edinburgh (Sci, *11*, 1036)

British Journal of Psychology
Publication announced (JoP, *1*, 28; Bull, *1*, 28)

British Medical Association
Meeting: Oxford (JoP, *1*, 420)
Meeting: Oxford, July 26-29 with Section E, Psychological Medicine (AJP, *15*, 463)

British Medical Journal
Tribute, Müller, J. (Sci, *10*, 620-621)

British Medical Research Council
Appointment: Bartlett, F. C. (SCI, *94*, 605)
Chair: Adrian, E. D., Committee on Mental Disorders (SCI, *79*, 383)

British Medico-Psychological Association
Lecture: Clarke, C. K., 1923 Congress (SCI, *56*, 331)

British Ministry of Health and the Assistance Board
Cooperating on Nuffield Foundation Trustees' survey on problems of aging and
care of old people (SCI, *99*, 363-364)

British Museum
Darwin, C., statue by Boehm (SCI°, 5, 471)

British National Institute of Industrial Psychology (*see also* National Institute of)
Appointment: Myers, C. S. (SCI, *55*, 451)
Election: Bingham, W. V. and Viteles, M. S., honorary correspondents (BULL,
26, 624; SCI, *69*, 449)
Miles, W. R. succeeds Myers, C. S. as director (SCI, *72*, 598)
Retirement: Myers, C. S. (SCI, *88*, 494-495)
Rockefeller grant (SCI, *71*, 504)

British Psychological Society
Election: Seashore, C. E. honorary member (SCI, *91*, 445)
Lecture: Bingham, W. V. (SCI, *66*, 537)
Lecture: Wolf, A., repression (JoP, *11*, 532)
List of papers presented (JoP, *8*, 448)
Meeting: joint Aristolelian Society/Mind Assoc., Univ. College, London (JoP,
10, 420)
Meeting: joint July 3-5, 1915 Aristotelian Society/Mind Assoc. (JoP, *12*, 448)
Meeting: joint June 7-8, 1913 Mind Assoc./Aristotelian Society (JoP, *10*, 308)
Meeting: joint with Aristotelian Society and Mind Assoc. (JoP, *7*, 420)
Meeting: July 3-6, 1914, Durham (JoP, *11*, 308, 532)
Participation in the Congress of Philosophy, 1920 (JoP, *17*, 391)

Britt, Steuart Henderson
Appointment: George Washington Univ, Wash. D.C. (SCI, *83*, 461; BULL, *33*, 578)
Appointment: Office of Psychological Personnel, executive director (SCI, *95*,
527-528)
Commissioned U.S. Naval Reserve (SCI, *97*, 576; SCI, *98*, 215)
Departure: Office of Psychological Personnel (BULL, *40*, 540)
Election: Wash.-Balt. Branch, APA, officer (BULL, *37*, 656-657; BULL, *36*, 712)
Lecture: Wash.-Balt. Branch of APA (J APP, *25*, 726)
Lecture: Wash.-Balt. Branch of APA, 1942 (BULL, *39*, 683)
Request for information on potential conscription of psychologist (J APP, *25*,
472)

Brochard, Victor
Death notice (JoP, 5, 56)

Brockway, Zebulon Reed
Publication: The care of criminals (Sci°, *13*, 141)

Brogan, Albert Perley
Promotion: Univ. of Texas (JoP, *14*, 504)

Brolver, Cecil R.
Promotion: Princeton Univ. (Sci, *74*, 146)

Bronk, Detlev Wulf
Vanuxem, Louis Clark Lectures at Princeton Univ., 1939 (Sci, *89*, 314)

Brooklyn Academy of Music (New York)
Conference on color vision, Ladd-Franklin, C. (JoP, *11*, 84)

Brooklyn Academy of Science (New York)
Opens reading room (Sci°, *14*, 8)

Brooklyn College (New York)
Announces name change of Office of War Service Counseling to Veterans' and War Counseling Office (Bull, *42*, 407)

Brooklyn Training School for Teachers (New York)
Appointment: Bell, J. C. (JoP, *4*, 392; Bull, *4*, 236; Sci, *26*, 32)
Departure: Bell, J. C. (Sci, *35*, 960)
Departure: Childs, H. G. (Bull, *11*, 116; JoP, *11*, 84)
Lecture: Witmer, L., gifted, children (Sci, *36*, 862)

Brotemarkle, Robert Archibald
Appointment: Univ. of Pennsylvania (Sci, *97*, 326; Bull, *40*, 539)
Editor: *Clinical Psychology-Studies in Honor of Lightner Witmer-Commemorating the Thirty-Fifth Anniversary of the First Psychological Clinic* (Sci, *75*, 75)
National Research Council conference, "Psychological factors on national morale" (Bull, *37*, 829)
National Research Council, Emergency Committee in Psychology (Bull, *37*, 755)

Brown, Andrew
Election: AAAP, clinical section chair (J App, *21*, 603, 713)
Election: Illinois Society of Consulting Psych., vice- president (Bull, *35*, 578)

Brown, Charles Henry
Death notice (Sci, *14*, 659)

Brown, Elmer Ellsworth
Appointment: U.S. Commissioner of Education (SCI, *24*, 381; JoP, *3*, 420)
Lecture: New York Univ. School of Pedagogy (SCI, *24*, 381)

Brown, Guy B.
Psychic research (SCI, *80*, 183)

Brown, Harold Chester
Psychological Index project, measure of public interest in psychology (BULL, *36*, 220)
Publication: military psychology (J APP, *25*, 358)

Brown, Judson Seise
Appointment: Yale Univ. (SCI, *94*, 62; BULL, *38*, 907)

Brown, Junius Flagg
Award: Board of National Research Fellowships (BULL, *26*, 380)

Brown, Robert Heath
Appointment: Clark Univ. (SCI, *85*, 354; BULL, *34*, 272; BULL, *35*, 334)

Brown University (Providence, Rhode Island)
Appointment: Beck, L. F. (BULL, *28*, 412)
Appointment: Carmichael, L. (SCI, *65*, 371; BULL, *24*, 380; J APP, *11*, 234)
Appointment: Colvin, S. S. (SCI, *35*, 926; BULL, *9*, 280; JoP, *9*, 364)
Appointment: Graham, C. H. (SCI, *93*, 591; BULL, *33*, 406)
Appointment: Hunter, W. S. (SCI, *83*, 367)
Appointment: Kemp, E. H. (SCI, *83*, 367)
Appointment: Meikeljohn, A. (JoP, *3*, 532)
Appointment: Ruggles, A. H. (BULL, *28*, 412)
Colloquium psych dept (BULL, *32*, 323)
Enlargement of psychology labs (BULL, *28*, 412)
Lecture: Miles, W. R. (BULL, *28*, 324)
Lecture: Sanford, E. C. (JoP, *4*, 196; BULL, *4*, 128)
Lecture: Yerkes, R. M. (SCI, *82*, 590)
Promotion: Carmichael, L.; Professor (BULL, *25*, 568)
Promotion: Graham, C. H. (BULL, *38*, 777)
Seminar: Miles, W. R., 1931 (SCI, *73*, 360)
Use of psych labs at Bradley Memorial Hospital, Providence (BULL, *28*, 412)

Brown, Warner
Appointment: APA committee, San Francisco program (SCI, *41*, 605)
Appointment: Univ. of California (SCI, *27*, 936; BULL, *5*, 244)
British Army, King's College (BULL, *12*, 364)
Election: National Research Council, Div of Anthropology and Psychology (BULL, *25*, 376)
Lecture: Swarthmore College (JoP, *13*, 308)
Preston School of Industry-California (J APP, *3*, 196)

Brown, William
Award committee for paper on Pearson's formula (JoP, *11*, 27-28)
Director Institute of Experimental Psych, Oxford (BULL, *33*, 849; SCI, *83*, 349)
Election: British Assoc. for Advancement of Science, Section J President (BULL, *24*, 312)
Lecture: Child Study Society (JoP, *8*, 644)
Summary of proceedings of joint meeting of Aristotelian Society, British Psychological Society and the Mind Assoc. (JoP, *7*, 420)

Brown, William Moseley
Appointment: Washington and Lee Univ. (J APP, *10*, 393)

Browne, Buckston
Letter about Darwin, C. and Lyell, C. (SCI, *90*, 155)

Brownell, William Arthur
Appointment: Cornell Univ. (J APP, *10*, 394)

Brownell, William Crary
Paper: French traits (SCI°, *9*, 610)
Publication: the social instinct, *Scribner's Magazine* (SCI°, *9*, 610)

Bruce, Robert Hall
Conference on psychology of learning, Univ. of Colorado, 1939 (BULL, *36*, 583)

Bruetsch, Walter L.
Award: Laymen's League Against Epilepsy (SCI, *93*, 419)

Brumbaugh, Martin Grove
Appointment: Philadelphia Public Schools superintendent (SCI, *24*, 448)
Appointment: Swarthmore College (JoP, *3*, 336)

Brumbaugh, M. B.
Appointment: Puerto Rico (SCI, *11*, 957)

Bruner, Frank Gilbert
Leave of absence: Columbia Univ. (SCI, *20*, 480)
Paper: audibility (JoP, *2*, 280)
Paper: audition (JoP, *2*, 224)
Paper: color (JoP, *2*, 112)

Bruner, Jerome Seymour
Lecture: Wash-Balt Branch, APA (J APP, *25*, 726)

Bruno, Giordano, Life and Works of
Publication: Trübner, (SCI°, *8*, 480)

Brunswick, David
Award: Board of National Research Fellowship (BULL, *23*, 292)

Brunswik, Egon
International Congress for Unity of Sciences (JoP, *33*, 392)
Publication: *Journal of Unified Science* (JoP, *36*, 532)

Brunswik, Else Frenkel (*see* Frenkel-Brunswik, Else)

Brush, Edward Nathaniel
Resignation: *American Journal of Psychiatry*, editor (SCI, *74*, 34)

Brussels, University of (Belgium)
Dwelshauver, G. and Stroobant, P. in charge of laboratory (REV, *1*, 112)
Election: Joteyko, J. Neurological Society of Belgium, vice- president (JoP, *1*, 504)

Bryan, A. Hughes
Appointment: United Nations Relief and Rehabilitation Admin (SCI, *102*, 325)

Bryan, Alice Isabel
AAAP program chair (J APP, *25*, 265)
Data collected, School of Fine and Applied Arts, Pratts Inst., Brooklyn (BULL, *37*, 257)
Election: American Assoc for Applied Psychologists, executive secretary (SCI, *96*, 292)

Bryan, William Lowe
Appointment: Indiana Univ., President (SCI, *16*, 40, 80)
Election: American Psychological Assoc, president (SCI, *17*, 158; JoP, *1*, 28)
Installation as president Indiana Univ. (SCI, *17*, 160)
Lecture: Indiana Univ. Psych Lab, 50th anniversary (J APP, *23*, 630)
Lecture: Indiana Univ. symposium on learning, 1939 (BULL, *37*, 61)

Bryn Mawr College (Pennsylvania)
Appointment: Bakewell, C. M. (REV, *5*, 449)
Appointment: de Laguna, T. del (BULL, *4*, 370)
Appointment: Fernald, G. (BULL, *4*, 160)
Appointment: Ferree, C. E. (BULL, *4*, 160; BULL, *10*, 39; BULL, *14*, 143)
Appointment: Helson, H. (BULL, *25*, 444)
Appointment: Leuba, J. H. (SCI, *38*, 478; SCI, *7*, 637)
Appointment: Lukens, H. T. (REV, *3*, 706)
Appointment: Rogers, A. L. (SCI, *61*, 339)
Award: Sarah Berliner fellowship to Rand, G., work on psychology of vision (JoP, *9*, 168)
Bequest: Thorne, P. A., associate professorship of education and model school (JoP, *8*, 392)
Celebration 25th anniversary (JoP, *7*, 616)
Course: Kellogg, C. E. (BULL, *11*, 190)
Course: Leuba, J. H. (REV, *5*, 449)
Course: Wilm, E. (BULL, *11*, 190)

Course: Witmer, L. (REV, *3*, 356)
Death: Irons, D., Jan 24, 1907 (SCI, *25*, 198)
Departure: Bakewell, C. M. (REV, *7*, 428)
Establishment: graduate school of education (JoP, *10*, 616)
Laboratory in experimental psych (BULL, *9*, 440; JoP, *10*, 56)
Laboratory opening (BULL, *3*, 184)
Leave of absence: Irons, D. (BULL, *1*, 94)
Leave of absence: Leuba, J. H. (BULL, *4*, 160; BULL, *11*, 190; BULL, *18*, 56)
Lecture: Chan, W. T. (JoP, *40*, 560)
Lecture: Lowell, A. L. (JoP, *7*, 616)
Lecture: Remsen, I. (JoP, *7*, 616)
Lecture: Russell, B., postulates of scientific methods (JoP, *40*, 560)
Meeting: Eastern Psychological Assoc (AJP, *52*, 473- 475)
Promotion: Ferree, C. E. (SCI, *45*, 361; JoP, *9*, 700; BULL, *9*, 440; JoP, *14*, 252)
Promotion: Kam, G. (SCI, *39*, 721)
Promotion: Rand, G. (BULL, *11*, 190)
Research: color stimuli (JoP, *1*, 166)

Buchanan, Scott
Appointment: Univ. of Chicago (JoP, *33*, 560)

Buchner, Edward Franklin
Appointment: Johns Hopkins Univ. (SCI, *27*, 440; BULL, *5*, 96)
Course: Univ. of Kansas (BULL, *12*, 403)
Election: Société Libre pour l'Étude Psychologique de l'Enfant (SCI, *13*, 155)
Election: SSPP, council member (JoP, *8*, 84)
Election: SSPP, president (SCI, *31*, 22; JoP, *7*, 56)
Election: SSPP, secretary-treasurer (SCI, *27*, 596; JoP, *1*, 168)
Lecture: SSPP (JoP, *8*, 84)
Resignation: New York Univ. (REV, *8*, 336)

Buck, Albert Francis
Appointment: Univ. of Chicago (REV, *5*, 109)

Buckel Foundation, Stanford University (California)
Established at Stanford Univ. (BULL, *11*, 191)
Ordahl, G., work with children (JoP, *13*, 448)

Buckingham, Burdette Ross
Bureau of Educational Research, Illinois, director (J APP, *3*, 196-197)

Bucknell University (Lewisburg, Pennsylvania)
Appointment: Hadley, L. S. (BULL, *42*, 407)
Degree: Humm, D. G. (BULL, *42*, 582)

Budapest University (Hungary)
Honorary doctorate, Wundt, W. (SCI, *3*, 865)

Buenos Aires, University of (Argentina) (*see also* Psychological Society of)
Appointment: Krueger, F. (BULL, 3, 148)

Buena Vista College (Storm Lake, Iowa)
Appointment: Andrew, M. (BULL, 14, 366)

Buffalo, University of (New York)
Appointment: Bensley, M. L. (BULL, 42, 791)
Appointment: Leary, D. B. (BULL, 16, 258; JoP, 16, 700; SCI, 50, 161)
Appointment: Stoke, S. M. (J APP, 10, 288)
Election: Scofield, C. E., officer, Sigma Xi (SCI, 93, 324)
Leave of absence: Jones, E. S. (BULL, 42, 792)
Lecture: Angell, J. R. (SCI, 89, 579)

Bugental, James Frederick Thomas
Appointment: Georgia School of Technology (BULL, 42, 64)

Bugg, Eugene Gower
Discussion: Binocular color phenomenona (AJP, 51, 769)

Buhl Foundation of Pittsburgh
Grant to Univ. of Pittsburgh (BULL, 38, 304)

Bühler, Charlotte
Appointment: Clark Univ. (SCI, 93, 537; BULL, 38, 777)
Summer courses, Univ. of Vienna, 1937 (BULL, 34, 410)

Bühler, Karl
Appointment: Clark Univ. (SCI, 93, 537; BULL, 38, 777)
Appointment: Johns Hopkins Univ. (SCI, 65, 495)
Appointment: Harvard Univ. (SCI, 67, 343; BULL, 25, 307)
Appointment: Stanford Univ. (BULL, 24, 380)
Appointment: St. Scholastica, Duluth, 1939-40 (BULL, 36, 218)
Appointment: Univ of Bonn (BULL, 6, 368)
Appointment: Univ. of Chicago, Summer 1929 (SCI, 69, 379)
Summer courses, Univ. of Vienna, 1937 (BULL, 34, 410)

Bulletin de l'Institut Général Psychologique
List of articles (JoP, 12, 588)

Bulletin of Menninger Clinic (Topeka, Kansas)
Contributions of clincial psych in psychiatric clinic (J APP, 27, 475)

Bulletin of the National Research Council
Industrial research labs (J APP, 5, 192)

Bulletin of the University of Wyoming
Study by Downey, J. E. (J App, *3*, 195)

Bullis, Harold Edmund
National Committee on Mental Hygiene (Bull, *36*, 711; Sci, *89*, 337)

Bullough, Edward
Paper: aesthetics of color (JoP, *7*, 420)

Bumstead, Charles Heath
Appointment: Knox College (Bull, *41*, 603)

Bunch, Cordia C.
Death notice (Bull, *39*, 681)

Burden Neurological Institute
Appointment: Golla, F. L. (Sci, *89*, 242)
Inskip, T. (Sci, *89*, 242)

Bureau for Psychological Services (Minnesota)
Appointment: Mitchell, M. B. (Bull, *39*, 325)

Bureau of Child Guidance of the New York City School System
Celebration decennial, 1941 (Bull, *38*, 778-779)
Zachry, C. B. nominated for director (Sci, *94*, 537)

Bureau of Child Guidance (Southern Illinois University, Carbondale)
Appointment: Parry, D. (Sci, *98*, 239)

Bureau of Education, United States
Appointment: Angell, J. R. (Bull, *12*, 481)
Circular on prison congress (Sci°, *3*, 640)
Publication: pamphlet concerning examination and licensing of teachers (Sci°, *2*, 28)
Publication: results of inquiry on effects of co-educating the sexes (Sci°, *2*, 117)
Publication: training methods (J App, *1*, 396)
Research on shorthand-writing (Sci°, *4*, 266-267)

Bureau of Educational Experiments (New York, New York)
Appointment: Emerson, R. P. (J App, *3*, 196)
Appointment: Johnson, B. J. (Bull, *15*, 176; Sci, *47*, 363; JoP, *15*, 280)

Bureau of Educational Research (Illinois)
Establishment: Univ. of Illinois (J App, *3*, 196-197)

Bureau of Efficiency
Job vacancy for psychological investigator (Sci, *52*, 11)

Bureau of Human Heredity
Gates, R. R. solicitation for contributions of information (J App, *21*, 474)

Bureau of Instructional Research (University of Nebraska)
Appointment: Cox, H. M. (Sci, *89*, 148; Sci, *92*, 8)
Appointment: Guilford, J. P. (Sci, *89*, 148)
Establishment (Sci, *89*, 148)

Bureau of Juvenile Research (Ohio)
Appointment: Goddard, H. H. (Sci, *47*, 264; Bull, *15*, 98)

Bureau of Medicine and Surgery (*see* Aviation Section of)

Bureau of Mental Tests
Headed by Gordon, K. (JoP, *13*, 112)

Bureau of Naval Personnel
Appointment: Bremner, M. (Bull, *40*, 231)

Bureau of Personnel Administration (*see* Carnegie Institute of Technology Bureau of Salesmanship Research)

Bureau of Salesmanship Research (*see* Carnegie Institute of Technology)

Bureau of Statistics
Paper: Wright, C. D., "the condition of working girls" (Sci°, *4, 450*)

Bureau of Training, War Manpower Commission
Studies need for trained vocational counselors (J App, *28*, 352-353)

Burks, Barbara Stoddard
Award: Guggenheim Fellowship (Bull, *40*, 540)
Death notice (AJP, *56*, 610-612; Bull, *40*, 539)
Establishment of memorial fund (Bull, *41*, 200)

Burlingame, Clarence Charles
Chief, Neuro-psychiatric Institute of the Hartford retreat 1940 (J App, *24*, 371)
Report of Neuro-psychiatric Institute of Hartford on psychiatry service in war (J App, *26*, 245)

Burlingham, Dorothy Tiffany
Problems of war children (J App, *25*, 597)
Report issued monthly on psychological care of children (J App, *27*, 207)

Burnham, Paul Sylvester
Appointment: Yale Univ. (Sci, *96*, 225)

Burnham, William Henry
Death notice (AJP, *54*, 611-612; BULL, *38*, 777)

Burr, Charles Walts
Appointment: Univ. of Pennsylvania (SCI, *14*, 784)
Will left endowment fund and library to Univ. of Pennsylvania (SCI, *99*, 425)

Burr, Emily Thorp
Appointment: Vocational Adjustment Bureau (J APP, *10*, 393)

Burt, Benjamin Chapman
Appointment: Clark Univ. (SCI°, *14*, 215, 437)

Burt, Cyril Lodowic
Appointment: Univ. College, London (SCI, *74*, 169)
Discussion: correlation technique (AJP, *52*, 122-124)
Honorary degree, Univ. of Aberdeen (SCI, *90*, 79)
Paper: British Psychological Society (JoP, *8*, 448)
Psychic research (SCI, *80*, 183)

Burton, Arthur
Appointment: California Youth Authority (BULL, *43*, 485)

Burts, Richard C.
Appointment: Denison Univ. (BULL, *42*, 791)

Burtt, Harold Ernest
Appointment: Harvard Univ. (SCI, *47*, 364; JoP, *15*, 252; BULL, *15*, 256)
Appointment: Ohio State Univ. (SCI, *91*, 100, SCI, *88*, 254)
Conducts psychological tests for the Aviation Corps (J APP, *1*, 300)
Election: AAAP, chair, industrial and business psychology (J APP, *21*, 603, 713)
Election: AAAS, Section I (BULL, *40*, 458)
Election: Alpha Psi Delta psychological fraternity, president (BULL, *19*, 586)
Election: Section on Psychology of AAAS, secretary (BULL, *42*, 191)
Lecture: Univ. of Cincinnati Chapter of the Society of the Sigma Xi on scientific
    crime detection (SCI, *94*, 582)
Legal psych radio broadcast (BULL, *32*, 323)
Promotion (BULL, *20*, 172)

Business, psychology of
Lecture: Kitson, H. D., New York Univ. (SCI, *55*, 593)

Business Training Corporation (New York)
Production methods course (J APP, *3*, 396)

Butler, John Simpkins
Publication: curability of insanity and the individualized treatment of the insane
    (SCI°, *9*, 482)

Butler, Nicholas Murray
Appointment: Columbia Univ., President (REV, *8*, 656; SCI, *14*, 584)
Editor: series of books for teachers (REV, *6*, 344)
Lecture: 50th anniversary of founding lab at Columbia Univ. (SCI, *95*, 190)
Lecture: pedagogics, Columbia Univ. (SCI°, *8*, 585)
National Advisory Board on Radio in Education (SCI, *74*, 411)
Publication announcement (JoP, *8*, 560)

Butler, Nicholas Murray Gold Medal Award
Croce, B. (JoP, *17*, 364)
Cubberly, E. P. (JoP, *12*, 335-336)
Hook, S. (JoP, *42*, 224)
Marshall, H. R. (JoP, *17*, 364)
Santayana, G. (JoP, *42*, 224)
Thorndike, E. L. (BULL, *22*, 504)

Buxton, Claude Elmo
Appointment: Northwestern Univ. (SCI, *90*, 391)
Research Assoc., Swarthmore College (SCI, *90*, 391)

Byrne, Inspector
Publication: professional criminals of America (SCI°, *8*, 432)

Byrne, W. P.
Member: Royal Commisssion on the Care of the Feeble-Minded (SCI, *22*, 510)

Bystroff, [?]
Research: headaches (SCI°, *8*, 187)

C

Cabot, Philippe Sidney de Q.
Appointment: United Drug Co; Director of personnel research (BULL, *41*, 343)
Resignation: Simmons College (BULL, *41*, 343)

Cahn, Bertram J.
Money given for erection of Scott Hall at Northwestern Univ. (SCI, *89*, 219)

Caird, Edward
Nominated Glasgow Univ. Gifford lecturer (SCI, *11*, 597)
Resignation: Balliol College, Oxford (JoP, *4*, 336)

Caius College (Cambridge University)
Fellowship offer to Myers, C. S. (BULL, *17*, 116)

Caldecott, Alfred
Lecturer: Kings College, London (SCI, *20*, 656; BULL, *1*, 488; JoP, *1*, 672)

Calderwood, Henry
Death notice (REV, *5*, 108)
Retirement: Edinburgh; Chair of moral philosophy (SCI, *2*, 48)

Caldwell, Verne Vincent
Appointment: General Extension Division of Oregon State System of Higher
Education (SCI, *92*, 307; BULL, *37*, 827)
Death notice (BULL, *41*, 409)

California, Academy of Sciences
Election: officers, 1887 (SCI°, *9*, 109)

California Association for Applied Psychologists
Formed: Northern, CA branch, Southern, CA branch, 1942 (J APP, *26*, 245)
Formed: requirements, 1942 (BULL, *39*, 327-328)

California Bureau of Juvenile Research
Appointment: (J App, *16*, 590)
Appointment: 1932 (Bull, *30*, 107)

California, Department of Research
Establishment: Santa Ana, CA Public School System (J App, *3*, 196)
Publication: mental testing (J App, *3*, 197)

California Institute of Technology at Pasadena
New home for *The American Journal of Psychology* (Sci, *102*, 221)

California Society for Mental Hygiene
Establishment: Martin, L. J. (J App, *2*, 386)

California (Southern) Psychological Association
Organized and list of officers (Bull, *42*, 583)

California State Board of Charities
Appointment: Gordon, K. (Bull, *16*, 257)

California State Board of Health
Provides for the establishment of a state psychopathic hospital (Bull, *14*, 116)

California, State Institutions of
Appointment: Rosanoff, A. J. (Sci, *89*, 174)

California State Normal School, Los Angeles
Appointment: Terman, L.; Professor of pedagogy (Sci, *24*, 96)

California State Psychopathic Hospital
Establishment: San Francisco (Bull, *14*, 116)

California Test Bureau of Los Angeles
Publication: California Test of Mental Maturity (J App, *26*, 571-572)

California Test of Mental Maturity
Publication: Intelligence test; California Test Bureau of Los Angeles (J App, *26*, 571-572)
Research: IQ (J App, *26*, 571-572)

California Test of Personality
Research: Los Angeles County Schools (J App, *26*, 571)
Research: Stott, L. (J App, *26*, 570-571)

California, University of (Berkeley) (*see also* Langley Porter Clinic)
APA preliminary program (Bull, *12*, 243)
Appointment: Adams, J. (JoP, *4*, 336)
Appointment: Bakewell, C. M. (Rev, *7*, 428)

Lecture: Ward, J. (JoP, *1*, 588; BULL, *1*, 94; JoP, *1*, 280; BULL, *1*, 133; BULL, *1*, 452)
Meeting: Philosophical Union centenary of Kant's death (JoP, *1*, 140)
Meeting; W.P.A. 21st (AJP, *54*, 607)
Philosophical Union, continuation of (BULL, *4*, 64)
Promotion: Ghiselli, E. E. (BULL, *41*, 603)
Promotion: Sanford, R. N. (BULL, *41*, 603)
Promotion: Sullivan, E. B. (J APP, *10*, 394)
Publication: announced in philosophy (JoP, *2*, 336)
Publication: commemoration of the semi-centennial of the Univ. (JoP, *15*, 252)
School for children with speech and motor defects (BULL, *22*, 260)

California, University of, Institute of Child Welfare
Appointment: Jones, H. E. (SCI, *66*, 255)
Grant: General Education Board, N.Y. (SCI, *92*, 236)

California, University of, Los Angeles
Anniversary 1st, program celebrating psych. building (BULL, *37*, 406)
Appointment: Dallenbach, K. M. (SCI, *91*, 311)
Appointment: Dorcus, R. M. (SCI, *86*, 218; BULL, *34*, 864)
Appointment: Dunlap, K. (SCI, *82*, 217)
Appointment: Fearing, F. (SCI, *82*, 386)
Appointment: Franz, S. I. (SCI, *60*, 315)
Appointment: Montague, W. P.; Visiting professorship, 1943 (JoP, *40*, 140)
Appointment: Wenger, M. A. (BULL, *42*, 583)
Dedication: lab, 1940 Dallenbach, K. M. (SCI, *91*, 311)
Paper: celebration of new psych building (SCI, *91*, 430)

California, University of, San Francisco
Establishment: psychopathic hospital (SCI, *45*, 163)

California, University of, School of Medicine
Appointments: Bridges, J. W. and May, M. A. (BULL, *29*, 460)

California Youth Correction Authority
Appointment: Castner, B. M. (BULL, *39*, 807)
Appointment: Fenton, N. (SCI, *97*, 65)
Opens diagnostic and classification clinic (BULL, *39*, 807)

Calkins, Mary Whiton
Appointment: Univ. of California (SCI, *44*, 18; JoP, *13*, 448)
Death notice (JoP, *27*, *168; BULL*, *27*, 240)
Degree: Columbia Univ. (BULL, *6*, 256)
Election: American Assoc. of Univ. Professors; Vice-president (SCI, *59*, 482)
Election: APA president (SCI, *21*, 37; JoP, *2*, 28)
Eulogized (JoP, *27*, 223)
Lecture: Columbia Univ. (JoP, *8*, 112; SCI, *33*, 214)
Lecture: England (SCI, *67*, 188)

Lecture: International Congress of Arts and Sciences, St. Louis (JoP, *1*, 420)
Lecture: Sanford, E. C. (J App, *9*, 87)
Lecture: Univ. of London conceptions of meaning and self psychology (BULL, *25*, 307)
Presiding over APA meeting (AJP, *17*, 144)
Publication: announcement (JoP, *8*, 560)
Resignation: Executive committee of American Philosophical Assoc. (JoP, *11*, 56)
Retirement (SCI, *69*, 666)
Retirement notice in *Boston Evening Transcript* (JoP, *26*, 531)

Calorimetric Experiments
Lecture: Rosenthal, I. at the Berlin Physiological Society (SCI°, *13*, 379)

Cambridge University (*see also* Caius College; Girton College; Gonville College) (England)
Anniversary celebration Darwin, C. (JoP, *6*, 420; BULL, *6*, 216)
Anthropological studies established (JoP, *1*, 364)
Appointment: Bartlett, F. C. (SCI, *56*, 43)
Appointment: Chambers, E. G. (SCI, *82*, 123)
Appointment: Fisher, R. A. (SCI, *98*, 58)
Appointment: Galton, F., Trinity College honorary fellow (SCI°, *16*, 917)
Appointment: Grindley, G. C. (SCI, *82*, 123)
Appointment: Jones, C. Girton College (SCI, *17*, 520)
Appointment: Myers, C. S. (BULL, *18*, 236)
Appointment: Rivers, W. H. R. (AJP, *9*, 250; SCI°, *16*, 840)
Appointment: Sorley, W. R. (SCI, *12*, 120; REV, *7*, 531)
Appointment: Ward, J. (REV, *4*, 229; AJP, *8*, 430)
Celebration, honor Darwin, C. (JoP, *5*, 168)
Degree: Galton, F. (SCI, *1*, 614)
Degree: Ward, J. (JoP, *6*, 532)
Degrees: instituted (JoP, *13*, 391)
Donation from Trinity College for physiology and experimental psychology buildings (JoP, *8*, 280; SCI, *33*, 526)
Endowment: Chair of mental philosophy and logic (REV, *3*, 588)
Establishment: experimental psychology dept (SCI, *5*, 729)
Experimental psychology professorship created (BULL, *28*, 80)
Laboratory, psychology erected (BULL, *8*, 146)
Laboratory, psychophysics proposed (SCI, *32*, 553)
Lecture: Bourtroux, E. religion and contemporaneous philosophy (JoP, *7*, 140)
Lecture: Prince, M. subconscious (SCI, *59*, 161)
Lecture: USA (JoP, *15*, 420)
Lecture: Ward, J., Univ. of California Philosophical Union (JoP, *1*, 588)
Lectureships established (BULL, *4*, 338)
Lectureship established experimental psychology (JoP, *4*, 448; REV, *4*, 567; REV, *4*, 452)

Medical Research Council for research in applied psychology established (BULL, *41*, 602; SCI, *99*, 531)

Meeting: Psychological Society (JoP, *1*, 616)

Publication: *Advanced Study and Research* a guide to students announced (JoP, *1*, 111)

Publication: *British Journal of Psychology* announced (JoP, *1*, 28)

Represented by Ward, J. at Oxford celebration of Bacon, R. (JoP, *11*, 336)

Resignation: Myers, C. S. (SCI, *55*, 451; BULL, *19*, 296)

Resignation: Sidgwick, H. (SCI *11*, 997)

Return: Ward, J. (JoP, *1*, 616)

Special Board for Moral Science states need for improving experimental psychology lab (BULL, 7, 75)

Studentships, Arnold Gerstenberg announced (JoP, *2*, 308)

Women student successes (SCI°, *16*, 21)

Cambridge University, Library of
Received Darwin's manuscripts, 1942 (SCI, *96*, 493)

Cambridge University Press
Publication: *Darwin and Modern Sciences* (JoP, *6*, 168)

Cameron, Donald Ewen
Appointment: McGill Univ. (SCI, *99*, 123-124)

Cameron, Edward Herbert
Appointment: Yale Univ.; Instructor (JoP, *3*, 196; SCI, *23*, 520; BULL, *3*, 147)

Course: Harvard Univ. (BULL, *12*, 403)

Paper: tones (JoP, *2*, 224)

Promotion: Yale Univ. (BULL, 7, 148; JoP, 7, 196, 252)

Cameron, Norman
Appointment: Cornell Univ. Medical College (SCI, *89*, 76)

Appointment: New York Hospital (SCI, *89*, 76; BULL, *36*, 218)

Appointment: Univ. of Wisconsin (SCI, *91*, 593; BULL, *37*, 656)

Departure: Cornell Univ. Medical College and New York Hospital (SCI, *91*, 593)

Departure: Johns Hopkins Medical School and Johns Hopkins Hospital (SCI, *89*, 76)

Resignation: editorial board of *Journal of Clinical Psychology* (BULL, *42*, 485)

Camp Jackson
Appointment: Morse, J. (JoP, *15*, 140)

Campbell, Albert Angus
Appointment: Social Science Research Council Fellow (BULL, *36*, 711)

Award: Social Science Research Council (BULL, *36*, 805)

Campbell, Charles Arthur

Lecture: Mind Assoc. and Aristotelian Society; "Is there an absolute good" (JoP, *34*, 252)

Campbell, Charles MacFie

Appointment: Harvard Medical School and Boston Psychopathic Hospital (SCI, *52*, 290; BULL, *17*, 351)

Appointment: Johns Hopkins Univ. (SCI, *40*, 25)

Election: American Board of Psychiatry and Neurology; Vice-president (SCI, *80*, 476)

Election: American Psychiatric Assoc.; President (SCI, *83*, 517)

Election: Massachusetts Psychiatric Society; President (SCI, *80*, 475)

Election: Massachusetts Society for Mental Hygiene; President (SCI, *65*, 11; SCI, *67*, 12)

Grant: Boston Psychopathic Hospital for clinics (SCI, *79*, 291)

Lecture: Gehrmann, Univ. of Illinois on abnormal (SCI, *75*, 262)

Lecture: Institute of Medicine of Chicago (SCI, *66*, 477)

Lecture: Lowell, Harvard (SCI, *76*, 462)

Lecture: Salmon, T. W. New York Acad of Medicine (SCI, *79*, 268)

Lecture: series (BULL, *30*, 107)

Resignation: Henry Phipps Psychiatric Clinic, Johns Hopkins Hospital (BULL, *17*, 351)

Campbell, Gabriel

Retirement: Dartmouth College (SCI, *31*, 949)

Campbell, Ivy Gertrude

Promotion: Wellesley College (BULL, *12*, 160)

Canadian National Committee for Mental Hygiene

Director: Clarke, C. K. (SCI, *58*, 463)

Canadian Psychological Association

Lecture: Bingham, W. V. (BULL, *42*, 485; SCI, *101*, 606-607)

Meeting: 1942 (BULL, *39*, 326)

Publication: *Bulletin of the Canadian Psychological Association* (BULL, *38*, 304)

Canady, Herman George

Promotion: West Virginia State College (BULL, *40*, 619)

Candolle, Alphonse de

Research: Production of a race of deaf-mutes (SCI°, *7*, 214)

Cannon, Walter Bradford

Award: distinguished service medal by War Dept (SCI, *56*, 683)

Death notice (BULL, *42*, 675)

Election: Barcelona Acad. of Medicine (BULL, *30*, 107)

Lecture: Harvard Medical Society (BULL, *28*, 80)

Lecture: Mayo Clinic (SCI, *56*, 105)

Cantril, Hadley
Appointment: Columbia Univ. (Sci, 82, 367)
National Research Council Conference "Psychological factors in national morale" (Bull, 37, 829)
President *Institute for Propaganda Analysis* (J App, 21 719)
Promotion: Princeton Univ. (Bull, 42, 581)

Capital punishment
Publication: Howard Assoc. (Sci, 12, 36)

Cappell, Daniel Fowler
Appointment: Univ. of Glasgow (Sci, 101, 60)

Capps, Harry Marcellus
Death notice (Sci, 95, 220; Bull, 39, 267)

Carl, George P.
Research: "Sympathomimetic" drugs, Inst. of the Penn. Hospital (Bull, 34, 636)

Carleton College (Northfield, Minnesota)
Appointment: Rautman, A. L. (Bull, 42, 793)
Appointment: Weigle, L. A. (JoP, 2, 280)

Carmichael, Leonard
Abstracts for papers of AAAS, Section I, 1940 (Sci, 92, 351-352)
Announcement: China Institute of Physiology and Psychology established (Sci, 93, 181)
Appointment: Brown Univ. (Sci, 65, 371; Bull, 24, 380; J App, 11, 234)
Appointment: Clark Univ. (Bull, 28, 503; Sci, 73, 609)
Appointment: Harvard (Bull, 32, 323; Sci, 81, 93; Sci, 82, 298)
Appointment: Tufts College (Sci, 87, 209, 549; Sci, 88, 398)
Appointment: Univ. of Rochester (Sci, 83, 367; Bull, 33, 405)
Appointment: Yale Laboratories of Primate Biology (Sci, 89, 266)
Chair: panel discussion APA, 1942 "Psychology in government service" (Sci, 95, 405)
Conference: National Research Council "Psychological factors in national morale" (Bull, 37, 829)
Conference: Psychologists on the Development of Morale in Childhood and Youth (Bull, 39, 267)
Degree: Boston Univ. (Bull, 35, 333; Sci, 87, 276)
Degree: St. Lawrence Univ., Canton, New York (Sci, 97, 462)
Departure: Univ. of Rochester (Sci, 87, 276)
Election: AAAS, Section I; Secretary (Bull, 34, 179; J App, 23, 630)
Election: APA; President (Sci, 90, 249)
Election: Tufts College President (Bull, 35, 259; Sci, 87, 184)
Grant: National Research Council (Bull, 33, 578)
Lecture: National Wartime Conference, 1943 (Sci, 97, 375)

Lecture: Tufts College Medical School, 50th anniversary (SCI, *98*, 260)

National Research Council, emergency committee in psychology (BULL, *37*, 755)

Promotion: Brown Univ. (BULL, *25*, 568)

Relationship between psychiatry and psychology (BULL, *37*, 122)

Resignation: National Roster of Scientific and Specialized Personnel of the War Manpower Commission (SCI, *100*, 447)

Washburn, M. F.; memorial conference at Vassar Coll. (BULL, *37*, 406)

Carnap, Rudolph

Appointment: Univ. of Chicago; Professor of philosophy (JoP, *33*, 560)

Editor: *Journal of Unified Science* (JoP, *36*, 532)

Carnegie, Andrew

Publication: *Triumphant Democracy* (SCI°, 7, 350)

Carnegie Corporation, New York

Appropriation: NAS (J APP, *4*, 112)

Appropriation: National Research Council (J APP, *4*, 112)

Election: Angell, J. R.; President (SCI, *51*, 411; BULL, *17*, 200; JoP, *17*, 308)

Grant: Yale Univ. Clinic of Child Development at School of Medicine (SCI, *95*, 192)

Carnegie Endowment for International Peace

Announcement: assist in preparation of a peace policy (JoP, *15*, 560)

Carnegie, Illinois Steel Corporation

Appointment: Husband, R. W. (SCI, *96*, 225; J APP, *26*, 712; BULL, *39*, 807)

Carnegie Institute of Technology (Pittsburgh, Pennsylvania)

Announcement: changes (JoP, *15*, 335-336)

Annual report-14th (J APP, *2*, 299)

Appointment: Baird, J. W. at Cornell Univ.; Research assistant (SCI, *17*, 677)

Appointment: Beatty, A. J. (JoP, *14*, 616)

Appointment: Bingham, W. V. (BULL, *12*, 160; JoP, *12*, 196)

Appointment: Charters, W. W. (J APP, *3*, 290; BULL, *16*, 257)

Appointment: Free, M. L. (JoP, *12*, 644; BULL, *12*, 403; SCI, *41*, 88)

Appointment: Gordon, K. (SCI, *43*, 133; JoP, *13*, 112; BULL, *13*, 108)

Appointment: made (BULL, *14*, 263)

Appointment: Miner, J. B. (JoP, *12*, 644; BULL, *12*, 403; SCI, *41*, 88)

Appointment: Ruml, B. (JoP, *14*, 616)

Appointment: Scott, W. D. (J APP, *2*, 299; JoP, *14*, 616)

Appointment: Thurstone, L. L. (JoP, *12*, 644; SCI, *41*, 88; JoP, *14*, 616; BULL, *12*, 403)

Appointment: Watson, J. B. (JoP, *9*, 112; SCI, *35*, 77)

Appointment: Whipple, G. M. (JoP, *15*, 335-336; JoP, *14*, 616; J APP, *2*, 196; BULL, *15*, 176)

Appointment: Wrinch, F. S. (REV, *10*, 344; SCI, *17*, 558)

Appointment: Yoakum, C. S. (JoP, *16*, 336; J App, *3*, 290)
Bureau of Salesmanship Research enlarged (J App, *3*, 197)
Bureau of Salesmanship Research opens (JoP, *13*, 139)
Election: Davenport, C. B., American Society of Naturalists; Vice-president
  (Sci, *21*, 37)
Election: Woodward, R. S.; President (JoP, *1*, 721)
Establishment: research assistantships (Rev, *10*, 224)
Grant: Jennings, H. S. (Sci, *17*, 635-636)
Grant: psychologists (Bull, *1*, 27)
Grant: Scripture, E. W. (Rev, *10*, 103; Sci°, *16*, 1039)
Leave of absence Gordon, K. (JoP, *15*, 336)
Leave of absence Ruml, B. (JoP, *15*, 336)
Lecture: Aikins, H. A., problems of psychotherapy (Sci, *49*, 118)
Lecture: Angell, J. R. (Sci, *50*, 480)
Lecture: Dodge, R. (Bull, *13*, 228)
Lecture: Schoen, M., psychology of music (Bull, *18*, 628)
Lecture: Strong, E. K., job analysis on army (Sci, *49*, 118)
Promotion: Gordon, K. (Bull, *16*, 257; J App, *3*, 290)
Promotion: Miner, J. B. (JoP, *15*, 336; Bull, *15*, 176)
Promotion: Scott, W. D. (Bull, *16*, 257)
Promotion: Thurstone, L. L. (JoP, *15*, 336; Bull, *15*, 176)
Promotion: Yoakum, C. S. (Bull, *16*, 257)
Resignation: Beatty, A. J. (JoP, *15*, 336)

Carnegie Institute of Technology, Bureau of Salesmanship Research

Appointment: Friedlaender, K. (Sci, *44*, 56; JoP, *13*, 476)
Appointment: Gould, R. L. (Sci, *44*, 56)
Appointment: Hoopingarner, D. L. (Sci, *44*, 56)
Appointment: Robinson, E. S. (Sci, *44*, 56)
Appointment: Scott, W. D. (Sci, *44*, 491; J App, *2*, 299; JoP, *13*, 140, 588)
Appointment: Stone, C. P. (Sci, *44*, 56)
Appointment: Student Fellows (JoP, *13*, 476; Bull, *13*, 296)
Appointment: Thurstone, L. L., Director (J App, *6*, 417)
Appointment: Whipple, G. M. (J App, *2*, 299)
Founded (JoP, *13*, 139, 196)
Name changed to Bureau of Personnel (J App, *3*, 196)
Psychological tests applied (JoP, *13*, 139)

Carnegie Institution of Washington

Appointment: Dodge, R., (Nutrition Lab) (Bull, *10*, 252; Sci, *36*, 591; JoP, *9*, 672)
Appointment: Watson, J. B. (Bull, *9*, 128)
Lecture: Angell, J. R. (Sci, *81*, 250)

Carnegie Laboratory of Education at Cold Spring Harbor

Departure: Basset, G. C. (Bull, *11*, 443)

Carpenter, Clarence Ray

Appointment: National Research Council (J App, *15*, 326)
Appointment: Pennsylvania State College (Sci, *92*, 307; Bull, *37*, 827)
Appointment: School of Tropical Medicine, San Juan, Puerto Rico (Sci, *92*, 307)
Collecting primates in Siam (Sci, *86*, 79)
Leave of absence (Sci, *86*, 98)
Promotion: Columbia Univ. (Sci, *86*, 98)
Research: Univ. of the School of Tropical Medicine, San Juan, Puerto Rico;
  psychobiology with primates (Sci, *86*, 79)
Santiago primate colonies (Bull, *37*, 827)

Carpenter, William Benjamin

Death notice (Sci°, *6*, 429)

Carr, [?]

Paper: examination of the social and political position of women among the
  Iroquois (Sci°, *3*, 668)

Carr, Harvey A.

Appointment: Pratt Institute (JoP, *3*, 532; Sci, *24*, 384; Bull, *3*, 319)
Appointment: Univ. of Chicago (Sci, *28*, 48; JoP, *5*, 392; Bull, *5*, 243)
Departure: Univ. of Chicago (Sci, *24*, 384)
Election: APA president (Sci, *63*, 41; Bull, *23*, 40, 112)
Election: MPA president, 12th annual meeting (Sci, *85*, 118; Sci, *83*, 517; Bull,
  34, 121)
Election: National Research Council Div of Anthropology and Psychology
  (Bull, *25*, 123)
Leave of absence: Univ. of Chicago (Bull, *32*, 322)
Lecture: president MPA 12th annual meeting (J App, *21*, 130)
Obituary: Robinson, II. A. (AJP, *49*, 489)
Promotion: Univ. of Chicao (Sci, *43*, 711; Sci, *63*, 454; Bull, *13*, 260; Bull, *23*,
  412; Sci, *58*, 67)
Retirement: Univ. of Chicago (Sci, *89*, 313; Bull, *36*, 499)

Carr, Herbert Wildon

Paper: abstract on instinct (JoP, *7*, 280)
Paper: instinct and intelligence (JoP, *7*, 420)
Paper: psychophysical parallelism in psychology (JoP, *8*, 280)

Carrel, Alexis

Director of Alexis Carrel Foundation for Study of Human Problems (Sci, *94*,
  559)

Carrier, Blanche

Appointment: San Jose State College (Bull, *42*, 255)

Carroll, Herbert Allen

Promotion: Univ. of New Hampshire (Bull, *40*, 539)

Carroll, Robert Sproul

Presentation: Highland Hospital for nervous and mental disorders (SCI, *89*, 555; SCI, *91*, 187)

Carrothers, George Ezra

Appointment: Rollins College, Dean (J APP, *10*, 288) *Carry On*
Editor: Wood, C. A. (BULL, *15*, 176)
Issued by the Office of the Surgeon General (J APP, *2*, 293-294)
Publication notice (J APP, *3*, 198)
Publication: Surgeon General of the Army (BULL, *15*, 176)

Carter, Harold Dean

Appointment: Social Science Research Fellow, Stanford Univ. (J APP, *15*, 326)

Carter, Jerry William, Jr.

Appointment: Wichita Child Guidance Center (BULL, *38*, 777; BULL, *37*, 406)

Carus Lecture

Mead, G. H. (SCI, *69*, 157)

Carus, Paul

Death notice (BULL, *16*, 222)

Case, Harry Walter

Course: military psychology, Univ. of Illinois (J APP, *26*, 392)
Publication: "The adjutant general's school and the training of psychological personnel for the army" (J APP, *26*, 392)

Case, Thomas

Election: Corpus Christi College, Fellow (JoP, *1*, 56)
Election: Corpus Christi College, President (JoP, *2*, 112)

Cason, Hulsey

Appointment: Univ. of Kansas (SCI, *55*, 675)
Appointment: Univ. of Rochester (J APP, *10*, 524; SCI, *65*, 397; BULL, *24*, 136)
Appointment: Univ. of Wisconsin (BULL, *27*, 564)
Paper: Organic nature of fatigue (AJP, *47*, 342)
Promotion: Syracuse Univ. (BULL, *22*, 260)
Promotion: Univ. of Kansas, Assistant professor (BULL, *19*, 462)
Promotion: Univ. of Rochester, Professor (BULL, *24*, 571; J APP, *11*, 319)
Research: Medical Center for Federal Prisoners, Springfield, Missouri (BULL, *38*, 305)

Cassirer, Ernst Alfred

Appointment: Yale Univ. (JoP, *38*, 168)
Death notice (JoP, *42*, 251)

Castle, William Ernst
Election: American Society of Naturalists; Secretary (SCI, *21*, 37)

Castner, Burton Menaugh
Appointment: Youth Correction Authority of the State of California (BULL, *39*, 807)

Departure: New Jersey Department of Institutions and Agencies (BULL, *39*, 807)

Castro, Matilde
Directs model school, Bryn Mawr College (JoP, *10*, 616)

Paper: sensation (JoP, *1*, 336)

Catholic University of America (Washington, DC)
Appointment: Commins, W.; Instructor (J APP, *15*, 326)

Appointment: Pace, E. A. (SCI°, *16*, 680)

Appointment: Shields, T. E. (REV, *9*, 644)

Appointment: Ulrich, J. L. (BULL, *10*, 292; SCI, *37*, 906; JoP, *10*, 504)

Laboratory opening (SCI°, *19*, 129)

Psychiatric clinic opens (BULL, *13*, 108)

Publication: Diastatic activity of the blood serum in mental disorders (J APP, *10*, 395)

Publication: Psychology of reasoning (J APP, *10*, 395)

Cattell, James McKeen
AAAS gives dinner for Cattell (SCI, *79*, 30)

Anniversary: 25th at Columbia Univ. (JoP, *11*, 251-252; AJP, *25*, 468)

Appointment: Cornell Univ. Medical College (SCI, *97*, 530; SCI, *83*, 572)

Appointment: National Research Council (JoP, *14*, 392; BULL, *14*, 191)

Appointment: Univ. of Pennsylvania (SCI°, *8*, 480)

Arranges reception for Lord Kelvin (SCI°, *15*, 637)

Attends meeting of British Assoc for Advancement of Science (BULL, *28*, 646)

Award: Society of Arts and Sciences, gold medal (SCI, *71*, 310)

Committee: APA/International Congress for Psychology (JoP, *8*, 196)

Committee: member Am. Society for Pharmacology and Experimental Therapeutics (SCI, *87*, 458)

Correspondence for *Psychological Review* (REV, *4*, 690)

Death notice (AJP, *57*, 270-275; BULL, *41*, 199; JoP, *41*, 84)

Degree: Lafayette College (BULL, *4*, 338)

Degree: Univ. of Arizona (SCI, *59*, 506)

Delegate American Scientific Congress, 7th (SCI, *82*, 217, 298)

Delegate to British Assoc. Centenary meeting, AAAS (SCI, *74*, 240, 409)

Dismissal: Columbia Univ. (SCI, *46*, 335; BULL, *14*, 366)

Editor: *School and Society* (BULL, *12*, 44)

Editor: *Science Series, The* (REV, *5*, 232)

Election: AAAS (SCI, *57*, 48)

Election: Affiliated Science Societies, President (SCI, *15*, 77-78)

Election: American Society of Naturalists; Member of executive committee (SCI, *17*, 78-79)

Election: APA, New York Branch (SCI, *77*, 364)

Election: declined Science Service, President (SCI, *85*, 475)

Election: Harvey Society; Secretary (SCI, *87*, 135)

Election: International Congress of Psychology (JOP, *8*, 196)

Election: International Congress of Psychology, 6th Vice-president (SCI, *30*, 202)

Election: National Acad. of Sciences (SCI, *71*, 478)

Election: New York Acad. of Sciences; President (SCI, *15*, 391-392)

Election: Psychological Corporation; Chairman of the board (J APP, *11*, 81)

Election: Science, President (SCI, *77*, 506)

Election: Sigma Xi, President (SCI, *37*, 55)

Election: symposium on feelings and emotions; Honorary chair (BULL, *24*, 620; JOP, *24*, 587)

Europe visit (SCI, *67*, 530)

Experimental psychologists holding dinner in honor of (JOP, *11*, 196)

Honor: dinner Univ. Club, Boston (BULL, *31*, 79)

Leave of absence: Columbia Univ. (BULL, *5*, 406)

Lecture: AAAS (REV, *5*, 677)

Lecture: APA meeting, 1935 (SCI, *82*, 298)

Lecture: apparatus (JOP, *1*, 224)

Lecture: Columbia Univ. (SCI, *95*, 190)

Lecture: Indiana Univ. (BULL, *9*, 96; JOP, *9*, 112)

Lecture: International Congress of Arts and Sciences, St. Louis (JOP, *1*, 419)

Lecture: Jastrow, J. on Cattell before N.Y. Branch of APA (SCI, *79*, 359)

Lecture: Johns Hopkins Univ. (SCI, *34*, 911; BULL, *9*, 96)

Lecture: Lafayette College (JOP, *9*, 112; SCI, *25*, 1014)

Lecture: Lehigh Univ. (BULL, *9*, 96; JOP, *9*, 112)

Lecture: Medical Institute of the Univ. of Toledo (SCI, *94*, 484)

Lecture: Michigan Academy of Sciences (BULL, *19*, 296; SCI, *55*, 512)

Lecture: New York State Assoc. of Consulting Psychologists meeting (BULL, *18*, 568)

Lecture: Scientific merit (JOP, *2*, 700)

Lecture: Sigma Xi (SCI, *43*, 423)

Lecture: Syracuse Univ. (SCI, *49*, 305)

Lecture: Taylor Society meeting (JOP, *21*, 700)

Lecture: training (JOP, *2*, 224)

Lecture: Twentieth Century Club (SCI, *45*, 498)

Lecture: Univ. of Arizona (SCI, *59*, 457)

Lecture: Univ. of Illinois (BULL, *9*, 96; JOP, *9*, 112)

Lecture: Yale Univ. (JOP, *13*, 224)

Meeting: 20th anniversary of Psychological Corp. (BULL, *39*, 196)

Portrait presented by colleagues and students (SCI, *75*, 661; BULL, *29*, 604)

Presentation: "Festschrift" by former students (SCI, *39*, 572)

Promotion: Columbia Univ. (REV, *9*, 328)

Publication: *A case in experimental psychology* (SCI°, *23*, 95)

Publication: *Biographical directory of leaders in education* released (J APP, *16*, 222)

Publication: contradicting Hall, G. S. (Sci, 2, 628)
Publication: critique of article by Baldwin, J. M. (Sci, 2, 271)
Publication: critique of pamphlet by Smith, E. (Sci, 2, 411)
Publication: note on evolution (Sci, 3, 668)
Publication: *School and society* (JoP, 12, 84)
Received Commander of the Legion of Honor (Sci, 86, 152)
Research: Cornell Univ. Medical College quinine and other alkaloids (Sci, 98, 59)
Resignation: Psychology Committee of the National Research Council (Bull, 14, 366)
Retirement: American Assoc. for Advancement of Science (Sci, 46, 336, 381)
Retirement: International Congress of Psychology (Sci, 76, 141)

Cattell, James McKeen Grants-in-Aid for Research

Awards announced (Bull, 39, 683; Bull, 40, 723; Bull, 41, 412; J App, 28, 79)
Offered Psychological Corp., 1942-43 (J App, 26, 389; Sci, 95, 573)

Cattell, Raymond Bernard

Appointment: Clark Univ. (Sci, 87, 276; Bull, 35, 333)
Appointment: Univ. of Illinois (Sci, 102, 299; Bull, 42, 793-794)
Degree: London Univ. (Bull, 36, 711)
Lecture: Psychological Supper Club, 1939-40 (Bull, 37, 656)
Publication: *Human affairs: An exposition of what science can do for man* (JoP, 34, 644)

Cavance Lectures

Ebaugh, F. G., 1940 (Sci, 91, 446)

Cavendish Lecture

Osler, W. (Sci, 9, 268)

Centenary Junior College (New Jersey)

Appointment: Garber, R. B. (Bull, 41, 679)
Appointment: Wright, C. A. (Bull, 41, 200)

Center for Psychological Service, Washington, D.C.

Interest inventory for elementary grades (J App, 25, 474)

Center, Stella Stewart

Publication: *Teaching high school students to read*, (J App, 21, 244)

Central Europe

Anglo-American libraries loan books (JoP, 17, 307-308)

Central Institute for the Deaf

Meyer, M. F., Research professor (Sci, 71, 583)

Central Kansas Teachers Association

Lecture: Judd, C. H., Salina, Mar 2, 1911 (Sci, 33, 420)

Century
Publication: Bean, R. B. "The negro brain" (JoP, 3, 615)

Century of Progress Exposition (Chicago, Illinois)
Köhler,W. AAAS guest (SCI, 77, 579)
Laird, D. A.; sleep and fatigue exhibit (SCI, 77, 348)
Mira, E. AAAS guest (SCI, 77, 579)
Piéron, H. AAAS guest (SCI, 77, 579)
Spearman, C. E. AAAS guest (SCI, 77, 579)

Cephalometry
Research: Peli, G. (AJP, 1, 205)

Cerebellar diseases
Research: Starr, A. (AJP, 1, 198)

Cerebral convolutions
Research: Pozzi, S.J. (AJP, 1, 205)

Cerebral hemisphere
Research: article on (AJP, 1, 198)

Cerebral localization
Research: Clevenger, S. V. (AJP, 2, 192)
Research: Hun, H. (SCI°, 9, 133)

Cerebrum, functions of
Lecture: Franz, S. I. (JoP, 7, 28)

Challman, Robert Chester
Appointment: Univ. of Connecticut (BULL, 41, 136)

Chamberlain, Alexander Francis
Death notice (AJP, 25, 470)

Chambers, Eric Gordon
Appointment: Univ. of Cambridge; Director industrial psych. (SCI, 82, 123)
Publication: Psychology in the industrial life of a nation (JoP, 34, 644)

Chambers, Will Grant
Appointment: State Normal School of Colorado, Greeley; Chair in psychology
(SCI, 20, 384; BULL, 1, 414)

Chan, Wing Tsit
Lecture: Bryn Mawr College (JoP, 40, 560)

Chance
Lecture: Sheldon, W. L. (JoP, 2, 224)

Chapin, Henry Dwight
Publication: The summer care of children in *Babyhood* (Sci°, *13*, 441)

Chapman College (Orange, California)
Promotion: Delp, P. S. (JoP, *33*, 560)

Chapman, Dwight Westley, Jr.
Appointment: Columbia Univ. (BULL, *34*, 635)
Appointment: Psychopathic clinic, city of Detroit (Sci, *84*, 13)
Publication: Attensity, clearness and attention (AJP, *45*, 156-165)
Publication: statistics, "The significance of matching with unequal series" (AJP, *48*, 169)

Chapman, James Crosby
Appointment: Western Reserve Univ. (BULL, *11*, 396)
Appointment: Yale Univ. (Sci, *59*, 398)
Death notice (Sci, *62*, 107)
Promotion: Yale Univ. (BULL, *21*, 360)

Chapman, Ross M.
Election: American Psychiatric Assoc., President (Sci, *83*, 517)

Chappell, Matthew Napoleon
Psychological Service Center, NY (BULL, *36*, 805)

Character and Personality
Publication: begins (J APP, *16*, 439; JoP, *29*, 644; BULL, *29*, 603)

Character Research Fund
Donation by Lilly, E. (BULL, *41*, 409-410)

Charcot, Jean-Martin
Election: Sociëtë de pychologie physiologique, President (Sci°, *6*, 360)

Charing-Cross Hospital Medical School (London, England)
Lecture: Pavlov, I. P. (Sci, *24*, 381)

Charpentier, Augustin
Death notice (BULL, *13*, 408)
Research: optical illusion (Sci°, *7*, 548)

Charters, Werrett Wallace
Appointment: Carnegie Institute of Technology (BULL, *16*, 257; J APP, *3*, 290)
Appointment: Univ. of Chicago, Professor (BULL, *22*, 260)
Appointment: War Manpower Commission (Sci, *97*, 87)
Retirement: Bureau of Educational Research of Ohio State Univ. (Sci, *95*, 271)

Chase, Harry Woodburn
Election: New York Univ., Chancellor (Sci, *77*, 165)

Election: Univ. of North Carolina, President (JoP, *16*, 588; Sci, *50*, 40)
Inaugurated president Univ. of North Carolina (Bull, *17*, 200)
Promotion: Univ. of North Carolina (Bull, *16*, 392)

Chase, Pliny Earle

Publication: photodynamics *Proceedings of the American Philosophical Society* (Sci°, *2*, 150)

Chase, Robert Howland

Lecture: Harvard, insanity (AJP, *2*, 190)

Chase, Susan F.

Committee member for New York State Teachers of Educational Psychology (JoP, *7*, 252)

Chassell, Clara Frances

Lecture: A test of ability to weigh forseen social consequences (JoP, *19*, 279)
Lecture: Psychology of play (JoP, *15, 140*)

Chautauqua

Appointment: Judd, C. H. (Sci, *27*, 759; JoP, *5*, 308)
Lecture: Judd, C. H. (Bull, *5*, 244)

Chautauquan, The

Publication: Brockway, Z. R. "The care of criminals" (Sci°, *13*, 141)
Publication: White, W. W. "Talks on memory" (Sci°, *12*, 250)

Chauveau, Auguste

Death notice (Bull, *14*, 80)

Chelpanov, Georgii Ivanovich

Commission: develop a psychological laboratory in Moscow (JoP, *8*, 335-336)
Lecture: Cornell Univ., status of psychology in Russia (JoP, *8*, 335-336)

Cheney, Clarence Orion

Appointment: Columbia Univ. (Sci, *74*, 308)
Appointment: New York Hospital (Sci, *92*, 76)
Retirement: American Psychiatric Assoc, President (Sci, *83*, 517)

Chervin, Arthur

Research: disabilities developed by the annual conscription (Sci°, *4*, 220)

Chevreul, Michel Eugene

Funeral (Sci°, *13*, 341)

Chicago and Northwestern Railway Company

Appointment: Ruckmick, C. A. (Sci, *99*, 404)

Chicago Bar Association

Recommendation: shut down of the Municipal Court of Chicago's psychopathic lab (BULL, *13, 296*)

Chicago Board of Education's Department of Child Study

Conclusions of examinations of the eyes of school children (SCI, *12, 815*)

Chicago Branch of Psychological Association (*see also* Midwestern Psychological Association)

Establishment (REV, *9, 432*)

Chicago Civilian Defense Office

Appointment: Ruckmick, C. A., committee chair (SCI, *99, 404*)

Chicago Community Trust

Disburse money from the will of Jones, G. H. for charities and educational institutions (SCI, *94, 112*)

Chicago Exposition

Publication: Harvard Univ. (REV, *1, 214*)

Chicago, Institute of Medicine

Lecture: Campbell, C. MacF. (SCI, *66, 477*)
Lecture: Gillespie, R. D. (SCI, *94, 323*)
Meeting: Assembly on Nervous and Mental Diseases and War (SCI, *100, 263, 311*)

Chicago Laboratory Supply Company

Manufacturer of stereoscopic vision card set to accompany E. B. Titchener's *Experimental Psychology*, (SCI, *24, 222*)

Chicago Medical Society

Meeting: directed at feeble mindedness (BULL, *13, 148*)

Chicago Musical College

Degree: Seashore, C. E. (SCI, *90, 59*; BULL, *36, 804*)

Chicago Neurological Society

Election: Donaldson, H. H., President (SCI, *17, 597*)
Lecture: Gillespie, R. D. (SCI, *94, 323*)

Chicago Normal School

Appointment: Scott, C. A. (SCI, *4, 170*; REV, *3, 706*)

Chicago Psychological Club

Lecture: Northwestern Univ. (BULL, *42, 332*)
Lecture: Sherman, M. (BULL, *40, 540*)
Lecture: Taylor, H. C. (BULL, *40, 540*)

Chicago Psychopathic Institute
Appointment: Adler, H., Director (BULL, *14*, 115)
Discontinued in the Municipal Court (BULL, *13*, 296)
Establishment (BULL, *14*, 115)
Resignation: Healy, W. (BULL, *14*, 32)
Work now connected with Juvenile Court under Cook County Authority (BULL,
   11, 232; BULL, *14*, 115)

Chicago, University of (Illinois)
Angell, J. R. relieved of duties (SCI, *46*, 407)
Anniversary, 50th, Lashley, K. S. member of roundtable discussion for
   conference on the training of biologists (SCI, *94*, 185-186)
Appointment: Andrews, G. T. (BULL, *41*, 603)
Appointment: Angell, J. R. (SCI, *59*, 422; BULL, *11*, 116; SCI, *33*, 770; BULL, *8*,
   222; SCI, *1*, 81; BULL, *21*, 360; BULL, *1*, 291; SCI, *33*, 770; REV, *1*, 440)
Appointment: Baldwin, B. T. (BULL, *6*, 184)
Appointment: Blatz, W. E. (SCI, *56*, 660)
Appointment: Buck, A. F. (REV, *5*, 109)
Appointment: Buhler, K. (SCI, *69*, 379)
Appointment: Carnap, R.; Professor of philosophy (JoP, *33*, 560)
Appointment: Carr, H. (SCI, *28*, 48; JoP, *5*, 392; BULL, *5*, 243)
Appointment: Charters, W. W. (BULL, *22*, 260)
Appointment: Conklin, E. S. (SCI, *72*, 649)
Appointment: Corey, S. M.; Director of audio-visual instruction center (BULL,
   42, 407)
Appointment: Dearborn, W. F. (SCI, *29*, 698; BULL, *6*, 184)
Appointment: Dewey, J. (REV, *1*, 440; SCI°, *15*, 920; SCI, *1*, 81)
Appointment: Downey, J. (REV, *5*, 109)
Appointment: Fite, W. (REV, *5*, 109)
Appointment: Franz, S. I. (BULL, *19*, 172)
Appointment: Freeman, F. N. (SCI, *89*, 313; BULL, *6*, 328)
Appointment: Grey, C. F. (SCI, *89*, 313)
Appointment: Haynes, R. (JoP, *3*, 532; BULL, *3*, 356)
Appointment: James, W. (SCI, *21*, 902)
Appointment: Judd, C. H. (JoP, *5*,588; SCI, *28*, 444; BULL, *27*, 674; SCI, *52*, 153;
   BULL, *5*, 347)
Appointment: Kantor, J. (SCI, *46*, 432; BULL, *14*, 420)
Appointment: Kingsbury, F. A. (BULL, *37*, 62)
Appointment: Kitson, H. D. (BULL, *16*, 257)
Appointment: Koffka, K. (BULL, *22*, 140; SCI, *61*, 257)
Appointment: Lashley, K. S. (SCI, *70*, 281)
Appointment: McLennan, S. F. (REV, *1*, 654; SCI, *1*, 81)
Appointment: Mead, G. H. (SCI, *1*, 81)
Appointment: Mullin, F. J. (SCI, *101*, 35)
Appointment: Rogers, C. R. (BULL, *42*, 486)
Appointment: Rosenow, C. (BULL, *14*, 420; SCI, *46*, 432)
Appointment: Stevens, H. C. (SCI, *40*, 408; JoP, *11*, 588)

Meeting: MPA, 1940 (BULL, *37*, 187)
Portrait of Angell, J. R. (SCI, *52*, 578)
Promotion: announced (REV, *1*, 552; SCI, *58*, 107)
Promotion: Carr, H. (SCI, *58*, 67; SCI, *63*, 454; BULL, *23*, 412; SCI, *43*, 711; BULL, *13*, 260)
Promotion: Freeman, F. N. (BULL, *36*, 499)
Promotion: Hayes, J. W. (BULL, *13*, 260; SCI, *43*, 711)
Promotion: Kingsbury, F. A. (BULL, *42*, 486)
Promotion: Thurstone, L. L. (SCI, *66*, 168; BULL, *27*, 620)
Promotion: Tufts, J. H. (REV, *7*, 324)
Psychology department transferred from biological sciences to social sciences (BULL, *36*, 499; SCI, *89*, 313)
Psychology made separate department (JoP, *1*, 336)
Research: Watson, J. B., in Dry Tortugas (SCI, *26*, 188)
Resignation: Angell, J. R. (SCI, *52*, 153)
Resignation: Dewey, J. (BULL, *1*, 291)
Resignation: Grinker, R. R. (SCI, *83*, 347)
Resignation: Mead, G. H. (BULL, *28*, 324)
Resignation: Tsai, L. S. (BULL, *28*, 79)
Retirement: Carr, H. (SCI, *89*, 313)

Chicago Veteran's Rehabilitation Center
Appointment: Shacter, H. (BULL, *42*, 127)

Child Clinic, Los Angeles, California
Appointment: Emery, E. V. N.; Director (J APP, *10*, 396)
Appointment: Mathews, J. (J APP, *10*, 396)

Child Development
Journal contents information (J APP, *22*, 540)

Child development
Univ. of Chicago Ph.D. program (J APP, *18*, 607)
Yale films on (J APP, *18*, 722)

Child Guidance Clinic, San Francisco, California
Appointment: Shirley, H. F. (SCI, *91*, 15)

Child Guidance, Institute for
Establishment (BULL, *24*, 136; SCI, *64*, 475)
Funding reduced (SCI, *76*, 81)
Grant: Commonwealth Fund (J APP, *16*, 336)

Child Health Program
Conference: psychological and psychiatric problems in children (SCI, *101*, 482)
Lecture: Plant, J. S. (SCI, *101*, 482)
Lecture: Waterman, J. H. (SCI, *101*, 482)

Child, Irvin Long
Grant: Social Science Research Council (BULL, *34*, 409)
Publication: military *Psychological Bulletin* (J APP, *25*, 359)

Child-life among savage and uncivilized peoples
Lecture: Mason, O. T. (SCI°, *3*, 56)

Child psychiatry
Establishment: Univ. of Utah (SCI, *102*, 273)
Meeting: International Congress of Child Psychiatry (BULL, *34*, 325)

Child psychology
Appointment: Lewin, K. Univ. of Iowa (BULL, *32*, 323)
Conference on education and the exceptional child, Child Research Clinic of
   the Woods School, Langhorne, PA (J APP, *22*, 215, 317)
Course: Merrill-Palmer School (J APP, *9*, 203)
Course: psychopathology (BULL, *6*, 72; JoP, *6*, 111)
Lab opens Iowa State Univ. (BULL, *18*, 628; SCI, *54*, 434)
Publication. Martin, L. J. and Gruchy, C. D. (J APP, *10*, 395)
Publication: Perez, (SCI°, *12*, 237)

Child research
Mooseheart Laboratory (AJP, *43*, 302)

Child Research Clinic of the Woods School
Conference: education and the exceptional child (J APP, *23*, 312)
Conference: exceptional child (J APP, *21*, 131, 344)
Institute on the Exceptional Child, 4th (J APP, *21*, 604)
Institute on the Exceptional Child, 7th (J APP, *24*, 855)

Child study
Announcement: Meeting of International Conference on Child Study (SCI, *9*,
   119)
Establishment: International Congress of Child Study (BULL, *3*, 116)
Fellowships from National Research Council (SCI, *63*, 303)
Grant: Univ. of Toronto from Laura Spelman Rockefeller fund (SCI, *62*, 10)
Publication: National Educational Assoc. *Proceedings* (REV, *6*, 240)
Report: findings by Chicago Board of Education on vision of school children
   (SCI, *12*, 815)

Child Study Association of America
Lecture: Glueck, B. (J APP, *9*, 319)
Lecture: Hinkle, B. (J APP, *9*, 319)
Lecture: Russell, J. E. (J APP, *9*, 319)
Lecture: Van Waters, M. (J APP, *9*, 319)
Lecture: Woolley, H. P. (J APP, *9*, 319)
Meeting (J APP, *16*, 438)
Meeting: New York, Oct 26-28, 1925 (J APP, *9*, 319)

Child Study Center of Maryland
Appointment: Beebe, R. W. (BULL, *41*, 409)

Child Study Department of Vassar College (Poughkeepsie, New York)
Research: normal personality development (BULL, *38*, 248)
Grant: General Education Board (BULL, *38*, 248)

Child Study Society, London
Lecture: announced (JoP, *8*, 644)

Child welfare
Appointment: Woods, E. L., Pasadena, California (BULL, *14*, 116)
Work done by Univ. of Iowa (BULL, *14*, 143)

Child Welfare Research Station (*see* Iowa Child Welfare Research Station)

Childhood Society of Great Britain
Meeting: London (AJP, *9*, 422)
Subscriptions announced by Galton, D. (SCI°, *5*, 549)

Children
Association formed for child-widows (SCI°, *13*, 358-359)
Grant: National Committee for Mental Hygiene by Commonwealth Fund (SCI, *100*, 122)
Lecture: Winch, W. H. (JoP, *7*, 420)

Children, retarded
Examination and classification Harvard Psychological Lab (JoP, *4*, 363)
Lecture: Lurton, F. E. (JoP, *7*, 223)
Lecture: Rogers, A. C. (JoP, *7*, 223)

Children, The Summer Care of
Publication: Chapin, H. D. in *Babyhood* (SCI°, *13*, 441)

Children's Service Bureau
Appointment: Hanson, J. M. (J APP, *3*, 289)
Appointment: Young, H. H. (J APP, *3*, 289)
Community Service Society, Ohio opens (J APP, *3*, 289)

Children's Year Leaflet No. 10
Publication notice (J APP, *3*, 198)

Childs, Herbert Guy
Appointment: Univ. of Indiana (BULL, *11*, 116; JoP, *11*, 84)
Departure: Brooklyn Training School for Teachers (BULL, *11*, 116; JoP, *11*, 84)

Chile
Order of merit award to Gotaas, H. B. (Sci, *101*, 663)

China
National Research Institute of Psychology (Bull, *28*, 79)
Psychology laboratories established (AJP, *44*, 372)
Request for psychology literature (Bull, *37*, 827)
Scholars sent to U.S. for year (Bull, *41*, 680)

China Institute of Physiology and Psychology
Appointment: Kuo, Z. Y. (Sci, *93*, 181)
Establishment: Chungking (Bull, *38*, 305; Sci, *93*, 181)

Chinese Journal of Psychology
Founded (AJP, *49*, 142)
Notes and news (AJP, *49*, 143)

Chou, Siegen K.
Publication: Optical illusion of personal magnetism (AJP, *51*, 574)
Publication: Psychology in China (AJP, *38*, 664)
Publication: What is the curve of forgetting (AJP, *45*, 348)

Chrislip, A. E.
Lecture: NY Branch APA/NYAS on memory (JoP, *9*, 167)

Chrysostom, John, Reverend
Death notice (Bull, *14*, 80; JoP, *14*, 252)

Chung-hua hsin li hsueh pao
Journal founded (AJP, *49*, 142-143)

Chunking University (*see* National Central University, and Physiology and Psychology, Institute of)

Church, Alonzo
Appointment: Editor of *Journal of Symbolic Logic* (JoP, *39*, 84)

Churchill, Ruth Dietz
Publication: military personnel, classification in *Psychological Bulletin* (J App, *25*, 358)

Cincinnati Society of Natural History
Darwin, C. birthday celebration (Sci°, *1*, 184)
Lecture: physiology and hygiene (Sci°, *6*, 359)

Cincinnati, University of (Ohio)
Appointment: Arlitt, A. H. (J App, *9*, 204)
Appointment: Bills, A. G.; Head psychology department (Bull, *34*, 325; Sci, *85*, 424)

Appointment: Breese, B. B. (SCI, 20, 192; JOP, 1, 476; BULL, 1, 372)
Appointment: Hines, H. C.; Head new psychology department (J APP, 10, 523)
Appointment: Judd, C. H. (SCI, 14, 232, 944; REV, 8, 552; SCI, 13, 1040)
Appointment: Montalto, F. D. (BULL, 42, 582)
Appointment: Pechstein, L. A. (SCI, 56, 387; BULL, 20, 172)
Appointment: Talbert, E. L. (JOP, 12, 504)
Appointment: Tawney, G. A. (BULL, 5, 348)
Appointment: Washburn, M. F. (REV, 9, 431; SCI, 15, 880)
Appointment: Weir, S. (SCI, 15, 160)
Appointment: Woolley, H. T. (JOP, 7, 644)
Departure: Judd, C. H. (SCI, 15, 360)
Departure: Washburn, M. F. (REV, 10, 344; SCI, 17, 440)
Lecture: Burtt, H. E., scientific crime detection (SCI, 94, 582)
Promotion: Piserens, C. M. (BULL, 42, 485)

City life
Injurious influences of (SCI°, 12, 36)

Civil Service Commission (*see also* United States Civil Service Commission)
Award: Bingham, W. V. D., exceptional service medal (SCI, 100, 400-401)

Civil Service Commission of Cook County, Illinois
Director position open at Psychopathic Institute (BULL, 11, 483)

Civil Service Commission of Wayne County, Michigan
Announcement: position for psychologist (BULL, 41, 410)

Civilization et philosophie au moyen age
Publication: Wulf, M. De (JOP, 15, 644)

Claparede, Edouard
Appointment: Institute for the Science of Education, Geneva (JOP, 9, 196)
Death notice (AJP, 54, 296-299; BULL, 38, 67)
Death notice, correction of date in *Bulletin* (BULL, 38, 248)
International Congress of Psychology, 11th, executive committee (J APP, 21, 242)
Resignation: correction of information (BULL, 12, 128)

Claparëde, Hugo
Dismissal: Univ. of Geneva (SCI, 40, 887; JOP, 12, 28)

Clapp, Hazel Scofield
Appointment: Briarcliff Junior College, NY (BULL, 40, 794; BULL, 41, 267)

Claremont Graduate School (California)
Promotion: Perkins, F. T. (BULL, 42, 191)

Clark, Eliza A.
Donation: Cleveland College for Women (Sci°, *13*, 298)

Clark, Helen
Appointment: Univ. of Illinois (Sci, *40*, 670; JoP, *11*, 721)

Clark, Jonas Gilman
Estate left to Clark Univ. (Rev, *7*, 427-428; Rev, *9*, 328)

Clark, Ruth Swan
Leave of absence: Smith College (Bull, *13*, 148)
Lecture (J App, *6*, 425)

Clark University (Worcester, Massachusetts)
Anniversary celebration: 20th (JoP, *6*, 419, 503, 559; Bull, *6*, 327)
Announcement: work to begin Oct, 1889 (Sci°, *13*, 360)
Appointment: Baird, J. W. (JoP, *7*, 84; Sci, *31*, 108)
Appointment: Bell, J. E. (Bull, *42*, 191)
Appointment: Boring, E. G. (Sci, *50*, 251; Bull, *16*, 257; JoP, *16*, 672)
Appointment: Bridges, J. W. (Sci, *64*, 39)
Appointment: Brown, R. H. (Sci, *85*, 354; Bull, *34*, 272; Bull, *35*, 334)
Appointment: Bühler, C. (Sci, *93*, 537; Bull, *38*, 777)
Appointment: Bühler, K. (Sci, *93*, 537; Bull, *38*, 777)
Appointment: Burt, B. C. (Sci°, *11*, 215, 437)
Appointment: Carmichael, L. (Sci, *73*, 609; Bull, *28*, 503)
Appointment: Cattell, R. B. (Sci, *87*, 276; Bull, *35*, 333)
Appointment: Cook, A. (Sci°, *14*, 215)
Appointment: Dennis, W. (Sci, *85*, 354; Bull, *34*, 272)
Appointment: Fernberger, S. W. (Bull, *9*, 440; Sci, *36*, 557; JoP, *9*, 700)
Appointment: Geissler, L. R. (Bull, *13*, 376; JoP, *13*, 588)
Appointment: Graham, C. H. (Sci, *73*, 609; Bull, *28*, 503)
Appointment: Hall, G. S. (Sci°, *12*, 34)
Appointment: Hunter, W. S. (Sci, *61*, 259; Bull, *22*, 260; J App, *9*, 90)
Appointment: Jones, V. A. (Sci, *64*, 39)
Appointment: Kakise, H. (Bull, *4*, 370)
Appointment: Köhler,W. (Sci, *61*, 183; Bull, *21*, 660; JoP, *22*, 56)
Appointment: McDonald, A. (Sci°, *14*, 215)
Appointment: McGeoch, J. A. (Sci, *84*, 387)
Appointment: Murchison, C. A. (Sci, *57*, 690)
Appointment: Porter, J. P. (Sci, *18*, 96)
Appointment: Pratt, C. C. (AJP, *32*, 160)
Appointment: Sanford, E. C. (Bull, *17*, 239; Bull, *6*, 368; Bull, *20*, 288)
Appointment: Super, D. E. (Sci, *87*, 276; Bull, *35*, 333)
Appointment: Tsanoff, R. A. (JoP, *9*, 588)
Bequest from Hall, G. S. (Sci, *54*, 422)
Celebration: second decade of work (AJP, *20*, 469)
Commemoration: life of Hall, G. S. (Sci, *60*, 380)

Conference: the Development of Morale in Childhood and Youth (BULL, 39, 267)

Course: Titchener, E. B., Knight, D. and Watson, J. B. (BULL, 21, 428)

Debate on psychical research held Nov 29-Dec 11, 1926 (J APP, 10, 522)

Degree: Conklin, E. S. (BULL, 37, 61)

Degree: Freud, S. (SCI, 30, 362)

Degree: Jennings, H. S. (SCI, 30, 362)

Degree: Jung, C. G. (SCI, 30, 362)

Degree: list of conferred (JOP, 6, 559)

Degree: Meyer, A. (SCI, 30, 362)

Degree: Titchener, E. B. (SCI, 30, 362)

Departure: Boring, E. G. (JOP, 19, 420)

Departure: Fernberger, S. (AJP, 32, 160)

Departure: Halverson, H. M. (JOP, 19, 532)

Departure: Weld, H. P. (BULL, 9, 407; (SCI, 36, 401; JOP, 9, 588)

Dinner given for Boring, E. G. (SCI, 55, 638)

Election: Hall, G. S. Assoc. of American Univ.; President (SCI, 21, 40)

Estate of Clark, J. G. left to Univ. (REV, 7, 427-428; REV, 9, 328)

Gift: Hall, G. S. library from son (SCI, 59, 483)

Lecture: Atwood, W. W. (J APP, 9, 87)

Lecture: Bentley, M. (SCI, 63, 65)

Lecture: Book, W. F. (J APP, 9, 88; SCI, 63, 162)

Lecture: Cook, A. psychology (SCI°, 14, 250)

Lecture: Dawson, G. E. genetic psychology (J APP, 9, 88)

Lecture: Ferry, F. C. (J APP, 9, 87)

Lecture: Gault, R. H. (J APP, 9, 87)

Lecture: Gesell, A. infant psychology (J APP, 9, 88)

Lecture: Hall, G. S. (SCI, 35, 100; JOP, 22, 140; SCI°, 14, 250)

Lecture: Jastrow, J. (SCI, 64, 554; SCI, 57, 173; J APP, 10, 522)

Lecture: Johnson, G. E. (J APP, 9, 87)

Lecture: Kohler, W. (J APP, 9, 87; SCI, 59, 460)

Lecture: Ladd-Franklin, C. (BULL, 10, 252)

Lecture: McDougall, W. (SCI, 62, 561)

Lecture: Porter, J. P. mental measurement (J APP, 9, 88)

Lecture: Prince, M. abnormal psychology (SCI, 60, 587)

Lecture: psychical research (BULL, 24, 204; JOP, 23, 700)

Lecture: psychology (SCI, 59, 574)

Lecture: Sanford, E. C. (JOP, 22, 140; SCI, 59, 437; SCI°, 14, 250)

Lecture: Swift, E. J. (J APP, 9, 87)

Lecture: Woodworth, R. (SCI, 62, 561)

Meeting: experimental psychologists (JOP, 1, 420)

Meeting: SEP (JOP, 2, 223)

Meeting: SEP (BULL, 33, 476)

Promotion: Bentley, R. C. (SCI°, 16, 80, 200)

Promotion: Nafe, J. P. (BULL, 25, 376)

Promotion: Porter, J. B. (BULL, 4, 337)

Promotion: Sanford, E. C. (SCI, 12, 936; SCI, 31, 108, 143)

Publication: *Studies in early graduate education* (J App, 23, 631)
Resignation: Hall, G. S. (Bull, 17, 239)
Resignation: Murchison, C. (Bull, 33, 849; Sci, 84, 326)
Resignation: Sanford, E. C. (Bull, 17, 239)
Retirement: Hall, G. S. (Sci, 52, 34)

Clark, Willis W.
California Capacity Questionnaire (J App, 25, 359)
California Test of Mental Maturity (J App, 21, 344)

Clarke, Charles Kirk
Death notice (Sci, 59, 210)
Lecture: British Medico-Psychological Assoc. (Sci, 56, 331)
Lecture: London psychiatry (Sci, 58, 463)

Claude, Henri
Appointment: Paris faculty of medicine (Sci, 55, 316)

Clayton, Alfred Stafford
Appointment: Illinois (Western) State Teachers College (Bull, 42, 675)
Appointment: Talladega College, Alabama (Bull, 40, 383)
Departure: Talladega College (Bull, 42, 675)

Cleveland Child Guidance Clinic (Ohio)
Appointment: Shumacher, H. C.; President (Sci, 65, 11)

Cleveland College for Women
Donation: Clark, E. A. (Sci°, 13, 298)

Cleveland Juvenile Court (Ohio)
Appointment: Rowland, E. H. (J App, 10, 396)

Cleveland Normal Training School (Ohio)
Appointment: Wallin, J. E. W. (Bull, 6, 32)

Cleveland, Public Schools (Ohio)
Appointment: Swift, W. B. (JoP, 16, 28)

Clevenger, Shobal Vail
Research: cerebral localization (AJP, 2, 192)

Clinical child psychology
Course: Buehler, C. (Sci, 93, 537)

Clinical psychology
Accreditation: APA (Sci, 55, 4)
American Assoc. of Applied Psychology, Clinical section (J App, 26, 108)
Commemorative volume presented to Witmer, L. 35th anniversary of 1st psych clinic (Sci, 75, 75)

Conference: clinical adjustment of behavior problems of school children, U.S. Dept. of Interior, 1938 (J APP, *22*, 317)

Conference: social work, Clinical Psychology Group, 6th annual session (J APP, *22*, 215)

Indiana Univ. Children Services (J APP, *22*, 106)

Institute on Professional Training, 1942 (J APP, *26*, 390)

Internships McLean Hospital (BULL, *42*, 795)

Internships Michael Reese Hospital (BULL, *41*, 136)

Internships New York State Institutions (BULL, *39*, 809-810)

Lecture: Huey, E. B. (SCI, *34*, 759)

Publication: Menninger Clinic contributions (J APP, *27*, 475)

Publication: Wallin, J. E. W. (J APP, *10*, 524)

Clinical Psychology Section, APA
Elections held (BULL, *23*, 112)

Clouston, Thomas Smith
Death notice (BULL, *12*, 244; SCI, *41*, 722)

Club for Research on Aging (*see* American Division of)

Coakley, John Diuguid
Appointment: Univ. of Rochester (SCI, *94*, 276)

Election: Sigma Xi, Univ. of Rochester (SCI, *101*, 556- 557)

Cobb, Margaret E.
Appointment: Army Medical Dept., Washington (JOP, *15*, 560)

Cobb, Stanley
Editor: *Psychosomatic Medicine* (J APP, *22*, 663)

Coblenz, Germany
Monument, Müller, J. (SCI, *10*, 540)

Cody, Sherwin
Publication: *Commercial tests and how to use them* (J APP, *3*, 194)

Coe College (Cedar Rapids, Iowa)
Appointment: Newell, F. S. (SCI, *30*, 709; BULL, *6*, 427)

Departure: Fracker, G. C. (JOP, *1*, 560)

Departure: Patton, C. K. (BULL, *41*, 679)

Leave of absence: Fracker, G. C. (BULL, *1*, 451; SCI, *20*, 480)

Resignation: Fracker, G. C. (SCI, *30*, 709)

Coe, George Albert
Appointment: Columbia Univ. (BULL, *20*, 288)

Publication: The psychology of religion (SCI, *44*, 307; *55*, 442-446)

Co-educating the sexes, effects of
Publication: Bureau of Education (Scɪ°, 2, 117)

Coefficient of correlation
Use in study of D-score for the level of aspiration (AJP, 55, 442-446)

Coffey, Alex B.
Appointment: College of William and Mary (JoP, 2, 560)

Coffin, Joseph Herschel
Appointment: Mount Holyoke College (BULL, 14, 116; JoP, 14, 168)

Coffman, Lotus Delta
Appointment: Univ. of Illinois (JoP, 9, 532, 588)
Departure: Eastern Illinois Normal School (JoP, 9, 532)

Coghill, George Ellett
Publication: "Space time as a pattern of psycho-organismal mentation" (AJP, 51, 759)

Cohen, Herman
Death notice (JoP, 15, 587-588)

Cohen, John
Publication: *"Human affairs: An exposition of what science can do for man"* (JoP, 34, 644)

Cohen, Morris Raphael
Lecture: human history (JoP, 42, 251)
Retirement: Columbia Univ. (Scɪ, 91, 236)

Cohn, Hermann Ludwig
Vision testing (AJP, 2, 186)

Cohoon, Elisha
Appointment: Massachusetts State Hospital, Psychopathic Dept. (Scɪ, 42, 415)

Colby College (Waterville, Maine)
Commemorated Copernicus, 400th anniversary (Scɪ, 98, 405)
Lecture: Stetson, H. T. commemorating Copernicus, 400th anniversary (Scɪ, 98, 405)

Colby, Martha Guernsey (*see* Guernsey, Martha)

Cole, Edwin M.
Course: Neurology of speech and reading (BULL, 39, 269)

Cole, Lawrence Wooster
Appointment: Univ. of Colorado (BULL, 7, 252; JoP, 7, 336)

Appointment: Wellesley College (JoP, 5, 616; Bull, 5, 379)
Departure: Wellesley College (Bull, 7, 252)
Publication: "Factors of human psychology" (J App, 10, 393)
Return: Univ. of Colorado (Sci, 50, 38)

Cole, William Harder
Director of Research Council, Rutgers Univ. (Bull, 41, 411)

Coleman, James Covington
Appointment: Univ. of Kansas (Bull, 42, 791)

Colgate University (Hamilton, New York)
Appointment: Estabrooks, G. H. (Sci, 65, 523)
Appointment: Ferguson, G. O. (JoP, 14, 140; Bull, 14, 115)
Appointment: Laird, D. A. (Sci, 60, 243; J App, 8, 450; Bull, 21, 660)
Appointment: Lake, H. (Sci, 72, 111, 421)
Appointment: Read, M. S. (JoP, 9, 532)
Appointment: Whitley, P. (Sci, 66, 151)
Degree: Stoddard, G. D. (Sci, 96, 314; Bull, 39, 895)
Departure: French, F. C. (Rev, 1, 552)
Election: Read, M. S., Vice-president (Bull, 9, 360)
Expands facilities (Bull, 27, 660)
Leave of absence: Berrien, F. K. (Bull, 42, 791)
Promotion: Laird, D. A. (Sci, 66, 151)
Psychology lab (Sci, 66, 351)
Research: effects of noise abatement (Bull, 42, 488)

Colgrove, Pitt Payson
Return: to State Normal School, Minn (Rev, 7, 640)

College and Normal School Teachers
Conference for teachers in Wisconsin and Michigan, 1906 (JoP, 3, 279)

College Curriculum Adjustments of the U.S. Office of Education Wartime Commission
APA committee formed for war preparation (Bull, 39, 895)

Collège de France
Appointment: Janet, P. (Rev, 9, 216; Bull, 10, 252; Sci, 15, 320)
Appointment: Ribot, T. (AJP, 1, 551)
Chair experimental psychology (AJP, 1, 551)
Departure: Janet, P. (Sci, 37, 785)
Departure: Ribot, T. (Sci, 15, 320)
Election: Tarde, G.; Chair (Rev, 7, 216)
Retirement: Ribot, T. (Rev, 8, 447; Sci, 13, 1000)

College Entrance Examination Board
Appointment: Gulliksen, H. O. (Bull, 42, 485)

College for the Training of Teachers (New York)
List of educational lectures given, 1890 (Sci°, *14*, 403)

College of Medical Evangelists, Los Angeles
Lecture: Miles, W. R. (Sci, *68*, 400)

College of Physicians and Surgeons, Boston
Lecture: Hall, G. S. (Sci, *27*, 1000)

College of Physicians and Surgeons, Columbia University (New York)
Appointment: Merrill, H. H. (Sci, *99*, 467)
Retirement: Goodhart, S. P. (Sci, *99*, 467)

College Personnel Association, Northwest
Election: Tyler, L. E. (Bull, *40*, 79)

Collier, Rex Madison
Appointment: U.S. Army (Sci, *97*, 199)

Collins, Mary
Election: British Assoc., Section J; President (Sci, *85*, 13)

Collins, Nancy Tappan
Election: Kentucky Psychological Assoc.; Secretary-treasurer (J App, *25*, 725)

Collip, James B.
Lecture: Assoc. for Research in Nervous and Mental Diseases (Sci, *84*, 551)

Colman, N. J.
Research: hypnotism (Sci°, *12*, 309)

Cologne, University of
Departure: Lindworsky, J. (Bull, *25*, 700)

Color vision (*see also* Vision)
Conference: Ladd-Franklin, C. (JoP, *11*, 84)
Establishment: Munsell Color Foundation (Bull, *41*, 268)
Explanation: Titchener, E. B. color equations in *Experimental Psychology* (JoP, *2*, 55)
Inter Society Color Council, color standards (Bull, *37*, 123)
Lecture: Bishop, H. G. (AJP, *34*, 469)
Lecture: British Assoc. (Sci°, *8*, 30)
Lecture: Bullough, E. (JoP, *7*, 420)
Lecture: congenital and acquired deficiencies (AJP, *55*, 573-576)
Lecture: Forbes, W. T. M. (AJP *40*, 52)
Lecture: Huntington, G. E. (AJP, *44*, 185)
Lecture: Judd, D. B. (AJP, *54*, 289-294)

Lecture: Ladd-Franklin, C., Chicago (JoP, *11*, 308)
Lecture: Ladd-Franklin, C., Columbia Univ. (Sci, *35*, 615; JoP, *9*, 252; Sci, *37*, 747; JoP, *10*, 364; Sci, *65*, 227)
Lecture: Ladd-Franklin, C., Cornell Univ. (JoP, *11*, 308)
Lecture: Ladd-Franklin, C., Harvard Univ. (Sci, *57*, 324; Sci, *61*, 16; Sci, *51*, 268; JoP, *17*, 224; Sci, *37*, 747)
Lecture: Ladd-Franklin, C., Univ. of Illinois (JoP, *11*, 308)
Lecture: Murray, E. (AJP, *42*, 117)
Lecture: Spiller, J., British Assoc., color blindness (Sci°, *14*, 267)
Lecture: Woodworth, R. S. (JoP, *1*, 224)
Lecture: Woodworth, R. S. and Bruner, F. (JoP, *2*, 112)
Meeting: Inter Society Color Council, 2nd annual (Sci, *76*, 462)
Meeting: Inter Society Color Council, 9th (Bull, *37*, 123)
Meeting: Inter Society Color Council, 1939 program (Bull, *36*, 141)
Publication: Boring, E. G. "Isochromatic contours" (AJP, *49*, 130)
Publication: Bugg, E. G. "A binocular color phenomenon" (AJP, *51*, 769)
Publication: Dunlap, K., color mixing (AJP, *57*, 559-563)
Publication: Dvorine, I. (AJP, *58*, 397-399)
Publication: *Engineer* (Sci°, *15*, 144)
Publication: Inter Society Color Council newsletter (Bull, *31*, 79)
Publication: König,A., color discrimination (Sci, *1*, 471)
Publication: Murray, E. (AJP, *58*, 253-261)
Publication: Murray, E. reply to Dvorine (AJP, *58*, 399-402)
Publication: Murray, E. "The Ishihara test for color- blindness: A point in ethics" (AJP, *47*, 511)
Publication: Pillsbury, W. B. and Schaefer, B. R. "Advancing and retreating colors, A note on" (AJP, *49*, 126)
Publication: psychological nature of black and white (AJP, *54*, 286-289)
Publication: Purdy, D. M. "The Bezold-Brücke phenomenon and contours for constant hue" (AJP, *49*, 313)
Publication: Stroop, J. R. "The basis of Ligon's theory" (AJP, *47*, 499)
Research: Bryn Mawr College (JoP, *4*, 166)
Research: Garth, T. R. on Indians (Sci, *71*, 414)
Research: Rayleigh, J. W. S. (Sci°, *16*, 203)
Von Hess, K. wins Helmholtz award (Bull, *21*, 360)

Colorado College (Colorado Springs, Colorado)
Appointment: Davies, A. E. (JoP, *16*, 504; Bull *16*, 392)
Appointment: Gerlach, F. M. (Bull, *12*, 280)
Appointment: Lancaster, E. G. (Rev, *5*, 232; Sci, *6*, 879; AJP, *10*, 165)
Appointment: Remmers, H. R. (Bull, *20*, 60)
Appointment: Ruger, H. A. (Bull, *1*, 451; JoP, *1*, 560)

Colorado Psychological Association
Election: Garth, T. R.; President (Sci, *76*, 31)

Colorado State Normal School (Greeley)

Appointment: Chambers, W. G. (Bull, *1*, 414; Sci, *20*, 384)
Departure: Dexter, E. G. (Rev, *7*, 216)
Lecture: Kirkpatrick, E. A. (JoP, *13*, 476)

Colorado, University of (Boulder)

Appointment: Allin, A. (Rev, *5*, 109; AJP, *9*, 250; Sci, *6*, 702)
Appointment: Bair, J. H. (Sci, *19*, 160; Bull, *9*, 94; JoP, *1*, 56)
Appointment: Cole, L. W. (Bull, *7*, 252; JoP, *7*, 336)
Appointment: Ebaugh, F. G. (Sci, *61*, 86)
Appointment: Farrand, L.; President (Bull, *11*, 116)
Appointment: Gilberston, G. N. (JoP, *6*, 588; Bull, *6*, 427)
Appointment: Henmon, V. (JoP, *6*, 588)
Appointment: Kennedy, F. (Rev, *5*, 449)
Appointment: Keyser, P. H. (Sci, *13*, 200)
Appointment: Russell, J. E. (Sci, *1*, 615)
Conference: Psychology of learning, 1939 (Bull., *36*, 583)
Death notice Allin, A. (JoP, *1*, 28)
Departure: Allee, W. L. (Bull, *42*, 485)
Director of conference on learning, Krechevsky, I. and Muensinger, K. F. (Sci, *89*, 483)
Fellowship: psychiatry (Sci, *71*, 13)
Leave of absence: Ebaugh, F. G. (Sci, *96*, 334)
Lecture: Krauss, W. W., Sigma Xi on race biology (Sci, *98*, 106)
Lecture: Stuart, M. (J App, *10*, 393)
Promotion: Kennedy, F. (Rev, *6*, 456)
Publication: Cole, L. W. factors of human psychology (J App, *10*, 393)
Return: Cole, L. from army (Sci, *50*, 38)

Colosi, Natale

Appointment: New York Commission of the Interstate Sanitation Commission (Sci, *101*, 297)

Columbia College

Course: Introduction of contemporary civilization (JoP, *16*, 448)
Lecture: list of 1889-1890 (Sci°, *14*, 387)

Columbia College for Women

Lecture: Baldwin, J. M. (Bull, *10*, 123)

Columbia College Philosophical Society

Lecture: Hall, G. S. (Sci°, *6*, 360)

Columbia Medical School

Appointment: Salmon, T. W. (Sci, *54*, 72)

Columbia University (*see also* Barnard College; College of Physicians and Surgeons; Knapp Foundation) (New York, New York)

Anniversary: Cattell, J. M.; Professor (JoP, *11*, 251- 252)
Anniversary: 50th of founding of lab (SCI, *95*, 190; BULL, *39*, 326)
Anniversary: Thorndike, E. 25th (BULL, *23*, 176)
Appointment: Adler, F.; Chair in social and political ethics (SCI, *21*, 600)
Appointment: Bair, J. H. (REV, *9*, 536)
Appointment: Bergson, H. (JoP, *9*, 112; JoP, *10*, 12)
Appointment: Butler, N. M.; President (REV, *8*, 656)
Appointment: Cantril, H. (SCI, *82*, 367)
Appointment: Chapman, D. W. (BULL, *34*, 635)
Appointment: Chene, C. O. (SCI, *74*, 308)
Appointment: Cunningham, B. (J APP, *9*, 319)
Appointment: Dallenbach, K. M. (SCI, *71*, 455; SCI, 72, 11, 336; BULL, *27*, 415)
Appointment: Dewey, J. (JoP, *1*, 280)
Appointment: Dodge, R. B. (SCI, *45*, 611; BULL, *14*, 264; BULL, *13*, 260; JoP, *13*, 336; JoP, *14*, 392)
Appointment: Fracker, G. C. (SCI, *20*, 480; JoP, *1*, 560)
Appointment: Franz, S. I. (REV, *3*, 356; REV, *4*, 452)
Appointment: Fullerton, G. S. (JoP, *1*, 28)
Appointment: Garrett, H. E. (SCI, *99*, 467; SCI, *93*, 493; SCI, *91*, 311)
Appointment: Gordon, K. (SCI, *23*, 832)
Appointment: Graham, C. H. (SCI, *101*, 112; BULL, *42*, 255)
Appointment: Hyslop, J. H. (REV, *2*, 534)
Appointment: Jastrow, J. (JoP, *6*, 700; BULL, *6*, 427)
Appointment: Jones, A. L. (BULL, *6*, 120)
Appointment: Keller, F. S. (SCI, *95*, 526)
Appointment: Kirby, G. H. (SCI, *65*, 471)
Appointment: Kitson, H. D. (SCI, *61*, 539; BULL, *22*, 504; J APP, *9*, 204)
Appointment: Krueger, P.: Kaiser Wilhelm Professor (SCI, *35*, 495)
Appointment: Marshall, H. R. (REV, *1*, 440)
Appointment: McWhood, L. B. (REV, *3*, 356)
Appointment: Miller, D. S. (AJP, *10*, 165; REV, *5*, 449)
Appointment: Montague, W. P. (BULL, *4*, 128; JoP, *2*, 224)
Appointment: Münsterberg, H. (BULL, *1*, 29; SCI, *18*, 800)
Appointment: Murphey, G. (SCI, *91*, 236)
Appointment: Ostwald, W. (BULL, *3*, 36; JoP, *2*, 721)
Appointment: Poffenberger, A. T. (SCI, *91*, 311)
Appointment: Spearman, C. E. (BULL, *29*, 91)
Appointment: Stone, C. P. (BULL, *42*, 486)
Appointment: Strong, C. A. (SCI, *3*, 99; REV, *3*, 244; REV, *10*, 344)
Appointment: Tawney, G. A. (JoP, *3*, 140; BULL, *3*, 116)
Appointment: Thorndike, E. L. (REV, *8*, 447)
Appointment: Titchener, E. B. (SCI, *26*, 845; BULL, *5*, 32; JoP, *5*, 56)
Appointment: Volkmann, J. (BULL, *34*, 635)

Appointment: Wells, F. L. (Sci, *32*, 863; Bull, *7*, 426; JoP, *7*, 721)

Appointment: Wissler, C. (Rev, *6*, 673)

Appointment: Woodbridge, F. J. E. (Sci, *15*, 440; Sci, *35*, 927; Sci, *17*, 800)

Appointment: Woolley, H. P.; Director Institute of Child Welfare Research (Bull, *22*, 612; J App, *9*, 319; Sci, *62*, 82)

Award: Croce, B.; Butler Medal (JoP, *17*, 364)

Award: Cubberly, E. P.; Butler Medal (JoP, *12*, 335- 336)

Award: Dewey, J.; emeritus (Sci, *78*, 382)

Award: Kruger, P.; Kaiser Wilhelm Professor (JoP, *9*, 224)

Award: Marshall, H. R.; Butler Medal (JoP, *17*, 364)

Award: Thorndike, E. L.; Butler Medal (Sci, *61*, 606; Bull, *22*, 504)

Birthday, Woodworth, R. S., 70th (Sci, *90*, 368)

Commemoration: Copernicus, Galileo and Newton, 1942 (JoP, *39*, 700)

Commemorative volume of selected papers, Woodworth R. S. (Bull, *37*, 61)

Conference: Dewey, J. (JoP, *10*, 252, 308)

Conference: Education of the gifted in memory of Hollingworth, L. S. (J App, *24*, 854)

Conference: Individual psychology (Bull, *11*, 152; Sci, *39*, 572; JoP, *11*, 251-252)

Course: Jastrow, J. at the Graduate School (Sci, *30*, 705)

Course: neuro-psychiatric nursing (J App, *26*, 857)

Course: Stone, C. (Sci, *101*, 375)

Course: summer session offerings (JoP, *16*, 475-476)

Course: Whipple, C. M. (Bull, *8*, 146)

Dedication ceremony for NY State Psychiatric Inst. (Sci, *70*, 578)

Degree: Angell, J. R. (Sci, *53*, 531)

Degree: Bennett, C. J. C. (Sci, *22*, 648)

Degree: Boutroux, E. (JoP, *7*, 224)

Degree: Calkins, M. W. (Bull, *6*, 256)

Degree: Thorndike, E. L. (Bull, *29*, 308)

Department of philosohpy and psychology divided (Sci, *91*, 236)

Departure: Andrews, G. T. (Bull, *41*, 603)

Departure: Bair, J. H. (JoP, *1*, 50)

Departure: Bingham, W. V. (JoP, *7*, 448)

Departure: Brown, W. (Sci, *27*, 936)

Departure: Dallenbach, K. (J App, *16*, 334; Bull, *29*, 460)

Departure: Davis, W. H. (JoP, *1*, 112)

Departure: Dearborn, W. F. (JoP, *2*, 448)

Departure: Evans, J. E. (Bull, *11*, 482)

Departure: Hollingworth, H. L. (Sci, *27*, 680)

Departure: Jackson, T. A. (Bull, *40*, 152)

Departure: Poffenberger, A. T. (Sci, *47*, 217)

Departure: Rejall, A. J. (Sci, *36*, 593)

Departure: Ruger, H. A. (JoP, *1*, 560)

Departure: Strong, E. K. (Sci, *39*, 325)

Dewey, J. portrait (Sci, *70*, 211)

Dismissal: Cattell, J. McK. (Sci, *46*, 335)

Division of Philosophy, Psychology, and Anthropology (JoP, *13*, 224)
Election: Dewey, J. American Philosophical Assoc. President (SCI, *21*, 37)
Election: Dewey, J.; Professor (SCI, *19*, 744)
Election: Woodworth, R. S., International Congress of Arts and Sciences, St. Louis (JoP, *1*, 532)
Election: Zubin, J., Sigma Xi (SCI, *93*, 276)
Endowed chair of psychology by Rockefeller, J. D. (AJP, *11*, 281; REV, *7*, 216)
Fellowship: established in memory of Hollingworth, L. S. by Hollingworth, H. L. (SCI, *100*, 383)
Fellowship: Messenger, J. F. (SCI, *13*, 680)
Fellowship: psychical research (BULL, *2*, 288)
Honor: dinner for Hollingworth, H. L. (SCI, *86*, 538)
Honor: Thorndike, E. L. (J APP, *10*, 129)
Kant, centenary of death of (JoP, *1*, 140)
Laboratory: alterations made to Schermerhorn Hall for psychology lab (SCI, *12*, 160)
Laboratory: established (SCI°, *19*, 172)
Laboratory: expansion of psychological lab (AJP, *11*, 281)
Leave of absence: Bruner, F. G. (SCI, *20*, 480)
Leave of absence: Fullerton, G. S. (JoP, *3*, 140; BULL, *4*, 370; BULL, *3*, 116)
Leave of absence: Gates, A. I. (BULL, *40*, 152)
Leave of absence: Poffenberger, A. T. (SCI, *91*, 311)
Leave of absence: Spence, R. B. (BULL, *40*, 152)
Leave of absence: Thorndike, R. L. (BULL, *40*, 152)
Leave of absence: Watson, G. (BULL, *40*, 152)
Leave of absence: Woodworth, R. S. (BULL, *9*, 95; JoP, *9*, 140)
Lecture: Angell, J. R. (SCI, *33*, 214; JoP, *12*, 280)
Lecture: Butler, N. M., pedagogics (SCI°, *8*, 585)
Lecture: Calkins, M. W., social psychology (SCI, *33*, 214)
Lecture: Cattell, J. McK. (JoP, *13*, 224)
Lecture: contemporary philosophic thought (JoP, *7*, 140)
Lecture: Dewey, J. (JoP, *1*, 224; SCI, *91*, 41)
Lecture: Dodge, R. (BULL, *13*, 188; JoP, *13*, 224)
Lecture: Economo, C., brain (SCI, *71*, 213)
Lecture: Hall, G. S. (BULL, *9*, 95; JoP, *9*, 56)
Lecture: James, W. (JoP, *4*, 84; BULL, *4*, 95)
Lecture: Jastrow, J., dream states (SCI, *33*, 214; JoP, *7*, 140)
Lecture: Judd, C. H. (J APP, *10*, 129)
Lecture: Judd, C. H. social psychology (SCI, *33*, 214)
Lecture: Krueger, F. (SCI, *36*, 591)
Lecture: Ladd-Franklin, C. (BULL, *10*, 252; SCI, *37*, 747; SCI, *35*, 615; JoP, *9*, 252; JoP, *14*, 308; JoP, *16*, 700; SCI, *65*, 227; JoP, *10*, 364; JoP, *12*, 224)
Lecture: Ladd, G. T., ontological problems in psychology (SCI, *33*, 214)
Lecture: Ladd, G. T. religion (JoP, *1*, 252)
Lecture: Loeb, J. (SCI°, *15*, 397)
Lecture: Miles, G. H. (J APP, *10*, 394)
Lecture: Morgan, C. L. (JoP, *1*, 644)

Lecture: Münsterberg, H. (JoP, *1*, 168)

Lecture: Ostwald, W. (Sci, *23*, 198; JoP, *3*, 112)

Lecture: Pillsbury, W. B. (Bull, *5*, 406; Sci, *33*, 214)

Lecture: problems of psychology (Bull, *8*, 78; Sci, *33*, 213; JoP, *8*, 112)

Lecture: psychology series (Sci, *66*, 350)

Lecture: Rogers, A., educational psychology (J App, *10*, 129)

Lecture: Royce, J., pragmatism (Sci, *33*, 214)

Lecture: Seashore, C. E., dreaming (Sci, *33*, 213)

Lecture: Sheldon, W. H., Woodbridge Memorial Lectures (JoP, *40*, 168)

Lecture: Southard, E. E. (Bull, *14*, 32)

Lecture: Thorndike, E. L. (Sci, *36*, 784)

Lecture: Thorndike, E. L., adult learning (J App, *10*, 129)

Lecture: Titchener, E. B. (JoP, *1*, 280; Sci, *27*, 318; Sci, *33*, 214; JoP, *5*, 140)

Lecture: Tufts, J. H., thought and moral philosophy (JoP, *17*, 336)

Lecture: Watson, J. B., animal behavior (Sci, *37*, 367; JoP, *10*, 196)

Lecture: Woodworth, R. S. (Sci, *26*, 485)

Meeting: announced experimental psychologists (JoP, *11*, 196)

Meeting: APA and NAS, New York Branch (JoP, *8*, 700)

Meeting: APA, New York Branch (JoP, *8*, 56)

Meeting: APA, 2nd (Rev, *1*, 214)

Meeting: APA, 23rd (JoP, *13*, 644)

Meeting: APS (JoP, *10*, 28; JoP, *9*, 615-616)

Meeting: conferences for the Division of Phil., Psych, and Anth. (JoP, *13*, 224)

Meeting: National Council of Women Psychologists (Bull, *42*, 487)

Meeting: NY Branch of APA (Bull, *8*, 78)

Meeting: NYAS/NY Branch APA (JoP, *8*, 280; JoP, *9*, 252; JoP, *10*, 251-252; JoP, *10*, 672; JoP, *11*, 280; JoP, *13*, 280)

Meeting: SEP (Bull, *40*, 539)

Nomination: professors to Dept. of Educational Research (JoP, *13*, 84)

Pageant to honor Bacon, R. postponed (JoP, *11*, 588)

Promotion: Butler, N. M.; President (Sci, *14*, 584)

Promotion: Carpenter, C. R. (Sci, *86*, 218)

Promotion: Cattell, J. McK. (Rev, *9*, 328)

Promotion: Farrand, L. (Sci, *13*, 440)

Promotion: Garrett, H. E. (Bull, *41*, 498)

Promotion: Gates, A. I. (JoP, *19*, 392)

Promotion: Hollingworth, H. L. (Bull, *13*, 187; JoP, *19*, 392; JoP, *11*, 336)

Promotion: Keller, F. S. (Bull, *39*, 423)

Promotion: McCall, W. A. (JoP, *19*, 392)

Promotion: Pitkin, W. B. (JoP, *9*, 336)

Promotion: Poffenberger, A. T. (Bull, *24*, 380; Bull, *19*, 350; JoP, *19*, 392)

Promotion: psychology dept. (Sci, *55*, 538)

Promotion: Sargent, S. S. (Bull, *41*, 498)

Promotion: Thorndike, E. L. (Sci, *13*, 440; Sci, *19*, 120)

Promotion: Woodworth, R. S. (Sci, *29*, 455; JoP, *2*, 196; Bull, *2*, 160; Sci, *21*, 480; JoP, *6*, 252; Bull, *6*, 152)

Publication: series on philosophy, psychology and education (Rev, *1*, 336)

Relieved: Poffenberger, A. T. of executive position (SCI, *93*, 493)
Removal: Cattell, J. McK. (BULL, *14*, 366)
Research: Thorndike, E. L., semantic word count (BULL, *36*, 141)
Resignation: Hyslop, J. H. (SCI°, *16*, 920)
Retirement: Cohen, M. R. (SCI, *91*, 236)
Retirement: Overstreet, H. A. (SCI, *91*, 236)
Retirement: Thorndike, E. L. (SCI, *91*, 381)
Retirement: Woodworth, R. S. (SCI, *95*, 476; BULL, *39*, 423)
Return: Dewey, J. (SCI, *54*, 376)
Visiting: Tufts, J. H. (BULL, *17*, 239)
Woodworth, R. S., laboratories at Louisiana Purchase Exposition (JoP, *1*, 84)

Columbia University Biological Series
Publication announced (REV, *1*, 552)

Columbia University, School of Optometry
Report: Treatment of strabismus (J APP, *26*, 858)

Columbia University, Teachers College (*see* Teachers College)

Colville, John
Election: International Congress of Psychology, 12th, honorary president (J APP, *23*, 530)

Colvin, Stephen Sheldon
Appointment: Brown Univ. (BULL, *9*, 280; SCI, *35*, 927)
Appointment: Univ. of Illinois (SCI, *14*, 232; REV, *8*, 552)
Chair, educational psychology, Brown Univ. (JoP, *9*, 364)
Death notice, 6-15-23 (BULL, *21*, 240)
Departure: Univ. of Illinois (BULL, *9*, 280)
Promotion: Univ. of Illinois (JoP, *4*, 448; BULL, *4*, 236)

Combe, George
Lectureship established Univ. of Edinburgh (JoP, *3*, 420)

Commercial Tests and How to Use Them
Publication: Cody, S. (J APP, *3*, 194)

Commins, William Dollard
Appointment: Catholic Univ. of America (J APP, *15*, 326)

Commonwealth Fund
Appropriation: Mental hygiene (SCI, *76*, 81)
Establishment: Institutes for Child Guidance (SCI, *64*, 475)
Fellowship: psychiatry (SCI, *71*, 13)
Fellowship: Univ. of Pennsylvania Medical School neuro- psychiatry (SCI, *62*, 11)
Grant: National Committee for Mental Hygiene (SCI, *100*, 122)

Grant: Stanford study of gifted children (Sci, 56, 510)
Grant: State Charities Aid Assoc. for Mental Hygiene (Sci, 98, 196)
Grant: Terman, L. and Freeman, F. (Sci, 60, 588)
Hosts Spearman, C. E., U.S. visit (Sci, 66, 616)

Communality
Discussion of relation to proaction and retroaction (AJP, 54, 280-283)

Comparative psychology (*see also* Animal)
Award: Wever, E. G. and Bray, C. W., H.C. Warren Medal for audition work
(Bull, 33, 476)
Course: Univ. of Chicago (JoP, 1, 336)
Election: Yerkes, R. M., Secretary International Congress of Arts and Sciences,
St. Louis (JoP, 1, 532)
Institute for the Study of Animal Behavior (Bull, 33, 580)
Lecture: Morgan, C. L. (JoP, 1, 616; Sci, 1, 693)
Lecture: Pierce, C. S. National Academy of Sciences (Sci°, 3, 524)
Lecture: Watson, J. B. (JoP, 5, 721)
Lecture: Yerkes, R. M. Johns Hopkins Univ. (Sci, 29, 853)
Publication: Bohn, G. (JoP, 6, 559)
Publication: Washburn, M. F. (Bull, 7, 324)
Publication: Yerkes, R. M. "Concerning the biology of the chimpanzee" (Sci,
82, 590)
Research: Morgan, C. L. (Rev, 1, 336)
Section C, Internationl Congress of Arts and Sciences, St. Louis (JoP, 1, 420)

Comparative Psychology Monographs
Announcement: New ownership Johns Hopkins Press (JoP, 25, 308; Bull, 25,
376; Sci, 67, 508)
Editor: named new board (Bull, 25, 376)
Publication: announcement (Sci, 55, 475)

Compton, Karl Taylor
Presides at dinner for Cattell, J. McK. (Bull, 31, 79)

Conant, James Bryant
Lecture: Tufts College (Sci, 88, 398)

Conditioned reflex
Award: Culler, E. K., Warren Medal (Bull, 35, 408)
Discussion: use in psychotherapeutic situation (AJP, 58, 391-392)
Grant: Girden, E., study on pupillary changes (Sci, 93, 473)
Lecture: Kupalov, P. S., Cornell Univ. (Sci, 69, 450)
Lecture: Volbroth, G. V. (Sci, 70, 402)
Publication: Ivanitskii, G. A. "From the conditioned reflex to
neuropsychodynamics" (AJP, 49, 676)

Conduct of Mind Series
Editor: Jastrow, J. (BULL, 7, 108)

Conference annuelle transformiste
Organization: advocates of evolution in Paris Anthropological Society (SCI°, 2, 91)

Conference on Mental Hygiene (*see* Mental Hygiene, Conference on)

Conference on Methods in Philosophy and the Sciences
Birthday celebration, Dewey J., symposium program (JoP, 36, 588)
Lecture: Hecht, S. Weber-Fechner law (JoP, 37, 224)
Lecture: Holt, E. B. (JoP, 35, 196)
Lecture: Kohler, W. (JoP, 40, 644)
Lecture: Lewin, K. (JoP, 35, 196)
Lecture: Nagel, E. "Authority in the sciences" (JoP, 41, 252)
Meeting (JoP, 40, 196; JoP, 42, 643; JoP, 38, 616; SCI, 87, 277; JoP, 35, 196; JoP, 39, 252; JoP, 41, 671-672)
Publication: proceedings (JoP, 34, 559)
Symposium: "Authority and freedom" (JoP, 41, 252)
Symposium: Dewey's, J., 80th birthday (SCI, 90, 326)
Symposium: naturalism and anti-naturalism, 1942 (JoP, 39, 644)
Symposium: 1943 (JoP, 40, 644)
Symposium: 1944 (JoP, 41, 252)

Conference on Science, Philosophy and Religion (*see* Science, Philosophy and Religion)

Conference of Teachers of Psychology in Normal Schools and Colleges (*see* Teachers of Psychology)

Congrès international de psychiatrie, de neurologie, de psychologie et d'assistance des aliénés
Meeting: announcement, 1907 (JoP, 4, 336)

Congress de neurologie et psychologie
Postponed due to war (JoP, 11, 672)

Congress for Experimental Psychology
Lecture: Martin, L. J. (SCI, 35, 772; JoP, 9, 336)
Meeting: Giessen (JoP, 1, 112; AJP, 15, 464; BULL, 1, 94, 292)
Meeting: 2nd, Paris announced (JoP, 9, 700)
Meeting: 4th, Innsbruck (BULL, 7, 75)

Congress of Arts and Sciences
Presentation: Ward, J. (JoP, 1, 280)

Congress of Arts and Sciences (St. Louis, Missouri) (*see* Saint Louis)

Congress of Evolutionists
Meeting: report of (Sci°, 22, 264)

Congress of German Men of Science and Physicians
Meeting: Vienna (JoP, *10*, 336)

Congress of Hygiene and Demography
Seventh International Congress, London (Sci°, *17*, 314)

Congress of Philosophy
Contributions: list of societies, 1920 (JoP, *17*, 391)
Meeting: announcement (JoP, *17*, 391-392)

Congress of Physiological Psychology (*see* Physiological Psychology)

Congress of Psychological Physiology (*see* Psychological Physiology)

Congress of the Royal Sanitary Institute (*see* Royal Sanitary Institute)

Congress of the Sanitary Institute (*see* Sanitary Institute)

Congress of the Society for Experimental Psychology
Meeting: 5th, Berlin, partial list of presentations (JoP, 9, 279)

Congreve, Richard
Death notice (Sci, *10*, 92)

Conklin, Edmund Smith
Anniversary commemorating Indiana Univ. psych lab, 50th (J App, *23*, 631)
Appointment: Indiana Univ. (Sci, *80*, 475)
Appointment: Univ. of Chicago (Sci, *72*, 649)
Appointment: Univ. of Oregon Graduate School: acting Dean (Bull, *20*, 60; Sci, *56*, 75)
Death notice (Bull, *39*, 807; AJP, *56*, 140-141)
Degree: Clark Univ. (Bull, *37*, 61)
Dinner: MPA, 1940 (J App, *25*, 266)
Election: MPA President (Bull, *36*, 304)
Lecture: MPA President (J App, *23*, 207; Sci, *89*, 150)

Conklin, Edwin Grant
Election: Science Service, President (Sci, *85*, 475)
Lecture: Rice Institute (Sci, *93*, 155, 396)

Conlen, Joseph J.
Death notice (SCI, *45*, 112; JOP, *14*, 252)

Connecticut Academy of Arts and Sciences
Election: officers (SCI, *102*, 559)

Connecticut College (formerly Connecticut College for Women) (New London, Connecticut)
Appointment: Gagne, R. M. (BULL, *37*, 656)
Appointment: Hoffman, G. (BULL, *34*, 498)
Appointment: Loewi, M. (BULL, *37*, 656)
Appointment: Ligon, E. M. (J APP, *11*, 165)
Appointment: McClelland, D. C. (BULL, *37*, 656)
Appointment: Seward, J. P. (BULL, *34*, 498)
Lab opened (BULL, *37*, 257; SCI, *91*, 188)
Lecture: Woodworth, R. S. Connecticut Valley Assoc. of Psychologists (SCI, *91*, 188; BULL, *37*, 257)
Resignation: Seward, G. H. (BULL, *42*, 583)
Resignation: Seward, J. P. (BULL, *42*, 582)
Return: Morris, F. E. (SCI, *49*, 281)

Connecticut Legislature
Bill for establishing a psychiatric hospital (SCI, *57*, 382)

Connecticut Prison Association
Clinic opened for inebriates (SCI, *99*, 99)

Connecticut Psychopathic Hospital
Funding and organization (SCI, *54*, 246)

Connecticut State Public Welfare Council
Appointment: Challman, R. C. (BULL, *41*, 136)
Appointment: Heiser, K. F. (BULL, *41*, 72; SCI, *98*, 404)
Appointment: Orbison, W. D. (BULL, *42*, 63)

Connecticut Valley Association of Psychologists
Election: officers (BULL, *38*, 191; BULL, *39*, 196)
Lecture: Woodworth, R. S. (BULL, *37*, 257; SCI, *91*, 188)
Meeting (BULL, *37*, 257; SCI, *91*, 188; BULL, *38*, 191; BULL, *39*, 196)

Connecticut Valley Student Scientific Conference
Meeting (SCI, *93*, 156)

Conner, Gervase J.
Award: Alvarenga Prize (SCI, *100*, 47)

Connolly, Cornelius Joseph
Meeting: APA Wash-Balt. Branch (BULL, *36*, 140)

Conrad, Herbert Spencer
Editor *Applied Psychology Monographs* (J App, 27, 115)

Conscience
Lecture: Palmer, G. H. (Bull, 4, 95)

Consciousness
Lecture: Boring, E. G., in siamese twins (AJP, 32, 448)
Lecture: Hodgson, S. (JoP, 4, 278)
Lecture: Jacks, L. P. Aristotelian Society (JoP, 10, 224)
Lecture: King, I. (JoP, 1, 644)
Lecture: Marshall, H. R. Union Theological Seminary, New York (JoP, 16, 196)
Lecture: Montague, W. P. (JoP, 2, 112)
Lecture: Münsterberg, H. (JoP, 1, 168)
Lecture: Woodbridge, F. J. E. (JoP, 1, 644)

Consciousness as Behavior
Publication: Marshall, H. R., criticism of Bode (JoP, 15, 559-560)

Conscription
Research: attitudes produced by; SPSSI (Bull, 37, 829)
Research: disabilities developed by (Sci°, 4, 220)
War dept. request information on psychologists subject to military call, National Research Council (J App, 25, 472)

Constantinople, University of (Turkey)
Appointment: Anschutz, G. (Bull, 12, 404)

Cook, Alfred
Appointment: Clark Univ. (Sci°, 14, 215)
Lecture: Clark Univ. (Sci°, 14, 250)

Cook County (*see* Civil Service Commission of)

Cook, Helen Dodd
Appointment: Wellesley College (Bull, 6, 400)
Award: Alice Freeman Palmer Fellowship (Sci, 25, 520; Sci, 26, 32)
Fellowship: Wellesley College (Bull, 4, 128)

Cook, Paul McCracken
Editor: *Educational Abstracts* (J App, 22, 107)

Cook, Sidney Albert
Appointment: Rutgers College (J App, 10, 523)
Death notice (Bull, 41, 409)
Promotion: Rutgers Univ. (Bull, 23, 412)

Cooper, Clara Chassell (*see* Chassell, Clara Frances)

Cooper, Emily M. Fletcher
Appointment: Harcum Junior College, Penn. (BULL, *41*, 267)

Cooper, Jacob
Death notice (BULL, *1*, 94)

Cooper, John Andrew
Appointment: Maryland State Teachers College (BULL, *40*, 230)

Cooper Union (New York, New York)
Appointment: Montague, W. P., Hewitt Lectures (JoP, *9*, 112)
Appointment: Watson, W. S. (SCI, *96*, 268)
Promotion: Watson, W. S. (BULL, *39*, 895)

Coote, C. R.
Lecture: National Institute of Industrial Psychology (SCI, *83*, 301)

Coover, John Edgar
Appointment: Johns Hopkins Univ. (SCI, *65*, 495)
Appointment: Stanford Univ. (BULL, *24*, 380)
Death notice (BULL, *35*, 259)
Obituary by Fearing, F. (AJP, *51*, 579)
Promotion: Stanford Univ. (JoP, *18*, 532; BULL, *18*, 236; SCI, *53*, 387)
Publication: monograph in Stanford Univ. library (BULL, *39*, 268)

Cope, Edward Drinker
Lecture: Origin of human physiognomy and character (SCI°, *3*, 342)

Copenhagen Academy of Sciences (Denmark)
Election: Ostwald, W. (SCI, *23*, 861)

Copenhagen, University of (Denmark)
Appointment: Brandt, F. (BULL, *20*, 416)
Appointment: Rubin, E. (BULL, *20*, 416)

Copernicus, Nikolaus
Anniversary, 400th (SCI, *97*, 398, 577; JoP, *39*, 700; SCI, *99*, 123; SCI, *98*, 58, 361, 405)
Lecture: Mizwa, S. P., Harvard (SCI, *99*, 123)
Lecture: Stetson, H. T. Colby College (SCI, *98*, 405)
Lecture: Stetson, H. T. Univ. of Maine (SCI, *97*, 398)

Corbusier, William H.
Research: emotional expressions of Apache Indians (SCI°, *9*, 212)

Corby, Philip G.
Psychological Corporation meeting with APA and AAAP, 1941 (J APP, *25*, 600)

Corey, Stephen Maxwell

Appointment: Univ. of Chicago Audio-visual Instruction Center; Director
   (BULL, *42*, 407)
Lecture: learning and memory (AJP, *44*, 191)
Publication: "Dependence upon chance factors in equating groups" (AJP, *45*,
   749)

Corfield, William Henry

Appointment: British Office of Works (SCI, *10*, 781)

Cornell College (Iowa)

Appointment: Scarborough, W. J. (BULL, *40*, 152)

Cornell University (Ithaca, New York)

Anniversary: Titchener, E. B., 25th (JoP, *14*, 420; BULL, *14*, 263 264)
Announcement: Summer Research Station (SCI, *91*, 430)
Appointment: Barnes, E. (REV, *5*, 344)
Appointment. Bentley, I. M. (SCI, *15*, 880; AJP, *9*, 135; AJP, *10*, 166; SCI, *67*,
   245; BULL, *25*, 307; JoP, *25*, 504; BULL, *39*, 807; SCI, *96*, 249)
Appointment: Bentley, I. M., N.R.C. Div. of Anthro. and Psych, Chair (SCI, *72*,
   11)
Appointment: Brownell, W. A. (J APP, *10*, 394)
Appointment: Cattell, J. McK. Pharmacology Medical College (SCI, *83*, 572)
Appointment: Dallenbach, K. M. (BULL, *13*, 407; BULL, *42*, 581; BULL, *18*, 236)
Appointment: Diethelm, O., Psychiatry (SCI, *83*, 228)
Appointment: Foster, W. S. (JoP, *13*, 308)
Appointment: Koffka, K. (BULL, *21*, 660)
Appointment: Kreezer, G. (SCI, *87*, 482)
Appointment: Lewin, K. (SCI, *78*, 278)
Appointment: Ogden, R. M. (JoP, *13*, 504; BULL, *13*, 407; SCI, *90*, 34; BULL, *36*,
   804)
Appointment: Parmenter, R. (SCI, *92*, 283)
Appointment. Pillsbury, W. B. (AJP, *8*, 430)
Appointment: Seth, J. (REV, *3*, 356)
Appointment: Thilly, F. (JoP, *3*, 308; BULL, *3*, 184)
Appointment: Titchener, E. B. (SCI, *36*, 556; BULL, *9*, 440; BULL, *7*, 36; JoP, *7*,
   84)
Appointment: Washburn, M .F. (SCI, *13*, 1000; REV, *7*, 428)
Appointment: Weld, H. P. (SCI, *36*, 401; BULL, *9*, 407; JoP, *9*, 588)
Appointment: Whipple, G. M. (AJP, *10*, 165-166)
Bentley, I. M., at Summer Research Station (SCI, *91*, 430)
Course: Kirkpatrick, E. A. (BULL, *8*, 146)
Departure: Bentley, I. M. (JoP, *9*, 588; BULL, *9*, 407; SCI, *36*, 401)
Departure: Dallenbach, K. M. (BULL, *39*, 807)
Departure: de Laguna, T. L. (JoP, *2*, 392)
Departure: Foster, W. S. (SCI, *50*, 65)
Departure: Geissler, L. R. (SCI, *34*, 484)

Departure: Guilford, J. P. (J App, *11*, 235)
Departure: Hoisington, L. B. (Bull, *25*, 700)
Departure: McGilvary, E. B. (JoP, *2*, 364)
Departure: Ruckmick, C. A. (JoP, *10*, 560)
Departure: Washburn, M. F. (Rev, *9*, 431; Sci°, *15*, 880)
Discussion: Summer Research Station (AJP, *53*, 297-298)
Election: Ogden, R. M.; Head, Dept. of Education (JoP, *13*, 308)
Establishment: Summer Research Station in Psychology (Sci, *89*, 532)
Grant: Liddell, H. S. Josiah Macy Jr. Foundation (Sci, *91*, 446)
Laboratory: Cornell Behavior Farm; psychobiology (Bull, *36*, 804)
Laboratory: expansion for smell and taste experiments (AJP, *9*, 250)
Laboratory: opening (Sci°, *19*, 129)
Laboratory: renovation (AJP, *43*, 295; Sci, *3*, 167)
Leave of absence: Bentley, I. M. (Bull, *32*, 323; Sci, *80*, 378)
Leave of absence: Creighton, J. H. (JoP, *7*, 252, 420)
Leave of absence: Weld, H. P. (Bull, *23*, 292)
Leave of absence: Whipple, G. M. (Bull, *9*, 280; JoP, *9*, 364)
Lecture: Chelpanov, G. I., status of psychology in Russia (JoP, *8*, 335-336)
Lecture: Hammond, W. A., International Congress of Arts and Sciences, St. Louis (JoP, *1*, 616)
Lecture: Koffka, K. (Sci, *61*, 181)
Lecture: Ladd-Franklin, C., color (JoP, *11*, 308)
Lecture: Little, C. C. (Sci, *102*, 665)
Lecture: Messenger Lecture Foundation; genetics, medicine and man (Sci, *102*, 665)
Lecture: Thomas W. Salmon Memorial (Sci, *76*, 13)
Lecture: Thorndike, E. L. (Bull, *26*, 120; Sci, *68*, 400)
Lecture: Titchener, E. B., mental health (Sci, *30*, 559)
Lecture: Webber, H. J., eugenics (Sci, *36*, 784)
Meeting: APA (AJP, *9*, 135; Rev, *4*, 339)
Meeting: Experimental Psychologists (JoP, *8*, 335-336; Bull, *1*, 213; Bull, *8*, 181)
Meeting: New York State Teachers of Educational Psychology (JoP, *7*, 252)
Portrait: Bentley, I. M. (Bull, *35*, 577; Sci, *88*, 31)
Portrait: Titchener, E. B. (Bull, *38*, 777)
Promotion: Bentley, I. M. (Rev, *9*, 432)
Promotion: Creighton, J. E. (Rev, *2*, 534)
Promotion: Pillsbury, W. B. (Rev, *4*, 340)
Promotion: Titchener, E. B. (Sci, *2*, 15; JoP, *9*, 644; Rev, *2*, 534)
Promotion: Whipple, G. M. (Bull, *8*, 406)
Psychology dept., new building (Rev, *3*, 243)
Psychology dept opens facilities (J App, *23*, 419)
Publication: acquisition of *American Journal of Psychology* (Sci, *53*, 114)
Publication: removed *American Journal of Psychology* (Sci, *102*, 221)
Publication: Titchener, E. B. (JoP, *5*, 252)
Research: Kupalov, P. S. and Lidell, H. S. conditioned reflex (Sci, *70*, 235)
Research: Simpson, S. and Lidell experimental neuroses (Sci, *86*, 221)

Resignation: McGilvary, E. B. (BULL, *2*, 224)
Resignation: Whipple, G. M. (BULL, *11*, 443)
Retirement: Bentley, I. M. (SCI, *88*, 31; SCI, *87*, 482)
Return: Dallenbach, K. M. (SCI, *75*, 581; BULL, *29*, 460)
Transfer: Anderson, O. D., psychology dept (BULL, *36*, 804)
Transfer: Liddell, H. S., psychology dept (BULL, *36*, 804)

Cornell University Medical College

Appointment: Cameron, N. (SCI, *89*, 76)
Appointment: Cattell, J. McK. (SCI, *97*, 530)
Appointment: Jacobsen, C. F. (BULL, *34*, 635)
Appointment: Meyer, A. (JoP, *1*, 588; BULL, *1*, 414; JoP, *3*, 168)
Departure: Cameron, N. (SCI, *91*, 593)
Establishment: Dept. of Psychopathology (JoP, *3*, 168)
Lecture: Kupalov, P. S., conditioned reflex (SCI, *69*, 450)
Research: Cattell, J. McK. quinine and other alkaloids (SCI, *98*, 59)
Resignation: Hamilton, A. McL. (JoP, *1*, 588)

Corps of Engineers

Appointment: Spaulding, E. G. (JoP, *15*, 392)

Corpus Christi College

Election: Case, T., Fellow (JoP, *1*, 56)
Election: Case, T., President (JoP, *2*, 112)
Election: McDougall, W., Fellow (JoP, *9*, 588; BULL, *9*, 360; SCI, *36*, 113)

Correlation (*see also* Coefficient of correlation)

Hull, C. L. establishes a correlation service (J APP, *10*, 523)
Publication: Burt, C. use of (AJP, *52*, 122-124)
Publication: Humm, D. G., product moment (AJP, *55*, 127-130)
Publication: Simplified Pearson product moment coefficients table (J APP, *22*, 218)

Cosmic Publishing Company, Chicago

Publication: *Mind in Nature* (SCI°, *5*, 243)

Cottingham, Charles E.

Retirement: Indiana Univ. School of Medicine, Bloomington (SCI, *91*, 616)

Couchoud, Paul Louis

Editor *Revue des Sciences Psychologiques* (JoP, *10*, 336)

Coues, Elliott

Lecture: Modern miracles (SCI°, *13*, 340)

Coulter, John Merle

Election: American Society of Naturalists, Vice-president (SCI, *21*, 37)

Counseling
Lecture: vocational counseling (AJP, *44*, 801)
Publication: employee counseling (J App, *28*, 80)

Counting, psychology of
Lecture: Science club, Univ. of Kansas (Sci°, *13*, 398)

Cournot, Antoine Augustin
Publication: *Revue de Métaphysique et de Morale* devoted to his life (JoP, *2*, 392)

Courtney, William Leonard
Lecture: Mind, its conditions and functions (Sci°, *10*, 250)

Courtroom psychology (*see also* Law and psychology)
Lecture: Münsterberg, H. (Sci, *31*, 187; JoP, *7*, 112)

Cowan, Edwina Abbott
Anniversary, 10th, Wichita Child Guidance Center (Bull, *38*, 126)
Retirement: Wichita Child Guidance Center (Bull, *38*, 777)

Cowdery, Karl Montague
Death notice (Bull, *41*, 602)

Cowles, Edward
Death notice (Bull, *16*, 258)

Cowles, Edward Spencer
Mental clinic, Church of St. Marks-in-the-Bouwerie (Sci, *76*, 622)
Resignation: McLean Hospital (Bull, *1*, 173)

Cowles, John Todd
Appointment: Univ. of Alabama, Director, psychology lab (Bull, *36*, 500)
Promotion: Univ. of Illinois (Bull, *42*, 793-794)

Cowley, William Harold
Appointment: Stanford Univ. (Sci, *100*, 424; Bull *42*, 63)
Resignation: Hamilton College (Sci, *100*, 381)

Cowling, D. J.
Appointment: Baker Univ., Kansas (JoP, *3*, 504; Bull, *3*, 288)

Cox, Catherine Morris (*see also* Miles, Catherine Cox)
Appointment: Stanford Univ. (J App, *11*, 404)

Cox, Charles Finney
Election: officer of NYAS (JoP, *9*, 28)

Cox, George Clarke

Appointment: Assistant Professor (JoP, *9*, 336)

Cox, Henry Miot

Appointment: Univ. of Nebraska; Bureau of Instructional Research (Sci, *89*, 148; Sci, *92*, 8; J App, *23*, 207; Bull, *36*, 304)

Coxe, Warren Winfred

Lecture: N.Y. A.A.P. (J App, *22*, 317)

Meeting: Assoc. of Consulting Psychologists, 8th (J App, *21*, 241)

Coy, Genevieve Lenore

Research: mental tests for selecting gifted children (J App, *1*, 298-299)

Research: Ohio State Univ., supernormal children (J App, *1*, 298-299)

Cracow, University of (Poland)

Gilman, D. C. represents Johns Hopkins Univ. at 500th anniversary (Sci, *11*, 877)

Craig, Wallace

Appointment: Univ. of Maine (Bull, *5*, 348)

Grant: American Philosophical Society (Bull, *42*, 581)

Lecture: Harvard Univ., animal psychology (Sci, *56*, 686)

Request for copy of Ehrenfels, *System der Werttheorie* (JoP, *15*, 252)

Resignation: Univ. of Maine (Bull, *19*, 410; Sci, *55*, 617)

Craik, Kenneth James Williams

Appointment: Univ. of Cambridge Medical Research Council (Sci, *99*, 531)

Crampton, Henry Edward

Election: officer NYAS (JoP, *9*, 28)

Crane, C. H.

Death notice (Sci°, *2*, 581)

Crane, Harry Wolven

Appointment: Univ. of North Carolina (Sci, *54*, 300, 408; Bull, *18*, 568; Sci, *89*, 55)

Departure: Division of Mental Hygiene of the North Carolina State Board of Charities and Public Welfare (Sci, *89*, 55)

Election: Alpha Psi Delta psychological fraternity, Secretary (Bull, *19*, 586)

Election: Univ. of Michigan, George S. Morris Fellowship in psych (JoP, *8*, 364; Sci, *33*, 892)
Resignation: Ohio State Univ. (Sci, *54*, 408)

Crawford, John Forsyth
Appointment: Princeton Univ. (Rev, *4*, 339; AJP, *8*, 584)

Crawford, Meredith Pullen
Appointment: Vanderbilt Univ. (Sci, *92*, 31; Bull, *37*, 656)
Departure: Barnard College (Sci, *92*, 31)

Creative intelligence
Publication announcement (JoP, *13*, 420)

Creative thought
Lecture: Patrick, C. (AJP, *54*, 128-131)

Creed, Isabel
Lecture: perception (JoP, *39*, 55-56)

Creegan, Robert Francis
Appointment: Univ. of Mississippi (JoP, *40*, 644)

Creighton, James Edwin
Editor: *Kantstudien* (JoP, *1*, 56)
Leave of absence: Cornell Univ. (JoP, *7*, 252, 420)
Promotion: Cornell Univ. (Rev, *2*, 534)

Crespi, Leo Paul
Promotion: Princeton Univ. (Bull, *42*, 581)

Crew, Francis Albert Eley
Election: International Congress for Sex Research, President (Sci, *70*, 552)
Information: International Society for the Investigation of Sex (Sci, *69*, 572)

Crime and psychology
Active interest (Bull, *13*, 296)
Appointment: National Committee on Prisons and Prison Labor (J App, *16*, 334)
Buenos Aires government prison opens institute (Sci, *27*, 320)
Care of criminals, Brockway, Z. R. *The Chautauquan* (Sci°, *13*, 141)
Criminality statistics and facts, Germany (Sci°, *14*, 215-216)
Identification of criminals (AJP, *1*, 205)
Lecture: Burtt, H. E., crime detection (Sci, *94*, 582)
Lecture: Goddard, H. (Bull, *12*, 403)
Lecture: Link, A. P., New York Electrical Society (Sci, *64*, 618)
Lecture: Mercier, C. A. (JoP, *1*, 420)
Lecture: Morelli (Sci, *38*, 124)
Lecture: Sikorskii, I. A., on suicide (Sci, *2*, 132)

Medical Correctional Assoc. contacts professionals (J App, *27*, 208)
Publication: Byrne, ?, professional criminals in America (Sci°, *8*, 432)
Publication: Gross, H. (JoP, *8*, 588)
Publication: Howard Assoc. (Sci°, *12*, 36)
Publication: Münsterberg, H. (JoP, *6*, 140)
Publication: Tulchin, S. H., intelligence and crime (J App, *23*, 744)
Senses of criminals (Sci°, *14*, 297)

Criminal Anthropology, International Congress of
Concern for criminal psychology (JoP, *8*, 532)
Meeting: Amsterdam, 1901 (Sci, *13*, 957)

Crispell, Raymond S.
Appointment: Duke Univ., Neuropsychiatry (Sci, *79*, 267)

Crissey, Orlo Lee
Publication: use of tests for personnel selection (Bull, *42*, 583)

Croce, Benedetto
Award: Butler Medal for *Filosofia dello spirito* (JoP, *17*, 364)

Crockett, Alex C.
Detroit General Aptitude Exam (J App, *23*, 420)

Crocodile habits
Publication: Voeltzkow, A. *Nature* (Sci°, *16*, 119)

Crofful, William Augustus
Research: hypnotism (Sci°, *12*, 309)

Crook, Mason Nelson
National Research Council Grant (Bull, *33*, 578)

Crooke, F. B.
Election: SSPP (JoP, *14*, 308)

Crosland, Harold Randolph
Appointment: Univ. of Arkansas (JoP, *14*, 504; Sci, *46*, 111; Bull *14*, 333, 420)

Crothers, Thomas Davison
Research: alcoholism (AJP, *1*, 362)

Crowd, psychology of
Research: Diall, G. H. (Sci, *4*, 73)

Cruze, Wendell Wayne
APA Wash-Balt. Branch (Bull, *37*, 657)

Cubberly, Ellwood Patterson
Award: Nicholas Murray Butler Medal (JoP, *12*, 335-336)

Cullen, Victor F.
Election: National Tuberculosis Assoc. (Sci, *101*, 635)

Culler, Elmer Augustine Kurtz
Appointment: Univ. of Rochester (Sci, *87*, 549)
Award: Warren, H. C. Medal (Sci, *87*, 362; Bull, *35*, 408)
Departure: Univ. of Illinois (Sci, *87*, 549)
Election: APA (Sci, *93*, 81)
Election: MPA President (J App, *25*, 128, 266; Bull, *38*, 191)
Lecture: National Research Council "Psychological factors in national morale"
   (Bull, *37*, 829)
Publication: offprint studies available (J App, *19*, 105)
Retirement: Univ. of Rochester (Sci, *101*, 219; Bull, *42*, 255)
Symposium: AAAS chair (Sci, *88*, 399)
Symposium: Indiana Univ., learning (Bull, *37*, 61)

Cullis, Winifred
Representative, Scientific Advisory Committee of the Trades Union (Sci, *88*, 398)

Culver, S. W.
Research: Educating the Negroes of the South (Sci°, *9*, 584)

Cummings, Carlos Emmons
Survey of exhibits at the World's Fair of New York (Sci, *89*, 339)

Cummings, Samuel Billings, Jr.
Departure: Kenyon College (Bull, *39*, 895)

Cunningham, Bess Virginia
Appointment: Columbia Univ. Teachers College (J App, *9*, 319)

Cupples, Upham and Co.
Publication: Proceedings of the American Society for Psychical Research (Sci°, *7*, 140)

Curtis, James Wylie
Election: Kentucky Psychological Assoc., Director (J App, *25*, 725)

Curtis, Josephine Nash (*see also* Foster, Josephine Curtis)
Death notice (Bull, *38*, 907)
Lecture: psychological examining (Bull, *13*, 407-408)
Marriage announcement to Foster, W. S. (Bull, *16*, 221)

Curtis, Josiah
Death notice (Sci°, *1*, 581)

Curwen, John
Death notice (SCI, *14*, 77)

Cushman, Herbert Ernest
Publication: history of philosophy (JoP, 7, 560)

Cutler, Anna A.
Promotion: Smith College (BULL, *2*, 427)

Cuyler, Eleanor and Thomas
Gift to George Peabody College for Teachers (BULL, *12*, 364)

D

Dabelstein, Donald Harold
Publication: expansion of program for vocational rehabilitation of handicapped
civilians, 1943 (J App, 27, 473-474)
Research: blind persons in private industry (J App, 28, 80)

D'Abernon, Lord
Election: National Institute of Industrial Psych.; President (Sci, 72, 498)

Dakota Wesleyan University (Mitchell, South Dakota)
Appointment: Emme, E. F. (Bull, 41, 343)

Dale, Edgar
Publication: *Propaganda analysis: An annotated bibliography* (J App, 24, 656)

Dalhousie College (Halifax, Nova Scotia)
Appointment: Schurman, J. G. (Sci°, 7, 74)

Dall, Charles Henry Appleton
Death notice (Sci°, 8, 123)

Dallenbach, Karl M.
Appointment: active military service (Sci, 96, 249; Bull, 39, 807)
Appointment: Columbia Univ. (Bull, 27, 415; Sci, 71, 455; Sci, 72, 11, 336)
Appointment: Cornell Univ. (Bull, 13, 407, Bull, 18, 236; Bull, 42, 581)
Appointment: National Research Council, Emergency Committee in
Psychology (Bull, 37, 755)
Appointment: Susan Linn Sage Professor of Psychology (Sci, 101, 663)
Appointment: Univ. of California, Los Angeles (Sci, 91, 311)
Courses: Univ. of California (J App, 24, 517)
Dedication: lab at Univ. of California, Los Angeles (Sci, 91, 311)
Departure: *AJP*, managing editor (AJP, 55, 583; Sci, 96, 249; Bull, 39, 807)
Departure: Columbia Univ. (J App, 16, 334)

Election: APA Council of Directors (BULL, 25, 123)
Lecture: A.A.A.S., Section I (BULL, 38, 908)
Lecture: A.A.A.S., temperature senses (J APP, 26, 107-108)
Lecture: A.A.A.S., "The psychology of magic" (SCI, 82, 591)
Lecture: APA, "Psychology in civilian service" (SCI, 95, 405)
Lecture: attention (SCI, 91, 311)
Lecture: Univ. of California, experimental psych. (SCI, 91, 311)
Publication: *American Journal of Psychology* (AJP, 48, 177)
Publication: counter-reply to Hollingworth, H. (AJP, 42, 458)
Publication: obituary, Geissler, L. R. (AJP, 45, 365-366)
Publication: obituary, Nichols, H. (AJP, 49, 320)
Publication: rebuttal to paper by Grace Adams (AJP, 41, 156)
Publication: rebuttal to paper by Wever, E. (AJP, 40, 337)
Publication: portraits useful to psychologists in teaching history of psychology
  (AJP, 45, 165-171)
Publication: "Professor Bentley retires from teaching" (AJP, 51, 579)
Publication: Society of Experimental Psychologists, the New Haven meeting of
  (AJP, 47, 344)
Publication: Society of Experimental Psychologists, the Philadelphia meeting of
  (AJP, 45, 539)
Publication: Society of Experimental Psychologists, the Worcester meeting of
  (AJP, 48, 526)
Publication: The pronunciation of liminal (AJP, 46, 142)
Publication: verbal imagery (AJP, 38, 667)
Return: Cornell Univ. (SCI, 75, 581; BULL, 29, 460)

Dalton, John Call
Death notice (SCI°, 13, 140)

Dana, Charles Loomis
Election: New York Psychiatric Society, President (SCI, 37, 172)

Dance
Publication: *Journal of Aesthetics and Art Criticism* (JoP, 38, 280)

Daniel, Robert Strongman
Indiana Univ. psych lab 50th anniversary commemoration (J APP, 23, 631)

Danish Academy of Sciences
Election: Ostwald, W.; foreign member (SCI, 23, 758; JoP, 3, 308)

Danish Royal Academy of Arts and Sciences
Award: Baldwin, J. M. (REV, 4, 340)
Competition: essay announced (BULL, 3, 148; JoP, 3, 196)

Danner, William Mason, Jr.
Appointment: Oberlin College (BULL, 42, 63)
Appointment: Oberlin College correction (BULL, 42, 256)

Darby, John Gordon
Publication: "Nineteenth-century sense: The paradox of spiritualism" (Sci°, *10*, 31-32)

Darley, John Gordon
Publication: Fields of applied psychology (J App, *24*, 370)

Darrow, Chester William
Course: Univ. of Chicago, physiological psychology (J App, *23*, 311)
Publication: Palmar galvanic skin reflex (sweating) and parasympathetic activity (AJP, *48*, 524)

Dartmouth College (Hanover, New Hampshire)
Angell, J. R., declines presidency (Sci, *28*, 558)
Appointment: Allport, G. W. (J App, *10*, 393)
Appointment: Bailor, E. M. (Bull, *22*, 672)
Appointment: Bingham, W. V. D. (Sci, *31*, 950; Bull, *7*, 220; JoP, *7*, 448; JoP, *9*, 224, Bull, *9*, 208)
Appointment: Cox, C. C. (JoP, *9*, 336)
Appointment: Franz, S. I. (Sci, *13*, 1000; Rev, *8*, 447)
Appointment: Horne, H. (Rev, *6*, 456)
Appointment: Johnston, C. H. (JoP, *3*, 616; Bull, *3*, 422)
Appointment: Josey, C. (JoP, *18*, 504)
Appointment: Karwoski, T. (JoP, *27*, 560; Bull, *27*, 496)
Appointment: Moore, H. T. (Bull, *12*, 243; JoP, *12*, 504)
Appointment: Stone, C. L. (Bull, *14*, 366)
Appointment: Urban, W. M. (Bull, *17*, 239)
Degree: Angell, J. R. (Sci, *83*, 180)
Departure: Allport, G. W. (JoP, *27*, 560; Bull, *27*, 496)
Departure: Bingham, W. V. D. (JoP, *12*, 196)
Departure: Franz, S. I. (JoP, *1*, 196)
Leave of absence: Bingham, W. V. D. (Bull, *11*, 152; JoP, *11*, 308)
Leave of absence: Horne, H. (JoP, *3*, 330)
Retirement: Campbell, G. (Sci, *31*, 949)

Darwin, Charles Robert
Birthday celebration by Cincinnati Society of Natural History (Sci°, *1*, 184)
Centennial celebration AAAS (JoP, *6*, 112)
Centennial celebration Cambridge Univ. (JoP, *5*, 168; JoP, *6*, 420; Bull, *6*, 216)
Centennial celebration Iowa State Univ. (Bull, *6*, 120)
Centennial celebration Univ. of Michigan (JoP, *6*, 112)
Centennial celebration voyage of the Beagle (Sci, *78*, 577)
Centennial commemorated, *Origin of Species* (Sci, *96*, 179)
Down House catalogues (Sci, *74*, 15)
Eulogy: Linnaean Society (Sci°, *11*, 277)
Grant: Univ. of Cambridge and British Association for Preservation at Down House; manuscripts (Sci, *96*, 493)

Lecture: Columbia Univ. (JoP, 6, 111)
Lecture: Instincts read at Linnean Society (SCI°, 2, 782)
Lecture: Jordan, D. S. at Indiana Academy of Sciences (SCI°, 7, 480)
Lecture: Jordon, D. S. at DePauw Univ. (SCI°, 9, 294)
Manuscripts received at Down House (SCI, 96, 493)
Memorial fund progress (SCI°, 2, 341)
Note in Sir Charles Lyell's *Elements of Geology* about Darwin's realization of *Origin of Species*, 1842 (SCI, 90, 155)
Paintings "Apotheosis of Science" (SCI, 93, 324)
Publication: bibliography of (SCI°, 7, 284)
Publication: *Biography* by son (SCI°, 8, 411-412; SCI°, 7, 284)
Publication: Cambridge Univ. Press (JoP, 6, 168)
Publication: dedicated to *Psychological Review* (JoP, 6, 308)
Publication: devoted to *Popular Science Monthly* (JoP, 6, 224)
Publication: his letters (SCI°, 16, 158)
Publication: Preservation of favored races in the struggle for life (SCI°, 12, 58)
Publication: The origin of species by means of natural selection (SCI°, 12, 58)
Statue British museum (SCI°, 5, 471)
Statue inscription suggestions (SCI, 10, 223)
Statue Oxford Univ. (SCI, 9, 917; SCI, 4, 915)
Statue South Kensington (SCI°, 6, 18)
Research: cruise of the Beagle continued (SCI, 90, 562)

Darwin, Francis

Lecture: Galton, F. (SCI, 39, 322)

Darwin, George Howard

Publication: *Bibliography of C. Darwin* (SCI°, 7, 284)

Darwin, Leonard

Election: International Congress of Eugenics, Honorary president (SCI, 76, 141)
Lecture: Eugenics Education Society (SCI, 44, 130)

Darwinian theory

Darwinism and the Christian Faith (SCI°, 11, 312-313)
Lecture: Whitney, W. D. Sheffield Scientific School (SCI°, 1, 293)
Publication: Baldwin, J. M. (JoP, 7, 644)

Dashiell, John Frederick

Appointment: Oberlin College (BULL, 14, 333)
Appointment: Univ. of North Carolina (JoP, 16, 588)
Bibliography for APS (JoP, 10, 472-476)
Election: Alpha Psi Delta Psychological Fraternity; Vice-president (BULL, 19, 586)
Election: APA Director (BULL, 27, 76; SCI, 71, 64)
Election: *Psychological Monographs*, Editor (BULL, 32, 862)
Promotion: Univ. of North Carolina (BULL, 32, 323)

Davenport, Charles Benedict
Election: American Society of Naturalists; Vice-president (Sci, *21*, 37)
Election: International Congress of Eugenics; President (Sci, *76*, 141)
Lecture: eugenics for Sigma Xi (Sci, *36*, 784)

Davidson, Thomas
Death notice (Rev, *7*, 639)

Davie, Maurice Rea
Election: Institute for Propaganda Analysis, Director (J App, *25*, 597)

Davies, Arthur Ernest
Appointment: Colorado College (JoP, *16*, 504; Bull, *16*, 392)
Promotion: Ohio State Univ. (Bull, *5*, 244; JoP, *5*, 336)

Davies, Elizabeth
Publication: psychophysics (AJP, *44*, 367)

Davies, Henry
Lecture: logic (JoP, *1*, 84)

Davis, D. Elizabeth
Appointment: Rochester Guidance Clinic, N.Y. (Bull, *36*, 841)

Davis, Edith Atwood
Publication: language "The tendency among children to avoid words with
unpleasant connotations" (AJP, *49*, 316)

Davis, Frank Cornelius
Appointment: Univ. of British Columbia (J App, *22*, 106)

Davis, Haim I.
Retirement: Univ. of Illinois (Sci, *80*, 114)

Davis, Hallowell
Editor *Psychosomatic Medicine* (J App, *22*, 663)
Publication: Auditory action currents (AJP, *45*, 358)

Davis, Katherine Bement Memorial Fellowship
Available Vassar College (Bull, *39*, 132)

Davis, Noah Knowles
Death notice (JoP, *7*, 336; Bull, *7*, 252)
Election: International Congress Arts and Science, St. Louis; Chair (JoP, *1*, 419)
Retirement: Univ. of Virginia (JoP, *3*, 476; Bull, *3*, 288)

Davis, Sturgiss Brown
Appointment: Swarthmore College (JoP, *15*, 140; Bull, *14*, 420)

Davis, Thomas K.

Election: Assoc. for Research in Nervous and Mental Diseases;
Secretary-treasurer (SCI, 79, 9)
Election: Assoc. for Research in Nervous and Mental Diseases; Vice-president
(SCI, 81, 42)

Davis, William Harper

Appointment: Lehigh Univ. (JoP, 1, 112; BULL, 2, 296; SCI, 21, 1000; JoP, 2, 364)
Appointment: Public Service Corp, New Jersey (JoP, 12, 280; SCI, 41, 678)
Announces opening office for book sales (JoP, 11, 721)
Degree: Univ. of Greifswald (SCI, 24, 286)
Election: APA Secretary (SCI, 21, 37; JoP, 2, 28)
Election: International Congress of Arts and Sciences, general psych. section;
Secretary (JoP, 1, 532)

Dawkins, Boyd

Lecture: Antiquity of man (SCI°, 2, 779)

Dawson, George Ellwsorth

Lecture: genetic and experimental psychology, Clark Univ. (J APP, 9, 88)

Dawson, Shepherd

Election: British Assoc. for the Advancement of Science, President (SCI, 78, 599)

Day, Lucy May

Appointment: Wells College (BULL, 11, 190)

Dayton, Neil Avon

Election: American Assoc. on Mental Deficiency, Vice-president (J APP, 22, 109)

Deaf

Indiana Inst. for the Deaf and Dumb (SCI, 5, 304)
Lecture: Bell, A.G. Wash. Phil. Society (SCI°, 2, 635)
List of people contributing funds for teaching of deaf (SCI°, 17, 215)
Teaching a deaf boy to read and write (SCI, 2, 780)
Wisconsin educates deaf mutes (SCI°, 5, 324)

Dearborn, George Van Ness

Appointment: Sargent School of Physical Education, Cambridge (BULL, 3, 392)
Courses: Tufts Medical School, Boston (SCI, 29, 335; BULL, 6, 152)
Death notice (BULL, 36, 218)
Publication: intellectual regression (J APP, 10, 394)
Publication: reaction to summary of APA paper (JoP, 3, 195)

Dearborn, Walter Fenno

Appointment: APA Committee on Certification (SCI, 51, 137)

Appointment: Univ. of Chicago (Sci, 29, 698; Bull, 6, 184)
Appointment: Univ. of Wisconsin (JoP, 2, 448)
Award: Milton fund, Harvard Univ. (Bull, 22, 672)
Lecture: Cattell jubilee (AJP, 25, 468)
Lecture: retinal local signs (JoP, 1, 84)
Promotion: Harvard Univ. (Sci, 45, 383; Bull, 14, 192, 264)
Resignation: Univ. of Wisconsin (Sci, 29, 698)

Death

Publication: MacDonald, A. (AJP, 38, 153)
Research: Death-rate and disease among whites and blacks in Alabama (Sci, 7, 140)
Research: Lähn, H. [Laehr, H.?] (AJP, 3, 148)

De Boer, Cecil

Appointment: Univ. of Arkansas (Bull, 25, 700)

De Burgh, William George

Death notice (JoP, 40, 616)

De Busk, Burchard Woodson

Appointment: Univ. of Oregon, Clinic for Atypical Children (J App, 21, 243)

de Laguna, Theodore de Leo

Appointment: American Philosophical Assoc. Executive Committee (JoP, 8, 27-28)
Appointment: Bryn Mawr College (Bull, 4, 370)
Appointment: Univ. of Michigan (JoP, 2, 392, 721)
Publication: concerning Franklin, C. F. (JoP, 9, 588)

De Sanctis, Sante

Director *Psiche* (JoP, 9, 56)
Election: International Congress of Psych., 5th; Vice-secretary general (JoP, 2, 56)
Obtains equipment for lab from estate of Traves, Z. (Bull, 8, 333)

de Vries, Hugo

Lecture: NYAS (JoP, 9, 672)

DeCamp, Joseph Edgar

Appointment: Univ. of California (Bull, 12, 440; JoP, 12, 721)
Appointment: Univ. of Illinois (JoP, 11, 721; Sci, 40, 670)
Departure: Univ. of Illinois (Bull, 12, 440)

Deception, psychology of

Publication: Jastrow, J. in *Popular Science Monthly* (Sci°, 12, 237)

Decroly, Ovide Jean
Publication: Binet-Simon tests (BULL, *11*, 191)

Defense program
Research money given by Josiah Macy, Jr. Foundation to Murphy, G. and
Barmack, J. E. (BULL, *38*, 779)

DeGraff, Harmon Opdyke
Dismissal: Univ. of Missouri (SCI, *69*, 379)
Dismissal: Univ. of Missouri, upheld (SCI, *69*, 399)

deGruchy, Clare
Publication: child psychology (J APP, *10*, 395)

Dejerine, Joseph Jules
Death notice (AJP, *28*, 313; BULL, *14*, 116)
Memorial research fund set up in his name (BULL, *17*, 116)

Delabarre, Edmund Burke
Appointment: Harvard Univ. (REV, *3*, 356; SCI, *3*, 406; AJP, *7*, 452)
Death notice (BULL, *42*, 406; AJP, *58*, 406-409)

Delacroix, Henri
Appointment: Oxford Univ. as Zaharoff Lecturer (SCI, *63*, 66; BULL, *23*, 176)

Delaware Division of Special Education and Mental Hygiene
Appointments: listed (BULL, *40*, 619-620)

Delaware, University of (Newark)
Appointment: Kitay, P. (BULL, *42*, 127)

Delboeuf, Joseph Remi Leopold
Death notice (AJP, *8*, 312)

Delbos, Victor
Publication: bibliography of French philosophy (JOP, *7*, 84)

Delinquency
Appointment: Fenton, N.; California Youth Correction Authority (SCI, *97*, 65)
Appointment: Haines, T. H., to bureau (BULL, *11*, 352)
Appointment: Lion, E. G., Director of psychiatric clinic (SCI, *97*, 65)
Psychiatric clinic organized by U.S. Public Health Services and San Francisco
Department of Public Health (SCI, *97*, 65)
Report: Wines, F. H. (SCI°, *8*, 254-255)

Delp, Paul S.
Promotion: Chapman College (JOP, *33*, 560)

Dementia praecox (*see also* Schizophrenia)
Lecture: Norman, C. (JoP, *1*, 420)
Research (J App, *19*, 496)
Research: Univ. of Pennsylvania (Sci, *91*, 68)

Denison University (Granville, Ohio)
Appointment: Burts, R. C. (Bull, *42*, 791)
Appointment: Lewis, T. A. (Bull, *11*, 444; JoP, *11*, 721)
C. L. Herrick Memorial Fund announced (JoP, *2*, 168)
Promotion: Steckle, L. C. (Bull, *40*, 723; Bull, *42*, 486)
Publication: *Journal of Comparative Neurology and Psychology* (JoP, *1*, 195)
Retirement: Lewis, T. A. (Bull, *40*, 723)

Dennis, Wayne
Appointment: Clark Univ. (Sci, *85*, 354; Bull, *34*, 272)
Appointment: Louisiana State Univ. (Sci, *95*, 220; Bull, *39*, 267)
Appointment: Social Science Research Council (Bull, *33*, 579)
Lecture: habit loss (AJP, *44*, 189)
Lecture: instinct, Sigma Xi (Sci, *79*, 180)
Publication: vision, "Desmonceaux's study of the newborn" (AJP, *49*, 677)

Denver, University of (Colorado)
Appointment: Garth, T. R., Department Head (Bull, *20*, 288)
Appointment: Mann, C. W. (Bull, *37*, 61)
Appointment: Meyers, C. E. (Bull, *39*, 895)
Departure: Mann, C. W. (Bull, *39*, 808)
National Opinion Research Center (J App, *27*, 475)
Research: Indian psychology (Sci, *59*, 438; Sci, *61*, 487)
Research: nature-nurture (J App, *17*, 342)

Department of Agriculture (*see* United States Department of Agriculture)

Department-Store Education...
Extracts (J App, *1*, 396)

DePauw University (Greencastle, Indiana)
Appointment: Bigham, J. (Rev, *2*, 642)
Appointment: Heston, J. C. (Bull, *41*, 679-680; Bull, *42*, 128)
Bureau of Testing and Research created (Bull, *41*, 679-680)
Lecture: Jordan, D. S. on 'Charles Darwin' (Sci°, *9*, 294)
Retirement: Bigham, J. (Rev, *5*, 449)

des Bancels, J. L. (*see* Larguier des Bancels, Jean)

Des Moines Health Center (Iowa)
Appointment: Sylvester, R. H. (Bull, *16*, 392; Sci, *50*, 326)

Descartes, Réné
International Congress of Philosophy, 9th (JoP, *33*, 140)
International Congress of Philosophy, 1944 (Sci, *100*, 284-285)
Lecture: by Balz, A. G. A. (JoP, *39*, 196)
Lecture on (JoP, *38*, 700)
Paintings, "Apotheosis of science" (Sci, *93*, 324)
Publication: addition to work of (JoP, *6*, 28)
Publication: complete edition of works (Rev, *3*, 706)

DeSilva, Harry Reginald
Appointment: Bureau of Street Traffic Research, Harvard Univ. (Sci, *83*, 347)
Appointment: Mass. State College (Sci, *76*, 119)
Appointment: Yale Univ. (Sci, *88*, 471; Bull, *36*, 140)
Departure: Harvard Univ. (Sci, *88*, 471)
Grant: body voltage research, American Academy of Arts and Sciences (Sci, *80*, 426)
Grant: body voltage research, Sigma Xi (Sci, *80*, 31)
Publication: military, *Psychological Bulletin* (J App, *25*, 358)
Research: automobile drivers, Yale Univ. (Sci, *88*, 471; J App, *22*, 664)
Research: Harvard Bureau for Street Traffic (Bull, *33*, 477)
Resignation: Mass. State College (Sci, *83*, 347)

Despert, Julliette Louise
Lecture: Institute of the Exceptional Child, 6th (J App, *23*, 746)

Dessoir, Max
Appointment: Univ. of Berlin (Sci, *6*, 736)
Promotion: Univ. of Berlin (Rev, *5*, 109)

Detroit, College of the City of (Michigan)
Appointment: Pyle, W. H. and Williams, G. (J App, *14*, 638)

Detroit General Aptitude Exam
Publication announcement (J App, *23*, 419-421)

Detroit (Michigan) (*see* Psychopathic Clinic of)

Detroit Teachers College (Michigan)
Appointment: Pyle, W. H. (Bull, *22*, 672; Sci, *62*, 306)

Deutsche, Jean Marquis
Publication: development of children's concepts of causal relations (J App, *21*, 719)

Development (*see also* Adolescence, Aging, Child)
Conference: Maternity and child welfare, 7th English-speaking (Bull, *34*, 325)
Grant: child study, Vassar College (Bull, *37*, 187)
Dennis, W., Social Science Research Council Fellow (Bull, *33*, 579)

Lecture: Wissler, C., growth of boys (Sci°, *15*, 627)
Publication: *Child Development* (J App, *22*, 540)
Publication: Deutsche, M. *The development of children's concepts of causal relations* (J App, *21*, 719)
Publication: Frazier, E. F., *Negro Youth at the Crossways* (J App, *24*, 655)
Publication: Gesell, A., The psychology of growth (Sci, *74*, 434)
Publication: *Monographs of the Society for Research in Child Development* (J App, *22*, 540)
Research: Gesell, A. (Sci, *101*, 87)
Witmer School at Devon (Bull, *34*, 635)

DeVoss, James Clarence

Appointment: Kansas State Normal School (Bull, *11*, 483; Sci, *40*, 446)

DeWeerdt, Ole Niehuis

Appointment: Beloit College (Sci, *58*, 465)

Dewey, John

Anniversary: 50th Univ. of Chicago, dinner (Sci, *94*, 296)
Appointment: Columbia Univ. (JoP, *1*, 280; Sci, *19*, 744)
Appointment: James, W. Lectureship (JoP, *27*, 140; Bull, *27*, 240)
Appointment: Johns Hopkins Univ. (Bull, *3*, 184)
Appointment: Michigan State Univ. (Sci°, *13*, 321)
Appointment: Univ. of Chicago (Sci, *1*, 81; Rev, *1*, 440; Sci, *15*, 920)
Award: Chinese order of the Jade, 1939 (Sci, *90*, 612)
Birthday, celebration of 80th, Progressive Education Assoc. (Sci, *90*, 350)
Birthday celebration, 85th (Sci, *100*, 381)
Birthday, 80th, American Philosophical Society honoring (Sci, *91*, 14; JoP, *36*, 336)
Birthday, 80th; commemorative symposium program (JoP, *36*, 588; Sci, *90*, 326)
Bust presented (Sci, *67*, 505)
Bust presented to Univ. of Chicago (Sci, *94*, 296; Sci, *93*, 14; JoP, *38*, 56)
Conference: City of New York College (JoP, *10*, 252, 308)
Conference: Columbia Univ. (JoP, *10*, 252, 308)
Conference: methods in philosophy and the sciences (Sci, *86*, 419-20; JoP, *34*, 559, 616; Sci, *90*, 326)
Correspondence about political philosophy in Germany (JoP, *12*, 584-588)
Course: modern philosophy (Bull, *20*, 172)
Degree: Johns Hopkins Univ. (JoP, *12*, 336)
Degree: L. L. D. conferred (JoP, *1*, 391, 448)
Degree: Univ. of Michigan (Sci, *38*, 151; JoP, *10*, 504)
Degree: Univ. of Paris (Sci, *72*, 497; Bull, *28*, 255)
Editor: *Journal of Social Psychology* (JoP, *27*, 84)
Election: American Philosophical Assoc.; President (Sci, *21*, 37; JoP, *2*, 28)
Election: APA; President (Sci, *9*, 38)
Election: Conference on Scientific Spirit and Democratic Faith; Honorary chair (Sci, *99*, 363)

Election: education as major subject (JoP, *13*, 84)
Election: Josiah Macy, Jr. Foundation; Board member (SCI, *92*, 553)
Lecture (JoP, *38*, 700)
Lecture: AAAS dinner in honor of Cattell, J. McK. (SCI, *79*, 30; BULL, *31*, 79)
Lecture: American Philosophical Assoc. (SCI, *56*, 416, 683)
Lecture: American Philosophical Assoc. Carus Lectures (JoP, *36*, 699)
Lecture: American Philosophical Assoc.; the philosophy of Whitehead (JoP, *33*, 700)
Lecture: Child Study Assoc. of America (J APP, *16*, 438)
Lecture: Columbia Univ. (JoP, *1*, 224; SCI, *91*, 41)
Lecture: Harvard Univ. (SCI, *21*, 798)
Lecture: James, W. (JoP, *38*, 616)
Lecture: James, W. Harvard Univ. (SCI, *71*, 212; SCI, *75*, 331)
Lecture: Johns Hopkins Univ. (BULL, *7*, 75; SCI, *31*, 212; JoP, *7*, 83)
Lecture: knowledge (JoP, *1*, 224)
Lecture: Mackay, D. S. (JoP, *39*, 55-56)
Lecture: Nelson, R. W.; "The logic of Jesus and John Dewey" (JoP, *34*, 721)
Lecture: NYU Philosophical Society on pragmatism (JoP, *11*, 84)
Lecture: N.Y. Univ.; "Time and individuality" (JoP, *35*, 252)
Lecture: philosophic reconstruction in Spain (JoP, *16*, 357-364)
Lecture: Scientific Spirit and Democratic Faith (JoP, *41*, 280)
Lecture: Smith College (BULL, *8*, 32)
Lecture: Univ. of Edinburgh (SCI, *68*, 11; SCI, *69*, 157)
Lecture: Univ. of Illinois (SCI, *26*, 685; BULL, *4*, 401)
Lecture: Univ. of North Carolina (JoP, *12*, 112)
Lecture: Univ. of Pennsylvania (SCI, *32*, 834)
Lecture: Yale Univ., religion (JoP, *30*, 336)
Letters from Japan printed (JoP, *16*, 588)
Nomination: Dept. of Educational Research at Columbia Univ. (JoP, *13*, 84)
Portrait, history of Columbia (SCI, *70*, 211)
Promotion: Columbia Univ., Emeritus (SCI, *78*, 382)
Publication: Messrs Henry Holt and Co. (JoP, *13*, 420)
Publication: *Reconstruction in Philosophy* (JoP, *17*, 336)
Resignation: Univ. of Chicago (BULL, *1*, 291)
Return to Columbia from Orient (SCI, *54*, 376)
Return to N.Y. (BULL, *18*, 628)
Univ. of Peking requests an extended stay (JoP, *17*, 364)
Work in China (BULL, *16*, 258)

DeWolf, L. Harold
Appointment: Boston Univ. (JoP, *34*, 83)

Dexter, Edwin Grant
Appointment: Univ. of Illinois (REV, *7*, 216; BULL, *2*, 360)
Departure: Colorado State Normal College (REV, *7*, 216)
Research: mortality of graduates at Yale (SCI°, *5*, 530)

Diagnosis, methods of psychological
Lecture: Yerkes, R. M., Univ. of Minnesota Sigma Xi (Sci, *45*, 138)

Dial, The
Announcement: new establishment in New York (JoP, *15*, 448)

Diall, Gideon H.
Research: crowd study (Sci, *4*, 73)

Dickinson, Charles Alexius
Appointment: Univ. of Maine (Bull, *24*, 136; Sci, *65*, 299)

Dickinson College (Carlisle, Pennsylvania)
Appointment: Norcross, W. H. (JoP, *14*, 56; Bull, *13*, 448)
Appointment: Waugh, K. T.; President (Sci, *74*, 408)

Dickinson, W. H.
Appointment: Royal Commission on the Care of the Feeble-Minded (Sci, *22*, 510)

Dictionary of Philosophy
Controversy over editorial responsibility (JoP, *39*, 195-196)
Correction: Fredericks, S. F. misinformation on Runes, D. D. (JoP, *39*, 195)
Publication announcement (Rev, *5*, 345)

Dictionary of Philosophy and Psychology
Publication announcement (Rev, *3*, 467; Sci, *3*, 702; AJP, *7*, 579)

Diethelm, Oskar
Appointment: Cornell Univ. (Sci, *83*, 228)

Dietze, Alfred Godfrey
Appointment: Univ. of Pittsburgh (J App, *10*, 522)
Promotion: Univ. of Pittsburgh (Bull, *42*, 581)

Differential limen for pitch
Lecture: Boring, E. G. (AJP, *53*, 450-455)

Dillinger, Claude Maurice
Appointment: Illinois State Normal Univ. (Bull, *41*, 807)
Promotion: Southwest Missouri State Teachers College (Bull, *40*, 459)

Dilthey, Wilhelm Christian Ludwig
Death notice (JoP, *8*, 615-616)

Dimmick, Forrest Lee
Election: Inter-Society Color Council meeting; Chair (Bull, *36*, 141)

Dimmick, Graham Bennett
Appointment: Kentucky (SCI, 72, 315)

Directory of Applied Psychologists
Publication (BULL, 38, 304)

Disabilities developed by the annual conscription
Research: Chervin, A. (SCI°, 4, 220)

Diserens, Charles Murdoch
Promotion: Univ. of Cincinnati (BULL, 42, 485)

Disher, Dorothy Rose
Grant: Social Science Research Council (BULL, 36, 805)

Dissertations
Numbers reported for psychology for 1934-1942 (BULL, 40, 540)

Distraction
Publication: Jenkins, J. G.; "The effects of distraction" (AJP, 45, 173-174)
Publication: Skaggs, E. B. (AJP, 41, 162)

Diven, Kenneth
Publication: "Dandy's radical extirpation of brain tissue in man" (AJP, 46, 503)

Dix, D.
Appointment: Univ. of Toronto (BULL, 3, 36)

Dixey, Frederick Augustus
Lecture: Elementary physiology (SCI°, 10, 250)

Dixon, Edward Travers
Courses: Univ. College, London (AJP, 10, 165; REV, 5, 554)

Dixon, Roland Burrage
Election: AAAS, section H; Vice-president (BULL, 7, 75; JOP, 7, 84)

Dobson, Mary MacFarlane
Appointment: Nebraska Central College (BULL, 41, 268)

Dockeray, Floyd Carlton
Appointment: Univ. of Michigan (BULL, 5, 379)
Election: Ohio College Assoc., Psychology section (BULL, 26, 624)
Promotion (SCI, 37, 906)
Promotion: Univ. of Kansas (BULL, 13, 407)

Dodd, Stuart
Lecture: Franklin Institute, Philadelphia (SCI, 63, 65)

Dodge, Raymond

Appointment: AAAS; Vice-president and chair (BULL, *19*, 63)
Appointment: Carnegie Institute, Nutrition lab (JoP, *9*, 672; Sci, *36*, 591)
Appointment: Columbia Univ. (JoP, *13*, 336; BULL, *14*, 264; JoP, *14*, 392)
Appointment: Columbia Univ.; Ernest Adams Fellowship (Sci, *45*, 611; JoP, *14*, 392; BULL, *13*, 260; Sci, *43*, 708)
Appointment: Council of National Defense, Industrial Fatigue Committee (Sci, *46*, 109)
Appointment: National Research Council (Sci, *45*, 477; BULL, *14*, 191; JoP, *14*, 392)
Appointment: U.S. Navy Lieutenant Commander (Sci, *48*, 596)
Appointment: Wesleyan Univ. (REV, *5*, 449; AJP, *11*, 130)
Appointment: Yale Univ. (J APP, *8*, 450)
Death notice (AJP, *55*, 584-600; BULL, *39*, 325)
Degree: Wesleyan Univ., Ph.D. (Sci, *73*, 697)
Degree: Williams College (Sci, *47*, *634*)
Degree: Yale Univ. (BULL, *28*, 503)
Departure: Wesleyan Univ. (JoP, *9*, 672)
Election: APA office (BULL, *13*, 40)
Election: APA President, 1916 (Sci, *43*, 17)
Election: National Academy of Sciences (Sci, *59*, 418; BULL, *21*, 360)
Election: National Research Council, Chair (BULL, *19*, 350)
Grant: AAAS, $400.00 (BULL, *19*, 171)
Leave of absence (BULL, *10*, 252)
Lecture: APA "The laws of relative fatigue" (Sci, *44*, 673)
Lecture: Carnegie Institute of Technology (BULL, *13*, 228; Sci, *43*, 710)
Lecture: Columbia Univ. (BULL, *13*, 188; Sci, *43*, 459; JoP, *13*, 224)
Lecture: eye movements (JoP, *2*, 223)
Lecture: Middletown Scientific Assoc., fatigue (Sci, *29*, 809)
Lecture: NYAS, alcohol (BULL, *12*, 160)
Lecture: NY Branch APA/NYAS (JoP, *12*, 196)
Portrait presented to Yale Univ. (BULL, *33*, 581; Sci, *83*, 571)
Promotion: Wesleyan Univ. (REV, *6*, 344; Sci, *15*, 720)
Publication: commemorative volume of scientific articles (Sci, *83*, 571)

Doll, Edgar Arnold

Appointment: Bonnie Brae Farm for Boys (N.J.) (BULL, *40*, 539; Sci, *97*, 420)
Appointment: New Jersey State Psychiatric Clinic (J APP, *4*, 112-113)
Appointment: Princeton Univ. (BULL, *14*, 366; BULL, *15*, 24)
Appointment: Vineland Training School (BULL, *9*, 360; JoP, *9*, 532; Sci, *36*, 47)
Departure: Vineland Training School (BULL, *40*, 539)
Lecture: American Assoc. for Applied Psychology, "Scientific freedom" (Sci, *94*, 230)
Lecture: American Assoc. on Mental Deficiency, 1938 (J APP, *22*, 109)
Lecture: mental deficiency (AJP, *54*, 116-124)
Lecture: Taylor Society, prison psychology (J APP, *9*, 428)
Vineland lab 25th anniversary (Sci, *74*, 286)

Donahue, Wilma Thompson
Appointment: Michigan Psychological Services (BULL, 42, 581-582)
Appointment: Univ. of Michigan (SCI, 102, 115)

Donaldson, Charles Durward
Death notice (BULL, 40, 152)

Donaldson, Henry Herbert
Election: Chicago Neurological Society, President (SCI°, 17, 597)
Election: Univ. of Chicago, Sigma Xi, President (SCI°, 17, 838)
Lecture: nervous system (JoP, 2, 280)
Lecture: neurology (JoP, 1, 336)

Donkin, Horatio Bryan
Appointment: Royal Commission on the Care of the Feeble-minded (SCI, 22, 510)

Donnan, Frederick George
Reception for the Society of Visiting Scientists (SCI, 101, 15)

Doob, Leonard William
Appointment: Yale Univ. (SCI, 80, 137)
Lecture: National Research Council conference, "Psychological factors in national morale" (BULL, 37, 829)

Dorcus, Roy Melvin
Appointment: Univ. of California (SCI, 86, 218; BULL, 34, 864)
Departure: Johns Hopkins Univ. (SCI, 86, 218)

Dorley, John E.
Publication: pragmatism *New York Medical Journal* (JoP, 5, 82)

Dotterer, Ray Harbaugh
Appointment: Franklin and Marshall College (JoP, 23, 420; SCI, 64, 324)

Douglas, Claude Gordon
Award: Osler Memorial Award of the Univ. of Oxford (SCI, 102, 114)

Dove, Claude Clifford
Conference on Psychology of Learning, Univ. of Colorado, 1939 (BULL, 36, 583)

Down House (*see* British Association for Preservation, and Darwin, C. R.)

Downey, June Etta
Appointment: Univ. of Chicago (REV, 5, 109)
Appointment: Univ. of Wyoming (REV, 7, 216, 324)
Death notice (JoP, 29, 616; AJP, 45, 362; BULL, 30, 107)
Dedication: seminar, 1943 by Univ. of Wyoming and Psi Chi (J APP, 27, 363; BULL, 40, 540)

Leave of absence Univ. of Wyoming (JoP, *19*, 476; Bull, *18*, 111; Bull, *11*, 268; Sci, *56*, 73; Bull, *19*, 410; JoP, *11*, 721)
Library fund ceremonies held, Univ. of Wyoming (AJP, *56*, 449)
Research: will-profile study (J App, *3*, 195)

Downing, A. B.
Election: National Educational Assoc. (Sci, *9*, 339-340)

Drake, Charles Arthur
Appointment: Assoc. of Consulting Psychologists Committee, 8th annual meeting (J App, *21*, 241)

Drake, Durant
Appointment: Univ. of Illinois (JoP, *8*, 532)

Draper, Andrew Sloan
Builds a pedagogical library (Sci°, *9*, 155)

Dreams
Lecture: Farquhar, E. J., Wash. Phil. Society (Sci°, *1*, 472)
Lecture: Jastrow, J., Columbia Univ. (Sci, *33*, 214)
Lecture: Seashore, C. E., Columbia Univ (Sci, *33*, 213)
Research: Monroe, W. S. (AJP, *10*, 326-327)

Dreese, Mitchell
APA, Wash-Balt Branch, 3rd meeting, 1939 (Bull, *36*, 500)
Interest inventory for elementary grades (J App, *25*, 474)

Dresslar, Fletcher Bascom
Appointment: Univ. of Alabama (Bull, *5*, 348)

Drever, James
Appointment: Univ. of Edinburgh (Bull, *16*, 222; Sci, *49*, 495)
Election: International Congress of Psychology, 12th; President (J App, *24*, 245)
Lecture: Points of view in psychology (Sci, *69*, 450)

Drewry, Patrick H., Jr.
Appointment: Medical College of Virginia, Richmond (Sci, *89*, 313)
Fellowship: Rockefeller Foundation (Sci, *89*, 313)

Drexel Institute of Technology (Philadelphia, Pennsylvania)
Appointment: Sones, A. M. (Bull, *39*, 681)

Driesch, Hans Adolf Eduard
Leipzig, Honorariums (Sci, *73*, 609)

Drowsiness
Lecture: Hollingworth, H. L. (JoP, *7*, 700)

Drugs

Appointment: Cattell, J. McK. American Society for Pharmacology, committee member (Sci, 87, 458)

Lecture: Hollingworth, H., on susceptibility (AJP, 43, 139)

Lecture: Kolb, L., on addiction (Sci, 89, 289)

Lecture: Rivers, W.H.R., on fatigue (Bull, 3, 248)

Report: Tucker, W. G. (Sci°, 9, 31)

Research: effects of on sense of taste in Italy (Sci°, 8, 54)

Dry Tortugas

Research: Watson, J. B., studying habits of sea-gulls (Sci, 26, 188)

Dualism in psychology

Lecture: Wright, H. W. (AJP, 53, 121-128)

Dublin, University of (Ireland)

Appointment: Johnston, S. P. (Rev, 5, 450)

Dugas, Ludovic

Research: memory and mental disturbance (JoP, 15, 615-616)

Duhamel, Georges

Appointment: Academy of Sciences, Paris (Sci, 101, 196)

Duke University (Durham, North Carolina)

Appointment: Crispell, R. S. (Sci, 79, 267)

Appointment: Lyman, R. S. (Sci, 91, 187)

Appointment: McDougall, W. (Bull, 24, 204; Sci, 65, 139)

Appointment: Stern, W. (Bull, 32, 376)

Courses: Wallin, J.E.W., mental hygiene (J App, 21, 130)

Department of Psychiatry and Mental Hygiene connected with Highland Hospital, Asheville, N.C. (Sci, 91, 187)

Editorship: *Journal of Parapsychology* returns (Sci, 95, 322-323; Bull, 39, 325)

Grant: Rockefeller Foundation for Psychiatry and Mental Hygiene Department (Sci, 91, 187)

Highland Hospital for nervous and mental disorders (Sci, 89, 555; Sci, 91, 187)

Lecture: Meyer, A. (Sci, 93, 38)

Publication: *Character and Personality* (Bull, 29, 603; J App, 16, 439; JoP, 29, 644)

Dumville, Benjamin

Lecture: philosophical education (JoP, 4, 447)

Dunbar, Helen Flanders

Editor *Psychosomatic Medicine* (J App, 22, 663)

Duncan, David

Requests letters of Spencer, H. for biography (JoP, 1, 111)

Duncan, George Martin
Appointment: Yale Psychological Laboratory, Advisory Council (JoP, *1*, 28)
Promotion announced (REV, *1*, 552)

Dunford, Ralph Emerson
Appointment: Univ. of Tennessee, Dean of students (BULL, *41*, 603)

Dunlap, Charles B.
Death notice (SCI, *63*, 615)

Dunlap chronoscope
Evaluation by Fernberger, S. (AJP, *44*, 582)

Dunlap, Jack Wilbur
Appointment: Univ. of Rochester; Director of testing (BULL, *34*, 498)
Commission: U.S. Navy (BULL, *40*, 539; SCI, *97*, 327)
Election: AAAP, Treasurer (BULL, *36*, 500)
Leave of absence: Univ. of Rochester (SCI, *97*, 327)
Lecture: Psychometric Society, "The psychometric society roots and powers" (SCI, *94*, 230)
Lecture: standard error of a difference (AJP, *44*, 581)
Publication: Recent advances in statistical theory and application (AJP, *51*, 571)
Publication: statistics (AJP, *54*, 583-601)
Resignation: National Research Council (BULL, *40*, 539; SCI, *97*, 327)

Dunlap, Knight
Appointment: Government Service (BULL, *14*, 366)
Appointment: Johns Hopkins Univ. (SCI, *23*, 928; BULL, *3*, 216; JoP, *3*, 364)
Appointment: Johns Hopkins Univ.; directs Psychology Dept. (BULL, *13*, 260; JoP, *13*, 532)
Appointment: Nela Research Lab (SCI, *39*, 866)
Appointment: Univ. of California (SCI, *86*, 218; BULL, *21*, 360)
Appointment: Univ. of California, Los Angeles (SCI, *82*, 217; SCI, *81*, 171)
Associated with Dorcus, R. M. at Univ. of California, Los Angeles (BULL, *34*, 864)
Comments on technique of negative practice by Peak, H. (AJP, *55*, 576-580)
Departure: Johns Hopkins Univ. (SCI, *86*, 218)
Editor *Journal of Animal Behavior Psychology* (BULL, *17*, 435)
Editor *Journal of Comparative Psychology* (JoP, *17*, 672)
Editor *Psychobiology* (JoP, *14*, 532; BULL, *14*, 115)
Editor *Psychology Classics* (BULL, *13*, 482; JoP, *14*, 56; BULL, *19*, 172; SCI, *55*, 315)
Election: AAAS, Vice-president, section I (BULL, *24*, 80)
Election: APA office (BULL, *13*, 40)
Election: National Research Council (SCI, *65*, 495)
Election: Social Science Research Council, APA representative (BULL, *24*, 80)
Election: SSPP (JoP, *14*, 308)
Johns Hopkins Univ. farewell dinner (SCI, *83*, 77)

Leave of absence: Johns Hopkins Univ. (SCI, 65, 495)
Lecture: Clark Univ. (SCI, 59, 574)
Lecture: emotions (AJP, 44, 572)
Lecture: SSPP, 35th annual meeting (JoP 37, 196)
Lecture: West Virginia Univ. (SCI, 65, 181)
Promotion: Johns Hopkins Univ. (BULL, 7, 324; BULL, 8, 302; SCI, 44, 238; JoP, 7, 560; JoP, 8, 420; SCI, 33, 992)
Publication: binocular color mixing (AJP, 57, 559-563)
Publication: negative practice (AJP, 55, 270-273)
Publication: psychological terminology papers sent to APA members (BULL, 13, 260)
Publication: *Psychology Classics* (JoP, 19, 224)
Research: memory work material (BULL, 31, 80)

Dunlop, James Craufurd
Royal Commission on the Care of the Feeble-minded (SCI, 22, 510)

Dunn, William H.
Publication: war neuroses *Psychological Bulletin* (J APP, 25, 359)

Durham, University of
Lecture: Pear, T. H.; Riddell Memorial Lecturer (SCI, 83, 619)

Durkheim, Emile
Lecture: judgment, International Congress of Philosophy, 4th (BULL, 7, 251)
Publication: social contract *The Revue de Métaphysique et de Morale* (JoP, 15, 196)

Durost, Walter Nelson
Publication: Simplified chart, Pearson product moment coefficient (J APP, 22, 218)

Durr, Georg Ernst
Death notice (AJP, 25, 319)

Dusenberry, Ida Smoot
Leave of absence: Brigham Young (BULL, 28, 410)

Dusser De Barenne, Johannes Gregorius
Lecture: Brown Univ. (BULL, 32, 323)

Duval, Mathias
Lecture: mutual relations of evolution and the embryology of the eye (SCI°, 2, 91)

Dvorine, Israel
Comments on color perception charts (AJP, 58, 397-399)

Dwelshauvers, Georges
Laboratory at Univ. of Brussels (REV, *1*, 112)

Dyer, W. T. Thiselton
Eulogy on Bentham, G. at Linnaean Society (SCI°, *11*, 277)

Dynamic psychology
Lecture: Dodge, R. (SCI, *43*, 459; JOP, *13*, 224)
Lecture: Woodworth, R. S., American Museum of Natural History (SCI, *44*, 745)

Dysinger, Donald Warren
Appointment: Univ. of Nebraska (SCI, *91*, 616; J APP, *24*, 518)

E

Ear, inner
Slides of Meyer, M. (BULL, 5, 406)

Eastern Branch of the American Psychological Association (*see also* New York Branch of the American Psychological Association)
Election: Lashley, K. S., President (SCI, 85, 380)
Lecture: Rogers, H. W., 1936 (AJP, 49, 486)
Meeting: 1937, Vassar College (SCI, 85, 331; BULL, 34, 121)
Meeting: 1938 (SCI, 87, 297)

Eastern Psychological Association (*see also* Eastern Branch; New York Branch of the APA)
Election: Helson, H., Secretary, 1940 (BULL, 36, 841)
Election: Hunter, W. S., President (SCI, 91, 402)
Election: Murphy, G., President (SCI, 93, 395)
Lecture: Allport, G., 1943 presidential (SCI, 97, 374)
Meeting: 10th Bryn Mawr College (AJP, 52, 473-475; SCI, 89, 265)
Meeting: 11th (BULL, 36, 841; AJP, 53, 462-464)
Meeting: 12th (AJP, 54, 441-443; SCI, 93, 373)
Meeting: 13th Providence, R.I. (AJP, 55, 447-449)
Meeting: 14th Hunter College (AJP, 56, 607-609; SCI, 97, 374)
Meeting: 15th Boston Univ. (AJP, 57, 575-576)
Meeting: 16th College of the City of New York (AJP, 58, 402-404)
Publication: Oberly, H. S.; "The ninth annual meeting of the Eastern Psychological Assoc." (AJP, 51, 577)

Eastern Washington College of Education (Cheney, Washington)
Leave of absence: Hall, W. E. (BULL, 42, 582)

Eaton, Ralph Monroe
Death notice (JoP, 29, 280)

Ebaugh, Franklin Gessford
Appointment: Univ. of Colorado (Sci, 61, 86)
Appointment: Eighth Service Command (Sci, 96, 334)
Leave of absence: School of Medicine of the Univ. of Colorado and
    Psychopathic Hospital (Sci, 96, 334)
Lecture: Cavanee (Sci, 91, 446)
Lecture: Rogers memorial (Sci, 92, 235)
Research: suicide; psychoanalytic case studies (J App, 22, 108)

Ebbinghaus, Hermann
Accepts chair at Univ. of Breslau (Rev, 1, 440)
Appointment: Univ. of Halle (JoP, 2, 644; Bull, 2, 427)
Death notice (Sci, 29, 451; JoP, 6, 196; Bull, 6, 152; AJP, 20, 472)
Discussion: interpretation of retention values (AJP, 54, 283-286)
Editor: *Zeitschrift f. Psychologie* (Bull, 3, 116)
Fails to attend International Congress of Arts and Sciences (JoP, 1, 615)
Laboratory Univ. of Breslau (AJP, 7, 152)
Lecture: International Congress of Arts and Sciences, St. Louis (JoP, 1, 420)
Publication: *Psychologie* (AJP, 8, 430)

Ecole de Psychologie de Paris
Anniversary: 40th (Sci, 71, 338)

Economic Psychology Association
Meeting: 2nd annual (J App, 1, 97)

Economo, Constantin von
Columbia Univ. Psychiatry (Sci, 71, 213)

Edgell, Beatrice
Appointment: Univ. of London (Bull, 24, 312)
Lecture: memory, Aristotelian Society (JoP, 9, 363-364)
Retirement: Univ. of London (Bull, 31, 80; Sci, 78, 576)

Edgerton, Harold Asahel
Leave of absence: Ohio State Univ. (Bull, 32, 323)

Edinburgh Review
Article: Kay, D. "Memory—what it is and how to improve it" (Sci°, 12, 237)

Edinburgh, University of (Scotland)
Anniversary: Fraser, A. C. (Bull, 3, 422)
Appointment: Bergson, H., Gifford lecturer (JoP, 9, 56)
Appointment: Drever, J. (Sci, 49, 495; Bull, 16, 222)
Appointment: James, W. (Rev, 5, 344; Sci, 7, 634)

Appointment: Kemp-Smith, N. (BULL, *16*, 257)
Appointment: Robertson, G. M. (SCI, *51*, 62)
Appointment: Seth, J. (REV, *5*, 450)
Appointment: Smith, W. G. (BULL, *8*, 333; JoP, *3*, 504; BULL, *3*, 320)
Candidate: Tuke, J. B. for parliamentary representative (SCI, *11*, 756)
Degree: James, W. (REV, *9*, 328, 431)
Degree: Newcomb, S. (SCI°, *19*, 100)
Degree: Sorley, W. R. (SCI, *11*, 717)
Degree: Thorndike, E. L. (BULL, *33*, 849; SCI, *83*, 321, 367)
Lecture: Bosanquet, B.; Gifford lecturer (JoP, *7*, 140)
Lecture: Dewey, J. (SCI, *68*, 11)
Lecture: Dewey, J., Gifford lectures (SCI, *69*, 157)
Lecture: established, Combe, G. (JoP, *3*, 420; BULL, *3*, 248)
Lecture: James, W., Gifford lectures (SCI, *15*, 675; SCI, *13*, 876; REV, *8*, 335)
Retirement: Calderwood, H. (SCI, *2*, 48)

Education (*see also* General Education Board)

Appointment: Mackintosh, H K , U.S. Office of Education (J APP, *22*, 107)
College for the training of teachers, 1890 (SCI°, *14*, 403)
Conference: educational, 8th; speakers announced (J APP, *23*, 530)
Conference: educ. broadcasting, national, 2nd (BULL, *34*, 637)
Conference: educational production, motion pictures (BULL, *36*, 140)
Conference for the education of the gifted, Columbia Univ.; in memory of
    Hollingworth, L. S. (J APP, *24*, 854; BULL, *38*, 192)
Conference: Stanford education, 1938 (J APP, *22*, 107)
Educational motion picture project of the American Council on Education
    (BULL, *36*, 499)
Election: Fraser, ?, Royal Society (SCI, *69*, 349)
Instruction of higher education (SCI, *2*, 253)
International conference on (SCI, *4*, 266; BULL, *2*, 158; BULL, *11*, 3, 267)
Lecture: Angell, J. R., Penrose memorial (SCI, *95*, 219)
Lecture: Ashbaugh, E. J., problems learning to read (J APP, *26*, 108)
Lecture: Clark, H. F., diet and learning (J APP, *26*, 107)
Lecture. Clark, R., on guidance (J APP, *6*, 425)
Lecture: Hall, G. S. (SCI, *34*, 754, 755; JoP, *9*, 28, 140)
Lecture: Hall, G. S., Johns Hopkins Univ. (SCI°, *9*, 360)
Lecture: King, I. (JoP, *7*, 222)
Lecture: Meltzer, H., mental hygiene and learning (J APP, *26*, 107)
Lecture: School of Pedagogy, New York Univ. (SCI, *11*, 318)
Lecture: Southwestern Philosophical Conference (JoP, *42*, 723-724)
Lecture: "Teacher education in a democracy at war" (J APP, *26*, 714)
Meeting: National Education Assoc., National education week program, 1938
    (J APP, *22*, 107)
Meeting: World Federation of Education Assoc., 8th Biennial Congress, 1939
    (BULL, *36*, 304)
Men of science publication (SCI, *9*, 856)

National Coordinating Committee on Education and Defense, APA (BULL, 37, 828)

Negroes of the South, education of (SCI°, 9, 584)

Publication: American Council on Education "Selected educational motion pictures: A descriptive encyclopedia" (J APP, 26, 570)

Publication: Cattell, J. McK. *Biographical Directory of Leaders in Education* (J APP, 16, 222)

Publication: continuing educ., catalogue of the Army Institute (J APP, 27, 114)

Publication: National Advisory Board on Radio in Education, Weekly Psych and Economics Broadcasts (SCI, 74, 411)

Publication: Rural education series, problems in rural areas (J APP, 26, 109)

Publication: "Youth in the CCC" (J APP, 26, 570)

Report of 1884 (SCI°, 13, 401)

Research: Psychological Institute (J APP, 19, 106)

Science examination prize announcement (SCI°, 2, 385)

Special Training, Committee created by the War Department (BULL, 15, 97-98)

Statistics from Japan (SCI°, 4, 266)

Symposium: AAAS (BULL, 38, 908)

Symposium: AAAS, 1941-42 interrelatedness of education and psychology (J APP, 26, 107)

Tests: college entrance exam, Toops, H. (BULL, 32, 324)

Educational Abstracts

Editor: Cook, P.M. (J APP, 22, 107)

Editor: Stumpf, W. A., Associate (J APP, 22, 107)

Phi Kappa Delta, new owners (J APP, 22, 107)

Publication: first issue (BULL, 33, 147)

Educational and Psychological Measurement

Publication: first issue (AJP, 54, 294-295)

Publication: founded, editor and associates (J APP, 25, 265)

Educational Conference

Meeting: 3rd (J APP, 7, 188)

Meeting: 7th (AJP, 38, 315)

Meeting: 8th (J APP, 23, 530)

Meeting: 10th (BULL, 38, 780)

Educational psychology

Appointment: Guilford, J. P., Bureau of Instructional Research, Univ. of Nebraska, Director (BULL, 36, 304)

Appointment: Super, D. E., Clark Univ. (BULL, 35, 333)

Course: Pyle, W. H., Univ. of Indiana (JOP, 14, 140)

Course: Simpson, B. R. (JOP, 7, 336)

Course: Univ. of Georgia (JOP, 7, 336)

Lecture: Baltimore (BULL, 3, 392)

Lecture: Judd, C. H. (J APP, 10, 129)

Lecture: King, I. (JoP, 7, 222)
Lecture: Ladd, G. T. Western Reserve Univ. (Sci, 28, 481)
Lecture: Rogers, A. (J App, 10, 129)
Lecture: Thorndike, E. L., retardation (Sci, 37, 302)
Lecture: Thorndike, E. L., semantic word count, Columbia Univ. (Bull, 36, 140)

Edwards, Austin Southwick

Appointment: Univ. of Georgia (Bull, 13, 376; JoP, 13, 588)
Lecture: suggestibility in school children (JoP, 7, 223)

Edwards, Richard H.

Appointment: Keuka College, NY (Bull, 41, 200)

Eeden, Frederik Van

Lecture: Univ. of Wisconsin (Sci, 29, 450, 541)

Efficiency

Lecture: Marsh, H D. (JoP, 1, 224)
Lecture: Munsterberg, H., industrial efficiency (Sci, 35, 925)

Egan, James

Appointment: Northwestern Univ. (Sci, 88, 471)

Egger, Victor

Death notice (Bull, 6, 120)

Egotism in German Philosophy

Boutroux, E., writes preface (JoP, 15, 112)

Ehrenfels, Christian J. L. K., Freiherr von (see System der Werttheorie)

Eidetic imagery

Publication: Finkestein, S. "The visual imagery of a lightning calculator" (AJP, 45, 353)
Publication: Helson, H., Child's spontaneous reports of imagery (AJP, 45, 360)

Eighth Service Command

Appointment: Ebaugh, F. G.; Chief psychiatric consultant (Sci, 96, 334)

Elder, James Harlan

Appointment: Louisiana State Univ. (Sci, 95, 220, 351; Bull, 39, 325)
Appointment: War Department, Washington, D.C. (Bull, 40, 619; Sci, 98, 12)
Departure: Univ. of Virginia (Sci, 95, 351)
Leave of absence: Louisiana State Univ. (Sci, 98, 12; Bull, 40, 619)

Electric currents in the skin

Research: Tarkhanov, I. R. (Sci°, 15, 72-73)

Electro-encephalogram
Publication: Kreezer, G. "The electro-encephalogram and its use in psychology" (AJP, *51*, 737)

Electromyographic technique
Research: use in recording eyelid movement (AJP, *58*, 112-113)

Elementary Psychology of Feeling and Attention
Publication: Titchener, E. B. (JoP, *5*, 252)

Elhardt, Walter Phillipp
Publication: relationship of pain to emotive conditions (AJP, *58*, 392-394)

Elkin, William Baird
Appointment: Hamilton College (REV, *6*, 673)

Elliott, Aaron Marshall
Publication: philological expedition to Canada; Johns Hopkins Univ. Circular (Sci°, *5*, 119-120)

Elliott, Edward C.
Retirement (Sci, *101*, 35, 403)

Elliott, Richard Maurice
Appointment: Yale Univ. (BULL, *12*, 243; JoP, *12*, 504)
Award: Sheldon Fellowship (BULL, *10*, 292; Sci, *37*, 628)
Departure: Harvard College (BULL, *12*, 243; JoP, *12*, 504)
Publication: *Explorations in Personality* (AJP, *52*, 453-462)

Ellis, Alexander Caswell
Appointment: Univ. of Texas, Director of lab (REV, *6*, 673)
Election: APA, Vice-president (BULL, *8*, 32)
Election: SSPP council member (Sci, *31*, 22; JoP, *7*, 56; JoP, *1*, 168)
Election: SSPP Vice-president (JoP, *8*, 84)

Ellis, Alexander John
Death notice (Sci°, *16*, 287)

Ellis, William John
Anniversary: 25th Vineland lab (Sci, *74*, 286)
Appointment: New Jersey State Psychiatric Clinic (J APP, *4*, 112-113)

Ellis, Willis Davis
Death notice (BULL, *39*, 681)
Lecture: ethics in psychology (AJP, *44*, 365)

Emerson, Charles P.
Election: National Committee for Mental Hygiene, President (Sci, *72*, 557)

Emerson College (Boston, Massachusetts)
Course: speech disorders (J App, *19*, 221)

Emerson, William Robie Patten
Appointment: Bureau of Educational Experiments, New York City (J App, *3*, 196)

Emery, E. Van Norman
Appointment: Child Clinic, Los Angeles, California (J App, *10*, 396)

Emme, Earle Edward
Appointment: Dakota Wesleyan Univ. (Bull, *41*, 343)
Departure: Morningside College (Bull, *41*, 343)

Emmert's Law
Discussion: Boring, E. G., optical geometry of (AJP, *53*, 293-295)

Emminghaus, Hermann
Death notice (Bull, *1*, 174)

Emory University (Atlanta, Georgia)
Promotion: Langhorne, M. C. (Bull, *40*, 794)
Promotion: Martin, H. W. (Bull, *40*, 794)
Promotion: Workman, W. G. (Bull, *40*, 794)

Emotion (*see also* Feelings)
Lecture: Cannon, W. B., Mayo Clinic (Sci, *56*, 105)
Lecture: Dunlap, K. (AJP, *44*, 572)
Lecture: Jastrow, J., expression (Sci, *43*, 529)
Lecture: Jastrow, J., New School for Social Research (Bull, *27*, 620; Sci, *66*, 278)
Lecture: Monin, L. C. (JoP, *2*, 280)
Lecture: Ruckmick, C. A. (Bull, *29*, 248)
Lecture: Ruckmick, C. A., facial expression of emotion (Sci, *73*, 416)
Lecture: Ruckmick, C. A., Galvanic response (Sci, *73*, 416)
Lecture: Ruckmick, C. A., Iowa (Sci, *75*, 262)
Publication: Forbes, T. W. and Landis, C. "Critique of Crosland's measurement of emotion" (AJP, *45*, 522)
Publication: Hunt, W. A. "Ambiguity of descriptive terms for feeling and emotion" (AJP, *47*, 165)
Publication: Martin, L. J. (J App, *2*, 386)
Publication: Ruckmick, C. A., "McCosh on the emotions" (AJP, *46*, 506)
Research: Corbusier, W. H., expressions in Apache indians (Sci°, *9*, 212)
Research: Washburn, M. F. (Bull, *17*, 239)
Symposium: Wittenberg College (AJP, *40*, 170)

Empiricism
Fellowship: Hofstadter, A., John Simon Guggenheim Memorial Foundation (JoP, *40*, 224)

Lecture: Bakewell, C. M. (JoP, *2*, 700)
Lecture: Judd, C. H. (JoP, *2*, 112)
Lecture: Ruckmick, C. A. (AJP, *40*, 166)

Employee counseling
Publication: *Personnel Adminstration*, 1943 (J App, *28*, 80)

Employment Stabilization Research Institute of Univ. of Minnesota
Research: wartime problems (J App, *26*, 713)

Emporia State University (*see* Kansas State Normal School)

Encyclopedia Britannica
Publication: philosophy (Sci°, *8*, 482)
Publication: Ward, J., psychology (Sci°, *7*, 304)
Publication: Whitney, W. D. and Sievers, E. "Philology" (Sci°, *5*, 162)

Encyclopedia of Psychology
Publication plans (Bull, *41*, 499)

Engelhart, N. L., Jr.
Research: air-age education (J App, *28*, 80)

Engineering Aptitude Test
Thurstone, L. L. (J App, *3*, 197)

Engineering Defense Training
Publication: Moore, B. V. (J App, *26*, 106-107)

Engineering Woman's Club
Election: Gilbreth, L. M. (Sci, *91*, 334)

England
Progress in experimental psychology (AJP, *8*, 583)

English and foreign philosophical library
Publication: "The life and work of Giordano Bruno" (Sci°, *9*, 190)

English, Horace Bidwell
Appointment: Antioch College (Bull, *24*, 312)
Appointment: Ohio State Univ. (Sci, *74*, 453; Bull, *27*, 564; Sci, *71*, 556)
Appointment: Univ. of Nebraska (Bull, *32*, 324)
Appointment: Wellesley College (Bull, *17*, 279)
Appointment: Wesleyan Univ. (Bull, *22*, 444; Sci, *61*, 489)
Attends AAAP organizational meeting (Bull, *34*, 864-865)
Election: AAAP Executive secretary (J App, *21*, 603, 713)
Election: Assoc. of Applied Psychologists; President (Sci, *90*, 613)
Election: MPA President (J App, *17*, 97)

Election: Ohio College Assoc. President, psychology section (BULL, 27, 415)
Election: Ohio College Assoc. Sect/Treas, psychology section (BULL, 26, 624)
Lecture: National Research Council Conference: "Psychological factors in national morale" (BULL, 37, 829)
Lecture: West Virginia Academy of Science "Psychology in the post-war world" (SCI, 99, 405)
Publication: *Dictionary of Psychological Terms* (J APP, 11, 528)
Publication: illusion and error in personalistic act psychology (AJP, 57, 563-565)
Return: Antioch College (J APP, 11, 165)

English Society for Psychical Research
Meeting: New York members, April, 1891, Columbia College (SCI°, 17, 228)
Resignation: Moses, W. S. (SCI°, 9, 10)

Enriques, Federigo
Election: Fourth International Congress of Philosophy, President (JoP, 7, 420)
International Congress for the Unity of Science (JoP, 33, 196)

Epilepsy
Appointment: Wallin, J. E. W.: Director of lab (BULL, 7, 324)
Award: Bruetsch, W. L., Laymen's League Against Epilepsy (SCI, 93, 419)
Award: Peterson, F. (SCI°, 14, 702)

Epiphenomenalism
Lecture: on Huxley by McGilvary, E. B. (JoP, 7, 223)

Epistemology
Lecture: Külpe, O. (JoP, 7, 504)

Equilibration
Lecture: Robinson, E. S. (AJP, 41, 153)

Erdmann, Benno
Appointment: Univ. of Berlin (JoP, 6, 560, 700; BULL, 6, 368)
Death notice (AJP, 33, 155)

Ergograph
Research: Wissler, C. (SCI, 15, 547)

Ericksen, Stanford Clark
Appointment: Univ. of Arkansas (BULL, 35, 796)

Erickson, Milton Hyland
Promotion: Wayne State Univ. College of Medicine (BULL, 42, 128)

Eriksen, Richard
Election: Norwegian Psychological Assoc., Vice-president (AJP, 46, 511)

Erikson, Erik Homburger
Appointment: Univ. of California (BULL, *36*, 304)

Erkenntnis
Changed to *Journal of Unified Science* (JoP, *36*, 532)

Escola Politechnica of Sao Paulo (Brazil)
Establishment: psychology department (BULL, *42*, 486)
Exchange professor, Klineberg, O. (SCI, *101*, 428)

Esper, Erwin Allen
Appointment: Univ. of Washington (BULL, *24*, 508; SCI, *65*, 595; J APP, *11*, 405)

Esso Research Club, Standard Oil Company, New Jersey
Affiliation: Society of Sigma Xi (SCI, *99*, 123)

Esso Safety Foundation
Grant: Yale Univ. auto driver research (BULL, *36*, 140)

Estabrooks, George Hoben
Appointment: Colgate Univ. (SCI, *65*, 523)

Esthetics (*see* Aesthetics)

Ethics
Lecture: Ellis, W. D., psychology (AJP, *44*, 365)
Lecture: Lloyd, A. H. (JoP, *1*, 224)
Lecture: O'Shea, M. V. (JoP, *2*, 280)
Publication: APA notice of animal legislation (BULL, *30*, 183)
Publication: Murray, E.; "The Ishihara test for color-blindness: A point in ethics" (AJP, *47*, 511)
School formed, London (REV, *5*, 110)

Ethnology
International Congress of Ethnology (AJP, *11*, 280; SCI, *10*, 981; SCI, *11*, 318)
Lecture: International Congress of Ethnology, ethnographical psychology (AJP, *11*, 280)

Étude de Psychologie
Publication begun (BULL, *10*, 490)

Eucken, Rudolf
Publication: "Prolegomena zu forschungen über der einheit desgeisteslebens" (SCI°, *6*, 452)

Eugenics (*see also* American Eugenics Society; Human Betterment Foundation)
American Eugenics Society moves headquarters (SCI, *83*, 573)

Appointment: Allan, W., Dept of Eugenics, Bowman Gray School of Medicine (SCI, *94*, 111)

Appointment: Basset, G. C., Station for Experimental Evolution (JoP, *10*, 503-504)

Appointment: Fisher, R. A., Galton Chair (SCI, *78*, 32)

Appointment: Lenz, F., Kaiser Wilhelm Institute for Anthropology; Director (SCI, *79*, 157)

Appointment: Pearson, K., Univ. of London, Eugenics chair (SCI, *34*, 150)

Award: Pearson, K.; Rudolph-Virchow Medal, Berlin Anthro. Soc. (SCI, *77*, 16)

Bequest: Univ. of London from Galton, F. (SCI, *33*, 370)

California Sterilization Program, Human Betterment Foundation (J APP, *23*, 745)

Conference: Inheritance of mental qualities, London, 1922 (SCI, *56*, 41)

Endowment: Oberlin College Library (SCI, *35*, 816)

Fellowship: London Univ. (BULL., *1*, 488; JoP, *1*, 672)

Grant: Mears, J. E., Harvard Eugenics Research (SCI, *69*, 668)

Grant: Mears, J. E., Harvard refuses (SCI, *72*, 168)

International Congress of Eugenics, 2nd (SCI, *53*, 160; SCI, *54*, 150, 219, 244, 296)

International Congress of Eugenics, 3rd (SCI, *74*, 626)

International Congress of Eugenics, 1932 (SCI, *76*, 141)

International Federation of Eugenics (SCI, *70*, 13)

Italian Congress of Eugenics, 2nd (SCI, *70*, 190)

Italian Eugenics Society, Mjoen, J. A., elected correspondent (SCI, *77*, 486)

Lecture: Davenport, C., Sigma Xi (SCI, *36*, 784)

Lecture: Galton, F., Huxley (SCI, *14*, 701)

Lecture: Galton, F., Oxford Univ. (SCI, *25*, 757)

Lecture: Mjoen, J. A., American Eugenics Society (SCI, *71*, 282)

Lecture: Pearson, K. (SCI, *36*, 113; SCI, *37*, 174)

Lecture: Thomson, J. A., Galton (SCI, *73*, 124)

Lecture: Webber, H. J., Cornell Univ. (SCI, *36*, 784)

Promotion: Günther, F. K., Univ. of Jena (SCI, *72*, 421)

Publication: Blacker, C. P., "Eugenics and social progress" (JoP, *34*, 644)

Publication: Gosney, E. S., Human Betterment Foundation; *Effects of Eugenic Sterilization as Practiced in California* (J APP, *21*, 476)

Publication: Inheritance of feeble-mindedness (SCI, *22*, 189)

Publication: Jennings, ?, "What can we hope from eugenics?" (SCI, *69*, 136)

Publication: Journals established; *Genesis* and *Eugenics* (SCI, *74*, 511)

Publication: Southern California Branch of American Eugenics Society, newsletter (J APP, *18*, 722)

Research: Bureau of Human Heredity (J APP, *21*, 474)

Research: Pearson, K. (BULL., *4*, 128)

Retirement: Pearson, K., Univ. of London (SCI, *79*, 30, 426)

Eugenics Education Society

Courses: Herne Bay College (SCI, *52*, 105)

Lecture: Darwin, L., presidential (SCI, *44*, 130)

Eugenics, International Congress of
Meetings (Sci, *54*, 150, 219, 244, 296; Sci, *74*, 626; Sci, *76*, 141; Sci, *91*, 289; Sci, *58*, 347)

Eugenics Record Office, at Cold Spring Harbor, Long Island (New York)
Name change to Genetics Record Office (Sci, *90*, 155)

Eugenics Research Association
Election: Meyer, A., President (Sci *43*, 923)
Election: Snyder, L. H., President (Sci, *86*, 218)
Essay contest: Decline of Nordic birth rate (Sci, *70*, 164)
Meeting announcement (Sci, *45*, 612)
Meeting: annual (Sci, *52*, 58; Sci, *59*, 316; Sci, *61*, 310; Sci, *71*, 338; Sci, *75*, 533; Sci, *77*, 424; Sci, *79*, 290; Sci, *81*, 251, 533; Sci, *83*, 257; Sci, *85*, 425; Sci, *87*, 412)
Research (Sci, *70*, 164)
Research: Androp, S., contest winner (Sci, *82*, 513)
Research: genetics on mental disorders (Sci, *81*, 483)
Research: probability of commitment for a mental disorder based on individual family history (Sci, *78*, 144)
Research: survey planned (Bull, *28*, 255)

Eugenics Society, London
Galton celebration dinner and lecture, 1938 (Sci, *87*, 210)

Eurich, Alvin Christian
Promotion: Stanford Univ. (Bull, *41*, 409)

Europe, Central
Anglo-American libraries loan books (JoP, *17*, 307-308)

European war
Suspension of foreign scientific publications (Bull, *11*, 352)

Euthenics
Vassar Institute of Euthenics, 15th annual session (J App, *24*, 245)

Evans, Herbert M.
Lecture: Assoc. for Research in Nervous and Mental Diseases (Sci, *84*, 551)

Evans, John Ellis
Appointment: Ohio State Univ. (Bull, *11*, 482)
Departure: Columbia Univ. (Bull, *11*, 482)

Evans, Soloman David
Death notice (Bull, *41*, 267)

Evenden, Edward Samuel
Lecture: "Teacher education in democracy at war" (J App, *26*, 714)

Everett, Joseph David
Death notice (Sci, *20*, 286)

Everett, Walter Goodnow
Death notice (JoP, *34*, 531)

Evolution (*see also* Congress of Evolutionists, and Darwinian Theory)
Appointment: Basset, C. C., Station for Experimental Evolution (Bull, *10*, 291; JoP, *10*, 503-504)
Lecture: Angell, J. R., Yale Univ. (Sci, *54*, 546)
Lecture: Jennings, H. S. (Sci, *69*, 136)
Lecture: Methods in philosphy and the sciences (JoP, *41*, 671-672)
Lecture: Univ. of Minnesota (JoP, *5*, 252)
Meeting: Congress of Evolutionists (Sci°, *22*, 264)
Publication: Baldwin, J. M., *The American Naturalist* (Sci, *1*, 139)
Publication: Stanley, H. M. (Rev, *2*, 432)
Teleology method research, Stanley, H. M. (Sci°, *2*, 634)

Ewall, Jack R.
Promotion: Univ. of Texas School of Medicine at Galveston (Sci, *100*, 245)

Ewart, J. Cossar
Award: Neill prize (Sci, *10*, 259)

Ewer, Bernard Capen
Lecture: James, W. (JoP, *39*, 84)
Lecture: naturalistic approach to philosophy (JoP, *7*, 223)

Ewert, Peter Harry
Death notice (Bull, *34*, 864)

Ewing Christian College (India)
Appointment: Manry, J. C. (Sci, *58*, 514)

Examinations
And licensing of teachers: Publication, Bureau of Education pamphlet (Sci°, *2*, 28)
Appointment: civil (Bull, *14*, 333)
Program of the New Jersey State Prison (J App, *4*, 113-114)
Psychological: Thurstone, L. L. (J App, *3*, 197)
Publication: Fernberger, S. (AJP, *38*, 155)

Examiners, psychological
Trained under Ogden, R. M. (Bull, *14*, 365)

Exceptional children (*see also* Gifted children)
Child Research Clinic Conference, Penn. (J App, *19*, 221)
Institute on Exceptional Children (J App, *18*, 721; J App, *23*, 745; J App, *24*, 855)
Meeting: National Assoc. for the Study and Education of Exceptional Children, New York Univ. (Sci, *34*, 712)
Minnesota Psychological Conference (JoP, *9*, 364)

Experimental groups
Publication: Corey, S. M.; "The dependence upon chance factors in equating groups" (AJP, *45*, 749)

Experimental inference
Lecture: Fullerton Philosophical Club of Penn., 1945 (JoP, *42*, 251)
Lecture: Preston, M. (JoP, *42*, 251)

Experimental neuroses
Award: Petrova, M. K.; Pavlov prize (Sci, 92, 450)
Research: Simpson, S. and Liddell, H. Cornell Univ. (Sci, 86, 221)

Experimental phonetics (*see also* Phonetics)
Lecture: Krueger, E., German Society of Experimental Psychology (Sci, 22, 727)

Experimental Psychologists (*see* Society of Experimental Psychologists)

Experimental psychology
Conference: International Bibliographical (Rev, 3, 588)
Department established at London County Council Asylums (Rev, 8, 447; Sci, 13, 877)
Election: Woodworth, R. S. International Congress of Arts and Sciences; Section secretary (JoP, *1*, 532)
England, progress in (AJP, 8, 583)
Fisher, R. A.; guest professor, Iowa State Univ., design and statistics (Sci, 82, 590)
History of, in Italy (JoP, 2, 448)
Institute of Experimental Psychology, Turin, Italy (Bull, *17*, 280)
International Congress of Experimental Psychology, 1892 (Sci°, *19*, 44)
Laboratory: Bryn Mawr College, Ferree, C. E. (Bull, 9, 440)
Laboratory: Florence (Bull, *1*, 172)
Laboratory: King's College, London (Rev, 9, 536)
Laboratory: opening of (Sci°, *19*, 129)
Lecture: Hall, G. S. (JoP, 2, 223)
Lecture: 4th congress (JoP, 7, 83)
Lecture: MacDougal, R. International Congress of Arts and Sciences, St. Louis (JoP, *1*, 616)
Lecture: Meyer, C. S., King's College, London (JoP, *1*, 672)
Lecture: Scripture, E. W., Yale Univ. (Sci, *1*, 722)

Lecture: Titchener, E. B., history of (BULL, *22*, 444)
Lecture: Yoakum, C. S., personnel problems (J APP, *9*, 204)
Lectureship: Cambridge Univ. (JoP, *4*, 448; REV, *4*, 567)
Lectureship: Univ. of Liverpool (SCI, *22*, 160; BULL, *2*, 296)
Meeting: International Congress of Arts and Sciences, St. Louis (JoP, *1*, 420)
Organization: German Society formed (BULL, *1*, 29, 293)
Oxford Univ. discussion on establishing dept. (REV, *10*, 223-224)
Oxford, Univ. of, Institute of Experimental Psychology founded (SCI, *83*, 433)
Oxford, Univ. of, Institute of Experimental Psychology proposed (SCI, *83*, 349)
Protest against by philosophers (JoP, *10*, 363)
Publication: Cattell, J. McK. (SCI°, *23*, 95)
Publication: Coover, J. E. (BULL, *39*, 268)
Publication: Flournoy, T. (REV, *4*, 106)
Publication: Martius, G. (SCI°, *11*, 169)
Publication: Titchener, E. B., color-equations (JoP, *2*, 55)
Research: mental processes (AJP, *9*, 420-421)
Required subject at the Univ. of Geneva (BULL, *14*, 115)

Explorations in Personality

Publication: Elliott, R. M. (AJP, *52*, 453-462)

Extirpation

Publication: Diven, K.; "Dandy's radical extirpations of brain tissue in man" (AJP, *46*, 503)

Eye (*see also* Binocular fusion; Color vision; Vision)

Lecture: Dodge, R., movement (JoP, *2*, 223)
Lecture: Duval, M., evolution and embryology of the eye (SCI, *2*, 91)
Publication: observation of wave-lengths, *London, Dublin and Edinburgh Philosophical Magazine* (SCI, *13*, 419)
Publication: Stempel, L. F., strabismus (J APP, *26*, 857-858)
Publication: Yale Psychological Laboratory, movement (JoP, *1*, 84)
Research: eyesight, Amherst College Physical Educ. Dept. (SCI°, *7*, 414)
Research: movement patterns in reading different color combinations of print and background (AJP, *57*, 93-94)

Eyre, Mary Brooks

Retirement: Scripps College (BULL, *41*, 499)

F

Facial expression
Publication: Ruckmick, C. A., "Facial expression of emotion" (SCI, 73, 416)
Research. Corbusier, W. H. (SCIᵛ, 9, 212)

Factor theory
Publication: Spearman, C. (AJP, 42, 645)

Faculty psychology
Publication: Lehmann and Witty, "Faculty psychology and personality traits" (AJP, 46, 486)

Fajarnes, Antonio Hernandez
Death notice (JoP, 6, 308)

Family life
Research: Leland, S., family life adjustment (J APP, 26, 570-571)

Family relations
Course: Individual study on counseling (J APP, 28, 80)

Fano, G.
Election: International Congress of Psychology, experimental psychology section; President (JoP, 2, 56)

Farabee, William Curtis
Research: headwaters of the Amazon (JoP, 3, 364)

Farago, Ladislas
Publication: *German Psychological Warfare* (J APP, 25, 359)

Faris, Ellsworth
Appointment: Univ. of Iowa (BULL, 12, 244; JoP, 12, 504)
Departure: Univ. of Chicago (BULL, 12, 244)

Farnsworth, Paul Randolph
Appointment: Stanford Univ. (SCI, *96*, 423)
Appointment: Univ. of Wisconsin (J APP, *22*, 106)
Conference: National Research Council; "Psychological factors in national morale" (BULL, *37*, 829)
Election: Sigma Xi, Stanford Univ. (SCI, *102*, 116)

Farquhar, E. J.
Lecture: Wash. Phil. Soc.; Dreams in their psychological relation (SCI°, *1*, 472)

Farrand, Livingston
Appointment: Columbia College (REV, *1*, 112)
Appointment: Univ. of Colorado; President (BULL, *11*, 116)
Death notice (AJP, *53*, 302)
Promotion: Columbia Univ. (SCI, *13*, 440)

Farrar, Clarence B.
Appointment: Johns Hopkins Univ. (JoP, *1*, 252; BULL, *1*, 172)
Appointment: Princeton Univ. (SCI, *43*, 169)
Editor: *American Journal of Psychiatry* (SCI, *74*, 34)

Farrow, Ernest Pickworth
Lecture: behaviorism (AJP, *38*, 660)

Fatigue (*see also* Industrial fatigue)
Lecture: Bitterman, M. E. (AJP, *57*, 569-573)
Lecture: Cason, H.; "The organic nature of fatigue" (AJP, *47*, 337)
Lecture: Dodge, R. (SCI, *44*, 673; SCI, *29*, 809)
Lecture: Ryan, T. A. (AJP, *57*, 565-569)

Fear
Publication: Stanley, H. M. (AJP, *9*, 418-419)

Fearing, Franklin
Appointment: Northwestern Univ. (J APP, *11*, 404)
Appointment: Ohio Wesleyan Univ. (J APP, *10*, 394, 523)
Obituary by Coover, J. E. (AJP, *51*, 582)
Leave of absence: Northwestern Univ. (SCI, *82*, 386)

Feathermann, Americus
Publication: "The Melanesians" (SCI°, *9*, 515)
Publication: "The Nigritians" (SCI°, *9*, 515)

Fechner, Gustav Theodor
Lecture: Hall, G. S. (SCI, *35*, 101; JoP, *9*, 56)
Portrait of (AJP, *9*, 422)

Federal Advertising Agency of New York
Appointment: Wulfeck, W. H. (SCI, *96*, 512; J APP, *26*, 857)

Federal Board for Vocational Education
Publication: *Vocational Summary* (BULL, *15*, 176)

Federal Security Agencies (*see* Vocational Rehabilitation)

Federal Works Agency
Appointment: Nyswander, D. B. (BULL, *39*, 895)

Feeble-mindedness
Appointment: Goddard, H. H., New Jersey Training School for Feeble-minded
    Girls and Boys (SCI, *23*, 798)
Course: Neurological Institute of Frankfort on Main (BULL, *0*, 72)
Course: on feeble-minded and psychopathic children (AJP, *20*, 296)
Course: Pathological Institute, Wards Island, NY (JoP, *6*, 111)
Course: special classes (J APP, *8*, 256)
Fellowship under Terman, L. (SCI, *39*, 506)
Lecture: Chicago Medical Science meeting (BULL, *13*, 148)
Lecture: Curtis, J. N. (BULL, *13*, 407-408)
Lecture: Huey, E. B. (SCI, *34*, 759)
Massachusetts School (BULL, *13*, 407)
Publication: Legal certification of feeblemindedness (BULL, *19*, 586)
Publication: Royal Commission (JoP, *5*, 615)
Royal Commission on the Care of the Feeble-minded named (SCI, *22*, 510)

Feelings (*see also* Emotion)
Lecture: expression of simple feelings, Titchener, E. B. (AJP, *34*, 149)
Lecture: Münsterberg, H. (JoP, *1*, 168)
Publication: Warner, F. (AJP, *1*, 200)
Symposium: feelings and emotions announcement of participants (BULL, *24*,
    620; BULL, *27*, 620; JoP, *24*, 587)

Fehlman, Charlotte
Appointment: Adelphi College (BULL, *42*, 255)

Fehrer, E. V.
Rejoinder by Wilcox, W. W. (AJP, *44*, 578)

Feinberg, Henry
Election: National Conference of Social Work, Clinical Psychology Group
    (J APP, *22*, 215)

Feldman, Shammai
Publication: "The magnetic eye illusion" (AJP, *51*, 575)

Felix, Robert Hanna
Appointment: U.S. Public Health Service, division of mental hygiene (SCI, *100*, 447)

Fellows, G. S. and Company
Publication: Middleton, A. E., "Memory systems, new and old" (SCI°, *12*, 107)

Fenton, Norman
Appointment: California Youth Correction Authority (SCI, *97*, 65)
Appointment: Ohio Univ. (J APP, *10*, 287)
Departure: Arizona State Teachers College (J APP, *10*, 287)

Feral children
Discussion: baboon boy of South Africa (AJP, *53*, 128-133, 455-462)
Publication: Dennis, W., significance of (AJP, *54*, 425-432)
Publication: Kellogg, W. N. (AJP, *43*, 508)
Publication: Kellogg, W. N. "A further note on the "Wolf children of India" (AJP, *45*, 149)
Publication: Zingg, R. M., reply to Dennis, W. (AJP, *54*, 432-435)

Féré, Charles
Death notice (BULL, *4*, 338)

Ferguson, George Oscar, Jr.
Appointment: Colgate Univ. (BULL, *14*, 115; JoP, *14*, 140)

Ferguson, Leonard Wilton
Appointment: Connecticut State College (BULL, *36*, 406)

Fernald, Frederick A.
Publication: criticizes Bell's, A. M., visible-speech letters (SCI°, *2*, 452)

Fernald, Grace Maxwell
Appointment: Bryn Mawr College (BULL, *4*, 160)
Clinic for atypical children established Univ. of Oregon (J APP, *21*, 243)
Organization: School for Children with Speech and Motor Defects (BULL, *22*, 260)

Fernald, Mabel Ruth
Appointment: Army Medical Dept, Washington (JoP, *15*, 560)

Fernald, Walter Elmore
Lecture: Conference on Mental Hygiene, care of feeble-minded (J APP, *3*, 396)

Fernau, L.
Publication: *Sphinx* (SCI°, *7*, 139-140)

Fernberger, Samuel Weiller
Appointment: Clark Univ. (BULL, *9*, 440; JoP, *9*, 700; SCI, *36*, 556)

Appointment: Officers' Reserve Camp (BULL, *14*, 191)

Appointment: Univ. of Pennsylvania (SCI, *52*, 636; BULL, *18*, 110; AJP, *32*, 160)

Departure: Univ. of Pennsylvania (JoP, *9*, 700)

Editor: *Psychological Bulletin* (JoP, *21*, 56; SCI, *59*, 60)

Election: APA representative (SCI, *69*, 36)

Election: APA Secretary (BULL, *23*, 112)

Election: Eastern Branch, APA 1937 meeting, President (SCI, *85*, 331)

Election: National Research Council; APA representative (BULL, *26*, 56)

Election: Society of Experimental Psychologists, Chair (AJP, *45*, 539)

Election: Society of Experimental Psychologists, Secretary (AJP, *47*, 334)

Promotion: Univ. of Pennsylvania (BULL, 7, 364; SCI, *66*, 14; JoP, *8*, 84)

Publication: bluffing on exams (AJP, *38*, 155)

Publication: on the number of articles of psychological interest published in the different languages: 1926-1935 (AJP, *48*, 680)

Publication: *Psychological Bulletin*, military (J APP, *25*, 359)

Publication: Sanford chronoscope (AJP, *37*, 154)

Research: Dunlap chronoscope (AJP, *41*, 582)

Research: peyote (AJP, *34*, 616)

Research: Psychological Index project, measure of public interest in psychology (BULL, *36*, 220)

Ferrari, Giulio Cesare

Appointment: International Congress of Psychology (JoP, *2*, 56)

Editor: *Rivista di Psicolgia Applicata alla Pedagogia ed alla Psicopatologia* (BULL, *2*, 120)

Research: experimental psychology in Italy (JoP, *2*, 448)

Ferree, Clarence Errol

Appointment: American Medical Assoc. Subcommittee on the Hygiene of the Eye (BULL, *9*, 486)

Appointment: Bryn Mawr College; Director of lab (BULL, *10*, 39; JoP, *10*, 56; BULL, *4*, 160)

Death notice (AJP, *56*, 137-140; BULL, *39*, 681)

Lecture: American Philosophical Society of Philadelphia, on the eye (BULL, *10*, 252; JoP, *10*, 336)

Lecture: flicker method (JoP, *11*, 140)

Lecture: Illuminating Engineering Society (BULL, *11*, 80; BULL, *10*, 490)

Lecture: International Congress on School Hygiene, 4th (JoP, *10*, 672)

Lecture: NYAS (BULL, *11*, 482-483; JoP, *11*, 672)

Promotion: Bryn Mawr College (BULL, *9*, 440; SCI, *45*, 361; JoP, *9*, 700; BULL, *14*, 143; JoP, *14*, 252)

Publication: "Perception of depth in the after-image" (AJP, *46*, 329)

Ferrero, Felice

Lecture: Northwestern Univ., history of science (JoP, *14*, 364)

Ferrier, David
Publication: "The functions of the brain" (Sci°, 8, 480)

Ferry, Frederick C.
Lecture: Clark Univ. (J App, 9, 87)

Feuerbach, Ludwig
Lecture: Lowie, R. H. (JoP, 7, 700)

Fick, Adolf
Death notice (Sci, 14, 422)

Field Museum (*see* Magellanic expedition)

Field of Philosophy, The
Publication: announcement (JoP, 15, 308)

Fields, Paul Eldon
Appointment: Stanford Univ, National Research Council Fellow (J App, 15, 326)
Appointment: Ohio Wesleyan Univ., Dept Head, Psychology (Bull, 34, 121;
  Sci, 84, 504)
Election: Ohio Academy of Science; Vice-president (J App, 25, 128)
Grant: National Research Council (Bull, 33, 578)

Filter, Raymond Otto
Appointment: Univ. of Pittsburgh (Bull, 22, 140; Sci, 60, 291; J App, 8, 450)

Finan, John Lincoln
APA, Wash-Balt. Branch, 1939 (Bull, 36, 712)

Finch, Glen
Award: Fellowship (Sci, 81, 482)

Findley, Warren George
New York State Assoc. for Applied Psych. (Bull, 37, 405)

Finger, Frank Whitney
Lecture: Virginia Sigma Xi meeting (Bull, 42, 791; Sci, 102, 420)

Finkelstein, Salo
Publication: Bousfield, W. A. and Barry, Jr., H. "The visual imagery of a
  lightning calculator" (AJP, 45, 353)

Fischer, Kumo
Death notice (Bull, 4, 338)
Retirement announced (JoP, 1, 28)
Retirement correction (Bull, 1, 174)

Fischer, Robert Paul
Appointment: Univ. of Illinois (BULL, *40*, 794)
Research: sense of smell (SCI°, 7, 547)

Fisher, Charles
Appointment: Swarthmore College (JoP, *15*, 140; BULL, *14*, 420)

Fisher, Irving
American Eugenics Society founder (SCI, *83*, 573)

Fisher, Mary Shattuck
Appointment: personality research, Director (BULL, *38*, 248)
Research: Vassar College, child study (BULL, *37*, 187)

Fisher, Ronald Aylmer
Appointment: Cambridge Univ. (SCI, *98*, 58)
Appointment: Galton Chair of Eugenics (SCI, *78*, 32)
Degree: Iowa State College (SCI, *84*, 81)
Lecture: Iowa State College, Experimental design and statistics (SCI, *82*, 590)
Lecture: Yale Univ., neurological study (SCI, *84*, 457)
Publication: *Design of Experiments* (SCI, *82*, 590)

Fisher, Sarah Carolyn
Publication: Critique of Köhler (AJP, *43*, 131)

Fiske, John
Death notice (SCI, *14*, 76)

Fitch, Florence Mary
Appointment: Oberlin College (BULL, *1*, 488)

Fitch, Frederic Brenton
Lecture: Eastern Division of the American Philosophical Assoc. (JoP, *35*, 699)

Fite, Warner
Appointment: Indiana Univ. (SCI, *24*, 384; BULL, *3*, 288, 319; JoP, *3*, 504, 532)
Appointment: Univ. of Chicago (REV, *5*, 109)
Departure: Univ. of Texas (SCI, *24*, 384; JoP, *3*, 504, 532)
Publication: translated into Japanese (JoP, *4*, 616)

Flechsig, Paul
Election: Psycho-Neurological Academy of Lenningrad (SCI, *67*, 291)

Fleming, Virginia Van Dyne
Death notice (BULL, *41*, 72)

Fletcher, John Madison
Appointment: Tulane Univ. (BULL, *40*, 152; SCI, *96*, 492; BULL, *9*, 408; JoP, *9*, 700)

Appointment: Vanderbilt Univ. (J App, *10*, 523)
Death notice (Bull, *42*, 127; AJP, *58*, 267-272)
Retirement: Tulane Univ. (Sci, *87*, 504)

Flexner, Eleanor
Appointment: Institute for Propaganda Analysis (J App, *25*, 597)

Flick, Walter A.
Appointment: Washington and Lee Univ. (J App, *10*, 393)

Flint Visiting Professorship
Appointment: Montague, W. P. Univ. of California, Los Angeles (JoP, *40*, 140)

Florida Academy of Sciences
Meeting: 1941 (Sci, *94*, 485)

Florida, University of (Gainesville)
Appointment: Thompson, W. R. (Bull, *42*, 331)
Research: Progress test program, IBM test scoring machine (J App, *23*, 531)

Flournoy, Henri
Departure: Johns Hopkins Phipps Psychiatric Clinic (Sci, *40*, 407)
Publication: book on psychoanalysis (JoP, *21*, 560)

Flournoy, Théodore
Death notice (Sci, *52*, 579; JoP, *18*, 110; Bull, *18*, 56; AJP, *32*, 154)
Publication: experimental psychology (Rev, *4*, 106)

Flower, William Henry
Eulogy on C. Darwin at Linnaean Society (Sci°, *11*, 277)

Flügel, Otto
Death notice (Bull, *12*, 128)

Flugel, John Carl
Appointment: Univ. College, London (Bull, *16*, 257)
Research: psychic phenomena (Sci, *80*, 183)

Flying
Award: Armstrong, H. G., physiological and psychological effects (Sci, *95*, 93)

Fochs, Ernest
Award: Hygienic Congress (Sci°, *4*, 364)

Fol, Hermann
Publication: Variations of personality in *Journal de Genève* (Sci°, *5*, 532)

Fol'bort, Georgii Vladimirovich
Publication: conditioned reflexes (Sci, *70*, 402)

Foley, John Porter, Jr.
APA, Wash-Balt, Branch, 1939 meeting (BULL, *36*, 140)

Folsom, Angela Townsend
Appointment: Director of internships in clinical psychology (BULL, *39*, 809-810)
Appointment: New York Rockland State Hospital (BULL, *40*, 618)

Food habits
Publication: National Research Council (J APP, *26*, 858)

Forbes, George M.
Appointment: committee member for New York State Teachers of Educational Psychology (JoP, *7*, 252)

Forbes, Theodore Watson
Publication: A critique of Crosland's measurement of emotion (AJP, *45*, 522)

Ford, Adelbert
Publication: *Psychological Cinema Record* founded (J APP, *23*, 633)
Resignation. Univ. of Michigan (BULL, *28*, 646)

Fordham University (New York, New York)
Appointment: McNemar, Q. (J APP, *21*, 474; BULL, *34*, 498)
Centennial celebration (SCI, *94*, 254)
Degree: Jung, C. (SCI, *36*, 398)

Fordyce, Charles
Appointment: Nebraska Central College (BULL, *41*, 136)
Appointment: Nebraska Central College correction (BULL, *41*, 268)

Forel, August
Resignation: Univ. of Zurich (REV, *5*, 109)

Forgetting (*see also* Memory)
Lecture: McGeoch, J. A., retroactive inhibition (AJP, *42*, 455)
Meeting: repression in forgetting (JoP, *11*, 532)
Publication: Bancels, D. reply to Chou; "The forgetting curve" (AJP, *45*, 758)
Publication: Chou, S. K.; "What is the curve of forgetting?" (AJP, *45*, 348)
Publication: Purdy, D. M.; "The theory of forgetting" (AJP, *46*, 339)
Research: Snoddy, G. S., Indiana Univ. (J APP, *23*, 530)

Forlano, George
Publication: *Aspects of Personality* (J APP, *22*, 318)

Fort Washington
Lecture: Ligon, E. M. (SCI, *96*, 81)

Fortschritte der Psychologie und ihrer Andwendugen
Editor: Marbe, K. (BULL, *9*, 359)
Publication: Marbe, K. and Peters, W. (JoP, *9*, 699-700)

Forum, The
Editor: Metcalf, L. S. (SCI°, *7*, 213)

Foster, [?]
Research: short-sightedness (SCI°, *13*, 481)

Foster children
Research: Terman, L. and Freeman, F. (SCI, *60*, 589)

Foster, Josephine Curtis (*see also* Curtis, Josephine Nash
Death notice (BULL, *38*, 907)

Foster Parent's Plan for War Children, Inc. (New York)
Publication: monthly report on psychological care of children (J APP, *27*, 207)

Foster, William Silliman
Appointment: Cornell Univ. (JoP, *13*, 308)
Appointment: Univ. of Minnesota (SCI, *50*, 65; BULL, *16*, 257)
Death notice (SCI, *63*, 42; BULL, *23*, 112)
Marriage announcement to Curtis, J. N. (BULL, *16*, 221)
Promotion: Univ. of Minnesota (SCI, *59*, 398)

Foston, Hubert Marshall
Publication: *The Mutual Symbolism of Activity and Intelligence* abstracted (JoP, *6*, 279)

Fouillée, Alfred
Death notice (JoP, *9*, 559-560)

Fowler, Thomas
Death notice (BULL, *2*, 36)

Fracker, George Cutler
Appointment: Columbia Univ. (SCI, *20*, 480; JoP, *1*, 560)
Appointment: State Normal School of Marquette, Mich. (SCI, *30*, 709; BULL, *6*, 427)
Appointment: Univ. of Arkansas (BULL, *21*, 660; SCI, *60*, 13, 40)
Leave of absence: Coe College (SCI, *20*, 480; BULL, *1*, 451)
Lecture: transference (JoP, *2*, 224)
Resignation: Coe College (SCI, *30*, 709)

Fränkel, M. O.
Publication: German translation of Tamburini and Seppilli hypnotism (SCI°, *5*, 303)

Fragapane, Salvatore
Death notice (JoP, 7, 84)

France, Collège de (*see* Collège de France)

France, Institute of
Election: James, W., member (Rev, 5, 344)

Frank, Benjamin
APA, Wash-Balt Branch, 1940 (Bull, 37, 405)

Frankfort-on-Main Neurological Institute (*see* Neurological Institute)

Frankfurt, University of (Germany)
Course: feeble-minded and psychopathic children (AJP, 20, 296)
Course: Schumann, F. (JoP, 12, 196)
Psychology grouped with natural sciences (Bull, 12, 243)

Franklin and Marshall College (Lancaster, Pennsylvania)
Appointment: Dotterer, R. H. (JoP, 23, 420; Sci, 64, 224)
Departure: Dotterer, R. H. (JoP, 27, 560)

Franklin, Fabian
Resignation: editor New York *Evening Post* (JoP, 14, 224)

Franklin Institute (Philadelphia, PA)
Lecture: Dodd, S. C. (Sci, 63, 65)

Frantz, Angus M.
Election: Assoc. for Research, in Nervous and Mental Diseases; Sec-Treas. (Sci, 85, 42; Sci, 81, 42)

Franz, Shepherd Ivory
Appointment: Cattell Portrait Committee (Sci, 75, 661)
Appointment: Columbia Univ. (Rev, 3, 356; Rev, 4, 452)
Appointment: Dartmouth College (Sci, 13, 1000; Rev, 8, 447)
Appointment: George Washington Medical School (JoP, 4, 28)
Appointment: George Washington Univ. (Sci, 27, 840; JoP, 5, 336; Bull, 4, 32; Bull, 3, 422; Sci, 25, 400)
Appointment: Government Hospital for the Insane (Washington, D.C.); Director (Bull, 7, 75; JoP, 4, 28; Sci, 30, 964; Bull, 4, 32)
Appointment: Harvard Medical School (Rev, 6, 673)
Appointment: McLean Hospital for the Insane (Bull, 1, 173; JoP, 1, 196)
Appointment: National Research Council (JoP, 14, 392; Bull, 14, 191)
Appointment: Univ. of California (Bull, 21, 552)
Appointment: Univ. of California, Los Angeles (Sci, 60, 315)
Death: obituary by Woodworth, R. S. (AJP, 46, 151)

Degree: George Washington Univ. (BULL, *12*, 244)
Degree: Waynesbury College (BULL, *12*, 244)
Editor: *Bull* issue on psychopathology (BULL, *10*, 252)
Editor: *Psychological Bulletin* (BULL, *11*, 152; JoP, *11*, 308)
Editor: *Psychological Monographs* (SCI, *59*, 60)
Election: APA office (JoP, *17*, 56; SCI, *51*, 41)
Election: SSPP President (BULL, *8*, 32; JoP, *8*, 84)
Election: SSPP Vice-president (JoP, *7*, 56; SCI, *31*, 22)
Lecture: Boston Psychiatric Hospital (BULL, *13*, 40)
Lecture: St. Louis Medical Society (JoP, *11*, 84)
Lecture: SSPP functions of cerebrum (JoP, *7*, 28)
Lecture: Swarthmore College (JoP, *13*, 308)
Lecture: Univ. of Chicago (BULL, *19*, 172)
Lecture: Wellesley College (BULL, *13*, 40)
Organization: School for Children with Speech and Motor Defects (BULL, *22*, 260)
Represents AAAS at the Cardiff meeting of the British Assoc. (BULL, *17*, 351)
Resignation: George Washington Univ. and St. Elizabeth's Hospital (SCI, *60*, 315; BULL, *21*, 552)
Resignation: *Psychological Bulletin* editorship (SCI, *59*, 60; JoP, *21*, 21, 56)
Returns from London (BULL, *17*, 435)

Fraser, Alexander Campbell
Anniversary: Univ. of Edinburgh (BULL, *3*, 422)
Lecture: John Locke (JoP, *2*, 672)

Frazier, Charles H.
Election: Assoc. for Research in Nervous and Mental Diseases, Vice-president (SCI, *81*, 42)

Frazier, Edward Franklin
Publication: *Negro Youth at the Crossways*, personality development (J APP, *24*, 655)

Free association
Lecture: Wells, F. L. (JoP, *7*, 700)

Free, Margaret
Appointment: Carnegie Inst. of Technology (SCI, *42*, 88; BULL, *12*, 403; JoP, *12*, 644)

Freeman, Ellis
Rejoinder to Ferree and Rand (AJP, *44*, 370)

Freeman, Frank Nugent
Appointment: Univ. of California (SCI, *90*, 268; BULL, *36*, 841)
Appointment: Univ. of Chicago (SCI, *89*, 313; BULL, *6*, 328)
Appointment: Washington College, Chesteton, MD (BULL, *4*, 370; JoP, *4*, 616)

Award: Educational research, "Twins, a study in heredity and environment"
(Sci, *91*, 287)
Departure: Univ. of Chicago (Sci, *90*, 268)
Grant: Commonwealth Fund, foster child study (Sci, *60*, 588)
Promotion: Univ. of Chicago (Bull, *36*, 499)
Publication: *Mental Tests* (revised edition) (J App, *23*, 421)
Research: adult handwriting (J App, *1*, 298)

Freeman, Graydon LaVerne

Appointment: Northwestern Univ. (Bull, *28*, 411)
Fellowship: Board of National Research Fellowships (Bull, *26*, 380)
Fellowship: Guggenheim (Bull, *42*, 791)
Leave of absence: Northwestern Univ. (Bull, *40*, 310)
Promotion: Northwestern Univ. (Sci, *88*, 471)
Publication: "The research laboratory in psychophysiology at Northwestern
Univ." (AJP, *51*, 176)

Freeman, Walter Jackson

American Board of Psychiatry and Neurology (Sci, *80*, 476)
Publication. Watts, J. W., "Psychosurgery" (Sci, *96*, 36)

Freiberg, Albert Daniel

Grant: Psychological Corp. announced (J App, *28*, 79)
Psychological Corporation meeting with APA and AAAP, secretary (J App, *25*,
600)

French Academy of Moral and Political Sciences

Appointment: Baldwin, J. M. (JoP, *7*, 420; Sci, *32*, 108; Bull, *7*, 251)
Appointment: James, W. (JoP, *7*, 140)
Appointment: Janet, P. (Sci, *37*, 785; JoP, *10*, 336)
Election: officers (Sci, *17*, 478)

French Academy of Sciences

Appointment: Langley, S. P., Corresponding member (Sci°, *12*, 36)
Lecture: Bergson, M. H. (JoP, *15*, 196)

French Association for the Advancement of Science

Election: Piéron, M. H., President (Bull, *36*, 804; Sci, *90*, 248)
Meeting (Sci°, *2*, 117; Sci°, *3*, 670; JoP, *6*, 504)

French, Ferdinand Courtney

Appointment: Vassar College (Rev, *1*, 552)
Election: WPA Vice-president (JoP, *2*, 308)
Lecture: religion (JoP, *2*, 252)
Lecture: virtue (JoP, *7*, 223)

French, J. M.
Publication: "Infant mortality and the environment" in *Popular Science Monthly* (Sci°, *12*, 237)

French journals
Publication: announced (Bull, *1*, 92)

French, Robert Linton
Appointment: Yale Univ. (Sci, *93*, 62; Bull, *38*, 907)

French Society of Psychology
Election: Stern, W. (Sci, *67*, 505)

French traits
Lecture: Brownell, W. C. (Sci°, *9*, 610)

Frenkel-Brunswik, Else
Award: Social Science Research Council, 1942-43 (Bull, *39*, 682)
Lecture: International Congress for the Unity of Sciences (JoP, *35*, 504; JoP, *38*, 504)

Freud, Anna
Appointment: Foster Parents Plan for War Children, Nursery director (J App, *25*, 597)
Attends father at Royal Society ceremony (Bull, *35*, 796)
Publication: psychological care of children (J App, *27*, 207)

Freud, Sigmund
Award: City of Vienna honorary citizenship (Bull, *23*, 455)
Award: Goethe prize (Bull, *27*, 636; Sci, *72*, 166)
Birthday celebration (Sci, *63*, 497; Sci, *73*, 491; Sci, *83*, 460; Bull, *35*, 796)
Death notice (AJP, *53*, 134-138; Bull, *36*, 841)
Degree: Clark Univ. (Sci, *30*, 362)
Departure: Vienna to London (Sci, *87*, 526; Bull, *35*, 796)
Editor: *Imago* (Bull, *9*, 208)
Election: Royal Society (Bull, *35*, 796; Sci, *84*, 36)
Freudian psychology criticized (JoP, *14*, 364)
Frink, H., work in Vienna (Sci, *53*, 211)
Honor: International Medical Congress for Psychotherapy (Sci, *88*, 164)
Memorial Fellowships for Psychoanalytic Training, Boston Psychoanalytic Institute (Bull, *37*, 827)
Publication: *Imago* (JoP, *9*, 335)
Publication: Wittells, F.; "Revision of a biography" (AJP, *45*, 745)
Research: Infirmity (Bull, *35*, 796)
Royal Society; roll of membership brought to his home (Sci, *88*, 105)
Surgery performed (Sci, *58*, 346)

Frey, Max von
Appointment: Univ. of Würzburg (AJP, *11*, 130)
Death notice (BULL, *29*, 248; AJP, *44*, 584)

Friedlaender, Kurt Theodor
Appointment: Bureau of Salesmanship Research (JoP, *13*, 476; SCI, *44*, 56)

Friends University (Wichita, KS)
Anniversary: Wichita Child Guidance Center (BULL, *38*, 126)

Frink, Horace Westlake
Work with Freud, S. in Vienna (SCI, *53*, 211)

Frisbee, Willis H., Jr.
Publication: *Psychological Bulletin,* military (J APP, *25*, 358)

Fritz, Martin Frederick
Collection and Presentation of Statistical Data in Psychology and Education
(J APP, *23*, 421)

Frost, Elliott Park
Appointment: Univ. of Rochester (BULL, *20*, 60; SCI, *56*, 167)
Appointment: Univ. of Tennessee (BULL, *11*, 443; JoP, *11*, 721)
Appointment: Yale Univ. (BULL, *7*, 220; JoP, *7*, 560)
Death notice (J APP, *10*, 524; BULL, *24*, 136; SCI, *64*, 246)
Departure: Princeton Univ. (BULL, *7*, 220)
Departure: Yale Univ. (BULL, *11*, 443)

Fry, Clements Collard
Appointment: Yale Univ. Clinic for Inebriates (SCI, *99*, 99)

Fryer, Douglas Henry
Election: AAAP, President (J APP, *21*, 603, 713; BULL, *34*, 865)
Lecture: Assoc. of Consulting Psychologists (J APP, *21*, 241)
Tour of Europe (SCI, *64*, 63)

Fuh Tan University, Kiangwan (Shanghai, China)
Grant: $100,000 for a psychology building (BULL, *22*, 140; SCI, *60*, 314)

Fullerton, George Stuart
Appointment: Columbia Univ. (JoP, *1*, 28)
Death notice: March 23, 1925 (BULL, *22*, 260)
Election: London Society for Psychical Research, corresponding member (SCI°, *5*, 62)
Leave of absence: Columbia Univ. (BULL, *4*, 370; BULL, *3*, 116; JoP, *3*, 140)
Research in Munich (JoP, *1*, 28)
Return: Univ. of Pennsylvania (REV, *6*, 673; SCI, *10*, 422)
Spends the summer in Munich, Germany (SCI, *17*, 836)

Fullerton Philosophical Club of Pennsylvania
Meeting: 1945 (JoP, *42*, 251)

Functional psychology
Publication: Adams, E. K. (JoP, *3*, 721)

Furman University (Greenville, South Carolina)
Appointment: Steele, W. M. (Bull, *1*, 333; JoP, *1*, 364)

Furry, William Davis
Lecture: SSPP, Genetic and social psychology (JoP, *7*, 28)

Furst, Clyde
Lecture: NYAS/APA meeting, mental hygiene (JoP, *7*, 700)

Furtmüller, Carl
Editor: *Zeitschrift für Individual-Psychologie* (Bull, *11*, 232)

G

Gagne, Robert Mills
Appointment: Connecticut College (BULL, 37, 656)

Gahagan, Lawrence
Resignation: Univ. of California, Los Angeles (SCI, 85, 97)

Galilei, Galileo
Commemoration: Columbia Univ. (JoP, 39, 700)
Symposium: Tercentenary of death; Eastern Division of the Amer. Phil. Assoc. (JoP, 39, 698-699)

Gallup, George Horace
Conference: National Research Council; "Psychological factors in national morale" (BULL, 37, 829)
Publication: psychology of marketing bulletin (J APP, 23, 310)

Galton, Douglas
Death notice (SCI, 9, 421)
Election: Childhood Society of Great Britain, Chairman (AJP, 9, 422)
Subscription announced: Childhood Society (SCI, 5, 549)

Galton, Francis
Appointment: Oxford Univ. (JoP, 4, 308)
Appointment: Trinity College, Cambridge Univ., honorary fellow (SCI, 16, 917)
Award: Knighthood (JoP, 6, 560)
Bequeathment: Univ. of London, study of eugenics (SCI, 33, 370)
Death notice (SCI, 33, 184; BULL, 8, 78; JoP, 8, 111)
Degree: Cambridge Univ. (SCI, 1, 614)
Fellowship: London Univ., founded (BULL, 1, 488; JoP, 1, 672)
Lecture: Congress of Psychological Physiology (SCI°, 14, 195)
Lecture: Huxley, eugenics (SCI, 14, 701)
Lecture: Oxford Univ., eugenics (SCI, 25, 757)

Lecture: subject of; anniversary (SCI, 39, 322)
Lecture: subject of; Harris, A. J. (SCI, 37, 172)
Lecture: subject of; Univ. of Michigan, McMurrich, J. P. (SCI, 33, 924)
Lecture: Twin research by Baron von Verschner (SCI, 89, 579)
Publication: memoir by Pearson, K. (SCI, 34, 755)
Publication: *Memoirs of My Life* (JoP, 6, 560)
Publication: "On the advisability of assigning marks for bodily efficiency of candidates for the public service" (SCI°, 14, 266)

Galton Lecture
Thomson, J. A., eugenics, 1931 (SCI, 73, 124)

Galton Society
Announcement of formation (SCI, 47, 484)

Galton whistle
Lecture: Pattie, F. A., blower for (AJP, 35, 308)

Galvanic response
Publication: Darrow, C. W., "The Palmar Galvanic skin reflex (sweating) and parasympathetic activity" (AJP, 48, 522)
Publication: DeSilva, H. R., body voltage research (SCI, 80, 31, 426)
Publication: Ruckmick, C. A., and emotion (SCI, 73, 416)

Gamble, Eleanor Acheson McColloch
Appointment: Wellesley College (AJP, 10, 166)
Death notice (BULL, 31, 79; AJP, 46, 154)
Leave of absence: Wellesley College (SCI, 59, 274; BULL, 21, 360)
Lecture: Wellesley College Faculty Science Club (SCI, 13, 358)

Gamma Alpha Graduate Scientific Fraternity
Lecture: Miles, W. R., History of Science (psychology) (SCI, 90, 614)

Garber, Robert Burnett
Appointment: Centenary Junior College (BULL, 41, 679)

Gardiner, Harry Norman
Leave of absence: Smith College (BULL, 6, 400)
Summering aboard (REV, 6, 456)

Gardner, William A.
Publication: "Influence of the thyroid gland on the consciousness of time" (AJP, 47, 701)

Garman, Charles Edward
Death notice (BULL, 4, 64)

Garrett, Emma
Resignation: Pennsylvania Oral School for the Deaf (SCI°, 17, 214)

Garrett, Henry Edward
Appointment: Columbia Univ. (SCI, *99*, 467; SCI, *91*, 311; SCI, *93*, 493)
Election: APA (SCI, *76*, 251; SCI, 77, 364; SCI, *102*, 299)
Election: New York State Assoc. for Applied Psych. (BULL, *37*, 405)
Promotion: Columbia Univ. (BULL, *41*, 498)
Publication: ethics (AJP, *44*, 580)
Publication: methods in checking representativeness of a sample (AJP, *55*, 580-581)

Garrison, Sidney Clarence
Death notice (BULL, *42*, 255)

Garth, Thomas Russell
Appointment: Univ. of Denver (BULL, *20*, 288)
Appointment: Univ. of Texas (BULL, *17*, 116)
Death notice (AJP, *52*, 479; BULL, *36*, 711)
Election: Colorado Branch, APA, President (SCI, *76*, 31)
Grant: $150.00 from AAAS (BULL, *18*, 111)
Grant: Social Science Research Council (BULL, *31*, 380)
Lecture: "Race psychology" (BULL, *29*, 180; SCI, *75*, 101)
Publication: "Riddles as a mental test" (AJP, *47*, 344)
Research: color vision (SCI, *71*, 414)
Research: Indian psychology (SCI, *59*, 438; SCI, *61*, 487)

Gaskell, Walter Holbrook
Award: Royal Society medal, cardiac physiology work (SCI°, *14*, 367)

Gaskill, Harold Vincent
Appointment: Iowa State College (SCI, *88*, 32; BULL, *35*, 578)

Gates, Arthur Irving
Appointment: Teachers College (BULL, *19*, 350)
Election: APA Council (BULL, *23*, 112)
Leave of absence (BULL, *40*, 152)
Lecture: Columbia Univ. conference for the education of the gifted (J APP, *24*, 854)
Promotion: Teachers College Columbia Univ. (JoP, *19*, 392)
Publication: Gates reading survey (J APP, *23*, 420)

Gates, Elmer
Endorses International Society of the Psychical Institute (SCI, *12*, 238)

Gates, Georgina Ida Stickland
Lecture: NYAS/NY Branch of APA (JoP, *15*, 140)

Gates, R. Ruggles
Election: Bureau of Human Heredity, President; soliciting contributions of information (J APP, *21*, 474)
Research: Bureau of Human Heredity, genetics (BULL, *34*, 637)

Gault, Robert Harvey
Appointment: George Washington Univ. (SCI, *60*, 99)
Appointment: Northwestern Univ. (BULL, *6*, 216)
Course: New York Univ. (BULL, *13*, 296)
Editor: *American Journal of Criminology* (SCI, *34*, 488; BULL, *8*, 406)
Editor: *Journal of Criminal Law and Criminology* (JoP, *11*, 140; BULL, *9*, 408)
Fellowship: Univ. of Pennsylvania (SCI, *17*, 640)
Grant: Barker Foundation of Chicago; touch and language research (SCI, *74*, 264; BULL, *28*, 645)
Grant: Teletactor (BULL, *33*, 223)
Leave of absence: Northwestern Univ. (BULL, *21*, 428)
Lecture: Baconian, Univ. of Iowa (SCI, *73*, 123)
Lecture: Clark Univ. (J APP, *9*, 87)
Lecture: SSPP, size-weight illusion (JoP, *7*, 28)
Promotion: Northwestern Univ. (SCI, *34*, 488; BULL, *11*, 116; JoP, *11*, 140; BULL, *15*, 176; BULL, *8*, 406)

Gauss and Weber
Monument: Göttingen (SCI, *10*, 126)

Gaw, Esther Allen
Resignation: Ohio State Univ. (BULL, *41*, 267)

Gayle, R. Finley
Promotion: Univ. of Virginia Medical College (SCI, *88*, 278)

Gaylord, Joseph S.
Lecture: learning (JoP, *7*, 222)

Geddes, Patrick
Lecture: International Assoc. for the Advancement of Science, Arts and Education (SCI, *11*, 519)

Gegenbaur, Carl
Award: The Wohlbrecht's Foundation Univ. of Göttingen (SCI, *11*, 716-717)

Gehrmann Lecture
Campbell, C. M., Univ. of Illinois, abnormal psychology (SCI, *75*, 262)

Gehuchten, Arthur Van
Death notice (BULL, *12*, 44)

Geiger, J. C.
Award: Order of Merit of Juan Pablo Duarte (SCI, *102*, 349)
Award: Portuguese Government (SCI, *101*, 427)

Geiger, Moritz
Lecture: Congress for Experimental Psychology, 4th (JoP, *7*, 83)

Geiger, Moritz A.
Death notice (JoP, *34*, 559)

Geissen Congress of Experimental Psychology
Committee announced (BULL, *1*, 94, 292)

Geissler, Ludwig Reinhold
Appointment: Clark College (JoP, *13*, 588; BULL, *13*, 376)
Appointment: Committee on Publications in Applied Psychology (J APP, *2*, 196)
Appointment: National Electronic Lamp Assoc. (BULL, *8*, 406; SCI, *34*, 484; JoP, *8*, 616)
Appointment: Randolph Macon College for Women (BULL, *17*, 351)
Appointment: Univ. of Georgia (JoP, *9*, 504; BULL, *9*, 360; SCI, *36*, 115)
Death: obituary by Dallenbach, K. M. (AJP, *45*, 365)
Editor: *Journal of Applied Psychology* (JoP, *14*, 252)
Election: Virginia Academy of Science (SCI, *69*, 571)
Publication: *Journal of Applied Psychology* (BULL, *13*, 482)
Resignation: National Electronic Lamp Assoc. (BULL, *9*, 360; JoP, *9*, 504)

Geisteswissenschaften, Die
Publication: announced (JoP, *11*, 336)

Geldard, Frank Arthur
Lecture: Sigma Xi (SCI, *93*, 520)
Promotion: Army Air Forces (BULL, *40*, 231)

Gemelli, Agostino
Consiglio Nazionale delle Ricerche of Italy; Applied Psychology (BULL, *37*, 329)
National Board of Researches, Permanent Commission for the Application of Psychology (BULL, *36*, 713)

General Education Board, New York
Appropriation: Whipple, G. M. (BULL, *13*, 407)
Grant: Univ. of California Institute of Child Welfare (SCI, *92*, 236)
Fellowship: Brewer, J. E. Univ. of Illinois (BULL, *37*, 827)

General psychology
Election: Davis, W. M., International Congress of Arts and Sciences, St. Louis; section secretary (JoP, *1*, 532)
International Congress of Arts and Sciences (JoP, *1*, 419)
Lecture: Münsterberg, H., on scope of psychology (JoP, *1*, 168)

Genetic psychology (*see also* Heredity)
Course: Bühler, K. (SCI, *93*, 537)
International Human Heredity Committee (BULL, *34*, 637)
Lecture: Book, W. F., Clark Univ. (J APP, *9*, 88; SCI, *63*, 162)
Lecture: Dawson, G. E. in relation to the public school clinic (J APP, *9*, 88)
Lecture: Furry, W. D. (JoP, *7*, 28)

Lecture: genetic logic Baldwin, J. M. (BULL, 2, 159; BULL, 3, 83)
Lecture: "Genetics, Medicine and Man", Messenger Lecture Foundation,
   Cornell Univ. (SCI, 102, 665)
Research: genetic factors of intelligence and emotional variance, Little, C. C.
   (SCI, 101, 482)

Genetic Psychology Monographs
Publication: Dallenbach, K. (AJP, 37, 311)
Publication: *The Pedagogical Seminary* and *Journal of Genetic Psychology*,
   Clark Univ. (JoP, 22, 700; SCI, 62, 396)

Geneva Congress of Psychology
Meeting (BULL, 6, 256)

Geneva, Institute for the Science of Education
Appointment: Claparéde, E. (JoP, 9, 196)

Geneva, University of (Switzerland)
Appointment: Ladame, C. (SCI, 61, 489)
Course: Psychology of religion (JoP, 22, 308)
Degree: Baldwin, J. M. (JoP, 6, 560; BULL, 6, 328)
Dismissal: Claparéde, H. (SCI, 40, 887; JoP, 12, 28, 112)
Laboratory opening (SCI°, 19, 129)

Genoa, University of (Italy)
Anniversary: 40th, Morselli, E., chair of psychiatry (SCI, 53, 135)
Death: Morselli, E. (SCI, 69, 469)

Gentry, John Robert
Appointment: Ohio Univ. (SCI, 101, 112; J APP, 8, 451)
Election: MPA Secretary, 1941 (J APP, 25, 128)
Promotion: Ohio Univ. (BULL, 42, 255)

George Peabody College (see Peabody College)

George Washington University (Washington, DC)
Anniversary, 200th commemoration of John Locke (JoP, 1, 672)
Appointment: Britt, S. H. (BULL, 33, 578; SCI, 83, 461)
Appointment: Franz, S. I. (SCI, 27, 840; BULL, 3, 422; JoP, 5, 335; BULL, 4, 32;
   SCI, 25, 400)
Appointment: Gault, R. H. (SCI, 60, 99)
Appointment: Hough, W. S. (SCI, 27, 840; JoP, 5, 280, 335; BULL, 2, 296; BULL,
   5, 168; SCI, 22, 256)
Appointment: Metcalf, J. T. (SCI, 52, 107; BULL, 17, 280)
Appointment: Metzner, C. A. (BULL, 41, 72)
Appointment: Moss, F. A. (BULL, 18, 439; SCI, 54, 73)
Appointment: Percy, M. (BULL, 42, 792)
Appointment: Raymond, G. L. (JoP, 3, 140; BULL, 2, 159)

Appointment: Ruediger, W. C. (SCI, *27*, 840; JoP, *5*, 336; JoP, *12*, 700; JoP, *10*, 364; BULL, *10*, 252)
Degree: Franz, S. I. (BULL, *12*, 244)
Degree: Southard, E. E. (BULL, *14*, 263)
Meeting: Society for Philosophical Inquiry (JoP, *7*, 280)
Meeting: Washington-Baltimore Branch of APA (BULL, *38*, 67)
Promotion: Hunt, T. (BULL, *41*, 603)
Promotion: Ruediger, W. C. (SCI, *34*, 345; BULL, *8*, 374)
Psychology department established (SCI, *27*, 840; BULL, *5*, 244; JoP, *5*, 335)
Research: Binet tests started (BULL, *12*, 244)

Georgetown University (Washington, DC)
Appointment: Sullivan, H. S. (SCI, *90*, 536)
Departure: Hickling, D. P. (SCI, *90*, 536)
Resignation: Sullivan, H. S. (SCI, *90*, 588)

Georgia Normal College
Appointment: Parks, M. M., acting president (JoP, *1*, 616)

Georgia Normal Industrial College
Appointment: Beals, A. H. (SCI°, *18*, 297)

Georgia School of Technology (Atlanta)
Appointment: Bugental, J.E.T. (BULL, *42*, 64)
Appointment: Moore, J. E. (BULL, *42*, 332)
Establishment Psychology Department (BULL, *42*, 63-64)

Georgia State Woman's College
Appointment: Pistor, F. (BULL, *40*, 383)

Georgia, University of (Athens)
Appointment: Edwards, A. S. (JoP, *13*, 588; BULL, *13*, 376)
Appointment: Geissler, L. R. (JoP, *9*, 504; SCI, *36*, 115; BULL, *9*, 360)
Course: Simpson, B. R. (JoP, *7*, 336)
Donation: Straus, D., experimental psychology (SCI, *14*, 623; REV, *9*, 103)

Gerlach, Frederick M.
Appointment: Colorado College (BULL, *12*, 280)

Germain Cebrián, José
Publication: *Normal Psychology and Pathology* (BULL, *42*, 791)

German
Vocabulary translation of terms (AJP, *8*, 584)

German Academy of Natural Sciences at Halle
Election: Spearman, C. E., member (SCI, *89*, 31)

German Congress for Experimental Psychology
Meeting: announced (JoP, *2*, 720)
Meeting: report of (JoP, *1*, 335)

German Medical Congress for Psychotherapy
Discussion of 3rd (AJP, *40*, 672)

German Military Psychology
Positions open (Bull, *37*, 779; Bull, *39*, 267-268)

German philosophy (*see* Egotism in German Philosophy)

German Society for Psychology
Election: Spearman, C. E.; Honorary member (Sci, *80*, 67)

German Society of Experimental Psychology
Lecture: Krueger, E., experimental phonetics (Sci, *22*, 727)
Lecture: Külpe, O., experimental esthetics (Sci, *22*, 727)
Lecture: Schumann, F., psychology of reading (Sci, *22*, 727)
Lecture: Sommer, K. R., psychiatry and individual psychology (Sci, *22*, 727)
Meeting (Bull, *2*, 427; Sci, *22*, 727; JoP, *9*, 279)
Organization formed (Bull, *1*, 292; Bull, *3*, 392; Bull, *4*, 31)

German universities
Enrollment: 1889 (Sci°, *14*, 196)

Germany, Physiotechnical Institute
Acquires library of Helmholtz, H. (Sci, *1*, 333)

Gerontological Society
Publication: *Journal of Gerontology* (Sci, *102*, 173)

Gerontology
Appointment: Kaplan, O. J., Editorial board of *Gerontology* (Bull, *42*, 792)
Appointment: Moore, R. A., Editor of *Gerontology* (Bull, *42*, 792)
Appointment: Shock, N. W., Experimental program director (Bull, *39*, 196; Sci, *94*, 605)
Laboratory: Baltimore City Hospitals (Sci, *94*, 605)

Gerty, Francis J.
Appointment: Univ. of Illinois (Sci, *93*, 565)

Gesell, Arnold Lucius
Association with *Journal of Delinquency* (JoP, *13*, 392)
Election: APA Director (Bull, *27*, 76; Sci, *71*, 64)
Lecture: Assoc. for Childhood Education (J App, *17*, 97)
Lecture: Clark Univ. on infant psychology (J App, *9*, 88)
Lecture: Laity "Creative behavior in child and adult" (Sci, *94*, 484)
Lecture: Massachusetts Society for Mental Hygiene (Sci, *92*, 399)

Lecture: New School for Social Research, "The psychology of growth" (SCI, *74*, 434)

Lecture: school standings (JOP, *2*, 223)

Research: Ontogenetic dev. of behavior in infants and young children (SCI, *101*, 87)

Vineland Lab, 25th anniversary (SCI, *74*, 286)

Gestalt psychology

Lecture: Boring, E. G., psychology and movement (AJP, *42*, 308)

Lecture: Koffka, K., Cornell Univ. (SCI, *61*, 181)

Lecture: Koffka, K., New School for Social Research (SCI, *69*, 156)

Lecture: Metzger, W., concepts (AJP, *40*, 162)

Lecture: Moore, M. G., vs. experience (AJP, *42*, 453)

Lecture: Taylor, H. (AJP, *44*, 356)

Publication: Hulin, W. S. and Katz, D. eye-movements and the Phi-phenomenon (AJP, *46*, 332)

Publication: Odgen, R. M., "Gestalt psychology and behaviorism" (AJP, *45*, 151)

Publication: Ogden, R. M., "Sociology and Gestalt psychology" (AJP, *46*, 651)

Publication: Squires, D. C., "Beethoven's concept of the 'whole'" (AJP, *48*, 684)

Publication: stepwise phenomenon (AJP, *52*, 125-127)

Publication: Thouless, R. H., *A Manual of Psychology* Stout, G. F. (J APP, *22*, 664)

Publication: Wertheimer translation of *Social Research* (BULL, *41*, 268)

Gettysburg College (Pennsylvania)

Appointment: Bassett, G. C. (SCI, *72*, 315)

Ghiselli, Edwin E.

Appointment: Univ. of California (BULL, *36*, 804)

Election: APA Wash-Balt Branch, Secretary (BULL, *36*, 712)

Lecture: "Oreganic amnesia and relearning" (AJP, *51*, 169-170)

Promotion: Univ. of California (BULL, *41*, 603)

Gibb, Jack Rex

Promotion: Brigham Young Univ. (BULL, *39*, 681)

Gibbs, Frederic Andrews

Appointment: Illinois Neuropsychiatric Institute, Univ. of Illinois College of Medicine (SCI, *99*, 530)

Gibson, William Ralph Boyce

Appointment: Univ. of Melbourne (JOP, *9*, 84)

Departure: Univ. of Liverpool (JOP, *9*, 84)

Giessen, University of (Germany)

Lecture: Juridical psychology and psychiatry (BULL, *4*, 32)

Gifford Lecturer
Alexander, S. Glasgow Univ., space, time and deity (JoP, *14, 224)*
Balfour, A. J. (JoP, *9, 336)*
Bergson, H., Univ. of Edinburgh (JoP, *9,* 56)
Caird, E., Glasgow Univ. (SCI, *11,* 597)
Dewey, J., Univ. of Edinburgh (SCI, *69,* 157)
James, W., Edinburgh (SCI, *15,* 675)
Seth Pringle-Pattison, A., Univ. of Aberdeen (JoP, *9,* 448)

Gifted children (*see also* Exceptional children)
Lecture: Terman, L., Stanford Medical School (SCI, *57,* 82)
Lecture: Witmer, L. (SCI, *36,* 862)
Research: Henry, T. S., classroom problems (J APP, *1,* 298-299)
Research: Stanford Univ. (SCI, *56,* 510)
Research: Urbana, IL (J APP, *1,* 298-299)
Research: Whipple, G..M., problems of (J APP, *1,* 298-299)

Gilbert, Joshua Allen
Appointment: Univ. of Iowa (REV, *2,* 534)

Gilbertson, Albert Nicolay
Appointment: Univ. of Colorado (JoP, *6,* 588; BULL, *6,* 427)
Appointment: Univ. of Minnesota (JoP, *10,* 588; BULL, *8,* 373)

Gilbreth, Frank Bunker
Lecture: Taylor Society (J APP, *9,* 204)

Gilbreth, Lillian Moller
Appointment: Purdue Univ. (SCI, *81,* 268)
Election: Engineering Woman's Club, member (SCI, *91,* 334)
Lecture: Taylor Society meeting on industrial psychology (J APP, *9,* 204, 428)

Gildea, Edwin F.
Appointment: Washington Univ. School of Medicine, St. Louis (SCI, *96,* 511)

Gildermeister, Theda
Lecture: thought method (JoP, *7,* 223)

Gilles de la Tourette, George Albert Edouard Brutus
Research: walking (SCI°, *8,* 631; SCI°, *7,* 548)

Gillespie, Robert Dick
Lecture: Chicago Institute of Medicine (SCI, *94,* 323)
Lecture: Chicago Neurological Society (SCI, *94,* 323)
Lecture: Illinois Psychiatric Society, Chicago (SCI, *94,* 323)
Lecture: Salmon Memorial Lectures (SCI, *94,* 323, 436; J APP, *25,* 726)
Lecture: San Francisco, CA (SCI, *94,* 323)
Lecture: Toronto, Ontario (SCI, *94,* 323)

Lecture: Weir Mitchell Oration, 9th "Psychoneurosis in peace and war and the future of human relationships" (Sci, *94*, 605)

Gillette, Annette Lillian

Rochester Guidance Clinic, NY, mental hygiene (Bull, *36*, 841)

Gilliland, Adam Raymond

Appointment: Northwestern Univ. (Bull, *21*, 428)

Gillingham, John Benton

Award: Social Science Research Council (Bull, *39*, 682)

Gilman, Benjamin I.

Lecture: psychology of aesthetics (Sci°, *19*, 33)

Gilman, Daniel Coit

Leave of absence: Johns Hopkins Univ. (Sci, *11*, 159)
Portrait: Johns Hopkins Univ. (Sci, *11*, 717)
Publication: the origin and organization of Johns Hopkins Univ. (Sci°, *17*, 187)
Representative: Johns Hopkins Univ., 500th anniversary of the Univ. of Cracow (Sci, *11*, 877)
Tribute: Baltimore (Sci, *11*, 38-39)

Gilson, Etienne

Lecture: James, W. (Sci, *84*, 371)

Gini, Corrado

Election: Italian Congress of Eugenics, 2nd President (Sci, *70*, 190)

Ginn and Company

Publication: July, 1888 (Sci°, *11*, 312-313)

Girden, Edward

Grant: Elizabeth Thompson Science Fund (Sci, *93*, 473)

Girton College (Cambridge, England)

International Congress of the Unity of Science, program, 1938 (JoP, *35*, 503)

Glasgow, University of (Scotland)

Appointment: Cappell, D. F. (Sci, *101*, 60)
Appointment: Thouless, R. (Bull, *23*, 455; Sci, *63*, 499)
Degree: Baldwin, J. M. (Sci, *14*, 37; Rev, *8*, 552)
Degree: Paton, H. J. (Sci, *90*, 134)
Degree: Wenley, R. M. (Rev, *8*, 552)
Lecture: Gifford lectures, Alexander, S. (JoP, *14*, 224)
Lecture: Gifford lectures, Boutroux, E. (Rev, *9*, 328)
Lecture: Gifford lectures, Caird, E. (Sci, *11*, 597)
Memorial: Hutcheson, F. (JoP, *3*, 56)
Return: Watt, H. J. from Germany (Bull, *12*, 403)

Glaze, John Arthur

Appointment: Texas Christian Univ., Department head (BULL, 25, 307)

Glenmore Summer School of the Culture Sciences

Lecture: Baldwin, J. M. (BULL, 1, 334)

Glueck, Bernard

Appointment: New School for Social Research (SCI, 65, 156)

Appointment: Sing Sing Prison, NY; Director of Psychopathic Research Dept. (BULL, 13, 296)

Course: New School for Social Research, psychoanalysis (BULL 24, 312)

Lecture: Child Study Assoc. of America (J APP, 9, 319)

Goddard, Henry Herbert

Appointment: Amer. Assoc. of Clinical Psychologists (SCI, 48, 598)

Appointment: Ohio Bureau of Juvenile Research (J APP, 2, 293; SCI, 47, 264; BULL, 15, 98)

Appointment: Ohio State Univ. (BULL, 20, 60, 172; JoP, 19, 588; SCI, 56, 279)

Appointment: The New Jersey Training School for Feeble-minded Boys and Girls, Head Department of Research (SCI, 23, 798)

Appointment: West Chester (PA) State Normal School (BULL, 3, 216)

Association with *Journal of Delinquency* (JoP, 13, 392)

Course: Berkeley, CA (BULL, 12, 403)

Degree: Ohio State Univ. (SCI, 97, 505-506)

Election: American Assoc. for the Study of the Feeble-minded, President (BULL, 11, 268)

Lecture: Crime, psychology of (BULL, 12, 403)

Lecture: Educational Conference, 3rd annual (J APP, 7, 188)

Lecture: NY Branch of APA/NYAS, heredity of mental traits (JoP, 9, 167)

Lecture: Univ. of Hawaii (SCI, 61, 564; BULL, 22, 504)

Vineland lab, 25th anniversary celebration (SCI, 74, 286)

Goddard, Pliny Earle

Lecture: NYAS, social organization (JoP, 13, 616)

Goethe Prize

Award: Freud (SCI, 72, 166)

Göttingen, University of (Germany)

Appointment: Pilzecker, A. (AJP, 7, 152)

Award: Gegenbaur, C., Wohlbrecht's Foundation (SCI, 11, 716-717)

Monument: Weber and Gauss (SCI, 10, 126)

Goldblatt, Harry

Grant: Western Reserve Univ. (SCI, 93, 37)

Goldmeier, Erich

Appointment: Wheaton College, (BULL, 36, 711)

Goldstein, Kurt
Appointment: Harvard Univ, William James Lecturer (Sci, 87, 482)

Golla, Frederick Lucien
Appointment: Burden Neurological Institute (Sci, 89, 242)

Gomperz, Theodor
Death notice (JoP, 9, 588)

Gonville and Caius College (Cambridge, England)
Election: Myers, C. S., Fellow (Sci, 82, 35)

Goodenough, Florence Laura
Appointment: Stanford Univ. (J App, 22, 106)
Election: AAAS Vice-president (Bull, 42, 191)

Goodhart, S. Philip
Retirement: Columbia Univ. College of Physicians and Surgeons (Sci, 99, 467)

Goodman, Louis S.
Research: anticonvulsants and analgesic compounds (Sci, 101, 197)

Goodrich, B. F. Company (Akron, Ohio)
Appointment: Johnson, H. M. (Bull, 17, 351)

Gordon, Kate
Appointment: Bryn Mawr College; Director graduate college (JoP, 10, 616)
Appointment: Bureau of Mental Tests (JoP, 13, 112)
Appointment: California State Board of Charities (Bull, 16, 257)
Appointment: Carnegie Institute of Technology (Bull, 13, 108; Sci, 43, 133; JoP, 13, 112)
Appointment: Columbia Univ. Teachers College (Sci, 23, 832; Bull, 3, 184; JoP, 3, 364)
Appointment: Mt. Holyoke (JoP, 9, 168)
Appointment: Stanford Univ. (J App, 10, 394)
Departure: Bryn Mawr College (JoP, 13, 112)
Election: WPA President (J App, 10, 395)
Leave of absence: Carnegie Institute of Technology (JoP, 15, 336)
Lecture: School of Applied Design (JoP, 13, 112)
Promotion: Carnegie Institute of Technology (J App, 3, 290; Bull, 16, 257)
Resignation (Bull, 3, 216)

Gordy, John Pancoast
Death notice (Bull, 6, 72)

Gordy, Margaret D.
Research: survey tests and their use in occupational adjustment (Bull, 41, 343)

Gore, J. Howard
Endorsement: International Society of the Psychical Institute (SCI, *12*, 238)

Gore, Willard Clark
Lecture: sensation (JOP, *1*, 336)
Research: origin of word (SCI°, *1*, 499)

Gorham, Donald Rex
Appointment: Keuka College, NY (BULL, *40*, 619)

Gosney, Ezra Seymour
Human Betterment Foundation, President; *Effects of eugenic sterilization as practiced in California* (J APP, *21*, 476)

Gotaas, Harold B.
Award: Order of Merit by the Chilean Government (SCI, *101*, 663)

Goucher College (Baltimore, Maryland)
Appointment: Adams, G. K. (BULL, *21*, 240)
Appointment: Ball, R. S. (BULL, *42*, 791)
Appointment: Bentley, M. (SCI, *94*, 38)
Appointment: Bowman, E. (JOP, *14*, 644; BULL, *17*, 279)
Appointment: Helfrich, D. (BULL, *42*, 791)
Appointment: Shaffer, G. W. (BULL, *42*, 63; SCI, *100*, 353)
Meeting: APA Wash.-Balt. Branch (BULL, *35*, 188)
Promotion: Bowman, E. (BULL, *20*, 172)

Gould, Rosalind
Award: Social Science Research Council (BULL, *39*, 683)

Gould, Russell L.
Appointment: Bureau of Salesmanship Research (JOP, *13*, 476; SCI, *44*, 56; BULL, *13*, 296)

Government College, Tsing Hua, China
Appointment: Walcott, G. D. (BULL, *14*, 115; JOP, *14*, 224)

Government Hospital for the Insane, Washington, D.C.
Appointment: Franz, S. I. (SCI, *30*, 964; JOP, *4*, 28; BULL, *4*, 32; BULL, *7*, 75)
Appointment: Sutherland, A. H. (BULL, *6*, 368)
Departure: Sutherland, A. H. (BULL, *7*, 75)
Publication: *Bulletin* (JOP, *6*, 446)

Government service
Research: psychologists surveyed (J APP, *26*, 391)

Gowers, William Richard
Death notice (BULL, *12*, 244)

Gradenigo, Giuseppe

Research: senses in criminals (Sci°, *14*, 297)

Grades

Lecture: Cattell, J. McK., Indiana (JoP, 9, 112)
Research: GRE scores and college marks (J App, *26*, 114)

Graduate Record Examination

Publication: Langmuir, C. R., and college marks (J App, 27, 114)
Publication: Learned, W. S. (J App, *26*, 114)

Graff, Peter

Endowment: Pennsylvania College; professorship of hygiene and physical
culture (Sci°, *14*, 333)

Graham, Clarence Henry

Appointment: Brown Univ. (Sci, 93, 591; Bull, *33*, 406)
Appointment: Clark Univ. (Sci, 73, 609; Bull, 28, 503)
Appointment: Columbia Univ. (Sci, *101*, 112; Bull., 42, 255)
Award: Howard Crosby Warren Medal (Sci, 93, 324; Bull, 38, 304; J App, 25,
267)
Election: American Academy of Arts and Sciences; Fellow (Bull, *34*, 409)
Election: National Research Council Fellow; Univ. of Penn. (Sci, 73, 609)
Promotion: Brown Univ. (Bull, 38, 777)
Research: human retina (Bull, *38*, 304)

Graham, James Larmour

Appointment: Lehigh Univ. (Sci, 72, 315)
Appointment: Univ. of Kentucky (J App, *10*, 522; Sci, *64*, 448)
Appointment: Univ. of Wisconsin (Bull, *24*, 136)
Publication: Normal probability curve (AJP, *52*, 293-296)

Graham Brown, Thomas

Paper: British Psychological Society (JoP, *8*, 448)

Grants

American Academy of Arts and Sciences: Body voltage research, DeSilva, H.
(Sci, *80*, 425)
Barker Foundation of Chicago: Gault's perception research (Sci, 74, 264)
Board of National Research Fellowships in the Biological Sciences: fellowships,
1935 (Sci, *81*, 482)
British National Institute of Industrial Psychology: from Rockefeller
Foundation (Sci, 71, 504)
Carnegie: Bryan, A. I. (Bull, 37, 187)
Carnegie Foundation: Bentley, M., abnormal psychology research (Sci, 75, 189)
Commonwealth Fund, Mental Hygiene Program (Sci, 76, 81)
Esso Safety Foundation (Bull, *36*, 140)

Freud, S., Memorial Fellowship for Psychoanalytic Training; Boston
Psychoanalytic Institute (BULL, 37, 827)
General Education Board Fellowship: Brewer, J. E. (BULL, 37, 827)
Harvard Eugenics Research: Mears, J. E. (SCI, 69, 668)
Heckscher Foundation: Kupalov, P. S., conditioned reflex (SCI, 70, 235)
National Research Council (BULL, 33, 578; SCI, 80, 585; SCI, 81, 14; SCI, 82, 568)
Oxford Univ.: establish Institute of Experimental Psychology (SCI, 83, 433;
BULL, 33, 578)
Research Council on Problems of Alcohol from Carnegie Corp., American
Philosophical Society, Dazian Foundation for Medical Resesarch (BULL, 37,
61)
Rockefeller Foundation: Institute of Experimental Psychology, Oxford Univ.
(SCI, 83, 433)
Rockefeller Foundation: Massachusetts General Hospital, Psychiatric Unit (SCI,
79, 291)
Sigma Xi: DeSilva, H. R.; body voltage research (SCI, 80, 310)
Social Science Research Council (BULL, 33, 579; BULL, 34, 409; BULL, 36, 805;
BULL, 37, 829)
Soviet government: Pavlov, I. (SCI, 70, 351)
Virginia Academy of Science: McGinnis, J. M. (SCI, 76, 590)
Wesleyan Univ. Faculty Committee on Research: Langlie, T. A. (SCI, 85, 14)
Whitney, W. Foundation: Society for the Psychological Study of Social Issues
(BULL, 36, 499)

Graphology (see also Handwriting)
Publication: Hearns, R. S.; open letter to American psychologists (J APP, 25, 357)

Grasset, Joseph
Award: Grand Prix Broquette Gonin of the Academie Francaise (JoP, 10, 420)

Grave, Charlotte Easby
Lecture: Conference on Education and the Exceptional Child, 5th (J APP, 23,
312)

Graves, William Washington
Award: St. Louis Medical Society (SCI, 90, 34, 488)

Gray, Clarence Truman
Research: eye movements as correlated to reading ability (J APP, 1, 298)

Gray, Landon Carter
Death notice (SCI, 11, 795)

Great Britain (see also British)
Institute proposal (BULL, 16, 258)
National Council of Mental Hygiene (SCI, 58, 263)

Greece
Publication: Mahaffy, J. P., social life of (Sci°, 9, 483)
Punishment for murder (Sci°, 7, 235)

Green Mountain Junior College (Poultney, Vermont)
Appointment: Seibert, E. W. (Bull, 42, 191)

Greenawalt, E. Guy
Appointment: Panzer College of Physical Education (Bull, 42, 792)

Greene, Edward Barrows
Appointment: Wesleyan Univ. (Bull, 22, 672)
Election: AAAP; Treasurer (J App, 21, 603, 713)
Publication: Michigan Vocabulary Profile Test (J App, 23, 745)

Greene, Harold D.
Appointment: Wake Forest College (Sci, 101, 268)

Greene, Harry Andrew
Publication: Iowa Silent Reading Test (J App, 23, 633)

Greenwood, Joseph Albert
Editor: *Journal of Parapsychology* (Bull, 39, 325; Sci, 95, 322-323)

Greenwood, M.
Retirement: Univ. of London School of Hygiene (Sci, 102, 7)

Gregory, Menas Sarkas
Appointment: Bellevue Hospital; Director psychological lab (Bull, 13, 376;
   JoP, 13, 476)
Bequeathal: New York Univ. College of Medicine (Sci, 95, 405)

Gregory, Wilbur Smith
Appointment: Univ. of Nebraska (Bull, 34, 634; J App, 24, 518; Sci, 91, 616)

Greifswald, University of
Degree: Davis, W. H. (Sci, 24, 286)

Grey, Charles F.
Appointment: Thurstone, L. L. as Grey Professor (Sci, 87, 387; Bull, 35, 408)
Appointment: Univ. of Chicago (Sci, 89, 313)

Griffin, Edward H.
Appointment: Johns Hopkins Univ. (Sci°, 14, 57)
Death notice (Sci, 69, 136)

Griffing, Harold
Death notice (Rev, 7, 639)

Griffith, Coleman Roberts
Award: Guggenheim Memorial Fellowship (Bull, 22, 504)
Lecture: St. Louis Univ. (Sci, 75, 332)

Griffith, William
Election: Oregon Psychological Assoc.; Chair (Sci, 85, 518)
Election: Psychologists of the State of Oregon; Chair (Sci, 83, 323)

Grindley, Gwilym Cuthbert
Appointment: Cambridge Univ. (Sci, 82, 123)

Grinker, Roy R.
Resignation: Univ. of Chicago (Sci, 83, 347)

Grinnell College (*see* Iowa College)

Grinsted, Alan Douglas
Leave of absence: Louisiana State Univ. (Sci, 95, 220; Bull, 39, 325)

Groen, Peter
American Catholic Phil. Assoc., 11th annual meeting (JoP, 33, 28)

Gross, Hans Gustav Adolf
Death notice (Bull, 13, 108)
Publication: criminal psychology (JoP, 8, 588)

Grot, N. Ia
Death notice (Sci, 10, 302; Rev, 6, 571; AJP, 11, 130)

Grove, William Richard
Promotion: Univ. of Pittsburgh (Bull, 42, 581)

Grünbaum, Anton Abram
Death notice (AJP, 44, 816; Bull, 29, 308)

Gruenberg, Sidonie Matsner
Conference on Education and the Exceptional Child (J App, 23, 312)

Grundriss der Psychologie
Publication: Judd, C. H. (Sci, 3, 775)
Publication: Praechter, K., 11th edition (JoP, 17, 532)
Publication: Wundt, W., book (Sci, 3, 353)

Günther, Hans F. K.
Promotion: Univ. of Jena, eugenics (Sci, 72, 421)

Guernsey, Martha
Fellowship: Social Science Research Council (Bull, 24, 136)

Guest, Lester Philip
APA, Wash.-Balt. Branch, 1939 (BULL, *36*, 712)

Guggenheim Fellowship
Award: Adams, D. K. (BULL, *34*, 499)
Award: Asch, S. E. (BULL, *40*, 540)
Award: Burks, B. S. (BULL, *40*, 540)
Award: Freeman, G. L. (BULL, *42*, 791)
Award: Griffith, C. R. (BULL, *22*, 504)
Award: Schneirla, T. C. (BULL, *42*, 485; BULL, *41*, 409; SCI, *100*, 517)
Award: Skinner, B. F. (BULL, *39*, 423)
Endowment announced (J APP, *9*, 89)
Fellowships (JoP, *40*, 224)

Guidance
Conference: Guidance Mental Hygiene (J APP, *21*, 475)

Guidance and Personnel Association
Meeting (J APP, *27*, 207)

Guild, Stacy R.
APA Wash.-Balt. Branch, 1940 (BULL, *37*, 657)

Guilford, Joy Paul
Appointment: Univ. of Kansas (J APP, *11*, 235)
Appointment: Univ. of Nebraska (SCI, *68*, 110; BULL, *25*, 444; BULL, *36*, 304; J APP, *23*, 207)
Appointment: Univ. of Nebraska Bureau of Instructional Research (SCI, *89*, 148)
Appointment: Univ. of Southern California (SCI, *92*, 8; J APP, *24*, 518)
Departure: Univ. of Nebraska (SCI, *92*, 8)
Election: MPA; Exec. Council (SCI, *83*, 517)
Election: MPA President (J APP, *23*, 96, 419; J APP, *21*, 717; BULL, *37*, 187)
Grant: Social Science Research Council (BULL, *34*, 409)
Lecture: Midwestern Psychological Assoc., 13th (AJP, *51*, 576; SCI, *91*, 68)
Lecture: Psychometric Society (SCI, *88*, 277)
Publication: Personality; "Unitary traits of personality and factor theory" (AJP, *48*, 680)
Publication: Statistics; discussion by Garrett, H. E. (AJP, *49*, 679, 683)
Publication: Statistics; reply to Garrett, H. E. (AJP, *49*, 680)

Gulliksen, Harold Oliver
Appointment: College Entrance Examination Board (BULL, *42*, 485)
Appointment: Princeton Univ. (BULL, *42*, 485)
Course: Univ. of Chicago (J APP, *23*, 311)
Departure: Univ. of Chicago (BULL, *42*, 485)

Gum-chewer's paralysis
Research: neurosis (SCI°, *14*, 215)

Gundlach, Ralph Harrelson
Appointment: Univ. of California, Berkeley (BULL, *41*, 72)
Appointment: Univ. of Washington (J APP, *11*, 405)

Gunther, Erna
Publication: right handedness (AJP, *35*, 465)

Gurnee, Herbert
Publication: "Some observations on after-images of bodily movement" (AJP, *45*, 528)

Gurney, Edmund
Death notice (SCI°, *12*, 22)
Publication: "Phantasms of living" (SCI°, *8*, 364)

Gustavus Adolphus College (St. Peter, Minnesota)
Appointment: Siebrecht, E. B. (BULL, *42*, 675)

Guthrie, Edwin Ray
Degree: Univ. of Nebraska (BULL, *42*, 484)
Publication: development of the art of numeration (SCI, *5*, 39)

Guthrie, Riley H.
Appointment: Saint Elizabeth's Hospital, Washington, D.C. (SCI, *89*, 125)
Departure: Boston Psychopathic Hospital (SCI, *89*, 125)

Guttmann, Eric
Grant: Oxford Univ. (SCI, *94*, 111)
Research: Oxford Univ., brain injuries (SCI, *94*, 111)

H

Habbe, Stephen
Publication: Guidebook, National Training School for Boys (BULL, *40*, 310-311)

Habit
Lecture: Dennis, W., habit loss (AJP, *44*, 189)
Lecture: Dunlap, K., technique of negative practice (AJP, *55*, 270-273)
Lecture: Eaton, T. (AJP, *40*, 665)
Lecture: Galton, F. W., Congress of Psychological Physiology (SCI°, *14*, 195)
Lecture: Judd, C. H. (JoP, *1*, 224)
Lecture: Lough, J. E., habit curve (JoP, *1*, 224)
Lecture: Lubbock, J., Linnean Society, of ants, bees, and wasps (SCI°, *10*, 320)
Lecture: MacDougal, R. (JoP, *2*, 112)
Research. Watson, J. B., seagulls (BULL, *4*, 337)

Hadley, Loren S.
Appointment: Bucknell Univ. Testing Bureau (BULL, *42*, 407)
Departure: Ohio State Univ. (BULL, *42*, 407)

Haeckel, Ernst Heinrich
Award: renounces honors conferred by English Univ. (JoP, *11*, 588)
Death notice (BULL, *16*, 258)
Memorial letter: Montague, W. P. (JoP, *16*, 503-504)
Resignation: Univ. of Jena (JoP, *6*, 56)

Haggard, Howard W.
Promotion: Yale Univ. (SCI, *87*, 482)

Haggerty, Melvin Everett
Appointment: National Research Council (JoP, *16*, 672; J APP, *3*, 393)
Appointment: Univ. of Minnesota (JoP, *12*, 644)
Commission: Sanitary Corps (JoP, *15*, 364; BULL, *15*, 98)
Death notice (BULL, *34*, 864)

Duties in the Army (BULL, *15*, 24)
Election: AAAS Vice-president, section Q (BULL, *23*, 112)
Leave of absence: Indiana Univ. (JoP, *12*, 644)
Promotion: Indiana Univ. (BULL, *9*, 280; SCI, *35*, 984; JoP, *9*, 448)

Hahn, Milton Edwin
Appointment: Syracuse Univ. (BULL, *41*, 603)

Haines, Thomas Harvey
Appointment: National Committee for Mental Hygiene and the Rockefeller
Foundation (BULL, *14*, 114-115)
Appointment: National Committee for Mental Hygiene; Consultant (BULL, *20*,
288)
Appointment: Ohio State Board, Juvenile Delinquent Bureau, Chief (SCI, *40*,
445; BULL, *11*, 352)
Association: *Journal of Delinquency* (JoP, *13*, 392)
Course: Smith College (BULL, *11*, 115; JoP, *11*, 196)
Leave of absence: Ohio State Univ. (BULL, *9*, 440; JoP, *9*, 700)
Promotion: Ohio State Univ. (SCI, *14*, 504; BULL, *5*, 244; JoP, *5*, 336)

Hall, Calvin Springer
Appointment: Western Reserve Univ. (SCI, *86*, 118; BULL, *34*, 326)
Election: Psychologists of the State of Oregon; Secretary (SCI, *83*, 323; BULL,
33, 406)

Hall, Everett Wesley
Election: American Phil. Assoc.; Secretary-treasurer (JoP, *33*, 56)

Hall, Granville Stanley
Appointment: Brown Univ. (BULL, *33*, 406)
Appointment: Clark Univ. (SCI°, *12*, 34)
Appointment: Johns Hopkins Univ. (SCI°, *3*, 524)
Appointment: National Research Council (JoP, *14*, 392; BULL, *14*, 191)
Bequest: Clark Univ. (SCI, *59*, 422)
Commemorative meeting in his honor (J APP, *9*, 87)
Commemoration of life at Clark Univ. (SCI, *60*, 380)
Course: Univ. of Pittsburgh (BULL, *12*, 403)
Death notice (BULL, *21*, 360; SCI, *59*, 395)
Degree: Univ. of Maryland (BULL, *4*, 200)
Editorship: *American Journal of Psychology* passed to Titchener, E. B. (BULL,
18, 110)
Election: APA President (SCI, *59*, 13)
Election: Association of American Universities; President (SCI, *21*, 40)
Election: London Society for Psychical Research (SCI°, *5*, 62)
Election: National Academy of Sciences (SCI, *41*, 640)
Editor: *Journal of Applied Psychology* (JoP, *14*, 252)
International committee, 5th International Congress of Psychology (JoP, *2*, 56)
Lecture: Clark Univ. (JoP, *22*, 140)

Lecture: Clark Univ., honoring Story, W. E. (Sci, *32*, 13)
Lecture: Clark Univ., psychology founders (Sci, *35*, 101)
Lecture: College of Physicians and Surgeons, Boston (Sci, *27*, 1000)
Lecture: Columbia College Phil. Society (Sci°, *6*, 360)
Lecture: Columbia Univ. (Bull, *9*, 95; JoP, *9*, 56)
Lecture: "Educational efficiency" (JoP, *9*, 28)
Lecture: experimental psychology (JoP, *2*, 223)
Lecture: International Congress of Arts and Sciences, St. Louis (JoP, *1*, 419)
Lecture: Johns Hopkins Univ. (Sci, *14*, 1021)
Lecture: Johns Hopkins Univ., education (Sci°, *9*, 360)
Lecture: Johns Hopkins Univ., student life at (Sci°, *5*, 19-20)
Lecture: Pittsburg, KS, educational efficiency (Sci, *34*, 755)
Lecture: State Manual Training School, Kansas, inauguration of Myers, G. M.
   (JoP, *9*, 140; Sci, *34*, 754; Bull, *9*, 95)
Lecture: "The high school as the people's college versus fitting schools" (Sci,
   15, 198)
Lecture: Twentieth Century Club of Boston, education (Sci, *14*, 781-782)
Lecture: Univ. of Chicago (Sci, *26*, 188)
Lecture: Univ. of Illinois (Sci, *27*, 280)
Lecture: Univ. of Maryland, centennial celebration (Sci, *25*, 879)
Lecture: Univ. of Tennessee (JoP, *1*, 280; Bull, *1*, 173)
Letters: Bowditch, H. P. (AJP, *41*, 326)
Publication: Festschrift volume for Hall, announcement (Sci, *17*, 558)
Publication: functions of docent at Clark Univ. (Sci°, *14*, 250)
Publication: introductory note in the manuscripts of Bridgman, L. (Sci°, *9*, 435)
Publication: *Journal of Applied Psychology*, (Bull, *13*, 482)
Publication: rebuttal to James, W., Ladd, G. T., Baldwin, J. M. and Cattell, J.
   McK. (Sci, *2*, 735)
Retirement: Clark Univ. (Sci, *52*, 34; Bull, *17*, 239)

Hall, Robert G.
Donation: Clark Univ., father's furniture (Bull, *21*, 360)
Donation: Clark Univ., Hall, G. S. library (Sci, *59*, 483)

Hall, Roscoe Willis
Election: American Psychiatric Assoc.; President (Sci, *91*, 520)

Hall, William Edward
Appointment: Univ. of Nebraska (Bull, *42*, 582)
Leave of absence: Eastern Washington College of Education (Bull, *42*, 582)

Halle, University of (Germany)
Appointment: Ebbinghaus, H. (Bull, *2*, 427)
Appointment: Meumann, E. (JoP, *6*, 700; Bull, *6*, 368)
Award: Gold medal given to Pavlov, I. P. for work on digestion (Sci, *17*, 518,
   597)
Death notice: Ebbinghaus, H. (Sci, *29*, 451)

Departure: Krueger, P. (SCI, *35*, 495)
Departure: Riehl, A. (JOP, *2*, 644)
Pedagogy: 1st professorship (JOP, *10*, 616)
Resignation: Hitzig, E. (SCI, *17*, 438)

Halleck, Rueben Post
Election: SSPP, Council (JOP, *1*, 168)

Halliburton, William Dobinson
Experimental psychology at King's College, London (SCI, *16*, 280)
Lecture: Kings College, London, histological psychology (SCI, *20*, 656; JOP, *1*, 672; BULL, *1*, 488)

Hallowell, Alfred Irving
Lecture: Institute on the Exceptional Child, 6th; Woods School (J APP, *23*, 744)

Hallucinations
Publication: Kandinskii, V. K. (AJP, *1*, 363)
Report of (AJP, *3*, 435)
Research: James, W. (AJP, *3*, 292)

Halstead, Ward Campbell
Election: American Neurological Assoc. (BULL, *40*, 619)
Fellowship awarded (SCI, *81*, 482)

Halverson, Henry Marc
Appointment: MacMurray College (BULL, *39*, 807)
Appointment: Univ. of Maine (JOP, *19*, 532; BULL, *19*, 410; SCI, *55*, 617)
Departure: Yale Univ. (BULL, *39*, 807)
Resignation: Clark Univ. (SCI, *55*, 617)

Hamburg, University of (Germany)
Appointment: Stern, W. (SCI, *43*, 208; BULL, *13*, 108)

Hamilton, Allan McLane
Election: Royal Society of Edinburgh (SCI, *9*, 380)
Publication: "Spiritualism and like delusions" in *The American Magazine* (SCI°, *11*, 312-313)

Hamilton College (Clinton, New York)
Appointment: Elkin, W. B. (REV, *6*, 673)
Appointment: Squires, W. H. (SCI, *13*, 837)
Leave of absence: Squires, W. H. (REV, *6*, 673)
Resignation: Cowley, W. H. (SCI, *100*, 381)

Hamilton, Francis Marion
Lecture: reading (JOP, *2*, 700)

Hamilton, Gilbert Van Tassel
Death notice (BULL, *41*, 409)

Hamilton, Hughbert Clayton
Grant: Temple Univ. Research Fund (BULL, *42*, 255-256)

Hamilton, Margaret
Appointment: Univ. of Southern California; Psych. clinic (JoP, *15*, 112)

Hamilton, Samuel W.
Appointment: Hospital for Mental Diseases, Philadelphia (SCI, *52*, 152)

Hamlin, Alice Julia
Appointment: Mt. Holyoke College (AJP, *7*, 579)

Hamline University (St. Paul, Minnesota)
Leave of absence: Walcott, C. D. (SCI, *45*, 162; JoP, *14*, 224)

Hammond, William Alexander
Death notice (SCI, *11*, 159)
Lecture: International Congress of Arts and Sciences, St. Louis (JoP, *1*, 616)

Hancock, J. W.
Appointment: Parsons College (SCI, *92*, 450)

Hancock, John A.
Lecture: mental association (JoP, *7*, 222)

Handedness
Lecture: Gunther, E. (AJP, *35*, 465)
Publication: Harriman, P. L.; "Intelligence and handedness" (AJP, *45*, 526)
Publication: Levine, K. N.; "A note on the relation of the dominant thumb in clasping to handedness" (AJP, *47*, 704)

Handicapped children
Course: MacMurray College (BULL, *39*, 807)

Handwriting (*see also* Graphology)
Research: Freeman, F. N. (J APP, *1*, 298)

Hanfmann, Eugenia
Grant: Social Science Research Council (BULL, *31*, 380)

Hanks, Lucien Mason, Jr.
Appointment: Bennington College (BULL, *39*, 808)
Departure: Univ. of Illinois (BULL, *39*, 808)
Grant: Social Science Research Council (BULL, *36*, 805)

Hannahs, Elizabeth Helen
Death notice (JoP, *14*, 672)

Hanson, J. M.
Appointment: Children's Service Bureau (J App, *3*, 289)

Hantz, Harold
Entered: Military Service (JoP, *40*, 644)

Harding, D. W.
Appointment: Bedford College (Sci, *102*, 219-220)

Hardwick, Rose Standish
Lecture: Mass. School for Feeble-minded (Bull, *13*, 407-408)

Hare, Clarence H.
Election: Assoc. for Research in Nervous and Mental Diseases; Secretary (Sci, *81*, 42; Sci, *85*, 42)

Harlem Valley State Hospital (New York)
Appointment: Kutash, S. B. (Bull, *42*, 63)

Harlow, Margaret (*see* Kuenne, Margaret Ruth)

Harrell, Thomas Willard
Appointment: American Assoc. for Applied Psychology, Section of Military Psychology; officer (Sci, *99*, 34)
Leave of absence: Univ. of Illinois (Sci, *97*, 136)
Promotion: Army Air Forces (Bull, *40*, 383; Sci, *97*, 136)
Promotion: Univ. of Illinois (Bull, *42*, 793-794)
Publication: *Psychological Bulletin*, military (J App, *25*, 358)

Harriman, Philip Laurence
Publication: relationship of intelligence and handedness (AJP, *45*, 526-528)

Harris, Arthur J.
Lecture: Sigma Xi, Galton, F. (Sci, *37*, 172)

Harris, James H.
Lecture: written composition (JoP, *7*, 223)

Harris, Marjorie S.
Election: SSPP President (Sci, *90*, 105)
Lecture: SSPP 35th annual meeting (JoP, *37*, 196)

Harris, William Torrey
Death notice: (JoP, *6*, 672)
Degree: Univ. of Iowa (Sci, *9*, 421)
Election: SSPP council (JoP, *1*, 168)

Memorial meeting of Society for Philosophical Inquiry (JoP, 7, 280)
Retirement: U.S. Commission of Education (JoP, 3, 420)

Harrison, Frederic
Herbert Spencer lecture, 1st (JoP, 2, 196)

Harsh, Charles Maxfield
Appointment: Bureau of Instructional Research, Univ. of Nebraska (BULL, 37, 755)

Hartley, Raymond Ellis, Jr.
Appointment: Univ. of Kansas (BULL, 42, 792)

Hartmann, Eduard von
Lecture: Hall, G. S., Columbia Univ. (JoP, 9, 56; SCI, 35, 101)

Hartmann, George Wilfried
Lecture: APA, 47th annual meeting (JoP, 36, 476)
Publication: SPSSI yearbook: The psychology of industrial conflict (BULL, 35, 61)
Rejoinder to Ogden's paper on insight (AJP, 44, 576)

Hartog, Marcus Manuel
Publication: *Nature*, inheritance of characters (SCI°, 13, 236-237)

Hartshorne, Edward Yarnall
Visits Harvard Univ. (BULL, 42, 407)

Hartson, Louis Dunton
Publication: "Real movements, apparent movements, and perceptions" (AJP, 49, 126)

Hartwick College (Oneonta, New York)
Election: Arnold, H. J.; President (BULL, 36, 712)

Harvard Medical School (Cambridge, Massachusetts)
Appointment: Beck, S. J. (BULL, 29, 603; J APP, 16, 438; SCI, 76, 97)
Appointment: Campbell, C. M. (BULL, 17, 351; SCI, 52, 290)
Appointment: Franz, S. I. (REV, 6, 673)
Appointment: Solomon, H. C. (SCI, 98, 321)
Appointment: Wells, F. L. (SCI, 53, 363; BULL, 18, 236)
Endowment: Rockefeller Foundation for Psychiatry (SCI, 52, 174)
Lecture: Pierre, J., hysteria (JoP, 3, 644)
Lecture: Southard, E. E., mapping the brain (SCI, 34, 914)
Lecture: Tuttle, G. T., mental illness (SCI, 34, 914)

Harvard Medical Society
Lecture: Cannon, W. B. (BULL, 28, 80)

Harvard Psychological Clinic (Cambridge, Massachusetts)
Appointment: Barker, R. G. (BULL, *34*, 634)
Appointment: Lewin, K. (SCI, *87*, 482)
Appointment: Murray, H. A. (BULL, *34*, 634)

Harvard University (Cambridge, Massachusetts)
Appointment: Allport, F. H. (SCI, *50*, 345; JoP, *27*, 560; BULL, *27*, 496; BULL, *16*, 391-392)
Appointment: Bakewell, C. M. (REV, *3*, 356)
Appointment: Berrien, F. K. (BULL, *42*, 791)
Appointment: Boring, E. G. (BULL, *19*, 350; AJP, *33*, 450; JoP, *19*, 420; SCI, *55*, 538)
Appointment: Bühler, K. (SCI, *67*, 343; BULL, *25*, 307)
Appointment: Burtt, H. E. (JoP, *15*, 252; BULL, *15*, 256; SCI, *47*, 364)
Appointment: Carmichael, L. (BULL, *32*, 323; SCI, *82*, 298; SCI, *81*, 93)
Appointment: Delabarre, E. B. (AJP, *7*, 452; REV, *3*, 356; SCI, *3*, 406)
Appointment: DeSilva, H. R., Bureau for Street Traffic Research (SCI, *83*, 347)
Appointment: Dewey, J., first James, Wm. Lectureship (JoP, *27*, 140; BULL, *27*, 240; SCI, *75*, 331)
Appointment: Goldstein, K., James, W. lecturer, 1938-39 (SCI, *87*, 482)
Appointment: Holt, E. B. (SCI, *14*, 424; BULL, *2*, 224; REV, *8*, 656-657; SCI, *21*, 840)
Appointment: James, W., professorship of philosophy at Stanford Univ. (SCI, *21*, 400)
Appointment: James, W., Stanford Univ. (SCI, *23*, 118)
Appointment: James, W., Univ. of Chicago (SCI, *21*, 902)
Appointment: Janet, P. (JoP, *3*, 392; SCI, *23*, 959; BULL, *3*, 248)
Appointment: Jenness, A. F. (BULL, *34*, 634)
Appointment: Katzenellenbogen, E. (SCI, *30*, 524)
Appointment: Kitson, H. D. (BULL, *12*, 440)
Appointment: Köhler, W. (BULL, *31*, 380; SCI, *61*, 465; SCI, *80*, 334; BULL, *22*, 444; JoP, *22*, 252)
Appointment: Langfeld, H. (SCI, *50*, 345; BULL, *19*, 350; AJP, *33*, 450; BULL, *16*, 391- 392; SCI, *42*, 527)
Appointment: Lashley, K. S. (SCI, *81*, 335; BULL, *34*, 409; SCI, *85*, 516; BULL, *32*, 376)
Appointment: Lough, J. E. (REV, *3*, 356; SCI, *3*, 558)
Appointment: Lovejoy, A. O. (JoP, *29*, 252; SCI, *75*, 331)
Appointment: MacDougall, R. (AJP, *10*, 165)
Appointment: McDougall, W. (JoP, *16*, 588; BULL, *16*, 391-392; SCI, *50*, 304)
Appointment: Mayo, E. (BULL, *23*, 455; SCI, *64*, 89)
Appointment: Messenger, J. F. (REV, *7*, 428)
Appointment: Miller, D. S. (SCI, *9*, 821)
Appointment: Münsterberg, H., Graduate School of Arts and Sciences; Administrative Board Member (SCI, *24*, 512)
Appointment: Ogden, R. M. (BULL, *20*, 288)
Appointment: Pratt, C. C. (AJP, *33*, 450; BULL, *19*, 350; SCI, *55*, 617)

Leave of absence: Holt, E. B., 1911-1912 (SCI, *34*, 435; BULL, *8*, 374)

Leave of absence: James, W. (SCI, *9*, 821)

Leave of absence: Münsterberg, H. (SCI, *24*, 788; SCI, *31*, 380; JoP, *4*, 28; BULL, *4*, 32)

Leave of absence: Royce, J. (JoP, *9*, 168)

Lecture: Boutroux, E. (JoP, *7*, 140)

Lecture: Campbell, C. M.; Lowell Lecture (SCI, *76*, 462)

Lecture: Chase, R. H. (AJP, *2*, 190)

Lecture: Dewey, J.; 1st James, W. lecture (SCI, *71*, 212)

Lecture: Dewey, J., "Knowledge and action" (SCI, *21*, 798)

Lecture: Gilson, E.; James, W. (SCI, *84*, 371)

Lecture: James, W. (BULL, *5*, 380; SCI, *4*, 50; JoP, *5*, 672; SCI, *28*, 642, 679)

Lecture: Koffka, K. (SCI, *60*, 587)

Lecture: Ladd-Franklin, C. (JoP, *17*, 224; SCI, *57*, 324; SCI, *65*, 520; SCI, *37*, 747; BULL, *10*, 252; SCI, *61*, 16)

Lecture: Ladd-Franklin, C., symbol logic, postponed (JoP, *15*, 280)

Lecture: Lovejoy, A.; James, W. lecturer (BULL, *29*, 308)

Lecture: Royce, J. on James, W. (JoP, *8*, 447-448)

Lecture: Royce, J., social psychology (SCI, *6*, 841)

Lecture: Ruckmick, C. A., psychology of music (BULL, *12*, 403)

Lecture: Starch, D. (JoP, *16*, 644)

Lecture: Thorndike, E. L., James, W. lectures (BULL, *39*, 896)

Lecture: Wallace, C., animal psychology (SCI, *56*, 686)

Lecture: Wells, F. L. (BULL, *10*, 124; JoP, *10*, 336)

Lectureship: established honor of James, W. (BULL, *27*, 240; JoP, *27*, 139)

Meeting: American Philosophical Assoc. announced (JoP, *8*, 503-504)

Meeting: American Philosophical Society, Eastern Division, 1936 (JoP, *33*, 280)

Meeting: APA announced (JoP, *2*, 699)

Meeting: experimental psychologists (BULL, *5*, 128)

Münsterberg, H. declines chair in philosophy at Univ. of Königsberg (SCI, *21*, 628; JoP, *2*, 252)

Münsterberg, H., German trip (SCI, *21*, 903)

Münsterberg, H. heads fund drive for Emerson Hall (SCI, *15*, 240; REV, *9*, 216)

Münsterberg's, H. library accepted (JoP, *14*, 252)

Promotion: Allport, G. W. (SCI, *83*, 518)

Promotion: Dearborn, W. (SCI, *45*, 383; BULL, *14*, 192, 264)

Promotion: Holt, E. B. (JoP, *2*, 336)

Promotion: Langfeld, H. (SCI, *55*, 538; BULL, *12*, 364)

Promotion: Stevens, S. S. (SCI, *87*, 482)

Promotion: Woods, J. H. (BULL, *5*, 244)

Promotion: Yerkes, R. M. (BULL, *5*, 244; SCI, *27*, 904)

Psychological laboratory director, Boring, E. G. (SCI, *60*, 429; BULL, *21*, 660)

Publication: exhibit at Chicago Exposition (REV, *1*, 214)

Research: examination and classification of backward children (JoP, *4*, 363)

Resignation: Holt, E. B. (JoP, *15*, 392; BULL, *15*, 98; SCI, *47*, 267)

Resignation: James, W. (JoP, *4*, 84)

Resignation: McDougall, W. (BULL, *24*, 204; SCI, *65*, 139)

Retirement: James, W., Jan 22, 1907 (SCI, *25*, 237; BULL, *4*, 64)
Returns: James, W. (SCI, *14*, 541)
Returns: Münsterberg, H. (JoP, *4*, 140; SCI, *5*, 584)
Transfer: Royce, J., Alford professorship (JoP, *11*, 308)
Visit: Hartshorne, E. Y. (BULL, *42*, 407)

Harvard University Press
Publication: Sheldon, W. H., duality (JoP, *15*, 280)

Harvey Society
Andrew, ?, relationship between physiology and medicine (SCI, *16*, 272)
Lecture: Alexander, F.; "Psychoanalysis and medicine" (SCI, *73*, 64)
Lecture: Jastrow, J., Univ. of Wisconsin, subconsciousness (SCI, *27*, 237)
Lecture: Jennings, H. S. (SCI, *34*, 376)
Lecture: Lashley, K. S.; "Mass action and localization of functions in cerebral cortex" (SCI, *72*, 499)
Lecture: Richter, C. P.; "Total homeostasis" (SCI, *96*, 445)
Meeting: 1938 (SCI, *87*, 135)

Haslerud, George Martin
Appointment: Univ. of New Hampshire (BULL, *42*, 792)

Haunted house
Publication: *Journal of the Society for Psychical Research* (SCI°, *8*, 367)

Hauptman, Leo M.
Appointment: Kalamazoo College (BULL, *42*, 63)

Hawaii Academy of Science
Lecture: announced (SCI, *102*, 6-7)

Hawaii, University of (Honolulu)
Appointment: Bernreuter, R. G. (J APP, *11*, 404)
Appointment: Pressey, S. L. (J APP, *21*, 241)
Lecture: Goddard, H. H. (SCI, *61*, 564; BULL, *22*, 504)

Hawthorne, Joseph Wyman
Resignation: Washington Univ., St. Louis (BULL, *32*, 324)

Haycraft, John Berry
Research: Royal Society of Edinburgh, voluntary muscular contraction (SCI°, *15*, 245)

Hayes, Joseph Wanton
Promotion: Univ. of Chicago (BULL, *13*, 260; SCI, *43*, 711)

Hayes, Samuel Perkins
Appointment: Mt. Holyoke College (SCI, *23*, 832; BULL, *6*, 256; BULL, *3*, 216; JoP, *3*, 364)

Appointment: Pennsylvania Institute for the Blind (JoP, *14*, 168; BULL, *14*, 32)
Grant: Social Science Research Council (BULL, *34*, 409)
Leave of absence: England (SCI, *35*, 304)
Leave of absence: Mount Holyoke Coll. (JoP, *14*, 168; BULL, *9*, 95; JoP, *9*, 168)
Request replacement psych literature for Mt. Holyoke Coll. (JoP, *15*, 280)

Haynes, Rowland
Appointment: Univ. of Chicago (JoP, *3*, 532; BULL, *3*, 356)
Appointment: Univ. of Minnesota (JoP, *4*, 392; BULL, *4*, 337)
Lecture: psychotherapy (JoP, *7*, 223)

Hays, Mary
Lecture: mental tests (J APP, *6*, 425)

Head, Henry
Death notice (AJP, *54*, 444-446)

Headaches
Research: Bystroff, [?] (SCI°, *8*, 187)

Health and education exhibit
Proposal: South Kensington, 1884 (SCI°, *2*, 839)

Healy, William
Appointment: Committee on Conservation of Child Life (SCI, *46*, 35)
Appointment: Judge Baker Foundation (J APP, *1*, 98; BULL, *14*, 32)
Appointment: Juvenile Court, Boston, MA (J APP, *1*, 98)
Association with *Journal of Delinquency* (JoP, *13*, 392)
Award: Janeway Medal, American Radium Society (SCI, *96*, 57)
Lecture: Janeway, 1942 (SCI, *96*, 57)
Lecture: New York Academy of Science; Salmon Memorial, personality (SCI, *85*, 355)
Resignation: Juvenile Psychopathic Institute, Chicago, Directorship (BULL, *14*, 32)

Hearing theories (*see also* Acoustics; Audition; Sound)
Lecture: Bray, C. W. and Wever, E. G. (AJP, *44*, 192)
Lecture: Kreezer, G. (AJP, *43*, 659)

Hearns, Rudolph S.
Publication: Graphology (J APP, *25*, 357)

Heath, D. C. and Co.
Publication: laboratory course in psychology (REV, *1*, 336)

Heathers, Louise Bussard
Promotion: Smith College (BULL, *42*, 331)

Heaviside, Oliver
Election: American Academy of Arts and Sciences (Sci, *9*, 118)

Hebb, Donald Olding
Editor: *Bulletin of the Canadian Psychological Assoc.* (Bull, *38*, 304)

Hedonism
Publication: Hunt, W. A.; "The meaning of pleasantness and unpleasantness" (AJP, *45*, 345)

Hegge, Thorleif Gruner
Appointment: Univ. of Michigan (Bull, *27*, 496; J App, *14*, 304)
Appointment: Wayne County Training School Director of Research (J App, *14*, 304)

Heidbreder, Edna
Appointment: Wellesley Coll. (Bull, *31*, 380; Sci, *80*, 31)
Lecture: Brown Univ. (Bull, *32*, 323)

Heidelberg (Germany)
Committee formed to erect monument to Helmholtz, H. (Sci, *13*, 475)

Heidelberg College (Tiffin, Ohio)
Retirement: Jones, J. W. L. (Bull, *40*, 723)

Heidelberg, University of (Germany)
Laboratory: opening (Sci*, *19*, 129)
Promotion: Nissl, F. (Sci, *13*, 400)
Retirement: Fisher, K. (JoP, *1*, 28)

Heilbronner, Karl
Death notice (Bull, *11*, 396)

Heilman, Jacob Daniel
Research: spelling and reading (J App, *3*, 195)

Heimann, G.
Death notice (Bull, *12*, 440)

Heinrich, Wladyslaw
Comments by Titchener, E. B. on research on fluctuation of tones (AJP, *11*, 436)

Heinze, Max
Election: Berlin Academy of Sciences (Rev, *7*, 323)

Heiser, Karl Florien
Appointment: Connecticut Public Welfare Council (Bull, *41*, 72; Sci, *98*, 404; Bull, *41*, 267)

Held, Omar Conrad
Appointment: St. Lawrence Univ. (Sci, *102*, 420; Bull, *42*, 792)
Appointment: Univ. of Pittsburgh (J App, *10*, 522)
Called to active duty (Sci, *93*, 565)
Resignation: Univ. of Pittsburgh (Bull, *42*, 792)

Helfrich, Dorothy
Appointment: Goucher College (Bull, *42*, 791)

Hellmer, Leo Aloysius
Appointment: Wichita Child Guidance Center (Bull, *39*, 196)
Leave of absence: Wichita Child Guidance Center (Bull, *40*, 79)

Hellpach, Willy
Appointment: State of Baden; Culture Minister (Bull, *20*, 416)

Helmholtz, Anna von
Death notice (Sci, *10*, 942)

Helmholtz Gold Medal
Award: Hess, C. Von for work on color vision (Bull, *21*, 360)

Helmholtz, Hermann von
Biography prepared by Königsberger, L. (Sci, *15*, 438; Rev, *9*, 328)
Bust erected, Wilhelm's Military Academy, Berlin (Sci, *28*, 392)
Death notice (Sci, *1*, 55; Rev, *1*, 654)
Lecture: Hall, G. S. (JoP, *9*, 56; Sci, *35*, 101)
Library acquired by Physio-Technical Institute (Sci, *1*, 333)
Memorial erected in Berlin (Sci, *1*, 499)
Memorial fund donation (Sci, *1*, 612, 722)
Monument: Heidelberg, committee formed (Sci, *13*, 475)
Publication: revised works (Sci, *2*, 162)
Publication: two volumes of speeches and addresses (Sci, *4*, 481-482)
Unveils statue, Univ. of Berlin (Sci, *9*, 157, 917)

Helson, Harry
Appointment: Bryn Mawr College (Bull, *25*, 444)
Appointment: Univ. of Kansas (J App, *10*, 522)
Lecture: Inter-Society Color Council (Bull, *40*, 459)
Meeting: Eastern Psych. Assoc. (Bull, *36*, 841)
Meeting: Inter-Society Color Council (Bull, *36*, 142)
Publication: "A child's spontaneous reports of imagery" (AJP, *45*, 360)
Reaction to Dr. Wilcox on "The role of form in perception" (AJP, *45*, 171-173)
Reply to Wells, E. F. (AJP, *43*, 691)

Henderson, Ernest Norton
Transfer: Adelphi College (JoP, *6*, 644; Bull, *6*, 427)

Henderson, Herman
Course: Oberlin College, psychology (JoP, 9, 224)

Henmon, Vivian Allen Charles
Appointment: Barnard College, Columbia Univ. (BULL, 3, 248)
Appointment: Univ. of Colorado (JoP, 6, 588)
Appointment: Univ. of Wisconsin (BULL, 7, 148; JoP, 7, 224)
Appointment: Yale Univ. (SCI, 63, 425)
Lecture: Cattell jubilee (AJP, 25, 468)
Lecture: Education Conference, 7th, testing (J APP, 22, 440-441)
Lecture: perception (JoP, 1, 224)
Meeting: APA, Wash.-Balt. Branch, 1940 (BULL, 37, 405)

Henri, Victor
Editor: *Intermédiaire des Biologistes* (AJP, 9, 250)
Research: memory (AJP, 7, 303)
Student: Wundt, W. (AJP, 7, 152)

Henry, Charles
Death notice (BULL, 24, 312)

Henry, Edwin Ruthvan
Course: New York Univ., personnel psychology (SCI, 98, 299)

Henry Holt and Company
Publication: James, W. Talks to Teachers on Psychology (SCI, 12, 349-350)

Henry, Mary Bess
Appointment: Public School System, Santa Ana, CA (J APP, 3, 197)

Henry, Theodore Spafford
Research: classroom problems of gifted children (J APP, 1, 298-299)

Heredity (see also Genetic psychology)
Lecture: Beard, J. (JoP, 1, 420)
Lecture: Goddard, H. H., heredity and mental traits, NY Branch of APA/NYAS (JoP, 9, 167)
Lecture: Jennings, H. S., heredity and personality American Society of Naturalists (SCI, 34, 870)
Lecture: Koenig, W. (AJP, 15, 463)
Lecture: Woodworth, R. S., heredity and environment (SCI, 92, 451)
Meeting: inheritance of acquired characteristics (SCI°, 16, 314)
Publication: Hartog, M. M., inheritance of characteristics (SCI°, 13, 236-237)

Hering, Ewald
Appointment: Univ. of Leipzig (REV, 3, 120)
Death notice (BULL, 15, 97, 176)
Election: Munich Academy of Sciences (SCI, 15, 557)

Election: St. Petersburg Academy of Sciences (BULL, *3*, 83)
Retirement: Univ. of Leipzig (BULL, *12*, 404)

Hering tissue papers
Ordering of (JoP, *2*, 56)

Hermann, Ludimar
Death notice (BULL, *11*, 268)

Herndon, Audell
Appointment: Wichita Child Guidance Center (BULL, *40*, 79)

Heron, William Thomas
Appointment: Univ. of Kansas (BULL, *21*, 240)
Appointment: Univ. of Minnesota (J APP, *10*, 522; BULL, *23*, 455)
Editor: *Psychological Bulletin* (BULL, *21*, 552)

Herrick, Charles Judson
Lecture: APA (JoP, *8*, 699-700)

Herrick, Clarence Luther
C. L. Herrick Memorial Fund announced at Denison Univ. (JoP, *2*, 168)
Death notice (SCI, *20*, 413; BULL, *1*, 413; JoP, *1*, 560)
Editor: *Journal of Comparative Neurology and Psychology* (SCI, *20*, 413; JoP, *1*, 195)
Lecture: Lotze's outline of psychology offered (JoP, *3*, 476)
Memorial fund subscription (BULL, *2*, 160)

Herrmann, Esther
Donation: Scientific Alliance of New York City (SCI, *9*, 188)

Herter, Christian Archibald
Publication: *Popular Science Monthly*, "Hypnotism: What it is, and what it is not" (SCI°, *12*, 131)

Herter, Ernst
Helmholtz statue (SCI, *9*, 157)

Hertz, Henriette Trust
Lecture: Santayana, G. (JoP, *15*, 280)

Hertz, Marguerite Rosenberg
Course: Rorschach method (BULL, *38*, 305)
Course: Western Reserve Univ., Rorschach (J APP, *25*, 266)

Hertzberg, Oscar Edward
Appointment: New York State Teachers College (BULL, *41*, 72; SCI, 72, 315)

Hertzman, Max
    Publication: "Two equations for the study of variability", (AJP, *51*, 571)

Herzen, Alexander
    Research: Vivisection and the senses (SCI°, *8*, 433)

Hess, Carl von
    Award: Helmholtz Gold Medal (BULL, *21*, 360)

Hess, H.
    Appointment: Univ. of Berlin; Director of eye clinic (SCI, *35*, 215)

Heston, Joseph Carter
    Appointment: DePauw Univ. (BULL, *41*, 679-680; BULL, *42*, 128)

Hewitt Lectures
    Appointment. Montague, W. P. (JOP, *9*, 112)

Heyl, Paul R.
    Lecture: Washington Academy of Sciences and Philosophical Society of
        Washington, "Cosmic emotion" (SCI, *95*, 429)

Heymans, Gerardus
    Death notice (BULL, *27*, 415)
    Election: International Congress of Psychology, 8th; President (BULL, *22*, 504)

Hibben, John Grier
    Inauguration: Princeton Univ.; President (JOP, *9*, 112)
    Spending year aboard (REV, *7*, 640)

Hibler, Francis Warren
    Appointment: Stevens, Jordan and Harrison; Management engineers (BULL, *41*,
        498)
    Resignation: Illinois State Normal Univ. (BULL, *41*, 498)

Hickling, Daniel Percy
    Departure: Georgetown Univ. School of Medicine (SCI, *90*, 536)

Hickman, J. E.
    Lecture: New York Branch APA/NYAS, influence of narcotics on children (JOP,
        9, 167)

Hicks, George Dawes
    Appointment: Univ. College, London (JOP, *1*, 280; BULL, *1, 174*)
    Lecture: attention (JOP, *7*, 420)
    Lecture: G. E. Moore on the subject matter of psychology (JOP, *7*, 251)

Hicks, Henry
    Death notice (SCI, *10*, 863)

Hickson, Joseph William Andrew
Appointment: McGill Univ. (BULL, 2, 296)

Hickson, William
Appointment: Court of Domestic Relations of Chicago (BULL, 11, 232)
Appointment: Vineland Training School (SCI, 36, 113)
Departure: Vineland Training School (BULL, 11, 232)

Higgins, H. H.
Fund raiser (SCI°, 7, 370)

Higginson, Glenn Devere
Lecture: movement, visual perception of (AJP, 37, 629)

Highland Hospital for Nervous and Mental Disorders (Asheville, North Carolina)
Connected with department of psychiatry and mental hygiene, Duke Univ. (SCI, 91, 187)
Presented to Duke Univ. by Carroll, R. S. (SCI, 89, 555)

Hildreth, Gertrude Howell
Lecture: Assoc. of Consulting Psychologists (J APP, 21, 241)
Publication: *Bibliography of Mental Tests and Rating Scores* (J APP, 23, 421)

Hilgard, Ernest Ropiequet
Anniversary: Univ. of California, Los Angeles psychology building (BULL, 37, 406)
Appointment: Committee of Intersociety Constitutional Convention; Chair (J APP, 27, 365)
Appointment: Stanford Univ. (SCI, 96, 423; J APP, 17, 341)
Award: Social Science Research Council (BULL, 39, 683)
Award: Warren Medal (BULL, 37, 405; SCI, 91, 334)
Election: AAAS, Section I, personality symposium, chair (J APP, 25, 727)
Grant: National Research Council (BULL, 33, 578)
Leave of absence: Stanford Univ. (BULL, 40, 79)
Lecture: "Experimental psychology" (SCI, 91, 430)
Promotion: Stanford Univ. (BULL, 40, 79)
Publication: "The saving score as a measure of retention" (AJP, 46, 339)
Research: morale, conducted for government (SCI, 96, 423)

Hill, Albert Ross
Appointment: Univ. of Nebraska (REV, 4, 567; SCI, 6, 132; AJP, 9, 135)
Departure: Oshkosh Normal School (AJP, 9, 135; REV, 4, 567)

Hill, David Spence
Appointment: Tulane Univ. (SCI, 34, 714; JoP, 8, 588)
Appointment: Univ. of Tennessee (BULL, 8, 374)
Departure: Peabody College for Teachers, Tennessee (BULL, 8, 374)

Departure: Univ. of Tennessee (Sci, *34*, 714)
Election: Univ. of New Mexico; office (Bull, *16*, 257)
Election: SSPP office (Bull, *13*, 40; Sci, *31*, 22; JoP, *13*, 112; JoP, *8*, 84; JoP, *7*, 56)
Lecture: SSPP, Binet-Buzenet Aesthesiometer (JoP, *7*, 28)

Hill, Frank Ernest

Report: American Youth Commission, "Youth in the CCC" (J App, *26*, 570)

Hill, George E.

Appointment: Macalester College (Bull, *40*, 724)

Hill, Leonard Erskine

Course: Physiological psychology (Rev, *1*, 216)

Hill, Richard E.

Appointment: Assistant to Koffka, K. (Bull, *25*, 123)

Hillebrand, Franz

Appointment: Univ. of Vienna (Rev, *2*, 534)

Hillsdale College (Michigan)

Departure: Ray, W. S. (Bull, *41*, 409)

Hincks, Clarence Meredith

Appointment: National Committee for Mental Hygiene Research; Director (Sci, *72*, 557; Bull, *36*, 711)
Departure: National Committee for Mental Hygiene, Division of Community Clinics (Sci, *89*, 337)
National Committee for Mental Hygiene, 25th anniversary (Sci, *80*, 446)

Hines, Harlin Cameron

Appointment: Univ. of Cincinnati; Director of psychology dept. (J App, *10*, 523)

Hinkle, Beatrice

Lecture: Child Study Assoc. of America (J App, *9*, 319)

Hinman, Edgar Lenderson

Appointment: Univ. of Nebraska (AJP, *7*, 579)
Lecture: introductory courses in philosophy (JoP, *7*, 223)
Promotion: Univ. of Nebraska (Rev, *4*, 567)
Symposium: Spencer, H. (JoP, *1*, 224)

Hinshaw, Robert Patton

Appointment: Kenyon College (Bull, *39*, 895)
Appointment: Pomona College (Bull, *42*, 331)
Departure: Princeton Univ. (Bull, *39*, 895)
Departure: Univ. of Illinois (Bull, *42*, 331)

Hippocrates
Paintings "Apotheosis of Science" (Sci, 93, 324)

Hiscock, Ira V.
Appointment: Yale Univ. (Sci, 101, 242)

Histological psychology
Course: Halliburton, Kings College, London (Sci, 20, 656; JoP, 1, 672)

History
Meeting: Society of Experimental Psychologists, 1904-1938 (AJP, 51, 410)
Publication: Dallenbach, K. and Bergman, G. "Portraits useful to the psychologist" (AJP, 25, 165)
Publication: Kantor, J. R.; "Concerning physical analogies in psychology" (AJP, 48, 153)

History of Medicine, International Congress of the
Meeting, 1938 Yugoslavia (Sci, 87, 164)

History of psychology
Lecture: Miles, W. R. (Sci, 90, 614)
Review: 1887-1889 (AJP, 2, 675)

History of Science, International Congress for the
Meeting: announced (Bull, 5, 31)
So. Kensington, London, 2nd (JoP, 28, 280)

History of science lectures
Ferrero, F., Northwestern Univ. (JoP, 14, 364)

History of University Education in Maryland, The
Publication: Steiner, B. C. (Sci°, 17, 187)

Hitzig, Eduard
Lecture: London Neurological Society, Hughlings Jackson Lecture (Sci, 12, 854, 975-976)
Resignation: Clinic for Nervous Diseases at Halle; Director (Sci, 17, 438)

Hoagland Laboratory (New York)
Appointment: Kemp, G. T. (Sci°, 14, 131, 437)

Hobart and William Smith Colleges (Geneva, New York)
Appointment: Boswell, F. P. (Sci, 28, 922; Bull, 6, 32)
Degree: Stoddard, G. D. (Sci, 96, 578)
Fellowship: Hubbard, M. (Bull, 34, 864)
Lecture: Phi Beta Kappa (Sci, 96, 578)

Hoch, August
Appointment: Bloomington Asylum, White Plains, New York (Bull, 2, 260)

Hocking, William Ernest
Appointment: Yale Univ. (BULL, *4*, 128)
Lecture: Ethics and international relations (JoP, *14*, 698-700)
Lecture: James, W. (JoP, *39*, 84)

Hodgson, Richard
Death notice (SCI, *22*, 886; SCI, *23*, 319; BULL, *3*, 36; JoP, *3*, 56)
Letter: regarding Mrs. Piper, a medium and her use of trances (AJP, *11*, 436-438)
Publication: reply by Sinnett, A. P. of report to Society of Psychical Research (SCI°, *7*, 306)

Hodgson, Shadworth Holloway
Lecture: consciousness (JoP, *4*, 278)
Lecture: Kant (JoP, *2*, 672)

Höber, Rudolf
Editor: *Pflüger's Archiv* (BULL, *17*, 200)

Höffding, Harald
Death notice (BULL, *29*, 91; SCI, *76*, 141; AJP, *44*, 583)
Election: International Congress of Psychology, 10th President (SCI, *70*, 254)
Lecture: International Congress of Arts and Sciences, St. Louis (JoP, *1*, 419)

Höfler, Alois
Election: Philosophical Society, Univ. of Vienna; President (SCI°, *12*, 23)

Hoen, Thomas I.
Appointment: New York Medical College (SCI, *90*, 613)

Hoernlé, Reinhold Friedrich Alfred
Death notice (JoP, *40*, 448)
Election: John Locke Scholarship (JoP, *1*, 56)
Lecture: Aristotelian Society, volition (JoP, *10*, 196)

Hofstadter, Albert
Fellowship: Guggenheim, J. S. Memorial Foundation, "Studies in the history of empiricism" (JoP, *40*, 224)

Hogg, James
Death notice (SCI, *9*, 692)

Hoisington, Louis Benjamin
Appointment: Univ. of Oklahoma; Professor and Dept. Head (BULL, *25*, 700)
Tranfer: Univ. of Oklahoma (SCI, *95*, 322)

Holden, Francis
Promotion: New York Univ. (SCI, *74*, 240)

Holder, Charles Frederick

Publication: "Marvels of animal life" (SCI°, 7, 6)

Holland, Kenneth

Report: American Youth Commission, "Youth in the CCC" (J APP, 26, 570)

Hollands, Edmund Howard

Appointment: Princeton Univ. (JoP, 3, 420)

Hollingworth, Harry Levi

Appointment: Committee on Publications in Applied Psychology (J APP, 2, 196)
Appointment: Univ. of Nebraska (SCI, 27, 680; BULL, 5, 168)
Degree: Univ. of Nebraska, honorary (SCI, 88, 9; BULL, 35, 577)
Editor: *Bulletin*, issue on race and individual psychology (BULL, 9, 408)
Election: APA office (BULL, 14, 32)
Election: APA president (BULL, 24, 80)
Election: National Research Council, Div. of Anthropology and Psychology
    (BULL, 25, 123)
Fellowship: Columbia Univ. in memory of Hollingworth, L. S., established (SCI,
    100, 383; BULL, 42, 63)
Honorary dinner given by Barnard College (SCI, 86, 538)
Lecture: Cattell jubilee (AJP, 25, 468)
Lecture: NYAS/APA, drowsiness (JoP, 7, 700)
Lecture: NYAS/NY Branch of APA meeting, redintegrative mechanisms (JoP,
    15, 140)
Lecture: psychology's relation to medicine and law (BULL, 9, 486)
Lecture: Society of Medical Jurisprudence, psychology and law (JoP, 9, 672)
Promotion: Barnard College (JoP, 11, 336; BULL, 19, 350; SCI, 55, 538; JoP, 19,
    392; SCI, 43, 641; BULL, 11, 232)
Promotion: Columbia Univ. (BULL, 13, 187; JoP, 13, 280)
Publication: reply to Freiberg, Dallenbach and Thorndike (AJP, 42, 457)

Hollingworth, Leta Stetter

Appointment: American Assoc. of Clinical Psychologists; Secretary (SCI, 48,
    598)
Appointment: APA Committee on Certification (SCI 51, 137)
Appointment: Bellevue Hospital (JoP, 13, 476)
Appointment: Teachers College (BULL, 19, 350)
Conference: Education of the Gifted, Teachers College, in memory of (J APP,
    24, 854; BULL, 38, 192)
Death notice (AJP, 53, 299-301; BULL, 37, 187)
Degree: Univ. of Nebraska, honorary (SCI, 88, 9; BULL, 35, 577)
Election: New York State Assoc. of Consulting Psychologists; Executive
    Committee (SCI, 54, 112)
Fellowship: established by Hollingworth, H. L. (BULL, 42, 63; SCI, 100, 383)
Lecture: NYAS, echolalia (JoP, 13, 700)
Photographs: Speyer School, gifted classes (J APP, 21, 605)

Promotion: Teachers College (SCI, *55*, 538; JoP, *19*, 392; BULL, *16*, 258)
Research: Bellevue Hospital psychological lab (BULL, *13*, 376)

Holman, Henry
Lecture: Child Study Society (JoP, *8*, 644)

Holmes, Arthur
Appointment: Pennsylvania State College (BULL, *9*, 208; JoP, *9*, 224; SCI, *35*, 371)
Appointment: Univ. of Pennsylvania (SCI, *56*, 447)
Departure: Univ. of Pennsylvania (BULL, *9*, 208)
Promotion: Univ. of Pennsylvania (BULL, *7*, 364; JoP, *8*, 84)

Holmes, Samuel Jackson
Honorary dinner: American Eugenics Society (SCI, *88*, 494)

Holmgren, Frithiof
Death notice (AJP, *9*, 135)

Holsopple, James Quinter
Appointment: Western Reserve Univ. (JoP, *23*, 420)
Lecture: Assoc. of Consulting Psychologists (J APP, *21*, 241)

Holt, Edwin Bissell
Appointment: Harvard Univ. (REV, *8*, 656-657; BULL, *2*, 224; SCI, *14*, 424; SCI, *21*, 840)
Leave of absence: Harvard Univ. (BULL, *8*, 374; SCI, *34*, 435)
Lecture: Conference on Methods in Philosophy and the Sciences (JoP, *35*, 196; SCI, *87*, 277)
Lecture: New School for Social Research (SCI, *64*, 446)
Lecture: New School for Social Research, psychology of response (BULL, *24*, 204)
Lecture: Princeton Univ., social psychology (J APP, *11*, 405)
Promotion: Harvard Univ. (JoP, *2*, 336)
Resignation: Harvard Univ. (SCI, *47*, 267; BULL, *15*, 98; JoP, *15*, 392)

Holway, Alfred Harold
Publication: "Normal equations and the phi-hypothesis" (AJP, *47*, 337)

Homeostasis
Lecture: Richter, C. P., Harvey Society (SCI, *96*, 445)

Hood, Frazer
Death notice (BULL, *41*, 602)

Hook, Sidney
Award: Nicholas Murray Butler Award (JoP, *42*, 224)

Hoopingarner, Dwight Lowell
Appointment: Carnegie Institute of Technology, Bureau of Salesmanship
Research (Sci, *44*, 56; JoP, *13*, 476; Bull, *13*, 296)

Hoopingarner, Newman Leander
Promotion: New York Univ. (Bull, *28*, 645; Sci, *74*, 240)

Hopkins, C. L.
Lecture: Biological Society, sense of smell in buzzards (Sci°, *10*, 319)

Hopkins House of Commons
Revived (Sci°, *17*, 242)

Hopkins, John
Member: Belgian Scholarship Committee (JoP, *13*, 167)

Hopkins, Mark
Williams College (JoP, *33*, 644)

Hoover, Herbert
American Philosophical Society (Sci, *69*, 66)
First International Congress on Mental Hygiene (Sci, *70*, 32)

Horace Mann-Lincoln Institute
Appointment: Super, D. E. (Bull, *42*, 486)

Horne, Herman Harrel
Leave of absence: Dartmouth College (JoP, *3*, 336)
Appointment: Dartmouth College (Rev, *6*, 456)

Horney, Karen
Appointment: Assoc. for the Advancement of Psychoanalysis; Dean (J App, *25*, 473)
Psychological Supper Club (Bull, *37*, 656)

Horse and Rider Puzzle
Demonstration of insight (AJP, *54*, 437-438)

Horsley, John, Memorial Prize
Award: Watts, J. W., "Psychosurgery" (Sci, *96*, 36)

Horsley, Victor Alexander Harden
Death notice (Bull, *13*, 296)

Horst, Paul
Lecture: suppressor variables (AJP, *58*, 550-554)
Publication: "The prediction of personal adjustment" (Bull, *39*, 132)

Horton, George Plant
Appointment: Univ. of Washington (BULL, *32*, 324)

Horton, Lydiard Heneage Walter
Death notice (BULL, *42*, 255)

Hoskins, Roy Graham
Appointment: Salmon Memorial Lecturer (SCI, *101*, 243)
Lecture: Academy of Medicine, New York City, "The biology of schizophrenia" (SCI, *102*, 397; SCI, *101*, 243)
Lecture: Laity lecture, mental diseases (SCI, *89*, 175)

Hough, Williston Samuel
Appointment: George Washington Univ. (SCI, 27, 840; JoP, 5, 280, 335; BULL, 2, 296; BULL, 5, 168; SCI, 22, 256)
Death notice (JoP, 9, 588)
Publication: *Logic* (SCI, *23*, 96)

Houghton College (New York)
Promotion: Ashton, P. F. (BULL, *41*, 267)

Houghton, Mifflin and Company
Publication: Cushman, H. E., book (JoP, 7, 560)
Publication: Rand, B., The classical psychologists (JoP, 9, 56)

Hovey, Edmund Otis
Election: NYAS officer (JoP, 9, 28)

Hovland, Carl Iver
Appointment: Yale Univ. (SCI, *94*, 62; BULL, *38*, 907)

Howard Association
Publication: Books on crime and punishment (SCI°, *12*, 36)

Howard, Charles W.
Appointment: Lewis and Clark College (BULL, *42*, 128)
Departure: Whitman College (BULL, *42*, 128)

Howard College
Appointment: Jones, J. H. (BULL, *42*, 792)

Howell, Annette
Test for the employment of proofreaders (J APP, *1*, 298)

Howison, George Holmes
Appointment: Univ. of California (BULL, *6*, 328)
Travels abroad (SCI, *10*, 341; REV, *6*, 456)

Howitt, Alfred William
Publication: Transactions of the Royal Society of Victoria, organization of Australian tribes (Sci°, *16*, 91)

Hrdlicka, Aleš
Lecture: brains (JoP, *3*, 476)

Hsiao, Hsiao Hung
Request for new psychological literature, National Central Univ., Chungking, China (Bull, *37*, 827; Sci, *92*, 308)

Huang, I.
Death notice (Bull, *41*, 807)

Hubbard, Margaret R.
Appointment: Hobart College (Bull, *34*, 864)

Hubbard, Ruth Marilla
Lecture: Clinical Psychology Group of the National Conference of Social Work (J App, *22*, 215)

Huber, Kurt
Death notice (Bull, *40*, 794)

Hudson, Jay William
Lecture: philosophy of history (JoP, *7*, 223)

Hübbe-Schleiden, T. U.
Editor: *Sphinx* (Sci°, *7*, 139-140)

Huey, Edmund Burke
Appointment: Illinois State Institution for the Feeble-minded (Bull, *6*, 427)
Appointment: Johns Hopkins Univ. (JoP, *8*, 721; Sci, *34*, 759; Bull, *9*, 95; Bull, *8*, 182)
Appointment: Lincoln State School, Illinois; Director (Sci, *30*, 557)
Appointment: Western Univ. of Pennsylvania (Bull, *1*, 452; JoP, *1*, 616)
Death notice (Sci, *39*, 137; AJP, *25*, 319; Bull, *11*, 80)
Leave of absence: Univ. of Pittsburgh (Sci, *28*, 483; Bull, *5*, 380)
Lecture: Johns Hopkins Univ. (Sci, *34*, 759)
Resignation: Illinois State Institute for the Feeble-minded (Bull, *8*, 192; Sci, *33*, 607)

Hughes, D. E.
Death notice (Sci, *11*, 399)

Hughes, Percy
Appointment: Lehigh Univ. (Bull, *4*, 337)
Promotion: Lehigh Univ. (JoP, *6*, 392; Bull, *6*, 256; JoP, *28*, 700)

Hulin, Wilbur Schofield
Publication: "Eye-movements and the phi-phenomenon" (AJP, *46*, 334)

Hull, Clark Leonard
Award: Warren, H. C. Medal (BULL, *42*, 406; SCI, *101*, 402)
Correlation Service established with his newly invented correlation machine
(J APP, *10*, 523)
Editor: *Psychosomatic Medicine* (J APP, *22*, 663)
Election: APA President (SCI, *82*, 247)
Election: NAS member (SCI, *83*, 430; BULL, *33*, 578)
Lecture: Critique APA address by Martin, M. F. (AJP, *49*, 310)
Lecture: International Congress for the Unity of Science (JoP, *38*, 504)
Lecture: MPA (SCI, *87*, 434-435)

Human Betterment Foundation (*see also* Eugenics)
California sterilization program (J APP, *23*, 745)
Publication: Gosney, E. S.; "Effects of eugenic sterilization as practiced in
California" (J APP, *21*, 476)

Human Heredity Committee, International
Bureau of Human Heredity (BULL, *34*, 637)

Human nature
Lecture: Cohen, M. R., human history (JoP, *42*, 251)
Lecture: Jastrow, J., Ohio State Univ. (SCI, *45*, 407; JoP, *14*, 364)
Lecture: Koffka, K., human behavior (SCI, *91*, 499-500)
Lecture: Lovejoy, A. O. (JoP, *39*, 139)

Humanism
Lecture: Jebb, R. C., Oxford, Romanes Lecture, humanism and education (SCI,
9, 461)
Publication: MacKenzie, J. S. (JoP, *4*, 308)

Humboldt Library
Receipt of series and contents (SCI°, *15*, 273)

Hume, David
Lecture: on by Jackson, A. C. (JoP, *42*, 56)
Lecture: on by Montague, W. P. (JoP, *1*, 224)

Hume, James Gibson
Appointment: Univ. of Toronto (SCI°, *14*, 437)

Humm, Doncaster George
Degree: Bucknell Univ. (BULL, *42*, 582)
Lecture: Southern California Junior College Assoc., Psychology-Philosophy
Section (J APP, *26*, 712)

Publication: criticism of statistical procedure by Johnson, H. M. (AJP, *56*, 111-116)

Publication: product-moment correlations (AJP, *55*, 127-130)

Publication: reply to Johnson's criticisms (AJP, *56*, 116-118)

Humm-Wadsworth Temperament Scale
Recognition of Humm, D. G. by Bucknell Univ. (BULL, *42*, 582)

Humphreys, Herbert Haynes
Appointment: Univ. of Kentucky (BULL *42*, 582)

Departure: Michigan State College (BULL, *42*, 582)

Humphreys, Lloyd Girton
Appointment: Northwestern Univ. (SCI, *90*, 391)

Appointment: Yale Univ., National Research Fellow (SCI, *90*, 391)

Humpstone, Henry Judson
Appointment: Univ. of North Dakota (BULL, *17*, 351)

Hun, Henry
Research: cerebral localization (SCI°, *9*, 133)

Hunt, Thelma
APA, Wash.-Balt. Branch, 3rd meeting (BULL, *36*, 500)

Promotion: George Washington Univ. (BULL, *41*, 603)

Hunt, William Alvin
Appointment: Northwestern Univ. (BULL, *42*, 792)

Chair: bimonthly meeting, 12 American and 12 foreign psychologists (BULL, *38*, 191)

Grant: National Research Council (BULL, *33*, 578)

New York State Psychiatric Institute and Hospital (BULL, *34*, 498)

Organized International Seminar in Psychology (BULL, *38*, 191)

Publication: "Ambiguity of descriptive terms for feeling and emotion" (AJP, *47*, 166)

Publication: "Systematic differences in introspection" (AJP, *46*, 660)

Publication: "The meaning of pleasantness and unpleasantness" (AJP, *45*, 345)

Publication: "The reality of bright and dull pressure" (AJP, *46*, 336)

Hunter, Walter Samuel
Appointment: Brown Univ. (BULL, *33*, 406; SCI, *83*, 367)

Appointment: Clark Univ, G. S. Hall chair in genetic psychology (J APP, *9*, 90; BULL, *22*, 260; SCI, *61*, 259)

Appointment: Univ. of Kansas (BULL, *13*, 296, 376; SCI, *44*, 132; JOP, *13*, 504)

Appointment: Univ. of Texas (SCI, *37*, 57; BULL, *10*, 39; JOP, *10*, 84)

Departure: Univ. of Chicago (JOP, *10*, 84)

Editor: *Bulletin* issues (BULL, *12*, 364; BULL, *13*, 376; BULL, *14*, 332; BULL, *15*, 324; BULL, *16*, 221)

Election: APA council (AJP, *32*, 157)
Election: EPA President (Sci, *91*, 402)
Election: NAS (Bull, *32*, 524)
Election: NRC Committee on Aging; member (Bull, *42*, 332)
Election: NRC, Emergency Committee in Psychology (Bull, *37*, 755)
Election: SEP Chair (Bull, *33*, 476; AJP, *47*, 344)
Lecture: APA Presidential (Sci, *74*, 170)
Lecture: EPA, "Professional training of psychologists" (Sci, *93*, 373)
Lecture: National Research Council Conference, "Psychological factors in national morale" (Bull, *37*, 829)
Promotion: Univ. of Texas (Bull, *11*, 396)
Resignation: *Psychological Bulletin*, cooperating editor (Bull, *21*, 552)
Resignation: Univ. of Kansas (Bull, *22*, 260)
Tour of Europe (Sci, *64*, 423)

Huntington, C. E.
Lecture: color vision (AJP, *44*, 185)

Huntington College (Indiana)
Appointment: Aleck, A. W. (Bull, *42*, 791)

Huntington, Thomas W.
Lecture: Nazi civil propaganda (J App, *24*, 520)
Publication: Psychological aspects of war and social aggression (Bull, *38*, 248)

Huntley, Charles William
Appointment: Adelbert College, Western Reserve Univ. (Sci, *94*, 512; Sci, *93*, 615)
Appointment: Mather College (Sci, *93*, 615)
Promotion: Adelbert College Western Reserve Univ.; Dean (Bull, *38*, 777)

Hurd, Henry M.
Appointment: Johns Hopkins Hospital (Sci°, *14*, 58)
Appointment: Johns Hopkins Univ. (Sci°, *14*, 351)
Appointment: Maryland State Lunacy Commission (Sci, *28*, 301)
Birthday celebration (Sci, *57*, 635; Sci, *59*, 481; Sci, *61*, 512)
Leave of absence: Johns Hopkins Medical School (Sci, *24*, 542)
Portrait presented by Johns Hopkins Medical School staff (Sci, *24*, 671)

Husband, Richard Wellington
Appointment: Carnegie-Illinois Steel Corporation (Sci, *96*, 225; Bull, *39*, 807; J App, *26*, 712)
Appointment: Pennsylvania State College (Bull, *38*, 304; Sci, *93*, 301)
Appointment: Univ. of Illinois (J App, *13*, 415)
Conference: Psychology of learning, Univ. of Colorado (Bull, *36*, 583)
Departure: Pennsylvania State College (Bull, *39*, 807)
Leave of absence: Univ. of Wisconsin (Bull, *38*, 304)

Hutcheson, Francis
Memorial: in honor at Glasgow Univ. (JoP, 3, 56)

Hutchinson, Eliot Dole
Fellowship: Board of National Research Fellowships (BULL, 23, 292)

Hutten, Ernest
Lecture: perception and propositions (JoP, 39, 55-56)

Hutton, Laurence (Mrs.)
Publication: letter from Keller, H. (REV, 6, 238)

Huxley, Julian Sorell
Election: Institute for the Study of Animal Behavior; President (BULL, 33, 580)
Lecture: Switzerland (SCI, 102, 350)

Huxley Lecture
Bartlett, F. C., Royal Anthropological Institute (SCI, 98, 512)
Galton, F. (SCI, 14, 701)
Pavlov, I. P., Charing-cross Medical School (SCI, 24, 381)

Huxley, Thomas Henry
Death notice (REV, 2, 534)
Election: American Academy of Arts and Sciences, foreign honorary member
(SCI°, 1, 237)
Publication: reply of H. Wace's criticism of "Agnosticism" (SCI°, 13, 299)

Huxley's epiphenomenalism
Lecture: McGilvary, E. B. (JoP, 7, 223)

Hyde, William DeWitt
Publication: announcement (JoP, 8, 560)

Hydrophobia
Research: progress of Pasteur's work (SCI°, 4, 122)

Hygiene (see also Mental hygiene)
Appointment: Abbott, A. C., Hygienic Institute, PA (SCI°, 17, 339)
Appointment: Koch, R., Hygienic Institute (SCI°, 4, 410)
Founded: Posen, Prussia, Hygienic Institute (SCI, 9, 341)
Koch, R. opens Museum of Hygiene (SCI°, 8, 513)
Lecture: Billings, J. S. at Johns Hopkins Univ., science of hygiene (SCI°, 5, 101)
Lecture: Cincinnati Society of Natural History, hygiene and physiology (SCI°,
6, 359)
Meeting: The Hague (SCI°, 4, 74)
Ostend, Belgium (SCI°, 12, 9)
Paris, Palace of Industry, hygiene exhibition (SCI°, 12, 9)
Penn College establishes professorship of hygiene by Graff, P. (SCI°, 14, 333)

Report: Riche, A., Council of Hygiene (Scı°, 5, 412
Univ. of Berlin, hygienic laboratory (Scı°, 5, 204; Scı°, 6, 360)

Hylan, John Perham
Appointment: Univ. of Illinois (AJP, 9, 135; Scı, 6, 257; Rev, 4, 567)

Hypertension
Lecture: Page, I. H., Janeway, E. G. Lecture (Scı, 93, 37-38)
Grant: Beaumont, L. D. to Goldblatt, H. (Scı, 93, 37)

Hypnotism
Exhibitions forbidden (Scı°, 14, 235)
Hypnotic story (Scı°, 6, 451)
Lecture: Janet, P. (JoP, 1, 616)
Lecture: Seppilli, G. (Scı°, 5, 303)
Lecture: Tamburini, A. (Scı°, 5, 303)
Publication: Frankel, Tamburini and Seppilli, German translation of (Scı°, 5, 303)
Publication: Herter, C. A. *Popular Science Monthly* (Scı°, 12, 131)
Publication: released, 4th edition (Rev, 5, 110)
Publication: vanLoon, F.G.H. and Thouless, R. H. (AJP, 38, 315)
Research: Croffut, W. A. and Colman, N. J. (Scı°, 12, 309)
Research: Kaan, H. (Scı°, 6, 280)
Resolutions adopted by the International Congress on Hypnotism (Scı°, 14, 216)

Hypnotism, International Congress on
Adoption of resolutions (Scı°, 14, 216)
Held: Paris, Aug 12-16, 1900 (Scı, 10, 542; Scı, 1, 755)

Hyslop, James Hervey
Appointment: Columbia College (Rev, 2, 534)
Appointment: Society for Psychical Research; Secretary (Scı, 23, 158)
Death notice (Bull, 17, 279)
Fellowship: American Society for Psychical Research, in memory of (Bull, 39, 71)
Offer: secretaryship of American Branch of the Society of Psychical Research (JoP, 3, 84)
Publication: Borderland of psychical research (JoP, 3, 588)
Publication: critique of critique of Jastrow (JoP, 5, 250)
Publication: Death of Hodgson, R. (Scı, 23, 319)
Resignation: Columbia Univ. (Scı, 16, 920)

Hyslop-Prince Fellowship
Award: Taves, E. (Bull, 39, 423)

Hysteria

Course: Janet, P., Harvard Univ. (Sci, *23*, 959)
Lecture: Janet, P., Harvard Medical School (JoP, *3*, 644)
Publication: Bianchi, L. (AJP, *1*, 202)
Publication: Janet, P. (Bull, *4*, 236)
Research: (Sci°, *18*, 256)
Research: report of (AJP, *1*, 204)

I

Ibison, Richard Arthur
Internship: Wichita Child Guidance Center (BULL, *40*, 310)

Idaho, University of (Moscow)
Appointment: Barton, J. W. (BULL, *19*, 171)
Appointment: Lindley, E. H. (J APP, *3*, 290; BULL, *16*, 257)
Appointment: Lindley, E. H. (JoP, *14*, 644)
Appointment: Reed, H. B. (JoP, *12*, 532)
Election: Lindley, E. H., president (BULL, *14*, 264)
Promotion: Barton, J. W. (SCI, *55*, 262)

Illinois Association for Applied Psychology
Name changed from Illinois Society of Consulting Psychologists (BULL, *40*, 230)
Officers listed (BULL, *42*, 584)
Sponsors law to provide education for educable mentally handicapped children
  (BULL, *42* 407)

Illinois College (Jacksonville)
Degree: Angell, J. R. (SCI, *70*, 375)

Illinois Committee on Social Legislation
Appointment: Tufts, J. H., chair (JoP, *10*, 112)

Illinois Eastern Hospital Bulletin
Publication begun (AJP, 9, 135)

Illinois Eastern Hospital for the Insane
Appointment: Krohn, W. O. (REV, *4*, 689; AJP, 9, 135)
Laboratory: experimental psychology opens (REV, *4*, 689)

Illinois Institute of Technology (Chicago)
Appointment: Speer, G. S. (BULL, *42*, 793)

Illinois Normal School (Eastern)
Departure: Kaufman, L. D. (JoP, 9, 532)

Illinois Normal University (Southern), Bureau of Child Guidance
Appointment: Parry, D. (BULL, 40, 310, 723)

Illinois Psychiatric Society
Lecture: Gillespie, R. D. (SCI, 94, 323)

Illinois Psychopathic Institute
Director position open (BULL, 11, 483)
Former patients (BULL, 37, 329)

Illinois Society of Consulting Psychologists
Election: officers, 1938-39 (SCI, 88, 53; BULL, 35, 578)
Name changed to Illinois Assoc. for Applied Psychologists (BULL, 40, 230)

Illinois State Civil Service Commission
Psychologist position at Lincoln State School and Colony (BULL, 12, 160)

Illinois State Institution for the Feeble-minded
Appointment: Huey, E. B. (BULL, 6, 427)
Resignation: Huey, E. B. (BULL, 8, 182)

Illinois State Normal University (Normal)
Appointment: Dillinger, C. M. (BULL, 41, 807)
Resignation: Hibler, F. W. (BULL, 41, 498)

Illinois, University of (Champaign-Urbana)
Appointment: Adler, H. M. (BULL, 16, 392)
Appointment: Anderson, L. (SCI, 30, 709; BULL, 6, 427)
Appointment: Baird, J. W. (SCI, 23, 864; BULL, 3, 184)
Appointment: Bentley, M. (BULL, 9, 407; SCI, 36, 401; JoP, 9, 588)
Appointment: Buckingham, B. R. (J APP, 3, 196-197)
Appointment: Campbell, C. M., Gehrmann Lecturer, abnormal psychology, medical school (SCI, 75, 262)
Appointment: Cattell, R. B. (SCI, 102, 299; BULL, 42, 793-794)
Appointment: Clark, H. (SCI, 40, 670; JoP, 11, 721)
Appointment: Coffman, L. D. (JoP, 9, 588)
Appointment: Colvin, S. S. (SCI, 14, 232; REV, 8, 552)
Appointment: DeCamp, J. E. (JoP, 11, 721; SCI, 40, 670)
Appointment: Dexter, E. G. (REV, 7, 216; BULL, 2, 360)
Appointment: Drake, D. (JoP, 8, 532)
Appointment: Fischer, R. P. (BULL, 40, 794)
Appointment: Gerty, F. J., medical school (SCI, 93, 565)
Appointment: Gibbs, F. A. and Mrs. Gibbs, F. A. (SCI, 99, 530)
Appointment: Husband, R. W. (J APP, 13, 415)

Lecture: Whipple, G. M. (BULL, 9, 360; SCI, 36, 211)
Lecture: Wilhelm, K. (JoP, 10, 252)
Meeting: Midwestern Psych. Assoc., 12th (BULL, 34, 121)
Personnel Bureau available to Illinois veterans (BULL, 41, 680)
Promotion: Baird, J. W. (JoP, 4, 448; BULL, 4, 236)
Promotion: Colvin, S. S. (JoP, 4, 448; BULL, 4, 236)
Promotion: Cowles, J. T. (BULL, 42, 793-794)
Promotion: Harrell, T. W. (BULL, 42, 793-794)
Promotion: McCulloch, W. S. (SCI, 102, 300)
Promotion: McQuitty, L. L. (BULL, 42, 793-794)
Promotion: Pennington, L. A. (BULL, 42, 793-794)
Promotion: Whipple, G. M. (BULL, 12, 440)
Psychology dept. new building (JoP, 4, 448)
Research: assistantship available (BULL, 42, 487)
Research: asst. in psychology position open (BULL, 40, 460)
Resignation: Esper, E. (BULL, 24, 508)
Resignation: Whipple, G. M. (J APP, 2, 196; BULL, 15, 176)
Retirement: Davis, H. I. (SCI, 80, 114)
Return: Pennington, L. A. (BULL, 42, 682)

Illinois (Western) State Teachers College (Macomb)
Appointment: Clayton, A. S. (BULL, 42, 675)

Illinois Woman's College
Appointment: Weber, P. H. (JoP, 17, 588)

Illuminating Engineering Society
Lecture: Ferree, C. E. (BULL, 11, 80)

Illusions (see also Optical illusions)
Lecture: Gault, R. H., size-weight (JoP, 7, 28)
Lecture: Steele, W. M. (JoP, 2, 56)
Lecture: Wells, E. F. (AJP, 43, 136)
Publication: English, H. B., personalistic act psychology (AJP, 57, 563-565)
Publication: Guilford, J. P., illusory movement (AJP, 41, 686)

Imageless thought
Lecture: Angell, J. R., Columbia Univ. (SCI, 33, 214)

Imagery (see also Eidetic imagery)
Lecture: Dallenbach, K. M. (AJP, 38, 667)

Imago
Editor: Freud, S. (BULL, 9, 208; JoP, 9, 335)
Publication: begun in Vienna (BULL, 9, 208)

Immortality
Lecture: Johnson, T. M. (JoP, 1, 224)

Imperial University (Tokyo, Japan)
Lecture: Dewey, J., philosophical reconstruction (JoP, *16*, 357-364)

India (*see also* Indian)
Expedition: Rivers, W. H. R. (SCI, *15*, 675)

India Institute of Applied Psychology
Interested in psychology materials (BULL, *42*, 487)

Indian Journal of Psychology
Publication notice (AJP, *38*, 156)

Indian psychology
Research: Univ. of Denver (SCI, *59*, 438)

Indian Science Congress
Election: Atreya, B. L., president of Psych. and Educ. Section (SCI, *96*, 12)

Indiana Academy of Science
Call for papers on war (BULL, *40*, 620)
Election: Kerr, W. A. (BULL, *40*, 152)
Election: officers, 1890 (SCI°, *14*, 436-437)
Lecture: Jordan, D. S., on Darwin (SCI°, *7*, 480)
List of papers to be read (SCI°, *14*, 436-437)
Meeting: 1st (SCI°, *7*, 435)
Meeting (SCI°, *8*, 387; SCI°, *11*, 205; SCI°, *13*, 338)

Indiana, Governor of
Research: commissioned, mental deficiency (BULL, *12*, 404)

Indiana Institution for the Deaf and Dumb (Indianapolis)
Object-teaching to deaf-mutes (SCI°, *5*, 304)

Indiana Society of Natural History
List of papers, 1887 (SCI°, *9*, 315)

Indiana State Normal School (Indiana, Pennsylvania)
Appointment: Skinner, C. E. (BULL, *17*, 200)

Indiana State Teachers Association
List of papers read, Dec. 1886, Indianapolis (SCI°, *9*, 52-53)

Indiana University (Bloomington)
Appointment: Beier, D. C. (BULL, *42*, 791)
Appointment: Bergstram, J. A. (REV, *2*, 432)
Appointment: Book, W. F. (BULL, *9*, 407-408; JoP, *9*, 588)
Appointment: Boyd, Jr., D. A., medical school (SCI, *90*, 369)
Appointment: Bryan, W. L., president (SCI, *16*, 40, 80)
Appointment: Childs, H. G. (BULL, *11*, 116; JoP, *11*, 84)

Appointment: Conklin, E. S. (SCI, *80*, 475)
Appointment: Fite, W. (SCI, *24*, 384; BULL, *3*, 288, 319)
Appointment: Jackson, T. A. (BULL, *40*, 152)
Appointment: Kitson, H. D. (SCI, *50*, 161; J APP, *3*, 290)
Appointment: Leuba, C., guest professor (BULL, *38*, 248)
Appointment: Louttit, C. M. (J APP, *15*, 324)
Appointment: Nowlis, V. (BULL, *41*, 603; SCI, *100*, 96-97)
Appointment: Roff, M. (BULL, *32*, 323; J APP, *19*, 105)
Appointment: Skinner, B. F. (BULL, *42*, 191)
Appointment: Todd, J. W. (BULL, *13*, 148)
Appointment: Young, H. (BULL, *19*, 462)
Clinical services for children (J APP, *22*, 106)
Course: Pyle, W. H., educational psych. (JoP, *14*, 140)
Departure: Jessup, W. A. (BULL, *9*, 408; JoP, *9*, 588)
Departure: Kitson, H. D. (J APP, *9*, 204)
Installation: Bryan, W. L., president (SCI, *17*, 160)
Laboratory, 50th anniversary commemoration (J APP, *23*, 630)
Leave of absence: Bergstram, J. A. (SCI, *13*, 598)
Leave of absence: Haggerty, M. E. (JoP, *12*, 644)
Lecture: Beach, F. A., neural and hormonal factors involved in reproductive
    behavior (SCI, *99*, 168)
Lecture: Cattell, J. McK. (BULL, *9*, 96; JoP, *9*, 112; SCI, *35*, 178)
Lecture: Jastrow, J. (BULL, *13*, 188; JoP, *13*, 280)
Lecture: Newman, H. H., use of twins in heredity vs. environment (SCI, *94*, 136)
Lecture: Perry, R. B., Mahlon Powell Foundation (JoP, *34*, 84)
Lecture: Powell, ?, philosophy (JoP, *33*, 224)
Lecture: Titchener, E. B. (BULL, *8*, 110; SCI, *33*, 420)
Promotion: Haggerty, M. E. (BULL, *9*, 280; SCI, *35*, 984; JoP, *9*, 448)
Psychology dept. separates from philosophy dept. (JoP, *26*, 308)
Publication: Kellogg, W. N., the Indiana conditioning laboratory (AJP, *51*, 174)
Research: Kinsey, A. C., sex (BULL, *41*, 603; SCI, *100*, 96-97)
Research: Snoddy, G. S., forgetting (J APP, *23*, 530)
Retirement: Book, W. F. (SCI, *80*, 475)
Retirement: Cottingham, C. E., medical school (SCI, *91*, 616)
Return: Book, W. F. from world tour (SCI, *67*, 578)
Return: Roff, M. (BULL, *42*, 582)
Symposium: apparatus exhibition, learning, 1939 (BULL, *37*, 61)
Symposium: Bryan, W. L., learning (BULL, *37*, 61)
Symposium: Culler, E. K., learning (BULL, *37*, 61)
Symposium: Kellogg, W. N., learning (BULL, *37*, 61)
Symposium: McGeoch, J. A., learning (BULL, *37*, 61)

Individual differences

Lecture: Bingham, W., British Psychological Society (SCI, *66*, 537)
Lecture: Thorndike, E. L., Univ. of Illinois (SCI, *31*, 575)
Publication: Fernberger, S. (AJP, *42*, 646)

Appointment: Miles, ?, British Inst. of Industrial Psych. (Sci, 72, 598)
Appointment: Ruckmick, C. A., C. H. Stoelting Co. (Bull, 37, 122)
Appointment: Solomon, R. S., Personnel Institute, director (Bull, 36, 712)
Conference: Univ. of Kentucky (Bull, 41, 199-200, 499)
Course: industrial statistics Massachusetts Institute of Technology (Sci, 94, 136)
Course: National Institute of Industrial Psychology, Great Britain (J App, 23, 312)
Grant: British National Institute of Industrial Psych. Rockefeller grant (Sci, 71, 504)
Election: D'Abernon, ?, National Institute of Industrial Psych., president (Sci, 72, 498)
Election: Viteles, M. S., Personnel Research Council (Sci, 77, 256)
Lecture: Bingham, W. V., MIT (Sci, 75, 355)
Lecture: Gilbreth, L. M., Taylor Society (J App, 9, 428)
Lecture: Münsterberg, H. (Sci, 29, 23)
Lecture: Taylor Society (JoP, 21, 700)
Meeting: Berlin (Sci, 57, 51)
Organization: Assoc. for Advancement of Science in Marketing, officers (Sci, 74, 336)
Organization: British National Institute of Industrial Psychology (Sci, 69, 449; Sci, 50, 110)
Organization: Industrial Conference, Personnel Research Federation (Sci, 69, 492)
Organization: International Conference of Industrial Psych. (Sci, 72, 599; Sci, 79, 521)
Organization: International Management Congress (Bull, 35, 797)
Organization: National Research Council, Committee on Selection and Training of Aircraft Pilots (Bull, 37, 827)
Organization: Research Lab and Registration Bureau, Personnel, Belgium (Sci, 70, 190)
Promotion: Hoopingarner, N.L., New York Univ., Professor of business (Sci, 74, 240)
Publication: Chambers, E., psychology in the industrial life of a nation (JoP, 34, 644)
Publication: clerical employees (J App, 26, 714)
Publication: Kornhauser, A. W. and Lazarsfeld, P., the techniques of market research from the standpoint of a psychologist, American Management Assoc. (Sci, 81, 589)
Publication: Lukens, S. J., the selection and development of foremen (J App, 22, 540)
Publication: SPSSI, *The Psychology of Industrial Conflict* (Bull, 35, 61)
Publication: Uhrbrock, R. S., a psychologist looks at wage incentives, American Management Assoc. (Sci, 81, 589)
Research: British farms (Sci, 66, 168)
Research: industrial fatigue (Sci, 69, 423)
Research: White, J. G., personal data blank (J App, 22,318)

Seminar: National Institute of Industrial Psychology, Exeter College, Oxford, 1936 (Sci, *83*, 301)
Symposium: AAAS (J App, *16*, 334)

Infancy, psychology of
Lecture: Gesell, A., Clark Univ. (J App, *9*, 88)

Infant Mortality and the environment
Publication: French, J. M., *Popular Science Monthly* (Sci°, *12*, 237)

Infantry Journal
Publication: National Research Council (J App, *27*, 475)

Ingenieros, José
Death notice (Sci, *62*, 540)

Inheritance (*see* Heredity)

Insanity
Congress on care of insane (Sci, *16*, 358, 479)
Exhibit: mental hygiene (Sci, *37*, 330)
Law prohibiting marriage, Minnesota Senate (Sci, *13*, 600)
Lecture: Chase, R. H. (AJP, *2*, 190)
Lecture: McLane, A., Academy of Medicine, New York, legal regulations governing the insane (Sci, *25*, 398)
Lecture: Tuke, H. (AJP, *1*, 361)
Publication: Butler, J. S., the curability of insanity and the individualized treatment of the insane (Sci°, *9*, 482)
Publication: *New York Medical Journal* (JoP, *4*, 503)
Publication: Tuke, H., care of lunatics (AJP, *1*, 200)
Research: Dutch East Indies natives (JoP, *1*, 112)
Research: *Journal of Mental Science* statistics (Sci, *4*, 113)
Research: Kraepolin, E. (Bull, *1*, 173)
Research: physiological conditions (JoP, *1*, 196)
Treatment: New York (AJP, *3*, 291)

Insight
Demonstration: Horse-and-rider puzzle (AJP, *54*, 437-438)
Lecture: Ogden, R. M. (AJP, *44*, 350)

Inskip, Thomas
Opened Burden Neurological Institute (Sci, *89*, 242)

Instinct
Lecture: Darwin, C., Linneaen Society (Sci°, *2*, 782)
Lecture: Dennis, W., Sigma Xi (Sci, *79*, 180)
Lecture: Hartman, C. G., Iowa State College (Sci, *97*, 114)

Lecture: Lashley, K. S., Eastern Branch of APA (Sci, 87, 297)
Lecture: Loeb, J. (Bull, 4, 370)

Instinct and intelligence
Lecture: Carr, H. A. (JoP, 7, 280; JoP, 7, 420)
Lecture: Marshall, H. R., APA (Sci, 34, 680)
Lecture: McDougall, W. (JoP, 7, 420)
Lecture: Morgan, C. L. (JoP, 7, 420)
Lecture: Myers, C. S. (JoP, 7, 420)
Lecture: Stout, G. F. (JoP, 7, 420)

Institut de Psychologie Appliquée et de Recherches Psychologiques Collectives
Establishment: Berlin (JoP, 3, 721)

Institute Esser de Chirurgie
Purpose: for aiding the gravely crippled, afflicted with an inferiority complex (Bull, 38, 907)

Institute for Mental Hygiene (see Mental Hygiene, Institute for)

Institute for Propaganda Analysis
Publication: monthly letter, officers (J App, 21, 719; Bull, 34, 865; J App, 25, 361)

Institute for Science and Labor (see Science and Labor)

Institute of Experimental Medicine (see Medicine)

Institute of Experimental Psychology, Moscow (see Moscow Institute of)

Institute of Human Relations (see Yale University)

Institute of Medical Psychology (see Medical Psychology)

Institute of Natural Science (see Natural Science)

Institute of Paper Chemistry (see Paper Chemistry)

Institute of Psychology, Paris (see Paris)

Instituto di Studi Superiori (Florence, Italy)
Laboratory founded (Bull, 1, 172)

Instruments (see also Apparatus)
Scientific Apparatus Makers of America (Sci, 69, 376)

Intelligence (*see also* Binet-Simon tests)
   Conference: National Institute of Industrial Psychology, Vocational and
      Educational Conference (J App, *23*, 744)
   Conference: National Research Council, superior college students (Sci, *55*, 70)
   Lecture: Dearborn, G. V. N., intellectual regression (J App, *10*, 394)
   Lecture: Foston, H., abstract (JoP, *6*, 279)
   Lecture: Gengerelli, J. A., stability of IQ (AJP, *53*, 610-614)
   Lecture: Mendel, L. B., animal intelligence (Sci, *15*, 117)
   Lecture: Norsworthy, N. (JoP, *2*, 224)
   Lecture: Terman, L. M. (JoP, *2*, 223)
   Publication: California Test of Mental Maturity, short form (J App, *23*, 419)
   Publication: creative intelligence (JoP, *13*, 420)
   Publication: Freeman, F., intercorrelation of intellligence tests (AJP, *40*, 349)
   Publication: Harriman, P. L., intelligence and handedness (AJP, *45*, 526)
   Publication: Sullivan, Clark and Tiegs, California Test of Mental Maturity
      (J App, *21*, 344)
   Publication: Terman-Merrill revision of Binet-Simon (J App, *23*, 312)
   Publication: *Test Service Bulletin*, books and tests (J App, *23*, 420)
   Publication: Tulchin, S. M., *Intelligence and crime* (J App, *23*, 744)
   Research: California Test of Mental Maturity (J App, *26*, 571-572)
   Research: inheritance, university grades of parents and children (AJP, *52*,
      634-638)
   Use of intelligence tests for U.S. immigration proposed (Sci, *57*, 22)

Inter-America
   English publication notice (JoP, *14*, 672)

Inter-American affairs
   Appointment: Peter, W. W. (Sci, *101*, 581)

Inter-American Conference of Philosophy
   Meeting: Yale Univ., 1st, 1943 (JoP, *40*, 280)

Intermëdiaire des Biologistes
   Publication: edited by Binet, A. and Simon, H. (AJP, *9*, 250)

International American Scientific Congress
   Meeting: Buenos Aires (Bull, *7*, 180)

**International Association for Psychology and
Techno Psychology**
   Organization of (Sci, *64*, 15)

**International Association for the Advancement of Science, Arts,
and Education**
   Lecture: Geddes, P. (Sci, *11*, 519)

International Association of Medical Psychology and Psychotherapy
Meeting: Vienna (Sci, *37*, 748; JoP, *10*, 336)

International Conference of Technopsychology (*see* Technopsychology)

International Congress for Research on Sex (*see* Sex, International Congress)

International Congress for the Scientific Study of Population Problems (*see* Population problems)

International Congress for the Unity of Science
Language (JoP, *35*, 112, 504)
Lecture (JoP, *33*, 392; JoP, *35*, 504; JoP, *38*, 503)
Meeting: announced, 2nd (JoP, *33*, 196)
Meeting: 4th, Girton College, Cambridge (JoP, *35*, 503; Bull, *35*, 259)
Meeting: 5th (Sci, *89*, 218, 555; Bull, *36*, 499)
Meeting: 6th (Sci, *93*, 38; JoP, *38*, 56; JoP, *38*, 504)
Meeting: tentative program, 6th (JoP, *38*, 504)

International Congress of Applied Psychology
Meeting: announcement (Bull, *25*, 308; JoP, *25*, 420; J App, *15*, 102)
Meeting: Postponement (JoP, *25*, 616)

International Congress of Arts and Sciences (St. Louis)
Meeting: announcement (JoP, *1*, 418; Bull, *1*, 333)
Program changes (JoP, *1*, 615)
Program listing (AJP, *15*, 463-464)
Publication: proceedings (Bull, *2*, 360)
Report of (Bull, *1*, 412)
Section secretaries, announcement of (JoP, *1*, 532)

International Congress of Individual Psychology
Lecture: Adler, A., 4th (Sci, *66*, 57; Sci, *72*, 167)
Meeting: Düsseldorf, 3rd (Sci, *64*, 222)

International Congress of Mental Hygiene (*see* Mental Hygiene, International Congress of)

International Congress of Neurology, Psychiatry, Medical Electricity and Hypnology (*see* Neurology, Psychiatry, Medical Electricity, ...)

International Congress of Neurology, Psychiatry and Psychology (*see* Neurology, Psychiatry and Psychology)

International Congress of Pedology (*see* Pedology)

International Congress of Philosophy
Lecture: Durkheim, E., judgment (BULL, 7, 251)
Lecture: list of (JoP, 8, 84)
Meeting: announcement, 3rd (BULL, 5, 96, 284; JoP, 5, 140)
Meeting: announcement, 4th (JoP, 7, 420; JoP, 8, 28; BULL, 5, 379; BULL, 8, 146)
Meeting: announcement, 9th (JoP, 33, 140)
Meeting: Geneva, 2nd (REV, 10, 591; AJP, 15, 463)
Meeting: London, 5th (BULL, 11, 191; JoP, 10, 364; JoP, 8, 392)
Meeting: Oxford (SCI, 52, 153)
Meeting: Paris, 1st (REV, 7, 216; SCI, 10, 981)
Meeting: postponed, 5th (JoP, 11, 644)
Meeting: subject Descartes (SCI, 100, 284-285)
Program information, 9th (JoP, 34, 364)

International Congress of Physiologists (*see* Physiologists)

International Congress of Psychology, III (Munich, Germany)
Meeting: announced, 3rd (REV, 3, 239; AJP, 7, 448)
Meeting: report of (REV, 3, 588; AJP, 8, 142; 312; SCI, 2, 660)
Organization: committee membership (REV, 3, 242)
Paper: announced, 3rd (REV, 3, 355)
Paper: summary of, 3rd (SCI, 4, 196)

International Congress of Psychology, IV (Paris, France)
Election: James, W., 4th (SCI, 11, 39)
Election: Ladd, G. T., 4th (SCI, 11, 39)
Meeting: Paris, 4th (SCI, 12, 380; REV, 10, 591; SCI, 10, 31; REV, 6, 571; J APP, 11, 234; AJP, 11, 128-129)

International Congress of Psychology, V (Rome, Italy)
Election: Sergi, G., 5th president (SCI, 21, 77)
Meeting: announcement, 5th (BULL, 2, 36; JoP, 1, 721; AJP, 16, 144; JoP, 2, 420)
Officers announced, 5th (JoP, 2, 56)

International Congress of Psychology, VI (Geneva, Switzerland)
Meeting: announced, 6th (JoP, 5, 280; BULL, 5, 128; JoP, 6, 392, 419; BULL, 6, 72, 119; AJP, 20, 469; AJP, 19, 286-288)
Meeting: report of 6th (JoP, 6, 504, 532; BULL, 6, 256)
Speakers announced, 6th (SCI, 30, 202)

International Congress of Psychology, VII (Oxford, England)
Announcement: 7th (AJP, 35, 148; BULL, 6, 327)
Appointment: officers, 7th (BULL, 6, 327)
Meeting: Oxford, 7th (JoP, 20, 336)

Officers: list of (JoP, *8*, 196)
Resignation: Baldwin, J. M. (BULL, *7*, 108)

International Congress of Psychology, VIII (Groningen, Holland)
Meeting: announcement, 8th (BULL, *23*, 112; AJP, *37*, 155; J APP, *9*, 204; BULL, *22*, 504; JoP, *22*, 420; SCI, *64*, 201; AJP, *38*, 153)
Participants: list (JoP, *23*, 224)

International Congress of Psychology, IX (New Haven, Connecticut)
Foreign psychologists named who will present, 9th (BULL, *26*, 340)
Meeting: announced, 9th (SCI, *69*, 11)
Meeting: announced and list of officers, 9th (JoP, *25*, 140, 671; AJP, *40*, 351; AJP, *41*, 684; SCI, *70*, 254)
Participant list expands (JoP, *26*, 392)

International Congress of Psychology, X (Copenhagen, Denmark)
Appointment: delegates, 10th (SCI, *76*, 119)
Meeting: announced, 10th (J APP, *13*, 533; BULL, *29*, 180; JoP, *29*, 364, 447)
Retirement: Cattell, J. McK., president (SCI, *76*, 141)

International Congress of Psychology, XI (Paris, France)
Election: Langfeld, H. S., 11th, executive committee (SCI, *86*, 34)
Election: Mira, L., 11th president (SCI, *76*, 269)
Lecture: Dallenbach, K. M., 11th (AJP, *49*, 142)
Meeting: announced, 11th (JoP, *33*, 168; BULL, *32*, 862; BULL, *33*, 303, 581; BULL, *34*, 59; SCI, *82*, 299; SCI, *86*, 34; J APP, *21*, 242)
Meeting: postponed, 11th (SCI, *83*, 619; JoP, *34*, 112; SCI, *86*, 34; SCI, *84*, 531)

International Congress of Psychology, XII (Edinburgh, Scotland)
Election: Colville, J., 12th honorary president (J APP, *23*, 530)
Election: Thomson, G., 12th secretary (J APP, *23*, 530)
Meeting: Edinburgh, 12th (SCI, *90*, 61; BULL, *36*, 500, 805; SCI, *89*, 433)
Meeting: postponed, 12th (AJP, *53*, 298; J APP, *24*, 245; BULL, *37*, 329; SCI, *91*, 188)

International Congress of Religious Psychology (*see* Religious Psychology)

International Congress of School Hygiene (*see* School Hygiene)

International Congress on Morale Education (*see* Morale Education, International Congress on)

International Congress on Technical Education (*see* Technical Education)

International Course for Psychology and Psychiatry (*see* Psychology and Psychiatry)

International Exhibition Congresses
Dates in 1889 to be held in Paris (SCI°, *13*, 361)

International Health Exhibition (London)
Health and education at South Kensington in 1884 (SCI°, *2*, 839)
Lecture: International Conference on Education listed in *Nature* (SCI°, *4*, 266)

International Journal of Individual Psychology
Publication: announcement (J APP, *19*, 353)

International Management Congress (*see* Management)

International Medical Congress (*see* Medical Congress)

International Medical Congress for Psychotherapy (*see* Medical Congress)

International Medical Society of Psychotherapy (*see* Medical Society)

International Neurological Congress (*see* Neurological Congress)

International Record of Charities and Correction
Editor: Wines, F. H. (SCI°, *7*, 306)
Publication: Putnam's Sons (SCI°, *7*, 306)

International Scientific Congress (*see* Scientific Congress)

International Seminar in Psychology (*see* Psychology)

International Society for Sexual Research (*see* Sexual Research)

International Society for the Investigation of Sex (*see* Sex, International)

International Society of the Psychical Institute (*see* Psychical Institute)

Internships
Announcement: Western State Psychiatric Hospital (BULL, *41*, 344)
Available: Letchworth Village, clinical psychology (BULL, *39*, 809-810)
Available: McLean Hospital (BULL, *42*, 795)

Available: New Hampshire State Hospital (BULL, *42*, 407)
Available: Worcester State Hospital (BULL, *42*, 408)

Inter-Society Color Council

Color standards for science, art and industry (BULL, *37*, 123)
Lecture: Helson, H. (BULL, *40*, 459)
Meeting: New York (BULL, *40*, 459)
Meeting: 2nd annual (SCI, *76*, 462)
Meeting: 13th, New York City (BULL, *42*, 128; AJP, *52*, 130)
Meeting: 1939, program (BULL, *36*, 141)
Meeting: 1941 (BULL, *38*, 191)
Publication: color research (BULL, *31*, 79)
Symposium: color tolerance, 1939 (BULL, *37*, 61)

Intersociety Constitutional Convention

Adoption: new by-laws (J APP, *28*, 530)
Cooperation among psychological societies, 1943 (J APP, *27*, 365)

Introspection

Lecture: Baird, J. W. (JOP, *2*, 56)
Research: Secor, W. B., utilizes (AJP, *11*, 435)
Publication: Hunt, W. A. and Landis, C., systematic differences in introspection
  (AJP, *46*, 659)

Iowa Academy of Sciences

Lecture: list, 1890 (SCI°, *16*, 147)
Meeting: Ames, 1883 (SCI°, *2*, 607)
Meeting: 1944 (SCI, *99*, 489)

Iowa Central College

Appointment: Williams, N. (BULL, *14*, 366)

Iowa Child Welfare Research Station (Iowa City)

Appointment: Baldwin, B. T. (BULL, *14*, 365)
Appointment: Lewin, K. (BULL, *32*, 323)
Appointment: Sears, R. R. (BULL, *39*, 682; SCI, *96*, 57-58)
Appropriation: National Women's Christian Temperance Union (J APP, *3*, 394-395)
Departure: Stoddard, G. D. (SCI, *94*, 297)
Grant: received (BULL, *22*, 444)
Grant: Laura Spelman Rockefeller Fund (SCI, *61*, 467)
Laboratory: organized, child psychology (J APP, *5*, 381; SCI, *54*, 434)

Iowa College (Grinnell)

Lecture: Royce, J. (SCI, *15*, 920)

Iowa College of Agriculture and Mechanic Arts

Appointment: Vance, T. F. (BULL, *12*, 44)

Iowa, Conference of Teachers of Psychology
Meeting: list of officers (BULL, 7, 147)

Iowa Silent Reading Test
Publication: new edition, 1939 (J APP, 23, 633)
Research: Lennon, L. J. (J APP 27, 363-364)

Iowa State University (formerly Iowa State College, Ames)
Appointment: Mount, G. H. (BULL, 9, 208)
Award: Fisher, R. A., honorary degree (SCI, 84, 81)
Lecture: Fisher, R. A., experimental design and statistics (SCI, 82, 590)
Lecture: Hartman, C. G., instinctive behavior (SCI, 97, 114)
Lecture: Miles, W. R., Sigma Xi (BULL, 41, 498; SCI, 99, 382)
Lecture: Starch, D. (SCI, 88, 144)
Promotion: Gaskill, H. V. (BULL, 35, 578; SCI, 88, 32)

Iowa, University of (Iowa City) (see also Iowa Child Welfare Research Station)
Appointment: Baldwin, B. T. (BULL, 14, 365)
Appointment: Faris, E. (BULL, 12, 244; JoP, 12, 504)
Appointment: Gilbert, J. A. (REV, 2, 534)
Appointment: Jessup, W. A. (JoP, 9, 588; BULL, 9, 408)
Appointment: King, I. (JoP, 6, 560; BULL, 6, 327)
Appointment: Köhler, W. (BULL, 32, 376)
Appointment: Metfessel, M. (BULL 26, 120)
Appointment: Miner, J. B. (JoP, 1, 476; BULL, 1, 372)
Appointment: Morgan, J. D. (SCI, 53, 186; BULL, 18, 236)
Appointment: Seashore, C. E. (SCI, 96, 10, 58; AJP, 9, 135; SCI, 16, 280; REV, 4, 452; SCI, 27, 520; SCI, 21, 640; BULL, 39, 682)
Appointment: Spence, K. W. (SCI, 96, 57; BULL, 39, 682)
Appointment: Starbuck, D. (JoP, 3, 420; BULL, 3, 247)
Appointment: Starch, D. (BULL, 3, 247)
Appointment: Stoddard, G. D. (SCI, 87, 504; SCI, 84, 326)
Appointment: Stroud, J. B. (BULL, 35, 796)
Appointment: Travis, L. (BULL, 34, 325; BULL, 24, 312; SCI, 85, 310)
Appointment: Travis, L., psychopathic hospital (SCI, 65, 229)
Appointment: VanEpps, C. (BULL, 5, 379)
Appointment: Whiting, P. W. (SCI, 54, 355)
Appointment: Williams, M. C. (BULL, 4, 370)
Award: Judd, C. H., honorary degree (BULL, 20, 664)
Award: Thorndike, E. L, honorary degree (SCI, 57, 580; BULL, 20, 664)
Child psychology lab opens (BULL, 18, 628)
Darwin centennial celebration (BULL, 6, 120)
Department of philosophy and psychology name change (BULL, 3, 247)
Departure: Malamud, W. (SCI, 90, 204)
Departure: Miner, J. B. (SCI, 23, 480)
Departure: Reymert, M. L. for Norway (BULL, 17, 280)

Departure: Stoddard, G. D. (Sci, *94*, 297)
Departure: Sylvester, R. H. (Sci, *50*, 326)
Editor: Ruckmick, C. A., *Studies in Psychology* (Bull, *24*, 508)
Editor: Seashore, C. E., *Studies in Psychology* (Sci, *69*, 212)
Election: Seashore, C. E., department chair (Rev, *9*, 536)
Election: Seashore, C. E., NAS member (Bull, *19*, 296)
Fellowships in psychology of music (Bull, *24*, 312; J App, *11*, 80)
Leave of absence: Meier, N. C. (Bull, *42*, 486)
Leave of absence: Patrick, G. T. W. (Sci, *21*, 640)
Leave of absence: Starbuck, E. D. (JoP, *9*, 504)
Lecture: Gault, R. H., audition (Sci, *73*, 123)
Lecture: Koffka, K. (Sci, *62*, 106)
Lecture: Points of view in psychology (Sci, *69*, 450)
Lecture: Ruckmick, C. A., emotion (Sci, *75*, 262)
Lecture: Titchener, E. B. (Bull, *8*, 110)
Lecture: Ward, J. (Bull, *1*, 173)
Meeting: APA, 1930 (Sci, *72*, 599)
Meeting: Board of Regents (JoP, *2*, 252)
Meeting: North Central Section of APA (Bull, *7*, 108)
Meeting: Western Philosophical Assoc., North Central Section of the APA and
   the Teachers of Psychology in Iowa (JoP, *7*, 112, 222-223)
Promotion: Ruckmick, C. A. (Bull, *21*, 360; Sci, *59*, 378)
Promotion: Seashore, C. E. (Bull, *5*, 64)
Promotion: Williams, M. C. (Bull, *7*, 324; JoP, *7*, 560)
Research: child welfare (Bull, *14*, 143)
Resignation: Lewin, K. (Bull, *42*, 191)
Resignation: Shirley, H. F. (Sci, *91*, 15)
Resignation: Stoddard, G. D. (Sci, *96*, 10)
Retirement: Seashore, C. E. (Sci, *84*, 326)
Retirement: Woods, A. H. (Sci, *94*, 297)
Seashore, C. E., bronze bust presented (Sci, *90*, 510)
Seashore, C. E., commemoration of 25 years of service (Bull, *26*, 120)
Seashore, C. E., 7th annual commemorative concert (Sci, *79*, 474)

Ireland, Merritte W.
Award: William Freeman Snow Medal (Sci, *101*, 349)

Irons, David
Death notice (JoP, *4*, 112; Sci, *25*, 198; Bull, *4*, 64)
Leave of absence: Bryn Mawr College (Bull, *1*, 94)

Irving, John Allan
Appointment: Univ. of Toronto (Bull, *42*, 485; JoP, *42*, 364)
Resignation: Univ. of British Columbia (Bull, *42*, 485; JoP, *42*, 364)

Isaacs, Schachne
Appointment: clinical psychology internships, director (Bull, *39*, 809-810)

Appointment: Government Service (BULL, *14*, 366)
Appointment: Mineola, Long Island Aviation Camp (JoP, *15*, 112)
Commissioned: Sanitary Corps (JoP, *15*, 112, 364; BULL, *15*, 97)
Fellowship: French universities (BULL, *17*, 32)
Fellowship: Psychology (SCI, *51*, 319)

Ishihara, Shinobu

Publication: Murray, E., the Ishihara test for color-blindness: a point in ethics (AJP, *47*, 511)

Isis

Printing of (JoP, *38*, 140)

Italian Congress of Eugenics

Mussolini (SCI, *70*, 190)

Italy

Research: Drug effects on taste (SCI°, *8*, 54)

Ivanitskii, G. A.

Publication: conditioned reflex (AJP, *49*, 677)

J

Jacks, Lawrence Pearsall
Lecture: Aristotelian Society, consciousness (JoP, *10*, 224)

Jackson, A. C.
Lecture: Hume, D. (JoP, *42*, 56)

Jackson, John Hughlings
Death notice (BULL, *8*, 406)

Jackson, Theodore Andrew
Appointment: Indiana Univ. (BULL, *40*, 152)
Appointment: New York Univ. (SCI, *74*, 240)
Appointment: Stevenson and Kellogg, Ltd. (BULL, *42*, 331)
Departure: Columbia Univ. (BULL, *40*, 152)

Jacobi, Abraham
Celebration: 70th anniversary (SCI, *11*, 794)

Jacobsen, Carlyle Ferdinand
Appointment: Cornell Medical College (BULL, *34*, 635)
Appointment: Washington Univ., St. Louis, Dept. of Neuropsychiatry (BULL, *35*, 577)
Award: Warren Medal recipient, 1939 (BULL, *36*, 499)
Lecture: NYAS, lobotomy (SCI, *77*, 85)

James, George F.
Election: Univ. of Minnesota, School of Education, Dean (SCI, *22*, 888)

James, Harold Ernest Oswald
Appointment: Univ. of Manchester (BULL, *23*, 455)

James, Henry, Jr.
Publication: Biography of James, W. (SCI, *35*, 651)
Publication: James, W. collecting letters (JoP, *9*, 279-280, 308, 335)

James, Maud Merrill (*see* Merrill, Maud)

James, William
    Abroad at this time (REV, 7, 639)
    Anniversary: New School for Social Research, 100th (JoP, 38, 616)
    Anniversary: Scripps College, 100th (JoP, 39, 84)
    Anniversary: Univ. of Wisconsin (JoP, 38, 616)
    Anniversary: Vassar College, 100th (JoP, 38, 308)
    Appointment: International Congress of Psychology, International Committee,
        5th (JoP, 2, 56)
    Appointment: Stanford Univ. (BULL, 2, 160; SCI, 21, 400; JoP, 2, 140)
    Appointment: Univ. of Edinburgh (SCI, 7, 634; REV, 5, 344)
    Award: tribute to (JoP, 7, 700)
    Course: Harvard Univ., religious life (SCI, 13, 918)
    Death notice (SCI, 32, 303, 659; BULL, 7, 324; JoP, 7, 504)
    Degree: Oxford Univ. (SCI, 27, 869)
    Degree: Univ. of Edinburgh (REV, 9, 328, 431)
    Election: American Philosophical Assoc., president (SCI, 23, 38)
    Election: American Society of Naturalists, president (SCI, 21, 37; JoP, 2, 56)
    Election: APA, president (JoP, 1, 28)
    Election: Berlin Academy of Sciences (REV, 7, 323; SCI, 11, 556)
    Election: British Academy (BULL, 4, 338; SCI, 26, 94; JoP, 4, 448)
    Election: French Academy of Moral and Political Science (JoP, 7, 140)
    Election: International Congress of Psychology (SCI, 11, 39)
    Election: International Congress of Psychology, 6th (SCI, 30, 202)
    Election: Institute of France (REV, 5, 344)
    Election: Institute Psychique International, notes unauthorized use of his name
        as member (REV, 7, 640)
    Health better (REV, 8, 112, 222)
    Invites Myers, F.W.H. to Rome (SCI, 13, 237)
    Leave of absence: Harvard Univ. (SCI, 9, 821)
    Lecture: Columbia Univ. (JoP, 4, 84; BULL, 4, 95; SCI, 25, 237)
    Lecture: Edinburgh, Gifford (SCI, 13, 876; SCI, 15, 675; REV, 8, 335)
    Lecture: Harvard Univ. (SCI, 4, 50; BULL, 5, 380; JoP, 5, 672; SCI, 28, 642, 679)
    Lecture: Harvard Univ., established in honor of (JoP, 27, 139; BULL, 27, 240)
    Lecture: Manchester New College (BULL, 5, 168)
    Lecture: nature of activity (JoP, 2, 28)
    Lecture: Stanford Univ. (BULL, 3, 83; JoP, 3, 84; SCI, 23, 118)
    Lecture: subject American Philosophical Assoc. (JoP, 37, 699)
    Lecture: subject, Ewer, B. C., 1942 (JoP, 39, 84)
    Lecture: subject, Hocking, W. E., 1942 (JoP, 39, 84)
    Lecture: subject, Moore, E. C., 1942 (JoP, 39, 84)
    Lecture: subject, Royce, J., Phi Beta Kappa oration, James as philosopher (JoP,
        8, 447-448)
    Lecture: subject, Univ. of Indiana, Powell Foundation Lecture (JoP, 34, 84)
    Lecture: Univ. of Chicago (JoP, 2, 304; SCI, 21, 902)

Meeting: Society for Psychical Research, American Branch, presides (Sci°, *15*, 144)

Meeting: Univ. of Chicago (JoP, *1*, 140)

Portrait presented (JoP, *7*, 112)

Publication: announcement (JoP, *8*, 280, 532, 672)

Publication: Boutroux, E. (JoP, *8*, 560)

Publication: comments by James, Jr., H. on book issued by Longmans, Green, and Co. (JoP, *8*, 336)

Publication: critique of (JoP, *5*, 112)

Publication: exhibition at Harvard Univ. (JoP, *17*, 194-195)

Publication: *Hegel and his method* (JoP, *5*, 643)

Publication: influenced writings of Stein, G. (AJP, *54*, 124-128)

Publication: James' biography call for correspondence (Sci, *35*, 651)

Publication: James, Jr., H. letter's collected (JoP, *9*, 279-280, 308, 335)

Publication: letter concerning the death of Hodgson, R. (Sci, *23*, 319)

Publication: letter to the editor about Hall, G. S. (Sci, *2*, 626)

Publication: *The meaning of truth* (JoP, *6*, 588)

Publication: Royce, J. on James, W. (JoP, *8*, 560)

Publication: translation into Italian (JoP, *4*, 196)

Publication: *Varieties of Religious Experience*, translation into French (Rev, *10*, 591)

Research: hallucinations (AJP, *3*, 292)

Retirement: Harvard Univ. (Bull, *4*, 64; JoP, *4*, 84; Sci, *25*, 237)

Returns: Cambridge from England (Sci, *28*, 556)

Returns: Harvard Univ. (Sci, *14*, 541)

Returns: Oxford, England (JoP, *5*, 644)

Sails for Greece and International Congress of Psychology at Rome (JoP, *2*, 224)

Symposium: Eastern Div. of American Philosophical Assoc. (JoP, *38*, 700)

James, William, Club

Lecture: Titchener, E. B. (Bull, *19*, 296)

James, William, Lecture

Dewey, J., 1st (Sci, *71*, 212; Sci, *75*, 331)

Endowment: Pierce, E. (Sci, *75*, 331)

Gilson, E., "The unity of the philosophical experience" (Sci, *84*, 371)

Köhler, W. (Sci, *80*, 334; Sci, *79*, 314)

Lovejoy, A. O. (Sci, *75*, 331)

Russell, E. (Sci, *91*, 165)

Thorndike, E. L. (Sci, *96*, 467; Bull, *39*, 896)

Janet, Paul

Death notice (Sci, *10*, 582; Rev, *6*, 673)

Publication: "The teaching of psychology", *Popular Science Monthly* (Sci°, *11*, 312-313)

Janet, Pierre
Appointment: Collège de France (REV, *9*, 216; SCI, *15*, 320; BULL, *10*, 252)
Appointment: Editorial board, *Character and Personality* (J APP, *16*, 439)
Appointment: French Academy of Moral and Political Science (SCI, *37*, 785;
    JoP, *10*, 336)
Appointment: Harvard Univ. (JoP, *3*, 392; BULL, *3*, 248; SCI, *23*, 959)
Appointment: Univ. of Paris, nominated lecturer (SCI, *8*, 707)
Election: International Congress of Psychology, 11th, honorary president (JoP,
    34, 112; SCI, *84*, 531)
Election: Société de psychologie physiologique, 1st vice-president (SCI°, *6*, 360)
Lecture: Bloomingdale Hospital, New York, centenary celebration (SCI, *53*, 532)
Lecture: Harvard Medical School, hysteria (JoP, *3*, 644)
Lecture: Harvard Tercentary Conference of Arts and Sciences (J APP, *20*, 519)
Lecture: International Congress of Arts and Sciences, St. Louis (JoP, *1*, 420)
Lecture: Johns Hopkins Univ. (JoP, *4*, 28; SCI, *24*, 788)
Lecture: psychoanalysis (SCI, *38*, 124)
Lecture: Univ. College, Bristol, England (JoP, *1*, 616)
Lecture: Univ. of London (SCI, *51*, 590)
Lecture: Univ. of Pennsylvania (BULL, *22*, 672)
Lecture: U.S. tour (SCI, *62*, 368)
Publication: hysteria (BULL, *4*, 236)

Janeway, Edward Gamaliel, Lecture
Page, I. H., hypertension (SCI, *93*, 37-38)

Jansen, M.
Appointment: Univ. of Toronto (BULL, *4*, 32)

Japanese Imperial Education Society
Lecture: Ladd, G. T., educational methods (SCI, *21*, 933)

Japanese Journal of Psychology
Beginning of (AJP, *34*, 149)

Japanese Society for Child Study
Congress held (AJP, *20*, 156)

Jaqua, Ernest James
Research: need for trained vocational counselors (J APP, *28*, 352-353)

Jasper, Herbert Henry
Appointment: McGill Medical School and Montreal Neurological Institute
    (BULL, *35*, 796)

Jastrow, Joseph
Anniversary: Univ. of Wisconsin, foundation of lab (SCI, *87*, 435)
Appointment: Columbia Univ. (JoP, *6*, 700; BULL, *6*, 427)
Award: APA resolution honoring (SCI, *59*, 253)

Award: MPA honored (Bull., *35*, 188)
Course: Columbia Univ. Graduate School (Sci, *30*, 705)
Course: Univ. of Wisconsin, mental evolution (Sci, *15*, 216)
Death notice (AJP, *57*, 581-585; Bull., *41*, 136)
Editor: *Conduct and Mind Series* (Bull., 7, 108; JoP, 7, 140; Sci, *31*, 212)
Election: APA representative to American Society of Naturalists (Rev, 7, 104)
Election: N.Y. Branch of APA, president (Sci, *81*, 67; Sci, *79*, 359)
Invention: aesthesiometer (AJP, *1*, 552)
Leave of absence: Univ. of Wisconsin (J App, *10*, 523)
Lecture: AAAS, Lancaster Branch (Sci, *88*, 449)
Lecture: Clark Univ. (AJP, *10*, 522; Sci, *57*, 173; Sci, *64*, 555)
Lecture: Columbia Univ. (JoP, 7, 140; Sci, *66*, 350; JoP, *8*, 112)
Lecture: Indiana Univ. (JoP, *13*, 280; Bull., *13*, 188)
Lecture: Kansas Normal School, Emporia (Sci, *35*, 772)
Lecture: MPA (Sci, *87*, 434-435)
Lecture: National Academy of Sciences with Pierce, C. S. (Sci°, 3, 524; Sci°, 4, 408-409)
Lecture: New School for Social Research, emotions (Sci, *66*, 278; Bull., 27, 620)
Lecture: New York Academy of Medicine (JoP, 5, 140)
Lecture: Ohio State Univ., human nature (Sci, 45, 407; JoP, *14*, 364)
Lecture: Purdue Univ. (Bull., *13*, 188)
Lecture: Sigma Xi, emotion expression (Sci, *43*, 529)
Lecture: subconscious (JoP, 9, 28; Sci, *34*, 755)
Lecture: theory and practice (Sci, *39*, 280)
Lecture: tour of colleges and universities (Sci, *61*, 412)
Lecture: Univ. of California (Sci, *36*, 48; JoP, 9, 476)
Lecture: Univ. of Missouri (JoP, *11*, 140; Bull., *11*, 116)
Lecture: Univ. of Wisconsin (Bull., 9, 359; Bull., 8, 438; Sci, *34*, 755; Sci, 27, 237)
Publication: "The psychology of deception," *Popular Science Monthly* (Sci°, *12*, 237)
Publication: the psychology of stereoscopic vision (Sci, 24, ???)
Publication: rejoinder to critiuqe of Hyslop (JoP, 5, 250)
Publication: subconscious, French translation (Sci, 27, 677)
Publication: *The Subconscious*, Japanese translation (Sci, 52, 635)
Publication: translated in *Revue Scientifique* (Sci, 4, 47)
Retirement: Univ. of Wisconsin (Sci, *66*, 148)
Returns: Univ. of Wisconsin (Rev, 6, 456)
Trip: Europe (Bull., *1*, 173; Sci, *19*, 317)

Jebb, Richard Claverhouse
Lecture: Oxford Univ., "Humanism and education" (Sci, 9, 461)

Jefferson Medical College
Appointment: Strecker, E. A. (Sci, *62*, 12, 396)
Grant: Eugenics (Sci, *69*, 668)

Jegi, John I.
Death notice (Sci, *19*, 517; Bull, *1*, 174)

Jelliffe, Smith Ely
Appointment: *New York Medical Journal* (JoP, *14*, 224)
Election: New York Psychiatric Society, president (Sci, *55*, 204)
Election: Vienna Society of Psychiatry and Neurology, member (Sci, *63*, 633)
Visits psychiatric clinic in Europe (Sci, *62*, 454)

Jellinek, Elvin Morton
Appointment: School of Alcohol Studies, director (Sci, *97*, 441)

Jena, University of
Appointment: Günther, F. K. (Sci, *72*, 421)
Course: Autumn, 1889 (Sci°, *14*, 195)
Degree: Harris, W. T. (Sci, *9*, 421)
Resignation: Haeckel, E. H. (JoP, *6*, 56)

Jenkins, John Gamewell
Appointment: Cornell Univ. (Sci, *72*, 11)
Appointment: National Research Council, Committee on Selection and Training of Aircraft Pilots (Bull, *37*, 827; Sci, *93*, 37)
Appointment: Univ. of Maryland (Bull, *37*, 864)
Lecture: National Research Council, "Psychological factors in national morale" (Bull, *37*, 829)
Lecture: perception, "Paradoxical warmth" (AJP, *45*, 350)
Meeting: Assoc. of Consulting Psychologists, 8th (J App, *21*, 241)
Publication: Effects of distraction (AJP, *45*, 173-174)

Jenkins, Thomas Nicholas
Fellowship: Board of National Research (Bull, *23*, 292)

Jenkins, William Leroy
Election: Lehigh Univ. Chapter of the Society of Sigma Xi, secretary (Sci, *95*, 573)
Publication: Nafe's vascular theory (AJP, *51*, 763; AJP, *52*, 462-465)

Jenness, Arthur Freeman
Appointment: Harvard Univ. (Bull, *34*, 634)
Appointment: Univ. of Nebraska, Chair Psych. Dept. (J App, *24*, 518; Bull, *37*, 656)
Returns: Univ. of Nebraska (Bull, *42*, 485)

Jennings, Herbert Spencer
Appointment: Johns Hopkins Univ. (Sci, *23*, 896)
Appointment: Johns Hopkins Univ., Henry Walters Chair in Zoology (Sci, *31*, 949)

Appointment: *Journal of Comparative Neurology and Psychology*, editorial board (JoP, *1*, 195)

Appointment: Zoological Station, Naples, Italy (SCI°, *17*, 798)

Degree: Clark Univ. (SCI, *30*, 362)

Election: American Society of Naturalists, president (SCI, *33*, 22)

Eugenics (SCI, *69*, 136)

Grant: Carnegie Institution (SCI, *17*, 635-636)

Lecture: American Society of Naturalists, heredity and personality (SCI, *34*, 870; SCI, *34*, 709)

Lecture: Harvey Society (SCI, *34*, 376)

Lecture: International Congress of Psychology, 6th (SCI, *30*, 202)

Lecture: Univ. of California, Sigma Xi Society, "The behavior of some animals of the seashore" (SCI, *24*, 381)

Lecture: Wagner Institute, Westbrook Lectures, heredity and evolution (JoP, *14*, 224)

Jensen, Kai

Appointment: Ohio State Univ. (BULL, *27*, 736)

Jensen, Milton B.

Appointment: Central State Teachers College (J APP, *13*, 415)

Election: Kentucky Psychological Assoc., chair (J APP, *25*, 725)

Jensen, Reynold A.

Establishment: Univ. of Utah's Child Psychiatry Program (SCI, *102*, 273)

Lecture: Univ. of Utah (SCI, *102*, 245)

Jessup, Walter Albert

Appointment: Univ. of Iowa (BULL, *9*, 408; JoP, *9*, 588)

Departure: Indiana Univ. (BULL, *9*, 408; JoP, *9*, 588)

Jesup Psychological Laboratory (Nashville, Tennessee) (*see also* Peabody College)

Builds new lab (SCI, *40*, 344; JoP, *12*, 504)

Construction begun (BULL, *11*, 443)

Donation: $8,500 for lab equipment (SCI, *42*, 186)

Jewett, Frank B.

Election: Sigma Xi National Executive Committee (SCI, *101*, 13)

Jewett, Stephen P.

Appointment: New York Medical College (SCI, *94*, 15)

Election: Assoc. for the Advancement of Psychoanalysis, treasurer (J APP, *25*, 473)

Joad, Cyril Edwin Mitchinson

Research: psychic phenomena (SCI, *80*, 183)

Job analysis
Lecture: Strong, E. K., Carnegie Institute of Technology (Sci, *49*, 118)

Jodl, Friedrich
Publication: *Lehrbuch der Psychologie* (Rev, *1*, 336; AJP, *8*, 430)

John Carroll University (Cleveland, Ohio)
Meeting: American Catholic Philosophical Assoc. (JoP, *33*, 27)

Johns Hopkins Hospital
Appointment: Hurd, H. M. (Sci°, *14*, 58)
Appointment: Osler, W. (Sci°, *12*, 215)
Appointment: Whitehorn, J. C. (Sci, *94*, 275; Sci, *93*, 493)
Departure: Cameron, N. (Sci, *89*, 76)
Opening (Sci°, *13*, 140, 217)
Opens Phipps Psychiatric Clinic (JoP, *10*, 308; Bull, *10*, 164)
Publication: progress, 1889 (Sci°, *14*, 298)
Retirement: Meyer, A. (Sci, *94*, 275; Sci, *93*, 493)

Johns Hopkins Press
Publication: Gilman, D. C., origin and organization of Johns Hopkins Univ.
   (Sci°, *17*, 187)
Publication: *Psychology Classics* (JoP, *14*, 56; Bull, *13*, 482)
Publication: Steiner, B. C., "The history of university education in Maryland"
   (Sci°, *17*, 187)

Johns Hopkins University (Baltimore, Maryland) (*see also*
Phipps Psychiatric Clinic)
Anniversary, 10th (Sci°, *7*, 415)
Appointment: Abbott, A. C. (Sci°, *14*, 351)
Appointment announced (JoP, *1*, 252)
Appointment: Baird, J. W. (Bull, *1*, 413)
Appointment: Baird, J. W., *The Psychological Review*, business manager (JoP,
   2, 672)
Appointment: Baldwin, B. T. (Bull, *13*, 407; JoP, *13*, 700)
Appointment: Baldwin, J. M. (Rev, *10*, 690; Sci, *18*, 352)
Appointment: Buchner, E. F. (Bull, *5*, 96; Sci, *27*, 440)
Appointment: Bühler, K. (Sci, *65*, 495)
Appointment: Campbell, C. (Sci, *40*, 25)
Appointment: Coover, J. E. (Sci, *65*, 495)
Appointment: Dewey, J. (Bull, *3*, 184)
Appointment: Dunlap, K. (Sci, *23*, 928; JoP, *3*, 364; Bull, *3*, 216)
Appointment: Farrar, C. B. (Bull, *1*, 172)
Appointment: Gilman, D. C., 500th anniversary of Univ. of Cracow,
   representative (Sci, *11*, 877)
Appointment: Griffin, E. H. (Sci°, *14*, 57)
Appointment: Hall, G. S. (Sci°, *3*, 524)

Appointment: Huey, E. B. (Sci, *33*, 607; Sci, *34*, 759; Bull, *9*, 95; Bull, *8*, 182; JoP, *8*, 721)

Appointment: Hurd, H. M. (Sci°, *14*, 351)

Appointment: Jennings, H. S., Henry Walters Chair in Zoology (Sci, *31*, 949)

Appointment: Johnson, B. J. (Bull, *17*, 280)

Appointment: Kafka, G., visiting prof. (Sci, *69*, 450; Bull, *26*, 624)

Appointment: Ladd-Franklin, C. (Bull, *1*, 172)

Appointment: list of (Sci°, *14*, 351)

Appointment: list of fellowships (Sci°, *2*, 341)

Appointment: list of gradutes (Sci°, *14*, 58, 437)

Appointment: list of men from Johns Hopkins (Sci°, *14*, 251)

Appointment: Lovejoy, A. O. (JoP, *7*, 308; Bull, *7*, 220)

Appointment: Meyer, A. (Sci, *28*, 14; JoP, *5*, 392; Bull, *5*, 243)

Appointment: Morgan, C. T. (Bull, *40*, 79; Sci, *96*, 444)

Appointment: Nichols, H. (Rev, *3*, 120; AJP, *7*, 452; Sci, *2*, 850)

Appointment: Nuttall, G. H. F. (Sci°, *17*, 339)

Appointment: Osler, W. (Sci, *11*, 439; Sci, *12*, 215)

Appointment: Scripture, E. W. (Bull, *1*, 172)

Appointment: Stebbins, E. L. (Sci, *102*, 420)

Appointment: Stratton, G. M. (Bull, *1*, 172)

Appointment: Watson, J. B. (Sci, *27*, 440; Bull, *5*, 96; Bull, *2*, 159; JoP, *5*, 196)

Appointment: Wertheimer, F. I., psychiatric clinic staff (Bull, *20*, 172)

Appointment: Wightman, A. C. (Sci°, *14*, 351)

Award: Riley, I. W., Henry E. Johnston scholarship (JoP, *2*, 140)

Clinic, Phipps Psychiatric, opening (Sci, *37*, 406)

Clinic, psychiatric to be constructed (Sci, *27*, 999)

Commemoration of death, Locke, J. (JoP, *1*, 616; Bull, *1*, 413, 451)

Course: Baldwin, B. T. (Bull, *12*, 403; Sci, *29*, 788)

Course: offered summer (Bull, *12*, 128)

Degree: Bachelor of Science in Education established (JoP, *12*, 504)

Degree: Dewey, J. (JoP, *12*, 336)

Degree: Ladd-Franklin, C. (Bull, *23*, 236; Sci, *63*, 276)

Degree: master's established (Bull, *5*, 243)

Department of Education established separate from philosophy and psychology dept. (JoP, *12*, 448; Bull, *12*, 243)

Departure: Baird, J. W. (Sci, *23*, 864)

Departure: Cameron, N., Medical School (Sci, *89*, 76)

Departure: Dorcus, R. M. (Sci, *86*, 218)

Departure: Dunlap, K. (Sci, *86*, 218)

Departure: Stratton, G. M. (Sci, *27*, 240)

Departure: Ulrich, J. L. (Bull, *10*, 292)

Departure: Watson, J. B. (JoP, *9*, 112)

Dunlap, K., farewell dinner (Sci, *83*, 77)

Election: Stratton, G. M., council of APA (JoP, *2*, 28)

Election: Welch, W. H., president (Sci, *72*, 625)

Endowment: psychiatric clinic (JoP, *5*, 391)

Fellowship: list of appointments, 1883 (Sci°, *2*, 341)

Grant: study of venerial disease, psych. lab (Sci, *50*, 110)
Lab, experimental physiology opens (Sci°, *2*, 209)
Laboratory: new building for psych. (Sci, *64*, 648)
Leave of absence: Boas, G. (Sci, *98*, 469)
Leave of absence: Gilman, D. C. (Sci, *11*, 159)
Leave of absence: Hurd, H. M., Medical School (Sci, *24*, 542)
Lecture: Baldwin, J. M. (Bull, *3*, 36)
Lecture: Billings, J. S., the science of hygiene in a liberal education (Sci°, *5*, 101)
Lecture: Cattell, J. McK. (Sci, *34*, 911; Bull, *9*, 96)
Lecture: Dewey, J. (Bull, *7*, 75; JoP, *7*, 83; Sci, *31*, 212)
Lecture: Hall, G. S. (Sci°, *9*, 360; Sci°, *5*, 19-20)
Lecture: Huey, E. B. (Sci, *34*, 759)
Lecture: instruction in the higher institutions of learning (Sci°, *2*, 253)
Lecture: Janet, P. (JoP, *4*, 28; Sci, *24*, 788)
Lecture: list of Nov. 15, 1884 (Sci°, *5*, 19-20)
Lecture: Münsterberg, H., psych. of labor (Sci, *37*, 478)
Lecture: Scripture, E. W. cancelled (Bull, *2*, 159)
Lecture: Thorndike, E. L. (Bull, *10*, 124; Sci, *37*, 302)
Lecture: Tufts, J. H. (Bull, *7*, 147)
Lecture: Yerkes, R. M., comparative psych. (Sci, *29*, 853)
Meeting: SSPP, 1st (JoP, *2*, 56)
Meeting: SSPP, 1913 (JoP, *10*, 280; Bull, *10*, 123)
Portrait of Gilman, D. C. (Sci, *11*, 717)
Promotion: Dunlap, K. (Bull, *7*, 324; Sci, *44*, 238; Bull, *8*, 302; JoP, *7*, 560; JoP, *8*, 420; Sci, *33*, 992)
Psych. Dept. temporary division (JoP, *13*, 532; Bull, *13*, 260)
Publication: Gilman, D. C., origin and organization (Sci°, *17*, 187)
Publication: midsummer circular (Sci°, *2*, 341)
Publication: original investigations in various subjects (Sci°, *2*, 147)
Publication: Phipps, Henry, Psychiatric Ward (JoP, *6*, 558)
Publication: statement of 1882 work and 1883-84 course offerings (Sci°, *2*, 92)
Research: effects of motion picture films (Bull, *16*, 258)
Resignation: Abbott, A. C. (Sci°, *17*, 339)
Resignation: Baldwin, J. M. (Sci, *30*, 81; JoP, *6*, 448; Bull, *6*, 256)
Resignation: Dorcus, R. M. (Sci, *86*, 218)
Resignation: Wang, G. H. (Bull, *24*, 380)
Retirement: Johnson, B. J. (Sci, *86*, 394; Bull, *35*, 61)

Johnson, Buford Jennette

Appointment: Bureau of Educational Experiments, New York (Sci, *47*, 363; JoP, *15*, 280; Bull, *15*, 176)
Appointment: Johns Hopkins Univ. (Bull, *17*, 280)
Resignation: Laboratory of Social Hygiene, New York (Sci, *47*, 363; JoP, *15*, 280; Bull, *15*, 176)
Retirement: Johns Hopkins Univ. (Sci, *86*, 394; Bull, *35*, 61)

Johnson, Donald McEwen
Discovery of optical illusion (AJP, *56*, 604-607)

Johnson, Frederick Ernest
Election: Institute for Propaganda Analysis, vice-president (J APP, *25*, 361)

Johnson, George Ellsworth
Lecture: Clark Univ. (J APP, *9*, 87)

Johnson, George S.
Appointment: Stanford Univ., prof. of neuropsychiatry (SCI, *78*, 278)

Johnson, Harry Miles
Appointment: Goodrich, B. F. Co., Akron, Ohio (BULL, *17*, 351)
Appointment: National Electric Lamp Assoc. (BULL, *9*, 280; SCI, *35*, 889)
Appointment: Tulane Univ., dept. head (SCI, *87*, 504)
Appointment: Univ. of Pittsburgh (J APP, *10*, 522; SCI, *62*, 177)
Fellowship: Univ. of Pittsburgh (BULL, *22*, 612)
Lecture: pseudo-mathematics in the mental and social sciences (AJP, *48*, 342-351)
Lecture: Univ. of North Carolina (SCI, *72*, 598)
Publication: criticism of Humm's non-linear product-moment correlation (AJP, *56*, 111-116)
Publication: rejoinder to Humm, D. G. (AJP, *56*, 118-120)
Publication: some neglected principles in aptitude-testing (AJP, *47*, 165)
Research: factory lighting (BULL, *17*, 351)
Research: Simmons investigation of sleep (SCI, *67*, 450)

Johnson, [Roger Bruce Cash ?]
Appointment: Princeton Univ., preceptor (JoP, *2*, 336)

Johnson, Thomas M.
Lecture: immortality in Plato (JoP, *1*, 224)

Johnson, W. Smythe
Appointment: Natchitoches State Normal School (SCI, *13*, 280)

Johnson, William Ernest
Appointment: King's College, Cambridge (REV, *5*, 109)

Johnston, Charles Hughes
Appointment: Dartmouth College (JoP, *3*, 616; BULL, *3*, 422)
Appointment: Univ. of Kansas, dean (JoP, *7*, 224; BULL, *7*, 180)
Appointment: Univ. of Michigan (JoP, *4*, 420; BULL, *4*, 337)
Death notice (JoP, *14*, 700; BULL, *14*, 420)

Johnston, G. H.
Resignation: Univ. of Minnesota (BULL, *3*, 147)

Johnston, Swift Paine
Appointment: Univ. of Dublin (Rev, 5, 450)

Johnstone, Edward Ransom
Anniversary, 25th, Vineland Laboratory (Sci, 74, 286)

Jolly, Friedrich
Death notice (Sci, 19, 157; Bull, 1, 174)

Jones, Adam Leroy
Appointment: Columbia Univ. (Bull, 6, 120)
Appointment: Princeton Univ., preceptor (JoP, 2, 336)

Jones, Constance
Appointment: Girton College, Cambridge Univ. (Sci, 17, 520)

Jones, Edward Safford
Appointment: Oberlin College (Bull, 14, 366)
Leave of absence: Univ. of Buffalo (Bull, 42, 792)

Jones, Elmer Ellsworth
Appointment: Virginia State Normal School (Rev, 9, 536)

Jones, Fred Nowell
Publication: organic amnesia and relearning (AJP, 51, 170)

Jones, George Herbert
Bequeathal, charities and educational institutions (Sci, 94, 112)

Jones, Grace
Appointment: Univ. of Pittsburgh (J App, 10, 522)

Jones, Harold Ellis
Appointment: National Research Council (Sci, 94, 62)
Appointment: Univ. of California, director Institute of Child Welfare (Bull, 27, 620; J App, 11, 405; Sci, 66, 255)
Election: APA Council of Directors (Sci, 82, 247)
Election: National Social Science Research Council, Board of Directors (Sci, 99, 167)
Grant: Social Science Research Council (Bull, 31, 380)

Jones, Henry
Trip, USA (JoP, 5, 588)

Jones, John Hall
Appointment: Howard College (Bull, 42, 792)
Lecture: National Institute of Industrial Psychology (Sci, 83, 301)

Jones, Joseph William Lester
Retirement: Heidelberg College (BULL, *40*, 723)

Jones, Llewelyn Wynn
Election: British Assoc. for the Advancement of Science, Psych. Sect., president
(SCI, *80*, 583)
Lecture: "Points of view in psychology" (SCI, *69*, 450)

Jones, Percy L. General Hospital
Government managed, name was Battle Creek Sanitarium (SCI, *96*, 133)

Jones, Vernon Augustus
Appointment: Clark Univ. (SCI, *64*, 39; BULL, *35*, 334)

Jones, Walter Benton
Conference, industrial psychology, 10th (SCI, *69*, 492)

Jordan, Arthur Melville
Appointment: Univ. of Arkansas (JoP, *16*, 504)
Return: Univ. of Arkansas (SCI, *50*, 136)

Jordan, David Starr
Lecture: DePauw Univ., Charles Darwin (SCI°, *9*, 294)
Lecture: Indiana Academy of Sciences, Darwin (SCI°, *7*, 480)

Jordanburgh Nerve Hospital
Psych. Dept. organized, Drever, J. (SCI, *70*, 497)

Jorgensen, Albert Nels
Publication: Iowa Silent Reading Test (J APP, *23*, 633)

Josey, Charles Conant
Appointment: Dartmouth College (JoP, *18*, 504)
Appointment: Univ. of South Dakota (JoP, *20*, 448)

Jost, Hudson
Appointment: Univ. of Tennessee, Memphis (BULL, *42*, 582; SCI, *102*, 147)

Joteyko, Jozefa
Death notice (BULL, *25*, 700)
Election: Neurological Society of Belgium, vice-president (JoP, *1*, 504; BULL,
1, 334)

Journal de Genève
Publication: Fol, H., variations of personality (SCI°, *5*, 532)

Journal de Psychologie
Publication: resumes, Jan. 1920 (JoP, *17*, 196)

Journal de Psychologie pour la France et pour l'E'tranger
Publication: projected (REV, *10*, 591-592)

Journal des Sociétés Scientifiques
Publication (SCI°, *5*, 122)

Journal für Psychologie und Neurologie
Continuation of *Zeitschrift fur Hypnotismus* (REV, *10*, 103)

Journal of Abnormal and Social Psychology
Editor: Allport, G. W. (BULL, *34*, 179, 272)

Journal of Abnormal Psychology
Editor: Prince, M. (BULL, *3*, 148; JoP, *3*, 251)
Publication: announced (BULL, *3*, 148; JoP, *3*, 251)

Journal of Abnormal Psychology and Social Psychology
Name change to *Journal of Abnormal and Social Psychology* (JoP, *22*, 364)

Journal of Aesthetics and Art Criticism
Announcement of new quarterly (JoP, *38*, 279-280)
Appointment: Staff (JoP, *42*, 252)
Ownership: American Society for Aesthetics (JoP, *42*, 252)

Journal of Animal Behavior
Consolidation *Psychology* (BULL, *17*, 435)
Merged with *Psychobiology* to become *The Journal of Comparative Psychology* (JoP, *17*, 672)
Publication: announced (BULL, *7*, 425)

Journal of Applied Psychology
Mental testing column started (J APP, *22*, 215)
Ownership change (J APP, *6*, 301)
Plans made to begin (BULL, *13*, 482)
Publication: notice (JoP, *14*, 252)
Special issue announced, radio, Lazarsfeld, P. F. (J APP, *25*, 128)
Subscription price increase (J APP, *18*, 721)

Journal of Clinical Psychology
Publication announced (BULL, *41*, 603-604; J APP, *28*, 531; SCI, *100*, 167)
Resignation: Cameron, ?, and Beck, ?, from editorial board in protest (BULL, *42*, 485)

Journal of Comparative Neurology
Name change (JoP, *1*, 195; BULL, *1*, 28)

Journal of Comparative Neurology and Psychology
Address change (BULL, *4*, 336)
Death notice: Herrick, C. L. (SCI, *20*, 413; JoP, *1*, 560)

Name change (JoP, *1*, 195; BULL, *1*, 28)
Reorganization of editorial board (JoP, *1*, 195)

Journal of Comparative Psychology
Developed under the merger of *Psychobiology* and *The Journal of Animal Behavior* (JoP, *17*, 672)

Journal of Consulting Psychology
Photo volumes of applied psychologists (BULL, *36*, 500)
Publication: first issue (BULL, *34*, 273)

Journal of Criminal Law and Criminology
Editor: Gault, R. H. (JoP, *11*, 140; BULL, *9*, 408)
Election: Whipple, G. M., board (BULL, *8*, 222)

Journal of Criminal Psychopathology
Founding quarterly (BULL, *36*, 842)

Journal of Delinquency
Editor: Nelles, F. C. (BULL, *13*, 296)
Editor: Williams, J. H. (BULL, *13*, 296)
Publication notice (BULL, *13*, 296; JoP, *13*, 392)

Journal of Education
Statistics, defective sight (SCI°, *16*, 342)

Journal of Education (London)
Notes the lack of psychological labs in England (SCI, *3*, 776)

Journal of Educational Psychology
Editors announced (JoP, *6*, 700; BULL, *6*, 427)
Publication: announcement (JoP, *6*, 700; BULL, *6*, 427; J APP, *3*, 198)
Resignation: Bell, J. C. as editor (JoP, *9*, 364)

Journal of Experimental Psychology
Added to Psychological Review Publications (JoP, *13*, 336)
Discontinued (JoP, *16*, 56)
Editor: Bentley, M. (SCI, *63*, 88)
Editor: consulting appointed (BULL, *36*, 711)
Publication: announcement (JoP, *11*, 448)
Publication: monthly (BULL, *33*, 849)
Resignation: Watson, J. B. (SCI, *63*, 88)
Size increase (BULL, *28*, 79)

Journal of Gerontology
Establishment: Gerontological Society (SCI, *102*, 173)

Journal of Mental Science
Index: Turner, J., prepares (REV, *6*, 344)

Publication: announcement (SCI, *1*, 418)
Publication: statistics on insanity (SCI, *4*, 113)

Journal of Nervous and Mental Diseases
Appointment: editorial board (SCI, *15*, 226-227)
Editor: Lewis, N. D. C. (SCI, *101*, 171)
Editors announced (SCI, *5*, 144)
Publication: Peckham. G., "A critical digest of the proceedings of the English Psychical Society" (SCI°, *6*, 360)
Symposium: Jelliffe, S. E., anniversary of editorship, neuro-psychiatric (SCI, *87*, 296)

Journal of Neurophysiology
First edition (BULL, *35*, 334)
Psychological abstracts accepted (SCI, *86*, 467)

Journal of Parapsychology
Editor: Greenwood, J. A.; Pratt, J. G.; Rhine, J. B.; Stuart, C. E. (BULL, *39*, 325)
Editorship returns to Duke Univ., 1942 (SCI, *95*, 322-323)

Journal of Pedagogy
Format change (SCI°, *12*, 70)

Journal of Personnel Research
Editor: Bingham, W. V. D. and Thurstone, L. L. (SCI, *58*, 347)
Publication begins (BULL, *19*, 462)

Journal of Philosophy
Appointment: Randall, Jr., J. H., Board of Editors (JOP, *34*, 280)
Editor: Nagel, E. (JOP, *36*, 420)
Editor: staff for book (JOP, *37*, 392; JOP, *40*, 392)
Publication: Neild, J., physical vs. psychological mechanisms of the mind (JOP, *40*, 139-140)

Journal of Philosophy, Psychology and Scientific Method
Name changed to *The Journal of Philosophy* (JOP, *18*, 26)
Publication: announced (BULL, *1*, 92)

Journal of Psychology
Prospectus issued (REV, *10*, 464)

Journal of Social Philosophy: A Quarterly Devoted to a Philosophic Synthesis of the Social Sciences
Editorial board founded (AJP, *48*, 174)

Journal of Social Psychology
Formation announced (JOP, *27*, 84)

Journal of Social Science

Publication: Noyes, W., modern view of the criminal type (Sci°, *11*, 217)

Journal of Symbolic Logic

Editor: Church, A. (JoP, *39*, 84)
Editor: McKinsey, J. C. C. (JoP, *39*, 84)

Journal of the History of Ideas

Publication: monograph series (JoP, *41*, 56)

Journal of the National Institute (British) of Industrial Psychology

Publication: begins (J App, *6*, 81)

Journal of the Society for Psychical Research

Publication: Barrett's trip to Amer. and the formation of Amer. Society (Sci°, *5*, 62)
Publication: Myers, G. C., Notes on the unconscious self (Sci°, *7*, 415)
September issue (Sci°, *8*, 367)

Journal of Unified Science

Name changed from *Erkenntnis*; Vol. VIII (JoP, *36*, 532)

Journal Press, The

Editor: Murchison, C. (Bull, *34*, 635; Sci, *86*, 239)

Journals

Publication: American photofile of psychology; microfilm and photoprints, journals, abstracts, manuscripts (Bull, *37*, 407)
Publication: Boring, E. G., "The lag of publication in journals of psychology" (AJP, *49*, 137)
Publication: Fernberger, S. W., "On the number of articles of psychological interest published in the different languages. 1920-1935" (AJP, *48*, 680)
Publication: Schultz, R. S. and Pallister, H., "Book reviews in psychological periodicals" (AJP, *46*, 508)
Research: Committee on Scientific Aids to Learning, microfilming project (Bull, *37*, 187)

Judd, Charles Hubbard

Appointment: Chautauqua summer lecturer (Sci, *27*, 759; JoP, *5*, 308; Bull, *5*, 244)
Appointment: National Youth Administration (Sci, *92*, 125)
Appointment: New York Univ. (Rev, *5*, 449; Sci, *7*, 713; AJP, *10*, 165)
Appointment: Univ. of California, Berkeley (Sci, *96*, 10)
Appointment: Univ. of Chicago (Sci, *28*, 444; JoP, *5*, 588; Bull, *27*, 674; Sci, *52*, 153; Bull, *5*, 347)
Appointment: Univ. of Cincinnati (Sci, *13*, 1040; Sci, *14*, 232, 944; Rev, *8*, 552)

Appointment: War Dept. at the Army School for Special Service, consultant (BULL, *40*, 231)
Appointment: Wesleyan Univ. (REV, *3*, 468; AJP, *7*, 579)
Appointment: Yale Psychological Laboratory (JoP, *1*, 28)
Appointment: Yale Summer School (SCI, *22*, 848; BULL, *3*, 36; JoP, *3*, 56)
Appointment: Yale Univ. (JoP, *4*, 252; SCI, *15*, 360)
Degree: Iowa State Univ. (BULL, *20*, 664)
Departure: New York Univ. School of Pedagogy (SCI, *14*, 944)
Departure: Univ. of Cincinnati (SCI, *15*, 360)
Departure: Wesleyan Univ. (REV, *5*, 449)
Editor: *Monograph Supplements* (JoP, *1*, 280; BULL, *1*, 213)
Election: Kappa Delta Pi (BULL, *42*, 484)
Lecture: AAAS, Lancaster Branch (SCI, *88*, 449)
Lecture: APA (JoP, *8*, 699-700; SCI, *34*, 680)
Lecture: Central Kansas Teachers' Assoc. (SCI, *33*, 420)
Lecture: Columbia Univ. (J APP, *10*, 129; SCI, *33*, 214; JoP, *8*, 112)
Lecture: empiricism (JoP, *2*, 112)
Lecture: habits (JoP, *1*, 224)
Lecture: movements (JoP, *2*, 224)
Lecture: visual perception and eye movement (BULL, *6*, 32; SCI, *29*, 23)
Lecture: Washington Academy of Sciences, visual perception (SCI, *24*, 792)
Promotion: Yale Univ. (BULL, *4*, 95; SCI, *25*, 360)
Publication: *Grundriss der Psychologie* translation of (AJP, *7*, 579; SCI, *3*, 775)
Resignation: New York Univ. (REV, *8*, 336)
Resignation: New York Univ. resolution from graduate students (SCI, *13*, 760)
Resignation: Yale Univ. (BULL, *5*, 347)

Judd, Deane Brewster
Appointment: Inter-Society Color Council (BULL, *37*, 123)
Appointment: National Bureau of Standards (J APP, *10*, 395)

Judgment
Lecture: Pillsbury, W. B. (JoP, *2*, 252)

Jung, Carl Gustav
Appointment: editorial board, *Character and Personality* (J APP, *16*, 439)
Course: nervous and mental diseases (SCI, *36*, 369)
Degree: Clark Univ. (SCI, *30*, 362)
Degree: Fordham Univ. (SCI, *36*, 398)
Degree: Oxford Univ. (BULL, *35*, 578; SCI, *88*, 52, 211)
Endowment: Higher Technical School of Zurich for Psycho-Analyses (SCI, *81*, 67)
Lecture: Harvard Tercentary Conference of Arts and Sciences (J APP, *20*, 518; BULL, *33*, 476)
Lecture: Institute of Medical Psychology, London (SCI, *82*, 348)
Lecture: Yale Univ. (SCI, *86*, 395; SCI, *85*, 541)
Presides over International Medical Congress, Oxford Univ. (SCI, *88*, 212)

Junior colleges (*see also* Psychology in Junior Colleges, Committee on)

Appointment: Amer. Assoc. of Junior Colleges, committee to study psychology in (AJP, *54*, 436-437)

Jurgensen, Clifford Eugene

Appointment: Minneapolis Gas Light Co. (Sci, *101*, 581; Bull, *42*, 485)

Justice

Lecture: Tufts, J. H. (JoP, *10*, 252)

Juvenile delinquency (*see also* Delinquency)

Appointment: Haines, T. H. to bureau (Bull, *11*, 352)

Juveniles

Psychological examiner sought by Los Angeles County Civil Service Commission for study of (Sci, *95*, 600)

K

Kaan, Hans
Research: hypnotism (SCI°, 6, 280)

Kafka, Gustav
Appointment: Johns Hopkins Univ. (SCI, 69, 450; BULL, 26, 624)

Kaiser, Albert D.
Appointment: Univ. of Rochester (SCI, 101, 481)
Award: Rochester Civic Medal (SCI, 102, 172)

Kaiser Wilhelm Institute for Anthropology
Appointment: Lenz, F., eugenics and racial hygiene (SCI, 79, 157)
Appointment: Scholz, W., director, German Research Institute of Psychiatry
    (SCI, 84, 288)

Kakise, Hikozo
Appointment: Clark Univ. (BULL, 4, 370)

Kalamazoo College (Michigan)
Appointment: Hauptman, L. M. (BULL, 42, 63)

Kallen, Horace Meyer
Letter concerning book on James, W. and Bergson, H. (JoP, 12, 615-616)

Kam, Gertrude
Promotion (SCI, 39, 721)

Kandinskii, Viktor Khrisanfovich
Publication: hallucinations (AJP, 1, 363)

Kansas Academy of Science
Election: Peterson, J. C., Kansas Psych. Assoc., president (SCI, 71, 505)

Lecture: list of (SCI°, *10*, 286; SCI°, *16*, 301)
Meeting: program of Nov, 1886 (SCI°, *8*, 537)

Kansas State Manual Training School
Lecture: Hall, G. S., educational efficiency (JOP, *9*, 140; SCI, *34*, 754)

Kansas State Normal School (Emporia)
Appointment: DeVoss, J. C. (SCI, *40*, 446; BULL, *11*, 483)
Lecture: Hall, G. S., inauguration of Myers, G. E. (JOP, *9*, 28)
Lecture: Jastrow, J. (SCI, *35*, 772)

Kansas State Teachers College (Pittsburg)
Departure: Small, G. D. (BULL, *42*, 583)
Promotion: Murphy, P. (BULL, *42*, 331)

Kansas, University of (Lawrence)
Appointment: Adams, H. F. (BULL, *7*, 148; JOP, *7*, 280)
Appointment: Coleman, J. C. (BULL, *42*, 791)
Appointment: Guilford, J. P. (J APP, *11*, 235)
Appointment: Hartley, R. (BULL, *42*, 792)
Appointment: Helson, H. (J APP, *10*, 522)
Appointment: Heron, W. T. (BULL, *21*, 240)
Appointment: Hunter, W. S. (SCI, *44*, 132; JOP, *13*, 504; BULL, *13*, 296, 376)
Appointment: Ogden, R. M. (BULL, *11*, 352; JOP, *11*, 560)
Appointment: Pepinsky, H. B. (BULL, *41*, 603)
Appointment: Rosenow, C. (SCI, *51*, 513; BULL, *17*, 200)
Appointment: Squires, P. C. (BULL, *25*, 568)
Appointment: Templin, O. (REV, *3*, 120)
Appointment: Wheeler, R. H. (BULL, *22*, 444)
Conference: Menninger Clinic, psychoanalysis and experimental psych. (BULL, *33*, 579)
Course: Buchner, E. F. (BULL, *12*, 403)
Departure: Guilford, J. P. (BULL, *25*, 444)
Departure: Helson, H. (BULL, *25*, 444)
Departure: Heron, W. T. (BULL, *23*, 455)
Departure: Hunter, W. S. (J APP, *9*, 90)
Departure: Rogers, D. C. (BULL, *11*, 190; SCI, *39*, 606; JOP, *11*, 308)
Election: Johnston, C. H., Dean School of Ed. (BULL, *7*, 180; JOP, *7*, 224)
Election: Lindley, E. H. (BULL, *17*, 435)
Lab: experimental psych. (SCI, *2*, 692)
Lecture: list of (SCI°, *13*, 398; SCI°, *7*, 480)
Lecture: Nichols, E. L., Sigma Xi (SCI, *11*, 634)
Lecture: Palmer, G. H. (JOP, *4*, 112; BULL, *4*, 95)
Lecture: Seashore, C. E., music (SCI, *51*, 268; JOP, *17*, 168)
Lecture: "The psychology of counting" (SCI°, *13*, 398)
Lecture: Titchener, E. B. (BULL, *8*, 110)
Meeting: MPA, 10th (SCI, *81*, 94)

Promotion: Cason, H. (BULL, *19*, 462)
Promotion: Dockeray, F. C. (BULL, *13*, 407)
Promotion: Psych. Dept. (SCI, *55*, 675)
Promotion: Rosenow, C. (BULL, *19*, 462)
Removal: Ogden, R. M. (JoP, *13*, 504)

Kant, Immanuel
Centenary of death celebrations (JoP, *1*, 139, 168; BULL, *1*, 133)
Commemoration of death *Revue de Métaphysique et de Morale* (BULL, *1*, 413)
Income record Univ. of Königsberg (JoP, *3*, 588)
Lecture: Cassirer, E., Yale Univ., philosophy of (JoP, *38*, 168)
Lecture: Hodgson, S. (JoP, *2*, 672)
Lecture: Lovejoy, A. O. (JoP, *1*, 224)
Meeting: Society for Philosophical Inquiry, Kant Centennial (JoP, *1*, 196)
Monument: Berlin plans to erect (SCI, *17*, 677)
Publication: monograph on (JoP, *41*, 56)

Kantgesellschaft
Competition announced (JoP, *5*, 532)
Contest: Kant study (JoP, *17*, 504)
Contest: postponement (JoP, *13*, 364)
Formation (JoP, *1*, 56)

Kantor, Jacob Robert
Appointment: Univ. of Chicago (SCI, *46*, 432; BULL, *14*, 420)
Editor: *Psychological Record* (BULL, *36*, 806)
Publication: "Concerning physical analogies in psychology" (AJP, *48*, 164)

Kaplan, Oscar Joel
Appointment: *Gerontology* editorial board (BULL, *42*, 792)

Kappa Delta Pi
Election: Judd, C. H., Laureate Chapter (BULL, *42*, 484)
Election: Seashore, C. E., Laureate Chapter (BULL, *42*, 484)

Kardiner, Abraham
Lecture: New York Philosophical Society, psychoanalysis (JoP, *35*, 616)

Karn, Harry Wendell
Research: relation between nutrition and pathological disturbances in behavior (BULL, *38*, 304)

Karwoski, Theodore
Appointment: Dartmouth College (JoP, *27*, 560; BULL, *27*, 496)
Grant: National Research Council (BULL, *33*, 578)

Kasanin, Jacob Sergi
Lecture: Rockefeller Foundation, U.S. Army Hospitals, psychosomatic medicine (Sci, *98*, 298)

Katona, George
Appointment: Univ. of Chicago, Committee on Price Control and Rationing (Bull, *40*, 231)
Publication: *Organizing and Memorizing* reply to Melton's review (AJP, *55*, 273-275)

Katz, Daniel
Promotion: Princeton Univ. (Sci, *74*, 146)
Publication: "Eye-movements and the phi-phenomenon" (AJP, *46*, 334)
Publication: "Psychological needs" (JoP, *34*, 644)

Katzenellenbogen, Edwin
Appointment: Harvard Univ. (Sci, *30*, 524)

Kaufman, Ralph
Appointment: Boston Psychoanalytic Institute, chair, education committee (Bull, *37*, 828)
Research: suicide, psychoanalysis as treatment (J App, *22*, 108)

Kay, David
Publication: *Edinburgh Review*, "Memory, what is it and how to improve it" (Sci°, *12*, 237)

Keen, William Williams
Election: American Philosophical Society, president (Sci, *27*, 117)

Keller, Fred Simmons
Appointment: Columbia Univ. (Sci, *95*, 526)
Promotion: Columbia Univ. (Bull, *39*, 423)

Kelley, Noble Henry
Appointment: Kentucky Psychological Assoc., director (J App, *25*, 725)

Kelley, Truman Lee
Appointment: Office of the Surgeon General (J App, *1*, 395; Bull, *14*, 334)
Appointment: Univ. of Texas (Bull, *11*, 444)
Election: Psychometric Society, president (Sci, *88*, 277)

Kelley, Victor Harold
Publication: Iowa Silent Reading Test (J App, *23*, 633)

Kellogg, Chester Elijah
Course: Bryn Mawr College (Bull, *11*, 190)

Kellogg, E. Ruth
Death notice (BULL., *41*, 807)

Kellogg, John Harvey
Award: Battle Creek Chamber of Commerce and County Medical Society (SCI, *95*, 298)

Kellogg, Robert James
Publication: *Studies in Linguistic Psychology* (JoP, *10*, 56)

Kellogg, Vernon Lyman
Publication: war, science, and the National Research Council (J APP, *3*, 393-394)

Kellogg, Winthrop Niles
Anniversary: 50th, Indiana Univ. Psych. Lab (J APP, *23*, 631)
Fellowship: Board of National Research (BULL., *26*, 380)
Fellowship: Social Science Research Council (BULL., *28*, 567)
Publication: "A further note on the 'Wolf Children' of India" (AJP, *45*, 149)
Publication: "The Indiana conditioning laboratory" (AJP, *51*, 174)
Symposium: Indiana Univ., learning, 1939 (BULL., *37*, 61)

Kelly, E. Lowell
Appointment: Purdue Univ. (BULL., *36*, 406)

Kelman, Harold
Election: Assoc. for the Advancement of Psychoanalysis, secretary (J APP, *25*, 473)

Kemmerer, Mabel Clare Williams (*see* Williams, Mabel Clare)

Kemp, Edward Harris
Appointment: Brown Univ. (SCI, *83*, 367)
Fellowship: awarded (SCI, *81*, 482)
Lecture: Brown Univ. (BULL., *32*, 323)

Kemp, George T.
Appointment: Hoagland Laboratory, New York (SCI°, *14*, 131, 437)

Kendall, Otis
Death notice (SCI, *9*, 78)

Kennedy, Foster
Lecture: neuroses in warfare (SCI, *97*, 374)
Moderator: Postgraduate Assembly on Nervous and Mental Diseases and War (SCI, *100*, 311)

Kennedy, Francis
Appointment: Princeton Univ. (REV, *4*, 690; AJP, *9*, 250)
Appointment: Univ. of Colorado (REV, *5*, 449)

Death notice (REV, 8, 224)
Promotion: Univ. of Colorado (REV, 6, 456)

Kennedy-Fraser, David
Election: Royal Society of Edinburgh (SCI, 69, 349)

Kent State University (Ohio)
Appointment: Bach, G. R. (BULL, 42, 581)

Kentucky Academy of Science
Meeting (SCI, 95, 298)

Kentucky Psychological Association
Meeting (BULL, 42, 487; J APP, 25, 725)
Permanent organization founded (J APP, 25, 725)

Kentucky State University (Frankfort)
Appointment: Simrall, J. P. (BULL, 16, 392)

Kentucky, University of (Lexington)
Appointment: Bassett, G. C. (J APP, 10, 522; BULL, 24, 136)
Appointment: Beaumont, H. (SCI, 72, 315)
Appointment: Dimmick, G. B. (SCI, 72, 315)
Appointment: Graham, J. L. (J APP, 10, 522; BULL, 24, 136)
Appointment: Humphreys, H. H. (BULL, 42, 582)
Appointment: Newberry, E. (SCI, 72, 315)
Appointment: psych. dept. (SCI, 64, 448)
Appointment: Ruckmick, C. A. (BULL, 19, 236)
Appointment: White, M. M., head of psych. (BULL, 40, 539; SCI, 72, 315)
Conference: industrial psychology (BULL, 41, 499)
Industrial psychology program announcement (BULL, 41, 199-200, 499)
Leave of absence: Tigert, J. J. (JOP, 15, 308; SCI, 47, 484)

Kenyon College (Gambier, Ohio)
Appointment: Hinshaw, R. P. (BULL, 39, 895)
Departure: Cummings, S. (BULL, 39, 895)

Keppel, Frederick Paul
Cattell Portrait Committee (SCI, 75, 661)

Kerr, Willard Augusta
Appointment: RCA Manufacturing Co., Inc., personnel research (BULL, 39, 681)
Departure: Purdue Univ. (BULL, 39, 681)
Election: Indiana Academy of Science (BULL, 40, 152)

Keuka College (Keuka Park, New York)
Appointment: Edwards, R. H. (BULL, 41, 200)
Appointment: Gorham, D. R. (BULL, 40, 619)

Key, [Axel ?]
 Research: effects of overwork in schools (Sci°, *15*, 40)

Keyser, P. H.
 Appointment: Univ. of Colorado (Sci, *13*, 200)

Kidd, Benjamin
 Death notice (Bull, *13*, 448; JoP, *13*, 643)

Kiev, University of (Ukraine)
 New psych. lab (Sci, *2*, 850)

Killeffer, David Herbert
 Chair: National Research Council, location of new and rare instrument (Sci, *96*, 58)

Kilmer, Elmer Kinsey
 Appointment: Muhlenberg College (Bull, *40*, 459)

Kilpatrick, William Heard
 Lecture: Stanford Education Conference, 1938 (J App, *22*, 108)

Kinder, Elaine Flitner
 Appointment: New York State Institutions, Director of Internships in Clinical
  Psych. (Bull, *39*, 809-810)
 Election: AAAP, clinical chair (J App, *25*, 265)
 Grant: Social Science Research Council (Bull, *36*, 805)
 Leave of absence: New York Rockland State Hospital (Bull, *40*, 618)
 Lecture: American Assoc. on Mental Deficiency, 1938 (J App, *22*, 109)

Kindred, John J.
 Appointment: Stetson Univ. (Sci, *75*, 306)

King, Irving
 Appointment: Iowa State Univ. (JoP, *6*, 560; Bull, *6*, 327)
 Appointment: Univ. of Michigan (JoP, *3*, 532; Bull, *3*, 240, 319; Sci, *24*, 384)
 Appointment: Pratt Institute, Brooklyn (Sci, *18*, 160)
 Departure: Pratt Institute (JoP, *3*, 532; Sci, *24*, 384)
 Lecture: Baltimore (Bull, *3*, 392)
 Lecture: consciousness (JoP, *1*, 644)
 Lecture: psychology of education (JoP, *7*, 222)
 Lecture: religion (JoP, *1*, 84)

King, Natalie A.
 Rochester Guidance Clinic, New York; Mental Hygiene (Bull, *36*, 841)

King's College (Cambridge, England)
 Appointment: Johnson, W. E. (Rev, *5*, 109)
 Degree: Sorely, W. R. (JoP, *2*, 420)
 Election: Pearson, K., honorary fellow (JoP, *1*, 56)

King's College (London, England)
Appointment: Myers, C. S. (SCI, *24*, 96; JoP, *3*, 476; SCI, *18*, 704; JoP, *1*, 28; BULL, *3*, 288; BULL, *1*, 134)
Departure: Smith, W. G. (BULL, *1*, 134; JoP, *1*, 28)
Laboratory experimental psych. opening (SCI, *16*, 280; REV, *9*, 536)
Lecture: Caldecott, A. (SCI, *20*, 656; BULL, *1*, 488; JoP, *1*, 672)
Lecture: Halliburton, W. D. (SCI, *20*, 656; BULL, *1*, 488; JoP, *1*, 672)
Lecture: Myers, C. S. (BULL, *1*, 488; SCI, *20*, 656)

Kingsbury, Forest Alva
Appointment: Univ. of Chicago (BULL, *37*, 62)
Course: Univ. of Chicago (J APP, *23*, 311)
Editor: *Educational and Psychological Testing* (J APP, *25*, 266)
Election: MPA (BULL, *37*, 187; J APP, *23*, 96)
Promotion: Univ. of Chicago (BULL, *42*, 486)

Kingsford, A. Beresford
Lecture: Child Study Society (JoP, *8*, 644)

Kinsey, Alfred Charles
Grant: National Research Council, Committee for Research on Problems of Sex (SCI, *95*, 600)
Research: Indiana Univ., Nowlis, V., associate (BULL, *41*, 603)
Research: Indiana Univ., sex behavior (SCI, *100*, 97)

Kirby, George Hughes
Appointment: Columbia Univ. (SCI, *65*, 471)
Election: New York Society for Clinical Psychiatry, president (SCI, *57*, 80)

Kirkpatrick, Edwin Asbury
Appointment: Bellingham State Normal College (JoP, *14*, 224)
Course: Cornell Univ. (BULL, *8*, 146)
Death notice (AJP, *49*, 489)
Lecture (JoP, *13*, 476)
Photograph collection of psychologists (BULL, *11*, 115; SCI, *39*, 422; BULL, *9*, 440; JoP, *9*, 644; JoP, *10*, 252)

Kirkpatrick, Forrest Hunter
Appointment: Department of State by Hull, C. (BULL, *41*, 679)
Promotion: RCA Manufacturing Co. (BULL, *41*, 409)

Kirkpatrick, Milton E.
Lecture: Child Health Program Conference (SCI, *101*, 482)

Kirschmann, August
Appointment: Univ. of Toronto (AJP, *11*, 130; REV, *6*, 673; REV, *1*, 112)

Kitay, Philip Morton
Appointment: Univ. of Delaware (BULL, *42*, 127)

Kitson, Harry Dexter
Appointment: Columbia Univ. (J APP, *9*, 204; BULL, *22*, 504; SCI, *61*, 539)
Appointment: Harvard Univ. (BULL, *12*, 440)
Appointment: Indiana Univ. (SCI, *50*, 161; J APP, *3*, 290)
Appointment: New York Univ. (SCI, *55*, 593; BULL, *19*, 410)
Appointment: Univ. of Chicago (BULL, *16*, 257)
Course: Teachers College, Columbia, vocational counseling (BULL, *42*, 794)
Lecture: National Vocational Guidance Assoc. (J APP, *6*, 425)
Publication: empathy (JoP, *17*, 644)
Publication: referred to the Committee on Terminology (JoP, *17*, 644)
Research: psychology of proofreading (J APP, *1*, 298)
Return from Europe (BULL, *18*, 568)

Kitzmiller, Albanus Blaine
Publication: "Memory of raccoons" (AJP, *46*, 512)

Klemm, Otto
Appointment: Alberta Univ. (SCI, *39*, 423; BULL, *11*, 192; JoP, *11*, 224)
Death notice (AJP, *52*, 308-309)

Kline, Linus Ward
Lecture: writing process (JoP, *7*, 223)
Resignation: Skidmore College (SCI, *81*, 149)

Klineberg, Otto
Appointment: Escola Politechnia of São Paulo (SCI, *101*, 428; BULL, *42*, 486)

Klinik für Psychische und Nervöse Krankheiten
Publication announced (BULL, *3*, 148)

Klopfer, Bruno
Appointment: City College of New York (BULL, *42*, 582)
Lecture: Institute on the Exceptional Child, 6th; Woods School (J APP, *23*, 744)
Publication: Rorschach record blank (J APP, *23*, 420)

Kluver, Heinrich
Fellowship: Social Science Research Group (BULL, *24*, 136)

Knapp Foundation, Columbia University
Appointment: Rand, G. (BULL, *40*, 459)

Knight, William Angus
Death notice (JoP, *13*, 224)
Publication: in *Philosophical Classics for English Readers* (SCI°, *8*, 512)
Resignation: Univ. of St. Andrews (REV, *10*, 103)

Knowledge
Lecture: Dewey, J. (JoP, *1*, 224)
Research: theory of, Will, F. L. (JoP, *42*, 308)

Knox College (Galesburg, Illinois)
Appointment: Bumstead, C. (BULL, *41*, 603)

Koch, Helen Lois
Election: Illinois Society of Consulting Psych., secretary-treasurer (BULL, *35*, 578)

Koch, Robert
Appointment: Hygienic Institute (SCI°, *4*, 410)
Election: Belgian Academy of Sciences (SCI, *9*, 420)
Museum of hygiene, Berlin opens (SCI°, *8*, 513)
Publication: *Zeitschrift für hygiene* (SCI°, *7*, 284)

Koenig, W.
Lecture: heredity (AJP, *15*, 463)

Koffka, Kurt
Appointment: Cornell Univ. (BULL, *21*, 660)
Appointment: Smith College (BULL, *29*, 603)
Appointment: Smith College, Neilson, W. A. Chair (JoP, *24*, 420; J App, *11*, 166; BULL, *24*, 380)
Appointment: Univ. of Chicago (SCI, *61*, 257; BULL, *22*, 140)
Appointment: Univ. of Wisconsin (BULL, *23*, 456; J App, *10*, 523; SCI, *64*, 118; JoP, *23*, 504)
Arrival in U.S. (BULL, *25*, 123; SCI, *67*, 13)
Death notice (BULL, *39*, 267; AJP, *55*, 278-281)
Election: SEP, chair (BULL, *34*, 273)
Lecture: Cornell Univ., gestalt psychology (SCI, *61*, 181)
Lecture: gestalt psychology (SCI, *69*, 156)
Lecture: Harvard Univ. (SCI, *60*, 587)
Lecture: human behavior (SCI, *91*, 499-500)
Lecture: Univ. of Iowa (SCI, *62*, 106)
Research: Russian scientific expedition (SCI, *75*, 510)

Kohl, Clayton Charles
Appointment: New York Univ. (BULL, *12*, 280)
Departure: Mount Holyoke College (BULL, *12*, 280)

Köhler, Wolfgang
Appointment: Berlin Psychological Laboratory (SCI, *55*, 313)
Appointment: Clark Univ. (SCI, *61*, 183; JoP, *22*, 56; BULL, *21*, 660)
Appointment: Harvard Univ. (JoP, *22*, 252; BULL, *31*, 380; BULL, *22*, 444; SCI, *61*, 465)

Appointment: Harvard Univ., William James Lecturer (Sci, *79*, 314; Sci, *80*, 334)
Appointment: Swarthmore College (Sci, *82*, 298)
Appointment: Univ. of Iowa (Bull, *32*, 376)
Course: Swarthmore College (Bull, *41*, 72)
Exposition: Century of Progress (Sci, *77*, 579)
Lecture: Clark Univ. (J App, *9*, 87; Sci, *59*, 460)
Lecture: Conference on Methods in Philosophy and the Sciences (Bull, *41*, 72; JoP, *40*, 644)
Lecture: intelligence of apes (Bull, *22*, 444)
Lecture: phenomenology (JoP, *42*, 55-56)
Lecture: points of view in psych. (Sci, *69*, 450)
Lecture: Rutgers Univ., Sigma Xi (Sci, *81*, 196)
Return to Berlin (Sci, *63*, 161)

Kohlrausch, Friedrich Wilhelm Georg
Appointment: Physico-Technical Institute (Sci, *1*, 109)

Kohs Block Designs Test
Publication: Hutt's revised scoring system (AJP, *54*, 131-132)

Kolb, Lawrence
Lecture: "Drug addictions" (Sci, *89*, 289)
Retirement: U.S. Public Health Service (Sci, *100*, 447)

Koldewey, Friedrich
Publication: "Monumenta Germaniae Pedagogica" (Sci°, *9*, 362)

König, Arthur Peter
Death notice (Sci, *14*, 1022; Rev, *9*, 104)
Death notice: correction about (Sci, *14*, 863)
Publication: discrimination of colors (Sci, *1*, 471)

König, Rudolf
Death notice (Rev, *9*, 104; Sci, *14*, 660)

Königsberg, University of
Appointment: Münsterberg, H., declined (Bull, *2*, 191; Sci, *21*, 638; JoP, *2*, 252)
Kant, celebrated centenary of death of (JoP, *1*, 139, 168)
Kant, I., income record (JoP, *3*, 588)

Königsberger Hartungsche Zeitung
Publication: centenary of death of Kant (JoP, *1*, 196)

Königsberger, Leo
Publication: biography of Helmholtz, H. (Rev, *9*, 328; Sci, *15*, 438)

Kopeloff, Nicholas
Return: Psychiatric Institute, New York (Sci, 60, 330)

Köppen, Max
Death notice (Bull, 13, 188)

Koppisch, Enrique
Leave of absence: Univ. of Puerto Rico (Sci, 101, 86)

Kornhauser, Arthur William
Election: Illinois Society of Consulting Psychologists, president (Bull, 35, 578)
Lecture: Taylor Society (J App, 9, 204)
Meeting: Psychological Corporation, APA, and AAAP, 1941 (J App, 25, 600)
Publication: American Management Assoc., "The techniques of market research
from the standpoint of a psychologist" (Sci, 81, 589)

Kraepelin, Emil
Death notice (Bull, 24, 312)
Departure: teaching, to devote time to research (Bull, 19, 462)
Departure: Univ. of Munich (Sci, 55, 673)
Editor: *Psychologische Arbeiten* (Rev, 2, 216)
Research: insanity (Bull, 1, 174; JoP, 1, 112)
Restoration of Italian villa (Sci, 56, 415)
Return: Germany from the U.S. (Sci, 28, 403)
Trip: Dutch East Indies (Sci, 19, 358)

Krafft-Ebing, Richard von
Retirement: Vienna, chair of psychiatry (Sci, 15, 320)

Krakow, University of (Poland)
Gilman, D. C. represents Johns Hopkins Univ. at 500th anniversary (Sci, 11,
877)

Krasno, Louis
Appointment: Northwestern Univ. (Sci, 88, 471)

Krauss, William W.
Lecture: Univ. of Colorado, race biology (Sci, 98, 106)

Krechevsky, Isadore (Krech, David)
Conference: Univ. of Colorado, Summer School, learning (Sci, 89, 483; Bull,
36, 583)

Kreezer, George L.
Appointment: Cornell Univ. (Sci, 87, 482)
Appointment: Vineland Training School, New Jersey (Sci, 77, 255)
Departure: Vineland Training School, New Jersey (Sci, 87, 482)
Publication: "Electro-encephalogram and its use in psychology" (AJP, 51, 737)

Publication: "Electro-physiological methods and their use in the investigation of growth and development" (AJP, *49*, 483)

Kreidl, Alois

Lecture: Congress for Experimental Psychology, 4th (JoP, *7*, 83)

Kremser, Victor Felix Karl

Research: mortality and temperature (Sci°, *16*, 203)

Krishnavarma, Shyamáji

Endowed lectureship (JoP, *1*, 56)
Offers to establish Herbert Spencer Indian fellowships (JoP, *2*, 196)

Krohn, William Otterbein

Appointment: Illinois Eastern Hospital for the Insane (Rev, *4*, 689; AJP, *9*, 135)
Departure: Univ. of Illinois (Rev, *4*, 689)

Kronecker, Hugo

Death notice (Bull, *11*, 268)

Krueger, Felix

Appointment: Buenos Aires (Bull, *3*, 148; JoP, *3*, 196)
Lecture: Columbia Univ. (Sci, *36*, 591)
Lecture: German Society of Experimental Psychology, experimental phonetics (Sci, *22*, 727)
Lecture: inaugural (JoP, *9*, 644)
Lecture: Univ. of Illinois (JoP, *10*, 252; Sci, *37*, 407)
Lecture: Univ. of Wisconsin (JoP, *10*, 252; Sci, *37*, 407)
Nomination: Columbia Univ., Kaiser Wilhelm professor (JoP, *9*, 224; Sci, *35*, 495)

Kuder, George Frederic

Editor: *Educational and Psychological Measurement* (J App, *25*, 265)
Preference record now scoreable on IBM test scoring machine (J App, *23*, 531)

Külpe, Oswald

Appointment: Univ. of Bonn (JoP, *7*, 84; JoP, *6*, 560; Bull, *6*, 368)
Appointment: Univ. of Munich (Bull, *10*, 212; Sci, *37*, 788; JoP, *10*, 364)
Appointment: Univ. of Wurzburg (Rev, *2*, 104; AJP, *7*, 152)
Death notice (Sci, *43*, 207; AJP, *27*, 296; Bull, *13*, 108; JoP, *13*, 112)
Lecture: Assoc. of German Scientific Men and Physicians, epistemology (JoP, *7*, 504)
Lecture: German Society of Experimental Psychology, experimental esthetics (Sci, *22*, 727)
Promotion: announced (Rev, *1*, 336)
Publication: *Einleitung in der Philosophie*, translation (Rev, *3*, 588)
Publication: English translation (Sci, *4*, 269)

Kuenne, Margaret Ruth
Appointment: Univ. of Minnesota (BULL, *42*, 331)

Kuhlen, Raymond Gerhardt
Leave of absence: Syracuse Univ. (BULL, *41*, 603)

Kuhlmann, Frederick
Appointment: Univ. of Illinois (JoP, *4*, 448; BULL, *4*, 236)
Appointment: Univ. of Wisconsin (BULL, *2*, 296)
Death notice (AJP, *54*, 446-447)
Lecture: American Assoc. on Mental Deficiency, 1938 (J APP, *22*, 109)
Lecture: apparatus to study memory and light/color sense in animals (JoP, *7*, 223)
Lecture: licensing psychologists (AJP, *56*, 120-129)
Publication: Minnesota Chapter of Psi Chi, last paper (J APP, *25*, 359)
Publication: *Tests of Mental Development* (J APP, *23*, 420)

Kunz, George F.
Election: NYAS, committee member (JoP, *9*, 28)

Kuo, Zing-Yang
Appointment: China Institute of Physiology and Psychology (SCI, *93*, 181; BULL, *38*, 305)
Arrival: California, furthering cultural relations (SCI, *93*, 471)
Fellowship: Yale Univ. (BULL, *34*, 499)
Visit: England, invitation of universities' China Committee in London (SCI, *94*, 411, 605; BULL, *39*, 196)

Kupalov, Peter Stepanovich
Cornell Univ., Summer School (SCI, *69*, 471)
Pavlov associate (SCI, *69*, 450)
Research: conditioned reflex, Cornell Univ. (SCI, *70*, 235)

Kurtz, Albert Kenneth
Appointment: Yale Univ. (SCI, *96*, 225)

Kutash, Samuel Benjamin
Appointment: Harlem Valley State Hospital, New York (BULL, *42*, 63)

Kuznets, George
Appointment: Stanford Univ. (J APP, *21*, 474; BULL, *34*, 499)
Grant: Social Science Research Council (BULL, *34*, 409)

L

Labor, psychology of
Lecture: Münsterberg, H., Johns Hopkins Univ. (Sci, 37, 478)

Laboratory
Anniversary: Indiana Univ., 50th (J App, 23, 630)
Anniversary: Univ. of Nebraska, 50th commemorated at MPA, 1939 (J App, 23, 207; Bull, 36, 304)
Anniversary: Univ. of Wisconsin, 50th celebrated at MPA, 1938 (J App, 22, 106)
Appointment: Cameron, N. Payne Whitney Clinic (Bull, 36, 248)
Cornell Behavior Farm (Bull, 36, 804)
Destroyed: Stellensbosch Univ. (Capetown) (Sci, 79, 539)
Established: Bellevue Hospital (Bull, 13, 376; JoP, 13, 476)
Established: Boston City (Bull, 13, 408; JoP, 13, 560)
Established: Boston Police Court (Bull, 13, 296)
Established: Michigan, biology and hygiene (Sci°, 9, 213)
Established: Moscow, Russia (JoP, 8, 335-336)
Established: Tufts Univ. (Bull, 35, 259)
Established: Univ. of Alabama (Bull, 36, 500)
Established: Univ. of California, physiological (Sci, 16, 1000)
Organized: Iowa Child Welfare Research Station, child psychology (J App, 5, 381)
Pavlov's new equipment (Sci, 62, 395)
Publication: Freeman, G. L., "The research laboratory in psychophysiology at Northwestern Univ." (AJP, 51, 176)
Publication: Kellogg, W. N., "The Indiana conditioning laboratory" (AJP, 51, 174)

Laboratory Manual of Experimental Psychology
Publication: Titchener, E. B. (Rev, 6, 344)

Laboratory of Social Hygiene (Bedford Hills, New York)
Resignation: Johnson, B. J. (JoP, 15, 280)

LaBrant, Lou L.
Appointment: New York Univ. (BULL, 39, 681)
Departure: Ohio State Univ. (BULL, 39, 681)

Lacey, Oliver Lilburn
Correction in abstract (BULL, 39, 684)

Lachelier, Jules
Death notice (JoP, 15, 224)
Election: Paris Institute (REV, 3, 355)

Ladame, Charles
Appointment: Univ. of Geneva (SCI, 61, 489)

Ladd, George Trumbull
Appointment: Adelbert College (JoP, 3, 140)
Appointment: Western Reserve Univ. (SCI, 21, 933; JoP, 2, 364; BULL, 2, 296)
Appointment: Yale Psychological Laboratory (JoP, 1, 28)
Attendance at commemorative for Zeller, E. (SCI°, 8, 452)
Course: Western Reserve Univ. (BULL, 5, 380)
Death notice (SCI, 54, 151)
Election: International Congress of Psychology (SCI, 11, 39)
Eulogized (AJP, 32, 601)
International Congress of Psychology, International Committee, 5th (JoP, 2, 56)
Leave of absence (SCI, 9, 421)
Lecture: Columbia Univ. (JoP, 8, 112; SCI, 33, 214; JoP, 1, 252)
Lecture: India (SCI, 9, 421)
Lecture: plans in Japan (JoP, 2, 364; SCI, 9, 421)
Lecture: Univ. of Chicago (REV, 3, 356)
Lecture: Western Reserve Univ., educational psych. (SCI, 28, 481)
Monument: Japan (SCI, 55, 512)
Publication: *Philosophy of Knowledge*, announced (REV, 4, 340; SCI, 5, 582)
Publication: *Physiological Psychology* (SCI°, 9, 294)
Publication: Japanese morals (JoP, 5, 420)
Reception: Yale Assoc. of Japan (SCI, 24, 671; JoP, 4, 28; BULL, 3, 422)
Resignation: Yale Corporation (BULL, 1, 333; SCI, 20, 96)
Resignation: Yale Univ. (JoP, 1, 336, 420; BULL, 2, 296; SCI, 21, 933)
Return: U.S. from Japan and India (SCI, 12, 533; REV, 7, 639; BULL, 5, 32; SCI, 26, 805)
Trip: Korea from Japan (SCI, 25, 558)
Trip: Japan (SCI, 21, 933)

Ladd-Franklin, Christine
Appointment: Johns Hopkins Univ. (BULL, 1, 172; JoP, 1, 252)
Conference: color vision (JoP, 11, 84)
Death notice (JoP, 27, 168; SCI, 71, 281; BULL, 27, 415)
Degree: Johns Hopkins Univ. (BULL, 23, 236; SCI, 63, 276)

Lecture: APA, New York Branch, correction (JoP, *10*, 720)
Lecture: APA/NYAS (JoP, *13*, 280)
Lecture: Clark Univ., color vision (BULL, *10*, 252)
Lecture: Columbia Univ. (JoP, *12*, 224)
Lecture: Columbia Univ., color vision (BULL, *10*, 252; SCI, *35*, 615; SCI, *65*, 227; JoP, *9*, 252; JoP, *10*, 364; SCI, *37*, 747)
Lecture: Columbia Univ., logic (JoP, *16*, 700; JoP, *14*, 308)
Lecture: Cornell Univ., color (JoP, *11*, 308)
Lecture: Harvard Univ. (JoP, *17*, 224; SCI, *65*, 520, SCI, *81*, 16; SCI, *37*, 747; BULL, *10*, 252; SCI, *51*, 268; SCI, *57*, 324)
Lecture: Harvard Univ., symbolic logic, postponed (JoP, *15*, 280)
Lecture: series cancelled because of WWI (SCI, *47*, 414)
Lecture: Univ. of Chicago (SCI, *39*, 683; JoP, *11*, 308)
Lecture: Univ. of Illinois, color (JoP, *11*, 308)
Publication: deLaguna, T. (JoP, *9*, 588)
Publication: psychological logic, comments on (JoP, *24*, 476)

Lafayette College (Easton, Pennsylvania)
Appointment: Mecklin, J. M. (BULL, *3*, 36)
Appointment: Rogers, H. W. (SCI, *60*, 221)
Degree: Cattell, J. McK. (BULL, *4*, 338)
Degree: Münsterberg, H. (BULL, *4*, 338)
Lecture: Cattell, J. McK. (JoP, *9*, 112; SCI, *25*, 1014)
Lecture: Münsterberg, H. (JoP, *4*, 420; SCI, *25*, 1014)
Resignation: Mecklin, J. M. (JoP, *10*, 504, 559-560)

Lähn, H. [Laehr, Heinrich ?]
Research: death rates, psychiatry (AJP, *3*, 148)

Lahy, Jean Maurice
International Congress of Technopsychology, 6th (SCI, *69*, 423)

Laird, Donald Anderson
Appointment: Colgate Univ. (SCI, *60*, 243; J APP, *8*, 450, BULL, *21*, 660)
Appointment: Century of Progress Exposition, sleep and fatigue (SCI, *77*, 348)
Appointment: Personnel Analysis Bureau of Chicago, chief of scientific staff (J APP, *13*, 93)
Editor: *Industrial Psychology* (J APP, *9*, 204; J APP, *10*, 129)
Exhibit: Century of Progress Exposition (J APP, *17*, 212)
Promotion: Colgate Univ. (SCI, *66*, 151)
Publication: *Psychology of Medicine*, sleep and fatigue chapter (J APP, *14*, 505)

Laity Lectures
Brill, A. A., "The Freudian Epoch" (SCI, *94*, 484)
Gesell, A., "Creative Behavior in Child and Adult", 1942 (SCI, *94*, 484)
Lecture: McGraw, M. (BULL, *39*, 895)
Program: 1942 (SCI, *96*, 334)
Putnam, T. J., "The mechanisms of the mind", 1941 (SCI, *94*, 484)

Lake Erie College (Painesville, Ohio)
Anniversary: 75th (SCI, *80*, 30)
Degree: Woodworth, R. S. (SCI, *80*, 30)

Lake Forest College (Illinois)
Appointment: Stewart, H. W. (BULL, *1*, 413)
Leave of absence: Smith, W. (BULL, *1*, 413)

Lake, H.
Appointment: Colgate Univ. (SCI, 72, 111, 421)

LaMar, Norvelle C.
American Orthopsychiatric Assoc. (BULL, *36*, 140; BULL, *35*, 125)

Lamarck, Jean Baptiste Pierre Antoine de Monet
Memorial postponement (JoP, *6*, 56)
Monument: in honor of (JoP, *4*, 336)

Lancaster, Ellsworth Gage
Appointment: Colorado College (SCI, *6*, 879; REV, *5*, 232; AJP, *10*, 165)

Landis, Agnes Thorson
Promotion: Tulane Univ. (BULL, *42*, 675)

Landis, Carney
Appointment: New York State Psychiatric Institute (J APP, *14*, 304; BULL, *27*, 415)
Appointment: Wesleyan Univ. (BULL, *23*, 412; BULL, *24*, 620; J APP, *11*, 405; J APP, *10*, 394)
Election: New York State Assoc. for Applied Psych., vice- president (BULL, *37*, 405)
Leave of absence: Wesleyan Univ. (J APP, *13*, 93)
Publication: constant blood pressure (AJP, *34*, 470)
Publication: "Critique of Crosland's measurement of emotion" (AJP, *45*, 522)
Publication: "Systematic differences in introspection" (AJP, *46*, 660)
Research: sleep (J APP, *10*, 394)
Research: with Lashley, K., Institute for Juvenile Research, Chicago (J APP, *13*, 93)

Lane, R. E.
Appointment: Univ. of Manchester (SCI, *101*, 324)

Lane, William C.
Publication: "The Books of Science" (SCI°, 2, 342)

Lang, H. Beckett
Leave of absence: New York State, Assistant Commissioner of Mental Hygiene (SCI, *98*, 447)

Lang, Johannes

Appointment: *Character and Personality* editorial board (J App, *16*, 439)

Langfeld, Herbert Sidney

Appointment: Harvard Corporation (Sci, *42*, 527)

Appointment: Harvard Univ. (AJP, *33*, 450; Bull, *16*, 391-392; Sci, *48*, 317; Sci, *50*, 345)

Appointment: Princeton Univ. (Sci, *87*, 411; Bull, *21*, 428; Sci, *59*, 576)

Appointment: Yale Univ. (Sci, *45*, 63; JoP, *14*, 84)

Editor: *Psychological Review* (Sci, *79*, 247)

Election: APA office (JoP, *17*, 56; Bull, *14*, 32; Sci, *71*, 64; Bull, *27*, 76; Sci, *77*, 364; Sci, *72*, 599)

Election: APA representative, National Research Council (Bull, *24*, 80)

Election: International Congress of Psych., 10th, delegate (Sci, *76*, 119)

Election: International Congress of Psych., 11th, executive committee (J App, *21*, 242; Sci, *86*, 34)

Election: SEP, president (Sci, *87*, 342)

Lecture: Brown (Bull, *32*, 323)

Promotion: Harvard Univ. (Bull, *12*, 364; Sci, *55*, 538; JoP, *19*, 420)

Publication: obituary of Stumpf, C. (AJP, *49*, 320)

Publication: obituary of Warren, H. C. (AJP, *46*, 340)

Langford, Cooper Harold

Election: Assoc. of Symbolic Logic, president (JoP, *40*, 196)

Langhorne, Maurice Curtis

Promotion: Emory Univ. (Bull, *40*, 794)

Langley Porter Clinic, Medical School of the University of California

Appointment: Bowman, K. L. (Sci, *94*, 322)

Langley, Samuel Pierpont

Election: Fench Academy of Science, corresponding member (Sci°, *12*, 36)

Election: Smithsonian Institution (Sci°, *10*, 264)

Lecture: American Assoc., copy of (Sci°, *10*, 80-81)

Langlie, Theos Alvin

Appointment: Wesleyan Univ. (J App, *11*, 405)

Grant: Wesleyan Univ., Faculty Committee on Research (Sci, *85*, 14)

Langmuir, Charles Ruggles

Lecture: Carnegie Foundation for the Advancement of Teachers, 37th annual report (J App, *27*, 114)

Languages

Lecture: Brinton, D. G., Lowell Inst., Boston, American aborigines (Sci°, *4*, 522)

Lecture: Orton, S. T., New York Acad. of Medicine (SCI, *83*, 389)

Lecture: Thorndike, E. L., Columbia Univ., semantic word count (BULL, *36*, 141)

Meeting: International Congress for the Unity of Science, 4th; scientific language (JoP, *35*, 112, 504)

Meeting: New School for Social Research, 1945 announced (JoP, *42*, 223-224)

Publication: Davis, E. A., "The tendency among children to avoid words with unpleasant connotations" (AJP, *49*, 315)

Publication: structure of (SCI°, 5, 40)

Publication: terms used in research (AJP, *57*, 264-269)

Publication: Waters, R. H., "A case of environmental change with an accompanying loss of language" (AJP, *46*, 336)

Lanier, Lyle Hicks

Appointment: New York Univ. (AJP, *10*, 522)

Appointment: Vassar College (BULL, *35*, 259; SCI, *87*, 163)

Election: SSPP, president (SCI, *85*, 261)

Publication: "Southern Society for Philosophy and Psychology, the 31st annual meeting of the" (AJP, *48*, 689)

Publication: "Southern Society for Philosophy and Psychology, the 32nd annual meeting of the" (AJP, *49*, 485)

Research: child study project, Vassar (BULL, *37*, 187)

Lanza, Anthony J.

Award: Legion of Merit (SCI, *101*, 296)

Larguier des Bancels, Jean

Publication: curve of forgetting (AJP, *45*, 758)

Larrabee, Harold Atkins

Appointment: Univ. of Vermont (SCI, *60*, 429; BULL, *22*, 140)

Larson, John Augustus

Appointment: Psychopathic Clinic, City of Detroit (SCI, *84*, 13)

LaRue, Daniel Wolford

Research: Phonetic alphabet (BULL, *17*, 239)

Lashley, Karl Spencer

Appointment: *Acta Psychologica* board (AJP, *48*, 174)

Appointment: Harvard Univ. (SCI, *81*, 335; SCI, *85*, 516; BULL, *32*, 376; BULL, *34*, 409)

Appointment: National Research Council, Committee on Human Heredity (SCI, *92*, 146)

Appointment: Univ. of Chicago (SCI, *70*, 281)

Appointment: Univ. of Minnesota (JoP, *14*, 448, 644; SCI, *45*, 660)

Award: Warren Medal recipient (SCI, *85*, 354; BULL, *34*, 273)

Degree: Harvard Univ. (BULL, *33*, 675)

Degree: Univ. of Pittsburgh (Sci, *83*, 593)
Election: American Phil. Society (Bull, *35*, 408)
Election: APA council (Bull, *23*, 112)
Election: APA Eastern Branch, president (Sci, *85*, 380)
Election: APA, president (Bull, *26*, 56; Sci, *69*, 11, 36)
Election: National Academy of Sciences (Bull, *27*, 415; Sci, *71*, 478)
Election: National Research Council, APA representative (Bull, *24*, 80)
Election: New York Acad. of Sciences (Sci, *85*, 13)
International Congress for the Unity of Science, 2nd (JoP, *33*, 196)
Lecture: APA Eastern Branch (Sci, *87*, 297)
Lecture: Conference on the Training of Biologists, 1941 (Sci, *94*, 185-186)
Lecture: Harvey Society, 2nd (Sci, *72*, 499)
Lecture: Montreal Neurological Institute, Hughlings Jackson Lecturer (Sci, *85*, 381)
Lecture: Univ. of London (Bull, *28*, 502)
Lecture: Univ. of Rochester (Sci, *87*, 164)
Promotion: Univ. of Minnesota (Bull, *21*, 660; Sci, *60*, 40)
Research: Dry Tortugas to study noddy and sooty terns (Bull, *10*, 252)
Research: Landis, C., Institute of Juvenile Research (J App, *13*, 93)

Lasker, Albert D.

Election: National Committee for Mental Hygiene, board of directors (Sci, *99*, 34-35)

Lasker Award in Mental Hygiene

Award: Menninger, W. C., 1944 (Sci, *100*, 516)
Establishment: Albert and Mary Lasker Foundation, Inc. through National Committee for Mental Hygiene (Sci, *100*, 354)

Lasswell, Harold Dwight

Lecture: Conference on Science, Philosophy, and Religion (JoP, *37*, 448)

Lauer, Alvhh Ray

Lecture: Psychological Museum (Bull, *41*, 410)

Laughlin, Harry Hamilton

Appointment: International Congress of Eugenics, 3rd, chair, exhibits committee (Sci, *74*, 626)

Laurie, Simon Somerville

Death notice (JoP, *6*, 196, 224; Bull, *6*, 216)
Degree: St. Andrews Univ. (Sci°, *9*, 362)

Law and psychology

Conference on Methods in Philosophy and the Sciences, 2nd, New School for Social Research (Bull, *34*, 636)
Course: legal psychology and psychiatry (AJP, *20*, 296)
Lecture: Münsterberg, H., courtroom psychology (Sci, *31*, 187; JoP, *7*, 112)

Lecture: Münsterberg, H., law and psychology (SCI, 29, 23)
Lecture: radio broadcast (BULL, 32, 323)
Lecture: Robinson, E. S., Princeton Univ., law and psychology (BULL, 33, 147;
SCI, 83, 229)

Lawrence, William
Election: National Committee for Mental Hygiene, vice-president (SCI, 72, 557)

Laws of nature
Lecture: Richardson, E. E. (JOP, 7, 28)

Laymen's League against Epilepsy
Award: Bruetsch, W. L., research (SCI, 93, 419)

Lazarsfeld, Paul Felix
Publication: *J App*, special issue, radio (J APP, 25,128)
Publication: "The techniques of market research from the standpoint of a
psychologist" (SCI, 81, 589)
Research: Princeton radio research project (J APP, 22, 663)

Lazarus, Moritz
Death notice (SCI, 17, 718)

Learned, William Setchell
Publication: Carnegie Foundation for the Advancement of Teachers, 37th
report (J APP, 27, 114)
Publication: College grades compared to GRE scores (J APP, 26, 114)

Learning (*see also* Conditioned reflex)
Conference on the Psychology of Learning, 1939, Univ. of Colorado (BULL, 36,
583)
Grant: Hilgard, E. R., National Research Council (BULL, 33, 578)
Lecture: Book, W. F. (JOP, 2, 223)
Lecture: Corey, S. M., learning and memory (AJP, 44, 191)
Lecture: Gaylord, J. S. (JOP, 7, 222)
Lecture: Laslett, H. R., process (AJP, 40, 168)
Lecture: Stroud, J. B., learning curves (AJP, 43, 684)
Publication: Thorndike, E. L., "A note on assimilation and interference" (AJP,
49, 671)
Publication: Wiley's test of Thurstone (BULL, 33, 579)
Symposium: Bryan, W. L., Indiana Univ. (BULL, 37, 61)
Symposium: Culler, E. K., Indiana Univ. (BULL, 37, 61)
Symposium: Kellogg, W. N., Indiana Univ. (BULL, 37, 61)
Symposium: McGeoch, J. A., Indiana Univ. (BULL, 37, 61)

Leary, Daniel Bell
Appointment: Univ. of Buffalo (JOP, 16, 700; SCI, 50, 161; BULL, 16, 258)

L'École des Hautes Etudes, Sorbonne (Paris, France)
Appointment: Piéron, H. (JoP, *9*, 532)
Editor: *Renaissance* (JoP, *40*, 448)

LeConte, Joseph
Research: speech (AJP, *1*, 354)

Lee, Alfred McClung
Election: Institute for Propaganda Analysis, treasurer (J App, *25*, 361)

Lee, Dorothy
Appointment: Purdue Univ. (Sci, *54*, 463)

Lee, Frederic S.
Election: NYAS, committee member (JoP, *9*, 28)

Lefevre, Albert
Appointment: Univ. of Virginia (Bull, *2*, 328)
Degree: South Carolina College (Bull, *2*, 88)
Election: SSPP, vice-president (Sci, *27*, 596)
Lecture: SSPP (JoP, *7*, 28)

LeFleming, E. K.
Lecture: National Institute for Industrial Psychology (Sci, *83*, 301)

Legal psychology (*see* Law and psychology)

Legion of Merit
Award: Lanza, A. J. (Sci, *101*, 296)

Lehigh University (Bethlehem, Pennsylvania)
Appointment: Davis, W. H. (JoP, *1*, 112; Sci, *21*, 1000; Bull, *2*, 296; JoP, *2*, 364)
Appointment: Graham, J. L. (Sci, *72*, 315)
Appointment: Hughes, P (Bull, *4*, 337)
Appointment: Witmer, L. (Rev, *10*, 690)
Election: Davis, W. H., APA, secretary (Sci, *21*, 37; JoP, *2*, 28)
Election: Davis, W. M., International Congress Arts and Sciences (JoP, *1*, 532)
Election: Jenkins, W. L., secretary, Sigma Xi (Sci, *95*, 573)
Lecture: Cattell, J. McK. (Bull, *9*, 96; JoP, *9*, 112; Sci, *35*, 178)
Promotion: Hughes, P. (JoP, *6*, 392; Bull, *6*, 256; JoP, *28*, 700)

Lehman, Harvey Christian
Appointment: Ohio Univ. (J App, *11*, 405)
Grant: Social Science Research Council (Bull, *42*, 791)
Lecture: vocational counseling (AJP, *44*, 801)
Publication: "Faculty psychology and personality traits" (AJP, *46*, 500)

Lehmann, Alfred Georg Ludwig
Death notice: Sept. 26, 1921 (BULL, *18*, 628)

Lehrbuch der Psychologie
Publication: announced (AJP, *8*, 430; REV, *1*, 552)

Leidy, Joseph, Memorial Award
Wheeler, W. M., 1931 (BULL, *28*, 324)

Leighton, Joseph Alexander
Election: Ohio State Univ., chair of philosophy (JoP, *7*, 476)
Publication: *The Field of Philosophy* (JoP, *15*, 308)

Leipzig, University of (Germany)
Anniversary celebration (JoP, *5*, 588; SCI, *16*, 720)
Anniversary: Wundt, W., 50th (SCI, *22*, 806)
Anniversary: Wundt, W., 100th (BULL, *29*, 603; SCI, *76*, 230)
Appointment: Hering, E. (REV, *3*, 120)
Appointment: Meumann, E. (JoP, *7*, 308; AJP, *7*, 152)
Appointment: Shröder, P. (SCI, *60*, 382)
Award: Wundt, W., knighted (JoP, *9*, 224)
Degree: Loeb, J. (SCI, *30*, 236, 280)
Degree: Ward, J. (JoP, *6*, 700)
Departure: Klemm, O. (SCI, *39*, 423)
Donation: Meyer, H. (BULL, *8*, 110; JoP, *8*, 140; SCI, *33*, 299)
Equipment for Wundt's lab (SCI, *36*, 343)
Lecture: Allport, G. W., Congress of Psychology (AJP, *34*, 612)
Lecture: Wundt, W. (JoP, *6*, 560)
Promotion: Külpe, O. (REV, *1*, 336)
Promotion: Paulsen, F. (REV, *1*, 336)
Publication: Wundt, W., "Stiftung" (SCI, *36*, 271)
Retirement: Hering, E. (BULL, *12*, 404)
Retirement: Ostwald, W. (SCI, *23*, 862)

Lemmon, Martha Lou
Publication: "What is social psychology?" (AJP, *48*, 673)

Lenâpé
Publication: Brinton, D. G. (SCI°, *5*, 159)

Leningrad, USSR (*see* Psycho-neurological Academy)

Lennon, Lawrence J.
Research: Iowa Silent Reading Test Form (J APP, *27*, 363-364)

Lenz, Fritz
Appointment: Kaiser Wilhelm Univ., Racial Hygiene and Eugenics (SCI, *79*, 157)

Lewin, Kurt
Appointment: Cornell Univ. (Sci, 78, 278)
Appointment: Harvard Psych. Clinic (Sci, 87, 482)
Appointment: Massachusetts Institute of Technology (BULL, 42, 191)
Appointment: Stanford Univ. (J App, 16, 222)
Appointment: Univ. of Iowa (BULL, 32, 323)
Lecture: Conference on Methods in Philosophy and the Sciences (Sci, 87, 277; JoP, 35, 196)
Lecture: International Congress for the Unity of Science (JoP, 38, 504)
Lecture: tour, Japan, Russia and Germany (Sci, 77, 486)
Meeting: Menninger Clinic, Conference on Psychoanalysis and Psychology (BULL, 33, 579)
Meeting: Psychological Supper Club (BULL, 37, 656)
Nomination: Univ. of Naples (Sci, 33, 420)
Research: food habits (J App, 26, 858)
Resignation: Child Welfare Research Station, Univ. of Iowa (BULL, 42, 191)

Lewis and Clark College (Portland, Oregon)
Appointment: Howard, C. W. (BULL, 42, 128)

Lewis, Burdette G.
New Jersey's State Psychiatric Clinic (J App, 4, 112-113)

Lewis, Don
Publication: measures of musical talent (J App, 23, 634)

Lewis, Helen Block
Award: Social Science Research Council (BULL, 39, 683)

Lewis, Nolan Don Carpentier
Appointment: Committee for Internships in Clinical Psych. in New York State institutions (BULL, 39, 809-810)
Appointment: Salmon Memorial Lectures (Sci, 91, 382; Sci, 92, 426)
Editor: *The Journal of Nervous and Mental Disease* (Sci, 101, 171)
Editor: *The Psychoanalytic Review* (Sci, 101, 171)
Research: dementia praecox (J App, 19, 497)

Lewis, Thomas Albert
Appointment: Denison Univ. (BULL, 11, 444; JoP, 11, 721)
Retirement: Denison Univ. (BULL, 40, 723)

Lewis, Virginia Whitney
Appointment: Phoenix Public Schools, Child-guidance Clinic (BULL, 42, 127)
Rochester Guidance Clinic, New York, mental hygiene (BULL, 36, 841)

Lewis, William Draper
Publication: *Political Organization of a Modern Municipality* (Sci°, 19, 103)

Library

Donation: Münsterberg, H. to Harvard Univ. (JoP, *14*, 252)

Library of Congress

Appointment: Bentley, M. (SCI, *88*, 31)

Barrows, S. J., fails confirmation (SCI, *9*, 380)

Library of Historical Psychology, The

Publication: volumes added (BULL, *1*, 29)

Licensing of psychologists

Discussion: Kuhlmann, F. (AJP, *56*, 120-129)

Lichte, William Heil

Appointment: Southern Methodist Univ. (BULL, *38*, 304)

Licklider, Joseph Carl Robnett

Fellowship: National Research Council (BULL, *39*, 682)

Liddell, Howard Scott

Editor: *Psychosomatic Medicine* (J APP, *22*, 663)

Grant: Josiah Macy Jr. Foundation, experimental neuroses (SCI, *91*, 446)

Research: Cornell Univ., conditioned reflex (SCI, *70*, 235)

Research: Cornell Univ., experimental neuroses (SCI, *86*, 221)

Transfer: Cornell Univ., Psych. Dept. (BULL, *36*, 804)

Liebmann, Otto

Death notice (JoP, *9*, 168)

Liégeois, Jules

Commemorative monument (AJP, *21*, 180)

Life of Reason

Publication: Santayana, G. (JoP, *15*, 82-84)

Life Office Management Association

Committee on Tests prepare Clerical Employees Report (J APP, *26*, 714)

Liggett, John Riley

Death notice (BULL, *28*, 254)

Light

Lecture: Boswell, F. (JoP, *2*, 280)

Lecture: Kuhlmann, F., color sense in animals (JoP, *7*, 223)

Ligon, Ernest Mayfield

Appointment: Connecticut College (J APP, *11*, 165)

Appointment: Consultant to Secretary of War (SCI, *96*, 81)

Appointment: Union College (BULL, 26, 624)
Lecture: Fort Washington (SCI, 96, 81)

Likert, Rensis
Lecture: National Research Council, Conference on Psychological Factors in
National Morale (BULL, 37, 829)
Lecture: Washington-Baltimore Branch of APA (BULL, 39, 683)

Lincoln, Leroy Alton
Lecture: Metropolitan Life Insurance Co., personnel selection (J APP, 21, 242)

Lincoln State School (Illinois)
Appointment: Huey, E. B., director Clinical Psych. Dept. (SCI, 30, 557)
Examination for psychologist's position (BULL, 12, 160)
Resignation: Sabin, T. R. (BULL, 41, 498)

Lincoln University
Degree: Beckham, A. S. (BULL, 42, 791)

Linder, Forrest E.
Publication: "The accuracy of the constant method" (AJP, 47, 508)

Lindley, Ernest Hiram
Appointment: Univ. of Idaho (JOP, 14, 644; BULL, 16, 257; J APP, 3, 290)
Appointment: Univ. of Idaho, president (BULL, 14, 264)
Appointment: Univ. of Kansas (BULL, 17, 435)
Death notice (BULL, 37, 755)
Election: APA Council (JOP, 7, 56)

Lindsay, Alexander Dunlop
Publication: guide to philosophy of Bergson (JOP, 9, 84)

Lindworsky, Johannes
Appointment: Univ. of Prague (BULL, 25, 700)

Linguistics
Lecture: Wells, F. L. (JOP, 2, 224, 700)

Link, Henry Charles
Election: Psychological Corporation meeting with APA and AAAP, 1941,
vice-president and treasurer (J APP, 25, 600)
Research: sentiment toward war-time advertising (J APP, 27, 208)

Linnaean Society
Eulogy: On Darwin, C. (SCI°, 11, 277)
Lecture: Instincts by the late Darwin (SCI°, 2, 782)
Lecture: Lubbock, J., habits of ants, bees, and wasps (SCI°, 10, 320)
Tribute to centenary of Origin of Species (SCI, 96, 179)

Lion, Ernest George

Appointment: U.S. Public Health Service and San Francisco Department of Public Health, Psychiatric Clinic for Feminine Delinquency (SCI, *97*, 65)

Lippincott, J. B. Company

Publication: Darby, J., "Nineteenth-century sense: The paradox of spiritualism" (SCI°, *10*, 31-32)

Lipmann, Otto

Death notice (BULL, *31*, 79)

Editor: *Zeitschrift* (AJP, *18*, 529)

Obituary by Stern, W. (AJP, *46*, 152)

Lipps, Theodor

Appointment: Univ. of Munich, chair (REV, *1*, 336)

Death notice (AJP, *26*, 160; SCI, *40*, 812; BULL, *11*, 483; JoP, *11*, 721)

Literary and Philosophical Society

Election: honorary members, 1900 (SCI, *11*, 958)

Littauer, Lucius N.

Appointment: Wortis, S. B., to Littauer Chair New York Univ. College of Medicine (SCI, *96*, 293)

New York Univ. College of Medicine, funded chair of psychiatry named for him (SCI, *96*, 293)

Little, Clarence C.

Lecture: Cornell Univ. (SCI, *102*, 665)

Research: genetic factors of intelligence and emotional variance (SCI, *101*, 482)

Liu, T'ing-fang

Lecture: APA/NYAS, Chinese taboos (JoP, *13*, 280)

Liverpool, University of (England)

Appointment: Smith, W. G. (SCI, *18*, 704; BULL, *1*, 134; JoP, *1*, 28; BULL, *2*, 427; SCI, *22*, 648)

Degree: Angell, J. R. (SCI, *74*, 146)

Departure: Gibson, W. R. B. (JoP, *9*, 84)

Departure: Smith, W. G. (JoP, *3*, 504)

Establish: Dept. of Neurology by Nuffield Foundation (SCI, *101*, 141)

Lectureship: experimental psychology (BULL, *2*, 296; SCI, *22*, 160; JoP, *2*, 476)

Resignation: Smith, W. G. (BULL, *3*, 320)

Lloyd, Alfred Henry

Appointment: Univ. of Michigan (REV, *2*, 104)

Leave of absence: Univ. of Michigan (JoP, *8*, 364)

Lecture: ethics (JoP, *1*, 224)

Lloyd, Frances E.
Leave of absence: Teachers College, Columbia Univ. (SCI, *13*, 278)

Lloyd, James Hendrie
Publication: critique of concept of "moral insanity" (AJP, *1*, 198)

Lloyd-Jones, Esther McDonald
Appointment: Teachers College, Columbia Univ. (BULL, *42*, 794)

Lobotomy
Lecture: Jacobsen, C., NYAS (SCI, 77, 85)

Localization of cortical function
Lecture: Hitzig, E. (SCI, *12*, 975-976)

Locke, John
Commemoration of 200th anniversary of death (JOP, *1*, 616, 672, 697; BULL, *1*, 413, 451)
Endowed: Wilde, H., John Locke Scholarship (AJP, *10*, 165)
Lecture: Frazer, A. C. (JOP, *2*, 672)
Lecture: on his intelligence (JOP, *1*, 672)

Lodge, Oliver Joseph
Publication: *The Survival of Man: A Study in Psychical Research* (JOP, *6*, 588)
Resignation: Society for Psychical Research, presidency (JOP, *1*, 112)

Lodge, Rupert Clendon
Appointment: Univ. of Alberta (JOP, *12*, 336)
Departure: Univ. of Minnesota (JOP, *12*, 336)

Loeb, Jacques
Appointment: Rockefeller Institute (SCI, *31*, 139)
Death notice (SCI, *59*, 187)
Degree (SCI, *30*, 236, 280)
Election: Royal Acad. of Science, associate (SCI, *33*, 184)
Election: Société Royaledes Sciences Medicale et Naturelles of Brussels (SCI, *56*, 507)
Grant: study artificial parthenogenesis (SCI, *15*, 276)
Laboratory Univ. of California, physiological (SCI, *16*, 1000)
Lecture: American Philosophical Society, artificial parthenogenesis (SCI, *13*, 476)
Lecture: Columbia Univ. (SCI, *15*, 397)
Lecture: International Congress of Psychology, 6th (SCI, *30*, 202)
Lecture: Univ. of California (BULL, *4*, 370)
Meeting: American Physiological Society (SCI, *14*, 863)
Visiting San Francisco (SCI, *16*, 516)

Loemker, Leroy Earl
Lecture: SSPP, 35th meeting (JoP, *37*, 196)

Loewi, Otto
Lecture: Ohio State Univ. (Sci, *97*, 398)

Loftus, John J.
Publication: test entitled *Aspects of Personality* (J App, *22*, 318)

Logic
Lecture: Davies, H. (JoP, *1*, 84)
Lecture: Ladd-Franklin, C., Columbia Univ. (JoP, *14*, 308; JoP, *24*, 476)
Lecture: Stuart, H. W. (JoP, *1*, 224)
Publication: Hough, W. S. (Sci°, *23*, 96)

Lois Sociales, Les
Publication: Warren, H. C., English translation (Rev, *6*, 119)

Lombroso, Cesare
Award: funds for monument (Bull, *8*, 333)
Death notice (JoP, *6*, 644)
Election: International Congress of Psychology, 5th, president criminal, pedagogical, and social psych. section (JoP, *2*, 56)

London County Council Asylums
Establishment: Dept. of experimental psychology (Sci, *13*, 877; Rev, *8*, 447)

London, Dublin, and Edinburgh Philosophical Magazine
Publication: list of standard wave-lengths that can be observed with human eye (Sci°, *13*, 419)

London Health Exhibition
Attractions (Sci°, *3*, 744)
Success (Sci°, *4*, 410)

London Institute for the Advancement of Technical Education
Periodical report issued (Sci°, *4*, 425)

London Neurological Society
Lecture: Hitzig, E. (Sci, *12*, 854, 975-976)

London, University of (*see also* Birkbeck College)
Appointment: Edgell, B. (Bull, *24*, 312)
Appointment: Mace, C. A., Birkbeck College (Sci, *100*, 424)
Appointment: Mackintosh, J. M., School of Hygiene (Sci, *101*, 60)
Appointment: Pearson, K. (JoP, *8*, 476; Sci, *34*, 150)
Appointment: Read, C., professor emeritus (Bull, *18*, 439)
Degree: Cattell, R. B. (Bull, *36*, 711)
Degree: mental and moral science excluded (Rev, *5*, 345)

Degree: Pearson, K. (SCI, *80*, 612)
Degree: Spearman, C. (SCI, 75, 43)
Departments of psych. and philosophy separated (SCI, 67, 421)
Examination: change (AJP, *1*, 197)
Fellowship: eugenics (BULL, *1*, 488)
Fellowship: National Eugenics founded by Galton, F. (JoP, *1*, 672; BULL, *1*, 488)
Galton, F., bequest for study of eugenics (SCI, *33*, 370)
Lecture: Calkins, M. W. (BULL, *25*, 307)
Lecture: Janet, P. (SCI, *51*, 590)
Lecture: Lashley, K. S. (BULL, *28*, 412)
Lecture: religion as a social force (SCI, *88*, 495)
Lecture: Slaughter, J. W. (BULL, *3*, 320)
Meeting: Council for Psychical Research (SCI, *80*, 183)
Meeting: International Philosophical Congress, 5th, announcement (JoP, *8*, 392)
Meeting: Universal Races Congress (BULL, *7*, 425)
Research: eugenics (BULL, *4*, 128)
Retirement: Edgell, B. (BULL, *31*, 80; SCI, *78*, 576)
Retirement: Greenwood, M., School of Hygiene (SCI, *102*, 7)
Retirement: Pearson, K. (SCI, *79*, 30, 426)

Long, Cyril Norman Hugh
Lecture: Assoc. for Research in Nervous and Mental Diseases (SCI, *84*, 551)

Long Island College of Medicine (New York)
Appointment: Potter, H. W. (SCI, *98*, 278)

Longmans, Green, and Company
Publication: book by James, W. (JoP, *8*, 280, 336, 532, 672)
Publication: Boutroux, E., James, W. (JoP, *8*, 560)

Loomis, Elias
Death notice (SCI°, *14*, 131)

Loomis, Stuart D.
Appointment: Univ. of New Hampshire (BULL, *42*, 792)

Loos, Joseph
Publication: *Enzyklopädisches Handbuch der Erziehungskunde* (JoP, 6, 28)

Lord, [Arthur Ritchie ?]
Appointment: Rhodes Univ. College, Grahamstown, Cape Colony (JoP, 2, 392)

Lord, Elizabeth Evans
Appointment: Yale Univ. (BULL, *20*, 288; SCI, *56*, 602)
Death notice (BULL, *40*, 230)
Resolution of Massachusetts Society of Clinical Psychologists (BULL, *40*, 458)

Lorge, Irving
Appointment: economic competence study, director (BULL, *40*, 230)
Appointment: U.S. Dept. of Agriculture (BULL, *42*, 127)
Appointment: War Department (BULL, *42*, 127)
Election: NYAS (J APP, *21*, 717)

Los Angeles County Civil Service Commission
Research: psychological examiner sought for juveniles (SCI, *95*, 600)

Los Angeles County Schools
Research: California Test of Personality, child-parent relationships (J APP, *26*, 571)

Los Angeles, Division of Psychology
Appointment: Sutherland, A. H. (J APP, *2*, 194-195)
Description of work (J APP, *2*, 194-195)
Established under the direction of Shiels, A. (J APP, *2*, 194-195)

Los Angeles Public Schools
Appointment: Sutherland, A. H. (BULL, *14*, 143; JOP, *14*, 364)

Los Angeles State Normal School
Appointment: Moore, E. C. (JOP, *14*, 532)
Appointment: Terman, L. M. (JOP, *3*, 476)

Lottier, Stuart
Appointment: Psychopathic Clinic, City of Detroit (SCI, *84*, 13)

Lotze, Rudolf Hermann
Lecture: Hall, G. S. (SCI, *35*, 101; JOP, *9*, 56)
Publication: "Outline of Psychology" offered to estate of Herrick, C. L. (JOP, *3*, 476)

Loucks, Roger Brown
Anniversary: UCLA, psych bldg. (BULL, *37*, 406)
Lecture: "Physiological Psychology" (SCI, *91*, 430)

Lough, James Edwin
Appointment: Harvard Univ. (REV, *3*, 356; SCI, *3*, 558)
Appointment: New York Univ. (REV, *8*, 656-657; BULL, *11*, 352; SCI, *14*, 304; SCI, *18*, 768)
Leave of absence: New York Univ. (J APP, *10*, 522)
Lecture: habit curve (JOP, *1*, 224)
Promotion: New York Univ. (REV, *9*, 104)

Louisiana Purchase Exposition (*see* Saint Louis World's Fair)

Louisiana State University (Baton Rouge)
Appointment: Bennett, C. J. C. (SCI, *22*, 648; BULL, *2*, 427)

Appointment: Dennis, W. (BULL, *39*, 267; SCI, *95*, 220)
Appointment: Elder, J. H. (BULL, *39*, 325; SCI, *95*, 220, 351)
Appointment: Mann, C. W., Testing and Guidance Bureau (BULL, *39*, 808)
Appointment: Unsworth, H. R., Med. Center (SCI, *74*, 385)
Departure: Sisson, E. D. (BULL, *39*, 808)
Leave of absence: Elder, J. H. (BULL, *40*, 619; SCI, *98*, 12)
Leave of absence: Grinsted, A. D. (BULL, *39*, 325; SCI, *95*, 220)
Promotion: Young, P. C. (BULL, *41*, 72)

Louisville Psychology Club
Information on (BULL, *42*, 487)

Louttit, Chauncey McKinley
Anniversary: Indiana Univ. Psych. Lab, 50th, commemoration (J APP, *23*, 631)
Appointment: APA (SCI, *98*, 321)
Appointment: Indiana Univ. (J APP, *15*, 324)
Appointment: Ohio State Univ. (SCI, *102*, 643)
Editor: *Psychological Record* (BULL, *36*, 806)
Election: American Assoc. for Applied Psychology, president (SCI, *96*, 292)
Publication: directory of psychological associations (BULL, *36*, 220; J APP, *23*, 418)

Love, Augustus Edward Hough
Election: Queens College, honorary fellow (SCI, *20*, 856)

Love, Inez
Appointment: Univ. of Pittsburgh (J APP, *10*, 522)

Lovejoy, Arthur Oncken
Appointment: Harvard Univ., William James Lectureship (BULL, *29*, 308; SCI, *75*, 331; JOP, *29*, 252)
Appointment: Johns Hopkins Univ. (BULL, *7*, 220; JOP, *7*, 308)
Appointment: Stanford Univ. (REV, *6*, 456)
Appointment: Univ. of Missouri (JOP, *5*, 252; BULL, *5*, 168)
Appointment: Washington Univ. (SCI, *14*, 624)
Departure: Univ. of Missouri (JOP, *7*, 308)
Election: American Philosophical Assoc., chair, publication committee (JOP, *31*, 536)
Election: American Philosophical Assoc., vice-president (JOP, *7*, 28)
Election: WPA, secretary and treasurer (JOP, *2*, 308)
Leave of absence: Washington Univ. (BULL, *5*, 32)
Lecture: Kant, I. (JOP, *1*, 224)
Lecture: SSPP (JOP, *21*, 84)
Lecture: Swarthmore College, Cooper Foundation (JOP, *39*, 139)
Resignation: Stanford Univ. (SCI, *13*, 760)
Resignation: Washington Univ., St. Louis (JOP, *5*, 252)

Lowell, Abbott Lawrence
Lecture: Bryn Mawr College (JoP, 7, 616)

Lowell, Frances Erma
Appointment: Minnesota State School for Feeble-minded (BULL, *14*, 333)

Lowell Institute (Boston)
Lecture: Brinton, D. G., language of the American Aborigines (SCI°, *4*, 522)

Lowell Lecture (Harvard University)
Campbell, C. M. (SCI, 76, 462)
Münsterberg, H. (SCI, *14*, 741)
Titchener, E. B. (BULL, 7, 426)

Löwi, Moritz
Appointment: Connecticut College (BULL, 37, 656)
Death notice (BULL, *41*, 199)
Publication: reading comprehension (AJP, 56, 129-133)

Lowie, Robert Harry
Election: National Research Council, chair (SCI, 73, 610)
Lecture: NYAS/APA on Feuerbach, L. (JoP, 7, 700)
Lecture: NYAS, Hopi Clan (JoP, *13*, 616)

Lowrey, Lawson Gentry
Lecture: National Research Council Conference, "Psychological Factors in National Morale" (BULL, 37, 829)

Lowson, James Prain
Appointment: Univ. of Queensland, Brisbane (SCI, 55, 398)

Loyola University (Chicago, Illinois)
Appointment: Bowers, P. F. (SCI, 69, 11)
Appointment: Braceland, F. J., School of Medicine (SCI, 93, 325)
Resignation: Moorhead, L. D., School of Medicine (SCI, 93, 325)

Lubbock, John
Lecture: Linnean Society, habits of ants, bees, and wasps (SCI°, *10*, 320)

Luborsky, Lester Bernard
Appointment: Univ. of Illinois (BULL, *42*, 793-794)

Lucas, Frederick A.
Election: NYAS officer (JoP, 9, 28)

Luccio, Giovanni
Election: International Congress of Psychology, 5th, treasurer (JoP, 2, 56)

Luce and Company
Publication: McDougall, W., book (JoP, *8*, 336)

Luciani, Luigi
Election: International Congress of Psychology, 5th, honorary president (JoP, *2*, 56; JoP, *1*, 721)

Luckey, George Washington Andrew
Leave of absence: Univ. of Nebraska (Rev, *6*, 673)

Lugt, Maria Johanna Antonia van der
Appointment: Univ. of Vermont (Bull, *40*, 383; Sci, *97*, 199)

Lukens, Herman Tyson
Appointment: Bryn Mawr College (Rev, *3*, 706)

Lunatics (*see also* Insanity)
Publication: Tuke, H., care of (AJP, *1*, 200)

Lundberg, George Andrew
Appointment: *Sociometry* (Bull, *38*, 305)

Luriia, Aleksandr Romanovich
Election: New York Academy of Medicine, Salmon Memorial Lecturer (Sci, *89*, 433)
Lecture: brain pathology (Sci, *89*, 433)
Salmon Memorial Lectures postponed (Sci, *91*, 382)

Lurton, Freeman Ellsworth
Lecture: retarded children (JoP, *7*, 223)

Luys, Jules Bernard
Death notice (AJP, *9*, 135)

Lyell, Charles, Sir
Publication: *Elements of Geology*, copy of note about Darwin's *Origin of Species*, 1842 (Sci, *90*, 155)
Publication: *Elements of Geology* preserved as a national memorial in Darwin's home (Sci, *90*, 155)

Lyman, Richard S.
Appointment: Duke Univ. (Sci, *91*, 187)
Departure: Johns Hopkins Univ., Phipps Psychiatric Clinic (Sci, *91*, 187)

M

MacAdam, David L.
Inter-Society Color Council (BULL, *36*, 142)

Macalester College (Minnesota)
Appointment: Hill, G. F. (BULL, *10*, 724)

McAllister, Cloyd North
Appointment: Yale Univ. (SCI, *13*, 600)
Death notice (BULL, *31*, 79)
Promotion: Yale Univ. (REV, *8*, 447)

McAllister, Ward
Publication: "Society as I have found it" (SCI°, *16*, 47-48)

McCall, William Anderson
Appointment: Teachers College, Columbia Univ. (BULL, *19*, 350)
Promotion: Teachers College, Columbia Univ. (JoP, *19*, 392)

McCann, Willis Harrison
Appointment: Univ. of Missouri (BULL, *36*, 218)

McCartney, James Lincoln
Mental Hygiene, Connecticut (SCI, *70*, 189)

McClelland, David Clarence
Appointment: Connecticut College (BULL, *37*, 656)

McClure, Matthew Thompson
Promotion: Tulane Univ. (JoP, *13*, 364)

McClusky, Howard Y.
Appointment: Univ. of Michigan (SCI, *90*, 439)

McComas, Henry Clay
Appointment: Princeton Univ. (BULL, 6, 328)

McConnell, Thomas Raymond
Appointment: Univ. of Minnesota (SCI, 99, 340-341)

McCoy, Peter
Appointment: Purdue Univ. (SCI, 54, 463)

McCracken, Thomas Cooke
Lecture: MPA (J APP, 25, 266)

McCulloch, W. S.
Promotion: Univ. of Illinois (SCI, 102, 300)

McDaniel, Henry Bonner
Appointment: California State Director of Vocational Education (BULL, 41, 267)

MacDonald, Arthur
Appointment: Clark Univ. (SCI, 14, 215)
Publication: death in man (AJP, 38, 153)

MacDonald, Carlos
Election: American Medico-Psychological Assoc. (SCI, 37, 936)

McDonald, E. F., Jr.
Telepathy experiment, Zenith Foundation, televised (J APP, 21, 605)

MacDonald, George
Appointment: Ross Institute of Tropical Hygiene (SCI, 101, 60)

Macdonald, M. Stuart
Appointment: McGill Univ. (BULL, 5, 380)

Macdonald, W. C., Sir
Donation: fund for psych. lab, McGill Univ. (JOP, 2, 280)

MacDougall, Robert
Appointment: Harvard Univ. (AJP, 10, 165)
Appointment: New York Univ. (SCI, 14, 424; REV, 8, 447)
Appointment: Western Reserve Univ. (REV, 5, 232)
Death notice (AJP, 53, 142-143; BULL, 37, 122)
Departure: Harvard Univ. (SCI, 14, 424; REV, 8, 447)
Leave of absence: New York Univ. (J APP, 10, 522)
Lecture: habits (JOP, 2, 112)
Lecture: International Congress of Arts and Sciences, St. Louis (JOP, 1, 616)
Lecture: nervous system (JOP, 2, 112)
Lecture: senses (JOP, 2, 224)
Lecture: spelling (JOP, 1, 84)

McDougall, William

Appointment: *Acta Psychologica*, board (AJP, *48*, 174)
Appointment: British Assoc. for the Advancement of Science, head of
  psychology section (BULL, *21*, 188)
Appointment: *British Journal of Psychology*, board (JoP, *1*, 28)
Appointment: *Character and Personality*, editorial board (J APP, *16*, 439)
Appointment: Duke Univ. (BULL, *24*, 204; SCI, *65*, 139)
Appointment: Harvard Univ. (SCI, *50*, 304; JoP, *16*, 588; BULL, *16*, 391-392)
Appointment: Oxford Univ. (BULL, *1*, 29; JoP, *1*, 28)
Award: Milton Fund Award, Harvard Univ. (BULL, *22*, 672)
Award: New York State Assoc. of Consulting Psychologists (BULL, *18*, 568)
Course: Univ. of Birmingham, psychotherapy (BULL, *17*, 200)
Death notice (AJP, *52*, 303-307; JoP, *35*, 699; BULL, *36*, 140)
Departure: Univ. College, London (JoP, *1*, 28)
Election: Corpus Christi College, extraordinary fellow (BULL, *9*, 360; SCI, *36*,
  113; JoP, *9*, 588)
Lecture: British AAS (SCI, *60*, 130)
Lecture: Clark Univ. (SCI, *62*, 561)
Lecture: instinct and intelligence (JoP, *7*, 420)
Lecture: Univ. of Manchester (BULL, *28*, 567)
Publication: notice (JoP, *8*, 336)
Research: expedition to Torrey Straits and Borneo (AJP, *9*, 423)
Resignation: Harvard Univ. (SCI, *65*, 139)

Mace, Cecil Alec

Appointment: Birkbeck College (BULL, *42*, 63; SCI, *100*, 424)
Publication: *Manual of Psychology* (J APP, *22*, 664)
Psychic research (SCI, *80*, 183)

McFarland, Ross Armstrong

Degree: Park College (BULL, *39*, 682)
Lecture: Union College, "The psycho-physiological effects of high altitude on
  the human organism" (SCI, *92*, 552)
Symposium: AAAS, Section I, Psychology (J APP, *23*, 630)

McGarvey, Hulda Rees

Appointment: Mount Holyoke College (BULL, *34*, 499)

McGarvey, John W.

Appointment: Mount Holyoke College (BULL, *34*, 499)
Death notice (BULL, *36*, 218)

McGeoch, John Alexander

Appointment: Clark Univ. (SCI, *84*, 387)
Appointment: Stanford Univ. (J APP, *18*, 156)
Appointment: Univ. of Arkansas (BULL, *25*, 700)
Appointment: Univ. of Missouri (BULL, *27*, 636)
Appointment: Univ. of North Dakota (BULL, *25*, 307)

Appointment: Wesleyan Univ. (SCI, *81*, 397)
Death notice (AJP, *56*, 134-136)
Election: AAAS, section I, psychology, secretary (SCI, *84*, 371; SCI, *79*, 406)
Election: MPA, president (J APP, *18*, 860)
Election: MPA, secretary, 1934 (SCI, *79*, 76)
Publication: AAAS, section I, psychology, 1941-42 (J APP, *26*, 107-108)
Publication: Robinson, F., obituary (AJP, *49*, 321)
Symposium: Indiana Univ., learning, 1939 (BULL, *37*, 61)

McGill University (Montreal, Canada)

Appointment: Cameron, D. E. (SCI, *99*, 123-124)
Appointment: Hickson, J. W. (JoP, *2*, 560; BULL, *2*, 296)
Appointment: Jasper, H. H., Medical School (BULL, *35*, 796)
Appointment: MacDonald, M. S. (BULL, *5*, 380)
Donation: MacDonald, W. C., fund for Psych. Lab. (JoP, *2*, 280)
Establishment: Dept. of Psychiatry in assoc. with Royal Victoria Hospital,
    Institute for Research and Teaching (SCI, *98*, 446-447; SCI, *99*, 123-124)
Establishment: psychology dept. separate (SCI, *60*, 175)
Promotion: Tait, W. D. (BULL, *21*, 552)

McGilvary, Evander Bradley

Appointment: Univ. of Wisconsin (BULL, *2*, 224; JoP, *2*, 364)
Election: WPA, president (JoP, *7*, 308)
Lecture: APA/WPA/AAAS meeting (JoP, *8*, 55)
Lecture: Huxley's epiphenomenalism (JoP, *7*, 223)
Resignation: Cornell Univ. (BULL, *2*, 224)

McGinnis, John Marshall

Appointment: Beloit College (BULL, *41*, 72)
Grant: Virginia Academy of Science Research (SCI, *76*, 590)

McGrath, Fern

Election: Psychologists Club of San Francisco, secretary (J APP, *25*, 129)
Publication: Psychologists Club of the San Francisco Bay Region, study on
    creation of world federation (J APP, *26*, 108-109)

McGraw, Myrtle Byram

Lecture: Laity lectures (BULL, *39*, 895)

McGregor, Douglas Murray

Appointment: Mass. Inst. of Tech., first psychologist (BULL, *34*, 634)

Mach, Ernst

Appointment: Univ. of Vienna (SCI, *1*, 363; SCI, *2*, 692; REV, *2*, 328, 534)
Award: Bavarian Maximilian Award for science and art (SCI, *24*, 60; JoP, *3*, 476)
Death notice (BULL, *13*, 188)
Fund in his honor for the Technical High School, Brünn (SCI, *53*, 72)
Retirement: Univ. of Vienna (SCI, *14*, 302)

MacIntosh, W. H.
Appointment: Trinity College (SCI, *3*, 111)

Mackay, Donald Sage
Lecture: Dewey, J. (JOP, *39*, 55-56)

McKeag, Anna Jane
Course: Penn. Summer School for Teachers (BULL, *8*, 222)

Mackenzie, John Stuart
Publication: *Lectures in Humanism* (JOP, *4*, 308)

McKim, Margaret Grace
Appointment: Teachers College, Columbia Univ. (BULL, *40*, 459)

McKinley, John Charnley
Appointment: Univ. of Minnesota, School of Medicine (SCI, *98*, 81)

McKinney, Fred
Appointment: MPA program committee (J APP, *24*, 96; BULL, *37*, 187)

McKinsey, John Charles Chenoweth
Editor: *Journal of Symbolic Logic* (JOP, *39*, 84)

Mackintosh, Helen K.
Appointment: U.S. Office of Education (J APP, *22*, 107)

Mackintosh, James Macalister
Appointment: British Fuel and Power Advisory Council (SCI, *101*, 197)
Appointment: London School of Hygiene and Tropical Medicine (SCI, *101*, 60)

McLane, Allan
Lecture: legal regulations governing the insane (SCI, *25*, 398)

McLean Hospital (Massachusetts)
Appointment: Franz, S. I. (JOP, *1*, 196; BULL, *1*, 173)
Appointment: Wells, F. L. (JOP, *4*, 308, 420; BULL, *4*, 337)
Appointment: Wyatt, F. (BULL, *41*, 679)
Internships in clinical psychology available (BULL, *42*, 795)
Resignation: Cowles, E. (BULL, *1*, 173)

MacLennan, Simon Fraser
Appointment: Univ. of Chicago (REV, *1*, 654)
Appointment: Oberlin College (REV, *7*, 323; REV, *5*, 109; SCI, *6*, 446; AJP, *9*, 135)
Lecture: metaphysics (JOP, *1*, 336)

MacLeod, Robert Brodie
Appointment: Swarthmore College (SCI, *77*, 364)

Macmillan and Company
Publication: APA proceedings of 1st and 2nd meetings (REV, *1*, 335)
Publication: announcement (JoP, *8*, 560)
Publication: announcement for Boodin, J. E.; Pillsbury, W. B.; Thorndike, E. L. (JoP, *8*, 392)
Publication: announcement for Pearson, K. (JoP, *8*, 476)
Publication: fall list (JoP, *7*, 560)

McMillin, Emerson
Donation: AAAS (SCI, *10*, 301)
Election: NYAS officer (JoP, *9*, 28)

McMullen, Charles Bell
Appointment: Princeton Univ. (BULL, *3*, 356)

MacMurray College (Jacksonville, Illinois)
Appointment: Halverson, H. M. (BULL, *39*, 807)
Course: organized workers for handicapped children (BULL, *39*, 807)

MacMurray, J.
Psychic research (SCI, *80*, 183)

McMurtry, Herbert Crawford
Appointment: Willamette Univ. (BULL, *41*, 603)

McNairy, C. Banks
Appointment: North Carolina School for Feeble-minded (BULL, *11*, 268)

McNamara, Eric D.
Psychic research (SCI, *80*, 183)

McNemar, Quinn
Appointment: Fordham Univ. (J APP, *21*, 474; BULL, *34*, 498)
Appointment: Stanford Univ. (BULL, *35*, 408)
Editor: commemorative volume honoring Terman, L. M. (BULL, *39*, 268; SCI, *95*, 117-118)
Publication: sample in statistics, reply to Garrett, H. E. (AJP, *55*, 581-582)

McNulty, J. J.
Death notice (BULL, *5*, 168)

Macomber, Freeman Glenn
Appointment: WAAC training (BULL, *40*, 383)

MacPherson, John
Appointment: Univ. of Sidney (SCI, *55*, 675)

McQuitty, Louis Laforce
Promotion: Univ. of Illinois (BULL, *42*, 793-794)

Macran, Henry Stewart
Appointment: Trinity College, Dublin, fellow (SCI, *15*, 120)

McTaggart, John McTaggart Ellis
Appointment: Trinity College, Cambridge Univ. (REV, *5*, 109)
Appointment: Univ. of California, summer school (JOP, *4*, 336)

MacVannel, John Angus
Promotion: Teacher's College, Columbia (BULL, *1*, 134)

McWhood, Leonard B.
Appointment: Columbia Univ. (REV, *3*, 356)

Macy, Josiah, Jr., Foundation
Appointment: Dewey, J., board (SCI, *92*, 553)
Grant: Cornell Univ., experimental neuroses (SCI, *91*, 446)
Grant: Murphy, G. and Barmack, J. E. for research (BULL, *38*, 779)
Grant: National Committee for Mental Hygiene, distribute articles in
psychosomatic medicine on war problems (SCI, *98*, 59-60)

Madison University (Hamilton, New York)
Name changed to Colgate Univ. (SCI*, *13*, 501)

Madrid Government School of Science
Nomination: Simmara, G., chair (AJP, *8*, 584)

Magdsick, Winifred Katherine
Appointment: Washington Univ., St. Louis (BULL, *39*, 682)

Magellanic Expedition of the Field Museum of Natural History
Research: continued Darwin's, C., begun on cruise of the Beagle (SCI, *90*, 562)

Magic
Lecture: Mayser, C. W., AAAS (SCI, *82*, 591)
Publication: Dallenbach, K. M., "The psychology of magic" (SCI, *82*, 591)

Magnan, Valentin
Death notice (BULL, *13*, 482; SCI, *44*, 672)

Mahaffy, John Pentland
Publication: Greek social life (SCI*, *9*, 483)

Maier, Norman Raymond Fredrick
Award: prize by AAAS (SCI, *89*, 7, 313; BULL, *36*, 220)
Award: Univ. of Michigan, Henry Russel Award (SCI, *89*, 313; BULL, *36*, 499)
Conference: Psychology of Learning, Univ. of Colorado, 1939 (BULL, *36*, 583)
Election: MPA, council member (J APP, *23*, 419)

Maine, University of (Orono)
Appointment: Craig, W. (BULL, 5, 348)
Appointment: Dickinson, C. A. (SCI, 65, 299; BULL, 24, 136)
Appointment: Halverson, H. M. (JoP, 19, 532; BULL, 19, 410; SCI, 55, 617)
Promotion: Quinsey, D. L. (BULL, 42, 63)
Resignation: Craig, W. (BULL, 19, 410)

Mair, W.
Lecture: British Psychological Society (JoP, 8, 448)

Major, David R.
Appointment: Teacher's College, Columbia Univ. (REV, 5, 677)
Appointment: Univ. of Nebraska (REV, 6, 673)
Departure: Teachers College, Columbia Univ. (REV, 6, 673)
Letter to JoP editors on review of "Elements of Psychology" (JoP, 11, 83-84)

Makuen, George Hudson
Death notice (BULL, 14, 115)

Malamud, William
Appointment: Worcester State Hospital, Massachusetts (SCI, 90, 204)
Departure: State Univ. of Iowa, College of Medicine (SCI, 90, 204)

Mallery, Garrick
Research: sign language (SCI°, 1, 157)

Malmburg, Constantine Frithiof
Death notice (BULL, 42, 790)

Management Congress, International, 7th
Meeting: announced, 1938 (J APP, 22, 443; BULL, 35, 796)

Managerial psychology
Lecture: Tead, O., Taylor Society (J APP, 9, 428)

Manchester New College
Lecture: James, W. (BULL, 5, 168)

Manchester, University of (England)
Appointment: James, H. (BULL, 23, 455)
Appointment: Lane, R. E. (SCI, 101, 324)
Appointment: Thouless, R. H. (BULL, 18, 568)
Appointment: Wyatt, S. (SCI, 54, 575)
Departure: Thouless, R. (BULL, 23, 455)

Manitoba, University of (Canada)
Appointment: professor of philosophy in Dept. of Phil. and Psych. (JoP, 17, 307)

Mann, Cecil William
Appointment: Univ. of Denver (BULL, 37, 61)
Appointment: Louisiana State Univ., Testing and Guidance Bureau (BULL, 39, 808)
Departure: Univ. of Denver (BULL, 39, 808)
Promotion: Tulane Univ. (BULL, 42, 675)

Manry, James Campbell
Appointment: Ewing Christian College, India (SCI, 58, 514)

Manuel, Herschel Thurman
Lecture: Educational Conference, 7th, testing (J APP, 22, 441)
Research: talents in drawing (J APP, 1, 298-299)

Maple-Wood Farms, Sidis Psychotherapeutic Institute
Donation: estate (JoP, 6, 721)

Marbe, Karl
Appointment: Univ. of Bonn (AJP, 7, 152)
Appointment: Univ. of Würzburg (JoP, 7, 84; SCI, 17, 320; BULL, 6, 368)
Editor: *Fortschritte der Psychologie und inrer Andwendungen* (BULL, 9, 359)
Publication: Peters, W. (JoP, 9, 699-700)

Marburg University (Germany)
Appointment: Ach, N. (SCI, 25, 760; JoP, 4, 308; BULL, 4, 338)
Course: Scripture, E. W. (BULL, 2, 360)

Marey, Etienne Jules
Statue, Boulogne-sur seine (BULL, 11, 268)

Marie, A.
Death notice (BULL, 12, 128, 204)

Marie, Pierre
Appointment: Univ. of Paris (BULL, 14, 192)

Marketing
Research: Scott, W. D. (J APP, 2, 299)

Marquis, Donald George
Appointment: APA (SCI, 98, 321)
Appointment: Office of Psychological Personnel (BULL, 40, 618; SCI, 98, 215)
Appointment: Univ. of Michigan (BULL, 42, 406)
Appointment: Yale Univ. (SCI, 94, 62; BULL, 38, 907)
Departure: Yale Univ. (BULL, 42, 406)

Marriage and divorce
Research: Wright, C. D. (SCI, 9, 411)

Marsh, Clarence Stephen
Election: National Conference on Education Broadcasting, 2nd, executive secretary (BULL, *34*, 637)

Marsh, Howard Daniel
Death notice (BULL, *42*, 675)
Lecture: efficiency (JoP, *1*, 224)
Promotion: College of the City of New York (JoP, *14*, 56)

Marshall, Henry Rutgers
Appointment: Columbia College (REV, *1*, 440)
Appointment: Yale Univ. (SCI, *23*, 480)
Award: Butler Medal for *Mind and Conduct* (JoP, *17*, 364)
Course: Yale Univ. (BULL, *3*, 147)
Death notice (BULL, *24*, 380)
Election: APA council (JoP, *1*, 28; BULL, *4*, 32)
Election: APA, president (SCI, *25*, 37)
Lecture: APA, instinct and intelligence (SCI, *34*, 680)
Lecture: presentations (JoP, *1*, 84)
Lecture: Union Theological Seminary, consciousness and behavior (JoP, *16*, 196)
Publication: consciousness and behavior, Dr. Bode's view (JoP, *15*, 559-560)
Publication: *Pain, Pleasure, Aesthetics* (SCI°, *22*, 335; SCI°, *23*, 96)
Publication: use of subconscious (JoP, *5*, 111)
Symposium: APA (JoP, *8*, 699-700)

Marston, William Moulton
Appointment: American Univ., Washington, D. C. (BULL, *20*, 60; SCI, *56*, 195)
Appointment: Universal Pictures Corp. (SCI, *69*, 542)

Martin, Clyde Eugene
Research: human sex behavior, Kinsey, A. C. and Ramsey, G. (SCI, *95*, 600)

Martin, Henry Newell
Lecture: Peabody Institute of Behavior, minds of animals (SCI°, *2*, 782)

Martin, Hermon Wilkes
Promotion: Emory Univ. (BULL, *40*, 794)

Martin, Lillien Jane
Appointment: APA chair, San Francisco program (SCI, *41*, 605; JoP, *12*, 280)
Appointment: Mental Hygiene Clinic (BULL, *14*, 191)
Appointment: Stanford Univ. (JoP, *8*, 336; AJP, *11*, 280; SCI, *43*, 776; SCI, *33*, 657; BULL, *13*, 260; REV, *7*, 104; BULL, *12*, 481; JoP, *13*, 84)
Death notice (AJP, *56*, 453-454; BULL, *40*, 458)
Degree: Univ. of Bonn (BULL, *10*, 424; AJP, *25*, 147; SCI, *38*, 400; JoP, *10*, 616)
Establishment: California Society for Mental Hygiene (J APP, *2*, 386)

Lecture: Congress of Experimental Psychology, 5th (Sci, *35*, 772; JoP, *9*, 336; Bull, *9*, 208)
Lecture: Stanford Univ., mental hygiene (Sci, *43*, 20)
Promotion: Stanford Univ. (Bull, *8*, 182; Sci, *29*, 455; JoP, *13*, 336)
Publication: child psychology (J App, *10*, 395)
Publication: old age, printed as memorial (Bull, *42*, 192)
Publication: review of her work (J App, *1*, 97-98)
Publication: training of the emotions (J App, *2*, 386)

Martin, Mabel Florence
Appointment: Wichita Child Guidance Center (Bull, *42*, 582)
Publication: "Mind, mechanism and lexicographic behavior" (AJP, *49*, 313)
Publication: "Responses of animals to the airplane" (AJP, *45*, 530)

Martineau, James
Death notice (Sci, *11*, 159)

Martius, Götz
Death notice (Bull, *25*, 56)
Editor: *Beiträge zur Psychologie and Philosophie* (Rev, *3*, 355)
Publication: aims and results of experimental psych. (Sci°, *11*, 169)
Publication: German psychology journal (Sci, *3*, 354)

Marty, Anton
Death notice (Bull, *12*, 128)

Marvin, Walter Taylor
Appointment: Princeton Univ. (JoP, *2*, 336)
Appointment: Rutgers College (JoP, *7*, 252; Bull, *7*, 180)
Death notice (Bull, *41*, 498)
Declines service to the Amer. Philosophical Assoc. (JoP, *14*, 196)
Election: American Philosophical Assoc., vice-president (Sci, *33*, ??; JoP, *8*, 27-28)

Maryland Mental Hygiene Society
Appointment: Truitt, R. C. P. (Sci, *66*, 34)
Election: Meyer, A., president (Sci, *64*, 495)

Maryland Psychiatric Hospital Unit
Establishment of outpatient treatment (Sci, *46*, 139)

Maryland State Lunacy Commission
Appointment: Hurd, H. M. (Sci, *28*, 301)

Maryland State Teachers College
Appointment: Cooper, J. A. (Bull, *40*, 230)

Maryland, University of (College Park)
Appointment: Jenkins, J. G. (BULL, 34, 864)
Degree: Hall, G. S. (BULL, 4, 200)
Lecture: Hall, G. S., centennial celebration (SCI, 25, 879)

Mason, Otis Tufton
Lecture: Child-life among savage and uncivilized peoples (SCI°, 3, 56)

Massachusetts Department of Education
Course: psychology for national defense (BULL, 38, 779-780)

Massachusetts General Hospital (Boston)
Psychiatric unit established (SCI, 79, 291)

Massachusetts Institute of Technology (Cambridge)
Appointment: Lewin, K. (BULL, 42, 191)
Appointment: McGregor, D. M. (BULL, 34, 634)
Course: industrial statistics (SCI, 94, 136)
Lecture: Bingham, W. V. (BULL, 29, 308)

Massachusetts Psychiatric Society
Election: Campbell, C. M. (SCI, 80, 475)

Massachusetts School for Feeble-minded
Conference: psychological examining (BULL, 13, 407)

Massachusetts Society for Mental Hygiene
Conference: mental hygiene in Massachusetts (J APP, 3, 396)
Election: Campbell, C. M., president (SCI, 65, 11; SCI, 67, 12)
Lecture: Beers, L. W., 20th anniversary (SCI, 77, 423)
Lecture: Gesell, A. L. (SCI, 92, 399)

Massachusetts State College
Appointment: DeSilva, H. R. (SCI, 76, 119)
Promotion: Neet, C. C. (BULL, 39, 423)
Resignation: DeSilva, H. R. (SCI, 83, 347)

Massachusetts State Hospital
Appointment: Cohoon, E. H. (SCI, 42, 415)

Massachusetts State Normal School (Worcester)
Course: observation (AJP, 1, 354)
Resignation: Bolton, T. L. (SCI, 4, 142)

Mateer, Florence
Lecture: Mass. School for Feeble-minded (BULL, 13, 407-408)

Mather College
Appointment: Huntley, C. W. (SCI, 93, 615)

Mather, Kirtley Fletcher
Election: Institute for Propaganda Analysis, president (J App, *25*, 361, 597)

Mathews, Julia
Appointment: Child Clinic, California (J App, *10*, 396)

Mathieson, Anna
Election: APA, Wash.-Balt. Branch, president (Bull, *35*, 188)

Matsumoto, Matataro
Appointment: Imperial Normal School of Tokoyo, Japan (Sci, *13*, 280)
Appointment: Yale Psychological Laboratory (Rev, *4*, 452)

Mattson, Marion Louise
Death notice (Bull, *40*, 794)

Maudsley, Henry
Death notice (JoP, *15*, 168; Sci, *47*, 189; Bull, *15*, 24, 97)

Maudsley Hospital (London, England)
Appointment: Nevin, S. (Sci, *89*, 554)

Maxfield, Francis Norton
Appointment: Pennsylvania Dept. of Public Instruction (Bull, *17*, 435)
Appointment: Public School Clinic of Newark, N.J. (Bull, *15*, 24, 98)
Death notice (Bull, *42*, 790)
Promotion (Sci, *40*, 482)
Promotion: Univ. of Pennsylvania (JoP, *11*, 588; Bull, *11*, 483)
Research: psychological tests for the aviation corps (J App, *1*, 30)

May, Mark Arthur
Appointment: Univ. of California, School of Medicine (Bull, *29*, 460)
Election: APA, director (Sci, *82*, 247)
Return: Syracuse Univ. (J App, *10*, 393)

Mayer, Alfred Marshall
Death notice (AJP, *9*, 135)

Mayo, Elton
Appointment: Harvard Univ. (Bull, *23*, 455; Sci, *64*, 89)
Lecture: Taylor Society, industrial psychology (JoP, *21*, 700)

Mayo Foundation (Rochester, Minnesota)
Lecture: Volbarth, ? and Orbeli, L. A., conditioned reflex and sympathetic nervous system (Sci, *70*, 402)

Mayser, Charles W.
Lecture: AAAS, magic (Sci, *82*, 501)

Maze performance
Lecture: Elliott, M. H. (AJP, *42*, 315)

Mead, George Herbert
Appointment: Carus Lecturer, 1929 (SCI, *69*, 157)
Appointment: Univ. of Chicago (SCI, *1*, 81; REV, *1*, 552)
Death notice (JoP, *28*, 280; BULL, *28*, 410)
Editor: *Bulletin* issue, social and religious psychology (BULL, *8*, 438; BULL, *9*, 486)
Lecture: AAAS psychology of social consciousness (JoP, *7*, 308)
Resignation: Univ. of Chicago (BULL, *28*, 324)

Mead, Margaret
Course: Univ. of Chicago, comparative psychology (JoP, *1*, 336)

Meaning, conception of
Lecture: Calkins, M. W., Univ. of London (BULL, *25*, 307)

Mecklin, John Moffatt
Appointment: Lafayette College (BULL, *3*, 35)
Appointment: Univ. of Pittsburgh (JoP, *10*, 588)
Resignation: Lafayette College (JoP, *10*, 504, 559, 560)

Medical Center for Federal Prisoners (Springfield, Missouri)
Research: Cason, H. (BULL, *38*, 304)

Medical Congress for Psychotherapy, International
Tribute to Freud, S., 1938 (SCI, *88*, 164)

Medical Congress, International
Election: Jung, C. G., Univ. of Oxford, presided (SCI, *88*, 212)
Lecture: psychiatrists (SCI, *38*, 124)
Meeting: Paris (AJP, *11*, 279)

Medical Correctional Association
Establish contact with professionals interested in medical aspects of crime (J APP, *27*, 208)

Medical Journal (Brooklyn, New York)
Publication: physiological effects of saccharin (SCI°, *16*, 77)

Medical Jurisprudence, Society of
Lecture: Hollingworth, H. L. (JoP, *9*, 672)

Medical practice
Lecture: Franz, S. I., psychological factors (JoP, *11*, 84)

Medical Press
Suicide statistics for 1889 (SCI°, *14*, 199)

Medical Psychology, Institute of (London)
Lecture: Jung, G. C. (SCI, 82, 348)

Medical Research Council
Appointment: Craik, K. J. W., Cambridge Univ. (SCI, 99, 531)
Establishment: Cambrdige Univ., Unit of Applied Psychology (SCI, 99, 531)

Medical Society of Psychotherapy, International
Annual Congress, 10th (BULL, 35, 408)

Medicine
Lecture: Wells, F. L., NY Branch of APA/NYAS (JoP, 9, 167)

Medicine, Institute of Chicago (*see* Chicago Institute)

Medicine, Institute of Experimental
Appointment: Kupalov, P. S., Pavlov Assoc. (SCI, 69, 450)

Medico-Psychological Assoc. of Great Britain
Certificates: psychological medicine (AJP, 1, 197)
Meeting (SCI, 58, 439)

Medico-Psychological Society
Appointment: Preston, J. (SCI, 46, 357)

Medvednikova, M. M. E.
Donation: asylums and hospitals (SCI, 11, 239)

Meenes, Max
Election: APA Wash.-Balt. Branch, vice-president (BULL, 35, 188)

Mehrtens, H. G.
Grant: syphilis research (SCI, 69, 37)

Meier, Norman Charles
Appointment: American Institute of Public Opinion (BULL, 42, 486)
Leave of absence: State Univ. of Iowa (BULL, 42, 486)

Meiklejohn, Alexander
Appointment: Amherst College, president (JoP, 9, 336)
Appointment: Brown Univ. (JoP, 3, 532)

Melanesians
Publication: Feathermann, A. (SCI°, 9, 515)

Melbourne, University of (Australia)
Appointment: Gibson, W. R. B. (JoP, 9, 84)
Lecture: Berry, R. J. A. (SCI, 55, 125)

Melby, Ernest Oscar

Election: Institute for Propaganda Analysis, vice-president (J App, *21*, 719; Bull, *34*, 865)

Mellon Institute

Appointment: Wallin, J. E. W., Mellon Fellow (Bull, *9*, 486; JoP, *9*, 672)
Fellowship: two Simmons Fellowships (Bull, *23*, 456)

Melton, Arthur Weever

Appointment: Yale Univ. (Sci, *80*, 137)

Meltzer, Hyman

Appointment: Univ. of Oklahoma, Guidance Institute (J App, *21*, 719)
Research: stuttering (J App, *19*, 497)

Memory (*see also* Forgetting)

Lecture: Boring, E. G., experiments (AJP, *40*, 513)
Lecture: Chrislip, A. E., NY Branch APA/NYAS (JoP, *9*, 167)
Lecture: Edgell, B., Aristotelian Society (JoP, *9*, 363-364)
Lecture: Kuhlmann, F. (JoP, *7*, 223)
Lecture: Monroe, W. S. (JoP, *2*, 224)
Lecture: Ogden, R. M. (JoP, *1*, 224)
Lecture: Titchener, E. B., Columbia Univ., imagination (Sci, *33*, 214)
Lecture: Titchener, E. B., Indiana Univ., imagination (Sci, *33*, 420)
Lecture: Ward, J. (JoP, *9*, 700)
Publication: Bergson, H. (JoP, *7*, 644)
Publication: Chou, S. K. "What is the curve of forgetting" (AJP, *45*, 348)
Publication: Des Bancels reply to Chou's Curve of forgetting (AJP, *45*, 758)
Publication: Hilgard, E. R. "The saving score as a measure of retention" (AJP, *46*, 337)
Publication: Kay, D. *Edinburgh Review*, memory, what is it and how to improve it (Sci°, *12*, 237)
Publication: Kitzmiller, A. B., "Memory of raccoons" (AJP, *46*, 511)
Publication: Middleton, A. E., memory systems, new and old (Sci°, *12*, 107)
Publication: Simpson, R. M., color (AJP, *40*, 351)
Publication: White, W. W. *The Chautauquan* (Sci°, *12*, 250)
Research: Dugas, L., and mental disturbance (JoP, *15*, 615-616)
Research: Dunlap, K. (Bull, *31*, 80)
Research: Henri, M. V. (AJP, *7*, 303)
Research: Snoddy, G. S., Indiana Univ., 20 year longitudinal study (J App, *23*, 530)

Mendel, Lafayette Benedict

Lecture: Yale Univ., animal intelligence (Sci, *15*, 117)

Menninger Clinic (Topeka, Kansas)

Conference: Psycholoanalysis and Experimental Psychology (Bull, *33*, 579)

Menninger Foundation (Topeka, Kansas)
Organization: purpose (BULL, *39*, 197)

Menninger, William Claire
Award: Mental Hygiene, 1st Lasker Award (SCI, *100*, 516)

Mental Attitudes for National Defense
Meeting: Detroit, 1941 with Sigma Xi, Tau Beta Pi, Alpha Omega Alpha, Phi Beta Kappa (SCI, *93*, 372)

Mental deficiency
Fellowship to work with Terman. L. M. (BULL, *11*, 191)

Lecture: Doll, E. A. (AJP, *54*, 116-124)

Legislation: Illinois provides education for mentally handicapped children (BULL, *42*, 407)

Meeting: American Assoc. on Mental Deficiency (J APP, *21*, 241)

Research: commissioned by governor of Indiana (BULL, *12*, 404)

Research: mental retardation Division of Psychology at Los Angeles (J APP, *2*, 194-195)

Research: musical sense in idiots (SCI°, *17*, 353)

Mental development
Lecture: Wallin, J. E. W., NY Branch APA/NYAS (JoP, *9*, 167)

Publication: Baldwin, J. M., *Mental Development in the Child and the Race* (SCI°, *23*, 95)

Publication: Baldwin, J. M., *Mental Development: Methods and Processes* (3rd. ed.) (BULL, *3*, 392)

Symposium: Philadelphia Pathological Society (JoP, *10*, 671-672)

Mental health/mental illness
Course: Rorschach Test and mental disturbances (J APP, *27*, 207)

Grant: Cambridge Univ., research, mental pathology (SCI, *60*, 39)

Lecture: Laity lecture by Hoskins, R. G., mental diseases (SCI, *89*, 175)

Lecture: Tuttle, G. T., mental illness (SCI, *34*, 914)

Meeting: mental health in later maturity (BULL, *38*, 778)

Publication: Preston School of Industry, California, mental condition study (J APP, *3*, 196)

Publication: Störring, G., mental pathology (JoP, *4*, 308)

Research: Bassi, G., mental distress (SCI°, *18*, 88)

Research: Dugas, L., memory and mental disturbance (JoP, *15*, 615-616)

Research: Vassar College fellowships, "Graduate Division of Conservation" (BULL, *39*, 132)

Mental hygiene (*see also* Hygiene)
American Foundation for Mental Hygiene (SCI, *70*, 536)

Appointment: Bullis, H. E., National Committee on Mental Hygiene (BULL, *36*, 711)

Appointment: Fenton, N., California Youth Correction Authority, consultant (SCI, 97, 65)

Appointment: Peppard, S. H., Connecticut (SCI, 74, 434)

Appointment: Rochester Guidance Center, New York (BULL, 36, 841)

Appointment: Shaw, H. A., Harvard Univ. (SCI, 74, 481)

Appointment: Stevenson, G. S., National Committee on Mental Hygiene (BULL, 36, 711)

Appointment: Wallin, J. E. W., Psycho-Educational Examiner, director (J APP, 21, 717)

Appropriations: Commonwealth Fund (SCI, 76, 81)

Award: Beer, C. W., National Institute of Social Sciences, gold medal (SCI, 77, 423)

Course: Wallin, J. E. W., Duke Univ. (BULL, 35, 259; J APP, 21, 130)

Election: National Committee for Mental Hygiene, officers, 1933 (SCI, 77, 46)

Exhibit: International Congress of Hygiene, Philadelphia (SCI, 37, 330)

Lecture: Furst, C. (JoP, 7, 700)

Lecture: Gillespie, R. D., New York Academy of Medicine, Salmon Lecturer (J APP, 25, 726)

Lecture: Martin, L. J. (SCI, 43, 20)

Lecture: Myers, G. C., The parent problem (J APP, 22, 539)

Lecture: Treadway, W. L., Academy of Medicine, Interaction between man and his environment (SCI, 84, 530)

Meeting: Amer. Public Health Assoc. (SCI, 86, 99)

Meeting: International Congress on Mental Hygiene, 1st (SCI, 70, 32)

Meeting: National Committee for Mental Hygiene (SCI, 70, 536)

Meeting: National Committee for Mental Hygiene, problems of peace, rehabilitation of veterans, etc. (SCI, 100, 402)

Meeting: National Committee for Mental Hygiene, 25th anniversary dinner (SCI, 80, 446)

Meeting: National Council of Great Britain (SCI, 58, 263)

Publication: journal released (BULL, 14, 114)

Research: Hincks, C. M., National Committee for Mental Hygiene (SCI, 72, 557)

Research: National Committee on Mental Hygiene, national research plan (SCI, 72, 557)

Research: North Dakota (BULL, 20, 288)

U.S. Public Health Care Service, new division established (SCI, 46, 135)

Mental Hygiene Commission
Grant: Commonwealth Fund, aid to men rejected by armed forces (SCI, 98, 196)

Mental Hygiene, Conference on
Lecture: Fernald, W. S., care of feeble-minded (J APP, 3, 396)

Lecture: Southard, E. E., causes of mental illness (J APP, 3, 396)

Lecture: Stearns, A. W. aims of society (J APP, 3, 396)

Meeting: Massachusetts Society for Mental Hygiene (J APP, 3, 396)

Mental Hygiene, Institute for
Appointment: Smith, L. H. (SCI, *88*, 591)
Resignation: Bond, E. D. (SCI, *88*, 591)

Mental Hygiene International Congress
Meeting, 1st announced (SCI, *69*, 244; SCI, *70*, 32; BULL, *27*, 76; AJP, *42*, 147)

Mental illness (*see* Mental health/mental illness and Insanity)

Mental processes
Lecture: Hancock, J. A., mental association (JoP, *7*, 222)
Lecture: Montague, W. P. (JoP, *2*, 700)
Lecture: Pillsbury, W. B., Columbia Univ. (SCI, *33*, 214)
Lecture: Thorndike, E. L., mental dynamics (AJP, *54*, 132-133)
Reaction: Münsterberg and Scripture (AJP, *9*, 420-421)
Research: Speir, F. (SCI°, *3*, 426)

Mental tests
Alterness tests for freshmen at Northwestern Univ. (SCI, *56*, 331; BULL, *20*, 172)
Application: Bingham, W. V. (JoP, *17*, 82-83)
Appropriations: APA (REV, *5*, 344)
Lecture: Hays, M. (J APP, *6*, 425)
Lecture: Porter, J. P., mental measurement, Clark Univ. (J APP, *9*, 88)
Lecture: Woolley, H. T., mental levels (J APP, *6*, 425)
Publication: *Journal of Applied Psychology*, regular column on mental testing (J APP, *22*, 215)
Publication: *Military Mental Testing* (JoP, *18*, 420; JoP, *20*, 280)
Publication: Otis, A. A. test (J APP, *20*, 791)
Publication: Woodburne, A. S. (JoP, *21*, 364)
Research: Carnegie Institute of Technology at Pittsburgh, bureau established (BULL, *12*, 160)
Research: Coy, G. L., gifted children (J APP, *1*, 298-299)
Research: Peterson, J., mentality differences (BULL, *17*, 240)

Mercer, Margaret
Lecture: Pennsylvania Mental Hospital Assoc. (BULL, *42*, 792)

Mercer University (Macon, Georgia)
Departure: Thaxton, O. A. (JoP, *1*, 616)

Mercier, Charles Arthur
Death notice (BULL, *16*, 392)
Lecture: criminology (JoP, *1*, 420)

Mercier, Désiré Félicien François Joseph, Cardinal
Publication: nervous system and the mind (SCI°, *10*, 176-177)

Merrick, F. A.
Conference: 10th annual, industrial (SCI, 69, 492)

Merrill, Maud
Editor: commemorative volume to Terman, L. M. (SCI, 95, 117-118; BULL, 39, 268)

Merrill-Palmer School (Detroit, Michigan)
Appointment: Woolley, H. B. T., director (J APP, 9, 203, 319)
Course: child psychology, graduate (J APP, 9, 203)

Merritt, H. Houston
Appointment: College of Physicians and Surgeons, Columbia Univ. and
Montefiore Hospital (SCI, 99, 467)

Messenger, James Franklin
Appointment: Harvard Univ. (REV, 7, 428)
Appointment: Univ. of Vermont (SCI, 29, 656; JoP, 6, 308; BULL, 6, 184)
Fellowship: Columbia Univ. (SCI, 13, 680)

Messenger, Loren E.
Commission: Navy (BULL, 40, 383)

Metaphysics
Award: essay competition announced (JoP, 5, 532)
Conference: 1945 (JoP, 41, 588)
Lecture: Machennan, S. F. (JoP, 1, 336)
Lecture: Southwestern Philosphical Conference (JoP, 42, 723-724)
Publication: Lloyd, J. H., metaphysical abstraction (AJP, 1, 198)

Metcalf, John Trumbull
Appointment: George Washington Univ. (SCI, 52, 107; BULL, 17, 280)
Appointment: Princeton Univ. (BULL, 11, 267)
Appointment: *Psychological Bulletin*, cooperating editor (BULL, 26, 56)
Appointment: Smith College (BULL, 13, 148)
Appointment: Univ. of Vermont (SCI, 54, 73; BULL, 18, 439)
Resignation: George Washington Univ. (SCI, 54, 73)

Metcalf, Lorettus S.
Editor: *Forum* (SCI°, 7, 213)

Metcalf, Ruth Swan (*see* Clark, Ruth Swan)

Metfessel, Milton Franklin
Anniversary: UCLA Psych. Bldg. (BULL, 37, 406)
Appointment: State Univ. of Iowa (BULL, 26, 120)
Appointment: Univ. of Southern California (BULL, 35, 577)
Fellowship: Board of National Research (BULL, 23, 292)
Lecture: Criminal psychology (SCI, 91, 430)

Method (*see* Statistics, Research)

Metropolitan Volunteers (London)
Lecture: experiments with distance and sound (SCI°, *14*, 386)

Metzner, Charles Alfred
Appointment: George Washington Univ. (BULL, *41*, 72)

Meumann, Ernst
Appointment: Univ. of Halle (JOP, *6*, 700; BULL, *6*, 368)
Appointment: Univ. of Leipzig (JOP, *7*, 308; AJP, *7*, 152)
Appointment: Univ. of Zurich (AJP, *9*, 135)
Death notice (AJP, *26*, 472; BULL, *12*, 244; SCI, *41*, 860; JOP, *12*, 364)

Mexico City Board of Education
Lecture: Baldwin, J. M. (JOP, *6*, 308)

Mexico, National University of (Mexico City)
Appointment: Baldwin, J. M. (JOP, *7*, 672)
Course: Baldwin, J. M., psychosociology (BULL, *7*, 396)
Lecture: Baldwin, J. M., psychosociology (BULL, *9*, 208; JOP, *9*, 335)

Meyer, Adolf
Anniversary, 25th National Committee for Mental Hygiene (SCI, *80*, 446)
Appointment: Cornell Medical School (BULL, *1*, 414; JOP, *1*, 588; JOP, *3*, 168)
Appointment: Johns Hopkins Univ. (SCI, *28*, 14; JOP, *5*, 392; BULL, *5*, 243)
Appointment: New York State Hospital (SCI, *15*, 317-318; SCI, *14*, 1021; REV, *9*, 104)
Appointment: Univ. of Glasgow celebration, representative from Clark Univ. (SCI, *13*, 796)
Award: Salmon Memorial Lectureship (BULL, *28*, 254)
Birthday: 75th and 25th anniversary at Henry Phipps Psychiatric Clinic, Johns Hopkins Univ. (SCI, *85*, 259; BULL, *34*, 273)
Degree: Clark Univ. (SCI, *30*, 362)
Degree: Harvard Univ. (SCI, *95*, 621)
Editor: *Psychological Bulletin*, psychopathology issue (BULL, *7*, 148; BULL, *5*, 284; BULL, *9*, 208)
Election: Eugenics Research Assoc., president (SCI, *43*, 923)
Election: International Congress of Arts and Sciences, abnormal psychology section, secretary (JOP, *1*, 532)
Election: Mental Hygiene Society of Maryland, president (SCI, *64*, 495)
Election: Social Science Research Council (JOP, *26*, 336)
Lecture: Bloomington Hospital, New York, centenary celebration (SCI, *53*, 532)
Lecture: Clark Univ. (AJP, *7*, 449)
Lecture: "Conditions for psychiatric research" (SCI, *15*, 396)
Lecture: Duke Univ., 10th anniversary of School of Medicine and Hospital (SCI, *93*, 38)
Lecture: psychiatric clinic (SCI, *38*, 124)

Lecture: Salmon Memorial (SCI, 76, 13)
Neuro Psychiatric Clinic named for Meyer (BULL, 36, 57; SCI, 88, 423)
Retirement: Henry Phipps Psychiatric Clinic of Johns Hopkins Univ. Hospital
(SCI, 93, 493; SCI, 94, 275)
Trip: Europe (SCI, 28, 115; SCI, 57, 738)

Meyer, Hans
Donation: Univ. of Lepzig (BULL, 8, 110; SCI, 33, 299; JoP, 8, 140)

Meyer, Max Frederick
Appointment: research professor, deaf studies (SCI, 71, 582)
Appointment: Univ. of Missouri (REV, 7, 428; BULL, 27, 564)
Dismissal: Univ. of Missouri (SCI, 69, 379)
Ear, slides of (BULL, 5, 406)
Election: APA, council member (JoP, 9, 28)
Election: International Congress of Arts and Sciences, esthetics section
secretary (JoP, 1, 532)
Election: SSPP, president (SCI, 69, 379)
Leave of absence: Univ. of Missouri (SCI, 29, 809; JoP, 6, 308; BULL, 6, 216)
Lecture: alcohol, tobacco and tea (AJP, 34, 617)
Lecture: International Congress of Psychology, 6th (SCI, 30, 202)
Lecture: sensations (JoP, 2, 223)
Publication: lost (JoP, 5, 168; BULL, 5, 96)
Reinstatement: Univ. of Missouri (SCI, 69, 399)
Return from Europe (BULL, 7, 364)

Meyer, Rudolf
Election: American Psychiatric Assoc., president (SCI, 65, 612)

Meyerding, E. A.
Lecture: retardation (JoP, 7, 223)

Meyers, Charles Edward
Appointment: Univ. of Denver (BULL, 39, 895)

Meyerson, Ignace
Election: International Congress of Psychology, 11th, general secretary (JoP, 34, 112; SCI, 84, 531; J APP, 21, 242)

Meynert, Theodor
Vienna Univ. philosophical society (SCI°, 12, 23)

Mezes, Sidney Edward
Degree: Univ. of California (JoP, 9, 335)
Promotion: Univ. of Texas (REV, 7, 531)

Miami University (Ohio)
Appointment: Biel, W. C. (BULL, 37, 827)
Organization: Alpha Psi Delta Psychological Fraternity (BULL, 19, 586)

Michael Reese Hospital (Chicago, Illinois)
Appointment: Beck, S. J. (BULL, 34, 58)
Appointment: Grinker, R. R. (SCI, 83, 347)
Course: Beck, S. J., Rorschach (BULL, 39, 325-326; BULL, 40, 384; BULL, 36, 219; BULL, 41, 343; BULL, 42, 256; J APP, 27, 207; J APP, 23, 207; J APP, 24, 245)
Internship: clinical psychology (BULL, 41, 136)

Michigan
Laboratory established, biology and hygiene (SCI°, 9, 213)

Michigan Academy of Science, Arts, and Letters
Lecture: Cattell, J, McK. (BULL, 19, 296; SCI, 55, 512)
Thurstone, L. L., program for psychology section (BULL, 34, 274)

Michigan Central State Teachers College
Appointment: Jensen, M. B. (J APP, 13, 415)

Michigan Psychological Services
Appointment: Donahue, W. T. (BULL, 42, 581-582)

Michigan State College
Departure: Humphreys, H. H. (BULL, 42, 582)

Michigan State Normal School (Marquette)
Appointment: Fracker, G. C. (SCI, 30, 709; BULL, 6, 427)
Resignation: Anderson, L. S. (SCI, 30, 709)
Resignation: Mount, G. H. (BULL, 9, 208)

Michigan State Psychopathic Hospital
Appointment: Waggoner, R, W (SCI, 85, 14)

Michigan State University (East Lansing)
Appointment: Dewey, J. (SCI°, 13, 321)

Michigan, University of (Ann Arbor)
Anniversary: 100th, College of Literature, Sciences and the Arts (BULL, 39, 72)
Applications: fellowship announced (SCI, 102, 351; BULL, 42, 676)
Appointment: Adams, E. C. (BULL, 5, 379)
Appointment: Adams, H. F. (BULL, 8, 333; JoP, 8, 364)
Appointment: Angell, J. R., presidency (SCI, 49, 283)
Appointment: Bigham, J. (REV, 2, 104)
Appointment: Breed, F. S. (JoP, 7, 560; BULL, 7, 220)
Appointment: deLaguna, T. (JoP, 2, 392, 721)
Appointment: Dockeray, F. C. (BULL, 5, 379)

Appointment: Donahue, W. T. (Sci, *102*, 115)
Appointment: Hegge, T. G. (Bull, 27, 496; J App, *14*, 304)
Appointment: Johnston, C. H. (JoP, *4*, 392; Bull, *4*, 337)
Appointment: King, I. (Sci, *24*, 384; JoP, *3*, 532; Bull, *3*, 248, 319)
Appointment: Lloyd, A. H. (Rev, *2*, 104)
Appointment: Marquis, D. G. (Bull, *42*, 406)
Appointment: McClusky, H. Y. (Sci, *90*, 439)
Appointment: Perry, C. M. (JoP, *8*, 364)
Appointment: Pierce, E. (Rev, *3*, 120; Sci, *2*, 665)
Appointment: Pillsbury, W. B. (AJP, *8*, 584; Rev, *4*, 451; Sci, *96*, 355)
Appointment: Rebec, G. (Rev, *2*, 104)
Appointment: Shepard, J. F. (JoP, *15*, 504; Bull, *3*, 422)
Appointment: Wallin, J. E. W. (Sci, *16*, 920)
Appointment: Werner, H. (Sci, *78*, 359)
Appointment: Whipple, G. M. (Bull, *16*, 257)
Appointment: Yoakum. C. S. (Bull, *21*, 428)
Award: Maier, N. R. F., Henry Russel award (Sci, *89*, 313; Bull, *36*, 499)
Celebration: Darwin centennial (JoP, *6*, 112)
Changes in Dept. of Philosophy (Sci, *33*, 892)
Degree: Angell, J. R. (Sci, *73*, 490)
Degree: Dewey, J. (Sci, *38*, 151; JoP, *10*, 504)
Departure: Glaze, J. A. (Bull, *25*, 307)
Fellowship: established in name of Morris, G. S. (JoP, *3*, 28)
Leave of absence: Lloyd, A. H. (JoP, *8*, 364)
Leave of absence: Pillsbury, W. B. (Bull, *10*, 123; Sci, *57*, 466; Sci, *91*, 475)
Leave of absence: Thuma, B. D. (Sci, *85*, 405)
Leave of absence: Wenley, R. M. (Bull, *2*, 427)
Lecture: Angell, J. R., 100th anniversary of College of Literature, Science and the Arts (Bull, *39*, 72)
Lecture: "Points of view in psychology", 6 psychologists (Sci, *69*, 450)
Promotion: Adams, H. E. (JoP, *15*, 504)
Promotion: Pillsbury, W. B. (Rev, *7*, 428; Sci, *32*, 627; Bull, *7*, 364)
Promotion: Shepard, J. F. (Bull, *8*, 222; JoP, *3*, 644; JoP, *8*, 364)
Publication: Greene, E. B., Michigan Vocabulary Profile Test (J App, *23*, 745)
Resignation: Ford, A. (Bull, *28*, 646)
Retirement: Pillsbury, W. B. (Bull, *42*, 406; Bull, *39*, 807)

Michigan (Western) College of Education (Kalamazoo)
Appointment: West, W. D. (Bull, *42*, 331)

Middleton, A. E.
Publication: "Memory systems, new and old" (Sci°, *12*, 107)

Middletown Scientific Association
Lecture: Dodge, R., fatigue (Sci, *29*, 809)
Lecture: Thorndike, E. L., animal intelligence (Sci, *31*, 65)

Midwest Academy of Sciences
Meeting: Kansas City, MO, 1941 (Sci, *94*, 112)

Midwestern Experimental Psychologists
Meeting: announced (AJP, *37*, 463; J App, *15*, 228; Sci, *65*, 521)

Midwestern Psychological Association (*see also* North-Central Branch of APA, and Northwestern Branch of APA)
Anniversary: 50th, Wolfe's, H. K., psych. lab (Sci, *89*, 150)
Election: Carr, H. A., president (Sci, *83*, 517; Sci, *85*, 118; J App, *21*, 130)
Election: Guilford, J. P., chair (Bull, *37*, 187)
Election: Guilford, J. P., executive council (Sci, *83*, 517)
Election: McKinney, F., president (Bull, *37*, 187)
Election: officers (J App, *23*, 419; Sci, *89*, 555; Bull, *29*, 90)
Election: Pressey, S. L., president (Sci, *97*, 398)
Election: Ruckmick, C. A., president (Sci, *83*, 257)
Formation of Assoc. (Bull, *24*, 508)
Lecture: Bills, A. (J App, *22*, 107)
Lecture: Conklin, E. S., presidential (J App, *23*, 207)
Lecture: Guilford, J. P., presidential (Sci, *91*, 68; J App, *24*, 96)
Meeting: 3rd annual, 1928 (Bull, *25*, 307; Sci, *67*, 487; AJP, *40*, 520)
Meeting: 4th annual, 1929 (AJP, *41*, 511)
Meeting: 5th annual, 1930 (AJP, *42*, 650)
Meeting: 6th annual, 1931 (AJP, *43*, 520; Bull, *28*, 324)
Meeting: 7th annual, 1932 (AJP, *44*, 810)
Meeting: 8th annual, 1933 (Bull, *30*, 182; J App, *17*, 97)
Meeting: 9th annual, 1934 (Bull, *31*, 80; AJP, *46*, 660; Sci, *79*, 76; J App, *17*, 774)
Meeting: 10th annual, 1935 (Bull, *32*, 112; Sci, *81*, 94; J App, *18*, 860)
Meeting: 11th annual, 1936 (J App, *20*, 167; Bull, *33*, 303; Sci, *83*, 257)
Meeting: 12th annual, 1937 (Sci, *85*, 118, 261; Bull, *34*, 121; J App, *20*, 790)
Meeting: 13th annual, 1938 (Sci, *87*, 84, 435; J App, *22*, 106; Bull, *35*, 188; J App, *21*, 716)
Meeting: 14th annual, 1939 (AJP, *52*, 473-475; Sci, *89*, 150; Bull, *36*, 304)
Meeting: 15th annual, 1940 (Sci, *91*, 68; Bull, *37*, 187; AJP, *53*, 615-616)
Meeting: 16th annual, 1941 (AJP, *54*, 443; J App, *25*, 128, 266; Sci, *93*, 81; Bull, *38*, 191)
Meeting: 17th annual, 1942 (Sci, *95*, 221; Bull, *39*, 267; J App, *26*, 110, 390; AJP, *55*, 449)
Meeting: operations suspended until wartime restriction on travel removed (Bull, *40*, 384; AJP, *56*, 449-450; Sci, *97*, 398)
Publication: Bills, A. G., "The eleventh annual meeting of the MPA" (AJP, *48*, 525)
Publication: Bills, A. G., "The twelfth annual meeting of the MPA" (AJP, *49*, 485)
Publication: Guilford, J. P., "The thirteenth annual meeting of the MPA" (AJP, *51*, 576)

Publication: Ruckmick, C. A., "The eighth annual meeting of the MPA" (AJP, 45, 752)

Publication: Wheeler, R. A., "The tenth annual meeting of the MPA" (AJP, 47, 515)

Miles, Catherine Cox

Appointment: Stanford Univ. (BULL, 27, 564)

Appointment: Yale Univ. (SCI, 73, 491; BULL, 28, 412; SCI, 71, 600)

Lecture: Columbia Univ. (J APP, 10, 394)

Miles, Walter Richard

Appointment: National Research Council, Emergency Committee in Psychology (BULL, 37, 755)

Appointment: Prohibition Bureau's Advisory Research Council (BULL, 28, 410)

Appointment: Stanford Univ. (SCI, 55, 593; BULL, 19, 410; BULL, 20, 60; BULL, 27, 564; J APP, 6, 301)

Appointment: Univ. of California (SCI, 62, 201)

Appointment: Yale Univ. (SCI, 73, 491; SCI, 74, 308; BULL, 28, 412; SCI, 71, 600)

Election: APA, Council of Directors (BULL, 24, 80)

Election: APA representative (SCI, 69, 36)

Election: International Congress of Psych., 10th, delegate (SCI, 76, 119)

Election: National Research Council, APA representative (BULL, 26, 56)

Election: Psychological Corporation meeting with APA and AAAP, 1941, president (J APP, 25, 600)

Election: SEP, chair (AJP, 46, 511; AJP, 47, 344)

Lecture: Brown Univ. graduate seminar (BULL, 28, 324; SCI, 73, 360)

Lecture: College of Medical Evangelists, Los Angeles (SCI, 68, 400)

Lecture: Iowa State College, Chapter of the Society of Sigma Xi (BULL, 41, 498; SCI, 99, 382)

Lecture: National Research Council Conference, "Psychological factors in national morale" (BULL, 37, 829)

Lecture: Vanderbilt Univ., Society of the Sigma Xi (SCI, 99, 446)

Lecture: Yale Univ., history of science (SCI, 90, 614)

Resignation: Carnegie Institution, Washington (SCI, 55, 593)

Retirement: APA, president (SCI, 76, 251)

Symposium: visual fatigue (BULL, 36, 713)

Military psychology

Course: Psychology for National Defense, Univ. Extension Division of the Dept. of Education (J APP, 25, 472)

Course: Univ. of Illinois (J APP, 26, 392)

Degree: Germany Military Psychologist (BULL, 39, 267-268)

Establishment: American Assoc. for Applied Psychology, Military Psychology Section (BULL, 41, 267-268; SCI, 99, 34)

Lecture: American Psychiatry Assoc. (SCI, 99, 382-383)

Lecture: Miles, W. R., Iowa State College, Chapter of Sigma Xi, aviation (SCI, 99, 382)

Publication: emotional stability of 18-19 year olds serving (J APP, *26*, 711-712)
Publication: mental tests (JoP, *18*, 420; JoP, *20*, 280)
Publication: National Research Council, military psychology (J APP, *27*, 475)
Publication: Occupational Index reviews (J APP, *26*, 858)
Shortage of psychologists in Germany (BULL, *39*, 267-268; BULL, *37*, 779)
War Dept requests information on psychologists for conscription (J APP, *25*, 472)

Mill, John Stuart
Exhibition: Harvard Univ., manuscripts (JoP, *17*, 194-195)
Monument erected at Avignon (JoP, *8*, 448)

Miller, Clyde Raymond
Inst. for Propaganda Analysis (BULL, *34*, 865; J APP, *21*, 719; J APP, *25*, 361)

Miller, Dickinson Sergeant
Appointment: Columbia Univ. (REV, *5*, 449; AJP, *10*, 165)
Appointment: Harvard Univ. (SCI, *9*, 821)
Course: Harvard Univ. (REV, *6*, 456)
Election: American Philosophical Assoc., executive committee (JoP, *8*, 27-28)
Lecture: NYAS/APA, subjectifying the objective (JoP, *7*, 700)
Lecture: temperaments (JoP, *2*, 112)

Miller, Eleanor Olmstead
Award: Cattell, J. McK. grants-in-aid (BULL, *39*, 683)

Miller, J. C.
Appointment: AAAP, Committee on Psychology in Junior Colleges (J APP, *25*, 361)

Miller, Joseph
Appointment: (Ohio) Child Study Institute, director (BULL, *41*, 498)

Miller, Karl Greenwood
Appointment: Univ. of Pennsylvania (AJP, *10*, 395; BULL, *18*, 296)
Promotion: Univ. of Pennsylvania (SCI, *66*, 14; SCI, *53*, 556)

Miller, Wilford Stanton
Promotion: Univ. of Minnesota (BULL, *41*, 136)

Millikin University (Decatur, IL)
Election: White, J. H., president (SCI, *72*, 87)

Mills, Charles Wright
Publication: absolute vs. relative norms (JoP, *39*, 503-504)

Mills Foundation
Appointment: Calkins, M. W. (JoP, *13*, 448)

Mills, Thomas Wesley
Death notice (BULL, *12*, 128)

Milwaukee State Teachers College (Wisconsin)
Lecture: Ruckmick, C. A. (BULL, *41*, 343)

Mind
Appointment: Moore, G. E. (BULL, *17*, 435)
Reorganization: *Mind Assoc.* (REV, *8*, 224)
Resignation: Stout, G. F. (BULL, *17*, 435)
Titchener, E. B. to receive American correspondence (REV, *1*, 440)

Mind
Lecture: Courtney, W. L., condition and functions of mind (SCI°, *10*, 250)
Lecture: Keyser, L. S., argument (AJP, *40*, 156)
Lecture: Martin, H. N., Peabody Institute of Balitmore, animals (SCI°, *2*, 782)
Lecture: Putman, T. J., mechanisms of (SCI, *94*, 484, 582)
Lecture: Romanes, G. J., Owens College, England, dawn of the mind (SCI°, *3*, 639-640)
Lecture: Titchener, E. B., structure of (JOP, *7*, 643)
Lecture: Titchener, E. B., Univ. of Minnesota, types of (SCI, *33*, 367)
Lecture: Upton, I. H., Amherst College Science Assoc., relation of the mind to the body (SCI°, *6*, 100)
Publication: Neild, J., physical vs. psychological mechanisms (JOP, *40*, 139-140)

Mind Association
Meeting: Aristotelian Society (JOP, *34*, 252; JOP, *35*, 252; JOP, *33*, 252)
Reorganized: *Mind* (REV, *8*, 224)
Report: joint meeting with British Psychological Society and Aristotelian Society (JOP, *7*, 420)

Mind in Nature
Contents of the first number (SCI°, *5*, 264)
Publication: Cosmic Publishing Co., Chicago (SCI°, *5*, 243)

Mind-reading (*see also* Telepathy)
American Society for Psychical, research committee requests interested individuals (SCI°, *5*, 204)

Miner, James Burt
Appointment: Bureau of Salesmanship Research (JOP, *13*, 140)
Appointment: Carnegie Institute of Technology (BULL, *12*, 403; SCI, *42*, 88; JOP, *12*, 644)
Appointment: Committee on Publications in Applied Psychology (J APP, *2*, 196)
Appointment: Univ. of Illinois (BULL, *1*, 94)
Appointment: Univ. of Iowa (BULL, *1*, 372; JOP, *1*, 476)
Appointment: Univ. of Minnesota (JOP, *4*, 392; SCI, *23*, 480; JOP, *3*, 224; BULL, *3*, 147)

Death notice (BULL, *40*, 458)
Departure: Univ. of Iowa Philosophy Dept. (SCI, *23*, 480)
Election: SSPP, president (J APP, *10*, 285)
Leave of absence: Univ. of Minnesota (BULL, *10*, 123; JoP, *10*, 588)
Lecture: New York Academy of Sciences, Involuntary muscular responses to
   rhythmic stimuli (SCI, *15*, 547)
Promotion: Carnegie Institute of Tech. (JoP, *15*, 336; BULL, *15*, 176)
Publication: deficiency and delinquency (J APP, *3*, 197)

Minneapolis Gas Light Company
Appointment: Jurgensen, C. E. (SCI, *101*, 581)

Minnesota
Legislation prohibiting marriage of insane, epileptic, and idiotic persons (SCI,
   13, 600)

Minnesota Chapter of Psi Chi
Lecture: Wolfle, D. B. (BULL, *40*, 310)

Minnesota Child Study Association
Publication: handbook (REV, *5*, 110)

Minnesota Committee of the White House Conference on Children in a Democracy
Appointment: Anderson, J. E. (BULL, *39*, 267)

Minnesota Department of Education, Division of Vocational Rehabilitation
Placement: blind persons in private industry (J APP, *28*, 80)

Minnesota Psychological Conference
Meeting: Univ. of Minnesota (JoP, *7*, 223; BULL, *7*, 147; JoP, *8*, 252; BULL, *8*,
   146; JoP, *9*, 364; BULL, *12*, 160)

Minnesota State Normal School (Moorhead)
Departure: Chambers, W. G. (SCI, *20*, 384)
Return: Colgrove, P. P. (REV, *7*, 640)

Minnesota State Public School (Owatonna)
Appointment: Yager, J. L. (BULL, *39*, 325)

Minnesota State School for Feeble-minded
Appointment: Lowell, F. (BULL, *14*, 333)

Minnesota, University of (Minneapolis) (*see also* Employment Stabilization Research Institute)
Appointment: Anderson, J. E. (SCI, *62*, 34; BULL, *22*, 444)
Appointment: Angell, J. R. (REV, *1*, 112)

Appointment: Bills, A. G. (BULL, *23*, 455)
Appointment: Foster, W. S. (BULL, *16*, 257; SCI, *50*, 65)
Appointment: Gilbertson, A. N. (BULL, *8*, 373; JoP, *10*, 588)
Appointment: Haggerty, M. E. (JoP, *12*, 644)
Appointment: Haynes, R. (JoP, *4*, 392; BULL, *4*, 337)
Appointment: Heron, W. T. (J APP, *10*, 522; BULL, *23*, 455)
Appointment: Kuenne, M. R. (BULL, *42*, 331)
Appointment: Lashley, K. S. (JoP, *14*, 448, 644; SCI, *60*, 40; SCI, *45*, 660)
Appointment: McConnell, T. R. (SCI, *99*, 340-341)
Appointment: McKinley, J. C. (SCI, *98*, 81)
Appointment: Miner, J. B. (JoP, *3*, 224; SCI, *23*, 480; BULL, *3*, 147)
Appointment: Moore, H. T. (JoP, *14*, 448, 644; SCI, *45*, 660)
Appointment: Peterson, J. (BULL, *12*, 244; SCI, *41*, 862; JoP, *14*, 644; SCI, *42*, 374; JoP, *12*, 476)
Appointment: Rahn, C. L. (SCI, *34*, 602; BULL, *8*, 373)
Appointment: Raimy, V., testing bureau (BULL, *40*, 152)
Appointment: Swenson, D. (JoP, *11*, 280)
Appointment: Tinker, M. A. (J APP, *11*, 404)
Appointment: Trabue, M. S. (BULL, *28*, 411)
Appointment: Woodrow, H. H. (JoP, *14*, 644; BULL, *14*, 333; JoP, *7*, 223-224)
Appointment: Yerkes, R. M. (JoP, *14*, 392; SCI, *45*, 500; BULL, *14*, 191)
Course: Personnel work for government offices and armed forces (J APP, *26*, 713)
Death notice: Haggerty, M. E. (BULL, *34*, 864)
Departure: Crosland, H. R. (SCI, *46*, 111)
Departure: Lodge, R. C. (JoP, *12*, 336)
Departure: Peterson, J. (SCI, *48*, 444)
Departure: Schneidler, G. G., testing bureau (BULL, *40*, 152)
Departure: Skinner, B. F. (BULL, *42*, 191)
Depature: Woodbridge, F. J. E. (SCI, *15*, 440)
Election: James, G. F., Dean of the School of Education (SCI, *22*, 888)
Fellowship: five teaching (BULL, *16*, 221)
Grant: Laura Spellman Rockefeller Fund for child research (SCI, *62*, 218)
Laboratory destroyed by fire (JoP, *1*, 560)
Laboratory reopened (BULL, *4*, 337)
Leave of absence: Miner, J. B. (JoP, *10*, 588; BULL, *10*, 123)
Leave of absence: Van Wagenen, M. J. (BULL, *22*, 612)
Leave of absence: Wilde, N. (JoP, *11*, 280)
Leave of absence: Wrenn, C. G. (BULL, *39*, 808)
Lecture: evolution (JoP, *5*, 252)
Lecture: "Points of view in psychology", 6 psychologists (SCI, *69*, 450)
Lecture: Thorndike, E. L. (SCI, *61*, 113)
Lecture: Titchener, E. B. (JoP, *8*, 168; SCI, *33*, 367)
Lecture: Vincent, G. E., social psychology (SCI, *42*, 374)
Lecture: Yerkes, R. M., psych. methods of diagnosis, Sigma Xi (SCI, *45*, 138)
Medical clinic opens (BULL, *14*, 116)
Meeting: APA, 45th (SCI, *86*, 119)

Meeting: Minnesota Psychological Conference (BULL, 7, 147; JoP, 7, 223; BULL,
    8, 146; JoP, 8, 252; JoP, 9, 364; BULL, 12, 160)
Philosophical Club formation (JoP, 3, 614)
Promotion: Foster, W. S. (SCI, 59, 398)
Promotion: Lashley, K. S. (BULL, 21, 660)
Promotion: Miller, W. S. (BULL, 41, 136)
Psychology Dept. organized (BULL, 14, 263)
Research: mental development, organization of clinic (BULL, 7, 147)
Resignation: Johnston, G. H. (BULL, 3, 147)
Resignation: Peterson, J. (BULL, 15, 360)

Mintz, Alexander
Appointment: Assistant to Koffka, K. (BULL, 25, 123)

Mira y Lopez, Emilio
Appointment: Ohio Univ. (J APP, 13, 193)
Appointment: Salmon Lecturer, 1942 (SCI, 96, 378)
Lecture: 10th series, Salmon lectures (J APP, 26, 856-857)
Meeting: AAAS, Century of Progress Exposition (SCI, 77, 579)
Visit to world's fair (J APP, 16, 695)

Mirmow, Esther Lee
Promotion: Smith College (BULL, 42, 331)

Mississippi, University of (Oxford)
Appointment: Creegan, R. F. (JoP, 40, 644)
Appointment: Wolfe, J. B. (BULL, 33, 578)
Hantz, H. entered military service (JoP, 40, 644)

Missouri Society for Mental Hygiene
Organization (SCI, 53, 114)

Missouri State Penitentary
Appointment: Peters, H. N., director of classification (BULL, 36, 218)

Missouri State Teachers College (Springfield)
Leave of absence: Wilkinson, R. (BULL, 40, 459)
Promotion: Dillinger, C. M. (BULL, 40, 459)

Missouri, University of (Columbia)
Appointment: Bock, C. (BULL, 9, 408; JoP, 9, 616)
Appointment: Lovejoy, A. O. (JoP, 5, 252; BULL, 5, 168)
Appointment: McGeoch, J. A. (BULL, 27, 636)
Appointment: Meyer, M. (REV, 7, 428; BULL, 27, 564)
Appointment: Pyle, W. H. (BULL, 7, 364)
Appointment: Rogers, A. K. (JoP, 7, 448)
Departure: Lovejoy, A. O. (JoP, 7, 308)
Departure: Reeves, P. (BULL, 9, 408; JoP, 9, 700)

Departure: Weiss, A. P. (BULL, *9*, 408; JoP, *9*, 616)
Dismissal: DeGraff, H. O. (SCI, *69*, 379)
Dismissal: Meyer, M. (SCI, *69*, 379)
Election: Meyers, M., International Congress of Arts and Sciences, St. Louis, esthetics section, secretary (JoP, *1*, 532)
Leave of absence: Meyer, M. (SCI, *29*, 809; JoP, *6*, 308; BULL, *6*, 216)
Lecture: Jastrow, J. (BULL, *11*, 116; JoP, *11*, 140; SCI, *39*, 280)
Lecture: "Points of view in psychology", 6 psychologists (SCI, *69*, 450)
Meeting: Western Philosophical Assoc. (JoP, *1*, 224)
Promotion: Baskett, E. D. (SCI, *74*, 147)
Psychology grouped with the natural sciences (JoP, *12*, 504; BULL, *12*, 243-244)
Reinstatement: Meyer, M. (SCI, *69*, 379)
Research: Johnson, H. M., sleep (SCI, *69*, 450)
Research: Meyer, M. F., deaf (SCI, *71*, 582)

Missouri Valley College (Marshall, Missouri)
Appointment: Saupe, M. (BULL, *42*, 675)

Mitchell, David
Appointment: Univ. of Pennsylvania (JoP, *11*, 588)
Lecture: NY Branch of APA meeting (JoP, *18*, 672)
Promotion (SCI, *40*, 482)
Publication: bibliography of psychological tests (JoP, *16*, 28)
Publication: *Malnutrition and Health Education* (J APP, *3*, 196)

Mitchell, Mildred Bessie
Appointment: Bureau for Psychological Services of the State of Minnesota, 1941 (BULL, *39*, 325)

Mitchell, Weir Oration
Gillespie, R. D., psychoneurosis in peace and war and the future of human relationships (SCI, *94*, 605)

Mitrano, Anthony Joseph
Appointment: Psychological Test Bureau, Rochester (BULL, *38*, 907)
Resignation: Board of Education (BULL, *38*, 907)

Mizwa, Stephen P.
Lecture: Washington Academy of Sciences, celebration Copernicus Quadricentennial (SCI, *98*, 361)

Mjoen, Jon A.
Appointment: Italian Eugenics Society, correspondent (SCI, *77*, 486)
Lecture: American Eugenics Society (SCI, *71*, 282)

Möbius, Paul Julius August
Death notice (JoP, *4*, 168; BULL, *4*, 95)
Memorial fund proposed (BULL, *4*, 200)

Mohler, E.
Death notice (Sci°, *2*, 148)

Monakow, Constantin von
Editor: *Schweizer Archiv für Neurologie und Psychiatric* (Bull, *14*, 333)
Lecture: Congress for Experimental Psychology, 4th (JoP, *7*, 83)

Monin, L. C.
Lecture: emotions (JoP, *2*, 280)

Monism
Lecture: Montague, W. P. (JoP, *2*, 224)

Monograph Supplements of Psychological Review
Editor: Judd, C. H. (Bull, *1*, 213; JoP, *1*, 280)
Journal announced (Bull, *36*, 219)

Monomania
Publication: Parsons, R. L. (AJP, *1*, 199)

Monroe, Paul
Appointment: Yale Univ. (Bull, *3*, 422)

Monroe, Will Stanton
Lecture: memory (JoP, *2*, 224)
Lecture: smell discrimination (JoP, *?*, 700)
Research: dreams (AJP, *10*, 326-327)

Montague, William Pepperell
Appointment: Columbia Univ. (Bull, *4*, 128; JoP, *2*, 224)
Appointment: Cooper Union, Hewitt Lectures (JoP, *9*, 112)
Appointment: Univ. of California, Los Angeles (JoP, *40*, 140)
Election: American Philosophical Assoc., vice-president (Sci, *27*, 76)
Lecture: Adler, F., 1942 (JoP, *39*, 250)
Lecture: consciousness (JoP, *2*, 112)
Lecture: Hume (JoP, *1*, 224)
Lecture: mental processes (JoP, *2*, 700)
Lecture: monism (JoP, *2*, 224)
Lecture: Western Univ., London, Ontario, philosophy futurist (JoP, *15*, 168)
Lecture: Woman's Canadian Club, political outlook (JoP, *15*, 168)
Publication: memorial on Haeckel, E. (JoP, *16*, 503-504)

Montalto, Fannie De Pietro
Appointment: Univ. of Cincinnati (Bull, *42*, 582)

Montana State University (Bozeman)
Departure: Book, W. F. (Bull, *9*, 407-408; JoP, *9*, 644)

Montana, University of (Missoula)
Appointment: Ames, W. R. (BULL, 17, 116)
Appointment: Wolfe, H. K. (JoP, 2, 392; BULL, 2, 296; SCI, 21, 968)
Departure: Wolfe, H. K. (JoP, 3, 56)
Leave of absence: Bolton, T. L. (BULL, 12, 481)

Montefiore Hospital (New York, New York)
Appointment: Merritt, H. H. (SCI, 99, 467)

Montessori, Maria
Course: teacher training (J APP, 20, 790)

Montgomery, Edmund Duncan
Death notice (AJP, 22, 475)

Montgomery, Thomas Harrison
Publication: *Analysis of Racial Descent in Animals* (JoP, 3, 419)

Montreal Neurological Institute (Canada)
Lecture: Lashley, K. S., Hughlings Jackson lecture (SCI, 85, 381)

Montreal, University of (Canada)
Appointment: Brennan, R. E. (BULL, 40, 310)
Appointment: Jasper, H. H., medical school (BULL, 35, 796)

Monumenta Germaniae Pedagogica
Publication: Koldeway, F. (SCI°, 9, 362)

Mooney, Elizabeth
Publication: Interest Inventory for Elementary Grades (J APP, 25, 474)

Moore, Addison Webster
Course: Stanford Univ. (JoP, 7, 252)
Election: Northwestern Branch, APA, chair (JoP, 1, 336)
Leave of absence: Univ. of Chicago (JoP, 3, 532)
Lecture: pragmatism (JoP, 2, 280)

Moore, Barrington, Jr.
Appointment: Institute for Propaganda Analysis (J APP, 25, 597)

Moore, Bruce Victor
Publication: engineering defense training (J APP, 26, 106-107, 245)

Moore, Ernest C.
Appointment: Los Angeles State Normal School (JoP, 14, 532)
Appointment: Univ. of California, summer school, dean (JoP, 3, 252)
Lecture: James, W. (JoP, 39, 84)

358

Moore, George Edward
Appointment: *Mind* (BULL, *17*, 435)
Appointment: Swarthmore College (JoP, *40*, 140)
Lecture: Hicks, G. D., on Moore (JoP, *7*, 251)
Publication: "The subject-matter of psychology" (JoP, *7*, 55)

Moore, Henry Thomas
Appointment: Dartmouth College (BULL, *12*, 243; JoP, *12*, 504)
Appointment: Skidmore College, president (BULL, *22*, 612; SCI, *62*, 180, 264)
Appointment: Univ. of Minnesota (SCI, *45*, 660; JoP, *14*, 448, 644)
Departure: Simmons College (BULL, *12*, 243)
Editor: *Journal of Abnormal and Social Psychology* (JoP, *22*, 364)
Election: Social Science Research Council (BULL, *25*, 123)

Moore, Joseph Ernest
Appointment: Georgia Institute of Tech. (BULL, *42*, 332)

Moore, Merrill
Appointment: Washingtonian Hospital, Boston (SCI, *93*, 254)
Award: Bronze Star (SCI, *100*, 516)

Moore, Robert A.
Editor: *Gerontology* (BULL, *42*, 792)

Moore, Thomas Verner
Meeting: APA Wash.-Balt. Branch (BULL, *36*, 140)
Psychiatric clinic opens (BULL, *13*, 108)

Moore, Vida Frank
Death notice (JoP, *12*, 392)

Moorhead, Louis D.
Resignation: Loyola Univ., School of Medicine, Chicago (SCI, *93*, 325)

Moral philosophy
Publication: Witherspoon's lectures (JoP, *9*, 252)

Morale
Award: for best article on worker morale (J APP, *11*, 80)
Definition of by Barlingame, C. C. (J APP, *26*, 244)
Publication: bibliography of (BULL, *41*, 499)
Research: Hilgard, E. R. (SCI, *96*, 423)

Morale, National Committee for
German Psychological Warfare, Allport, Boring, Stevens, Beebe-Center, Young, Ruch, and Farago (J APP, *25*, 359)

Morale Education, International Congress on
Meeting: the Hague, 2nd (JoP, *9*, 448)

Morals
Meeting: Clark Univ., Conference of Psychologists on the Development of,
childhood and youth (BULL, 39, 267)
Publication: Ladd, G. T., Japanese (JoP, 5, 420)

More, Paul Elmer
Death notice (JoP, 34, 168)

Moreira, J.
Election: Brazilian Psychiatrical Neurological and Medical Society, president
(SCI, 27, 903)

Moreno, Jacob L.
Psychodramatic Institute (BULL, 37, 329)

Morgan, Clifford Thomas
Appointment: Johns Hopkins Univ. (BULL, 40, 79; SCI, 96, 444)

Morgan, Conway Lloyd
Appointment: Bristol Univ. (BULL, 17, 280)
Appointment: Univ. of Oxford, Herbert Spencer Lecturer (BULL, 10, 164)
Award: Univ. of Bristol, recogntion of his services (JoP, 7, 252, 336)
Award: Univ. College (England), library for service (BULL, 7, 252)
Death notice (JoP, 33, 336; BULL, 33, 406)
Degree: offered (JoP, 1, 252)
Gifts received from students (SCI, 31, 453)
Lecture: American tour (SCI, 1, 693)
Lecture: comparative psychology (JoP, 1, 616)
Lecture: instinct and intelligence (JoP, 7, 420)
Lecture: International Congress of Arts and Sciences, St. Louis (JoP, 1, 420)
Lecture: Locke, J. (JoP, 1, 616)
Lecture: Oxford Univ., Herbert Spencer Lecture (JoP, 10, 720)
Lecture: Psychological Journal Club of Columbia (JoP, 1, 644)
Lecture: Royal Society, Croonian Lecture (SCI, 13, 555)
Lecture: Univ. College, Bristol (JoP, 1, 616)
Lecture: Univ. of St. Andrews (JoP, 19, 504)
Publication: comparative psychology (REV, 1, 336)
Resignation: Univ. of Bristol (JoP, 6, 504; BULL, 17, 280)

Morgan, Jane D.
Appointment: Office of Psychological Personnel (SCI, 98, 215)
Appointment: Univ. of Iowa (SCI, 53, 186; BULL, 18, 236)

Morgan, John Jacob Brooke
Appointment: Princeton Univ. (BULL, 14, 115)
Appointment: Univ. of Southern California (J APP, 10, 396)
Death notice (BULL, 42, 581)
Election: APA, president (J APP, 17, 774; SCI, 79, 76)

Morningside College (Sioux City, Iowa)
Appointment: Thompson, M. (BULL, *14*, 366)
Departure: Emme, E. E. (BULL, *41*, 343)

Morrill, Justin Smith
Publication: self-consciousness of noted persons (SCI°, *8*, 344)

Morris, Frank Edward
Return: Connecticut College for Women (SCI, *49*, 281; BULL, *16*, 392)

Morris, George Sylvester
Fellowship: established at Univ. of Michigan (JoP, *3*, 28)
Grant: Crane, H. W., Morris Memorial Fellowship (JoP, *8*, 364)

Morse, Josiah
Appointment: Camp Jackson, South Carolina (BULL, *14*, 420; JoP, *15*, 140)
Appointment: Red Cross, South Carolina (JoP, *15*, 140; BULL, *14*, 420)
Course: Peabody College for Teachers (BULL, *12*, 403)
Election: SSPP, officer (JoP, *11*, 140)
Leave of absence: Univ. of South Carolina (JoP, *15*, 140)
Lecture: SSPP, psychology of prejudice (JoP, *7*, 28)

Morselli, Enrico Agostino
Anniversary: 40th, Univ. of Genoa, chair of psychiatry (SCI, *53*, 135)
Appointment: *Psiche*, director (JoP, *9*, 56)
Death notice (SCI, *69*, 469)
Election: International Congress of Psychology, 5th, pathological psych
    sectional president (JoP, *2*, 56)

Mortality
Research: Dexter, E. G. (SCI°, *5*, 530)
Research: Kremser, V.F.K., temperature (SCI°, *16*, 203)

Mortimer, Hector
Assoc. for Research in Nervous and Mental Diseases, speaker, 1936 (SCI, *84*,
    551)

Moscow Institute of Experimental Psychology
Research: primitive cultures (BULL, *29*, 90)

Moscow Naturalists' Society
Tribute: centenary of *Origin of Species* (SCI, *96*, 179)

Moscow State Institute of Psychology
Research: Koffka, K., isolated people (SCI, *75*, 510)

Moscow, University of (*see also* Psychological Society of)
New psych. lab (SCI, *2*, 850)

Mosely, John O.
Departure: Univ. of Tennessee, dean of students (BULL, *41*, 603)

Moser, Anna Catherine
Appointment: San Diego Public Schools, director of vocational guidance (BULL, *41*, 267)

Moses, William Stainton
Resignation: English Society for Psychical Research (SCI°, *9*, 10)

Moss, Fred August
Appointment: George Washington Univ. (SCI, *54*, 73; BULL, *18*, 439)

Motion pictures
Psychological Cinema Register founded (J APP, *23*, 632)

Motor strength
Lecture: Woodworth, R. S. (JoP, *1*, 644)

Motora, Yujiro
Death notice (SCI, *37*, 145; BULL, *10*, 124)

Mount, George Haines
Appointment: Iowa State Teachers College (BULL, *9*, 208)
Lecture: musical education, pitch discrimination (JoP, *7*, 223)
Resignation: Northern Michigan State Normal School (BULL, *9*, 208)

Mount Holyoke College (South Hadley, Massachusetts)
Accommodation after fire (BULL, *15*, 98)
Appointment: Bell, S. (SCI, *13*, 1000)
Appointment: Coffin, J. H. (JoP, *14*, 168; BULL, *14*, 116)
Appointment: Gordon, K. (JoP, *9*, 168)
Appointment: Hamlin, A. J. (AJP, *7*, 579)
Appointment: Hayes, S. P. (SCI, *23*, 832; JoP, *3*, 364; BULL, *6*, 256; BULL, *3*, 216)
Appointment: McGarvey, H. R. (BULL, *34*, 499)
Appointment: McGarvey, J. W. (BULL, *34*, 499)
Appointment: Muir, E. (AJP, *9*, 135)
Appointment: Reese, T. W. (BULL, *39*, 896)
Appointment: Scott, C. A. (BULL, *12*, 280)
Appointment: Simrall, D. V. (BULL, *42*, 793)
Burn notice (BULL, *15*, 24)
Departure: Kohl, C. C. (BULL, *12*, 280)
Departure: Rowland, E. H. (JoP, *9*, 168)
Laboratory established (REV, *9*, 432)
Leave of absence: Hayes, S. P. (BULL, *9*, 95; JoP, *9*, 168; JoP, *14*, 168)
Leave of absence: Warbeke, J. M. (JoP, *17*, 672)
Psych. literature: Hayes, S. P. request replacement (JoP, *15*, 280)
Resignation: Gordon, K. (BULL, *3*, 216)

Movement
Lecture: Higginson, G. D., visual perception (AJP, 37, 629)
Lecture: Judd, C. H. (JoP, 2, 224)
Research: Schaeffer, A. A., orientation and direction (BULL, 17, 240)

Mowrer, Orval Hobart
Publication: *Psychological Bulletin*, military psychology (J APP, 25, 359)

Muchow, Martha
Death notice (BULL, 31, 79)

Mudge, Evlyn Leigh
Appointment: Ohio State Univ. (BULL, 13, 482; JoP, 14, 56)

Müenzinger, Karl Friedrich
Conference on Psychology of Learning, Univ. of Colorado, 1939 (BULL, 36, 583; SCI, 89, 405)

Muhlenberg College (Allentown, Pennsylvania)
Appointment: Kilmer, E. K. (BULL, 40, 459)

Muir, Ethel Gordon
Appointment: Mt. Holyoke College (AJP, 9, 135; REV, 4, 567)

Müller, Georg Elias
Election: Congress for Experimental Psychology, German, 1st, president (JoP, 1, 335)
Election: Congress of the Gesellschaft für Experimentelle Psychologie, 5th, president (JoP, 9, 279)
Obituary by Boring, E. G. (AJP, 47, 344)

Müller, Herman
Death notice (SCI°, 2, 484)

Müller, Johannes
Monument unveiled at Coblentz (SCI°, 10, 540)
Tribute: *British Medical Journal* (SCI°, 10, 620-621)

Müller, Friedrich Max
Publication: *The Open Court* (SCI°, 9, 584)
Publication: science of thought (SCI°, 9, 132)

Müller, Wilhelm V.
Death notice (SCI°, 9, 525)

Mullin, E. J.
Appointment: Univ. of Chicago (SCI, 101, 35)

Mumford, Lewis
Stanford Education Conference, 1938 (J App, 22, 108)

Münchener Studien zur Psychologie und Philosophie
Publication begun (JoP, 11, 448)

Munich (Germany)
Institute for Research in Psychiatry (Sci, 54, 128)

Munich Academy of Sciences (Germany)
Bequest received (JoP, 1, 56)
Election: Hering, E. (Sci, 15, 557)
Election: Wundt, W., member (Sci, 12, 933)

Munich, University of (Germany)
Appointment: Becher, E. (Bull, 13, 448; JoP, 14, 56)
Appointment: Beringer, K. (Sci, 77, 209)
Appointment: Külpe, O. (Bull, 10, 212; Sci, 37, 788; JoP, 10, 364)
Appointment: Lipps, T. (Rev, 1, 336)
Award: essay competition announced (Rev, 4, 340)
Relieved of teaching duties: Kraeplin, E. (Bull, 19, 462)

Munn, Norman Leslie
Appointment: George Peabody College for Teachers (Bull, 33, 477; Sci, 83, 99)
Appointment: Vanderbilt Univ. (Sci, 87, 342; Bull, 35, 408)
Departure: Peabody College for Teachers (Sci, 87, 342)
Election: SSPP, secretary and teasurer (Sci, 90, 105)

Munsell Color Foundation
Research: color (Bull, 41, 268)

Munster, University of
Appointment: Becher, E. (JoP, 7, 84)

Münsterberg, Hugo
Apparatus: Univ. College, London (AJP, 9, 135)
Appointment: Amerika-Institut, Berlin (Bull, 7, 396)
Appointment: Berlin (Sci, 31, 380; Sci, 32, 51; Sci, 33, 212; Bull, 7, 147; JoP, 7, 168)
Appointment: Columbia Univ. (Bull, 1, 29; Sci, 18, 800)
Appointment: Harvard Univ., administrative board member for the graduate school of arts and sciences (Sci, 24, 512)
Death notice (JoP, 14, 28; Sci, 44, 887; J App, 1, 99; Bull, 14, 32)
Declines chair in philosophy, Univ. of Königsberg (Sci, 21, 638; Bull, 2, 191; JoP, 2, 252)
Degree: Harvard Univ. (Sci, 14, 36)
Degree: Lafayette College (Bull, 4, 338)

Donation: Harvard Univ., library (JoP, *14*, 252)

Election: American Philosophical Assoc., president (SCI, *27*, 76)

Election: APA, council (JoP, *1*, 28)

Election: delegate at the Univ. of Aberdeen, 400th anniversary celebration (SCI, *24*, 477)

Emerson Hall fund drive (SCI, *15*, 240; SCI, *17*, 880; REV, *9*, 216)

Executive Committee for APA/International Congress of Psychology (JoP, *8*, 196)

Guest: Psychological Journal Club of Columbia (JoP, *1*, 168)

International Committee of Psychology, 5th (JoP, *2*, 56)

Leave of absence: Harvard Univ. (SCI, *24*, 788; JoP, *4*, 28; BULL, *4*, 32)

Lecture: American Assoc. for Labor Legislation (JoP, *9*, 364)

Lecture: American Society of Naturalists (SCI, *16*, 1038)

Lecture: Canadian Club, prohibition movement (SCI, *29*, 23)

Lecture: Chicago Club, psychotherapy (SCI, *29*, 23)

Lecture: Columbia Univ. (JoP, *1*, 168)

Lecture: commercial psychology (SCI, *29*, 23)

Lecture: industrial efficiency (SCI, *35*, 925)

Lecture: Johns Hopkins, psychology of labor (SCI, *37*, 479)

Lecture: Lafayette Univ. (JoP, *4*, 420; SCI, *25*, 1014)

Lecture: M.I.T., Lowell Lectures (SCI, *14*, 741)

Lecture: Naval War College (Newport, R. I.) (JoP, *9*, 364; SCI, *35*, 924)

Lecture: Ohio State Univ., courtroom psychology (SCI, *31*, 187; JoP, *7*, 112)

Lecture: psychological laboratories (SCI, *29*, 23)

Lecture: psychology and law (SCI, *29*, 23)

Lecture: report of tour (JoP, *6*, 56)

Lecture: series (BULL, *6*, 32)

Lecture: Union College (BULL, *9*, 95; JoP, *9*, 168)

Lecture: Wellesley College (BULL, *5*, 379; JoP, *5*, 616)

Lecture: Yale Univ. (SCI, *23*, 439; JoP, *3*, 196)

Publication: announced (BULL, *2*, 260; JoP, *6*, 196)

Publication: *Aus Deutsch Amerika* (JoP, *5*, 700)

Publication: correction of announcement (JoP, *6*, 196)

Publication: English edition of *Grundzüge der Psychologie* (REV, *8*, 112)

Publication: exhibit at Chicago Exposition (REV, *1*, 214)

Publication: *Psychology and Crime* (JoP, *6*, 140)

Return: from Berlin (BULL, *8*, 333)

Return: to Harvard Univ. (SCI, *5*, 584; REV, *4*, 339; JoP, *4*, 140)

St. Louis World's Fair (SCI, *17*, 636)

Tribute after his death (JoP, *14*, 111)

Trip: Germany (SCI, *21*, 903; SCI, *17*, 915; JoP, *2*, 304; BULL, *2*, 260)

Murchison, Carl

Appointment: Clark Univ. (SCI, *57*, 690)

Degree (SCI, *86*, 239)

Degree: Univ. of Athens, centenary (BULL, *34*, 635)

Editor: *Journal of Social Psychology* (JoP, *27*, 84)

Resignation: Clark Univ. (Sci, *84*, 326; Bull, *33*, 849)
Resignation: Miami Univ. (Sci, *57*, 690)

Murphy, Arthur Edward

Election: American Phil. Assoc., Eastern Division, secretary- treasurer (JoP, *33*, 56)

Murphy, Gardner

Appointment: College of the City of New York (Bull, *37*, 405)
Appointment: Columbia Univ. (Sci, *91*, 236)
Departure: *Journal of Parapsychology* editorship (Sci, *95*, 322-323)
Election: APA, president (Sci, *98*, 321)
Election: EPA, president (Sci, *93*, 395)
Lecture: National Research Council Conference, Psychological Factors in National Morale (Bull, *37*, 829)
Research: defense program (Bull, *38*, 779)
Research: literature collection for Chinese psychologists (Bull, *37*, 329; J App, *24*, 246)
Research: post-war planning (J App, *27*, 114-115)
Research: SPSSI, attitudes produced by conscription (Bull, *37*, 829)
Resignation: *Sociometry* (Bull, *38*, 305)

Murphy, Paul Ghormley

Promotion: Kansas State Teachers College (Bull, *42*, 331)

Murray, Elsie

Appointment: Vassar College (Bull, *4*, 370)
Publication: color blindness (AJP, *58*, 253-261)
Publication: color perception charts, reply to Dvorine's comments (AJP, *58*, 399-402)
Publication: "The Ishihara test for color blindness: A point in ethics" (AJP, *47*, 513)

Murray, Henry Alexander, Jr.

Appointment: Harvard Psychological Clinic (Bull, *34*, 634)
Lecture: National Research Council Conference, Psychological Factors in National Morale (Bull, *37*, 829)

Murray, James Augustus Henry

Editor: *English Dictionary of Philological Society* (Sci°, *3*, 527)

Muscular contraction

Research: Haycraft, J. B., Royal Society of Edinburgh (Sci°, *15*, 245)

Music

Contest: APA, effects of (JoP, *17*, 671-672; Bull, *17*, 352)
Course: Seashore, C. E. (Sci, *45*, 657; Bull, *14*, 80; JoP, *14*, 448)
Fellowship: Univ. of Iowa (Bull, *24*, 312; J App, *11*, 80)

Lecture: Ruckmick, C. A., Harvard Univ. (BULL, *12*, 403)
Lecture: Schoen, M. (BULL, *18*, 628)
Lecture: Seashore, C. E., Univ. of Kansas (SCI, *51*, 268; JoP, *17*, 168)
Lecture: Vernon, P. (AJP, *42*, 127)
Publication: Squires, P. C., "Beethoven's concept of the whole" (AJP, *48*, 684)
Publication: Validity of Seashore's measure of talent (AJP, *52*, 638-640)
Research: music studies (J APP, *1*, 299-300)
Research: Wildermuth (K. ?), sense of idiots (SCI°, *17*, 353)

Mussolini, Benito
Italian Congress of Eugenics, 2nd (SCI, *70*, 190)

Myers, Charles Samuel
Appointment: *British Journal of Psychology*, board (JoP, *1*, 28)
Appointment: British National Institute of Industrial Psychology (SCI, *55*, 451)
Appointment: Kings College, London (SCI, *18*, 704; SCI, *24*, 96; JoP, *1*, 28; BULL, *1*, 134; BULL, *3*, 288; JoP, *3*, 476)
Appointment: Univ. of Cambridge (BULL, *18*, 236)
British Army, Cambridge Univ. (BULL, *12*, 364)
Degree: Univ. of Pennsylvania (SCI, *92*, 234)
Departure: British National Institute of Industrial Psychology, directorship (SCI, *72*, 598)
Election: British Assoc. Centenary, Psych. Section J, president (SCI, *73*, 62)
Election: Gonville and Caius College, Cambridge Univ., fellowship (SCI, *50*, 248; SCI, *82*, 35; BULL, *17*, 116)
Laboratory, Cambridge Univ. psychophysics, funds collected (SCI, *32*, 553)
Lecture: instinct and intelligence (JoP, *7*, 420)
Lecture: Kings College, London (SCI, *20*, 656; JoP, *1*, 672; BULL, *1*, 488)
Lecture: Oxford, Spencer (SCI, *69*, 570)
Located at hospital in France (BULL, *12*, 128)
Publication: selection of personnel (J APP, *27*, 207)
Research: Torres Straits and Borneo (AJP, *9*, 423)
Resignation: Cambridge Univ. (SCI, *55*, 451)
Retirement: British National Institute of Industrial Psychology (SCI, *88*, 494-495)

Myers, Edward D.
Appointment: Roanoke College (BULL, *42*, 486)
Departure: Trinity College (Connecticut) (BULL, *42*, 486)

Myers, Frederic William Henry
Death notice (REV, *8*, 223)
Glossary of psychical research terms (SCI, *4*, 140)
Lecture: phantasms of the dead (SCI°, *15*, 144)

Myers, Garry Cleveland
Commissioned: Sanitary Corps (JoP, *15*, 364; BULL, *15*, 97)
Editor: *Junior Home for Parent and Child* (J APP, *16*, 589)

Lecture: Conference on Education and the Exceptional Child, 5th (J App, *23*, 312)

Lecture: NYAS, visual images (JoP, *13*, 700)

Publication: Mental Hygiene, the parent problem (J App, *22*, 539)

Publication: notes on the unconscious self *Journal of the Society for Psychical Research* (Sci°, 7, 415)

Myers, George E.

Appointment: State Manual Training School (Kansas) (JoP, 9, 140)

Inauguration: Normal School in Pittsburgh, Kansas, principal (JoP, 9, 28)

Mysticism

Conference on Methods in Philosophy and the Sciences, 11th (JoP, 39, 252)

N

Näcke, Paul Adolf
Death notice (SCI, 38, 176)

Nafe, John Paul
Appointment: Washington Univ. (BULL, 28, 324; SCI, 73, 337)
Election: SSPP, president (SCI, 91, 354)
Lecture: SSPP (JoP, 38, 224)
Lecture: SSPP, "The quantification of psychology" (SCI, 93, 373)
Lecture: Virginia Chapter of Sigma Xi (SCI, 87, 411)
Promotion: Clark Univ. (BULL, 25, 376)
Publication: Jenkins, W. L. on the vascular theory of warmth and cold (AJP, 51, 763; AJP, 52, 462-465)
Publication: Obituary for Swift, E. J. (AJP, 45, 364)

Nagel, Ernest
Editor: *Journal of Philosophy* (JoP, 36, 420)
Lecture: Conference on Methods in Philosophy and the Sciences (JoP, 41, 252)

Nagel, Wilibald A.
Appointment: Rostock Univ. (BULL, 6, 120)
Death notice (BULL, 8, 78; JoP, 8, 140)
Vision test, use of (BULL, 5, 32)

Nakajima, Taizo
Death notice (BULL, 16, 392)

Nancy, University of (France)
Requests for contributions to aid in losses due to bomb (JoP, 17, 140)

Naples, University of (Italy)
Appointment: Bianchi, L., clinic director (JoP, 13, 448)
Nomination: Lewin, K. R. (SCI, 33, 420)

Narcotics
Lecture: Hickman, J. E., NY Branch APA/NYAS, influence on children (JoP, 9, 167)

Nation
Publication: compendium of the tenth census concerning age (Sci°, 2, 209)

National Ability Tests (see Ability Tests, National)

National Academy of Sciences
Appointment: Angell, J. R. (Sci, 51, 459; Bull, 17, 200)
Appropriation from the Carnegie Corporation, New York (J App, 4, 112)
Building site National Research Council (JoP, 17, 672)
Election: Cattell, J. McK. (Sci, 71, 478)
Election: Cattell, J. McK., delegate to American Scientific Congress, 7th (Sci, 82, 298)
Election: Dodge, R. (Bull, 21, 360; Sci, 59, 418)
Election: Hall, G. S. (Sci, 41, 640)
Election: Hull, C. L. (Sci, 83, 430; Bull, 33, 578)
Election: Hunter, W. (Bull, 32, 524)
Election: Lashley, K. S. (Bull, 27, 415; Sci, 71, 478)
Election: members posthumously, 1891-1900 (Sci, 13, 597)
Election: Seashore, C. E. (Bull, 19, 296)
Election: Stratton, G. M. (Bull, 25, 376)
Election: Terman, L. (Bull, 25, 376)
Election: Thorndike, E. L. (Bull, 14, 192)
Election: Thurstone, L. L. (Bull, 35, 408)
Election: Washburn, M. F. (Bull, 28, 410)
Election: Woodworth, R. S. (Bull, 18, 296)
Election: Wundt, W., foreign associate (Sci, 29, 694; JoP, 6, 184, 308, 504)
Lecture: Angell, J. R., NAS, Yale Univ., 1931 (Sci, 74, 481)
Lecture: list of (Sci°, 4, 408-409; Sci°, 5, 370; Sci°, 7, 391; Sci°, 8, 451-452; Sci°, 13, 320; Sci°, 14, 351; Sci°, 15, 259; Sci°, 16, 287)
Lecture: Peirce, C. S. and Jastrow, J., perceptible differences of sensation (Sci°, 3, 524)
Lecture: Peirce, C. S., comparative biography (Sci°, 3, 524)
Meeting: announcement (Sci°, 2, 581; Sci°, 3, 337-338; Sci°, 4, 329; Sci°, 5, 261; Sci°, 6, 382; Sci°, 7, 284; Sci°, 8, 345; JoP, 8, 700; Bull, 40, 540)
Members representing psychology (Bull, 17, 200)
National Research Council perpetuated (Bull, 15, 256)
Proceedings of: Editor, Wilson, E. B. (Bull, 12, 128)
Publication: annual report (Sci°, 7, 140)
Publication: report of psychological work in the US Army (J App, 5, 192)

National Advisory Council on Radio in Education
Broadcasts: Angell, J. R., weekly (Sci, 74, 411)
Election: Butler, N. M., chair (Sci, 74, 411)

National Association for Nursery Education (*see* Nursery Education)

National Board of Researchers

Permanent commission for the application of psychology (BULL, *36*, 713)

National Bureau of Standards

Appointment: Judd, D. B. (J APP, *10*, 395)

National Central University (Chunking, China)

Hsiao, H. H., request for psych. literature (BULL, *37*, 827)

National Committee for Mental Hygiene

Anniversary: 25th dinner (SCI, *80*, 446; SCI, 77, 423; SCI, *70*, 536)

Appointment: Bullis, H. E., business manager (BULL, *36*, 711)

Appointment: Haines, T. H. (BULL, *14*, 114-115)

Appointment: Hincks, C. M., research director (SCI, 72, 557)

Appointment: Pratt, G. K. (SCI, 61, 113)

Appointment: Stevenson, G. S. (SCI, *89*, 337; SCI, *99*, 319, 363; BULL, *36*, 711)

Appointment: Weiss, E., director of fund established for research in psychosomatic medicine (SCI, *99*, 319, 363)

Award: Lasker established (SCI, *100*, 354)

Award: Menninger, W. C., 1944, Lasker (SCI, *100*, 516)

Course: Summer Training School of Psychiatric Social Work (JoP, *15*, 671-672)

Departure: Hincks, C. M. (SCI, *89*, 337)

Election: Lasker, A. D., Board of Directors (SCI, *99*, 34-35)

Election: members (SCI, *100*, 215)

Election: officers (SCI, 72, 557; SCI, 77, 46)

Election: Preston, G., Board of Directors (SCI, *99*, 34-35)

Election: Welch, W. H., honorary president (SCI, 72, 557)

Election: Williams, F. E., director (SCI, *59*, 60)

Grant: research (SCI, *89*, 264; SCI, *91*, 68; SCI, *97*, 352; J APP, *16*, 336; SCI, *100*, 122)

Meeting: announced (SCI, *36*, 669; SCI, *67*, 35; SCI, *87*, 277; SCI, *100*, 402; BULL, *41*, 680)

Publication: *Mental Hygiene* journal (BULL, *14*, 114)

Publication: psychosomatic medicine on war problems (SCI, *98*, 59-60)

Research: dementia praecox (J APP, *19*, 496)

Research: plan announced (SCI, 72, 557)

Research: psychosomatic medicine, establishment of fund (SCI, *99*, 319, 363)

Research: survey conducted (BULL, *20*, 288; SCI, *56*, 534)

Retirement: Williams, F. E. (SCI, 72, 557)

Staff division of community clinics continues (SCI, *89*, 337)

National Committee for Morale (*see* Morale, National Committee for)

National Conference of Social Work (*see* Social Work, National
Conference of)

National Council of Mental Hygiene (Great Britain)
Meeting: first annual, 1923 (Sci, 58, 263)

National Council of Women Psychologists (*see* Women
Psychologists)

National Defense, Mental Attitudes for (*see* Mental Attitudes)

National Education Association
Election: Downing, A. B. (Sci, 9, 339-340)
Meeting: Wisconsin, July, 1884 (Sci°, 3, 466)
National Education week program, 1938 (J App, 22, 107)
Papers on child-study (Rev, 6, 240)

National Electric Lamp Association (Cleveland, Ohio)
Appointment: Geissler, L. R. (JoP, 8, 616; Bull, 8, 406)
Appointment: Johnson, H. M. (Bull, 9, 280; Sci, 35, 889)
Departure: Geissler, L. R. (Sci, 36, 115; Bull, 9, 360)

National Institute of Industrial Psychology (*see also* British
National Institute of)
Course: announced (J App, 23, 312)
Election: D'Abernon, president (Sci, 72, 498)
Meeting: Vocational and Educational Conference (J App, 23, 744)
Publication: annual report (Sci, 73, 526)
Publication: research report (J App, 26, 247-248)
Seminar: Exeter College, Oxford Univ., 1936 (Sci, 83, 301)

National Institute of Psychology
Election: officers (Sci, 94, 435; Bull, 39, 267)
Election: Tolman, E. C. (Bull, 27, 736)
Transfer: Woodworth, R. S., honorary membership (Bull, 27, 736)

National Institute of Social Science (*see* Social Science)

National Library
Appointment: Barrows, S. J. (Sci, 9, 267-268)

National Opinion Research Center at University of Denver
Report: reconversion period from war to peace (J App, 27, 475)

National Probation Association (*see* Probation)

National Research Council

Fellowships: Graham, C. H. (SCI, 73, 609)
Fellowships: Hutchinson, E. D. (BULL, 23, 292)
Fellowships: Jenkins, T. N. (BULL, 23, 292)
Fellowships: Kellogg, W. N. (BULL, 26, 380)
Fellowships: Licklider, J. C. R. (BULL, 39, 682)
Fellowships: Metfessel, M. F. (BULL, 23, 292)
Fellowships: Olsen, W. C. (BULL, 23, 292)
Fellowships: Rizzolo, A. (BULL, 26, 380)
Fellowships: Travis, L. E. (BULL, 23, 292)
Fellowships: Turner, W. D. (BULL, 26, 380)
Fellowships: Witkin, H. A. (BULL, 40, 539-540)
Fellowships: Young, P. T. (BULL, 23, 292)
Financial aid applications announced (BULL, 41, 200)
Financial aid information, Committee for Research in Problems in Sex (BULL, 40, 231; BULL, 42, 191; SCI, 93, 109; SCI, 91, 140; SCI, 95, 168; SCI, 197, 88; SCI, 99, 98; SCI, 101, 86)
Funds given to support Psychological Personnel, Office of (BULL, 40, 459-460)
Grant (BULL, 33, 147, 578; AJP, 44, 195; J APP, 5, 95)
Grant: Karwoski, T. (BULL, 33, 578)
Grant: Kinsey, A. C., Committee for Research on Problems of Sex (SCI, 95, 600)
Grant: request, Committee on Human Heredity (SCI, 92, 146)
Grant: Trimble, O. C., audition (SCI, 80, 585)
Lecture: Lowrey, L. G. (BULL, 37, 829)
Meeting: Division of Anthro. and Psych. (SCI, 95, 298)
Perpetuated by the NAS (BULL, 15, 256)
Publication: Dunlap, K., words and paralogs (BULL, 31, 80)
Publication: food habits (J APP, 26, 858)
Publication: military psychology text (J APP, 27, 475)
Publication: Psychology Committee, to the director of the Council of National Defense (J APP, 1, 394-395)
Publication: Yerkes, R. M., *Psychological Review*, report of the Psychology Committee (JoP, 16, 307-308)
Reorganization (JoP, 16, 671-672)
Research: army mental tests in schools (JoP, 16, 672)
Research: Bentley, M., mental disorders (SCI, 75, 189)
Research: Killeffer, D. H., Committee on the Location of New and Rare Instruments (SCI, 96, 58)
Research: sex and reproduction problems (SCI, 89, 126)
Resignation: Cattell, J. McK. (BULL, 14, 366)
Resignation: Dunlap, J. W. (BULL, 40, 539)
War effort: APA organizes a committee (JoP, 14, 504)
War effort: requests information on psychologists (J APP, 25, 472; BULL, 39, 132, 328)

National Research Institute of Psychology (China)

Appointment: Tsai, L. S. (BULL, 28, 79)

National Service
List of APA members enlisted (J App, 2, 294-295, 386)

National Society for the Study and Correction of Speech Disorder (*see* Speech Disorder)

National Tuberculosis Society (*see* Tuberculosis)

National Vocational Guidance Association War Service Committee (*see* War Service Committee)

National Wartime Conference (*see* Wartime Conference)

National Youth Administration
Appointment: Judd, C. H. (Sci, 92, 125)

Nation's Business, The
Excerpts from Kellogg, V. (J App, 3, 393-394)

Natural Science, Institute of
Lecture: Boring, E. G. (Bull, 28, 324)

Naturalism
Lecture: Ewer, B. C. (JoP, 7, 223)
Symposium: 1942 (JoP, 39, 644)

Nature
Publication: Hartog, M. M., inheritance of characters (Sci°, 13, 236-237)
Publication: education of men of science (Sci, 9, 856)
Publication: short-sightedness (Sci°, 17, 7)
Publication: Voeltzkow, M., crocodile habits (Sci°, 16, 119)
Research: Dutch Society of Sciences at Haarlem (Sci°, 16, 189)
Review of article on Pearson, K. (JoP, 3, 84)

Nature-Nurture
Research: Univ. of Denver (J App, 17, 342)

Naval War College
Lecture: Münsterberg, H. (Sci, 35, 924; JoP, 9, 364)
Lecture: Swift, E. J. (Sci, 55, 126)

Navy (*see* United States Navy)

Nebraska Central College
Appointment: Dobson, M. M. (Bull, 41, 268)
Appointment: Fordyce, C. (Bull, 41, 136)

Nebraska, University of (Lincoln) (*see also* Bureau of Instructional Research)

Anniversary: 50th, Wolfe, H. K. psych. lab (SCI, *89*, 150; J APP, *23*, 207)

Appointment: Alexander, H. B. (BULL, *5*, 244)

Appointment: Bolton, T. L. (SCI, *17*, 400; JoP, *1*, 364; BULL, *1*, 334; REV, *7*, 323-324)

Appointment: Cox, H. M. (J APP, *24*, 518)

Appointment: English, H. (BULL, *32*, 324)

Appointment: Gregory, W. S. (BULL, *34*, 634)

Appointment: Guilford, J. P. (BULL, *25*, 444; SCI, *68*, 110)

Appointment: Hall, W. E. (BULL, *42*, 582)

Appointment: Harsh, C. M., Bureau of Instructional Research (BULL, *37*, 755)

Appointment: Hill, A. R. (REV, *4*, 567; SCI, *6*, 132; AJP, *9*, 135)

Appointment: Hinman, E. L. (AJP, *7*, 579)

Appointment: Hollingworth, H. L. (SCI, *27*, 680; BULL, *5*, 168)

Appointment: Jenness, A. (SCI, *91*, 616; J APP, *24*, 518)

Appointment: Major, D. R. (REV, *6*, 673)

Appointment: staff, new psych. dept. (J APP, *24*, 518)

Appointment: Wolfe, H. K. (BULL, *2*, 426; JoP, *3*, 56)

Appointment: Worcester, D. A. (SCI, *66*, 78)

Degree: Bentley, M. (SCI, *82*, 34; BULL, *32*, 862)

Degree: Guthrie, E. R. (BULL, *42*, 484)

Degree: Hollingworth, H. L. (SCI, *88*, 9; BULL, *35*, 577)

Degree: Hollingworth, L. S. (SCI, *88*, 9; BULL, *35*, 577)

Degree: Pillsbury, W. B. (SCI, *79*, 537)

Departure: Guilford, J. P. (SCI, *92*, 8)

Establishment: Bureau of Instructional Research (SCI, *89*, 148; BULL, *36*, 304; J APP, *23*, 207)

Establishment: Department of Psychology (SCI, *91*, 616; BULL, *37*, 656)

Fellowship: established to honor Hollingworth, L. S. (BULL, *42*, 63; SCI, *100*, 383)

Laboratory expanded (SCI, *3*, 167)

Leave of absence: Luckey, G. W. A. (REV, *6*, 673)

Meeting: Midwestern Psychological Assoc. (AJP, *52*, 473-475)

Meeting: Western Philosophical Assoc., 5th (JoP, *2*, 252)

Memorial fund raising for Wolfe, H. K. (JoP, *16*, 672)

Promotion: Bolton, T. L. (SCI, *17*, 760)

Promotion: Hinman, E. L. (REV, *4*, 567)

Resignation: Wolfe, H. K. (REV, *4*, 452; AJP, *9*, 135)

Return: Jenness, A. (BULL, *42*, 485)

Neet, Claude Cassell

Promotion: Massachusetts State College (BULL, *39*, 423)

Negative practice

Publication: Peak, H. on K. Dunlap's technique (AJP, *55*, 576-580)

Negro
Education in the South, Culver, S. W. (Sci°, 9, 584)
Publication: Bean, R. B., negro brain (JoP, 3, 615)

Neild, James
Publication: *Journal of Philosophy*, physical vs. psychological mechanisms of the mind (JoP, 40, 139-140)

Neill Prize
Award: Ewart, J. C. (Sci, 10, 259)

Nela Research Lab
Appointment: Dunlap, K. (Sci, 39, 866)

Nelles, Fred C.
Editor: *Journal of Delinquency* (Bull, 13, 296; JoP, 13, 392)

Nelson, Ralph Waldo
Lecture: Southwestern Philosophical Conference, "Logic of Jesus and John Dewey" (JoP, 34, 721)

Nervous and Mental Diseases and War
Meeting: Institute of Medicine of Chicago (Sci, 100, 263, 311)
Meeting: Kennedy, F., moderator (Sci, 100, 311)

Nervous Child, The
Journal purchased by Harms, F. (Bull, 42, 795)

Neuberg, Maurice Joseph
Death notice (Bull, 41, 807)

Neurological Congress, International
Berne, Switzerland, 1931 (AJP, 44, 384)

Neurological Institute of Frankfort-on-Main
Course: Feeble-minded and Psychopathic Children (Bull, 6, 72; AJP, 20, 296)

Neurological Society of Belgium
Election: Joteyko, J. (Bull, 1, 334; JoP, 1, 504)

Neurological Society of London
Lecture: Hitzig, E. (Sci, 12, 854, 975-976)

Neurological Society of Paris
Research fund for neurology established (Bull, 17, 116)

Neurology
Course: Cole, E. M., neurology of speech and reading (Bull, 39, 269)
Lecture: Donaldson, H. H. (JoP, 1, 336; JoP, 2, 280)

Lecture: Ladd-Franklin, C., Columbia Univ., visibility of current (JoP, *13*, 280)
Lecture: MacDougall, R. (JoP, *2*, 112)
Paper: Stowell, T. B., cats (Sci°, *8*, 453)
Publication: Mercier, D. F. F. J., the mind (Sci°, *10*, 176-177)
Univ. of Liverpool established dept. of by Nuffield Foundation (Sci, *101*, 141)

Neurology, Psychiatry and Psychology, International Congress of
Meeting: announced (Sci, *39*, 719; Bull, *11*, 191)

Neurology, Psychiatry, Medical Electricity, and Hypnology, International Congress of
Meeting: announced, 1897 (AJP, *8*, 584)

Neuro-psychiatry
Appointment: Grinker, R. R., Michael Reese Hospital (Sci, *83*, 347)
Appointment: Jacobsen, C. F., Washington Univ. (Bull, *35*, 577)
Appointment: Meyer, A., Rhode Island State Hospital for Mental Diseases (Bull, *36*, 57)
Appointment: Rioch, D. M., Washington Univ. (Bull, *35*, 577)
Appointment: Whitehorn, J. C., Washington Univ. (Bull, *35*, 577)
Course: Columbia Univ., for neuro-psychiatric nursing (J App, *26*, 857)
Departure: Boyd, Jr., D. A., Neuropsychiatric Institute of the Univ. of Michigan (Sci, *90*, 369)
Establishment: Neuro-Psychiatric Clinic, Univ. of Rochester, Rivas, H. W. (Sci, *101*, 198)
Lecture: Strecker, E. A., neuropsychiatry of global war (Sci, *98*, 405)
Report: 118th annual, Burlingame, C. D. on psychiatry service in war (J App, *26*, 245)

Neurosis (*see also* Experimental neuroses)
Gum-chewers paralysis recorded (Sci°, *14*, 215)
Lecture: Kennedy, F., H. B., neuroses in warfare, Shmookler Memorial Lecture (Sci, *97*, 374)
Lecture: Maier, N. R. F., neurotic behavior (Sci, *89*, 7)

Nevin, Samuel
Appointment: Maudsley Hospital (Sci, *89*, 554)

New Hampshire State Hospital
Internships available (Bull, *42*, 407)

New Hampshire, University of (Durham)
Appointment: Haslerud, G. M. (Bull, *42*, 792)
Appointment: Loomis, S. D. (Bull, *42*, 792)
Appointment: Shaw, F. J. (Bull, *41*, 679)
Promotion: Carroll, H. A. (Bull, *40*, 539)

New Jersey (*see also* Bonnie Brae Farm for Boys)

New Jersey College for Women
Appointment: Sackett, R. S. (BULL, *29*, 603)

New Jersey Department of Institutions and Agencies
Departure: Castner, B. M. (BULL, *39*, 807)

New Jersey State Prison
Program of psychological examining (J APP, *4*, 113-114)

New Jersey State Psychiatric Clinic
Appointment: Doll, E. A. (J APP, *4*, 112-113)
Appointment: Ellis, W. J. (J APP, *4*, 112-113)
Extended: Lewis, B. G. (J APP, *4*, 112-113)

New Jersey Training School for Feeble-minded Girls and Boys
(*see* Vineland Training School)

New Mexico, University of (Albuquerque)
Appointment: Hill, D. S. (BULL, *16*, 257)
Appointment: Worcester, D. A. (BULL, *11*, 444; JOP, *11*, 560; SCI, *40*, 379)

New Orleans Child Guidance Clinic (Louisiana)
Position offered for extern, 1943 (J APP, *27*, 365)

New Psychology, The
Publication: Scripture, E. W. (SCI, *5*, 583)

New School for Social Research (New York, New York)
Appointment: Glueck, B. (SCI, *65*, 157)
Appointment: Holt, E. B. (SCI, *64*, 447)
Appointment: Wertheimer, M. (JOP, *31*, 532)
Conference: James, W. centenary (JOP, *38*, 616)
Conference: Methods in Philosophy and the Sciences (BULL, *41*, 72; JOP, *34*, 616; BULL, *34*, 363; SCI, *87*, 277; SCI, *86*, 419-420; JOP, *34*, 559; JOP, *37*, 224)
Course: Dewey, J., modern philosophy (BULL, *20*, 172)
Course: Glueck, B., psychoanalysis (BULL, *24*, 312)
Course: Watson, J. B., behavior psychology (BULL, *20*, 172)
Fellowship: social research (BULL, *17*, 32)
Lecture: Bentley, A. F. (SCI, *87*, 277)
Lecture: Gesell, A., psychology of growth (SCI, *74*, 434)
Lecture: Holt, E. B. (SCI, *87*, 277)
Lecture: Holt, E. B., response, psychology of (BULL, *24*, 204)
Lecture: Jastrow, J., emotions (SCI, *66*, 278; BULL, *27*, 620)
Lecture: Jastrow, J., introduces Gesell, A. (SCI, *74*, 434)
Lecture: Koffka's Gestalt psychology (SCI, *69*, 156)
Lecture: Köhler, W. (BULL, *41*, 72)

Lecture: Lewin, K. (Sci, 87, 277)
Publication: *Renaissance* (JoP, 40, 448)
Symposium: Dewey's J. 80th birthday (Sci, 90, 326; JoP, 36, 588)
Symposium: naturalism (JoP, 39, 644)

New York Academy of Medicine

Lecture: Gillespie, R. D., Salmon (J App, 25, 726)
Lecture: Hoskins, R. G., biology of schizophrenia (Sci, 102, 397)
Lecture: Hoskins, R. G., Laity (Sci, 89, 175)
Lecture: Jastrow, J. (JoP, 5, 140)
Lecture: Lashley, K. S., Harvey Society (Sci, 72, 499)
Lecture: Luria, A., Salmon (Sci, 89, 433)
Lecture: McGraw, M., Laity (Bull, 39, 895)
Lecture: McLane, A., legal regulations governing the insane (Sci, 25, 398)
Lecture: Putnam, T. J., Laity, the mechanisms of the mind (Sci, 94, 582)
Lecture: Strecker, E. A., Salmon (Sci, 89, 385)
Meeting: section of neurology and psychiatry (JoP, 9, 224)

New York Academy of Sciences

Election: Cattell, J. McK., president (Sci, 15, 391-392)
Election: Lashley, K. S., honorary member (Sci, 85, 13)
Election: Lorge, I. (J App, 21, 717)
Election: officers (Bull, 17, 116; Sci, 86, 418; JoP, 9, 28)
Election: Thorndike, E. L. (Sci, 50, 588; Bull, 18, 111)
Election: Thorndike, E. L., chair exhibition (Sci, 11, 636)
Election: Woodworth, R. S., vice-president (Bull, 18, 111)
Lecture: deVries, H. (JoP, 9, 672)
Lecture: Dodge, R., alcohol (Bull, 12, 160; JoP, 12, 196)
Lecture: Ferree, C. E. (Bull, 11, 482-483; JoP, 11, 672)
Lecture: Gates, G. I. S. (JoP, 15, 140)
Lecture: Healy, W., Salmon, personality (Sci, 85, 355)
Lecture: Jacobsen, C., lobotomy (Sci, 77, 85)
Lecture: Miner, J. B. (Sci, 15, 547)
Lecture: Watson, J. B. (Sci, 60, 402)
Lecture: Wissler, C. (Sci, 15, 547, 627)
Lecture: Woodworth, R. S., heredity and environment (Sci, 92, 451)
Meeting (JoP, 13, 112, 224, 280; JoP, 12, 700; Sci°, 12, 167; Sci, 10, 540)
Meeting: American Ethnological Society, Columbia Univ. (JoP, 13, 616, 700; JoP, 14, 644)
Meeting: American Museum of Natural History (JoP, 13, 224)
Meeting: APA (JoP, 11, 721)
Meeting: joint, New York Branch APA (JoP, 1, 84, 224, 644; Bull, 9, 486; JoP, 2, 112, 223; Bull, 10, 124; Bull, 7, 179; Bull, 11, 443; Bull, 8, 181; JoP, 3, 139; JoP, 7, 700; Bull, 12, 168; JoP, 14, 140; JoP, 8, 280; JoP, 12, 252, 721; JoP, 10, 112, 251-252, 672; JoP, 11, 168, 280; Bull, 1, 173; JoP, 15, 28, 140; JoP, 9, 167, 252, 699)
Meeting: report of (JoP, 3, 700; JoP, 13, 280; JoP, 9, 27-28; Sci, 15, 309-310)

Section formed: psychology, anthropology and philosophy (REV, *3*, 356; SCI, *3*, 402)

Proposal: 6th annual exhibition (SCI, *9*, 339)

New York Board of Education (Rochester)

Resignation: Mitrano, A. J. (BULL, *38*, 907)

New York Board of Examiners of the Board of Education

Announcement: exams for license of research assistants (BULL, *12*, 488)

New York Branch of American Psychological Association (see also Eastern Psychological Association)

Election: officers, 1933 (SCI, *77*, 364)

Lecture: Dodge, R., NYAS (JOP, *12*, 196)

Lecture: Jastrow, J., presidential (SCI, *81*, 67)

Lecture: Ladd-Franklin, C. (JOP, *10*, 720)

Lecture: list of (JOP, *10*, 112)

Meeting: announcement (JOP, *8*, 56; BULL, *8*, 78; BULL, *11*, 115; BULL, *15*, 93; JOP, *18*, 672, 723; SCI, *79*, 359; SCI, *81*, 290)

Meeting: joint NYAS (JOP, *15*, 28, 140; JOP, *12*, 168, 252, 721; JOP, *7*, 700; JOP, *11*, 168; JOP, *10*, 112, 672; BULL, *1*, 173; BULL, *7*, 179; BULL, *8*, 181; JOP, *2*, 112, 223; BULL, *9*, 486; JOP, *14*, 140; JOP, *1*, 84, 224, 644; BULL, *10*, 124; BULL, *11*, 443; JOP, *3*, 139; JOP, *8*, 280, 700; JOP, *9*, 167, 252, 699; JOP, *10*, 251-252)

New York City

Appointment: Bisch, L. E., police dept. (BULL, *13*, 188)

Appointment: Rowe, E. C. (BULL, *13*, 188)

New York City Schools (see Bureau of Child Guidance of)

New York College for the Training of Teachers

List of educational lectures given, 1890 (SCI°, *14*, 403)

New York, College of the City of

Appointment: Klopfer, B. (BULL, *42*, 582)

Appointment: Murphy, G. (BULL, *37*, 405)

Appointment: Sheldon, W. H. (JOP, *15*, 448)

Appointment: Turner, J. P. (JOP, *10*, 720)

Conference: Dewey, J. (JOP, *10*, 252, 308)

Course: offers graduate work (BULL, *41*, 499)

Laboratory alterations (BULL, *38*, 779)

Leave of absence: Blum, M. L. (BULL, *41*, 267)

Promotion: Marsh, H. D. (JOP, *14*, 56)

Promotion: Peatman, J. G. (BULL, *40*, 152; BULL, *41*, 679)

Retirement: Bell, J. C. (BULL, *40*, 310)

New York Hospital

Appointment: Cameron, N. (SCI, *89*, 76)

Appointment: Cheney, C. O. (Sci, *92*, 76)
Appointment: Wells, F. L. (Sci, *32*, 863)
Departure: Cameron, N. (Sci, *91*, 593)

New York Institute of Social Science
Lecture: list of 1886 (Sci°, *9*, 130-131)

New York Medical College
Appointment: Hoen, T, I, (Sci, *90*, 613)
Appointment: Jewett, S. P. (Sci, *94*, 15)

New York Medical Journal
Editor: Jelliffe, S. E. (JoP, *14*, 224)
Publication: insanity (JoP, *4*, 503)
Publication: pragmatism (JoP, *5*, 82)
Publication: psychiatry (JoP, *4*, 307)

New York Museum of Science
Paintings: "Apotheosis of Science" (Sci, *93*, 324)

New York Psychiatric Institute (*see* New York State Psychiatric Center)
Appointment: Wells, F. L. (Bull, 7, 426; JoP, 7, 721)
Research: Stone, C. (Sci, *101*, 375)
Return: Kopeloff, N. (Sci, *60*, 330)

New York Psychiatric Society
Election: Dana, C., president (Sci, *37*, 172)
Election: Jelliffe, S. E., president (Sci, *55*, 204)
Meeting: psychologist activities (JoP, *14*, 278-280)

New York Psychoanalytic Society
Election: officers (Sci, *94*, 135)

New York Psychological Service Center
Purpose of (J App, *16*, 589)
Research: stuttering (J App, *19*, 497)

New York Rockland State Hospital
Appointment: Folsom, A. (Bull, *40*, 618)
Leave of absence: Kinder, E. F. (Bull, *40*, 618)

New York Society for Clinical Psychiatry
Election: Kirby, G. H., president (Sci, 57, 80)

New York Society for Ethical Research
Lecture: Montague, W. P., Felix Adler Lecture (JoP, *39*, 250)

New York State

Appointment: Bigelow, N. J. T., Assistant Commissioner of Mental Hygiene (SCI, *98*, 447)

Leave of absence: Lang, H. B., Assistant Commissioner of Mental Hygiene (SCI, *98*, 447)

Treatment of insane (AJP, *3*, 291)

New York State Association for Applied Psychology

Election: officers (BULL, *37*, 405; BULL, *41*, 602)

Meeting (BULL, *41*, 268; J APP, *22*, 317; SCI, *89*, 433)

Reorganization of APA and dissolution of AAAP, resolutions proposed (BULL, *41*, 500)

New York State Association of Consulting Psychologists

Election: results (SCI, *58*, 28)

Election: Washburn, M. F., honorary president (BULL, *18*, 568)

Establishment (SCI, *54*, 112)

Meeting: organization (JOP, *18*, 504; BULL, *18*, 439)

New York State Commission on Lunacy

Directorship position open (SCI, *29*, 854)

New York State Commissioner of Education

Appointment. Stoddard, G. D. (SCI, *96*, 10, 58; SCI, *95*, 600)

New York State Department of Mental Hygiene

Internships in clinical psychology (BULL, *39*, 809-810)

New York State Normal College (Albany)

Appointment: Painter, G. S. (SCI, *36*, 593)

Appointment: Piez, R. K. (SCI, *12*, 616; REV, *7*, 640)

Appointment: Smith, M. K. (REV, *8*, 552; SCI, *14*, 40)

New York State Normal College (Cortland)

Resignation: Robertson, C. (SCI, *33*, 926)

New York State Pathological Institute

Departure: Meyer, A. (JOP, *1*, 588)

Election: Meyer, A., International Congress of Arts and Sciences, St. Louis, abnormal psychology section secretary (JOP, *1*, 532)

New York State Psychiatric Center (*see* New York Psychiatric Institute)

Appointment: Hunt, W. A. (BULL, *34*, 498)

Appointment: Landis, C. (J APP, *14*, 304; BULL, *27*, 415)

Dedicated: 1929 (SCI, *70*, 578)

New center (SCI, *60*, 588)

Research: Stone, C. P. (BULL, *42*, 486)

New York State Teachers College
Appointment: Hertzberg, O. E. (BULL, *41*, 72; SCI, 72, 315)
Retirement: Root, C. C. (BULL, *41*, 72)

New York State Teachers of Educational Psychology
Meeting: April 8-9, 1910, Cornell Univ. (BULL, 7, 179-180; JOP, 7, 252)

New York State Training School for Boys (Warwick, New York)
Internships in clinical psychology (BULL, 39, 809-810)

New York University (New York, New York)
Appointment: Angell, J. R., hall of fame (SCI, 99, 34)
Appointment: Chase, H. W. (SCI, 77, 165)
Appointment: Jackson, T. A. (SCI, 74, 240)
Appointment: Judd, C. H. (AJP, *10*, 165; REV, 5, 449; SCI, 7, 713)
Appointment: Kitson, H. D. (BULL, *19*, 410)
Appointment: Kohl, C. C. (BULL, *12*, 280)
Appointment: Lanier, L. H. (AJP, *10*, 522)
Appointment: Lough, J. E. (SCI, *14*, 302; REV, *8*, 656-657; SCI, *18*, 768)
Appointment: MacDougall, R. (SCI, *14*, 424; REV, *8*, 447)
Appointment: Shaw, C. G. (REV, *6*, 673)
Appointment: Stoddard, G. D., president and state commissioner of education (SCI, *94*, 296)
Appointment: Tomlinson, B. E. (BULL, *39*, 682)
Appointment: Wissler, C. (REV, *9*, 104)
Appointment: Wortis, S. B., College of Medicine (SCI, *96*, 293)
Bequeathal: Gregory, M. S., College of Medicine (SCI, *95*, 405)
Course: Gault, R. H. (BULL, *13*, 296)
Course: personnel psychology (BULL, *40*, 794; SCI, *98*, 299)
Course: Terman, L. M. (BULL, *13*, 296)
Degree: Angell, J. R. (SCI, *88*, 372-373)
Degree: Stoddard, G. D. (SCI, *97*, 550)
Grant: National Committee for Mental Hygiene, College of Medicine (SCI, *97*, 352)
Leave of absence: Benson, C. E. (BULL, *39*, 682)
Leave of absence: Lough, J. E. (J APP, *10*, 522)
Leave of absence: MacDougall, R. (J APP, *10*, 522)
Lecture: annual convocation of the regents, list of papers (SCI°, *9*, 558)
Lecture: Brill, A. A. (BULL, *12*, 128)
Lecture: Brown, E. E., U.S. Commissioner of Education (SCI, *24*, 381)
Lecture: Dewey, J. (JOP, *11*, 84)
Lecture: Dewey, J., time and individuality (JOP, *35*, 252)
Lecture: education (SCI, *11*, 318)
Lecture: Kardiner, A., Philosophical Society (JOP, *35*, 616)
Lecture: Kitson, H. D. (SCI, *55*, 593)
Lecture: MacDougall, R., International Congress of Arts and Sciences, St. Louis (JOP, *1*, 616)

Meeting: National Assoc. for the Study of Education of Exceptional Children
(JoP, *8*, 700; Sci, *34*, 712)
Meeting: Philosophical Society, 1938 (JoP, *35*, 616)
Occupational Index, Inc. (J App, *26*, 392)
Organization of dept. to train teachers of backward and defective children
(Bull, *11*, 352)
Promotion: Holden, F. (Sci, *74*, 240)
Promotion: Hoopingarner, N. L. (Bull, *28*, 645; Sci, *74*, 240)
Promotion: Lough, J. E. (Rev, *9*, 104)
Promotion: Tomlinson, B. E. (Bull, *42*, 331)
Resignation: Bowman, K., College of Medicine (Sci, *96*, 293)
Resignation: Buchner, E. F. (Rev, *8*, 336)
Resignation: Judd, C. H. (Rev, *8*, 336; Sci, *14*, 944)
Resignation: Judd, C. H., resolution from graduate students concerning (Sci,
13, 760)
Retirement: Benson, C. E. (Bull, *42*, 331)

New York World's Fairs
Research: Cummings, C. E. and Shaw, R. P. (Sci, *89*, 339)

Newark, (New Jersey) Public School Clinic
Appointment: Maxfield, F. N. (Bull, *15*, 24, 98)

Newberry, Edward
Appointment: Kentucky (Sci, *72*, 315)

Newcomb College School of Education, Tulane University
Appointment: Fletcher, J. M. (Bull, *9*, 408)
Appointment: Seago, D. W. (Sci, *74*, 564)

Newcomb, Simon
Degree: Univ. of Edinburgh (Sci°, *19*, 100)
Eulogy: report of (JoP, *6*, 532)
Return: New York after attending the French Assoc. for the Advancement of
Science (Sci°, *2*, 254)

Newcomb, Theodore Mead
Grant: Social Science Research Council (Bull, *36*, 805)
Publication: SPSSI yearbook, *The Psychology of Industrial Conflict* (Bull, *35*,
61)

Newell, F. S.
Appointment: Coe College (Sci, *30*, 709; Bull, *6*, 427)

Newhall, Sidney Merritt
Election: APA Wash.-Balt. Branch, president (Bull, *36*, 712; Bull, *37*, 406)
Election: APA Wash.-Balt. Branch, secretary (Bull, *35*, 188)

Meeting: Inter-Society Color Council (BULL, 36, 142)
Promotion: Yale Univ. (BULL, 27, 660)

Newlin, William James
Appointment: Amherst College (JoP, 4, 363; BULL, 4, 337)

Newman, Edwin Broomell
Conference: Psychology of Learning, Univ. of Colorado (BULL, 36, 583)
Publication: "On the method of disection and its relation to a loudness scale"
(AJP, 49, 137)
Publication: reply to paper by Wells, E. F. (AJP, 43, 506)

Newman, Horatio Hackett
Lecture: Indiana Univ., use of twins in heredity vs. environment (SCI, 94, 136)
Research: twin studies (SCI, 82, 567)

Newnham College
Lecture: physiology (SCI°, 14, 180)
Lecture: Ward, J., Henry Sidgwich Memorial (JoP, 9, 700)

Newton, Isaac
Commemoration: Columbia Univ. (JoP, 39, 700)
Symposium: Tercentenary of birth, Eastern Div. of American. Phil. Assoc. (JoP, 39, 698-699)

Nichol, C. C. W.
Appointment: Oberlin College (BULL, 14, 366)

Nichols, Edward L.
Lecture: Univ. of Kansas, Sigma Xi (SCI, 11, 634)
Research: sense of smell in different sexes (SCI°, 9, 294)

Nichols, Herbert
Appointment: Johns Hopkins Univ. (SCI, 2, 850; REV, 3, 120; AJP, 7, 452)
Obituary: Dallenbach, K. M. (AJP, 49, 320)
Publication: Our Notions of Numbers and Space (REV, 1, 440)

Nietzsche, Friedrich Wilhelm
Meeting: centenary, 1944 (JoP, 41, 671-672)

Niles, Walter L. Memorial Lecture
Strecker, E. A. (SCI, 98, 405)

Nineteenth Century
Publication: "Are animals happy?" (SCI°, 8, 255)
Publication: Huxley, T. H. replies to Wace's, H. criticism of "Agnosticism" (SCI°, 13, 299)

Nissl, Franz
Promotion: Univ. of Heidelberg (Sci, *13*, 400)

Nobel, Alfred
Death notice (Sci, *43*, 131)

Norcross, William Harrington
Appointment: Dickinson College (JoP, *14*, 56; Bull, *13*, 448)

Norman, Conolly
Lecture: dementia praceox (JoP, *1*, 420)

Norsworthy, Naomi
Lecture (JoP, *1*, 224)
Lecture: intelligence (JoP, *2*, 224)

North Carolina School for Feeble-minded
Opened July 1 (Bull, *11*, 268)

North Carolina State Board of Charities and Public Welfare
Departure: Crane, H. W., Mental Hygiene Division (Sci, *89*, 55)

North Carolina, University of (Chapel Hill)
Appointment: Allport, F. (JoP, *19*, 532; Bull, *19*, 410; Sci, *55*, 617)
Appointment: Bagby, E. (Bull, *22*, 504; Sci, *61*, 588)
Appointment: Chase, H., president (Sci, *50*, 40; JoP, *16*, 588; Bull, *17*, 200)
Appointment: Crane, H. W. (Bull, *18*, 568; Sci, *54*, 300, 408; Sci, *89*, 55)
Appointment: Dashiell, J. F. (JoP, *16*, 588)
Appointment: Stern, W. (Bull, *32*, 323)
Course: psychology as science elective (Bull, *24*, 80)
Leave of absence: Trabue, M. S. (Bull, *28*, 411)
Lecture: Dewey, J. (JoP, *12*, 112)
Lecture: Johnson, H. M. (Sci, *72*, 598)
Meeting: Society of Experimental Psychologists (Bull, *35*, 408)
Organization: Alpha Psi Delta, Psychological Fraternity (Bull, *19*, 586)
Promotion: Chase, H. W. (Bull, *16*, 392)
Promotions (Bull, *32*, 323)

North Central Branch, American Psychological Association (*see also* Northwestern Branch of APA, Midwestern Psychological Association)
Meeting: report of (JoP, *4*, 223; Bull, *5*, 406)
Meeting: Univ. of Chicago (JoP, *2*, 280)
Meeting: Western Philosophical Assoc. and Teachers of Psychology in Iowa (JoP, *7*, 112, 222-223; Bull, *7*, 108)

North Dakota, University of (Grand Forks)
Appointment: Humpstone, H. J. (Bull, *17*, 351)

Appointment: McGeoch, J. (BULL, 25, 307)
Appointment: Winter, J. (BULL, 13, 148)

Northeastern College
Laboratory established, Roback, A. A. (JoP, 16, 721)

Northwestern Branch of American Psychological Association
(*see also* North Central Branch of APA, Midwestern
Psychological Association)
Meeting: report of (BULL, 1, 291)
Meeting: Univ. of Chicago (JoP, 1, 336)

Northwestern University (Evanston, Illinois)
Acquires Boas Memorial Collection (BULL, 41, 411)
Anniversary: Scott, W. D., 10th as C.E.O. (SCI, 73, 490)
Appointment: Anderson, G. V. (BULL, 42, 791)
Appointment: Buxton, C. E. (SCI, 90, 391)
Appointment: Egan, J. (SCI, 88, 471)
Appointment: Freeman, G. (BULL, 28, 411)
Appointment: Gault, R. H. (BULL, 6, 216)
Appointment: Gilliland, A. R. (BULL, 21, 428)
Appointment: Humphreys, L. G. (SCI, 90, 391)
Appointment: Hunt, W. A. (BULL, 42, 792)
Appointment: Krasno, L. (SCI, 88, 471)
Appointment: Scott, W. D. (SCI, 12, 320; REV, 7, 531)
Appointment: Scott, W. D., president (SCI, 52, 441; JoP, 17, 672; BULL, 17, 435)
Appointment: Seashore, R. H. (SCI, 86, 218; BULL, 34, 498)
Appointment: Valentine, W. L. (SCI, 92, 169; BULL, 37, 755)
Appointment: Webb, L. W. (BULL, 14, 116)
Building: Scott Hall, in honor of Scott, W. D. (SCI, 89, 219)
Leave of absence: Fearing, F. (SCI, 82, 386)
Leave of absence: Freeman, G. L. (BULL, 40, 310)
Leave of absence: Gault, R. H. (BULL, 21, 428)
Lecture: Ferrero, F., history of science (JoP, 14, 364)
Lecture: Seashore, C. E. (SCI, 89, 458)
Lecture: Western Philosophical Assoc., list of (JoP, 10, 224)
Meeting: Chicago Psychological Club (BULL, 42, 332)
Meeting: MPA, 1936 (BULL, 33, 303)
Meeting: WPA/Western Philosophical Assoc. (JoP, 10, 140, 224)
Promotion: Freeman, G. L. (SCI, 88, 471)
Promotion: Gault, R. H. (SCI, 34, 488; BULL, 15, 176; BULL, 11, 116; BULL, 8, 406; JoP, 11, 140)
Publication: Freeman, G. L., "The research laboratory in psychophysiology at Northwestern Univ." (AJP, 51, 176)
Publication: mental alertness tests for incoming freshman (SCI, 56, 331; BULL, 20, 172)

Research: Snow, A. J., with Yellow Cab Co. selection of drivers (J App, *9*, 90)
Resignation: Scott, W. D. (Sci, *89*, 76; Sci, *90*, 368; Bull, *36*, 304)

Norton, Edwin Lee
Appointment: Univ. of Wisconsin (Bull, *1*, 488)

Norton, Helen Rich
Publication: training methods developed at the Boston School of Salesmanship
(J App, *1*, 396)

Norwegian Psychological Association
Organization (Bull, *31*, 450; AJP, *46*, 511)

Nourrisson, Jean Felix
Death notice (Sci, *9*, 917)

Nowlis, Vincent
Appointment: Indiana Univ. (Bull, *41*, 603; Sci, *100*, 96-97)

Noyes, William
Death notice (Sci, *42*, 688)
Publication: view of the criminal type (Sci°, *11*, 217)

Nuffield Foundation
Appointment: Rowntree, B., survey committee on aging and care for old people
(Sci, *99*, 363-364)
Establishment: dept. of neurology, Univ. of Liverpool (Sci, *101*, 141)
Research: problems of aging and care of old people (Sci, *99*, 363-364)

Nuffield Institute of Oxford University
Lecture: Koffka, K., human behavior (Sci, *91*, 500)

Numbers
Publication: Guthrie, E., art of numeration (Sci, *5*, 39)
Publication: Nichols, H. (Rev, *1*, 440)

Nunn, Thomas Percy
Lecture: perception (JoP, *7*, 420)

Nursery Education, National Association for
Conference: October 24-27, 1941 (Bull, *38*, 780)
Lecture: Olsen, W., Detroit conference (Bull, *39*, 269)

Nurse Testing Division
Potts, E., Psychological Corporation (J App, *23*, 421)

Nutrition
Publication: Mitchell, D. (J App, *3*, 196)

Research: Emerson, W. R. P. (J APP, *3*, 196)
Research: relation to pathological disturbances in behavior (BULL, *38*, 304)

Nutrition Laboratory of Carnegie Institution
Appointment: Dodge, R. (SCI, *36*, 591)
Equips experimental psychology laboratory (SCI, *36*, 591)

Nuttall, George H. F.
Appointment: Johns Hopkins Univ. (SCI°, *17*, 339)

Nygard, John Wallace
Death notice (BULL, *42*, 484)

Nyswander, Dorothy Bird
Appointment: War Public Service Projects of Federal Works Agency (BULL, *39*, 895)

O

Oberlin College (Ohio)
Appointment: Danner, W. E. (BULL, 42, 63)
Appointment: Dashiell, J. F. (BULL, 14, 333)
Appointment: Fitch, F. (BULL, 1, 488)
Appointment: Jones, E. S. (BULL, 14, 366)
Appointment: McLennan, S. F. (REV, 5, 109; REV, 7, 323; SCI, 6, 446; AJP, 9, 135)
Appointment: Nichol, C. C. W. (BULL, 14, 366)
Appointment: Stetson, R. H. (BULL, 6, 328)
Appointment: Wells, G. R. (BULL, 9, 360; SCI, 36, 115; JOP, 9, 476)
Course: Henderson, H. (JOP, 9, 224)
Departure: Wells, G. (SCI, 45, 431)
Endowment: library for eugenics books (SCI, 35, 817)
Promotion: Weaver, H. E. (BULL, 42, 583)
Promotion: Wells, G. R. (BULL, 11, 116, 482; SCI, 40, 519; JOP, 11, 196, 672)

Oberly, Henry Sherman
Publication: EPA, 9th annual meeting (AJP, 51, 577)

Objectivity (see Absolute objectivity)

Obourne, Constance
Rochester Guidance Clinic, NY, mental hygiene (BULL, 36, 841)

Observer
Publication: Nafe, J. P., trained (AJP, 41, 161)
Lecture: Bentley, M., subject argument (AJP, 41, 682)

Occult
Lecture: Jastrow, J., Clark Univ. (SCI, 57, 173)

Occupational Analysis and Manning Tables of the War Manpower Commission, Division of

Program: *Occupations: the Vocational Guidance Magazine*, 1944 (J APP, *28*, 351)

Occupational Index

Publication: review of military occupations (J APP, *26*, 858)

Occupational Index Inc., New York University

Publication: *Best Books of Nineteen Forty-one on Occupational Information, Guidance and Personnel administration* (J APP, *26*, 392)

Occupational psychology

Celebration, 10 year issue of *Occupations, The Vocational Guidance Magazine*, 1944 (J APP, *28*, 351)

Plan announced, Williamson, E. G., occupational rehabilitation of soldiers (J APP, *27*, 207)

Publication: selection of personnel (J APP, *27*, 207)

U.S. Civil Service Commisssion accepting applications for occupational therapy (BULL, *38*, 126-127)

O'Connor, Johnson

Grant: Social Science Research Council (BULL, *31*, 380)

Odbert, Henry Sebastian

Award: Social Science Research Council (BULL, *39*, 683)

Odegard, Peter H.

Appointment: Institute for Propaganda Analysis, Director (J APP, *25*, 597)

Odom, Charles Leonard

Appointment: Tulane Univ. (BULL, *42*, 486)

Odor (*see also* Smell)

Lecture: Boring, E. G., classification of (AJP, *40*, 345)

Office of Education (*see* United States Office of Education)

Office of Psychological Personnel

Appointment: Marquis, D. G., director (BULL, *40*, 618; SCI, *98*, 215)

Appointment: Morgan, J. D. (SCI, *98*, 215)

Appropriation: APA to National Research Council for support of (SCI, *98*, 470; J APP, *27*, 473)

Continued by APA (SCI, *96*, 294)

Departure: Britt, S. H. (BULL, *40*, 540; SCI, *98*, 215)

Establishment: by APA (SCI, *95*, 527-528)

Office of Scientific Research and Development
Institute established to carry on wartime work by Committee on Post-war Research of the War Production Board (Sci, *100*, 246)

Office of the Medical Division of the Office of Civilian Defense
Appointment: Vogel, V. H. (Sci, *96*, 11)

Ogburn, William Fielding
Stanford Education Conference, 1938 (J App, *22*, 108)

Ogden, Robert Morris
Appointment: AAAS (Bull, *10*, 424)
Appointment: Cornell Univ. (Sci, *90*, 34; Bull, *36*, 804; Bull, *13*, 407; JoP, *13*, 308)
Appointment: Harvard Univ. (Bull, *20*, 288, 416)
Appointment: Univ. of Kansas (Bull, *11*, 352; JoP, *11*, 560)
Conference: New School for Social Research, methods in philosophy and the sciences (JoP, *34*, 560)
Course: Peabody College for Teachers (Bull, *12*, 403)
Course: train psychological examiners (Bull, *14*, 365)
Departure: Univ. of Kansas (JoP, *13*, 504)
Departure: Univ. of Tennessee (Bull, *11*, 352)
Election: APA officer (JoP, *11*, 56; Bull, *8*, 32; Sci, *39*, 94; Bull, *13*, 40)
Election: SSPP, president (Bull, *9*, 40)
Election: SSPP, sec.-treas. (JoP, *7*, 56; JoP, *8*, 84; Sci, *31*, 22)
Lecture: Gestalt psychology and behaviorism (AJP, *45*, 151)
Lecture: insight (AJP, *44*, 350)
Lecture: International Congress of Psychology, 6th (Sci, *30*, 202)
Lecture: memory (JoP, *1*, 224)
Lecture: sociology and Gestalt psychology (AJP, *46*, 655)
Lecture: SSPP; experiments on the thought process (JoP, *7*, 28)
Lecture: Univ. of Tennessee (Bull, *15*, 176)
Promotion: Univ. of Tennessee (Bull, *7*, 148; JoP, *7*, 224; Sci, *31*, 500)
Publication: lost (JoP, *5*, 168; Bull, *5*, 96)
Resignation: *Psychological Bulletin* (Bull, *26*, 56)
Resignation: Univ. of Tennessee (JoP, *11*, 560)

Ohio Academy of Science
Election: Fields, P. E., vice-president, psychology (J App, *25*, 128)
Meeting (Bull, *18*, 568; J App, *16*, 695)
Radio talks (J App, *16*, 695)

Ohio Association for Applied Psychology
Meeting: 1942 (J App, *26*, 392)

Ohio Bureau of Juvenile Research
Appointment: Goddard, H. H. (J App, *2*, 293)
Establishment: Board of Administration (J App, *2*, 293)

Ohio Child Study Institute
Appointment: Miller, J. (BULL, *41*, 498)

Ohio College Association
Establishment: separate section of psychology (BULL, *26*, 624)
Election: officers (BULL, *26*, 624; BULL, *27*, 415)
Lecture: modern psychology and the aesthetics experience (JoP, *35*, 140)

Ohio Community Service Society
Children's Service Bureau open (J APP, *3*, 289)

Ohio State Institution Journal, The
Publication: Ohio Board of Administration (J APP, *2*, 293)

Ohio State University (Columbus, Ohio)
Anniversary: Arps, G. F., dinner (SCI, *72*, 165)
Appointment: announced, psychology dept. (SCI, *56*, 387)
Appointment: Arps, G. F. (BULL, *9*, 407; JoP, *9*, 560)
Appointment: Bates, M. (BULL, *20*, 172)
Appointment: Biel, W. C. (BULL, *34*, 499; J APP, *21*, 474)
Appointment: Burtt, H. E. (SCI, *91*, 499; SCI, *88*, 254)
Appointment: English, H. B. (SCI, *74*, 453; BULL, *27*, 564; SCI, *71*, 556)
Appointment: Evans, J. E. (BULL, *11*, 482)
Appointment: Goddard, H. H. (JoP, *19*, 588; BULL, *20*, 60, 172; SCI, *56*, 279)
Appointment: Jensen, K. (BULL, *27*, 736)
Appointment: Leighton, J. A. (JoP, *7*, 476)
Appointment: Loutitt, C. M. (SCI, *102*, 643)
Appointment: Mudge, E. L. (BULL, *13*, 482; JoP, *14*, 56)
Appointment: Shartle, C. L. (BULL, *42*, 127)
Appointment: Spearman, C. (BULL, *28*, 411)
Appointment: Weiss, A. P. (BULL, *9*, 408; JoP, *9*, 616)
Appointment: Williams, R. D. (BULL, *20*, 172)
Appointment: Zigler, M. J. (BULL, *23*, 176)
Conference: Educational production of motion pictures, 1938 (BULL, *36*, 140)
Conference: Human development in war time, 1942 (J APP, *26*, 389)
Conference: Visual problems, 1941 (SCI, *94*, 136)
Course: Program in personnel relations announced (BULL, *42*, 488)
Death: Scott, W. H., obituary (JoP, *34*, 83)
Degree: Goddard, H. H. (SCI, *97*, 505-506)
Departure: Hadley, L. S. (BULL, *42*, 407)
Departure: LaBrant, L. L. (BULL, *39*, 681)
Departure: Valentine, W. L. (SCI, *92*, 169)
Departure: Wissler, C. (REV, *6*, 673)
Leave of absence: Edgerton, H. (BULL, *32*, 323)
Leave of absence: Haines, T. H. (BULL, *9*, 440; JoP, *9*, 700)
Lecture: Jastrow, J., human nature (SCI, *45*, 407; JoP, *14*, 364)
Lecture: Loewi, O. (SCI, *97*, 398)

Lecture: Münsterberg, H. (JoP, *7*, 112; Sci, *31*, 187)
Meeting: AAAP, 1938 (JoP, *35*, 280)
Meeting: Ohio Assoc. for Applied Psychology, 1942 (J App, *26*, 392)
Meeting: Psychometric Society, 1938 (JoP, *35*, 280)
Meeting: SPSSI, 1938 (JoP, *35*, 280)
Organization: Alpha Psi Delta Psychological Fraternity Chapter (Bull, *19*, 586)
Promotion: announced, psych. dept. (Sci, *56*, 387)
Promotion: Burtt, H. E. (Bull, *20*, 172)
Promotion: Davies, A. E. (JoP, *5*, 336; Bull, *5*, 244)
Promotion: Haines, T. H. (Sci, *14*, 504; JoP, *5*, 336; Bull, *5*, 244)
Promotion: Rogers, A. S. (Bull, *20*, 172)
Radio broadcasts, legal psych. (Bull, *32*, 323)
Research: Coy, G. L., gifted children (J App, *1*, 298-299)
Resignation: Gaw, E. A. (Bull, *41*, 267)
Retirement: Charters, W. W., Bureau of Educational Research (Sci, *95*, 271)
Retirement: Scott, W. H. (JoP, *7*, 476)

Ohio University (Athens)

Appointment: Allin, A. (Rev, *3*, 468; Sci, *3*, 900)
Appointment: Anderson, A. C., head of committee to honor Porter, J. P. (Sci, *98*, 382)
Appointment: Beck, L. F. (J App, *20*, 421)
Appointment: Fenton, N. (J App, *10*, 287)
Appointment: Gentry, J. R. (Sci, *101*, 112; J App, *8*, 451)
Appointment: Lehman, H. (J App, *11*, 405)
Appointment: Mira, E. (J App, *13*, 193)
Appointment: Paulsen, G. B. (Sci, *101*, 112)
Appointment: Scott, T. C. (Sci, *101*, 112)
Appointment: Stoke, S. (J App, *11*, 405)
Appointment: Worcester, D. A. (J App, *10*, 288)
Departure: Carrothers, G. E. (J App, *10*, 288)
Establishment: Porter, J. P. loan fund in psychology (Bull, *40*, 618; J App, *27*, 475; Sci, *98*, 382)
Promotion: Gentry, J. R. (Bull, *42*, 255)
Promotion: Paulson, G. B. (Bull, *42*, 255)
Promotion: Scott, T. C. (Bull, *42*, 255)
Research: Tausch, E., questionnaire on theology (JoP, *2*, 364)
Retirement: Porter, J. P. (Sci, *98*, 382)

Ohio Wesleyan University (Delaware, Ohio)

Appointment: Fearing, F. (J App, *10*, 394, 523)
Appointment: Fields, P. A. (Sci, *84*, 504; Bull, *34*, 121)
Appointment: Thompson, L. A. (J App, *11*, 404; Sci, *77*, 304)
Appointment: Valentine, W. (J App, *10*, 523)
Appointment: Wells, G. R. (JoP, *14*, 308; Bull, *14*, 143, 264; Bull, *15*, 24; Sci, *45*, 431)
Departure: Fearing, F. (J App, *11*, 404)

Ohmann, Oliver Arthur
Appointment: Personnel Research Institute, Western Reserve Univ. (Sci, *94*, 208)
Appointment: Western Reserve Univ. (J App, *10*, 396)

Oklahoma Central State College (Edmond)
Leave of absence: Beck, R. L. (Bull, *41*, 409)

Oklahoma, University of (Norman, Oklahoma)
Appointment: Hoisington, L. B. (Bull, *25*, 700)
Appointment: Wilson, M. O. (Sci, *95*, 322; Bull, *39*, 423)
Departure: Woodrow, H. (Bull, *25*, 444)
Lecture: Meltzer, H., Guidance Institute (J App, *21*, 719)
Meeting: Guidance Institute (J App, *21*, 719)
Promotion: Hoisington, L. B. (Sci, *95*, 322)
Promotion: Wilson, M. O. (Bull, *24*, 380)

Oliver, James Edward
Obituary (AJP, 7, 152)

Olson, Willard Clifford
Election: APA secretary (J App, *22*, 443)
Fellowship: Board of National Research (Bull, *23*, 292)
Lecture: National Assoc. for Nursery Education, "Making the findings of research useful" (Bull, *39*, 269)

Omwake, Louise
Appointment: AAAP, Committee on Psychology in Junior Colleges, Chair (J App, *25*, 361; Bull, *38*, 779)

Ontology
Lecture: Ladd, G. T., Columbia Univ., problems in psychology (Sci, *33*, 214)

Open Court, The
Publication: Binet, M. A., "Sensation and the outer world" (Sci°, *13*, 217)
Publication: Müller, M. M. (Sci°, *9*, 584)

Open Court Publishing Company
Publication: Portraits of Psychologists (Rev, 5, 111, 450)

Operationism
Publication: Boring, E. G., "Temporal perception and operationism" (AJP, *48*, 519)
Publication: Stevens, S. S., "The operational basis of psychology" (AJP, *47*, 323)

Oppenheim, Nathan
Death notice (Bull, *13*, 188)

Optical Geometry of Emmert's Law
Discussion: Boring, E. G. (AJP, *53*, 293-295)

Optical illusions (*see also* Illusions)
  Discovery: Johnson, D. M. (AJP, *56*, 604-607)
  Lecture: Stadelmann, H. (AJP, *11*, 279)
  Publication: Chou, S. K., "An optical illusion of personal magnetism" (AJP, *51*, 574)
  Publication: Feldman, S., "The magnetic eye illusion" (AJP, *51*, 575)
  Publication: Hartson, L. D., "Real movements, apparent movements, and perception" (AJP, *49*, 121)
  Research: Charpentier, A. (SCI°, *7*, 548)

Orange Park, Florida Anthropoid Station (*see* Anthropoid Station)

Orbeli, Leon Abgarovich
  Appointment: Pavlov's laboratories, director (SCI, *84*, 482)
  Appointment: Permanent International Committee of the Physiological Congresses (SCI, *84*, 482)
  Research: Autonomic Nervous System (SCI, *70*, 499)
  Research: Conditioned reflexes (SCI, *70*, 402)

Orbison, William Dillard
  Appointment: Univ. of Connecticut (BULL, *12*, 63)

Orcutt, Anna Clippinger
  Appointment: Illinois Institute of Technology (BULL, *12*, 793)

Ordahl, George
  Appointment: Sonoma State Home (JOP, *13*, 448)
  Connection with the Buckel Foundation, Stanford (JOP, *13*, 448)

Order of Merit (Chile)
  Award: Gotaas, H. B. (SCI, *101*, 663)

Oregon Academy of Sciences
  Election: officers, 1945 (SCI, *101*, 34-35, 268)

Oregon Psychological Association
  Meeting: 2nd annual (SCI, *85*, 518; BULL, *34*, 410)

Oregon, Psychologists of the State of
  Meeting: founding (SCI, *83*, 323)

Oregon State System of Higher Education
  Appointment: Caldwell, V. V., dean of general extension division (BULL, *37*, 827)

Oregon State University (Corvallis, Oregon)
  Lecture: Kirkpatrick, E. A. (JOP, *13*, 476)

Oregon, University of (Eugene, Oregon)
Appointment: Conklin, E. S. (BULL, 20, 60)
Appointment: Young, K. (BULL, 20, 664)
Establishment: Clinic for atypical children (J APP, 21, 242)
Establishment: psychology lab (SCI, 41, 323; BULL, 12, 128; AJP, 37, 155; JoP, 12, 168)
Meeting: Psychologists of the State of Oregon, officers elected (SCI, 83, 323; BULL, 33, 406)
Promotion: Wheeler, R. H. (SCI, 46, 288)
Publication: notice Oregon Bulletin, University of (J APP, 3, 198)
Return: Wheeler, R. H. (SCI, 49, 145; BULL, 16, 222)
Return: Young, K. (SCI, 57, 556)

Origin of Species by Means of Natural Selection, The
Publication: Darwin, C. (SCI°, 12, 58)

Orthogenic Clinic
Appointment: Town, C. H. (BULL, 13, 407)

Orton, Edward
Memorial exercises (SCI, 10, 862)

Orton, Samuel Torrey
Lecture: New York Acad. of Medicine (SCI, 83, 389)

Osborn, Henry Fairfield
Lecture: International Congress of Eugenics (SCI, 76, 141)

O'Shea, Michael Vincent
Editor: Psychological Bulletin (BULL, 6, 152)
Leave of absence: Univ. of Wisconsin (BULL, 3, 148)
Lecture: ethics (JoP, 2, 280)

Oshkosh Normal School (Oshkosh, Wisconsin)
Appointment: Sherman, F. D. (AJP, 9, 135; REV, 4, 567; SCI, 6, 169)
Death: Quantz, J. O. (SCI, 17, 238-239)
Departure: Hill, A. R. (AJP, 9, 135; REV, 4, 567)

Osiris
Printing (JoP, 38, 140)

Osler Memorial Award
Douglas, C. G., Oxford Univ. (SCI, 102, 114)

Osler, William
Lecture: Cavendish Lecture (SCI, 9, 268)
Appointment: Johns Hopkins Univ. (SCI, 12, 215; SCI, 11, 439)

Ostend (Belgium)
  Hygiene exhibition, 1888 (SCI°, *12*, 9)

Ostwald, Wilhelm
  Appointment: Columbia Univ. (BULL, *3*, 36; JOP, *2*, 721)
  Election: Copenhagen Acad. of Sciences, honorary member (SCI, *23*, 861)
  Election: Danish Acad. of Sciences (JOP, *3*, 308; SCI, *23*, 758)
  Lecture: Columbia Univ. (SCI, *23*, 198; JOP, *3*, 112)
  Retirement: Univ. of Leipzig (SCI, *23*, 862)

Otis, Arthur Sinton
  Appointment: Office of the Surgeon General (J APP, *1*, 395; BULL, *14*, 334)
  Appointment: Training School of Vineland, N.J. (BULL, *14*, 366)
  Publication: *Manual of Directions for Administering the Otis Group Intelligence Scale, A Point Scale* (J APP, *3*, 194)
  Publication: mental ability tests (J APP, *20*, 791)
  Publication: *Normal Percentile Chart* (J APP, *22*, 54)

Otis Group Intelligence Scale
  Manual for administering (J APP, *3*, 194)

Otis, Jay Lester
  Appointment: Personnel Research Institute, Western Reserve Univ. (SCI, *94*, 208)

Ottolenghi, Salvatore
  Research: senses of criminals (SCI°, *14*, 297)

Outhwaite, Leonard
  Editor: *Journal of Personnel Research* (BULL, *19*, 462)

Outline of Psychology
  Publication: announced, 2nd ed. (AJP, *8*, 430)
  Publication: Wundt, W. (AJP, *7*, 452)

Overholser, Winfred
  Appointment: Boston Univ. Medical School (SCI, *62*, 371)
  Degree: Boston Univ. (SCI, *92*, 8)

Overstreet, Harry Allen
  Retirement: Columbia Univ. (SCI, *91*, 236)

Owen, Roberts Bishop
  Appointment: Division of Psychological Tests, Sanitary Corps (JOP, *15*, 168, 364)
  Commission: Sanitary Corps (JOP, *15*, 364)

Owens College (Manchester, England)
  Alexander, S. accepts chair (REV, *1*, 112)

Departure: Adamson, R. (REV, *1*, 112)
Lecture: Romanes, G. J., dawn of the mind, 1884 (SCI°, *3*, 639-640)

Oxford University (England) (*see also* Nuffield Institute)
Appointment: Baldwin, J. M., Herbert Spencer Lecturer (BULL, *12*, 204)
Appointment: Boutroux, M. E. (JoP, *14*, 588)
Appointment: Brown, N., Inst. of Experimental Psychology (SCI, *83*, 349)
Appointment: Delacroix, H., Zaharoff Lecturer (BULL, *23*, 176; SCI, *63*, 66)
Appointment: Galton, F. (JoP, *4*, 308)
Appointment: McDougall, W. (BULL, *1*, 29; JoP, *1*, 28)
Appointment: Morgan, L., Herbert Spencer Lecturer (BULL, *10*, 164)
Appointment: Stephenson, W., Inst. of Experimental Psychology (SCI, *84*, 81)
Appointment: Stout, G. F. (REV, *6*, 239)
Award: Douglas, C. G., Osler Memorial Award (SCI, *102*, 114)
Death notice: Romanes, G. J. (REV, *1*, 440)
Degree: Baldwin, J. M. (REV, *7*, 427)
Degree: James, W. (SCI, *27*, 869)
Degree: Jung, C. G. (SCI, *88*, 52, 211; BULL, *35*, 578)
Degree: Royce, J. (JoP, *10*, 195-196)
Degree: Ward, J. (JoP, *5*, 476; BULL, *5*, 316)
Departure: Stout, G. F. (SCI, *17*, 680)
Election: Case, T. (JoP, *1*, 56)
Election: Love, A. E. H. (SCI, *20*, 856)
Endowment: Wilde, H. (REV, *5*, 450)
Establishment of experimental psychology department (REV, *10*, 223-224)
Fellowship: Herbert Spencer (JoP, *2*, 196)
Grant: Institute of Experimental Psychology, founding gift and Rockefeller
   grant (SCI, *83*, 349, 433; BULL, *33*, 578)
Grant: Rockefeller Foundation, Guttmann, E. (SCI, *94*, 111)
Lecture: Baldwin, J. M., Herbert Spencer Lecture (JoP, *12*, 721)
Lecture: Boutroux, E., Herbert Spencer Lecture, thought and action (JoP, *15*,
   28)
Lecture: Harrison, F., Herbert Spencer Lecture (JoP, *2*, 196)
Lecture: in honor of Spencer, H. (JoP, *1*, 56)
Lecture: Myers, C. S., Herbert Spencer Lecture (SCI, *69*, 570)
Lecture: subjects announced, 1887 (SCI°, *9*, 53)
Meeting: British Medical Assoc. (JoP, *1*, 420)
Meeting: International Congress of Psychology (JoP, *20*, 336)
Meeting: International Medical Congress (SCI, *88*, 212)
Physiology success (SCI°, *5*, 283)
Statue of Darwin, C. (SCI, *4*, 915; SCI, *9*, 917)

P

Pace, Edward Aloyius
  Appointment: Catholic Univ., Director of the Institute of Psychology (Sci, *16*, 680)
  Election: International Congress of Arts and Sciences, St. Louis, chair (JoP, *1*, 420)
  Lecture: analysis (JoP, *2*, 56)
  Lecture: influence of Locke, J. (JoP, *1*, 672)

Pacific International Exposition, Panama
  Meeting: AAAS (JoP, *11*, 720)

Page, Irvine H.
  Lecture: Janeway, E. G., hypertension (Sci, *93*, 37-38)

Pain
  Lecture: relation to emotive conditions (AJP, *58*, 392-394)
  Lecture: variations in the strength of the stimuli (AJP, *55*, 275-276)
  Publication: Marshall, H. R., *Pain, Pleasure, and Aesthetics* (Sci°, *22*, 335; Sci°, *23*, 96)

Painter, George Stephen
  Appointment: New York State Normal College, Albany (Sci, *36*, 593)

Painter, William Issac
  Appointment: Univ. of Akron (Bull, *42*, 792)

Pall Mall Gazette
  Publication: instinct in a dog (Sci°, *17*, 200)

Pallister, Helen
  Publication: Book reviews in psychological periodicals (AJP, *46*, 511)

Palmer, Alice Freeman Fellowship
Award: Cook, H. D., $1000.00 (SCI, *25*, 520; SCI, *26*, 32)

Palmer, Courtlandt
Death notice (SCI°, *12*, 48)

Palmer, George Herbert
Appointment: Yale Univ. (JoP, *3*, 196)
Course: Yale Univ. (BULL, *3*, 147)
Degree: Harvard Univ. (JoP, *3*, 420)
Lecture: Univ. of California (JoP, *14*, 364)
Lecture: Univ. of Kansas (JoP, *4*, 112; BULL, *4*, 95)

Pan American Scientific Congress
Meeting: Washington (BULL, *12*, 364)

Panama, Pacific International Exposition
Meeting: AAAS (JoP, *11*, 720)

Panzer College of Physical Education
Appointment: Greenawalt, E. G. (BULL, *42*, 792)

Paper Chemistry, Institute of
Appointment: Todd, J. E. (BULL, *39*, 681)

Paralytic disorder
Publication: Starr, M. A. (AJP, *1*, 199)

Parapsychology (*see also* Psychical research)
Fellowship: American Society for Psychial Research (BULL, *39*, 71)

Parents
Lecture: Willoughby, R. R., intelligence and fertility (AJP, *40*, 671)
Parent education (J APP, *19*, 742)

Paris Academy of Medicine
Appointment: Raymond, F. (SCI, *10*, 30)

Paris Academy of Moral Sciences
Election: Ribot, Th. (SCI, *11*, 197; REV, *7*, 216)

Paris Academy of Sciences
Appointment: Dahamel, G. (SCI, *101*, 196)

Paris Anthropological Society
Organization: conference to discuss Darwin's evolution (SCI°, *2*, 91)

Paris Exhibition
Plans (SCI°, *13*, 280)

Progress (Sci°, *12*, 57-58)
Publication: official circular, congresses and conferences (Sci°, *13*, 381)

Paris Faculty of Medicine
Appointment: Claude, H. (Sci, *55*, 316)

Paris Institute of Psychology
Course: list of offerings (JoP, *17*, 616)
Election: council members (Bull, *17*, 351-352)
Election: Lachelier, J. (Rev, *3*, 355)
Election: Wundt, W. (Rev, *3*, 355)
Establishment: Univ. of Paris (Bull, *17*, 351-352; JoP, *17*, 616; AJP, *32*, 304; Sci, *52*, 361)
Governing board listed (JoP, *17*, 616)
Institute of psychology proposed (Bull, *3*, 248; JoP, *3*, 364)

Paris Neurological Society
Research fund established (Bull, *17*, 116)

Paris Palace of Industry
Exhibition: hygiene, July, 1888 (Sci°, *12*, 9)

Paris Society of Hypnotism and Psychology
Meeting: 7th annual announced (Sci, *6*, 127)
Proposed congress in 1900 in Paris (Sci, *4*, 755)

Paris, University of (*see* Paris Institute of Psychology)
Appointment: Marie, P. (Bull, *14*, 192)
Course: Institute of Psychology, list of offerings (JoP, *17*, 616)
Death notice: Binet, A. (Sci, *34*, 558)
Degree: Dewey, J. (Sci, *72*, 497)
Establishment: Institute of Psychology (Sci, *52*, 361; Bull, *17*, 351-352; JoP, *17*, 616)
Nomination: Angell, J. R., lecturer at the Sorbonne (JoP, *11*, 448)
Nomination: Janet, P., lecturer (Sci, *8*, 707)

Park College (Kansas City, Missouri)
Appointment: Bell, E. (Bull, *40*, 723)
Degree: McFarland, R. A. (Bull, *39*, 682)

Parkes Museum of Hygiene
Opening May 26, 1883 (Sci°, *1*, 588)

Parks, Marvin McTyoire
Appointment: Georgia Normal College (JoP, *1*, 616)

Parmenter, Richard
Appointment: Cornell Univ. (Sci, *92*, 283)

Parry, Douglas Farlow
Appointment: Southern Illinois Normal Univ., Bureau of Child Guidance
(BULL, *40*, 310, 723; SCI, *98*, 239)

Parsons College (Fairfield, Iowa)
Appointment: Hancock, J. W. (SCI, *92*, 450)

Parsons, John Herbert
Research: disinfection by heat (SCI°, *7*, 165)

Parsons, Ralph Lyman
Publication: monomania (AJP, *1*, 199)

Partridge, Ernest DeAlton
AAAP Committee, *Psychology as an occupation* (J APP, *22*, 311)

Paschal, Franklin Cressey
Appointment: Vanderbilt Univ. (SCI, *70*, 191)
Resignation: Vanderbilt Univ. (BULL, *41*, 679)

Pasteur Lecture
Strecker, E. A. (SCI, *100*, 263, 311)

Paterson, Donald Gildersleeve
Appointment: National Research Council, Division of Anthropology and
Psychology (SCI, *86*, 438)
Election: APA secretary (J APP, *21*, 243)
Election: Sigma Xi president (SCI, *76*, 31)
Publication: APA annual reports (AJP, *45*, 174; AJP, *46*, 151; AJP, *47*, 168; AJP,
48, 174; AJP, *49*, 142; AJP, *51*, 174)
Publication: eye-movement in reading different color combinations of print and
background (AJP, 57, 93- 94)
Symposium: Univ. of Minnesota, "measurement of man" (SCI, *72*, 88)

Pathological behavior
Lecture: Wells, F. L., Harvard Univ. (JoP, *10*, 336)
Research: relation of nutrition to pathology of behavior (BULL, *38*, 304)

Pathological Institute (Wards Island, New York)
Course: feeble-minded and psychopathic children (JoP, *6*, 111)

Paton, Herbert James
Degree: Univ. of Glasgow (SCI, *90*, 134)

Patrick, George Thomas White
Leave of absence (JoP, *2*, 252)
Leave of absence: Iowa State Univ. (SCI, *21*, 640)
Spending the year in Germany (SCI, *16*, 958)

Patten, Clarence A.
Election: Assoc. for Research in Nervous and Mental Diseases (SCI, 79, 9)

Patterson, E. J.
Lecture: National Institute of Industrial Psychology (SCI, 83, 301)

Pattie, Frank Acklen, Jr.
Publication: Galton whistle (AJP, 35, 308)
Publication: Psychological journals (AJP, 46, 149)

Patton, Francis Landey
Election: President, Princeton Theological Seminary (REV, 9, 644)
Summering abroad (REV, 6, 456)

Patton, George S.
Appointment: Princeton Univ. (REV, 9, 644; SCI, 16, 480)

Patton, Leslie K.
Appointment: USO (BULL, 41, 679)
Departure: Coe College (BULL, 41, 679)

Patton, Robert A.
Research: nutritional state in relation to pathological disturbances in behavior
  (BULL, 38, 304)

Paulsen, Friedrich
Death notice (BULL, 5, 348; JoP, 5, 504)
Exchange professor, Harvard Univ. (JoP, 2, 140)
Promotion: announced (REV, 1, 336)

Paulsen, Gaige Brue
Appointment: Ohio Univ. (SCI, 101, 112)
Promotion: Ohio Univ. (BULL, 42, 255)

Pavlicek, George
Lecture: paradoxical warmth perception (AJP, 45, 350)

Pavlov, Ivan Petrovitch
Appropriation: Soviet Government for building biological stations (SCI, 74, 481)
Award: Halle Univ., digestion research, gold medal (SCI, 17, 518, 597)
Birthday (SCI, 60, 264; SCI, 70, 138; SCI, 76, 230; SCI, 80, 309; SCI, 82, 122)
Death notice (SCI, 43, 273; BULL, 13, 148, 228)
Departure: United States (SCI, 70, 138, 351)
Election: International Congress of Physiology (SCI, 82, 122)
Lab equipment, new (SCI, 62, 395)
Lecture: Charing-Cross Hospital Medical School, Huxley Lecture (SCI, 24, 381)
Lecture: International Congress of Psychology, Copenhagen (BULL, 29, 604)
Lecture: International Physiological Congress, 9th (SCI, 82, 150)

Meeting: International Congress of Psychology (SCI, 76, 230)
Meeting: International Neurological Congress, 1935 (SCI, 82, 122)
Meeting: Royal Medico-Psychological Assoc. (SCI, 70, 162)
Scholarships (SCI, 80, 309)
Trip to Paris (SCI, 62, 507)

Pavlov, Ivan Petrovitch Prize
Award: Beritashvili, I. S. (SCI, 89, 124)
Award: Petrova, M. (SCI, 92, 450)

Payne, Bruce Ryburn
Appointment: George Peabody College for Teachers (JoP, 8, 308; BULL, 8, 222)
Election: SSPP, council member (SCI, 31, 22; JoP, 7, 56; JoP, 8, 84)

Paynter, Richard Henry
Appointment: Univ. of Pennsylvania (BULL, 23, 60; SCI, 62, 371)
Election: AAAP, consulting section chair (J APP, 21, 603, 713)
Meeting: AAAP (BULL, 34, 865)

Peabody, Francis Greenwood
Exchange professor to Berlin Univ. (JoP, 2, 140)

Peabody, George College for Teachers (Nashville, Tennessee)
(*see also* Jesup Psychological Laboratory)
Appointment: Boynton, P. L. (SCI, 72, 315)
Appointment: Munn, N. L. (SCI, 83, 99; BULL, 33, 477)
Appointment: Payne, B. (JoP, 8, 308; BULL, 8, 222)
Appointment: Peterson, J. (SCI, 48, 444; BULL, 15, 360)
Appointment: Rose, W. (JoP, 1, 588)
Appointment: Spearman, C. E. (BULL, 29, 91)
Appointment: Strong, E. K. (JoP, 11, 308; SCI, 39, 325; BULL, 11, 116)
Course: Morse, J. (BULL, 12, 403)
Course: Ogden, R. M. (BULL, 12, 403)
Departure: Boynton, P. (BULL, 39, 681)
Departure: Hill, D. S. (BULL, 8, 374)
Departure: Munn, N. L. (SCI, 87, 342)
Donation: Cuyler, E. and Thomas, ? (BULL, 12, 364)
Laboratory built (SCI, 40, 344; BULL, 11, 443)
Laboratory donation to equip Jesup psychology lab (JoP, 12, 504)

Peabody Institute (Baltimore, Maryland)
Lecture: Martin, H. N., minds of animals (SCI°, 2, 782)

Peak, Helen
Fellowship: Yale Univ., Sterling (BULL, 29, 460)

Pear, Tom Hatherly
Appointment: Univ. of Durham, Riddell Memorial Lecturer (SCI, 83, 619)

Pearce, Haywood Jefferson
Election: SSPP, council member (SCI, *31*, 22; JOP, *8*, 84; JOP, *7*, 56)
Election: SSPP, vice-president (BULL, *9*, 40)
Lecture: perception (JOP, *2*, 56)

Pearson, B. Jarne
Appointment: Univ. of Vermont (SCI, *101*, 60)

Pearson, Francena Leah
Appointment: Wichita Child Guidance Center (BULL, *42*, 582)

Pearson, Karl
Appointment: Francis Galton Laboratory for National Eugenics (SCI, *77*, 16)
Appointment: Univ. College, London (SCI°, *4*, 75)
Appointment: Univ. of London (JOP, *8*, 476; SCI, *34*, 150)
Award: Rudolf-Virchow Medal (SCI, *77*, 16)
Degree: Univ. of London (SCI, *80*, 612)
Election: honorary fellow (JOP, *1*, 56)
Election: Royal Society, fellow (SCI, *80*, 92)
Lecture: character reading from external signs (SCI, *17*, 160)
Lecture: Congress of the Royal Sanitary Institute (SCI, *36*, 113)
Lecture: Univ. College, London, eugenics (SCI, *37*, 174)
Publication: *Biometrica* proposed (REV, *8*, 223)
Publication: book (SCI, *5*, 513)
Publication: Galton memoir (SCI, *34*, 755)
Publication: *Grammar of Science*, 3rd ed. (JOP, *8*, 476)
Publication: *Nature*, about him (JOP, *3*, 84)
Research: eugenics (BULL, *4*, 128)
Retirement dinner (SCI, *79*, 426)
Retirement: Univ. of London, emeritus (SCI, *79*, 30)

Pearson's formula
Award: best paper on (JOP, *11*, 27-28)
Lecture: Thomson, G. T. (JOP, *17*, 140)

Peatman, John Gray
Promotion: City College, New York (BULL, *41*, 679; BULL, *40*, 152)

Pechstein, Louis Augustus
Appointment: Univ. of Cincinnati Teachers College (BULL, *20*, 172; SCI, *56*, 387)
Appointment: Univ. of Rochester (BULL, *15*, 98; SCI, *46*, 482; BULL, *14*, 420)

Peckham, Grace
Publication: a critical digest of the proceedings of the English Psychical Society
(SCI°, *6*, 360)

Pedagogical Seminary and Journal of Genetic Psychology
Publication: *Genetic Psychology Monographs* (JOP, *22*, 700)

Pedagogy

Establishment: dept., Univ. of Pennsylvania (Sci°, *14*, 26)
Establishment: professorship, Univ. of Halle (JoP, *10*, 616)
Lecture: Butler, N. M., Columbia College (Sci°, *8*, 585)
Library: Draper, A.S. is building in Albany (Sci°, *9*, 155)
Publication: Bennett, C. W. (Sci°, *22*, 254)
Publication: *Rivista di peadgogia e scienze affine* (Rev, *1*, 336)

Pedology, International Congress of

Meeting: Brussels (Bull, *8*, 333)

Peiffer, Herbert Claire, Jr.

Appointment: San Diego State College (Bull, *40*, 383)

Peirce, Charles Santiago Sanders

Lecture: NAS, biography (Sci°, *3*, 524)
Lecture: NAS, minimum differences of sensibility (Sci°, *4*, 408)
Lecture: NAS, with Jastrow, J., perceptible differences in sensation (Sci°, *3*, 524)
Lecture: Young, F. H., biographical (JoP, *42*, 672)
Meeting: Pike County Historical Society of Milford, Pennsylvania (JoP, *42*, 672)

Peking, University of (China)

Dewey, J. accepts a request for an additional year stay (JoP, *17*, 364)

Peli, Giuseppe

Research: cephalometry (AJP, *1*, 205)

Pencharz, Dorothy

Election: Psychologists Club of San Francisco, vice-president (J App, *25*, 129)

Pendulum

Lecture: Scott, W. D. (JoP, *2*, 280)

Penfield, Wilder

Election: Assoc. for Research in Nervous and Mental Diseases, president (Sci, *85*, 42)

Pennington, Leon Alfred

Appointment: Univ. of Illinois (Bull, *35*, 796)
Course: Univ. of Illinois, military psychology (J App, *26*, 392)
Promotion: Univ. of Illinois (Bull, *42*, 793-794)
Publication: The adjutant general's school and the training of psychological personnel for the Army (J App, *26*, 392)
Return: Univ. of Illinois (Bull, *42*, 582)

Pennsylvania Child Research Clinic

Conference: exceptional children (J App, *19*, 222, 625; J App, *20*, 165, 420)

Establishment (J APP, *18*, 722)
Lecture: unstable child (J APP, *18*, 859)

Pennsylvania College
Appointment: Sanders, C. F. (JoP, *4*, 28; BULL, *3*, 422)
Appointment: Staley, G. D. (SCI°, *14*, 333)
Endowment: Graff, P. professorship of hygiene and physical culture (SCI°, *14*, 333)

Pennsylvania Department of Public Instruction
Appointment: Maxfield, F. N. (BULL, *17*, 435)

Pennsylvania Hospital
Appointment: Smith, L. H. (SCI, *88*, 591)
Appointment: Turner, W. D. (BULL, *34*, 635; SCI, *86*, 98)
Research: Turner, W. D. and Carl, G. P., sympathomimetic drugs (BULL, *34*, 636)
Resignation: Bond, E. D. (SCI, *88*, 591)

Pennsylvania Institute for the Blind
Appointment: Hayes, S. P. (JoP, *14*, 168)

Pennsylvania Mental Hospital Association
Publication: Mercer, M., psychological tests (BULL, *42*, 792)

Pennsylvania Oral School for the Deaf
Resignation: Garrett, E. (SCI°, *17*, 214)

Pennsylvania State College (State College)
Appointment: Anderson, D. A. (BULL, *14*, 366, 420; SCI, *46*, 385)
Appointment: Carpenter, C. R. (SCI, *92*, 307; BULL, *37*, 827)
Appointment: Holmes, A. (SCI, *35*, 371; BULL, *9*, 208; JoP, *9*, 224)
Appointment: Husband, R. W. (SCI, *93*, 301; BULL, *38*, 304)
Appointment: Snyder, W. U. (BULL, *42*, 675)
Appointment: Van Riper, B. W. (JoP, *12*, 560)
Conference: reading instructions (J APP, *28*, 531)
Course: Institute on Professional Training for Clinical Psychologists (J APP, *26*, 390)
Departure: Artley, A. S., reading clinic (BULL, *39*, 896)
Departure: Dotterer, R. (JoP, *23*, 420)
Departure: Husband, R. W. (BULL, *39*, 807)
Departure: Ruch, F. L. (SCI, *86*, 263)
Leave of absence: Bernreuter, R. G. (SCI, *96*, 250; BULL, *39*, 807)
Leave of absence: Smith, K. R. (BULL, *39*, 896)
Retirement: Walton, A. (SCI, *96*, 155; BULL, *39*, 681)

Pennsylvania State Normal College (East Stroudsburg)
Appointment: Thaxton, O. A. (JoP, *1*, 616)
Appointment: Wallin, J. E. W. (JoP, *3*, 532; BULL, *3*, 319)

Pennsylvania, University of (Philadelphia)

Anniversary: psychological clinic (SCI, *65*, 11; SCI, *75*, 75)
Appointment: Blanchard, P. (BULL, *23*, 60)
Appointment: Brinton, D. G. (SCI°, *8*, 452)
Appointment: Brotemarkle, R. A. (SCI, *97*, 326; BULL, *40*, 539)
Appointment: Burr, C. (SCI, *14*, 784)
Appointment: Cattell, J. McK. (SCI°, *8*, 480)
Appointment: Fernberger, S. (AJP, *32*, 160; SCI, *52*, 636; BULL, *18*, 110)
Appointment: Holmes, A. (SCI, *56*, 447)
Appointment: Miller, K. G. (BULL, *18*, 296)
Appointment: Mitchell, D. (JOP, *11*, 588)
Appointment: Paynter, R. H. (BULL, *23*, 60)
Appointment: Preston, M. G., School of Social Work (BULL, *42*, 582)
Appointment: psychiatry, Medical School (SCI, *62*, 371)
Appointment: Reiter, F. H. (JOP, *11*, 588)
Appointment: Strecker, E. A. (SCI, *74*, 364, 384)
Appointment: Twitmyer, E. B. (SCI, *46*, 612)
Appointment: Wallin, J. E. W. (SCI, *24*, 288)
Appointment: Wendt, G. R. (SCI, *85*, 560; BULL, *34*, 498)
Appointment: Yoakum, D. (SCI, *24*, 448)
Assistantships available in training school (JOP, *4*, 700)
Conference: Bicentennial, multidiscipline plans announced (J APP, *24*, 517)
Degree: Angell, J. R. (SCI, *87*, 572)
Degree: Myers, C. S. (SCI, *92*, 234)
Departure: Fernberger, S. W. (JOP, *9*, 700; SCI, *36*, 556)
Departure: Holmes, A. (SCI, *35*, 371; BULL, *9*, 208)
Departure: Starr, H. (BULL, *25*, 444)
Departure: Thompson, A. S. (BULL, *42*, 486)
Election: Witmer, L., APA council (JOP, *2*, 28)
Endowment: Burr, C. W., library (SCI, *99*, 425)
Establishment: Dept. of Pedagogics (SCI°, *14*, 26)
Establishment: Personnel Index to aid in employment after the war (BULL, *41*, 343)
Fellowship: Gault, R. H. (SCI, *17*, 640)
Fellowship: in neuropsychiatry (SCI, *62*, 11)
Grant: National Committee on Mental Hygiene (SCI, *91*, 68)
Leave of absence: Witmer, L. (SCI, *46*, 612)
Lecture: Dewey, J. (SCI, *32*, 834)
Lecture: Janet, P. (BULL, *22*, 672)
Lecture: Witmer, L. (SCI, *12*, 735; JOP, *6*, 168; BULL, *6*, 120)
Meeting: Assoc. of Consulting Psychologists (SCI, *77*, 424)
Meeting: Experimental Psychologists (BULL, *4*, 128)
Promotion: announced (SCI, *40*, 482; SCI, *66*, 14)
Promotion: Brotemarkle, R. A. (BULL, *24*, 508; J APP, *11*, 234)
Promotion: Fernberger, S. W. (BULL, 7, 364; JOP, *8*, 84; BULL, *24*, 508; J APP, *11*, 234)
Promotion: Greenwood, K. (SCI, *53*, 556)

Promotion: Holmes, A. (Bull, *7*, 364; JoP, *8*, 84)
Promotion: Maxfield, F. N. (Bull, *11*, 483; JoP, *11*, 588)
Promotion: Miller, K. G. (Bull, *24*, 508; Sci, *53*, 556; J App, *11*, 234)
Promotion: Oberly, H. S. (J App, *11*, 234)
Promotion: Starr, H. E. (J App, *11*, 234; Bull, *24*, 508)
Promotion: Reiter, F. N. (Bull, *11*, 483)
Promotion: Twitmyer, E. B. (Bull, *11*, 483; JoP, *11*, 588)
Promotion: Urban, F. M. (Bull, *7*, 364; JoP, *8*, 84)
Promotion: Viteles, M. S. (Bull, *22*, 504)
Resignation: Reiter, F. H. (Sci, *52*, 635)
Retirement: Witmer, L. (Bull, *34*, 635)
Return: Fullerton, G. S. (Rev, *6*, 673; Sci, *10*, 422)

Penrose, Lionel Sharples

Appointment: Univ. College, London, Galton chair (Sci, *101*, 170)

Penrose Memorial Lecture

Angell, J. R. at American Philosophical Society (Sci, *95*, 219, 428)

Penzoldt, [?]

Research: sense of smell (Sci°, *7*, 547)

Pepinsky, Harold Brenner

Appointment: Univ. of Kansas (Bull, *41*, 603)

Peppard, Stanley H.

Appointment: Connecticut Health Dept., Mental Hygiene Director (Sci, *74*, 434)

Perception

Grant: Gault, R. H., Barker Foundation of Chicago (Sci, *74*, 264)
Lecture: Boring, E. G. (AJP, *55*, 423-435)
Lecture: Creed, I. (JoP, *39*, 55-56)
Lecture: Helson, H., Dr. Wilcox on the role of form in perception (AJP, *45*, 171)
Lecture: Hemmon, V. A. C. (JoP, *1*, 224)
Lecture: Hutten, E. (JoP, *39*, 55-56)
Lecture: Münsterberg, H. (JoP, *1*, 168)
Lecture: Nunn, T. P. (JoP, *7*, 420)
Lecture: Pavlicek, G. and Jenkins, J. G., paradoxical warmth (AJP, *45*, 350)
Lecture: Pearce, H. J. (JoP, *2*, 56)
Lecture: Russell, B., Bryn Mawr College (JoP, *40*, 560)
Lecture: Schiller, F. C. S. (JoP, *7*, 420)
Lecture: Stoops, J. D. (JoP, *2*, 280)
Publication: Boring, E. G., temporal perception and operationism (AJP, *48*, 519)
Publication: Ferree, C. E. and Rand, G., perception of depth in the after-image (AJP, *46*, 329)
Publication: Gurnee, H., some observations of after-images of bodily movement (AJP, *45*, 528)

Publication: Hunt, W. A., the reality of bright and dull pressure (AJP, *46*, 334)
Publication: Ruckmick, C. A., reality of bright and dull pressure (AJP, *47*, 330)
Research: NRC, analysis on research in United States (AJP, *54*, 435-436)

Percy, Mildred St. Martin
Appointment: George Washington Univ. (BULL, *42*, 792)
Election: APA Wash.-Balt., Branch, treasurer (BULL, *36*, 712; BULL, *35*, 188; BULL, *37*, 657)

Perez, Bernard
Publication: First three years of childhood (SCI°, *12*, 237)

Perkins, Francis Theodore
Promotion: Claremont Graduate School (BULL, *42*, 191)

Perrin, Fleming Allen Clay
Appointment: Univ. of Pittsburgh (SCI, *37*, 57; BULL, *10*, 39; JoP, *10*, 84)
Appointment: Univ. of Texas (SCI, *46*, 360; BULL, *14*, 334)
Death notice (BULL, *42*, 127)
Departure: Univ. of Chicago (JoP, *10*, 84)
Resignation: Univ. of Pittsburgh (BULL, *14*, 334)
Responds to McNutt, W. S. (J App, *14*, 303)

Perry, Charles Milton
Appointment: Univ. of Michigan (JoP, *8*, 364)

Perry, Ralph Barton
Editor: James', W. book of essays (JoP, *8*, 672)
Lecture: Indiana Univ., Powell Foundation Lectures (JoP, *34*, 84)

Personalist, The
Publication: new journal (JoP, *17*, 278-279)

Personality
Lecture: Blakeslee, A. F., Phi Beta Kappa (SCI, *95*, 220)
Lecture: differences in north and south (AJP, *58*, 555-557)
Lecture: Healy, W., New York Acad. of Science, Salmon Memorial Lectures (SCI, *85*, 355)
Meeting: American Orthopsychiatric Assoc. (BULL, *33*, 148)
Publication: Elliott, R. M., *Explorations in Personality* (AJP, *52*, 453-462)
Publication: Fol, H., *Journal de Genève*, variations (SCI°, *5*, 532)
Publication: Frazier, E. F., *Negro Youth at the Crossways* (J App, *24*, 655)
Publication: Guilford, J. P., unitary traits of personality and factor theory (AJP, *48*, 673)
Publication: Lehmann, H. C., commonwealth teacher-training study (AJP, *46*, 486)
Publication: Pintner, R., *Aspects of Personality* (J App, *22*, 318)
Publication: Ribot, Th., diseases of (SCI°, *23*, 97)

Publication: Terman, L. M., commemorative volume, studies in personality contributed in honor of (BULL, 39, 268)
Publication: Witty, P. A., faculty psychology and personality traits (AJP, 46, 486)
Research: psychotechnical methods (SCI, 69, 423)
Symposium: AAAS (J APP, 26, 107; BULL, 38, 908)
Symposium: Hilgard, E. R., AAAS, Section I (J APP, 25, 727)

Personnel

Appointment: Thurstone, L. L., Bureau of Personnel Service (SCI, 57, 81)
Course: New York Univ. (SCI, 98, 299)
Course: Yerkes, R., Army War College (SCI, 57, 145)
Establishment: Office of Psychological Personnel (SCI, 95, 527-528)
Lecture: Bell, H. M., matching youth and jobs, American Youth Commission (J APP, 24, 854)
Lecture: Lincoln, L. A., Metropolitan Life Insurance, selection (J APP, 21, 242)
Lecture: Yoakum, C. S. (J APP, 9, 204)
Meeting: American College Personnel Assoc., 1938 (J APP, 22, 106)
Meeting: American Council on Guidance and Personnel Assoc. (J APP, 24, 98)
Meeting: Personnel Research Federation, Conference on Labor Relations, 1937 (J APP, 21, 718)
Meeting: Society for Personnel Administration (J APP, 26, 712)
Publication: Committee on Classification of Personnel in the Army (J APP, 2, 384-385, J APP, 3, 106)
Publication: discontinued (J APP, 2, 385)

Personnel Institute, The

Appointment: Solomon, R. S., Personnel Control, Analyses and Vocational Guidance, director (BULL, 36, 712)

Personnel Research Council

Election: Viteles, M. S. (SCI, 77, 256)

Personnel Research Federation

Appointment: Achilles, P. S. (BULL, 22, 260)
Appointment: Bingham, W. V. (BULL, 22, 140)
Conference: 10th annual industrial (SCI, 69, 492)

Personnel Research Institute

Appointment: Ohmann, O. H., Western Reserve Univ., director (SCI, 94, 208)
Appointment: Otis, J. L., Western Reserve Univ., director (SCI, 94, 208)

Personnel Research Section, War Department

Appointment: Instructors, New York Univ., Personnel Psychology (SCI, 98, 299)

Persons, Gladys L.

Publication: teaching high school students to read (J APP, 21, 244)

Pestalozzi, Johann Heinrich
Publication: *Times* (SCI, 9, 120)

Peter, William W.
Appointment: Inter-American Affairs (SCI, 101, 581)
Resignation: Yale Univ. (SCI, 101, 504)

Peters, Henry Nelson
Appointment: Missouri State Penitentiary, director (BULL, 36, 218)

Peters, Wilhelm
Editor: *Zentrablatt* (BULL, 11, 232)
Publication: with Marbe, K. (JOP, 9, 699-700)

Peterson, [Hans Jordan ?]
Death notice (BULL, 39, 895)

Peterson, Joseph
Appointment: George Peabody College (SCI, 48, 444; BULL, 15, 360)
Appointment: Univ. of Minnesota (SCI, 42, 374; BULL, 12, 244; SCI, 41, 862; JOP, 12, 476; JOP, 14, 644)
Appointment: Univ. of Utah (JOP, 8, 616; BULL, 8, 373)
Death notice (SCI, 83, 99; BULL, 33, 477; AJP, 48, 175)
Editor: *Psychological Monographs* (SCI, 79, 247)
Election: APA, council of directors (BULL, 24, 80)
Election: Kansas Acad. of Science, Kansas Psychological Assoc. president, 1930 (SCI, 71, 504)
Publication: SSPP annual reports (AJP, 45, 530; AJP, 46, 513; AJP, 47, 515)
Research: mentality differences (BULL, 17, 240)
Resignation: Univ. of Minnesota (BULL, 15, 360)
Resignation: Univ. of Utah, in protest (BULL, 12, 160, 244; JOP, 12, 476)

Petite Fille, La
Publication: Perey, M. B. (SCI°, 9, 460)

Petrova, Mariia K.
Award: Pavlov Prize (SCI, 92, 450)

Petrullo, Luigi
Lecture: APA Wash.-Balt. Branch (J APP, 25, 726)

Pettenkofer, Max von
Election: Sciences and Arts (SCI, 11, 317)

Peyote
Lecture: Fernberger, S. W., observations of (AJP, 34, 616)

Pfaffmann, Carl
Rhodes scholar (BULL, 32, 324)

Pfleiderer, Otto
Publication: philosophy of religion (Sci°, 9, 54)

Pflüger's Archiv
Editor: change (Bull, 17, 200)

Phantasms
Lecture: of the dead, Podmore, F., American Branch of the Society for Psychical
   Research (Sci°, 15, 144)
Lecture: of the dead, Myers, F. W. H., American Branch of the Society for
   Psychical Research (Sci°, 15, 144)
Publication: of living, Gurney, F. (Sci°, 8, 364)

Phenomenological Society
Meeting: announced (JoP, 42, 55-56)

Phenomenology
Lecture: Köhler, W. (JoP, 42, 55-56)
Publication: Baillie J. B. (JoP, 7, 644)

Phi Beta Kappa
Meeting: Detroit, mental attitudes for national defense (Sci, 93, 372)
Lecture: Blakeslee, A. F., personality in relation to science and society (Sci, 95,
   220)

Phi Phenomenon
Publicationn: Hulin, W. S. and Katz, D., eye-movements and the
   phi-phenomenon (AJP, 46, 332)

Philadelphia Hospital for Mental Diseases
Appointment: Hamilton, S. W. (Sci, 52, 152)

Philadelphia Institution for the Blind
Appointment: Hayes, S. P. (Bull, 14, 32)

Philadelphia Neurological Society
Lecture: Meyer, A. (Sci, 15, 396)

Philadelphia Normal School
Laboratory established for psychology (Rev, 5, 109; Sci, 6, 483)

Philadelphia Pathological Society
Symposium: physical growth and mental development (JoP, 10, 671-672)

Philippi, E.
Publication: translation of Jastrow's, J. work on the subconscious into French
   (Sci, 27, 677)

Philological Society
Publication: English dictionary (Sci°, 3, 527)

Philology
Publication: Elliott, A. M., Johns Hopkins circular, expedition to Canada (Sci°, 5, 119-120)
Publication: Whitney, W. D. and Sievers, E., *Encyclopedia Britannica* (Sci°, 5, 162)

Philosophic Abstracts
Founding (JoP, 36, 700; Bull, 36, 713)
Publication: dictionary of philosophy (Bull, 37, 828)

Philosophical Society (University of Vienna) (*see also* Vienna Philosophical Society)
Election: Höfler, A., president (Sci°, 12, 23)
Formation: Univ. of Vienna (Sci°, 12, 23)
Meynert, T. H. aids in formation (Sci°, 12, 23)

Philosophical Society (Washington, DC)
Election: officers, 1929 (Sci, 69, 155)
Lecture: Heyl, P. R., cosmic emotion (Sci, 95, 429)

Philosophische Studien
Rename: *Archiv für die gesammte Psychologie* (Rev, 10, 103-104)

Philosophy
Course: Hinman, E. L. (JoP, 7, 223)
Course: Yale Univ., requirement abandoned (Sci, 11, 480)
Distinction made between philosophy and psychology (Bull, 12, 127)
Lecture: Boutroux, E. (JoP, 7, 140)
Lecture: Dewey, J., Japan reconstruction (JoP, 16, 357-364)
Lecture: Dumville, B., education (JoP, 4, 447)
Lecture: Hudson, J. W., history (JoP, 7, 223)
Lecture: Montague, W. P., Western Univ., London, Ontario, futurists (JoP, 15, 168)
Lecture: Santayana, G., British Acad., opinion (JoP, 15, 280)
Meeting: New School for Social Research, conference on methods (Bull, 34, 363; Bull, 41, 72; JoP, 34, 559, 616; JoP, 37, 224; Sci, 86, 419-420; Sci, 87, 277)
Meeting: Society for Philosophical Inquiry (JoP, 7, 280)
Protest: against experimental psychology (JoP, 10, 363)
Publication: Alexander, A. B. D., history of (JoP, 4, 364)
Publication: Andrews and Co., philosophical papers of the Univ. of Michigan (Sci°, 11, 265)
Publication: bibliography of French philosphy (JoP, 7, 84)
Publication: Cushman, H. E., history of (JoP, 7, 560)
Publication: Knight, W. A., on Hume (Sci°, 8, 512)

Publication: Ladd, G. T., knowledge (Sᴄɪ, 5, 582)
Publication: Pfleiderer, O., religion (Sᴄɪ°, 9, 54)
Publication: professors interested in promoting philosophy (JoP, 9, 419-420)
Publication: Schiller, F. C. D., humanism (JoP, 7, 644)

Phillips, Daniel Edward
Course: Washington Univ. (Bᴜʟʟ, 14, 264)

Phipps, Henry professorship
Appointment: Whitehorn, J. C. (Sᴄɪ, 94, 275)
Retirement: Meyer, A. (Sᴄɪ, 94, 275)

Phipps, Henry Psychiatric Clinic (see also Johns Hopkins University)
Anniversary: Meyer, A., 25th, 75th birthday (Sᴄɪ, 85, 259)
Appointment: Wertheimer, F. I. (Sᴄɪ, 56, 387)
Departure: Flournoy, H. (Sᴄɪ, 40, 407)
Departure: Lyman, R. S. (Sᴄɪ, 91, 187)
Division of psychology dept, at Johns Hopkins Univ. (Bᴜʟʟ, 13, 280; JoP, 13, 532)
Donation: Johns Hopkins Univ. psychiatric clinic (Sᴄɪ, 27, 999)
Opening: Johns Hopkins Univ. (Sᴄɪ, 37, 406, 596; JoP, 10, 308; Bᴜʟʟ, 10, 164)
Resignation: Campbell, C. M. (Bᴜʟʟ, 17, 351)

Phonetics
Course: Scripture, E. W., experimental (Bᴜʟʟ, 2, 360)
Lecture: Krueger, E., experimental phonetics (Sᴄɪ, 22, 727)
Research: LaRue, D. W., alphabet (Bᴜʟʟ, 17, 239)

Photographs
Publication: *Journal of Consulting Psychology*, photo volumes of pre-1939 applied psychologists (Bᴜʟʟ, 36, 500)
Publication: Kirkpatrick collection psychologists photos (JoP, 10, 252; Bᴜʟʟ, 10, 164; Bᴜʟʟ, 9, 440; Bᴜʟʟ, 11, 115; JoP, 9, 644)

Physical handicaps (see also Handicapped children)
Diagnosis and guidance of civilians and veterans (J Aᴘᴘ, 28, 79)
Publication: untapped value as governmental employees (J Aᴘᴘ, 28, 79)

Physical Reconstruction, Staff of the Division of
List of members (J Aᴘᴘ, 2, 294)

Physico-Technical Institute
Appointment: Kohlrausch, F.W.G. (Sᴄɪ, 1, 109)

Physiognomy
Lecture: Cope, E. D., origin of human physiognomy and character (Sᴄɪ°, 3, 342)

Physiological Psychology
Publication: Ladd, G. T. (SCI°, 9, 294)

Physiological Psychology, Congress of
Results of meeting, 1889 (SCI°, 14, 148)

Physiological Society
Meeting: Berlin, 1889 (SCI°, 13, 237)

Physiologists, International Congress of
Meeting: Berne, 1895 (SCI, 2, 68)

Physiology (*see also* Brain)
Course: Oxford Univ., success (SCI°, 5, 283)
Lecture: Cincinnati Society of Natural History, hygiene (SCI°, 6, 359)
Lecture: Dixey, F. A., at Oxford Univ. (SCI, 10, 250)
Lecture: Hill, L. E., psychology (REV, 1, 214)
Lecture: Newnham College (SCI°, 14, 180)
Meeting: AAAS, biochemistry and physiology relating to mental disease (SCI, 92, 552)
Publication: Gardner, W. A., influence on the thyroid gland on the consciousness of the passage of time (AJP, 47, 698)
Publication: laboratory, the Sorbonne (REV, 5, 345)
Publication: Titchener, E. B., psychology (JoP, 7, 644)
Publication: Wenley, R. M., psychology (JoP, 5, 448, 560)

Physiology and Psychology, Institute of (Chungking, China)
Kuo, Z. Y. requested to visit England by Chinese minister of Education (SCI, 94, 411, 605)

Physiotechnical Institute of Germany (*see* Germany, Physiotechnical Institute)

Pi Lambda Theta
Award: research (J APP, 28, 80, 531)

Piaget, Jean
Lecture: Harvard Tercentary Conference of Arts and Sciences (J APP, 20, 519)

Pick, Arnold
Death notice (BULL, 21, 660; SCI, 60, 38)
Publication: sensations (AJP, 1, 360)

Pickering, Edward Charles
Lecture: Amer. Society for Psychical Research, observations of thought-transference (SCI°, 5, 491)
Return from Europe (SCI°, 2, 254)

Pierce, Arthur Henry
Appointment: Smith College (REV, 7, 428)
Death notice (AJP, 25, 320; BULL, 22, 115; SCI, 39, 323; JOP, 11, 168)
Donation: Smith College, library (BULL, 11, 152; SCI, 39, 462)
Editor: *Psychological Bulletin* (JOP, 7, 280)
Election: APA office (JOP, 8, 55; JOP, 7, 56)

Pierce, Edgar
Appointment: Univ. of Michigan (REV, 3, 120)
Endowment: William James Lecture (SCI, 75, 331)
James Lecture Foundation, Harvard Univ. (SCI, 71, 212)

Pierce, Edward
Appointment: Univ. of Michigan (SCI, 2, 665)

Pierce, Watson O'Dell
Appointment: Office of the Secretary of War, Test Construction Advisor (BULL, 41, 136)
Grant: Social Science Research Council (BULL, 36, 805)

Piéron, Henri
Appointment: l'Ecole des Hautes Etudes of the Sorbonne (JOP, 9, 532)
Appointment: Sorbonne, director of lab (BULL, 10, 40; BULL, 9, 359)
Editor: *Année Psychologique* (BULL, 10, 40; BULL, 9, 359)
Election: American Acad. of Arts and Sciences, fellow (BULL, 34, 409)
Election: French Assoc. for the Advancement of Science, president (SCI, 90, 248; BULL, 36, 804)
Election: International Congress of Psychology, 11th, president (J APP, 21, 242; BULL, 34, 59, 121; JOP, 34; 112)
Meeting: AAAS, Century of Progress Exposition (SCI, 77, 579)
Meeting: International Congress of Psychology, 11th (SCI, 84, 531)
World's Fair visit (J APP, 16, 695)

Piez, Richard K.
Appointment: New York State Normal School (SCI, 12, 616; REV, 7, 640)

Pike County Historical Society (Milford, Pennsylvania)
Meeting: honoring Peirce, C. S. (JOP, 42, 672)

Pike, F. H.
Lecture: Washington Square College, Psi Chi Chapter (SCI, 81, 457)

Pilgram Trust
Grant: purchase of Darwin's manuscripts (SCI, 96, 493)

Pillsbury, Walter Bowers
Appointment: Cornell Univ. (AJP, 8, 430)
Appointment: Univ. of Michigan (AJP, 8, 584; REV, 4, 451; SCI, 96, 355)

Degree: Univ. of Nebraska (Sci, 79, 537)
Editor: *Bulletin*, experimental psychology (Bull, 8, 222; Bull, 9, 280)
Election: APA president (Sci, 31, 22; JoP, 7, 56; Bull, 7, 36)
Leave of absence: Univ. of Michigan (Sci, 91, 475, Sci, 57, 466; Bull, 10, 123)
Lecture: APA/WPA/AAAS (JoP, 8, 55)
Lecture: apperception (AJP, 9, 421)
Lecture: colors (AJP, 49, 130)
Lecture: Cornell Univ. (JoP, 8, 112; Bull, 5, 406; Sci, 33, 214)
Lecture: Cuba to San Antonia, observations (Sci°, 9, 87)
Lecture: Europe (Sci, 57, 466)
Lecture: intelligence (AJP, 52, 634-638)
Lecture: judgments (JoP, 2, 252)
Nomination: APA representative, National Research Council (AJP, 32, 157)
Promotion: Cornell Univ. (Rev, 4, 340)
Promotion: Univ. of Michigan (Rev, 7, 428; Sci, 32, 627; Bull, 7, 364)
Publication: hemeralopia, a case of (AJP, 46, 658)
Publication: Macmillan Co. announced (JoP, 8, 392)
Publication: psychology of reasoning (JoP, 7, 196)
Publication: translation by Külpe, O. (Sci, 4, 269)
Publication: Wundt centenary (AJP, 45, 176)
Retirement: Univ. of Michigan (Bull, 42, 406; Bull, 39, 807)

Pilzecker, Alfons
Appointment: Univ. of Göttingen (AJP, 7, 152)

Pinsent, [Ellen Frances Parker ?]
Royal Commission on the Care of the Feeble-minded (Sci, 22, 510)

Pinsent-Darwin Fund
Grant: Cambridge Univ., research in mental pathology (Sci, 60, 39)

Pintner, Rudolf
Appointment: Toledo Univ. (Bull, 9, 408; JoP, 9, 588; Sci, 36, 373)
Death notice (AJP, 56, 303-305; Bull, 39, 895)
Editor: *Psychological Bulletin* (Bull, 22, 444)
Lecture: Columbia Univ., Conference for the Education of the Gifted (J App, 24, 854)
Lecture: New York Branch of APA (JoP, 18, 672)
Publication: *Aspects of Personality* (J App, 22, 318)

Piper, Hans Edmund
Appointment: Berlin Univ. (Bull, 6, 120)
Death notice (Bull, 12, 440)

Pistor, Frederick
Appointment: Georgia State Woman's College (Bull, 40, 383)

Pitch

Award: Stevens, S. S., Howard Crosby Warren Medal, psychological (SCI, *97*, 373)
Lecture: Mount, G. H., discrimination (JOP, *7*, 223)
Lecture: Schaeffer, H. G., discrimination (JOP, *7*, 223)
Lecture: Woodrow, H., rhythm (JOP, *7*, 223)

Pitkin, Walter Boughton

Election: American Philosophical Assoc., committee member (JOP, *9*, 28)
Promotion: Columbia Univ. (JOP, *9*, 336)

Pittsburgh, University of (Pennsylvania)

Appointment: Basset, G. C. (BULL, *11*, 443)
Appointment: Dietze, A. G. (J APP, *10*, 522)
Appointment: Filter, R. O. (BULL, *22*, 140; J APP, *8*, 450; SCI, *60*, 291)
Appointment: Held, O. C. (J APP, *10*, 522)
Appointment: Johnson, H. M. (J APP, *10*, 522; SCI, *62*, 177)
Appointment: Jones, G. (J APP, *10*, 522)
Appointment: Love, I. (J APP, *10*, 522)
Appointment: Mecklin, J. M. (JOP, *10*, 588)
Appointment: Perrin, F. A. C. (JOP, *10*, 84; SCI, *37*, 57; BULL, *10*, 39)
Appointment: Reed, H. B. (BULL, *22*, 140; J APP, *8*, 450; SCI, *60*, 291)
Appointment: Rich, G. J. (BULL, *17*, 279)
Appointment: Robertson, C. B. (JOP, *8*, 392)
Appointment: Root, W. T. (SCI, *70*, 36)
Appointment: Rosenzweig, S. (BULL, *40*, 618-619)
Appointment: Seaton, J. T. (J APP, *10*, 522)
Appointment: Wallin, J. E. W. (BULL, *9*, 208; JOP, *9*, 167; SCI, *35*, 416)
Appointment: White, J. H. (SCI, *28*, 483; BULL, *5*, 380)
Course: Hall, G. S. (BULL, *12*, 403)
Degree: Lashley, K. S. (SCI, *83*, 593)
Departure: Graham, J. L. (BULL, *24*, 136)
Departure: Held, O. C. (SCI, *93*, 565)
Departure: Perrin, F. A. C. (SCI, *46*, 360)
Departure: Rahn, C. L. (SCI, *34*, 602)
Departure: Wallin, J. E. W. (SCI, *39*, 756)
Establishment: Dept. of Clinical Psychology (SCI, *35*, 416; JOP, *9*, 167)
Grant: Buhl Foundation of Pittsburgh (BULL, *38*, 304)
Grant: Research Corporation of New York (BULL, *38*, 304; BULL, *39*, 196-197)
Fellowship: Johnson, H. M. (BULL, *22*, 612)
Leave of absence: Huey, E. B. (SCI, *28*, 483; BULL, *5*, 380)
Lecture: points of view in psychology (SCI, *69*, 450)
Promotion: Basset, G. C. (BULL, *12*, 404)
Promotion: Dietze, A. G. (BULL, *42*, 581)
Promotion: Grove, W. R. (BULL, *42*, 581)
Promotion: Wheeler, E. T. (BULL, *42*, 581)

Resignation: Held, O. C. (BULL, *42*, 792)
Resignation: Perrin, F. A. C. (BULL, *14*, 334)

Plant, James Stuart
Lecture: Conference by Child Health Program (SCI, *101*, 482)

Platt, Walter B.
Publication: *Popular Science Monthly*, the injurious influences of city life (SCI°, *12*, 36)

Podmore, Frank
Lecture: phantasms of the dead (SCI°, *15*, 144)

Poey, Felipe
Death notice (SCI°, *17*, 103)

Poffenberger, Albert Theodore
Anniversary: 50th, Columbia Univ. (SCI, *95*, 190)
Appointment: Cattell Portrait Committee (SCI, *75*, 661)
Appointment: Columbia Univ. (SCI, *91*, 311)
Commission: Army, psychological examination of recruits (SCI, *47*, 217)
Commission: Sanitary Corps (BULL, *15*, 97; JOP, *15*, 364)
Departure: Columbia Univ. (SCI, *93*, 493)
Election: AAAP president, 1944 (J APP, *28*, 79)
Election: APA president, 1934 (SCI, *80*, 242)
Election: APA representative to National Research Council (BULL, *27*, 76)
Leave of absence: Columbia Univ. (SCI, *91*, 311)
Promotion: Columbia Univ. (BULL, *24*, 380; SCI, *55*, 538; BULL, *19*, 350; JOP, *19*, 392)
Meeting: AAAS, Section I (BULL, *34*, 179)
Research: Psychological Index project, measure of public interest in psychology (BULL, *36*, 220)

Polarity
Subject of Woodbridge Memorial Lectures, 1943 (JOP, *40*, 168)

Polish Institute of Arts and Sciences
Conference: Copernican Quadricentennial, pure and applied science (SCI, *97*, 399)

Politics
Lecture: Montague, W. P., political outlook, Woman's Canadian Club (JOP, *15*, 168)
Publication: Lewis, W. D., municipalities and political organization (SCI°, *19*, 103)

Pollock, Lewis J.
Election: American Neurological Association (SCI, *93*, 614-615)

Pollock, Martha
Appointment: Bradley Memorial Hospital of Providence (BULL, *28*, 411)

Pomona College (Claremont, California)
Appointment: Hinshaw, R. P. (BULL, *42*, 331)

Pond, Frederick Logan
Inventory of reading experiences (J APP, *24*, 855)

Poor, Charles Lane
Election: NYAS officer (JOP, *9*, 28)

Popular Science Monthly
Darwinism and the Christian faith (SCI°, *11*, 312-313)
Herter, C. A., hypnotism: what it is, and what it is not (SCI°, *12*, 131)
French, J. M., infant mortality and the environment (SCI°, *12*, 237)
Janet, P., the teaching of psychology (SCI°, *11*, 312-313)
Jastrow, J., the psychology of deception (SCI°, *12*, 237)
Platt, W. B., the injurious influences of city life (SCI°, *12*, 36)
Publication: devoted to Darwin, C. (JOP, *6*, 224)
Wace, H., opposes Huxley's agnosticism (SCI°, *13*, 299)
White, A. D., the warfare of science (SCI°, *13*, 299)

Population Problems, International Congress for the Scientific Study of
Lecture: psychology (SCI, *82*, 150)

Porter, James Pertice
Appointment: Clark College (SCI, *18*, 96)
Appointment: Univ. of Oregon (J APP, *20*, 421)
Election: MPA president (J APP, *25*, 266; BULL, *39*, 267)
Election: Ohio Acad. of Sciences (BULL, *27*, 415)
Establishment: Porter, J. P. Loan Fund in Psychology, Ohio Univ. (J APP, *27*, 475; BULL, *40*, 618; SCI, *98*, 382)
Lecture: Clark Univ., mental measurement (J APP, *9*, 88)
Lecture: MPA (SCI, *95*, 221)
Meeting: 4th International Conf. of Techno-psychology (BULL, *25*, 198)
Promotion: Clark College (BULL, *4*, 337)
Purchase: *Journal of Applied Psychology* (J APP, *6*, 301)
Retirement: Ohio Univ. (SCI, *98*, 382)

Porter, Samuel
Death notice (SCI, *14*, 422)

Portraits of psychologists
Series offered by Open Court Publishing Co. (AJP, *9*, 422; REV, *5*, 111, 450)

Posen (Prussia)
Erected: Hygienic Institute (Sci°, 9, 341)

Postman, Leo Joseph
Research: estimating time during a series of tasks (AJP, 57, 421-424)

Potter, Howard W.
Appointment: Long Island College of Medicine, Brooklyn (Sci, 98, 278)

Powell Foundation Lecture
Perry, R. B., in the spirit of William James (JoP, 34, 84)

Powell Lectures on Philosophy
Indiana Univ., annual lecture series announced (JoP, 33, 224)

Powell, Norman John
Editor: *The Psychological Exchange* withdrawn (J App, 17, 629)
Publication: educational abstracts (Bull, 33, 147)
Resignation: *The Psychological Exchange* editorship (Sci, 78, 307; Bull, 31, 79)

Powers, Grover F.
Editor: *Psychosomatic Medicine* (J App, 22, 664)

Pozzi, Samuel Jean
Research: cerebral convolutions (AJP, 1, 205)

Praechter, Karl
Publication: revision of Ueberweg's, F. *Grundriss*, 11th ed. (JoP, 17, 532)

Pragmatism
Lecture: Dewey, J. (JoP, 7, 83; JoP, 11, 84; Sci, 31, 212)
Lecture: James, W. (Sci, 25, 237; Bull, 4, 95)
Lecture: Lowie, R. H., on Feuerback, L. (JoP, 7, 700)
Lecture: Moore, A. W. (JoP 2, 280)
Lecture: Royce, J., Columbia Univ. (Sci, 33, 214)
Publication: Bawden, H. H. (JoP, 5, 447)
Publication: critique of (JoP, 5, 112)
Publication: Dorley, J. E. (JoP, 5, 82)

Prague, University of (Czechoslovakia)
Appointment: Lindworsky, J. (Bull, 25, 700)
Publication: Jodl, F., *Lehrbuch der Psychologie* (Rev, 1, 336)

Pratt, Carroll Cornelius
Appointment: Univ. of Ankara (Sci, 102, 374; JoP, 42, 616)
Appointment: Clark Univ. (AJP, 32, 160)
Appointment: Harvard Univ. (Sci, 55, 617; AJP, 33, 450)
Appointment: National Research Council, Emergency Committee in
Psychology (Bull, 37, 755)

Appointment: Princeton Univ. (Sci, *93*, 80)
Appointment: Rutgers Univ. (Bull, *34*, 236, 635)
Award: Howard Crosby Warren Medal to Graham, C. H. (Sci, *93*, 324)
Election: American Acad. of Arts and Sciences (Sci, *77*, 506)
Leave of absence: Rutgers Univ. (Bull, *42*, 792-793; Sci, *102*, 374; JoP, *42*, 616)
Promotion: Harvard Univ. (Bull, *19*, 350)
Resignation: Clark Univ. (Sci, *55*, 617)

Pratt, George Kenneth
Appointment: National Committee for Mental Hygiene, New York (Sci, *61*, 113)

Pratt Institute of Brooklyn (New York)
Appointment: Carr, H. (Sci, *24*, 384; Bull, *3*, 319; JoP, *3*, 532)
Appointment: King, I. (Sci, *18*, 160)
Departure: King, I. (JoP, *3*, 532; Sci, *24*, 384)
Research: Bryan, A. I., data colleced as psych. dept. head (Bull, *37*, 257)

Pratt, James Bissett
Appointment: Williams College (JoP, *14*, 392; Sci, *21*, 936; Bull, *14*, 191; JoP, *2*, 364)

Pratt, Joseph Gaither
Editor: *Journal of Parapsychology* (Sci, *95*, 322-323; Bull, *39*, 325)

Pratt, Marjory (see Bates, Marjory)

Prejudice
Lecture: Morse, J., psychology of (JoP, *7*, 28)

Prentiss, Elizabeth Severence Award
Winslow, C. E. A. (Sci, *102*, 642)

Prescott, Daniel Alfred
Research: Vassar College, child study project (Bull, *37*, 187)

Preservation of Favored Races in the Struggle for Life
Publication: Darwin, C. (Sci°, *12*, 58)

Press and Censorship Bureau
Appointment: Bartlett, F. C., Panel for censorship of scientific papers for journals (Sci, *91*, 288)

Pressey, Sidney Leavitt
Appointment: Univ. of Hawaii (J App, *21*, 241)
Election: MPA president (Sci, *97*, 398)
Grant: AAAS, $200 (Bull, *20*, 664)
Lecture: Mass. School for Feeble-minded (Bull, *13*, 407-408)
Publication: *Occupational Orientation Inquiry* (J App, *23*, 419-421)

Preston, George Heinrichs
Election: National Committee for Mental Hygiene (SCI, *99*, 34-35)

Preston, John
Appointment: Medico-Psychological Society (SCI, *46*, 356)

Preston, Malcolm Greenhough
Appointment: Univ. of Pennsylvania, School of Social Work (BULL, *42*, 582)
Lecture: experiment in psychology (JOP, *42*, 251)

Preston School of Industry (Waterman, California)
Diagnostic and classification clinic opens for troubled youth (BULL, *39*, 807)
Report: mental conditions study (J APP, *3*, 196)

Preston, Thomas
Death notice (SCI, *11*, 518)

Preyer, Wilhelm
Death notice (REV, *4*, 567; AJP, *9*, 135)

Price, Bronson
Appointment: Medico-Biological Institute at Moscow (J APP, *18*, 156)
Arrival: United States (BULL, *36*, 841)

Price, Harry
Research: psychic (SCI, *80*, 183)

Primates
Research: Univ. School of Tropical Medicine, San Juan, Puerto Rico,
  psychobiology (SCI, *86*, 79)

Primer of Psychology
Publication: Titchener, E. B. (AJP, *9*, 250)

Prince, Lucinda Wyman
Course: salesmanship (J APP, *1*, 396)

Prince, Morton
Appointment: Harvard Univ. (BULL, *23*, 292; SCI, *63*, 425)
Award: Cross of the Legion of Honor (BULL, *16*, 392)
Course: Tufts College Medical School (BULL, *6*, 152; SCI, *29*, 335)
Editor: *Journal of Abnormal Psychology* (BULL, *3*, 148; JOP, *3*, 251)
Lecture: abnormal psychology (JOP, *7*, 28; BULL, *7*, 75; SCI, *30*, 914; SCI, *60*, 587)
Lecture: Cambridge Univ., subconscious (SCI, *59*, 161)
Lecture: International Congress of Arts and Sciences, St. Louis (JOP, *1*, 420)

Prince, Walter Franklin
Fellowship: American Society for Psychical Research, in memory of (BULL, *39*,
  71)

Princeton Contributions to Psychology
Publication: announcement (Sci, *1*, 724)

Princeton University (New Jersey)
Appointment: assistant professors (JoP, *2*, 336)
Appointment: Baldwin, J. M. (Sci°, *21*, 187)
Appointment: Bray, C. W. (Sci, *87*, 411)
Appointment: Brigham, C. C. (Bull, *17*, 239)
Appointment: Crawford, J. F. (Rev, *4*, 339; AJP, *8*, 584)
Appointment: Doll, E. A. (Bull, *14*, 366; Bull, *15*, 24)
Appointment: Farrar, C. B. (Sci, *43*, 169)
Appointment: Gulliksen, H. O. (Bull, *42*, 485)
Appointment: Hollands, E. H. (JoP, *3*, 420)
Appointment: Johnson, [R.B.C.?] (JoP, *2*, 336)
Appointment: Kennedy, F. (Rev, *4*, 690; AJP, *9*, 250)
Appointment: Langfeld, H. S. (Bull, *21*, 428; JoP, *21*, 560; Sci, *87*, 411; Sci, *59*, 576)
Appointment: McComas, H. C. (Bull, *6*, 328)
Appointment: McMullen, C. B. (Bull, *3*, 356)
Appointment: Metcalf, J. T. (Bull, *11*, 267)
Appointment: Morgan, J. J. B. (Bull, *14*, 115)
Appointment: Patton, G. S. (Sci, *16*, 480; Rev, *9*, 644)
Appointment: Pratt, C. C. (Sci, *93*, 80)
Appointment: Reeves, P. (Bull, *9*, 408; JoP, *9*, 700)
Appointment: Shaw, W. J. (Rev, *8*, 656-657)
Appointment: Smith, C. K. (Rev, *8*, 112)
Appointment: Smith, N. (JoP, *3*, 504; Bull, *3*, 288)
Appointment: Tawney, G. (Rev, *3*, 706)
Appointment: Thilly, F. (Bull, *1*, 134)
Appointment: Thilly, F., Stuart chair in psychology (Sci, *19*, 480)
Appointment: Urban, W. M. (Rev, *4*, 452)
Appointment: Vaughan, C. L. (Bull, *4*, 336)
Appointment: Wallin, J. E. W. (Rev, *10*, 690; Bull, *1*, 414)
Appointment: Warren, H. C. (Rev, *1*, 112; Rev, *3*, 244; AJP, *7*, 452; Sci, *3*, 284)
Appointment: Weaver, E. G. (Sci, *93*, 419; J App, *11*, 405)
Appointment: Wedell, C. H. (Sci, *87*, 411)
Appointment: Woodrow, H. H. (JoP, *4*, 196; Bull, *4*, 64)
Appointment: Wrinch, F. S. (Rev, *9*, 644)
Appointment: Zener, K. E. (J App, *11*, 405)
Course: Warren, H. C. (AJP, *11*, 130)
Degree: Angell, J. R. (Sci, *54*, 11)
Departure: Carmichael, L. (Bull, *24*, 380)
Departure: Frost, E. P. (Bull, *7*, 220)
Departure: Hinshaw, R. P. (Bull, *39*, 895)
Departure: Wallin, J. E. W. (Sci, *24*, 288)
Departure: Wrinch, F. S. (Sci, *17*, 558)
Fellowship: Sherif, M. (Bull, *42*, 128; Sci, *100*, 516)

Inauguration: Hibben, J. G. (JoP, 9, 112)
Laboratory: new (AJP, 35, 465; SCI, 59, 63)
Leave of absence: Baldwin, J. M. (AJP, 11, 130; SCI, 10, 341)
Leave of absence: Warren, H. C. (SCI, 77, 408)
Lecture: Bronk, D. W., Vanuxem. L. C. Lectures (SCI, 89, 314)
Lecture: Jennings, H. S. (SCI, 34, 709)
Lecture: Robinson, E. A., psychology and the law (SCI, 83, 229)
Lecture: Russell, B., postulates of scientific method (JoP, 41, 55-56)
Lecture: Stafford Little Lectures (BULL, 33, 147)
Lecture: Titchener, E. B., association (SCI, 45, 360; JoP, 14, 364)
Lecture: Ward, J. (JoP, 1, 504)
Meeting: American Philosophical Assoc. (JoP, 8, 27-28)
Meeting: Experimental Psychologists (JoP, 13, 224)
Meeting: New York Branch APA/NYAS (JoP, 11, 168; BULL, 11, 115; SCI, 81, 67)
Meeting: SEP (SCI, 87, 342; AJP, 52, 302)
Promotion: announced (BULL, 28, 503)
Promotion: Bray, C. W. (BULL, 42, 581)
Promotion: Brolyer, C. R. (SCI, 74, 146)
Promotion: Cantril, H. (BULL, 42, 581)
Promotion: Crespi, L. P. (BULL, 42, 581)
Promotion: Katz, D. (SCI, 74, 146)
Promotion: Spaulding, E. G. (JoP, 11, 364)
Promotion: Stalnaker, J. M. (BULL, 41, 603)
Promotion: Warren, H. C. (REV, 9, 432; SCI, 15, 1000)
Psychological testing in admissions (SCI, 56, 42)
Resignation: Brigham, C. C. (BULL, 14, 115)
Resignation: Warren, H. C., *Psychological Review* (JoP, 2, 672)
Research: Lazarsfeld, P. F., radio research project (J APP, 22, 663)
Research: Radio research project, special issue of *J App* announced (J APP, 22, 663)
Resignation: Thilly, F. (BULL, 1, 134; BULL, 3, 248)

Principles of Sociology
Publication: Spencer translation by Alcan, M. (SCI°, 8, 510)

Pringle-Pattison, Andrew Seth (*see* Seth Pringle-Pattison, A.)

Pringsheim, [?]
Research: syllable durations, intensities and pitches (SCI°, 17, 315)

Prinzhorn, Hans
Visit: U.S., International Congress of Psychology and Physiology (SCI, 70, 325)

Prison Congress
Circular issued by the U.S. Bureau of Education, 1884 (SCI°, 3, 640)

Prison psychology
Lecture: Doll, E., Taylor Society (J App, 9, 428)

Probability
Lecture: Becknell, E. A. (AJP, 53, 604-609)

Lecture: Graham, J. L., normal probability curve (AJP, 52, 293-296)

Probation Association, National
1931 yearbook on scientific treatment of crime (J App, 16, 223)

Production methods
Course: Business Training Corporation, New York (J App, 3, 396)

Product-moment Correlation *(see also* Correlation)
Publication: Humm, D. G. (AJP, 55, 127-130)

Progressive Education Association
Celebration: Dewey's, J, 80th birthday (Sci, 90, 350)

Prohibition movement
Lecture: Münsterberg, H. (Sci, 29, 23)

Projective techniques
Research: Rosenzweig, S., study of personality (Bull, 42, 487)

Propaganda
Course: Dept. of Education, Univ. Extension Division of Psychology for National Defense (J App, 25, 472)

Election: Institute for Propaganda Analysis, officers (J App, 25, 361, 597; J App, 21, 719)

Lecture: Hays, W. H., renounces propaganda in motion pictures (J App, 22, 217)

Lecture: Huntington, T. W., Nazi civil propaganda (J App, 24, 519)

Organization: Institute of Propaganda Analysis (Bull, 34, 865)

Propaganda Analysis Bulletin
Outline schedule of issues, 1941 (J App, 25, 597)

Publication: Dale, E. and Vernon, N. W., propaganda analysis: an annotated bibliography (J App, 24, 656)

Publication: *German Psychological Warfare*, committee for national morale (J App, 25, 359)

Publication: *Institute for Propaganda Analysis* monthly letter, officers (J App, 21, 719; Bull, 34, 865)

Providence Hospital
Open: psychiatric clinic for Catholic Univ. of America (Bull, 13, 108)

Provisional International Committee
Excluded psychology from catalogue of scientific literature (Rev, 7, 104)

Prussia

Plans a hygienic institute at Berlin (SCI°, *4*, 410)
Publication: minister of instruction, opinion on the over work in schools (SCI°, *4*, 268)

Prussian Order of Merit

Award: Stumpf, C. (SCI, *70*, 63)

Psi Chi

Lecture: Pike, F. H., Washington Square College Chapter (SCI, *81*, 457)
Lecture: Wolfle, D. B., Univ. of Minnesota Chapter (BULL, *40*, 310)
Publication: Kuhlmann, F., Minnesota Chapter (J APP, *25*, 359)

Psiche

Publication: begun in Italy (BULL, *9*, 96; JoP, *9*, 56)
Publication: suspended temporarily (BULL, *13*, 40)

Psychiatry

Appointment: Bowman, K. M., Bellevue Hospital (SCI, *83*, 181)
Appointment: Burlingame, C. C., Neuro-psychiatric Institute of the Hartford Retreat (J APP, *24*, 371)
Appointment: Diethelm, O. A., Cornell Univ. (SCI, *83*, 228)
Appointment: Johnson, G. S., Stanford Univ. (SCI, *78*, 278)
Appointment: Scholz, W., Kaiser Wilhelm Institute, German Research Institute of Psychiatry (SCI, *84*, 288)
Appointment: Strecker, E. A., Univ. of Pennsylvania (SCI, *74*, 364, 384)
Birthday: Wagner-Jauregg, J. (SCI, *85*, 354)
Clinic opens, Moore, T. V. (BULL, *13*, 108)
Election: American Board of Psychiatry and Neurology, officers (SCI, *80*, 476)
Fellowship: the Commmonwealth Fund (SCI, *71*, 13)
Hospital: Bellevue replaced (SCI, *70*, 306)
Hospital: Connecticut to build one (SCI, *57*, 382)
Hospital: Massachusetts General, psychiatric unit established (SCI, *79*, 291)
Hospital: New York State Psychiatric Institute dedicated, 1929 (SCI, *70*, 578)
Hospital: Psychiatric Institute of the Illinois Research and Educational Hospitals (BULL, *37*, 329)
Lecture: Campbell, C. M., Salmon Memorial Lectures (SCI, *79*, 268)
Lecture: Carmichael, L., relationship between psychology and psychiatry (BULL, *37*, 122)
Lecture: Economo, K., Columbia Univ. (SCI, *71*, 213)
Lecture: Gillespie, R. D., New York Acad. of Medicine, Salmon Lecturer (J APP, *25*, 726)
Lecture: Meyer, A. (SCI, *15*, 396)
Lecture: Orton, S. T., New York Acad. of Medicine, language (SCI, *83*, 389)
Lecture: Sommer, R., German Society of Experimental Psychology (SCI, *22*, 727)
Meeting: International Congress of Child Psychiatry, 1st (BULL, *34*, 325)

Meeting: Massachusetts Psychiatric Society (SCI, *80*, 475)

Publication: Lost and found, journal for recovering patients announced (BULL, *37*, 329)

Publication: Neuro-psychiatric Institute of the Hartford Retreat, 116th annual report (J APP, *24*, 371)

Publication: *New York Medical Journal* (JoP, *4*, 307)

Resignation: Brush, E. N., *American Journal of Psychiatry* editor (SCI, *74*, 34)

Resignation: Grinker, R. R., Univ. of Chicago (SCI, *83*, 347)

Psychiatry, Institute for Research in, (Munich)

Gifts and bequests (SCI, *54*, 128)

Psychiatry, Neurology, Psychology and Care of the Insane, International Congress of

Meeting: announced, 1907 (BULL, *4*, 95)

Psychical Institute, International Society of the

Establishment: Janet, P. (REV, *7*, 532)

Establishment: Paris (SCI, *12*, 238)

Resignation: Baldwin, J. M., Committee of Patrons (REV, *8*, 112)

Psychical research (*see also* Parapsychology)

Establishment: Univ. of London, Council for Psychical Research (SCI, *80*, 183)

Fellowship: Columbia Univ. (BULL, *2*, 88)

Glossary of terms (SCI, *4*, 140)

Joad, C. E. M. (SCI, *80*, 183)

Lecture: Clark Univ. (BULL, *24*, 204; JoP, *23*, 700; J APP, *10*, 522)

Publication: Ramaer, I. N., analysis (AJP, *1*, 201)

Psychical Research Society

Publication: Nyers, W. H., glossary of terms (SCI, *4*, 140)

Psycho-Acoustic Laboratory (*see* Harvard University)

Continues Harvard Univ. Faculty of Arts and Sciences (SCI, *102*, 506)

Psychoanalysis

Course: American Institute for Psychoanalysis (BULL, *38*, 779)

Course: Glueck, B., New School for Social Research (BULL, *24*, 312; SCI, *65*, 156)

Lecture: Brill, A. A. (BULL, *12*, 128)

Election: Freud, Royal Society (BULL, *35*, 796)

Establishment: Assoc. for the Advancement of Psychoanalysis, officers (J APP, *25*, 473)

Fellowship: Boston Psychoanalytic Institute, Sigmund Freud Memorial Fellowships for Psychoanalytic Training (BULL, *37*, 827)

Grant: Jung, C. G., studies of psycho-analyses, Zurich (SCI, *81*, 67)

Lecture: Harvey Society, 4th (SCI, *73*, 64)

Lecture: Janet, P. (SCI, *38*, 124)

Lecture: Jung, C. G., Institute of Medical Psychology, London (SCI, *82*, 348)
Lecture: Kardiner, A., New York Univ. Philosophical Society (JoP, *35*, 616)
Lecture: Tannenbaum, S. A., Columbia Univ. (JoP, *13*, 280)
Meeting: Menninger Clinic conference with experiential psychology (BULL, *33*, 579)
Meeting: New York Acad. of Medicine (JoP, *9*, 224)
Publication: Baudouin, C., "LA Psychoanalyses" monograph (JoP, *36*, 392)
Publication: Committee for the Study of Suicide, annual report, 1938 (J APP, *22*, 108)
Publication: Flournoy, H. (JoP, *21*, 560)
Publication: *Imago* (JoP, *9*, 335)
Research: Benjamin, J., suicide (J APP, *22*, 108)
Research: Ebaugh, F. G., suicide (J APP, *22*, 108)
Research: Kaufman, M. R., suicidal patients (J APP, *22*, 108)

Psychoanalytic Review

Editor: Lewis, N. D. C. (SCI, *101*, 171)
Publication begun (BULL, *10*, 490; JoP, *10*, 616)

Psychobiology

Research: Carpenter, C. R., Univ. of the School of Tropical Medicine at San Juan, Puerto Rico, with primates (SCI, *86*, 79)

Psychobiology

Merge: *Journal of Animal Behavior* to become *The Journal of Comparative Psychology* (JoP, *17*, 672)
Publication: announced (JoP, *14*, 532; BULL, *14*, 115)

Psychodramatic Institute, The

Moreno, J. L. (BULL, *37*, 329)
Summer session, 1940 (BULL, *37*, 329)

Psychological Abstracts

Publication: notice (AJP, *38*, 316; J APP, *11*, 320)

Psychological articles

Research: analysis of articles published in 1939 (AJP, *53*, 295-297)

Psychological Bulletin

Appointment: Anderson, J. E. (BULL, *25*, 444; J APP, *26*, 392)
Appointment: cooperating editor change (BULL, *22*, 444)
Appointment: Fernberger, S. (SCI, *59*, 60)
Appointment: Franz, S. I. (BULL, *11*, 152; JoP, *11*, 308)
Appointment: Heron, W. T. (BULL, *21*, 552)
Appointment: Metcalf, J. (BULL, *26*, 56)
Appointment: Pierce, A. H. (JoP, *7*, 280)
Appointment: Robinson, E. S. (BULL, *23*, 112)
Editor: change (JoP, *21*, 56; BULL, *22*, 444)

Editor: Meyer, A., psychopathology issue (BULL, *7*, 148)
Issue: constitutional amendment of APA (BULL, *39*, 196)
Issue: guidance for handicapped of WWII (J APP, *28*, 79)
Issue: military science, special (J APP, *25*, 358)
Issue: psychologists in government service (J APP, *26*, 391)
Issue: psychology and the war (J APP, *26*, 391-392)
Price increase (BULL, *14*, 144)
Resignation: Franz, S. I. (SCI, *59*, 60)
Resignation: Hunter, W. S. (BULL, *21*, 552)
Resignation: Ogden, R. M. (BULL, *26*, 56)

Psychological Cinema Register
Founding (J APP, *23*, 632)
Purchase: Pennsylvania State College (BULL, *41*, 343-344)

Psychological Clinic, The
Publication: announced (BULL, *4*, 95; JoP, *4*, 167)

Psychological Corporation
Anniversary: 20th, honoring Cattell, J. McK., 1941 (BULL, *39*, 196)
Appointment: Chappel, M. N., Psychological Service Center, New York (BULL, *36*, 805)
Appointment: Potts, E., Nurse Testing Division, founded (J APP, *23*, 421)
Appointment: Wulfeck, W. H. (BULL, *36*, 805)
Award: advertising and selling (J APP, *27*, 207)
Departure: Wulfeck, W. H. (J APP, *26*, 857)
Election (BULL, *24*, 80; J APP, *11*, 80; J APP, *25*, 600)
Election: Achilles, P. S., secretary (J APP, *16*, 334)
Election: Board of Directors (SCI, *65*, 10)
Grants: Cattell, J. McK. grants-in-aid of research and applied psych. established (BULL, *39*, 683)
Grants: Cattell, J. McK. grants-in-aid of research in applied psychology available (SCI, *05*, 579; J APP, *26*, 389)
Grants: research awarded (J APP, *28*, 79)
Lecture (J APP, *17*, 341)
Meeting: annual (J APP, *11*, 80)
Meeting: APA and AAAP (J APP, *25*, 600)
Meeting: APA luncheon (J APP, *24*, 369, 517)
Publication: annual report (BULL, *42*, 408; J APP, *27*, 364-365)
Publication: Wonderlic Personnel Test (J APP, *27*, 207)
Research: Bregman, E., women secretaries (J APP, *10*, 393)
Research: English usage and vocabulary (BULL, *28*, 645)
Research: money set aside (BULL, *42*, 584)
Research: Schultz, R. S., on personnel selection (J APP, *21*, 242)
Research: Stoy, E. G., selection of key punch operators (J APP, *24*, 654)
Stock information (J APP, *6*, 213)

Psychological Exchange, The
Resignation: Powell, N. (SCI, *78*, 307)

Psychological Index
Editor: Bentley, M. (BULL, *12*, 403)
Publication: announced, 1896 (REV, *4*, 230)

Psychological Index Project
Works Progess Administration, measures of public interest in psychology (BULL *36*, 219)

Psychological Monographs
Editor: Angell, J. R. (BULL, *6*, 296)
Editor: change (JOP, *21*, 56)
Editor: Dashiell, J. F. (BULL, *32*, 862)
Editor: Franz, S. I. (SCI, *59*, 60)
Editor: Peterson, G. (SCI, *79*, 247)
Quantitative psychology articles, titles and authors, 1940 (J APP, *24*, 855)
Resignation: Angell, J. R. (SCI, *59*, 60)

Psychological Museum (Chicago, Illinois)
Lecture: Boder, D. P., apparatus (BULL, *41*, 410)
Lecture: Lauer, A. R. (BULL, *41*, 410)

Psychological Personnel, Office of (*see* National Research Council, and Office of Psychological Personnel)

Psychological Physiology, Congress of
Lecture: Galton, F. W., acquired habits, mental, scientific, or social (SCI°, *14*, 195)

Psychological Record, The
Publication: announced (J APP, *20*, 791; BULL, *34*, 409)
Subscription rate increased (BULL, *36*, 806)

Psychological Review (see also *Monograph Supplements of Psychological Review*)
Appointment: Bentley, M. (JOP, *12*, 644)
Appointment: Langfeld, H. S. (SCI, *79*, 247)
Appointment: Warren, H. C. (REV, *8*, 112)
Change of business manager (JOP, *2*, 672)
Editor: *Monograph Supplements* (JOP, *1*, 280)
Price increase (BULL, *14*, 144)
Publication: announced (JOP, *1*, 84)
Publication: Darwin, C., dedicated (JOP, *6*, 308)
Publication: *Philosophical Monographs* (JOP, *4*, 252)
Publication: psychological index for 1894 (SCI, *1*, 473)

Publication: psychology bibliography for 1895 (Sci, *3*, 354)
Resignation: Baldwin, J. M. (JoP, *7*, 140)

Psychological Review Publications
Adds: *The Journal of Experimental Psychology* (JoP, *13*, 336)
Appointment: Bentley, M. (Bull, *12*, 403)
Involved in war (Bull, *13*, 448)

Psychological Service Center (New York)
Appointment: Chappell, M. N. (Bull, *36*, 805)

Psychological Society
Establishment (JoP, *1*, 616)

Psychological Society of Buenos Aires (Argentina)
Driesch, H., honorary member (Sci, *73*, 609)

Psychological Society of Moscow (Russia)
Report (AJP, *3*, 592)

Psychological Supper Club
Monthly discussion group, program for 1940 (Bull, *37*, 656)

Psychological Test Bureau (Rochester)
Appointment: Mitrano, A. J. (Bull, *38*, 907)

Psychologie
Publication: Ebbinghaus, H. (AJP, *8*, 430)

Psychologie des Sentiments
Translation to English (Rev, *5*, 110)

Psychologische Arbeiten
Publication: announcement (Rev, *2*, 216)

Psychologische Forschung
Publication: begins (Bull, *18*, 628)

Psychologische Studien
Discontinuation announced (Bull, *18*, 110)
Publication: announced (JoP, *1*, 721)

Psychologists Club of San Francisco (*see* San Francisco)

Psychology
Course: Baldwin, J. M., National Univ. of Mexico, history of (JoP, *9*, 335)
Course: Columbia Univ. (JoP, *16*, 475-476)
Degree: American Doctorates, list of 1934-1942 (AJP, *57*, 94-96)
Degree: number of doctorates conferred (JoP, *4*, 532)

Editor: Baldwin, J. M., library volumes, history of (REV, *10*, 344)
Lecture: Angier, R. P., Yale Univ., history of (SCI, *52*, 384)
Lecture: Blayney, E. F., instruction of (JoP, *7*, 222)
Lecture: Columbia Univ., problems of (BULL, *8*, 78)
Lecture: Cook, A., Clark Univ. (SCI°, *14*, 250)
Lecture: Hall, G. S., Columbia Univ., founders of (JoP, *9*, 56)
Lecture: Moore, G. E., subject matter of (JoP, *7*, 55)
Lecture: Sanford, E. C., Clark Univ. (SCI°, *14*, 250)
Lecture: Skaggs, E. B., elementary courses (AJP, *38*, 153)
Lecture: Stratton, G. M., health and (SCI, *51*, 112)
Lecture: Weigle, L. A., philosophical implications (JoP, *7*, 223)
Publication: Chou, S. K., China (AJP, *38*, 664)
Publication: Leuba, J. H., card catalogue (SCI, *10*, 661)
Publication: Titchener, E. B. (JoP, *7*, 560)
Publication: volumes listed for Library of Historical Psychology (REV, *10*, 592)
Publication: Ward, J., *Encyclopedia Britannica* (SCI°, *7*, 304)

Psychology and Psychiatry, International Course for
Meeting: announced (BULL, *6*, 72)

Psychology and the Post-War World
Reprints available from APA (BULL, *42*, 332)

Psychology Classics
Editor: Dunlap, K. (JoP, *14*, 56; BULL, *13*, 482)
Publication: announcment (SCI, *55*, 315; BULL, *13*, 482; JoP, *14*, 56)

Psychology, Encyclopedia of
Publication: plans (BULL, *41*, 499)

Psychology for the Fighting Man
Textbook: National Research Council (J APP, *27*, 475)

Psychology in Junior Colleges, Committee on
Election: Omwake, L., chair, instruction investigation (J APP, *25*, 361)
Establishment: American Assoc. for Applied Psychology Committee on
  Instruction (BULL, *38*, 779)
Lecture: Miller, J. C., methods of instruction investigation (J APP, *25*, 361)

Psychology, International Seminar in
Organization: APA Committee on Displaced Foreign Psychologists (BULL, *38*,
  191)

Psychology of Child Development, The
King, I., new Bohemian translation (BULL, *9*, 359)

Psychometric Society
Election: Kelley, T. L., president (SCI, *88*, 277)

Lecture: Dunlap, J. W., the Psychometric Society roots and powers (Sci, *94*, 230)

Lecture: Guilford, J. P. (Sci, *88*, 277)

Meeting: APA (Sci, *91*, 500; Sci, *94*, 230)

Meeting: Ohio State Univ. (JoP, *35*, 280)

Psycho-neurological Academy of Leningrad (U.S.S.R.)

Election: Flechsig, P. (Sci, *67*, 291)

Institute opens, St. Petersburg (Bull, *5*, 168; JoP, *5*, 224)

Psychopathic Clinic of the Recorders Court of the City of Detroit

Appointments (Sci, *84*, 13)

Psychopathology

Course: Neurological Institute of Frankfort-on-Main, children (Bull, *6*, 72)

Course: Pathological Institute, Wards Island, New York, children (JoP, *6*, 111)

Course: Tufts College Medical School, Boston (Sci, *29*, 335)

Establishment: research dept., Sing Sing, New York (Bull, *13*, 296)

Psychopharmacology

Lecture: Hanzlik, P. J. (Sci, *87*, 253)

Psychophysics

Award: postponed due to war (JoP, *12*, 280; Bull, *12*, 204)

Lecture: Carr, H. W. (JoP, *8*, 280)

Lecture: Davies, E. and Babb, W. W. M. (AJP, *44*, 367)

Lecture: Linder, F. E., accuracy of the constant method (AJP, *47*, 504)

Lecture: Pearson's formula (JoP *11*, 27-28)

Lecture: Titchener, E. B. (JoP, *1*, 280)

Lecture: Volkman, J., single stimuli method (AJP, *44*, 808)

Psychoses

Lecture: Williams, T. A., traumatic neuresthenia (JoP, *7*, 20)

Meeting: Research Council on Problems of Alcohol (Bull, *37*, 61)

Psychosociology

Lecture: Baldwin, J. M., National Univ. of Mexico (JoP, *9*, 335)

Course: Baldwin, J. M., National Univ. of Mexico (Bull, *7*, 396)

Psychosomatic Medicine

Appointment: Board of Editors (J App, *22*, 663)

Publication: announced (Bull, *36*, 219; J App, *22*, 663)

Research: fund established by National Committee for Mental Hygiene (Sci, *99*, 319, 363)

Psychosomatic Problems, Society for Research in

Election: officers, 1943 (Sci, *98*, 258)

Psychosurgery
Award: Watts, J. W., John Horsley Memorial Prize (Sci, 96, 36)
Lecture: Taylor, J. W., trephining of Inca skull (Sci°, 7, 186)

Psychotechnic, International Conference of
Meeting (Bull, 26, 624; Bull, 27 240; J App, 14, 96; J App, 13, 413)
Meeting: postponed (Sci, 70, 306; J App, 13, 533)

Psychotechnology
Jenkins, J. G., Univ. of Maryland (Bull, 34, 864)

Psychotherapies
Publication: Münsterberg, H. (JoP, 6, 196)

Psychotherapy
German medical congress (AJP, 40, 672)
Lecture: Aikins, H. A., problems of (Sci, 49, 118)
Lecture: conditioning and reconditioning (AJP, 58, 391-392)
Lecture: Haynes, R. (JoP, 7, 223)
Lecture: International Congress of the History of Medicine, psychological
    disorders (Sci, 87, 164)
Lecture: Münsterberg, H. (Sci, 29, 23)
Meeting: International Med. Soc. of Psychotherapy, 10th (Bull, 35, 408)

Public Health Service (see United States Public Health Service)

Public Law 113
Expansion of program for vocational rehabilitation of handicapped civilians,
    1943 (J App, 27, 473-474)

Public relations
Civil service employment for psychologists, Forest Service, USDA (Sci, 85, 382)

Public service
Barnes, J. H., financial backer (J App, 3, 290)
Lecture: Galton, F., on the advisability of assigning marks for bodily efficiency
    of candidates for public service (Sci°, 14, 266)

Puerto Rico, University of (San Juan)
Appointment: Brumbaugh, M. B. (Sci, 11, 957)
Leave of absence: Koppisch, E. (Sci, 101, 86)
Lecture: Yerkes, R. M., School of Tropical Medicine (Sci, 87, 136-137)

Punishment
Greek custom (Sci°, 7, 235)

Purdue University (West Lafayette, Indiana)
Appointment: announced, psychology (Sci, 54, 463)
Appointment: Asher, E. J. (Bull, 42, 332)

Q

Quadfasel, Angela Folsom (*see* Folsom, Angela T.)

Quantitative psychology (*see* Statistics)

Quantz, John Oscar
Appointment: Wisconsin State Normal School (SCI, *14*, 744)
Death notice (SCI, *17*, 238-239; REV, *10*, 224)

Quarterly Journal of General Psychology
Publication notice (SCI, *66*, 617)

Quarterly Journal of Studies on Alcohol
Editor: Haggard, H. W. (BULL, *37*, 755)

Quebec, Province of (Canada)
Establishment: Dept. of Psychiatry, McGill Univ. and Royal Victoria Hospital
(SCI, *98*, 446-447; SCI, *99*, 123-124)

Queen, James W.
Death notice (SCI°, *16*, 104)

Queens College (Belfast)
Death notice: Everett, J. D. (SCI, *20*, 286)
Election: Love, A. E. H., honorary fellow (SCI, *20*, 856)

Queens College (Flushing, New York)
Appointment: Anastasi, A. (SCI, *90*, 439; BULL, *37*, 122)
Appointment: Razran, G. (BULL, *37*, 329)
Appointment: Spencer, D. (BULL, *37*, 329)
Appointment: Spragg, S. D. (BULL, *37*, 329)
Appointment: Young, K. (SCI, *91*, 138)
Promotion: Razran, G. S. (BULL, *42*, 486)
Promotion: Spragg, S. D. (BULL, *42*, 486)

Queensland, University of (Brisbane, Australia)
Appointment: Lawson, J. P. (Sci, 55, 398)

Quimby, Isaac F.
Retirement: Univ. of Rochester (Sci°, 4, 465)

Quinsey, Donald Leroy
Promotion: Univ. of Maine (Bull, 42, 63)

R

Race
Lecture: Garth, T. R., psychology (SCI, 75, 101; BULL, 29, 180)
Lecture: Krauss, W. W., Univ. of Colorado, biology (SCI, 98, 106)
Publication: Montgomery, T. H., racial descent (JoP, 3, 419)
Research: Candolle, A. de, deaf-mutes (SCI°, 7, 214)

Radcliffe College (Cambridge, Massachusetts)
Endowment: Helen Putnam Fellowship for Advanced Research (SCI, 100, 402)

Radio
Broadcast: National Advisory Council on Radio in Education, psychology and economics (SCI, 74, 411)
Publication: Lazarsfeld, P. F., J APP special issue (J APP, 25, 128)
Research: Princeton radio research project (J APP, 22, 663)

Raggi, [Antigonio ?]
Research: sound perception (SCI°, 7, 570)

Rahn, Carl Leo
Appointment: Univ. of Minnesota (BULL, 8, 373; SCI, 34, 602)
Appointment: Univ. of Wyoming (BULL, 11, 268; JoP, 11, 721)

Raimy, Victor
Appointment: Univ. of Minnesota, Testing Bureau (BULL, 40, 152)

Rall, Edward Everett
Election: SSPP office (BULL, 13, 40; JoP, 13, 112)

Ramaer, I. N.
Publication: psychical analysis (AJP, 1, 201)

Ramon y Cajal, Santiago
Award: gold medal (JoP, 5, 448)

Ramsdell, Donald Angus
Appointment: Univ. of Alabama, psych lab director (BULL, *36*, 500)

Ramsey, Glenn
Research: Kinsey, A. C. and Martin, C. E., human sex behavior (SCI, *95*, 600)

Rand, Benjamin
Death notice (JOP, *31*, 671)
Publication: the classical psychologists (JOP, *9*, 56)

Rand, Marie Gertrude
Award: Sarah Berliner fellowship (JOP, *9*, 168)
Appointment: Columbia Univ., Knapp Foundation (BULL, *40*, 459)
Degree: Wilson College (BULL, *40*, 619)
Promotion: Bryn Mawr College (BULL, *11*, 190)
Publication: perception of depth in the after-image (AJP, *46*, 329)

Randall, Jr., John Herman
Editor: *Journal of Philosophy* (JOP, *34*, 280)

Randels, George Basil
Death notice (BULL, *40*, 152)

Randolph Macon College for Women (Lynchburg, Virginia)
Appointment: Geissler, L. R. (BULL, *17*, 351)

Rank, Otto
Publication: *Imago* (JOP, *9*, 335)

Ranschburg, Paul
Lecture: Congress for Experimental Psychology, IV (JOP, *7*, 83)

Raskin, Evelyn
Grant: Social Science Research Council (BULL, *36*, 805)

Rasmussen, Andrew T.
Lecture: Assoc. for Research in Nervious and Mental Diseases (SCI, *84*, 551)

Rats
Grant: Univ. of Illinois, food preferences in (SCI, *95*, 600)
Lecture: Fernberger, S. W., unlearned behavior (AJP, *41*, 343)
Lecture: Rodhom, C., use in psychology (AJP, *58*, 262-266)

Rauh, Salomon Frédéric
Death notice (BULL, *6*, 216)

Rausch, Alfred
Seminar: Univ. of Halle (JOP, *10*, 616)

Rauth, John Edward, Reverend
Death notice (BULL, *42*, 406)

Rautman, Arthur Louis
Appointment: Carleton College (BULL, *42*, 793)

Ravaisson-Mollien, Felix
Death notice (SCI, *11*, 916)

Ravizza Prize
Competition: announced (JOP, *3*, 308)

Rawson, Edward B.
Appointment: Swarthmore College (JOP, *3*, 336)

Ray, Wilbert Scott
Appointment: Adelphi College (BULL, *41*, 409, 498)
Appointment: European School Center for American Servicemen (BULL, *42*, 582)
Departure: Hillsdale College, Mich. (BULL, *41*, 409)

Rayleigh, John William Strutt, Lord
Research: color vision (SCI[8], *16*, 203)

Raymond, Fulgence
Appointment: Paris Acad. of Medicine (SCI, *10*, 30)

Raymond, George Lansing
Appointment: George Washington Univ. (JOP, *3*, 140; BULL, *2*, 159)

Razran, Gregory Harry Solomon
Appointment: Queens College (BULL, *37*, 329)
Promotion: Queens College (BULL, *42*, 486)
Publication: the number of articles of psychological interest published in the Russian language (AJP, *49*, 316)
Publication: *Psychological Bulletin*, military (J APP, *25*, 358)

RCA Manufacturing Company, Inc.
Appointment: Kerr, W. A. (BULL, *39*, 681)

Reaction time
Passage from Wundt's *Vorlesungen* (AJP, *9*, 421-422)

Read, Carveth
Appointment: Univ. of London (BULL, *18*, 439)
Death notice (BULL, *29*, 89)
Lecture: comparative psychology (SCI, *36*, 473)

Read, Melbourne Stuart
Appointment: Colgate Univ. (BULL, 9, 360)
Promotion: Colgate Univ. (JoP, 9, 532)

Reading
Lecture: Hamilton, F. M. (JoP, 2, 700)
Lecture: Schumann, F., German Society of Experimental Psychology (SCI, 22, 727)
Lecture: Weigle, L. A. (JoP, 2, 224)
Research: Gray, C. T., ability and eye movements (J APP, 1, 298)
Research: Heilman, J. D. (J APP, 3, 195)
Research: Kitson, H. D., proofreading (J APP, 1, 298)

Reasoning (see also Thought)
Publication: Pillsbury, W. B., psychology of (JoP, 7, 196)

Rebec, George
Appointment: Univ. of Michigan (REV, 2, 104)

Reconstruction in Philosophy
Publication: Catholic Univ. (J APP, 10, 395)
Publication: Dewey, J. (JoP, 17, 336)

Red Wing Training School for Boys, Minnesota (see Training School for)

Reed College (Portland, Oregon)
Appointment: Rowland, E. H. (JoP, 9, 168)
Appointment: Sisson, E. D. (JoP, 9, 56)
Meeting: Oregon Psychological Assoc., 2nd (BULL, 34, 410)
Psychology lab improvements planned (BULL, 12, 403)

Reed, Homer Blosser
Appointment: Univ. of Idaho (JoP, 12, 532)
Appointment: Univ. of Illinois (SCI, 40, 670; JoP, 11, 721)
Appointment: Univ. of Pittsburgh (BULL, 22, 140; J APP, 8, 450; SCI, 60, 291)

Rees, John Rawlings
Lecture: Salmon, 1944 (SCI, 99, 531; SCI, 100, 402, 492)

Reese, Thomas Whelan
Appointment: Mount Holyoke College (BULL, 39, 896)

Reeves, Prentice
Appointment: Princeton Univ. (BULL, 9, 408; JoP, 9, 700)
Departure: Univ. of Missouri (BULL, 9, 408; JoP, 9, 700)

Reiter, Frank Horace

Appointment: Newark, New Jersey Public School System (BULL, *18*, 56; SCI, *52*, 635)

Appointment: State of Pennsylvania, Dept. of Education (BULL, *22*, 612)

Appointment: Univ. of Pennsylvania (JOP, *11*, 588)

Promotion: Univ. of Pennsylvania (BULL, *11*, 483; SCI, *40*, 482)

Resignation: Univ. of Pennsylvania (SCI, *52*, 635)

Rejall, Alfred Ernst

Appointment: Boston Univ. (JOP, *14*, 224)

Appointment: Columbia Univ. (SCI, *36*, 593)

Reliability

Crosland, H. R., experimental (AJP, *40*, 331)

Religion

Course: Ames, E. S., Univ. of Chicago, psychology of (JOP, *1*, 336)

Course: Armed Forces Institute (JOP, *41*, 305-306)

Course: Univ. of Geneva, psychology (JOP, *22*, 308)

Lecture (JOP, *42*, 56)

Lecture: Boutroux, E. (JOP, *7*, 140)

Lecture: Bryn Mawr College, Indian thought (JOP, *41*, 196)

Lecture: Dewey, J., Yale Univ. (JOP, *30*, 336)

Lecture: French, F. C. (JOP, *2*, 252)

Lecture: Jung, C. G. (SCI, *86*, 395)

Lecture: King, I. (JOP, *1*, 84)

Lecture: Ladd, G. T. (JOP, *1*, 252)

Lecture: Leuba, J. H., 8th International Congress of Psychology, psychology of (BULL, *23*, 176; SCI, *53*, 436)

Lecture: Purinton, D. B. (JOP, *2*, 56)

Library proposed, Bornhausen, K., psychology of (JOP, *10*, 84)

Meeting: Conference on methods in Philosophy and the Sciences, XI (JOP, *39*, 252)

Meeting: Conference on Science, Philosophy, and Religion in their Relation to the Democratic Way of Life (SCI, *92*, 76)

Meeting: International Congress, 1st, Vienna, psychology of (JOP, *28*, 196)

Meeting: Scientific Spirit and Democratic Faith (JOP, *41*, 279)

Publication: Coe, G., psychology of (SCI, *44*, 307)

Research: APA, relations of philosophy, science and religion (JOP, *40*, 587-588)

Research: society founded, psychology of (JOP, *11*, 700)

Religious Psychology, International Congress of, 1st

Meeting: announced (JOP, *27*, 672; BULL, *27*, 674; JOP, *28*, 196)

Remmers, Hermann Henry

Appointment: Colorado College (BULL, *20*, 60)

Remp, Martin
Election: Ohio College Assoc., secretary-treasurer (BULL, 27, 415)

Remsen, Ira
Lecture: Bryn Mawr College (JoP, 7, 616)

Renaissance
Edit: L'École Libre des Hautes Études, a branch of New School for Social Research (JoP, 40, 448)

Renouvier, Charles Bernard
Monument: honor of (JoP, 1, 223)

Renshaw, Samuel
Conference: Psychology of Learning, Univ. of Colorado, 1939 (BULL, 36, 583)

Replogle, Frederick Allen
Appointment: Stevenson, Jordan and Harrison, Inc. (BULL, 40, 794)

Repression in forgetting (*see also* Forgetting)
Meeting: British Psychological Society/Aristotelian Society/Mind Assoc. (JoP, 11, 532)

Reproductive behavior (*see also* Sex)
Lecture: Beach, F. A., Indiana Univ. (SCI, 99, 168)

Research
Conference: problems of method in psychology (SCI, 87, 277)
Lecture: Cattell, J. McK. (JoP, 13, 224)
Lecture: Fernberger, S., interests of American psychologists (AJP, 41, 163)
Lecture: history of methods, psychological (AJP, 55, 569-573)
Publication: terms used (AJP, 57, 424-426, 577-579; AJP, 58, 113-117)
Research: analysis of interests in psychology (AJP, 54, 605-607)

Research Bureau for Retail Training
Appointment: Charters, W. W. (J APP, 3, 290)

Research Corporation of New York
Grant: Univ. of Pittsburgh (BULL, 38, 304; BULL, 39, 196-197)

Research Council on Problems of Alcohol
Award: research (BULL, 40, 311-312; J APP, 27, 208)
Election: Bowman, K. M., chair (BULL, 37, 61)
Grant: Carnegie, APS, Dazian Foundation (BULL, 37, 62)
Meeting (SCI, 92, 126, 307; SCI, 94, 412; SCI, 96, 294)
Research: AAAS Assoc., program announced (BULL, 37, 61)

Response
  Lecture: Holt, E. B., New School of Social Research, psychology of (BULL, *24*, 204)

Retardation
  Lecture: Meyerding, E. A. (JoP, *7*, 223)
  Lecture: Thorndike, E. L. (SCI, *37*, 302)
  Lecture: Woodrow, H. H. (JoP, *7*, 223)

Retina
  Lecture: Dearborn, W. F., retinal local signs (JoP, *1*, 84)
  Research: Graham, C. H. (BULL, *38*, 304)

Retroactive inhibition (*see also* Forgetting; Memory)
  Lecture: McGeoch, J. A. (AJP, *42*, 455)

Review of Psychiatry, Neurology and Experimental Psychology
  Publication: announced (REV, *3*, 244; SCI, *3*, 98)

Review of the Science of Labor, The
  Publication (SCI, *70*, 190)

Revista de Criminología, Psiquiatría y Medicina-legal
  Publication: announced (BULL, *11*, 268)

Revista de Educacion
  Publication: notice (J APP, *3*, 198)

Revista de Filosofia
  Listing of Argentine books (JoP, *15*, 474-476)

Revista de Psiquiatría y Disciplinas Conexas
  Contents for the first number, July, 1918 (JoP, *15*, 504)
  Publication: notice (J APP, *3*, 198)

Revue de Métaphysique et de Morale
  Monument: memory of Renouvier, C. (JoP, *1*, 223)
  Publication: Cournot, A. A. (JoP, *2*, 392)
  Publication: Durkheim, E., social contract (JoP, *15*, 196)
  Publication: Protestant reformation, 1918 (JoP, *16*, 112)

Revue de Pédotechnie
  Publication: begun (BULL, *11*, 191)

Revue de Psychologie Concrete
  Announcement: inauguration (J APP, *13*, 317)

Revue des Revues
  Publication: laboratory at the Sorbonne (REV, *5*, 345)

Revue des Sciences Psychologiques
Publication: announcement (BULL, *10*, 292; JoP, *10*, 336)

Revue Philosophique
Publication: January, 1888 (SCI°, *11*, 45)

Revue Psychologique, La
Publication announced (BULL, *5*, 243)

Revue Scientifique
Editor: Toulouse, E. (JoP, *1*, 112)
Publication: animal morale (SCI°, *14*, 181)
Publication: Jastrow, J., translation from *Science* (SCI, *4*, 47)

Reymert, Martin Luther
Appointment: International Symposium on Feelings and Emotions (JoP, *24*, 587)
Appointment: Mooseheart, Illinois (BULL, *27*, 674)
Departure: Univ. of Iowa (BULL, *17*, 280)
Election: Ohio College Assoc., president (BULL, *26*, 624)
Establishment: Norwegian Psychological Assoc. (AJP, *46*, 511)

Reynolds, Chester L.
Rochester Guidance Clinic, New York, mental hygiene (BULL, *36*, 841)

Reynolds, Myra Memorial Fellowship
Vassar College, Graduate Division of Conservation (BULL, *39*, 132)

Rhine, Joseph Banks
Editor: *Journal of Parapsychology* (BULL, *39*, 325; SCI, *95*, 322-323)

Rhinehart, Jesse Batley
Appointment: Univ. of Illinois (BULL, *42*, 793-794)

Rhode Island State College (Providence)
Appointment: Bird, G. E. (BULL, *16*, 392)
Retirement: Bird, G. E. (BULL, *40*, 79)

Rhode Island State Hospital for Mental Diseases (Providence)
Neuro-psychiatric Clinic named for Meyer, A. (SCI, *88*, 423; BULL, *36*, 57)

Rhodes University College (Grahamstown, Cape Colony)
Appointment: Lord, A. R. (JoP, *2*, 392)

Ribot, Theodule Armand
Appointment: Collège de France (AJP, *1*, 551)
Election: Paris Acad. of Moral Sciences (SCI, *11*, 197; REV, *7*, 216)
Death notice (AJP, *28*, 312; BULL, *14*, 32)
Departure: Collège de France (SCI, *15*, 320)

Election: Société de psychologie physiologique, 1st vice- president (SCI°, *6*, 360)
Publication: *The Diseases of Personality* (SCI°, *23*, 97)
Publication: psychology of the emotions (SCI, *5*, 583)
Retirement: Collège de France (REV, *8*, 447; SCI, *13*, 1000)

Ricci, Corrado
Eugenics chair (SCI, *70*, 13)

Rice Institute (Houston, Texas)
Departure: Aldrich, V. C. (JOP, *41*, 532)
Lecture: Conklin, E. G., Sharp Foundation (SCI, *93*, 396)
Lecture: Conklin, E. G., "what is man" (SCI, *93*, 155)

Rich, Gilbert Joseph
Appointment: Univ. of Pittsburgh (BULL, *17*, 279)
Lecture: auditory analysis (AJP, *35*, 467)
Lecture: visual acuity (AJP, *34*, 615)

Richardson, Edward Elliott
Lecture: SSPP, concept of laws of nature (JOP, *7*, 28)

Richardson, Marion Webster
Course: New York Univ., personnel psychology (SCI, *98*, 299)
Course: Univ. of Chicago (J APP, *23*, 311)
Editor: *Educational and Psychological Measurement* (J APP, *25*, 266)

Richardson, Roy Franklin
The Psychology and Pedagogy of Anger (J APP, *3*, 197)

Richardson-Robinson, Florence (*see* Robinson, Florence Ella Richardson)

Riche, Alfred
Publication: Council of Hygiene (SCI°, *5*, 412)

Richot, Charles
Publication: Baldwin, M. (SCI, *2*, 187)

Richmond, Winifred Vanderbilt
Death notice (BULL, *42*, 581)
Lecture: Child Research Clinic of Woods School, exceptional child (J APP, *21*, 131)

Richter, Curt Paul
Grant: Sugar Research Foundation (BULL, *42*, 191)
Lecture: New York Acad. of Medicine (BULL, *40*, 79; SCI, *96*, 445)

Riddell Memorial Lecture
Pear, T. H., Univ. of Durham (SCI, *83*, 619)

Riddle, Oscar
Meeting: International Congress for Sex Research (Sci, 72, 395)

Rider College (Lawrenceville, New Jersey)
Promotion: Russo, S. (Bull, 40, 79)

Rieger, Conrad
Research: Will (Sci°, 6, 260)

Riehl, Alois
Appointment: Univ. of Berlin (JoP, 2, 644)

Riesen, Austin Herbert
Appointment: Yale Univ. (Sci, 96, 225)
Leave of absence: Yale Univ. (Bull, 40, 618)
Promotion: Yale Univ. (Bull, 39, 807)

Riess, Bernard Frank
Departure: *Journal of Parapsychology* (Sci, 95, 322-323)

Riker, Britten Littell
Appointment: Univ. of Vermont (Bull, 42, 582)

Riley, Gordon Lee
Rochester Guidance Clinic, New York, mental hygiene (Bull, 36, 841)

Riley, Issac Woodbridge
Appointment: Vassar College (Bull, 5, 168)
Award: Johnston, H. E., scholarship (JoP, 2, 140)
Lecture: American Medico-Psychological Assoc. (Sci, 29, 931; JoP, 6, 364)
Lecture: France (JoP, 17, 168)
Lecture: International Congress of Psychology, 6th (Sci, 30, 202)

Rioch, David M.
Neuropsychiatry, Washington Univ., St. Louis (Bull, 35, 577)

Ripman, Walter
Lecture: Child Study Society (JoP, 8, 644)

Rippmann, Walter (*see* Ripman, Walter)

Ritter, William Emerson
Lecture: Unification for Psychology and Biology, is man a rational animal (Sci, 71, 435)

Rivas, Helen W.
Establishment: Neuro-psychiatric Clinic, Univ. of Rochester (Sci, 101, 198)

Rivers, William Halse Rivers
Appointment: Cambridge Univ. (AJP, *9*, 250)
Appointment: St. John's College, Cambridge Univ. (Rev, *5*, 232; Sci, *6*, 958)
Appointment: St. John's College, Cambridge Univ., fellow (Sci, *16*, 840)
Appointment: Univ. College, London (Rev, *4*, 567; AJP, *9*, 135)
Death notice (Sci, *55*, 674)
Editor: *British Journal of Psychology* (JoP, *1*, 28)
Lecture: Royal College of Physicians, London (Bull, *3*, 248)
Research: Cambridge Univ. (Rev, *1*, 112)
Research: expedition for psychological study of the Todas of Southern India
    (Sci, *15*, 675; Rev, *9*, 328)
Research: expedition to Torres Straits and Borneo (AJP, *9*, 423)

Rivista di Filosofia, The
Bibliography of philosophical writings continued (JoP, *15*, 196)

Rivista di Pedagogia
Publication. announced (JoP, *3*, 364)

Rivista di psicologia applicata
Proposes formation of Assoc. of Italian Psychologists (JoP, *7*, 84)

Rivista Pedagogica Italiana
Publication: Veniali, F. (Sci°, *8*, 481)

Rivista quindicinale di psicologia, psichiatria, neuropatologia
Publication: begun (AJP, *9*, 135)

Rizzolo, Attilio
Fellowship: National Research Board (Bull, *26*, 380)

Roanoke College (Salem, Virginia)
Appointment: Myers, E. D. (Bull, *42*, 486)

Roback, Abraham Aaron
Appointment: Harvard Univ. (JoP, *17*, 560)
Course: psychology for national defense (Bull, *38*, 779-780)
Establishment: psych. lab, School of Liberal Arts of Northeastern College (JoP,
    16, 721)

Robbins, Samuel Dowse
Research: blood pressure (Bull, *17*, 239)

Robertson, Charles Barr
Appointment: Univ. of Pittsburgh (JoP, *8*, 392)
Resignation: Cortland, New York State Normal School (Sci, *33*, 926)

Robertson, George Matthew
Appointment: Univ. of Edinburgh (Sci, *51*, 62)

Robinson, Edward Stevens

Appointment: Carnegie Institute of Technology, Bureau of Salesmanship
Research (Sci, *44*, 56; Bull, *13*, 296; JoP, *13*, 476)
Appointment: Harvard Univ. (Bull, *23*, 455)
Appointment: Yale Univ. (Bull, *23*, 455; J App, *10*, 395; Bull, *24*, 380; J App,
11, 234)
Bequeathal: estate to Yale Univ. (Sci, *85*, 331)
Death notice: obituary by Carr, H. A. (AJP, *49*, 488; AJP, *48*, 177)
Editor: *Psychological Bulletin* (Bull, *23*, 112)
Election: AAAS (Bull, *26*, 56; Bull, *33*, 223)
Election: APA, director (Sci, *80*, 242)
Lecture: Princeton Univ., psychology and the law (Bull, *33*, 147; Sci, *83*, 229)

Robinson, Florence Ella Richardson

Death notice (AJP, *49*, 321; AJP, *48*, 177 Bull, *34*, 179)

Robinson, Phillip

Publication: *Psychological Bulletin*, military (J App, *25*, 358)

Robinson, Thomas Rutherford

Appointment: Univ. of Toronto (Bull, *3*, 35; Bull, *4*, 32)

Rochester, City of

Appointment: Kaiser, A. D. (Sci, *101*, 481)

Rochester Guidance Clinic (New York)

Appointment: Davis, D. E. (Bull, *36*, 841)

Rochester Psychology Society

Lecture: Bentley, M. (Sci, *94*, 38)

Rochester, University of (New York)

Appointment: Berry, W. (Bull, *19*, 586)
Appointment: Bouman, H. D. (Sci, *94*, 276)
Appointment: Carmichael, L. (Sci, *83*, 367; Bull, *33*, 405)
Appointment: Cason, H. (J App, *10*, 524; Bull, *24*, 136; Sci, *65*, 397)
Appointment: Coakley, J. D. (Sci, *94*, 276)
Appointment: Culler, E. A. (Sci, *87*, 549)
Appointment: Dunlap, J. W. (Bull, *34*, 498)
Appointment: Frost, E. (Bull, *20*, 60; Sci, *56*, 167)
Appointment: Kaiser, A. D. (Sci, *101*, 481)
Appointment: Pechstein, L. A. (Sci, *46*, 482; Bull, *15*, 98)
Appointment: Smith, K. U. (Bull, *33*, 405)
Appointment: Walls, G. L. (Bull, *42*, 675; Sci, *102*, 219)
Appointment: Wendt, G. R. (Bull, *42*, 255; Sci, *101*, 170)
Death notice: Frost, E. (J App, *10*, 524)
Departure: Carmichael, L. (Sci, *87*, 184)
Departure: Wellman, B. (Sci, *87*, 209)

Establishment: laboratory (BULL, *14*, 420; BULL, *15*, 98; SCI, *48*, 482)
Establishment: Neuro-psychiatric Clinic, Rivas, H. W. (SCI, *101*, 198)
Leave of absence: Dunlap, J. W. (SCI, 97, 327)
Lecture: Lashley, K. S., Sigma Xi (SCI, *87*, 164)
Promotion: Cason, H. (BULL, *24*, 571; J APP, *11*, 319)
Psychology department expanded (SCI, *46*, 482; BULL, *15*, 98)
Resignation: Culler, E. A. (BULL, *42*, 255; SCI, *101*, 219)
Retirement: Quimby, I. F. (SCI°, *4*, 465)

Rock, Robert Thomas, Jr.

Promotion: Army Air Forces (BULL, *40*, 231)

Rockefeller Foundation

Appointment: Haines, T. H. (BULL, *14*, 114-115)
Endowment: Harvard Medical School, psychiatry (SCI, *52*, 174)
Establishment: Psychopathic Institute, Chicago (BULL, *14*, 115)
Fellowship: Drewry, Jr., P. H., London (SCI, *89*, 313)
Lecture: Kasanin, J. S., U.S. Army Hospitals, psychosomatic medicine (SCI, *98*, 298)
Grant: American Philosophical Assoc., Commission on the Function of Philosophy in Liberal Education (JoP, *40*, 587-588)
Grant: Anthropoid Station Lab, Orange Park, Florida (SCI, *89*, 266)
Grant: Connecticut Psychopathic Hospital (SCI, *54*, 246)
Grant: Duke Univ., Dept. of Psychiatry and Mental Hygiene (SCI, *91*, 187)
Grant: McGill Univ., Dept. of Psychiatry, assoc. with Royal Victoria Hospital (SCI, *98*, 446-447; SCI, *99*, 123-124)
Grant: Oxford Univ. (SCI, *94*, 111)
Grant: research, genetic factors of intelligence and emotional variance (SCI, *101*, 482)
Grant: Univ. of Utah Child Psychiatry Program (SCI, *102*, 273)
Grant: Yale Laboratories of Primate Biology (SCI, *89*, 266)

Rockefeller Institute

Establishment: experimental biology lab, Loeb, J. director (SCI, *31*, 139)

Rockefeller, John D.

Endowment: Columbia Univ. (AJP, *11*, 281; REV, *7*, 216)

Rockefeller, Laura Spelman Fund

Grant: Blackett, M., industrial psych. research (SCI, *66*, 374)
Grant: Havard Univ., industrial psych. research (SCI, *65*, 13)
Grant: Iowa Child Welfare Research Station (SCI, *61*, 467)
Grant: Univ. of Minnesota, child research (SCI, *62*, 219)
Grant: Univ. of Toronto, child study (SCI, *62*, 10)

Rockland State Hospital

Internships: clinical psychology (BULL, *39*, 809-810)

Rocky Mountain Psychological Association
Meeting (BULL, 36, 500; BULL, 37, 657; AJP, 58, 117)

Rodger, Alec
Appointment: National Institute of Industrial Psychology (J APP, 23, 312)

Rodhom, C.
Lecture: rats use in psychology (AJP, 58, 262-266)

Roe, Anne
Appointment: Yale Univ., clinic for inebriates (SCI, 99, 99)

Roels, Franciscus Mattheus Joannes Agathos
Lecture: points of view in psychology (SCI, 69, 450)

Roff, Merrill Flagg
Appointment: Indiana University (BULL, 32, 323; J APP, 19, 105)
Return: Indiana Univ. (BULL, 42, 582)

Rogers, Agnes Low
Appointment: Bryn Mawr College (SCI, 61, 339)
Death notice (BULL, 40, 618)
Lecture: Columbia Univ., educational psychology (J APP, 10, 129)

Rogers, Anna Sophie
Appointment: Univ. of Illinois (JoP, 11, 721; SCI, 40, 670)
Promotion (BULL, 20, 172)

Rogers, Arthur Curtis
Death notice (BULL, 14, 32)
Lecture: backward and feeble-minded children (JoP, 7, 223)

Rogers, Arthur Kenyon
Appointment: Univ. of Missouri (JoP, 7, 448)

Rogers, Carl Ransom
Appointment: Univ. of Chicago (BULL, 42, 486)
Election: AAAP, president (J APP, 28, 530)
Lecture: Wichita Child Guidance Center, anniversary (BULL, 38, 126)
Rochester Guidance Clinic, New York, mental hygiene (BULL, 36, 841)

Rogers, David Camp
Appointment: Harvard Univ. (BULL, 5, 244)
Appointment: Smith College (SCI, 39, 606; JoP, 11, 308; BULL, 11, 190)
Departure: Univ. of Kansas (BULL, 11, 190; JoP, 11, 308)

Rogers, Herbert Wesley
Appointment: Lafayette College (SCI, 60, 221)
Appointment: Univ. of Vermont (SCI, 59, 552; BULL, 21, 428)

Rosanoff, Aaron Joshua
Appointment: California State Institutions (SCI, 89, 174)

Roscoe, Henry
Legislation: provisions in day-schools (SCI°, 9, 611)

Rose, Annelies Argelander
Promotion: Smith College (BULL, 42, 331)

Rose, Wickliffe
Election: Peabody Normal College for Teachers (JOP, 1, 588)

Rosenau, Milton Joseph
National Committee for Mental Hygiene, 25th anniversary (SCI, 80, 446)

Rosenow, Curt
Appointment: Univ. of Chicago (BULL, 14, 420; SCI, 46, 433)
Appointment: Univ. of Kansas (SCI, 51, 513; BULL, 17, 200)
Promotion: Univ. of Kansas (SCI, 55, 675; BULL, 19, 462)

Rosenthal, Isidor
Lecture: Berlin Physiological Society, calorimetric experiments (SCI°, 13, 379-380)

Rosenzweig, Saul
Appointment: Univ. of Pittsburgh, Western State Psychiatric Hopsital (BULL, 40, 618-619)
Establishment: International Seminar in Psychology (BULL, 38, 191)
Establishment: Psychological Supper Club (BULL, 37, 656)
Grant: Social Science Research Council (BULL, 36, 805)
Publication: projective approaches to the study of personality (BULL, 42, 487)

Ross Institute of Tropical Hygiene
Appointment: MacDonald, B. G. (SCI, 101, 60)

Ross, S. V.
Appointment: Univ. of California (BULL, 4, 370)

Rossy, C. S.
Lecture: Mass. School for Feeble-minded (BULL, 13, 407-408)

Rostock University (Germany)
Appointment: Nagel, W. A. (BULL, 6, 120)

Rothmann, Max
Death notice (BULL, 12, 404)

Rothney, John Watson Murray
Leave of absence: Univ. of Wisconsin (BULL, 39, 895)

Royal Society of Arts
Lecture: Myers, C. S. (BULL, *18*, 111)

Royal Society of Canada
Lecture: list (SCI°, *17*, 313)

Royal Society of Edinburgh
Election: British Honorary Fellows (SCI, *11*, 1036)
Election: Hamilton, A. M. (SCI, *9*, 380)
Election: Kennedy-Fraser, D. (SCI, *69*, 349)
Election: Pearson, K (SCI, *80*, 92)
Research: Haycraft, J. B., voluntary muscular contraction (SCI°, *15*, 245)

Royal Society of Lombardy
Election: Rowland, H. A. (SCI, *10*, 741)

Royal Society of Medicine (London)
Lecture: Sarkisov, S. (SCI, *98*, 150)

Royal Society of Victoria
Publication: Howitt, A. W., organization of Australian tribes (SCI°, *16*, 91)

Royce, Josiah
Appointment: Alford Professorship (JoP, *11*, 308)
Death notice (SCI, *44*, 420; JoP, *13*, 560; BULL, *13*, 407)
Degree: Oxford Univ. (JoP, *10*, 195-196)
Election: APA, president (SCI, *13*, 37)
Leave of absence: Harvard Univ. (SCI, *16*, 558; JoP, *9*, 168)
Lecture: Columbia Univ. (JoP, *8*, 112; SCI, *33*, 214)
Lecture: Harvard Univ., social psychology (SCI, *6*, 841)
Lecture: Iowa College (SCI, *15*, 920)
Lecture: Phi Beta Kappa oration, James, W. as a philosopher (JoP, *8*, 447-448)
Lecture: Univ. of California (SCI, *15*, 400)
Lecture: Univ. of Illinois (JoP, *4*, 140)
Lecture: Yale Univ. (BULL, *4*, 370)
Memorial fund establishment (JoP, *15*, 363-364)
Publication: announcement (JoP, *9*, 224)
Publication: James, W. (JoP, *8*, 560)

Rubin, Edgar John
Appointment: Univ. of Copenhagen (BULL, *20*, 416)

Ruch, Floyd Leon
Appointment: Univ. of Southern California (SCI, *86*, 263; BULL, *54*, 864)
Departure: Penn State College (SCI, *86*, 263)
Publication: *German Psychological Warfare* (J APP, *25*, 359)

Ruch, Giles Murrel

Appointment: Univ. of California (J App, *10*, 395)
Meeting: APA, Wash.-Balt. Branch (Bull, *37*, 405)

Ruckmick, Christian Alban

Appointment: Chicago and Northwestern Railway Co. (Bull, *42*, 255; Sci, *99*, 404)
Appointment: C. H. Stoelting Co. (Sci, *90*, 34; Bull, *37*, 122; J App, *23*, 530)
Appointment: Committee for Organization of Techniques, Office of Civilian Defense, Metropolitan District of Chicago (Sci, *99*, 404)
Appointment: Iowa State Univ. (Bull, *21*, 360; Sci, *59*, 378)
Appointment: Univ. of Illinois (Bull, *10*, 424; JoP, *10*, 560; Sci, *38*, 362)
Appointment: Univ. of Kentucky (Bull, *19*, 236)
Appointment: Wellesley College (JoP, *18*, 392; Bull, *18*, 438)
Departure: Cornell Univ. (JoP, *10*, 560)
Editor: Univ. of Iowa Studies in Psychology (Bull, *24*, 508)
Election: MPA, president (Bull, *33*, 303; Sci, *83*, 257)
Lecture: emotions (Bull, *29*, 248; Sci, *75*, 262)
Lecture: Harvard Univ., psychology of music (Bull, *12*, 403)
Lecture: Milwaukee State Teachers College (Bull, *41*, 343)
Lecture: 10 colleges (Sci, *73*, 416)
Lecture: tour of West and Pacific coast (Bull, *28*, 502)
Publication: anent the reality of bright and dull pressure (AJP, *47*, 333)
Publication: Gamble, E. A. M., obituary (AJP, *46*, 156)
Publication: McCosh, J. on the emotions (AJP, *46*, 508)
Publication: MPA, 8th annual meeting (AJP, *45*, 752)
Stumpf, C. A., photo and signature (AJP, *49*, 321)

Rudolph-Virchow Medal

Award: Pearson, K., Berlin Anthro. Society (Sci, *77*, 16)

Ruediger, William Carl

Appointment: George Washington Univ. (Sci, *27*, 840; JoP, *5*, 336; JoP, *12*, 700; Bull, *10*, 252; JoP, *10*, 364)
Election: SSPP (JoP, *8*, 84)
Election: SSPP, officer (JoP, *11*, 140; Bull, *9*, 40)
Promotion: George Washington Univ. Teachers College (Sci, *34*, 345; Bull, *8*, 374)

Ruesch, Jurgen

Appointment: Univ. of California, San Francisco, Medical School (Sci, *97*, 351)

Ruger, Henry Alford

Appointment: Colorado College (Bull, *1*, 451; JoP, *1*, 560)
Leave of absence: Teachers College, Columbia Univ. (Bull, *13*, 148)

Rugg, Harold Ordway

Appointment: Teachers College, Columbia Lincoln School (Bull, *16*, 392)

Ruggles, Arthur H.
Appointment: Brown Univ. (BULL, 28, 412)
Appointment: Yale Univ., Medical School (SCI, 62, 396)
Election: National Committee for Mental Hygiene, president (SCI, 80, 446)

Rumford, Benjamin Thompson, Count
Publication: life sketch by Tyndall, J. (SCI°, 2, 147)

Ruml, Beardsley
Appointment: Carnegie Institute of Technology (JoP, 14, 616; BULL, 14, 263)
Leave of absence: Carnegie Institute of Technology (JoP, 15, 336)
Lecture: applied psychology (JoP, 19, 279)
Research: trade test standardization division (JoP, 15, 336)

Russel, Henry Award
Maier, N. R. F., Univ. of Michigan (SCI, 89, 313; BULL, 36, 499)

Russell, Bertrand Arthur William
Lecture: Mind Assoc. and Aristotelian Society (JoP, 35, 252)
Lecture: postulates of scientific methods (JoP, 40, 560; JoP, 41, 55-56)

Russell, James Earl
Appointment: Teacher's College, Columbia Univ. (REV, 5, 109)
Appointment: Univ. of Colorado (SCI, 1, 615)
Death notice (JoP, 14, 140; BULL, 14, 115)
Lecture: Child Study Association of America (J APP, 9, 319)
Personal tribute (JoP, 14, 195-196)

Russell, Roger Wolcott
Appointment: Univ. of Nebraska (SCI, 91, 616; J APP, 24, 518)

Russell Sage College (Troy, New York)
Departure: Savides, A. P. (BULL, 42, 793)

Russell, William L.
Election: National Committee for Mental Hygiene, vice-president (SCI, 72, 557)
Lecture: Cornell Univ., Salmon Memorial (SCI, 76, 13)

Russia
Publication: Chelpanov, G. I., status of psychology (JoP, 8, 335-336)
Publication: percentage of psychology literature (BULL, 34, 179)
Publication: psychology journal announced (REV, 3, 244)
Publication: Razran, G. H. S., the number of articles of psychological interest
published in the Russian language (AJP, 49, 316)

Russian Academy of Science
Centennary anniversary, 1883 (SCI°, 2, 753)

Russian Scientific Association
Meeting: Odessa (SCI°, 2, 117)

Russo, Salvatore
Promotion: Rider College, New Jersey (BULL, 40, 79)

Rutgers University (New Brunswick, New Jersey)
Appointment: Cole, W. H. (BULL, 41, 411)
Appointment: Cook, S. A. (J APP, 10, 523)
Appointment: Marvin, W. T. (JoP, 7, 252; BULL, 7, 180)
Appointment: Pratt, C. C. (BULL, 34, 326, 635)
Appointment: Starr, H. E. (BULL, 25, 444; BULL, 41, 679; SCI, 68, 13, 156)
Degree: Angell, J. R. (SCI, 85, 601)
Establishment: research council (BULL, 41, 411)
Grant: Works Progress Admin., psych. building (BULL, 37, 257; SCI, 91, 140)
Leave of absence: Pratt, C. C. (BULL, 42, 792-793; SCI, 102, 374; JoP, 42, 616)
Promotion: Cook, S. A. (BULL, 23, 412)

Rutherford, Elizabeth Jane
Meeting: APA, Wash.-Balt. Branch (BULL, 37, 122)

Ryan, Thomas Arthur
Lecture: fatigue (AJP, 57, 565-569)

S

Sabine, George Holland
Election: American Philosophical Assoc., Eastern Divison, vice-president (JoP, 33, 56)
Leave of absence: Stanford Univ. (JoP, 7, 252)
Promotion: Stanford Univ. (BULL, 5, 348)

Saccharin
Publication: *Medical Journal*, physiological effects (SCI°, 16, 77)

Sachs, Bernard
National Committee for Mental Hygiene (SCI, 72, 557)

Sachs, Hanns
Publication: *Imago* (JoP, 9, 335)

Sackett, Robert See
Appointment: Educational Motion Picture Project of the American Council on Education (BULL, 36, 499)
Appointment: New Jersey College for Women (BULL, 29, 603)

Sacramento Junior College (California)
Appointment: Tyler, H. T. (BULL, 39, 895)

Saetveit, Joseph Gerhard
Publication: measures of musical talent (J APP, 23, 634)

Safety
Pubication: Safety Research Planning Committee, New York Univ., report on safety research program, 1940 (J APP, 24, 369)
Research: DeSilva, H. R., automobile driver research project, Yale Univ. (J APP, 22, 664)

Saffir, Milton A.
Announcement: movement of offices of Psychological Guidance Center (BULL, *41*, 498)

Sage Professorship
Appointment: Dallenbach. K. M., Cornell Univ. (BULL, *42*, 581; SCI, *101*, 663)

Saint Andrews, University of
Appointment: Stout, G. F. (SCI, *17*, 680; JoP, *1*, 28)
Appointment: Taylor, A. E. (JoP, *5*, 448; BULL, *5*, 316)
Appointment: Ward, J. (BULL, *3*, 116)
Candidate: Tuke, J. B., parliamentary representation (SCI, *11*, 756)
Degree: Laurie, S. S. (SCI°, *9*, 362)
Lecture: Morgan, C. L. (JoP, *19*, 504)
Lecture: Ward, J. (JoP, *5*, 196)
Resignation: Knight, W. (REV, *10*, 103)

Saint Elizabeth's Hospital (Washington, D. C.)
Appointment: Guthrie, R. H. (SCI, *89*, 125)

Saint Georges Hospital (London)
Death notice: Blanford, G. F. (SCI, *34*, 376)

Saint Johns College
Appointment: Rivers, W. (SCI, *6*, 958; REV, *5*, 232)

Saint Lawrence University (Canton, New York)
Appointment: Held, O. C. (BULL, *42*, 792; SCI, *102*, 420)
Degree: Carmichael, L. (SCI, *97*, 462)

Saint Louis Congress of Arts and Sciences (Missouri)
Announcement: corrections (BULL, *1*, 372)

Saint Louis Medical Society
Award: Graves, W. W. (SCI, *90*, 34, 488)

Saint Louis Psychiatric Clinic
Appointment: Swift, E. J. (SCI, *59*, 120; BULL, *21*, 360)

Saint Louis Public Schools, Psychoeducational Clinic
Announcment: opening (SCI, *39*, 756)
Appointment: Wallin, J. E. W. (BULL, *11*, 190-191)

Saint Louis World's Fair
Laboratories: Woodworth, R. S. (JoP, *1*, 84)
Meeting: Münsterberg, H., organizational (SCI, *17*, 636)
Trip: Münsterberg, H., seeks cooperation of German government (SCI, *17*, 915)

Saint Olaf College (Northfield, Minnesota)
Appointment: Boraas, H. (BULL, *42*, 191)

Saint Petersburg Academy of Sciences (Russia)
Election: Hering, E. (BULL, *3*, 83)
Election: Wundt, W. (SCI, *17*, 276)

Saint Petersburg, University of (Russia)
Lecture: Pavlov, I. P., Huxley Lecture, Charing-Cross Hospital Medical School
(SCI, *24*, 381)
Museum opens for psychiatry (REV, *5*, 109)
Psychology lab, new (SCI, *2*, 850)
Psycho-Neurological Institute opened, directed by Bechterev, V. (SCI, *27*, 320;
BULL, *5*, 168)

Saint Scholastica College (Duluth, MN)
Appointment: Bühler, K. (BULL, *36*, 218)

Salmon, Thomas William
Appointment: Columbia Univ. Medical School (SCI, *54*, 72)
Death notice (SCI, *66*, 190)

Salmon, Thomas William Memorial Lectures
Brill, A. A., 1943 (SCI, *98*, 383)
Campbell, C. M., New York Acad. of Medicine (SCI, *79*, 268)
Gillespie, R. D., psychoneuroses from war experience (SCI, *94*, 323, 436; J APP,
25, 726)
Healy, W., New York Acad of Science, personality (SCI, *85*, 355)
Hoskins, R. G., 1945 (SCI, *101*, 243)
Lewis, N. D. C. (SCI, *91*, 382; SCI, *92*, 426)
Luriia, A., New York Acad. of Medicine (SCI, *89*, 433)
Luriia, A., postponed (SCI, *91*, 382)
Meyer, A., first recipient (BULL, *28*, 254)
Mira, E. (SCI, *96*, 378; J APP, *26*, 856-857)
Rees, J. R., 1944 (SCI, *100*, 402, 492; SCI, *99*, 531)
Strecker, E. A., New York Acad. of Medicine, 1939 (SCI, *89*, 385)

Sampling
Gallup, G., subject of excerpt (J APP, *23*, 310)

Samson, A.
Bequest: donated (JoP, *1*, 56)

San Diego State College (California)
Appointment: Peiffer, H. C. (BULL, *40*, 383)

San Francisco Bulletin (California)
Review: Martin's, L. J. work (J APP, *1*, 97-98)

San Francisco Department of Public Health
 Organization: psychiatric clinic for feminine delinquency with U.S. Public
  Health Service (Sci, 97, 65)

San Francisco, Psychologists Club of
 Founded: officers (J App, 25, 129)
 Research: creation and functioning of an international or world federation
  (J App, 26, 108-109)

San Jose State College (California)
 Appointment: Carrier, B. (Bull, 42, 255)

San Juan School of Tropical Medicine (*see* Tropical Medicine,
 School of)

Sanatoria for Consumptives
 Publication: Central Committee for establishment (Sci, 9, 190)

Sanborn, Herbert Charles
 Lecture: SSPP (JoP, 21, 84)

Sanctis, Sante de (*see* De Sanctis, Sante)

Sanders, Charles Finley
 Appointment: Pennsylvania College (JoP, 4, 28; Bull, 3, 422)

Sandiford, Peter
 Death notice (Bull, 39, 71)

Sands, Benjamin Franklin
 Death notice (Sci°, 2, 581)

Sanford chronoscope
 Lecture: Fernberger, S. W., improvement of (AJP, 37, 154)

Sanford, Edmund C.
 Appointment: Clark Univ. (Bull, 6, 368; Bull, 20, 288; Sci, 56, 602; Bull, 17,
  239)
 Appointment: Committee for APA/International Congress for Psychology (JoP,
  8, 196)
 Commemorative meeting in his honor (J App, 9, 87)
 Death notice (AJP, 9, 87; Bull, 22, 140; Sci, 60, 587; JoP, 22, 27)
 Degree: Univ. of California (Bull, 9, 280; Sci, 35, 860; JoP, 9, 335)
 Editor: *American Journal of Psychology* (Rev, 2, 641)
 Editor: *Festschrift* volume for Hall, G. S. (Sci, 17, 558)
 Election: APA, president (Sci, 15, 78)
 Election: International Congress of Arts and Sciences, St. Louis, chair (JoP, 1,
  420)

Lecture: Brown Univ. (BULL, *4*, 128; JOP, *4*, 196)
Lecture: Clark Univ., commencement (SCI, *59*, 437)
Lecture: Clark Univ., honoring Story, W. E. (SCI, *32*, 13)
Lecture: Clark Univ., psychology (SCI°, *14*, 250)
Promotion: Clark Univ. (SCI, *12*, 936; SCI, *31*, 108, 143)
Publication: Experimental Psychology translated into French (REV, *7*, 640)
Publication: laboratory course (REV, *1*, 336)
Publication: manuscripts of Bridgman, L. (SCI°, *9*, 435)
Resignation: Clark Univ. (BULL, *17*, 239)

Sanford, Robert Nevitt
Promotion: Univ. of California (BULL, *41*, 603)
Psychological Supper Club (BULL, *37*, 656)

Sanitary Corps, U. S. Army
Commission: Angier, R. P., captain (JOP, *15*, 700)
Commission: APA members (BULL, *15*, 97)
Commission: Baldwin, B. T. (BULL, *15*, 98)
Commission: Haggerty, M. E. (BULL, *15*, 98; JOP, *15*, 364)
Commission: Myers, G. C. (JOP, *15*, 364)
Commission: Owen , R. B. (JOP, *15*, 364)
Commission: Poffenberger, A. T. (JOP, *15*, 364)
Commission: psychologists (JOP, *15*, 364)
Commission: Schachne, I. (JOP, *15*, 364)

Sanitary Institute, Congress of the
Election: Preece, W. H. (SCI, *9*, 756)
Meeting: Worcester, England, 1889 (SCI°, *14*, 112)

Santa Ana Public Schools (California)
Appointment: Henry, M. B. (J APP, *3*, 197)
Department of Research established (J APP, *3*, 197)

Santayana, George
Award: Nicholas Murray Butler (JOP, *42*, 224)
Lecture: British Acad., philosophy in America (JOP, *15*, 280)
Publication: excerpts from his book *Life of Reason* (JOP, *15*, 82-84)

Santiago Primate Colonies
Carpenter, C. R. (BULL, *37*, 827)

Sarason, Seymour Bernard
Appointment: Yale Univ. (BULL, *42*, 675)

Sarbin, Theodore Roy
Award: Social Science Research Council grant (BULL, *39*, 682)
Grant: postdoctoral research training fellowship (BULL, *38*, 777-778)
Resignation: Lincoln State School and Colony, Illinois (BULL, *41*, 498)

Sargent, Stephen Stansfeld
Promotion: Columbia Univ. (BULL, *41*, 498)

Sarkisov, Semon
Lecture: Royal Society of Medicine, London, 1943 (SCI, *98*, 150)

Sartain, Aaron Quinn
Appointment: North American Aviation (BULL, *41*, 603)
Appointment: Southern Methodist Univ. (BULL, *38*, 304)
Leave of absence: Southern Methodist Univ. (BULL, *41*, 603)

Sathianathan, Samuel
Death notice (JoP, *3*, 364)

Satiation (*see also* Appetite)
Effects of benzedrine sulfate upon (AJP, *52*, 297-299)

Saul, Leon Joseph
Publication: auditory action currents (AJP, *45*, 358)

Saupe, Mildred Winn
Appointment: Missouri Valley College (BULL, *42*, 675)

Savides, Antonio Panayotou
Appointment: Lesley College (BULL, *42*, 793)
Departure: Russell Sage College (BULL, *42*, 793)

Scarborough, William J.
Appointment: Cornell College, Iowa (BULL, *40*, 152)

Schaarschmidt, Carl Max Wilhelm
Appointment: *Philosophische monatshefte* (SCI°, *8*, 386)
Death notice (JoP, *7*, 84)

Schaefer, Benjamin Richard
Publication: a note on advancing and retreating colors (AJP, *49*, 130)

Schaeffer, Asa Arthur
Research: orientation and direction of movement (BULL, *17*, 240)

Schaeffer, Henry G.
Lecture: pitch discrimination (JoP, *7*, 223)

Schanck, Richard Louis
Grant: Social Science Research Council (BULL, *33*, 579)

Scheidemann, Norma Valentine
Publication: novel experiment with the negative after image (AJP, *45*, 361)

Scheidt, Philip Vernon
Meeting: APA Wash.-Balt. Branch (BULL, *36*, 304; BULL, *37*, 657)

Schiller, Ferdinand Canning Scott
Death notice (JoP, *34*, 559)
Lecture: Clark Univ. (AJP, *10*, 522)
Lecture: perception (JoP, *7*, 420)
Publication: riddles of the sphinx: a study in the philosophy of humanism (JoP, *7*, 644)

Schizophrenia (*see also* Dementia praecox)
Appointment: Turner, W. D., Institute of the Pennsylvania Hospital (SCI, *86*, 98)
Lecture: Hoskins, R. G., biology of (SCI, *101*, 243; SCI, *102*, 351)

Schjelderup, Harald Krabbe
Election: Norwegian Psychological Assoc., president (AJP, *46*, 511)

Schneck, Matthew Maximilian Ruprecht
Election: AAAS Southwestern Division, secretary (SCI, *75*, 101)

Schneider, Herbert Wallace
Meeting: American Philosophical Assoc. (JoP, *33*, 700)

Schneidler, Gwendolen Goette
Commission: WAVES (BULL, *40*, 152)
Departure: Univ. of Minnesota, Testing Bureau (BULL, *40*, 152)

Schneirla, Theodore Christian
Award: Guggenheim Fellowship (BULL, *42*, 128, 485; BULL, *41*, 409; SCI, *100*, 517)

Schoen, Max
Lecture: Carnegie Institute of Technology, psychology of music (BULL, *18*, 628)

Scholz, Willibald
Appointment: German Research Institute of Psychiatry, Kaiser Wilhelm Institute (SCI, *84*, 288)

Schöndorff, Bernhard
Resignation: *Pflüger's Archiv*, editorship (BULL, *17*, 200)

School and Society
Editor: Cattell, J. McK. (BULL, *12*, 44; JoP, *12*, 84)

School Hygiene, International Congress of
Appointment: Whipple, G. M. (BULL, *10*, 292)
Election: Terman, L. M. (JoP, *10*, 616)
Lecture: Binet-Simon tests and its revision (JoP, *10*, 560)

Lecture: Ferree, C. E. (JoP, *10*, 672)
Lecture: list of (JoP, *10*, 560)
Program: received (BULL, *4*, 32)

School psychologists

Announcement: examinations by Board of Education, New York (BULL, *41*, 499-500)

Schools

Lecture: Gesell, A. L. (JoP, *2*, 223)
Research: Key, [A.?], effects of overwork (SCI°, *15*, 40)

Schopenhauer, Arthur

Birthday celebration (SCI°, *9*, 293)

Schreier, Fritz

Lecture: International Congress for the Unity of Science, VI (JoP, *38*, 503)

Schröder, Conrad

Death notice (BULL, *12*, 128)

Schröder, Paul

Appointment: Univ. of Leipzig (SCI, *60*, 382)

Schüle, Heinrich

Death notice (BULL, *14*, 80)

Schultz, Richard Samuel

Conference: Psychological Corporation, Personnel Research Federation, labor relations, 1937 (J APP, *21*, 718)
Publication: book reviews in psychological periodicals (AJP, *46*, 511)
Publication: Psychological Corporation, personnel selection (J APP, *21*, 242)

Schultze, C. A. J. Fritz

Death notice (JoP, *5*, 560)

Schumacher, Henry Cyril

Appointment: Cleveland Child Guidance Clinic (SCI, *65*, 11)

Schumann, Friedrich

Appointment: Univ. of Berlin (AJP, *7*, 152)
Course: Univ. of Frankfurt, psychology (JoP, *12*, 196)
Editor: *Zeitschrift für Psychologie* (JoP, *6*, 700; BULL, *6*, 368)
Lecture: German Society of Experimental Psychology, psychology of reading (SCI, *22*, 727)
Publication: *Psychologische Studien* announced (JoP, *1*, 721)

Schurman, Jacob Gould

Appointment: Dalhousie College (SCI°, *7*, 74)

National Committee for Mental Hygiene, 25th anniversary (SCI, *80*, 446)
Travel: Philippines (SCI, *9*, 228)

Schuster, Edgar
Lecture: inheritance of feeble-mindedness (SCI, *22*, 189)

Schutz, Alfred
Lecture: Eastern Division of the American Philosophical Assoc., James, W.
(JOP, *37*, 699)

Schweizer Archiv für Neurologie und Psychiatrie
Editor: Monakow, C. V. (BULL, *14*, 333)
New journal (BULL, *14*, 333)

Sciamanna, Ezio
Editor: *Rivista quindicinale di psicologa, psichiatria, neuropathologia* (AJP, *9*, 135)

Science
Lecture: Cattell, J. McK., scientific merit (JOP, *2*, 700)
Lecture: Russell, B., postulates of scientific method (JOP, *41*, 55-56)
Lecture: Wendt, G., science challenges society (SCI, *101*, 140)
Lecture: Winslau, C. E. A., Sigma Xi, science and the post-war world (SCI, *101*, 14)
List, 1886 scientific works (SCI°, *7*, 304)
National Research Council, scientific research funds (J APP, *5*, 95)
Publication: Müller, M., science of thought (SCI°, *9*, 132)

Science
AAAS program detailed (JOP, *15*, 700)
Editor: Valentine, W. L. (BULL, *42*, 791)
Reviews scientific work of the leading nations (SCI°, *3*, 798-799)
Translation: Jastrow, J., article in *Revue Scientifique* (SCI, *4*, 47)

Science and Labor, Institute for
Psychological reports, industrial health from Japan (SCI, *89*, 78)

Science Philosophy and Religion, Conference on
Meeting (JOP, *37*, 448; SCI, *99*, 490)

Science Series
Publication: announced (REV, *5*, 232)

Science Service
Election: Conklin, E. G., president (SCI, *85*, 475)
Election: officers, 1937 (SCI, *85*, 475)

Scientific Advisory Committee of the Trades Union
Cullis, W., representative for psychology (SCI, *88*, 398)

Scientific Congress, International
List of signers (Sci°, *4*, 140)

Scientific Literature, Catalogue of
Election: Committee from the U.S. (Sci, *9*, 460)

Scientific management
Course: Orga Institut, Berlin (J App, *6*, 213)

Scientific Spirit and Democratic Faith
Conference: 1944 (JoP, *41*, 279-280)
Election: Dewey, J., chair (Sci, *99*, 363)
History of scientific thought, Eastern Division of American Philosophical Assoc.
 (JoP, *39*, 643-644)

Scofield, Carleton Forman
Appointment: Yale Univ. (Bull, *22*, 444)
Election: Univ. of Buffalo, Sigma Xi, officer (Sci, *93*, 324)

Scots Philosophical Club
Meeting: Mind Assoc. and Aristotelian Society (JoP, *33*, 252)

Scott, Colin Alexander
Appointment: Chicago Normal School (Sci, *4*, 170; Rev, *3*, 706)
Appointment: Mount Holyoke College (Bull, *12*, 280)
Departure: Boston Normal School (Bull, *12*, 280)
Lecture: Hall, G. S. (AJP, *9*, 87)

Scott, Thurman Carlisle
Appointment: Ohio Univ. (Sci, *101*, 112)
Promotion: Ohio Univ. (Bull, *42*, 255)

Scott, Walter Dill
Anniversary: Northwestern Univ., 10th (Sci, *73*, 490)
Appointment: APA Committee on Medical Education (JoP, *9*, 28)
Appointment: Bureau of Salesmanship Research, Carnegie Institute of Tech.
 (Sci, *44*, 491; Bull, *14*, 263; J App, *2*, 299; JoP, *13*, 140, 588; JoP, *14*, 616)
Appointment: Committee on Publication in Applied Psychology (J App, *2*, 196)
Appointment: National Research Council (Bull, *14*, 366)
Appointment: Northwestern Univ. (Sci, *12*, 320; Rev, *7*, 531)
Election: APA office (Bull, *16*, 32; JoP, *12*, 112)
Election: APA, president (Sci, *49*, 19)
Election: Northwestern Univ., president (JoP, *17*, 672; Sci, *52*, 441; Bull, *17*,
 435)
Election: Psychological Corporation, president (J App, *17*, 341)
Election: Psychological Corporation, vice-president (Bull, *24*, 80; J App, *11*, 80)
Lecture: pendulums (JoP, *2*, 280)
Lecture: Univ. of Chicago (Sci, *55*, 289)

Lecture: Univ. of Chicago, convocation (BULL, *19*, 171)
Meeting: Psychological Corporation, APA and AAAP (J APP, *25*, 600)
Northwestern Univ. erecting Scott Hall (SCI, *89*, 219)
Promotion: Carnegie Institute of Tech. (BULL, *16*, 257)
Research: human element problems in marketing (J APP, *2*, 299)
Resides in Evanston, Illinois (J APP, *3*, 290)
Resignation: Northwestern Univ. (SCI, *89*, 76; SCI, *90*, 368; BULL, *36*, 304)
Return: Carnegie Institute of Tech. (J APP, *2*, 196)

Scott, William Berryman
Lecture: Wagner Institute, Philadelphia (SCI, *13*, 237)

Scott, William Henry
Death notice (JoP, *34*, 83)
Retirement: Ohio State Univ. (JoP, *7*, 476)

Scribner's Magazine
Publication: Brownell, E. C., the social instinct (SCI°, *9*, 610)

Scribner's Sons, Charles
Baldwin, J. M., *Library of Historical Psychology* (SCI, *17*, 679-680)

Scripps College (Claremont, California)
Anniversary: James, W. 100th (JoP, *39*, 84)
Appointment: Stinchfield-Hawk, S. (BULL, *41*, 679)
Retirement: Eyre, M. B. (BULL, *41*, 499)

Scripture, Edward Wheeler
Appointment: Johns Hopkins Univ. (JoP, *1*, 252; BULL, *1*, 172)
Appointment: Yale Univ. (SCI°, *19*, 313)
Award: gold medal of Paris Exposition (SCI, *12*, 572)
Course: Univ. of Marburg (BULL, *2*, 360)
Editor: *American Journal of Psychology* (SCI°, *19*, 131)
Grant: Carnegie Institute (REV, *10*, 103; SCI, *16*, 1039)
Grant: study of phonetics (SCI, *15*, 276)
Leave of absence: Yale Univ. (BULL, *1*, 27)
Lecture: Germany (SCI, *53*, 136)
Lecture: Johns Hopkins Univ., canceled (BULL, *2*, 159)
Lecture: Yale Univ., experimental psychology (SCI, *1*, 722)
Promotion: Yale Univ. (SCI, *13*, 480)
Publication: *The New Psychology* (SCI, *5*, 583)
Resignation: Yale Univ. (REV, *10*, 690; SCI, *18*, 352)

Seago, Dorothy Wilson
Appointment: Newcomb College (SCI, *74*, 564)

Sealy, John Hospital (Galveston, Texas)
Appointment: Ewall, J. R. (SCI, *100*, 245)

Searles, Herbert Leon
Election: American Philosophical Assoc., vice-president (JoP, *33*, 56)
Lecture: Pacific Division of the American Philosophical Society (JoP, *36*, 722)

Sears, Robert Richardson
Appointment: Iowa Child Welfare Research Station (BULL, *39*, 682; SCI, *96*, 57-58)
Appointment: Univ. of Illinois (BULL, *29*, 603)

Seashore, Carl Emil
Appointment: National Research Council (JoP, *14*, 392; BULL, *14*, 191)
Appointment: State Univ. of Iowa (AJP, *9*, 135; REV, *4*, 452; SCI, *27*, 520; SCI, *16*, 280; SCI, *21*, 640; SCI, *96*, 10, 58; BULL, *39*, 682)
Award: American Speech Correction Assoc. (BULL, *42*, 485)
Award: Bronze bust and musical soirée by former students (SCI, *90*, 510)
Commemoration: State Univ. of Iowa, 25 years service (BULL, *26*, 120)
Commemorative concert, State Univ. of Iowa (SCI, *79*, 474)
Course: Univ. of California, psychology of music (SCI, *45*, 657; JoP, *14*, 448)
Degree: Chicago Musical College (SCI, *90*, 33, 59; BULL, *36*, 804)
Delegate: International Congress of Psychology, 10th (SCI, *76*, 119)
Editor: *Bulletin*, child and educational psychology (BULL, *10*, 424; BULL, *8*, 374)
Editor: *Journal of Educational Psychology* (JoP, *6*, 700; BULL, *6*, 427)
Election: APA, president (SCI, *33*, 22; BULL, *8*, 32; JoP, *8*, 55)
Election: British Psychological Society, member (SCI, *91*, 445)
Election: Kappa Delta Pi (BULL, *42*, 484)
Election: NAS, member (BULL, *19*, 296)
Election: State Univ. of Iowa, chair (REV, *9*, 536)
Election: Western Philosophical Assoc., president (JoP, *7*, 112)
Honor: Acoustical Society of America, luncheon (SCI, *90*, 510)
Lecture: Columbia Univ. (JoP, *8*, 112; SCI, *33*, 213)
Lecture: Northwestern Univ. (SCI, *39*, 458)
Lecture: tone quality (AJP, *55*, 123-127)
Lecture: Univ. of Kansas, psychology of music (SCI, *51*, 268; JoP, *17*, 168)
Lecture: validity of measures of musical talent (AJP, *52*, 638-640)
Lecture: Western Philosophical Assoc. (JoP, *7*, 223)
Musical talent and education, psychology of (BULL, *14*, 80)
Promotion: State Univ. of Iowa (BULL, *5*, 64; JoP, *2*, 252)
Publication: description of his psychology of music studio (J APP, *1*, 299-300)
Publication: measures of musical talent (J APP, *23*, 633)
Publication: studies in psychology, State Univ. of Iowa (SCI, *69*, 212)
Publication: *Vocational Guidance in Music* (J APP, *1*, 299-300)
Reorganization: State Univ. of Iowa (SCI, *72*, 576)
Retirement: State Univ. of Iowa (SCI, *84*, 326)

Seashore, Robert Holmes
Appointment: Northwestern Univ. (SCI, *86*, 218; BULL, *34*, 498)
Departure: Univ. of Southern California (SCI, *86*, 218)

Election: MPA, sec.-treas. (J App, *23*, 419; J App, *25*, 128)
Publication: APA meeting (Sci, *96*, 294)
Representative: Northwestern Univ., local committee on arrangements for
  convention of Society of the Sigma Xi at Chicago (Sci, *98*, 448)

Seaton, John Thomas
Appointment: Univ. of Pittsburgh (J App, *10*, 522)

Seattle Pacific College (Washington)
Return: Ashton, P. F. (Bull, *42*, 63)

Sebring, E.
Appointment: Teachers' College (Rev, *1*, 552)

Secor, W. B.
Publication: paper on reading (AJP, *11*, 435)

Secretary of State
Appointment: Bowman, I., advisor (Sci, *101*, 85)

Secretary of War
Appointment: Lignon, E. M., expert consultant (Sci, *96*, 81)

Seele des Kindes, Die
Translation: Preyer's book by Alcan, M. (Sci, *8*, 510)

Seguin, Edouard
Publication: reprint proposed (Bull, *4*, 160)

Seibert, Earl William
Appointment: Green Mountain Junior College (Bull, *42*, 191)

Seidenfeld, Morton Alfred
Appointment: Advisory Board on Clinical Psychology of the Office of the
  Adjutant General (Sci, *100*, 166)
Appointment: National Foundation for Infantile Paralysis, New York (Bull, *42*,
  793; Sci, *102*, 527)
Promotion (Bull, *38*, 777)

Selection
Research: Snow, A. J., of cab drivers (J App, *9*, 90)
Research: Stoy, E. G., key punch operators (J App, *24*, 654)

Selective Service Occupational Bulletin No. 11
Psychology no longer a shortage field (J App, *27*, 207-208)

Selective thinking (see also Thought)
Lecture: Baldwin, J. M., APA (AJP, *9*, 250)

Self-consciousness of noted persons
Publication: Morrill, J. S. (SCI°, 8, 344)
Publication: Ticknor and Company (SCI°, 8, 344)

Self, psychology of
Lecture: Calkins, M. W., Univ. of London (BULL, 25, 307)

Sellars, Roy Wood
Lecture: Dewey, J. (JoP, 38, 700)

Semantic word count
Thorndike, E. L., word count complete, Columbia Univ. (BULL, 36, 141)

Semantics
Congress: Ellensburg, Washington (BULL, 32, 324)

Sensation
Discussion: Boring, E. G., attributes of sensation (AJP, 35, 301)
Examination of sensation and cognition terms by the Committee on
  Terminology of the APA (JoP, 17, 139-140)
Lab established at Tufts College, sensory psychology (SCI, 87, 209)
Lecture: Castro, M. (JoP, 1, 336)
Lecture: Dallenbach, K. M., AAAS, temperature (J APP, 26, 107-108)
Lecture: Gore, W. C., Northwestern Branch of APA (JoP, 1, 336)
Lecture: MacDougall, R. (JoP, 2, 224)
Lecture: Meyer, M. (JoP, 2, 223)
Lecture: Münsterberg, H. (JoP, 1, 168)
Lecture: Pierce, C. S. and Jastrow, J., NAS, perceptible differences (SCI°, 3,
  524)
Lecture: Sanford, E. C. (BULL, 4, 128)
Lecture: Stratton, G. M., sensory discrimination (JoP, 2, 56)
Lecture: Tsukahara, M. (JoP, 2, 112)
Lecture: Washburn, M. F. (JoP, 1, 224)
Publication: Binet, A., sensation and the outer world (SCI°, 13, 217)
Publication: Coghill, G. E., space time as a pattern of psycho-organismal
  mentation (AJP, 51, 759)
Publication: Nafe, J. P., Dr. W. L. Jenkins on the vascular theory of warmth and
  cold (AJP, 51, 763)
Publication: Pick, A. (AJP, 1, 360)
Publication: Pierce, C. S. and Jastrow, J., NAS, minimum differences (SCI°, 4,
  408-409)
Research: Bloch, E. (AJP, 1, 550)
Research: Gradenigo, G., criminals (SCI°, 14, 297)
Research: Herzen, A., vivisections (SCI°, 8, 433)
Research: Ottolenghi, S., criminals (SCI°, 14, 297)
Symposium: American Physiological Society, special senses relating to war (SCI,
  97, 114)

Seppilli, Giuseppe

Lecture: hypnotism (SCI°, 5, 303)

Sergi, Giuseppe

Announcement: volume on pain and pleasure (REV, 1, 336)

Editor: *Journal of Pedagogy* (REV, 1, 336)

Editor: *Rivista quindicinale di psicologa, psichiatria, neuropathologia* (AJP, 9, 135)

Election: International Congress of Psychology, president (SCI, 21, 77; JoP, 2, 56)

Seth, James

Appointment: Cornell Univ. (REV, 3, 356)

Appointment: Edinburg Univ. (REV, 5, 450)

Seth Pringle-Pattison, Andrew

Lecture: Univ. of Aberdeen, Gifford Lectures (JoP, 9, 448)

Seward, Georgene Hoffman

Appointment: Connecticut College (BULL, 34, 498)

Appointment: Simmons College, Boston (BULL, 42, 583)

Resignation: Connecticut College (BULL, 42, 583)

Seward, John Perry

Appointment: Boston Univ. (BULL, 42, 582)

Appointment: Connecticut College (BULL, 34, 498)

Resignation: Connecticut College (BULL, 42, 582)

Sex

Appointment: Nowlis, V., Indiana Univ., behavior (SCI, 100, 96-97)

Appointment: Riddle, O. (SCI, 72, 395)

Award: diseases of human genital organs research (SCI, 89, 386)

Grant: Kinsey, A. C., NRC Committee for Research on Problems of Sex (SCI, 95, 600)

Lecture: Beach, F. A., reproductive behavior (SCI, 99, 168)

Lecture: Lehman, H. and Witty, P. A., differences (AJP, 42, 140)

Lecture: Wyatt, H. G., differences (AJP, 44, 361)

Meeting: International Congress for Sex Research (SCI, 72, 395; SCI, 70, 552)

Meeting: International Society for the Investigation of Sex (SCI, 69, 572)

Grant: Committee for Research in Problems of Sex, requests of applications (SCI, 93, 109)

Grant: National Research Council Committee, problems of (SCI, 89, 126)

Research: questionnaire (SCI, 69, 379, 399)

Sex, International Congress for Research on

Delegate: Riddle, O. (SCI, 72, 395)

Sex, International Society for the Investigation of
Meeting: 2nd (Sci, 69, 572; Sci, 70, 552)

Sexual Research, International Society for
Meeting: Berlin (Bull, 11, 267)

Shacter, Helen
Appointment: Chicago Veteran's Rehabilitation Center (Bull, 42, 127)

Shaffer, George Wilson
Appointment: Goucher College (Sci, 100, 353; Bull, 42, 63)
Meeting: APA Wash.-Balt. Branch (Bull, 36, 304)

Shaffer, Laurance Frederic
Appointment: Teachers College, Columbia (Bull, 42, 794)

Shand, Alexander Faulkner
Appointment: *British Journal of Psychology* (JoP, 1, 28)

Shapley, Harlow
Election: Society of the Sigma Xi, president (Sci, 101, 13)

Sharp, Agnes Arminda
Appointment: A. B. Dick Company (Bull, 42, 128)

Sharp Foundation
Lecture: Conklin, E. G., Rice Institute Lectures (Sci, 93, 396)

Shartle, Carroll Leonard
Appointment: AAAP Committee, psychology as an occupation (J App, 22, 311)
Appointment: Ohio State Univ. (Bull, 42, 127)
Meeting: APA Wash.-Balt. Branch (Bull, 37, 405)
Publication: sample occupational interview (J App, 27, 473)

Shaw, Charles Gray
Appointment: New York Univ. (Rev, 6, 673)

Shaw, Franklin Julius
Appointment: Univ. of New Hampshire (Bull, 41, 679)

Shaw, Henry A.
Appointment: Harvard Univ., mental hygiene (Sci, 74, 481)

Shaw, W. J.
Appointment: Princeton Univ. (Rev, 8, 656-657)

Shea, John Penfield
APA Wash.-Balt. Branch, 1940 (Bull, 37, 405)

Sheffield Lectures
Yale Univ., 36th annual (SCI, *15*, 117)

Sheffield Scientific School
Lecture: Whitney, W. D., Darwinian theory (SCI°, *1*, 293)

Sheldon Fellowship
Award: Elliott, R. M., Harvard Univ. (SCI, *37*, 628; BULL, *10*, 292)

Sheldon, Wilmon Henry
Appointment: College of the City of New York (JoP, *15*, 448)
Appointment: Princeton Univ. (JoP, *2*, 336)
Election: American Philosophical Assoc., executive committee (JoP, *7*, 28)
Election: APA officer (JoP, *11*, 56)
Lecture: chance (JoP, *2*, 224)
Lecture: Woodbridge Memorial (JoP, *40*, 168)
Publication: Duality, Harvard Univ. Press (JoP, *15*, 280)

Shepard, John Frederick
Appointment: Univ. of Michigan (JoP, *15*, 504)
Promotion: Univ. of Michigan (BULL, *8*, 222; JoP, *8*, 364; SCI, *33*, 897; BULL, *3*, 422; JoP, *3*, 644)

Shepherd, William Thomas
Lecture: SSPP, discrimination of articulate sound by raccoons (JoP, *7*, 28)
Resignation: Waynesburg College (BULL, *13*, 407)

Sherif, Muzafer (*see also* Basoglu, Muzaffer Serif)
Fellowship: Princeton Univ. (BULL, *42*, 128)
Fellowship: U.S. (SCI, *102*, 374; BULL, *42*, 792-793; JoP, *42*, 616)

Sherman, Frederic David
Appointment: Oshkosh Normal School (AJP, *9*, 135; SCI, *6*, 169; REV, *4*, 567)

Sherman, Mandel
Lecture: Chicago Psychological Club (BULL, *40*, 540)

Sherrington, Charles Scott
Appointment: *British Journal of Psychology* (JoP, *1*, 28)
Lecture: British Psychological Society (JoP, *8*, 448)
Meeting: Royal Medico-Psychological Assoc. (SCI, *70*, 162)

Shields, Thomas Edward
Appointment: Catholic Univ. of Washington (REV, *9*, 644)

Shiels, Albert
Appointment: Columbia Univ. (BULL, *20*, 288)
Directs the creation of a Divison of Psychology at Los Angeles (J APP, *2*, 194)

Shinn, Milicent Washburn
Death notice (BULL, 37, 755)
Publication: review, correction of (JoP, 6, 336)

Shirley, Hale F.
Appointment: Child Guidance Clinic, San Francisco (SCI, 91, 15)
Appointment: Stanford Univ., School of Medicine (SCI, 91, 15)
Resignation: State Univ. of Iowa, College of Medicine (SCI, 91, 15)

Shmookler, H. B. Memorial
Kennedy, F., neuroses in warfare, 1943 (SCI, 97, 374)

Shock, Nathan Wetherill
Appointment: National Institute of Health, U.S. Public Health Center (BULL,
39, 196; SCI, 94, 605)

Shorthand-writing
Research: Bureau of Education (SCI°, 4, 266-267)

Shortley, Michael J.
Publication: untapped manpower, handicapped as governmental employees
(J APP, 28, 79)

Short-sightedness
Publication: Nature (SCI°, 17, 7)
Research: Foster, [?] (SCI°, 13, 481)

Shpil'rein, Isaak Naftul'evich
Meeting: Industrial Psychology, 7th International Conference (SCI, 72, 599)

Sidgwick, Henry
Death notice (REV, 7, 639; SCI, 12, 380)
Resignation: Cambridge Univ. (SCI, 11, 997)

Sidgwick, Henry Memorial Lecture
Ward, J., Newnham College (JoP, 9, 700)

Sidis, Boris
Donation: estate and park for establishing private hospital (BULL, 7, 75)
Donation: Psychotherapeutic Institute, received (JoP, 6, 721)
Publication: response to review (JoP, 4, 699)

Sidis Psychotherapeutic Institute (see Maple-Wood Farms)

Siebrecht, Elmer Bradley
Appointment: Gustavus Adolphus College (BULL, 42, 675)

Sievers, Eduard
Publication: philology, Encyclopedia Britannica (SCI°, 5, 162)

Sight (*see* Vision)

Sigma Xi

Affiliation: Esso Research Club Assoc. with Standard Oil CO., N.J. (Sci, 99, 123)

Anniversary: 400th of death of Copernicus, Univ. of Oklahoma (Sci, 98, 58)

Appointment: Seashore, R. H., Chicago local committee on arrangements for convention, 1943 (Sci, 98, 448)

Election: Boder, D., Illinois Institute of Tech., vice- president (Sci, 95, 551)

Election: Cattell, J. McK., president (Sci, 37, 55)

Election: Coakley, J., Rochester Univ. (Sci, 101, 556-557)

Election: Jewett, F. B., National Executive Committee (Sci, 101, 13)

Election: Jones, M. C. K., National Membership Committee (Sci, 101, 13)

Election: officers, Cincinnati Chapter (Sci, 101, 455)

Election: officers, District of Columbia Chapter (Sci, 101, 60)

Election: officers, Louisiana State Chapter (Sci, 101, 14)

Election: officers, Smith Chapter (Sci, 101, 14)

Election: officers, Stanford Chapter (Sci, 102, 116)

Election: Shapley, H., president (Sci, 101, 13)

Grant: DeSilva, H. R., body voltage research (Sci, 80, 310)

Lecture: Bentley, M., Missouri and Kansas (Sci, 59, 14, 160)

Lecture: Cattell, J. McK. (Sci, 43, 423; JoP, 13, 224)

Lecture: Davenport, C. B., eugenics (Sci, 36, 784)

Lecture: Finger, F. W., Virginia, psychology, the war and after (Sci, 102, 420)

Lecture: Geldard, F. A. (Sci, 93, 520)

Lecture: Harris, A. J., on Galton, F. (Sci, 37, 172)

Lecture: Jastrow, J. (JoP, 13, 280; Bull., 13, 188)

Lecture: Jastrow, J., emotional expression (Sci, 43, 529)

Lecture: Lashley, K., Univ. of Rochester (Sci, 87, 164)

Lecture: Loewi, O., Ohio State Univ. (Sci, 97, 398)

Lecture: Nafe, J. P., Univ. of Virginia, temperature sense (Sci, 87, 412)

Lecture: Nichols, E. L., Univ. of Kansas (Sci, 11, 634)

Lecture: psychopharmacology (Sci, 87, 253)

Lecture: Stetson, H. T., Univ. of Maine (Sci, 97, 398)

Lecture: Winslow, C. E. A., Smith Coll. Chapter, science and planning in the post-war world (Sci, 101, 14)

Lecture: Yerkes, R. M., Univ. of Minnesota, psych. methods of diagnosis (Sci, 45, 138; JoP, 14, 168)

Meeting: Detroit, mental attitudes for national defense (Sci, 93, 372)

Meeting: Witmer, L. presides, 1915 (Sci, 41, 263)

Retirement: Snoddy, G. S., Indiana president (Sci, 90, 391)

Sign language

Research: Mallery, G. (Sci°, 1, 157)

Signal Office Reserve Corps

Appointment: psychologists (Bull, 14, 333)

Siipola, Elsa Margareeta
Promotion: Smith College (BULL, *42*, 331)

Sikorski, Ivan Alekseevich
Research: suicide and crime (SCI, *2*, 132)

Silverberg, William V.
Appointment: Assoc. for the Advancement of Psychoanalysis (J APP, *25*, 473)

Simett, A. P.
Publication: the occult world phenomena and the Society for Psychical
Research (SCI*, *7*, 306)

Simmara, G. [Simarro, Luis ?]
Nomination: Government School of Science, Madrid (AJP, *8*, 584)

Simmons College (Boston, Massachusetts)
Appointment: Seward, G. H. (BULL, *42*, 583)
Departure: Moore, H. T. (BULL, *12*, 243)
Resignation: Cabot, P. S. (BULL, *41*, 343)

Simoneit, Max
Announcement: open positions in German army (BULL, *38*, 779)

Simpson, Benjamin Roy
Course: Univ. of Georgia (JoP, *7*, 336)

Simpson, Ray Hamill
Appointment: Barnard College (BULL, *34*, 635)

Simpson, Sutherland
Research: Cornell Univ., experimental neuroses (SCI, *86*, 221)

Simrall, Dorothy V.
Appointment: Mount Holyoke College (BULL, *42*, 793)

Simrall, Josephine Price
Appointment: Kentucky State Univ. (BULL, *16*, 392)

Sinai, Nathan
Election: National Sanitation Foundation (SCI, *101*, 60)

Sinclair, Eileen Marie
Appointment: Univ. of Illinois, College of Medicine (BULL, *40*, 231)

Sing Sing Prison (Ossining, New York)
Psychopathic research dept. established (BULL, *13*, 296)

Singer, Edgar Arthur
Appointment: American Philosophical Assoc. (JoP, *9*, 28)
The Winston Simplified Dictionary with Lewis, W. D. (J App, *3*, 194)

Singer, H. Douglass
Election: American Board of Psychiatry and Neurology, president (Sci, *80*, 476)

Sisk, Thurman Kelley
Death notice (Bull, *41*, 807)

Sisson, Earl Donald
Appointment: Reed College (JoP, *9*, 56)
Armed Forces (Bull, *39*, 808)
Departure: Louisiana State Univ. (Bull, *39*, 808)

Size-weight illusion (*see also* Illusions; *and* Optical illusions)
Lecture: Gault, R. H. (JoP, *7*, 28)

Skaggs, Ernest Burton
Lecture: elementary psych. courses (AJP, *38*, 153)

Skandinavian Scientific Review
Discussion (AJP, *34*, 312)
Publication: announced (Bull, *20*, 416)

Skard, Aase G.
Election: Norwegian Psychological Assoc., secretary (AJP, *46*, 511)

Skidmore College (Saratoga Springs, New York)
Appointment: Smith, C. E. (Sci, *81*, 149)
Election: Moore, H. T., president (Bull, *22*, 612; Sci, *62*, 180, 264)
Psychology laboratory (AJP, *43*, 300)
Resignation: Kline, L. W. (Sci, *81*, 149)

Skillman (New Jersey)
Appointment: Wallin, J. E. W. (Bull, *7*, 324)

Skinner, Burrhus Frederic
Appointment: Indiana Univ. (Bull, *42*, 191)
Award: Guggenheim fellowship, 1942-43 (Bull, *39*, 423)
Award: Howard Crosby Warren Medal, Society of Experimental Psychologists
   (Bull, *39*, 325; Sci, *95*, 378)
Departure: Univ. of Minnesota (Bull, *42*, 191)
Editor: *Psychological Record* (Bull, *34*, 410)
Publication: quantitative analysis of Swinburne's poetry (AJP, *55*, 115-123)

Skinner, Charles Edward
Appointment: Indiana State Normal School (Bull, *17*, 200)

Slaughter, John Willis
Lecture: London Univ. (BULL, 3, 320)
Publication: *The Adolescent* (JoP, 7, 644)

Sleep
Century of Progress Exposition exhibit, sleep and fatigue (J APP, 17, 212)
Lecture: Johnson, H. M., Univ. of North Carolina (SCI, 72, 598)
Lecture: Laird, D. A., Century of Progress Exposition, sleep and fatigue (SCI, 77, 348)
Research: Johnson, H. M., Simmons investigation of sleep (SCI, 69, 450; SCI, 62, 177)
Research: Landis, C. (J APP, 10, 394)

Sletto, Raymond Franklin
Award: Social Science Research Council (BULL, 36, 805)

Sloan, Louise Littig
Meeting: APA Wash.-Balt. Branch (BULL, 37, 122)

Small, George D.
Appointment: Univ. of Tulsa (BULL, 42, 583)
Departure: Kansas State Teachers College (BULL, 42, 583)

Smell
Lecture: Boring, E. G., classification of odors (AJP, 40, 345)
Lecture: Hopkins, C. L., Biological Society, in buzzards (SCI°, 10, 318)
Lecture: Monroe, W. S., discrimination (JoP, 2, 700)
Research: Fischer, ? and Penzoldt, ?, sense of (SCI°, 7, 547)
Research: Nichols, E. L. and Bailey, E. H. S., sense of in different sexes (SCI°, 9, 294)
Research: Romanes, G. J., in dogs (SCI, 9, 360)

Smith, Anthony Joseph
Appointment: Univ. of Illinois (BULL, 42, 793-794)

Smith, Bruce Lannes
Publication: *Psychological Bulletin*, military psychology (J APP, 25, 359)

Smith, C. K.
Appointment: Princeton Univ. (REV, 8, 112)

Smith, Carl E.
Appointment: Skidmore College (SCI, 81, 149)

Smith College (Northampton, Massachusetts)
Appointment: Adams, E. K. (BULL, 2, 427)
Appointment: Bishop, H. G. (BULL, 22, 140, 260; SCI, 61, 117)
Appointment: Koffka, K. (BULL, 29, 603; J APP, 11, 166; JoP, 24, 420)

Appointment: Metcalf, J. T. (BULL, *13*, 148)
Appointment: Pierce, A. H. (REV, 7, 428)
Appointment: Rogers, D. C. (BULL, *11*, 190; SCI, *39*, 606; JoP, *11*, 308)
Appointment: Smith, W. G. (REV, 2, 642; AJP, 7, 452)
Appointment: Spencer, R. (BULL, 22, 140)
Course: Haines, T. H. (BULL, *11*, 115; JoP, *11*, 196)
Course: psychology accepted as a science elective (BULL, 24, 380)
Course: psychology classification as a science (J APP, *11*, 319)
Course: Summer Training School of Psychiatric Social Work (JoP, *15*, 671-672;
     J APP, 2, 384; BULL, *15*, 360)
Departure: Bishop, H. G. (BULL, 23, 456)
Departure: Bishop, M. K. (BULL, 23, 456)
Establishment: Neilson, W. A. Chair (J APP, *11*, 166)
Fellowship: advanced work in philosophy and psychology (SCI, *17*, 120)
Leave of absence: Clark, R. S. (BULL, *13*, 148)
Leave of absence: Gardiner, H. N. (BULL, 6, 400)
Lecture: Dewey, J. (BULL, 8, 32)
Library donated by Pierce, A. H. (BULL, *11*, 152; SCI, *39*, 462)
Meeting: Society of Experimental Psychologists (BULL, *34*, 273)
Promotion: Adams, E. K. (JoP, 9, 168)
Promotion: Cutler, A. A. (BULL, 2, 427)
Promotion: Heathers, L. B. (BULL, 42, 331)
Promotion: Mirmow, E. L. (BULL, 42, 331)
Promotion: Rose, A. A. (BULL, 42, 331)
Promotion: Sipola, E. M. (BULL, 42, 331)
Psychology and philosophy dept. combined (JoP, *13*, 224; BULL, *13*, 148)

Smith, Elliott Dunlap

Discussion: Taylor Society Meeting (JoP, *21*, 700)

Smith, Franklin Orion

Death notice (BULL, 38, 907)
Grant: AAAS, $300.00 (BULL, *19*, 171)
Resignation: Univ of Utah (BULL, *12*, 204)

Smith, G. A.

Visits U.S. (SCI°, 8, 364)

Smith, Henry Clay

Meeting: APA Wash.-Balt. Branch (BULL, 36, 304)

Smith, Henry Peter

Appointment: Syracuse Univ. (BULL, *41*, 603)
Departure: Arizona State Teachers College (BULL, *41*, 603)

Smith, James Lorrain

Lecture: British Psychological Society (JoP, 8, 448)

Smith, Josephine M.
Death notice (BULL, *41*, 409)

Smith, Karl Ulrich
Appointment: Univ. of Rochester (BULL, *33*, 405)

Smith, Kinsley Richard
Appointment: AAAP (J APP, *25*, 265)
Leave of absence: Pennsylvania State College (BULL, *39*, 896)
Research: U.S. Navy (BULL, *39*, 896)

Smith, Lauren H.
Appointment: Institute for Mental Hygiene and Pennsylvania Hospital (SCI, *88*, 591)

Smith, Margaret Keiver
Appointment: New York State Normal School (REV, *8*, 552; SCI, *14*, 40)

Smith, Norman Kemp
Appointment: Princeton Univ. (JOP, *3*, 504; BULL, *3*, 288)
Appointment: Univ. of Edinburgh (BULL, *16*, 257)
Election: American Philosophical Assoc., executive committee (JOP, *7*, 28)
Election: American Philosophical Assoc., officer (JOP, *9*, 28)

Smith, S. E.
Election: American Medico-Psychological Assoc. (SCI, *37*, 936)

Smith, Samuel George
Publication: announcement (JOP, *8*, 560)

Smith, Stevenson
Appointment: Univ. of Washington (BULL, *8*, 374; JOP, *8*, 616; BULL, *11*, 232)
Departure: Columbia Univ., Teachers College (BULL, *8*, 374)

Smith, Theodate Louise
Death notice (AJP, *25*, 320; BULL, *11*, 152)

Smith, Walter
Death notice (JOP, *4*, 140; BULL, *4*, 64)
Leave of absence: Lake Forest Univ. (BULL, *1*, 413)

Smith, William Benjamin
Appointment: Tulane Univ. (BULL, *3*, 319; JOP, *3*, 504)
Election: SSPP, council member (JOP, *8*, 84)

Smith, William G.
Appointment: *British Journal of Psychology* (JOP, *1*, 28)
Appointment: London County Council Asylums (REV, *8*, 447; SCI, *13*, 877)
Appointment: Smith College (REV, *2*, 642; AJP, *7*, 452)

Appointment: Univ. of Edinburgh (BULL, *8*, 333; BULL, *3*, 320)
Appointment: Univ. of Liverpool (SCI, *18*, 704; JoP, *1*, 28; SCI, *22*, 648; BULL, *2*, 427; BULL, *1*, 134)
Course: Kings College, London, experimental psychology (SCI, *16*, 280)
Departure: Kings College, London (BULL, *1*, 134; JoP, *1*, 28)
Departure: Univ. of Liverpool (JoP, *3*, 504; BULL, *3*, 319)

Smith, William George
Appointment: Univ. of Toronto (BULL, *3*, 35; BULL, *4*, 32)

Smithsonian Institution (Washington, DC)
Election: Langley, S. P. (SCI°, *10*, 264)
Publication: Bolton's catalogue of scientific and technical periodicals (SCI°, *2*, 91-92)
Publication: list in press (SCI°, *7*, 214)

Smithsonian Report
Summaries of scientific progress in the natural sciences, 1884 (SCI°, *7*, 371)

Smoking, psychology of
Research: Wallin, J. E. W. (BULL, *9*, 486; JoP, *9*, 672)

Sneath, Elias Hershey
Appointment: Yale Psychological Laboratory (JoP, *1*, 28)
Leave of absence: Yale Univ. (BULL, *3*, 36, 422)

Snoddy, George Samuel
Research: Indiana Univ., longitudinal forgetting (J APP, *23*, 530)
Retirement: Indiana Chapter of the Society of Sigma Xi, president (SCI, *90*, 391)

Snow, Adolph Judah
Appointment: Krenn and Dato Co. (J APP, *9*, 319)
Appointment: Yellow Cab Co. (J APP, *9*, 90)

Snow, William Freeman Medal
Award: Ireland, M. W. (SCI, *101*, 349)

Snyder, Laurence H.
Lecture: Yerkes Laboratories for Primate Biology, heredity in apes and humans (SCI, *97*, 398)

Snyder, Walter
Election: National Sanitation Foundation (SCI, *101*, 60)

Snyder, William Ulrich
Appointment: Pennsylvania State College (BULL, *42*, 675)

Soal, Samuel George
Research: psychic phenomena (SCI, *80*, 183)

Social and Ethical Interpretations
Publication: Baldwin, J. M., 4th ed. (Bull, 3, 392)

Social consciousness
Lecture: Mead, G. H. (JoP, 7, 308)

Social instincts
Lecture: Thorndike, E. L., Johns Hopkins Univ. (Sci, 37, 302)
Publication: Brownell, W. C., *Scribner's Magazine* (Sci°, 9, 610)

Social philosophy
Lecture: Talbert, E. L. (JoP, 7, 223)
School formed, London (Rev, 5, 110)

Social psychology
Fellowship: Sarbin, T. R. (Bull, 38, 777-778)
Fellowship: Sherif, M., Princeton Univ. (Sci, 100, 516)
Grant: Schanck, R. L., Social Science Research Council (Bull, 33, 579)
Lecture: Baldwin, J. M. (JoP, 1, 280)
Lecture: Calkins, M. W., Columbia Univ. (Sci, 33, 214)
Lecture: Judd, C. H., Columbia Univ. (Sci, 33, 214)
Lecture: Vincent, G., Univ. of Minnesota (Sci, 42, 374)
Publication: Lemmon, M. L., what is social psychology (AJP, 48, 665)
Research: Wright, C. D., sanitary and economic conditions of employed women
    (Sci°, 12, 227)

Social Research
Publication: translation of Max Wertheimer's Gestalt theory (Bull, 41, 268)

Social Science Abstracts
Publication: Social Science Research Council (Bull, 35, 334)
Reserved sales for libraries (Bull, 37, 657)

Social Science Congress
List of topics to be discussed at Birmingham (Sci°, 4, 92)
Meeting: notes, Birmingham, 1884 (Sci°, 4, 410)

Social Science, National Institute of
Award: Angell, J. R., gold medal (Sci, 85, 474)
Award: Beers, C. W., gold medal, mental hygiene (Sci, 77, 423)

Social Science Research Council
Appointment: Allport, G. W. (Sci, 82, 247)
Appointment: Barrett, L. (Bull, 37, 829)
Appointment: Campbell, A. A. (Bull, 36, 711)
Award: announced (Bull, 36, 805; Bull, 39, 682-683; Bull, 42, 64)
Election: Jones, H. E., Board of Directors (Sci, 99, 167)
Election: Meyer, A., member at large (JoP, 26, 336)

Meeting: London (JoP, *1*, 112)
Research: money raised to endow scholarship (JoP, *1*, 112; Bull, *1*, 174)

Society for Research in Child Development
Monographs completed (AJP, *52*, 477-478; J App, *22*, 540)

Society for Research in Psychosomatic Problems (*see* Psychosomatic Problems)

Society for Study of Psychology by Experimental Methods
Meeting: inaugural, held in London (Sci, *13*, 637)

Society for the Protection of Science and Learning
Appointment: Thomson, D. C. (Sci, *88*, 544)
Purpose (Sci, *88*, 544)
Reception: British Acad. and Royal Society for exiled scientists and scholars (Sci, *89*, 174)

Society for the Psychological Study of Social Issues
Course: problems of post-war world (Bull, *42*, 256)
Grant: Whitney, W. C. Foundation (Bull, *36*, 499)
Lecture: Allport, F. H., methods in the study of collective action phenomena (Sci, *94*, 230)
Meeting: APA (Sci, *91*, 500; Sci, *94*, 230)
Meeting: Ohio State Univ., 1938 (JoP, *35*, 280)
Meeting: post-war planning (J App, *27*, 114-115)
Organization: announcement (Bull, *34*, 274)
Publication: Yearbook, *The Psychology of Industrial Conflict* (Bull, *35*, 61)

Society for the Study of Development and Growth
Election: officers, 1945-1946 (Sci, *102*, 245)
Meeting: 1941, officers elected (Sci, *94*, 435)
Meeting: 1945 announced (Sci, *102*, 147)
Symposium: annual, 1942 (Sci, *95*, 573)

Society for Visiting Scientists
Reception: Donnan, F. G. (Sci, *101*, 15)

Society of Experimental Psychologists
Award: Culler, E. A., Warren medal (Sci, *87*, 362)
Award: Graham, C. H., Warren medal (Bull, *38*, 304; J App, *25*, 267; Sci, *93*, 324)
Award: Hull, C. L., Warren medal (Bull, *42*, 406; Sci, *101*, 402)
Award: Jacobsen, C. F., Warren medal (Bull, *36*, 499)
Award: Lashley, K. S., Warren medal (Sci, *85*, 354)
Award: Skinner, B. F., Warren medal (Sci, *95*, 378; Bull, *39*, 325)
Award: Stevens, S. S., Warren medal (Sci, *97*, 373)
Award: Warren, H. C. medal (Bull, *33*, 476; Bull, *35*, 408; Sci, *83*, 367)

Election: Langfeld, H. S., president (SCI, *87*, 342)

Lecture: Dallenbach, K. M. (AJP, *49*, 487)

Meeting: annual (BULL, *1*, 213; JoP, *1*, 420; BULL, *3*, 147; BULL, *4*, 128; BULL, *5*, 128; AJP, *19*, 288; AJP, *20*, 471; BULL, *7*, 179; JoP, *8*, 335-336; BULL, *8*, 181; BULL, *9*, 208; JoP, *9*, 336; BULL, *10*, 211-212; JoP, *10*, 364; JoP, *11*, 196; JoP, *13*, 224; BULL, *13*, 148; AJP, *44*, 582)

Meeting: 1st (AJP, *15*, 464)

Meeting: 2nd, Clark Univ. (JoP, *2*, 223)

Meeting: 8th (BULL, *33*, 476)

Meeting: 9th (BULL, *34*, 273)

Meeting: 23rd (AJP, *37*, 467; SCI, *63*, 474)

Meeting: 30th, Cambridge (AJP, *46*, 511)

Meeting: 31st (AJP, *47*, 344)

Meeting: 33rd (AJP, *49*, 487)

Meeting: 35th, Princeton Univ. (AJP, *52*, 302; SCI, *87*, 342)

Meeting: 36th, Philadelphia (AJP, *53*, 299; SCI, *91*, 334; BULL, *37*, 405)

Meeting: 37th, New Brunswick (AJP, *54*, 295)

Meeting: 38th New York Psychiatric Institute (AJP, *55*, 276-277)

Meeting: 39th, Columbia Univ. (AJP, *56*, 449; BULL, *40*, 539)

Meeting: 40th, Harvard Club (AJP, *57*, 426-427)

Meeting: 41st, Harvard Club (AJP, *58*, 405)

Publication: Chapel Hill meeting of the Society of Experimental Psychologists (AJP, *51*, 578)

Publication: Dallenbach, K. M., Philadelphia meeting, 29th (AJP, *45*, 539)

Publication: Dallenbach, K. M., Worcester meeting (AJP, *48*, 526)

Publication: history of (AJP, *51*, 410)

Society of Medical Jurisprudence (*see* Medical Jurisprudence)

Sociometry

Appointment: Lundberg, G. A. (BULL, *38*, 305)

First edition (BULL, *34*, 636)

Resignation: Murphy, G. (BULL, *38*, 305)

Solomon, Harry C.

Harvard Medical School and Boston Psychopathic Hospital (SCI, *98*, 321)

Solomon, Richard Samuel

Appointment: Standard Register Co. Ohio (BULL, *40*, 79)

Appointment: The Personnel Institute (BULL, *36*, 712)

Solomons, Leon Mendez

Death notice (REV, *7*, 216)

Sommer, Karl Robert

Exhibition of apparatus (JoP, *1*, 335)

Lecture: German Society of Experimental Psychology, individual psychology and psychiatry (SCI, *22*, 727)

Sones, A. Merlin
Appointment: Drexel Institute of Technology (BULL, 39, 681)

Sonoma State Home
Appointment: Ordahl, G. (JoP, 13, 448)

Sorbonne (Paris, France) (*see also* L'École des Hautes Études)
Appointment: Angell, J. R. (SCI, 40, 22)
Appointment: Piéron, H. (BULL, 9, 359; BULL, 10, 40)
Lecture: Angell, J. R. (BULL, 11, 268)
Lecture: Angell, J. R., postponed (JoP, 11, 721)
Lecture: Leuba, J. H., psychology of religion (SCI, 53, 436)

Sorley, William Ritchie
Appointment: Cambridge Univ. (SCI, 12, 120; REV, 7, 531)
Appointment: Univ. of Aberdeen (REV, 2, 104)
Degree: Univ. of Edinburgh (SCI, 11, 717; JoP, 2, 420)
Departure: Univ. of Aberdeen (SCI, 12, 120)

Sorrow
Publication: Wasmansdorff, E., forms of (SCI°, 6, 407)

Sound (*see also* Acoustics; Audition; Hearing; Tones)
Lecture: Bousfield, W. A., localization (AJP, 44, 805)
Lecture: Shepherd, W. T., discrimination (JoP, 7, 28)
Research: Raggi, A., perception (SCI°, 7, 570)

South Africa (*see* Baboon boy of; *and* Stellenbosch University)

South Carolina Academy of Science
Meeting: 1941 (SCI, 93, 472-473)

South Carolina, College of
Degree: Baldwin, J. M. (BULL, 2, 88)
Degree: Lefevre, A. (BULL, 2, 88)

South Carolina Red Cross
Appointment: Morse, J. (JoP, 15, 140)

South Carolina, University of (Columbia)
Lecture: Baldwin, J. M. (BULL, 10, 123)
Meeting: SSPP, 32nd annual (SCI, 85, 261)

South Dakota Academy of Science
Election: officers (SCI, 102, 7)

South Dakota, University of (Vermillion)
Appointment: Josey, C. C. (JoP, 20, 448)

South, Earl Bennett
Publication: *Dictionary of Terms in Measurement and Guidance* (J APP, 23, 421)

South Kensington (England)
International exhibition on health and education, 1884, proposal (SCI°, 2, 839)
Memorial statue: Darwin, C. (SCI°, 6, 18)

Southard, Elmer Ernest
Appointment: APA Committee on Medical Education (JoP, 9, 28)
Appointment: Boston Psychopathic Hopsital (SCI, 33, 60)
Award: Boston Psychopathic Hospital, bronze memorial (SCI, 60, 564)
Death notice (AJP, 32, 154)
Degree: George Washington Univ. (BULL, 14, 263)
Editor: *Bulletin*, psychopathology (BULL, 12, 280; BULL, 14, 263; BULL, 13, 260; BULL, 16, 221)
Lecture: Columbia Univ. (BULL, 14, 32)
Lecture: Conference of Mental Hygiene (J APP, 3, 396)
Lecture: mapping the brain (SCI, 34, 914)
Lecture: Mass. School for Feeble-minded (BULL, 13, 407-408)

Southern California Junior College Association
Lecture: Humm, D. G., 1942 (J APP, 26, 712)

Southern California, University of (Los Angeles)
Appointment: Guilford, J. P. (SCI, 92, 8)
Appointment: Metfessel, M. (BULL, 35, 577)
Appointment: Morgan, J. J. B. (J APP, 10, 396)
Appointment: Ruch, F. L. (SCI, 86, 263; BULL, 34, 864)
Appointment: Thorpe, L. P. (BULL, 39, 681)
Appointment: Travis, L. E. (BULL, 35, 577)
Appointment: Warren, N. (BULL, 35, 577)
Appointment: Whipple, G. M. (J APP, 10, 396)
Appointment: Zigler, M. J. (BULL, 24, 80)
Departure: Seashore, R. H. (SCI, 86, 218)
Leave of absence: Morse, J. (JoP, 15, 140)
Lecture: Ebaugh, F. G. (SCI, 91, 446)
Methods of psychoanalysis and reeducation, Psychological Clinic (JoP, 15, 112)
Psychological clinic headed by Hamilton, M. (JoP, 15, 112)

Southern Education Association
Meeting: SSPP (BULL, 7, 251)

Southern Illinois University (*see* Bureau of Child Guidance of)

Southern Methodist University (Dallas, Texas)
Appointment: Litchte, W. H. (BULL, 38, 304; J APP, 25, 265)
Appointment: Sartain, A. Q. (BULL, 38, 304)

Appointment: Sartain, A. Q. (J App, 25, 265)
Formation: Southern Philosophical Assoc., (JoP, 33, 112)
Leave of absence: Sartain, A. Q. (BULL, 41, 603)
Leave of absence: Yarborough, J. U. (BULL, 38, 304; J App, 25, 265)
Return: Yarborough, J. U. (BULL, 40, 539)

Southern Society for Philosophy and Psychology

Election: Buchner, E. F., president (SCI, 31, 22)
Election: Buchner, E. F., secretary-treasurer (SCI, 27, 596)
Election: Ellis, A. C., council member (SCI, 31, 22)
Election: Franz, S. I., president (BULL, 8, 32)
Election: Franz, S. I., vice-president (SCI, 31, 22)
Election: Harris, M., president (SCI, 90, 105)
Election: Harris, W. T., council member (JoP, 1, 168)
Election: Hill, D. S., council member (SCI, 31, 22)
Election: Lanier, L. H., president (SCI, 85, 261)
Election: Lefevre, A., vice-president (SCI, 27, 596)
Election: MacBride, J., president (SCI, 27, 596)
Election: members (JoP, 14, 308)
Election: Miner, J. B., president (J App, 10, 285)
Election: Munn, N. L., secretary-treasurer (SCI, 90, 105)
Election: Nafe, J. P., president (SCI, 91, 354)
Election: officers (BULL, 13, 40; BULL, 39, 423; SCI, 95, 429; JoP, 7, 56; JoP, 11, 140; BULL, 12, 44; BULL, 11, 28; BULL, 1, 134; JoP, 13, 112; JoP, 5, 195; JoP, 6, 56; BULL, 6, 32; BULL, 7, 36; BULL, 9, 40)
Election: Ogden, R. M., secretary-treasurer (SCI, 31, 22)
Election: Payne, B. R., council member (SCI, 31, 22)
Election: Pearce, H. J., council member (SCI, 31, 22)
Lecture: Balz, A. G. (JoP, 37, 196)
Lecture: Buchner, E. F., presidential address (JoP, 8, 84)
Lecture: Dunlap, K. (JoP, 37, 196)
Lecture: Harris, M., presidential address (JoP, 37, 196)
Lecture: Loemker, L. E. (JoP, 37, 196)
Lecture: Nafe, J. P., presidential address (JoP, 38, 224)
Meeting: 1st, AAAS (BULL, 2, 427)
Meeting: 1st, Montgomery, Alabama, 1906 (SCI, 24, 749; JoP, 3, 700; BULL, 3, 421)
Meeting: 1st postponed (BULL, 3, 35)
Meeting: 2nd, announcement (JoP, 4, 140)
Meeting: 3rd, announcement (BULL, 5, 32; JoP, 5, 84)
Meeting: 4th, announcement (BULL, 5, 379)
Meeting: 5th, announcement (JoP, 6, 700, 721; BULL, 6, 427)
Meeting: 5th, Baltimore (SCI, 28, 555; SCI, 31, 22)
Meeting: 6th, Southern Education Assoc. (BULL, 7, 251; JoP, 7, 392)
Meeting: 8th, Johns Hopkins Univ. (JoP, 10, 280; BULL, 10, 123; SCI, 37, 409)
Meeting: 9th, Philadelphia (BULL, 11, 443)
Meeting: 12th, Virginia (BULL, 14, 144; JoP, 14, 308)

Meeting: 13th, Nashville abandoned (JoP, *15*, 224; Sci, *47*, 363; Bull, *15*, 97)
Meeting: 19th, announcement (JoP, *21*, 84)
Meeting: 23rd (AJP, *40*, 515)
Meeting: 24th (AJP, *41*, 502)
Meeting: 25th (AJP, *42*, 459)
Meeting: 26th (AJP, *43*, 509)
Meeting: 27th, New Orleans (AJP, *44*, 374)
Meeting: 31st (JoP, *33*, 223)
Meeting: 32nd, Univ. of South Carolina (Sci, *85*, 261)
Meeting: 33rd, 1938 (Sci, *87*, 413)
Meeting: 35th, program (JoP, *37*, 196)
Meeting: 36th, 1941 (Sci, *93*, 373; AJP, *54*, 439, 441; JoP, *38*, 224)
Meeting: 37th, Nashville (AJP, *55*, 446-447; JoP, *39*, 196, 279)
Membership list (JoP, *7*, 334-336)
Officers announced (Bull, *5*, 32; JoP, *8*, 84)
Organization (Bull, *1*, 134; Sci, *19*, 478; JoP, *1*, 168)
Program listing (JoP, *7*, 28)
Publication: Lanier, L. H., 31st meeting (AJP, *48*, 688)
Publication: Lanier, L. H., 32nd meeting (AJP, *49*, 483)
Publication: Peterson, J., 28th meeting (AJP, *45*, 530)
Publication: Peterson, J., 29th meeting (AJP, *46*, 512)
Publication: Peterson, J., 30th meeting (AJP, *47*, 513)
Publication: report meeting (JoP, *8*, 84)
Publication: report 1st meeting (Bull, *2*, 36; JoP, *2*, 56)
Publication: report 3rd meeting (JoP, *5*, 167; JoP, *6*, 28)
Publication: status of philosophy teaching in the South (JoP, *33*, 672)

Southern University (Baton Rouge, Louisiana)
Appointment: Bayton, J. A. (Bull, *42*, 791)

Southwestern Philosophical Association
Formation (JoP, *33*, 112)
Meeting: 2nd annual (JoP, *34*, 721)

Space
Publication: Nichols, H. (Rev, *1*, 440)

Spain
Accounts of criminality (Sci°, *8*, 139-140)

Spanish Royal Academy of Sciences
Offer: premiums for papers on bird migrations and habits (Sci°, *7*, 414)

Spaulding, Edward Gleason
Announcement: American Philosophical Assoc. (JoP, *8*, 503-504)
Appointment: American Philosophical Assoc. (JoP, *14*, 196)
Appointment: Corps of Engineers (JoP, *15*, 392)
Appointment: Princeton Univ. (JoP, *2*, 336)

Election: American Philosophical Assoc., secretary-treasurer (JoP, *8*, 27-28; JoP, *7*, 28)

Meeting: American Philosophical Assoc./American Philosophical Society (JoP, *10*, 335)

Promotion: Princeton Univ. (JoP, *11*, 364)

Report: American Philosophical Society meeting (JoP, *10*, 167-168)

Spearman, Charles Edward

Appointment: Ohio State Univ. (BULL, *28*, 411)

Appointment: Univ. College, London (JoP, *4*, 476; BULL, *4*, 338; BULL, *25*, 376; SCI, *67*, 420)

Appointment: Univ. College, London, British Army (BULL, *12*, 364)

Death notice (BULL, *42*, 675; AJP, *58*, 558-560)

Degree: Univ. of London (SCI, *75*, 43; SCI, *74*, 169)

Election: German Academy of Natural Sciences, Halle, member (SCI, *89*, 31)

Election: German Society for Psychology (SCI, *80*, 67)

Guest: Century of Progress Exhibition (SCI, *77*, 579)

Retirement: Univ. College, London (SCI, *74*, 169)

Visiting professorships (BULL, *29*, 91)

Visits U.S. compliments of Commonwealth Fund (SCI, *66*, 616)

Visits World's Fair (J APP, *16*, 695)

Specht, Wilhelm

Publication: *Zeitschrift für Pathopsychologie* (JoP, *9*, 335)

Speech

Course: Emerson College, disorders (J APP, *19*, 221)

Grant: Scripture, E. W. (SCI, *16*, 1039)

Lecture: Swift, W. B., Boston Psychopathic Hospital, defects (BULL, *13*, 407)

Lecture: Swift, W. B., correction (J APP, *3*, 197)

Publication: Bell, A. M., teaching methods (SCI°, *2*, 30, 452)

Research: LeConte, J. (AJP, *1*, 355)

Speech Disorder, National Society for the Study and Correction of

Meeting (J APP, *3*, 197)

Speer, George Scott

Appointment: Illinois Institute of Technology (BULL, *42*, 793)

Speer, Robert K.

Election: Institute for Propaganda Analysis, treasurer (J APP, *21*, 719; BULL, *34*, 865)

Speir, Francis

Research: psychological questions concerning conscious mental activity (SCI°, *3*, 426)

Spelling
Lecture: MacDougall, R. (JoP, *1*, 84)
Research: Heilman, J. D. (J App, *3*, 195)

Spence, Kenneth Wartenbe
Appointment: State Univ. of Iowa (Bull, *39*, 682; Sci, *96*, 57)
Appointment: Yale Univ. (Sci, *96*, 268)

Spence, Ralph Beckett
Leave of absence: Columbia Univ. (Bull, *40*, 152)

Spence, Ruth Elizabeth
Appointment: Smith College (Bull, *22*, 140)

Spencer, Herbert
Birthday celebration: 81st (Sci, *13*, 716)
Death notice (Bull, *1*, 28)
Endowment: in memory of (JoP, *1*, 252)
Health report (Sci°, *9*, 54)
Lecture: Oxford Univ. (JoP, *1*, 56)
Lecture: sounds alarm over worries regarding civilization (Sci°, *3*, 56)
Publication: autobiography (Sci°, *14*, 234; JoP, *4*, 672)
Publication: biography author announced (JoP, *1*, 84)
Publication: biography, letters requested (JoP, *1*, 111)
Symposium: Hinman, E. L. (JoP, *1*, 224)
Trip: to U.S. results in poor health (Sci°, *3*, 771)
Will probated (JoP, *1*, 84)

Spencer Lectures, Herbert
Appointment: Baldwin, J. M. (Bull, *12*, 204; JoP, *12*, 336, 721)
Appointment: Boutroux, E. (JoP, *14*, 588; JoP, *15*, 28)
Appointment: Morgan, L., Oxford Univ. (Bull, *10*, 164; JoP, *10*, 720)
Appointment: Myers, C. S., Oxford Univ. (Sci, *69*, 570)
Delivered: Oxford Univ. (JoP, *13*, 308)

Spencer Lectures, Ichabod
Thorndike, E. L., Union College (JoP, *10*, 112)

Spencer, Llewellyn Truman
Promotion: Yale Univ. (Bull, *23*, 236; Sci, *63*, 279)

Spencer, W. Douglas
Appointment: New York State Assoc. for Applied Psychology (Bull, *37*, 405)
Appointment: Queens College (Bull, *37*, 329)

Speyer School (New York)
Photos: Anhalt, E., gifted classes (J App, *21*, 604)
Photos: Hollingworth, L. S., gifted classes (J App, *21*, 605)

Sphinx
Editor: Hübbe-Schleiden, T. U. (SCI°, 7, 139-140)
Publication: Fernau, L., issue (SCI°, 7, 139-140)

Spiesman, Anna (*see* Starr, Anna Spiesman)

Spiller, J.
Lecture: British Assoc., an experiment of color-blindness (SCI°, 14, 267)

Spindler, Frank Nicholas
Appointment: Wisconsin State Normal College (SCI, 14, 424; REV, 8, 656-657)

Spiritualism
Publication: Hamilton, A. M., *The American Magazine* (SCI°, 11, 312-313)

Spitzka, Edward Anthony
Death notice (SCI, 56, 306)

Spottiswoode, William
Death notice (SCI°, 2, 116)

Spragg, Sidney Durward Shirley
Appointment: Barnard College (BULL, 34, 635)
Appointment: Queens College (BULL, 37, 329)
Promotion: Queens College (BULL, 42, 486)
Publication: *Psychological Bulletin*, military psychology (J APP, 25, 359)

Springfield College (Massachusetts)
Leave of absence: Arsenian, S. (BULL, 41, 343)

Squires, Paul Chatham
Appointment: Univ. of Kansas (BULL, 25, 568)
Lecture: feral children (AJP, 38, 313)
Publication: Beethoven's concept of the whole (AJP, 48, 688)
Publication: Psychological loss in paretics and schizophrenics (AJP, 48, 172)

Squires, William H.
Appointment: Hamilton College (SCI, 13, 837)
Leave of absence: Hamilton College (REV, 6, 673)

Stadelmann, Heinrich
Lecture: optical illusions (AJP, 11, 279)

Stafford Little Lecture
Princeton (BULL, 33, 147)

Stagner, Ross
Conference: Psychology of Learning, Univ. of Colorado, 1939 (BULL, 36, 583)
Grant: Social Science Research Council (BULL, 36, 805)

Publication: bibliography of psychological aspects of war and social aggression
(BULL, *38*, 248)
Publication: *Psychological Bulletin*, military (J APP, *25*, 359)

Staley, George D.
Appointment: Pennsylvania College (SCI°, *14*, 333)

Stallo, John Bernard
Death notice (SCI, *11*, 238)

Stalnaker, John Marshall
Appointment: Stanford Univ. (BULL, *42*, 406-407)
Promotion: Princeton Univ. (BULL, *41*, 603)

Standard error of difference
Lecture: Dunlap, J. W. (AJP, *44*, 581)

Stanford University (Palo Alto, California) (*see also* Buckel Foundation)
Appointment: Boring, E. G. (BULL, *18*, 438)
Appointment: Bühler, K. (BULL, *24*, 380)
Appointment: Coover, J. E. (BULL, *24*, 380)
Appointment: Cowley, W. H. (BULL, *42*, 63; SCI, *100*, 424)
Appointment: Farnsworth, P. R. (SCI, *96*, 423)
Appointment: Goodenough, F. L. (J APP, *22*, 106)
Appointment: Gordon, K. (J APP, *10*, 394)
Appointment: Hilgard, E. R. (J APP, *17*, 341; SCI, *96*, 423)
Appointment: James, W. (BULL, *2*, 160; JoP, *2*, 140; SCI, *21*, 400)
Appointment: Johnson, G. S., medical school (SCI, *78*, 278)
Appointment: Kuznets, G. (J APP, *21*, 474; BULL, *34*, 499)
Appointment: Lewin, K. (J APP, *16*, 222)
Appointment: Lovejoy, A. E. (REV, *6*, 456)
Appointment: Martin, L. J. (SCI, *33*, 657; AJP, *11*, 280; BULL, *12*, 481; REV, *7*, 104; SCI, *43*, 776; JoP, *8*, 336)
Appointment: McNemar, Q. (BULL, *35*, 408)
Appointment: Miles, C. C. (BULL, *27*, 564; J APP, *11*, 404)
Appointment: Miles, W. R. (J APP, *6*, 301; BULL, *20*, 60; BULL, *19*, 410; SCI, *55*, 593; BULL, *27*, 564)
Appointment: Shirley, H. F., medical school (SCI, *91*, 15)
Appointment: Stalnaker, J. M. (BULL, *42*, 406-407)
Appointment: Stone, C. P. (BULL, *19*, 462; BULL, *20*, 60)
Appointment: Taylor, D. W. (BULL, *42*, 583; SCI, *102*, 193)
Appointment: Terman, L. M. (SCI, *56*, 108; SCI, *90*, 106; J APP, *6*, 301; BULL, *20*, 60)
Appointment: Walton, A. (J APP, *14*, 505)
Celebration: Angell, J. R., 70th birthday (SCI, *67*, 155)
Conference: social education, 1938 (J APP, *22*, 107)

Degree: Angell, J. R. (SCI, 79, 337)
Departure: Book, W. F. (JOP, 9, 588, 644)
Departure: Jensen, M. B. (J APP, 13, 415)
Departure: Sward, K. (J APP, 14, 505)
Fellowship: Buckel, ?, research established (BULL, 11, 191)
Fellowship: feeble-minded announced (SCI, 39, 506)
Fellowship: psychical research (BULL, 36, 57)
Leave of absence: Angell, F. (BULL, 12, 481)
Leave of absence: Hilgard, E. R. (BULL, 40, 79)
Leave of absence: Sabine, G. H. (JOP, 7, 252)
Lecture: Bingham, W. V. (SCI, 52, 152)
Lecture: James, W. (JOP, 3, 84; BULL, 3, 83; SCI, 23, 118)
Lecture: Orbelli, L. A., autonomic nervous system (SCI, 70, 499)
Lecture: Terman, L., gifted children (SCI, 57, 82)
Meeting: WPA (BULL, 21, 360)
Promotion: Coover, J. E. (JOP, 18, 532; BULL, 18, 236; SCI, 53, 387)
Promotion: Eurich, A. C. (BULL, 41, 409)
Promotion: Hilgard, E. R. (BULL, 40, 79)
Promotion: Martin, L. J. (SCI, 29, 455; BULL, 6, 152; BULL, 8, 182; BULL, 13, 260)
Promotion: Sabine, G. H. (BULL, 5, 348)
Promotion: Stuart, H. W. (BULL, 5, 348; BULL, 6, 152)
Publication: Coover, J. E. (BULL, 39, 268)
Recognition: Martin, L. J. (JOP, 13, 336)
Research: gifted children (SCI, 56, 510; SCI, 57, 380)
Resignation: Lovejoy, A. O. (SCI, 13, 760)
Resignation: Terman, L. M. (SCI, 96, 423)

Stanley, Hiram Miner
Publication: fear (AJP, 9, 418-419)
Publication: *Studies in Evolutionary Psychology* (REV, 2, 432)

Starbuck, Edwin Diller
Appointment: *The Beacon Press* (BULL, 9, 359)
Appointment: Iowa State Univ. (BULL, 3, 247; JOP, 3, 420)
Leave of absence: State Univ. of Iowa (JOP, 9, 504)
Lecture: attention value of magazines (JOP, 7, 223)

Starch, Daniel
Appointment: Harvard Univ. (SCI, 52, 174; BULL, 17, 280; BULL, 16, 257)
Appointment: Iowa State Univ. (BULL, 3, 247)
Appointment: Univ. of Wisconsin (JOP, 5, 644; BULL, 5, 379)
Appointment: Wellesley College (JOP, 4, 588; BULL, 4, 337)
Course: Univ. of Washington (JOP, 12, 280)
Leave of absence: Univ. of Wisconsin (JOP, 16, 644)
Lecture: adjustment (JOP, 7, 223)
Lecture: Harvard Univ. (JOP, 16, 644)

Lecture: Iowa State College (SCI, *88*, 144)
Lecture: Naval Acad., psychological tests (SCI, *57*, 297)
Promotion: Univ. of Wisconsin (SCI, *35*, 984)

Starr, Anna Spiesman

Appointment: Rutgers Univ. (BULL, *41*, 679)

Starr, Henry Etter

Appointment: Rutgers Univ. (SCI, *68*, 13, 156; BULL, *25*, 444)

Starr, Moses Allen

Election: International Congress of Arts and Sciences, chair (JoP, *1*, 420)
Publication: paralytic disorders (AJP, *1*, 199)
Research: cerebellar diseases (AJP, *1*, 197)

State Charities Aid Association

Grant: Commonwealth Fund for Mental Hygiene (SCI, *98*, 196)

State University of Iowa (*see* Iowa, University of)

Statistics (*see also* Correlation)

Caution in using matching (AJP, *53*, 614-615)
Lecture: Culler, E., methods (AJP, *40*, 432)
Lecture: Dunlap, J. W. (AJP, *54*, 583-601)
Lecture: Garrett, H. E. representativeness of sample (AJP, *55*, 580-581)
Lecture: Humm's non-linear product-moment correlation (AJP, *56*, 111-116)
Lecture: use in psychological experiments (AJP, *54*, 270-280)
Publication: Chapman, D. W., the significance of matching with unequal series
  (AJP, *48*, 167)
Publication: correlation chart simplified Pearson product moment coefficients
  (J APP, *22*, 218)
Publication: Dunlap, J. W., recent advances in statistical theory and application
  (AJP, *51*, 558)
Publication: Garrett, H. E., on interpretation of the standard error of
  measurement (AJP, *49*, 679, 683)
Publication: Guilford, J. P., reply to Garrett's, H. E. critique (AJP, *49*, 680)
Publication: Hertzman, M., two equations for the study of variability (AJP, *51*,
  571)
Publication: Holway, A. H., normal equations and the phi gamma hypothesis
  (AJP, *47*, 334)
Publication: Johnson, H. M., pseudo-mathematics in the mental and social
  sciences (AJP, *48*, 342)
Publication: McNemar, Q., reply to Garrett, H. E. discussion of
  representativeness of sample (AJP, *55*, 581-582)
Publication: quantitative psychology (J APP, *24*, 855)
Publication: rules for predicting selectivity of a test (AJP, *55*, 436-442)

Stead, William Henry
Celebration: occupational research (J App, *28*, 351)

Stearns, Albert Warren
Lecture: Conference on Mental Hygiene (J App, *3*, 396)

Stebbing, Susan
Death notice (JoP, *40*, 560)

Stebbins, Ernest Lyman
Appointment: Johns Hopkins Univ. (Sci, *102*, 420)

Stecher, Lorle Ida
Lecture: NYAS/New York Branch of APA meeting, math prodigy (JoP, *15*, 140)

Steckle, Lynde Charles
Promotion: Denison Univ. (Bull, *40*, 723; Bull, *42*, 486)

Stedman, Henry R.
Death notice (Sci, *63*, 227)

Steele, Asa George
Appointment: Temple Univ. (JoP, *11*, 84)

Steele, Warren Merrill
Appointment: Furman Univ. (JoP, *1*, 364; Bull, *1*, 333)
Lecture: illusion (JoP, *2*, 56)
Publication: Yale Psychological Laboratory (JoP, *1*, 84)

Stein, Ludwig
Editor: *Archiv für Geschichte der Philosophie* (Sci°, *9*, 583)

Steiner, Bernard C.
Publication: the history of university education in Maryland (Sci°, *17*, 187)

Steinmetz, Harry Charles
Award: Cattell, J. McK. grants-in-aid (Bull, *39*, 683)

Stellenbosch University (Capetown, South Africa)
Psychological lab destroyed by fire (Sci, *79*, 539)

Stempel, Lillian F.
Publication: treatment of strabismus (J App, *26*, 857-858)

Stenquist, John Langdon
Publication: review of mental tests (J App, *23*, 311)

Stephen F. Austin State Teachers College (Nacogdoches, TX)
Election: Boynton, P., president (Bull, *39*, 681)

Stephens College (Columbia, Missouri)
Appointment: Allee, W. L. (BULL, *42*, 485)
Appointment: Artley, A. S. (BULL, *39*, 896)

Stephens, John Mortimer
Meeting: APA Wash.-Balt, Branch (BULL, *37*, 122)

Stephenson, William
Appointment: Oxford Institute Experimental Psychology (SCI, *84*, 81)

Stereoscopic vision (*see also* Binocular fusion; Vision)
Lecture: Schlosberg, H., depth perception (AJP, *54*, 601-605)
Publication: Jastrow, J., *The Psychology of Stereoscopic Vision* (SCI, *24*, 222)
Publication: Titchener, E. B., stereoscope cards (BULL, *3*, 319; SCI, *24*, 222)

Stern variator
Lecture: Bishop, H. G. (AJP, *34*, 150)

Stern, William
Appointment: Duke Univ. (BULL, *32*, 376)
Appointment: Univ. of Hamburg (SCI, *43*, 208; BULL, *13*, 108)
Appointment: Univ. of North Carolina (BULL, *32*, 323; BULL, *32*, 376)
Death notice (BULL, *35*, 333)
Death notice: obituary by Allport, G. W. (AJP, *51*, 769)
Editor: *Beitrage zür Psychologie der Aussage* (REV, *10*, 464)
Election: French Society of Psychology (SCI, *67*, 505)
Publication: *Aussage* to the *Zeitschrift* (AJP, *18*, 529)
Publication: Lipmann, D., obituary (AJP, *46*, 153)

Sterrett, James Macbride
Election: SSPP, president (SCI, *27*, 596)

Stetson, Harlan True
Lecture: celebration, quadricentennial of death of Copernicus (SCI, *97*, 398)

Stetson, Raymond Herbert
Appointment: Oberlin College (BULL, *6*, 328)

Stetson University (Deland, Florida)
Appointment: Kindred, J. J. (SCI, *75*, 306)

Stevens, Herman Campbell
Appointment: Univ. of Chicago (SCI, *40*, 408; JoP, *11*, 588)
Appointment: Univ. of Washington (BULL, *2*, 427)
Departure: Univ. of Washington (JoP, *11*, 588)

Stevens Institute of Technology (Hoboken, New Jersey)
Appointment: Bingham, W. V. (BULL, *27*, 674)

Stevens, Norah
Appointment: Cottage School for Delinquent Girls, Quebec (BULL, 42, 255)

Stevens, Samuel Nowell
Appointment: Pillsbury Mills, Inc. (BULL, 42, 331)

Stevens, Stanley Smith
Appointment: Harvard Univ. (BULL, 34, 635)
Award: Howard Crosby Warren medal (BULL, 40, 539; SCI, 97, 373)
Promotion: Harvard Psych. Lab (SCI, 87, 482)
Publication: *German Psychological Warfare* (J APP, 25, 359)
Publication: on the method of bisection and its relation to a loudness scale (AJP, 49, 134)
Publication: operational basis of psychology (AJP, 47, 330)
Publication: spatial tones (AJP, 46, 145-147)

Stevenson, George Salvadore
Appointment: National Committee for Mental Hygiene (SCI, 99, 319, 363)
Appointment: National Committee for Mental Hygiene, Division of Community Clinics (SCI, 89, 337)
Appointment: National Committee for Mental Hygiene, medical affairs (BULL, 36, 711)

Stewart, Alexander
Publication: temperaments (AJP, 1, 356)

Stewart, H. W.
Appointment: Lake Forest Univ. (BULL, 1, 413)

Stickland, Georgina (*see* Gates, Georgina Ida Stickland)

Stilling, Jakob
Death notice (BULL, 12, 244)

Stinchfield-Hawk, Sara Mae
Appointment: Scripps College (BULL, 41, 679)

Stirling, James Hutchinson
Death notice (BULL, 6, 216)

Stoddard, George Dinsmore
Appointment: New York State Commission of Education (SCI, 96, 10, 58; BULL, 39, 682; SCI, 95, 600; SCI, 94, 297)
Appointment: State Univ. of Iowa (SCI, 84, 326; SCI, 87, 504)
Appointment: Univ. of Illinois (BULL, 42, 484)
Appointment: Univ. of the State of New York (SCI, 94, 297)
Degree: Colgate Univ. (BULL, 39, 895; SCI, 96, 314)
Degree: Hobart and William Smith Colleges (SCI, 96, 578)

Degree: New York Univ. (Sci, 97, 550)
Departure: Iowa Child Welfare Research Station, State Univ. of Iowa (Sci, 94, 297; Bull, 39, 682)
Lecture: Child Study Assoc. of America (J App, 16, 438)
Lecture: Hobart and William Smith Colleges, Phi Beta Kappa (Sci, 96, 578)
Resignation: State Univ. of Iowa (Sci, 96, 10)

Stoelting, Christian H.
Death notice (AJP, 56, 450; Bull, 40, 458)

Stoelting, C. H. Company of Chicago
Appointment: Ruckmick, C. A. (Sci, 90, 34; J App, 23, 530)

Störring, Gustav
Publication: mental pathology (JoP, 4, 308)

Stogdill, Emily Leatherman
Lecture: Assoc. of Consulting Psychologists (J App, 21, 241)

Stoke, Stuart M.
Appointment: Ohio Univ. (J App, 11, 405)
Appointment: Univ. of Buffalo (J App, 10, 288)

Stokes, George
Election: Berlin Acad. of Sciences (Sci, 10, 91)

Stone, Calvin Perry
Appointment: APA, Committee of the Precautions in Animal Experimentation (Sci, 77, 189)
Appointment: Bureau of Salesmanship Research (JoP, 13, 476; Sci, 44, 56; Bull, 13, 296)
Appointment: Columbia Univ. (Bull, 42, 486)
Appointment: Stanford Univ. (J App, 6, 301; Bull, 20, 60; Bull, 19, 462)
Course: Columbia Univ. (Sci, 101, 375)
Election: APA, president (Sci, 95, 405; Sci, 94, 253)
Election: APA, representative, National Research Council (Bull, 27, 76)
Election: International Congress for Sex Research, representative (Sci, 70, 552)
Lecture: AAAS, the endocrine system as related to behavior (J App, 21, 603)
Research: New York Psychiatric Institute and Hospital (Bull, 42, 486; Sci, 101, 375)

Stone, Charles Leonard
Appointment: Dartmouth College (Bull, 14, 366)

Stone, Lawrence Joseph
Research: Vassar Coll., child study project (Bull, 37, 187)
Personality research director (Bull, 38, 248)

Stoops, John Dashiell
Lecture: perception (JoP, 2, 280)

Storrs, Harry C.
Election: American Assoc. on Mental Deficiency, president (J APP, 22, 109)

Story, William Edward
Lecture: Clark Univ., in honor of Hall, G. S. and Sanford, E. C. (SCI, 32, 13)

Stott, Leland Hyrum
Research: California Test of Personality, family life adjustment (J APP, 26, 570-571)

Stout, George Frederick
Appointment: Oxford Univ. (REV, 6, 239)
Appointment: Univ. of Aberdeen (AJP, 8, 430; REV, 3, 588; SCI, 4, 199)
Appointment: Univ. of St. Andrews (SCI, 17, 680; JoP, 1, 28)
Death notice (JoP, 41, 672)
Degree: Univ. of Aberdeen (SCI, 9, 460)
Departure: Oxford Univ. (SCI, 17, 680)
Election: British Acad. of Science (SCI, 17, 635)
Lecture: instinct and intelligence (JoP, 7, 420)
Publication: *Manual of Psychology* (J APP, 22, 664)
Resignation: *Mind* (BULL, 17, 435)

Stowell, Thomas B.
Lecture: APS, nerves of the cat (SCI°, 8, 453)

Stoy, Edward Guthrie
Research: selection of keypunch operators, Psychological Corporation (J APP, 24, 654)

Strabismus (*see also* Eye; *and* Vision)
Publication: Stempel, L. F. (J APP, 26, 857-858)

Straeussler, Ernst
Taken custody by Nazis in Austria (SCI, 87, 319)

Strasbourg, University of
Appointment: Wollenberg, R. (SCI, 24, 352)
Formal opening: Nov. 21-22, 1919 (JoP, 17, 55)

Stratton, George Malcolm
Anniversary: Psych. Bldg. Univ. of California, Los Angeles (BULL, 37, 406)
Appointment: APA Committee, San Francisco program (SCI, 41, 605)
Appointment: Johns Hopkins Univ. (BULL, 1, 172)
Appointment: Univ. of California (JoP, 5, 140; SCI, 27, 240; BULL, 5, 64)
Election: APA council (JoP, 2, 28)

Election: National Acad. of Sciences (BULL, *25*, 376)
Lecture: San Francisco psychology and health (SCI, *51*, 112; BULL, *17*, 31)
Lecture: sensory discrimination (JoP, *2*, 56)
Lecture: social psychology (SCI, *91*, 430)
Nomination: APA representative, National Research Council (AJP, *32*, 157)
Psychological tests for the aviation corps (J APP, *1*, 300)

Straus, Oscar

Donation: Univ. of Georgia (SCI, *14*, 623; REV, *9*, 103)

Strecker, Edward Adam

Appointment: Commission for Changes in Qualifications for Admittance in Armed Forces (SCI, *99*, 13)
Appointment: Jefferson Medical College (SCI, *62*, 12, 396)
Appointment: Secretary of War for the Air Forces of the U.S. Army, consultant (SCI, *97*, 551)
Appointment: Univ. of Pennsylvania (SCI, *74*, 364, 384)
Lecture: Niles, W. L. Memorial, neuropsychiatry of global war (SCI, *98*, 405)
Lecture: Pasteur Lecture, 17th (SCI, *100*, 263, 311)
Lecture: Research Council on Problems of Alcohol (SCI, *94*, 412)
Lecture: Salmon, T. W. Lectures, New York Academy of Medicine (SCI, *89*, 385)

Strong, Charles Augustus

Appointment: Columbia Univ. (REV, *3*, 244; SCI, *3*, 99; REV, *10*, 344)
Death notice (AJP, *53*, 302)
Election: International Congress of Arts and Sciences, St. Louis, chair (JoP, *1*, 419)
Fellowship: trust fund established, science and philosophy (SCI, *91*, 166)

Strong, Edward Kellogg, Jr.

Appointment: Committee on Publications in Applied Psychology (J APP, *2*, 196)
Appointment: George Peabody College for Teachers (BULL, *11*, 116; SCI, *39*, 325; JoP, *11*, 308)
Election: SSPP office (BULL, *13*, 40; JoP, *13*, 112)
Lecture: Carnegie Institute of Tech. (SCI, *49*, 118)

Strong, Esther

Appointment: American Univ. (BULL, *42*, 793)

Strong, Margaret K.

Appointment: Univ. of Toronto (BULL, *3*, 36)

Strong, Oliver Smith

Appointment: *Journal of Comparative Neurology and Psychology* (JoP, *1*, 195)

Stroobant, Paul
Laboratory at Univ. of Brussels (REV, *1*, 112)
Publication: theory on estimation of the real size of heavenly bodies (SCI°, *5*, 222)

Stroop, John Ridley
Publication: Ligon's theory (AJP, *47*, 504)

Stroud, James Bart
State Univ. of Iowa (BULL, *35*, 796)

Structuralism
Lecture: Bentley, M., Clark Univ. (SCI, *63*, 65)
Lecture: Squires, P. C. (AJP, *42*, 134)
Lecture: Titchener, E. B., Wesleyan Univ. (SCI, *55*, 512)

Strümpell, Ludwig Adolf
Death notice (SCI, *9*, 789; REV, *6*, 456)

Struve, Henry K.
Death notice (JOP, *9*, 392)

Stuart, Charles Edward
Editor: *Journal of Parapsychology* (SCI, *95*, 322-323; BULL, *39*, 325)

Stuart, Henry Waldgrave
Lecture: logic (JOP, *1*, 224)
Promotion: Stanford Univ. (BULL, *5*, 348; BULL, *6*, 152)

Stuart, Mary
Lecture: Univ. of Colorado (J APP, *10*, 393)

Student life
Lecture: Hall, G. S., Johns Hopkins Univ. (SCI°, *5*, 19-20)

Studies in Linguistic Psychology
Publication: Kellogg, R. J. (JOP, *10*, 56)

Studies in Philosophy and the Social Sciences
Formerly *Zeitschrift für sozialforschung* (JOP, *37*, 504)

Stumpf, Carl
Appointment: Univ. of Berlin (JOP, *4*, 560; BULL, *4*, 338; REV, *1*, 112, 336)
Award: Prussian order of merit (SCI, *70*, 63)
Death notice: obituary by Langfeld, H. S. (AJP, *49*, 316)
Election: National Acad. of Sciences, foreign associate (BULL, *24*, 380)
Election: Univ. of Berlin, rector (SCI, *26*, 325)
Laboratory: Univ. of Berlin (AJP, *7*, 152)
Lecture: Titchener, E. B. (AJP, *32*, 156)

Photo and signature (AJP, *49*, 321)
Publication: reprinted in German journal (Rev, *2*, 534)

Stumpf, Wippert Arnot
Editor: *Educational Abstracts* (J App, *22*, 107)

Stutsman, Rachel (*see* Ball, Rachel Stutsman)

Subconscious
Lecture: Jastrow, J. (Sci, *34*, 755; JoP, *5*, 140; JoP, *9*, 28)
Lecture: Prince, M., Cambridge (Sci, *59*, 161)
Publication: use of (JoP, *5*, 111)
Research: Jastrow, J., work translated into French (Sci, *27*, 677)

Suggestibility (*see also* Hypnosis)
Lecture: Edwards, A. S. (JoP, *7*, 223)
Lecture: Stevick, P. R. (AJP, *44*, 807)

Suicide
Committee for Study of (J App, *20*, 273; J App, *22*, 108; Bull, *33*, 406)
Publication: *Medical Press*, statistics, 1889 (Sci°, *14*, 199)
Publication: The Washington Life Insurance Co. (Sci°, *14*, 131)
Research: Sikorskii, Russia (Sci, *2*, 132)

Sullivan, Elizabeth Teresa
Publication: California Capacity Questionnaire (J App, *25*, 359)
Publication: California Test of Mental Maturity (J App, *21*, 344)

Sullivan, Ellen Blythe
Promotion: Univ. of California (J App, *10*, 394)

Sullivan, Harry Stack
Appointment: Georgetown Univ., School of Medicine (Sci, *90*, 536)
Departure: Washington School of Psychiatry (Sci, *90*, 536)
Lecture: William Alanson White Memorial (Sci, *90*, 269)
Resignation: Georgetown Univ. (Sci, *90*, 588)

Sully, James
Death notice (Bull, *21*, 240)
Departure: Univ. College, London (JoP, *1*, 280; Sci, *17*, 520; Bull, *1*, 174)

Summers, Walter G.
Lecture: American Catholic Philosophical Assoc., bearing of recent psychology
upon a philosophy of education (JoP, *34*, 722)

Sumner, Francis Cecil
APA, Wash.-Balt. Branch, 1940 (Bull, *37*, 406)

Sun Yat-Sen University (China)
Appointment: Wang, G. H. (BULL, 24, 380)

Super, Donald Edwin
Appointment: Clark Univ. (SCI, 87, 276; BULL, 35, 333)
Appointment: Columbia Teachers College, vocational and guidance department (BULL, 42, 794)
Appointment: Horace Mann-Lincoln Institute (BULL, 42, 486)

Suppressor variables
Discussion of (AJP, 58, 550-554)

Surgeon General, United States Army
Appointment: Kelley, T. L. (BULL, 14, 334; J APP, 1, 395)
Appointment: Otis, A. S. (BULL, 14, 334; J APP, 1, 395)
Conference: National committee concerned with rejected men by induction boards for neuropsychiatric reasons (SCI, 98, 298)
Members of the Staff of the Division of Physical Reconstruction (J APP, 2, 294)
Publication: Carry On (BULL, 15, 176; J APP, 2, 293-294)
Opportunity of psychologists commissioned as officers (BULL, 38, 305-306)

Sutherland, Arthur Howard
Appointment: Government Hospital for the Insane (BULL, 6, 368)
Appointment: Los Angeles Division of Psychology (J APP, 2, 194-195)
Appointment: Los Angeles Public Schools (BULL, 14, 143; JoP, 14, 364)
Appointment: Univ. of Illinois (BULL, 7, 75; JoP, 7, 112)
Appointment: Yale Univ. (BULL, 11, 396)
Departure: Government Hospital for the Insane (BULL, 7, 75)
Departure: Univ. of Illinois (BULL, 11, 396)

Sward, Keith
Appointment: Western Reserve University (J APP, 14, 505)
Grant: Social Science Research Council (BULL, 31, 380)
Publication: SPSSI yearbook, the psychology of industrial conflict (BULL, 35, 61)

Swarthmore College (Pennsylvania)
Appointment: Baldwin, B. T. (SCI, 35, 303; BULL, 9, 128)
Appointment: Brumbaugh, M. G. (JoP, 3, 336)
Appointment: Buxton, C. E. (SCI, 90, 391)
Appointment: Davis, S. B. (JoP, 15, 140; BULL, 14, 420)
Appointment: Fisher, C. (JoP, 15, 140; BULL, 14, 420)
Appointment: Köhler, W. (SCI, 82, 298)
Appointment: Moore, G. E. (JoP, 40, 140)
Appointment: Rauson, E. B. (JoP, 3, 336)
Course: Köhler, W. (BULL, 41, 72)
Course: pedagogy established (JoP, 3, 336)
Leave of absence: Baldwin, B. T. (BULL, 6, 184)
Lecture: Angell, J. R. (SCI, 86, 371)

Lecture: Lovejoy, A. O., Cooper Foundation (JoP, *39*, 139)
Lecture: Thorndike, E. L. (Sci, *86*, 371)
Lecture: Weyl, H., Cooper, W. J. Foundation (Sci, 77, 17)
Psychology Dept. established (JoP, *9*, 168; Sci, *35*, 303)

Swedenberg, Carl
Appointment: Training School for Boys, Red Wing, Minnesota (Bull, *39*, 325)

Swenson, David
Fills in for Wilde, N. during leave of absence, Univ. of Minnesota (JoP, *11*, 280)

Swensson, Carl Aaron
Death notice (Bull., *1*, 134)

Swift, Edgar James
Appointment: St. Louis Psychiatic Clinic (Bull, *21*, 360; Sci, *59*, 120)
Appointment: Washington Univ., St. Louis (Sci, *18*, 128)
Death notice: obituary by Nafe, J. P. (AJP, *45*, 364)
Lecture: Clark Univ. (J App, *9*, 87)
Lecture: Naval War College (Sci, *55*, 126)
Lecture: U.S. Naval Acad. (Sci, *54*, 406; Bull, *18*, 111; Sci, *51*, 85; Sci, *53*, 89; Sci, *65*, 252; Sci *63*, 399)
Retirement: Washington Univ., St. Louis (Sci, *73*, 337; Bull, *28*, 324)

Swift, Fletcher Harper
Award: American Educational Research Assoc. (Sci, *93*, 346)

Swift, Walter Babcock
Appointment: Cleveland Ohio Public Schools (JoP, *16*, 28)
Lecture: Boston Psychopathic Hospital, speech defects (Bull, *13*, 407)
Speech correction, Cleveland (J App, *3*, 197)

Switzerland
Changes education dept. (Sci°, *9*, 362)

Sydney, University of (Australia)
Appointment: MacPherson, J. (Sci, *55*, 675)
Meeting: Australian Assoc. of Psychology and Philosophy (JoP, *35*, 448)

Syllable
Research: Pringsheim, [?]. durations, pitches and intensities (Sci°, *17*, 315)

Sylvester, Reuel Hull
Appointment: Health Center at Des Moines, Iowa (Sci, *50*, 326; Bull, *16*, 392)
Joins army in WWI (Sci, *46*, 167; Bull, *15*, 98)

Symbolic logic
Lecture: Ladd-Franklin, C., Columbia Univ. (JoP, *16*, 700)

Symonds, Percival Mallon

Appointment: AAAP Committee, Psychology as an Occupation (J APP, 22, 311)
Election: AAAP (J APP, 21, 603, 713)
Meeting: AAAP (BULL, 34, 865)

Syracuse University (New York)

Appointment: Allport, F. H. (BULL, 21, 660; SCI, 60, 200)
Appointment: Hahn, M. E. (BULL, 41, 603)
Appointment: Smith, H. P. (BULL, 41, 603)
Appointment: Thelin, E. (SCI, 74, 543)
Assistantships for graduate students in educational psychology available (BULL, 42, 676)
Establishment: Psychology Dept. (J APP, 16, 98; SCI, 74, 543)
Leave of absence: Kuhler, R. G. (BULL, 41, 603)
Lecture: Cattell, J. McK. (SCI, 49, 305)
Promotion: Cason, H. (BULL, 22, 260)
Promotion: Thelin, E. (BULL, 29, 90)
Return: May, M. (J APP, 10, 393)

System der Werttheorie of C. von Ehrenfels

Craig, W. requests a copy (JOP, 15, 252)

T

Taft, Charles P.
Appointment: Health, welfare, nutrition and recreation activities affecting national defense (Sci, *93*, 180)

Tait, William Dunlop
Promotion: McGill Univ. (Sci, *60*, 175; Bull, *21*, 552)

Talbert, Ernest Lynn
Appointment: Univ. of Cincinnati (JoP, *12*, 504)
Lecture: social philosophers (JoP, *7*, 223)

Talbot, Samuel A.
APA Wash.-Balt. Branch (Bull, *37*, 657)

Talladega College (Alabama)
Appointment: Clayton, A. S. (Bull, *40*, 383)
Departure: Clayton, A. S. (Bull, *42*, 675)

Tamburini, Augusto
Appointment: International Congress of Psychology (JoP, *2*, 56)
Lecture: hypnotism (Sci°, *5*, 303)

Tannenbaum, Samuel Aaron
Lecture: APA/NYAS, psychoanalysis and neuroses (JoP, *13*, 280)

Tanzi, Eugenio
Royal Medico-Psychological Assoc. (Sci, *70*, 162)

Tarde, Jean Gabriel de
Death notice (Sci, *20*, 287)
Election: Collège de France, chair (Rev, *7*, 216)
Publication: *Les Lois Sociales* translated by Warren, H. C. (Rev, *6*, 119)

Tarkhanov, Ivan Romanovich
Research: electric currents in the skin from mental excitation (Sci°, *15*, 72-73)

Taste (*see also* Appetite)
Research: Italy, drug effects (Sci°, *8*, 54)

Tastevin, Joseph
Editor: *Revue des Sciences Psychologiques* (JoP, *10*, 336)

Tau Beta Pi
Meeting: Detroit, mental attitudes for national defense (Sci, *93*, 372)

Tausch, Edwin
Questionnaire on experiences of existential perplexity and relation to God (JoP, *2*, 364)

Taves, Ernest
Fellowship: Hyslop-Prince, 1942-43 (Bull, *39*, 423)

Tawney, Guy Allan
Appointment: Beloit College (Rev, *4*, 106)
Appointment: Columbia Univ. (Bull, *3*, 116; JoP, *3*, 140)
Appointment: Princeton Univ. (Rev, *3*, 706)
Appointment: Univ. of Cincinnati (Bull, *5*, 348)
Promotion: Beloit College (Rev, *6*, 239)

Taylor, Alfred Edward
Appointment: Univ. of St. Andrews (JoP, *5*, 448; Bull, *5*, 316)

Taylor, Caroline
Appointment: Tulane Univ. (Bull, *41*, 807)

Taylor, Donald Wayne
Appointment: Stanford Univ. (Bull, *42*, 583; Sci, *102*, 193)

Taylor, Harold Claire
Lecture: Chicago Psychological Club (Bull, *40*, 540)

Taylor, Howard Rice
Lecture: Gestalt psychology (AJP, *44*, 356)
Meeting: Univ. of Oregon, Oregon Psychologists, chair (Bull, *33*, 406; Sci, *83*, 323)

Taylor, J. W.
Lecture: trephining of an Inca skull (Sci°, *7*, 186)

Taylor Society
Lecture: Doll, E. A., prison psychology (J App, *9*, 428)
Lecture: Gilbreth, F. B. (J App, *9*, 204)

Lecture: Gilbreth, L. M. (J App, *9*, 204, 428)

Lecture: Kornhauser, A. W. (J App, *9*, 204)

Lecture: Tead, O., managerial psychology (J App, *9*, 428)

Lecture: Yoakum, C. S., experimental psychology in personnel problems (J App, *9*, 204)

Meeting: announcement (J App, *9*, 204, 428)

Meeting: industrial psychology (JoP, *21*, 700)

Tea

Publication: Barr, G. W., *Therapeutic Gazette*, physiological effects (Sci°, *16*, 160)

Teachers College, Columbia University (New York, New York)

Appointment: Breeze, B. B. (Rev, *5*, 677)

Appointment: Colvin, S. S. (Bull, *20*, 288)

Appointment: Gates, A. I. (Bull, *19*, 350)

Appointment: Gordon, K. (JoP, *3*, 364; Bull, *3*, 184)

Appointment: Hollingworth, L. S. (Bull, *19*, 350)

Appointment: Majors, D. R. (Rev, *5*, 677)

Appointment: McCall, W. A. (Bull, *19*, 350)

Appointment: McKim, M. G. (Bull, *40*, 459)

Appointment: Rugg, H. O. (Bull, *16*, 392)

Appointment: Russell, J. E. (Rev, *5*, 109)

Appointment: Sebring, E. (Rev, *1*, 552)

Appointment: Shaffer, L. F. (Bull, *42*, 794)

Appointment: Thorndike, E. L. (Rev, *6*, 344)

Appointment: Wilde, N. (Rev, *5*, 109)

Departure: Major, D. R. (Rev, *6*, 673)

Departure: Smith, S. (Bull, *8*, 374)

Fellowship: announcement (Rev, *5*, 345)

Leave of absence: Lloyd, F. E. (Sci, *13*, 278)

Leave of absence: Ruger, H. A. (Bull, *13*, 148)

Meeting: proposal for APA (JoP, *13*, 644)

Promotion: Hollingworth, L. S. (Bull, *16*, 258)

Promotion: MacVannel, J. A. (Bull, *1*, 134)

Promotion: Thorndike, E. L. (Bull, *1*, 134; JoP, *1*, 56)

Promotion: Whitley, M. T. (JoP, *11*, 308)

Teachers College, Detroit, Michigan (*see* Detroit Teachers College)

Teachers College, George Washington University (*see* George Washington University)

Teachers of Psychology in Iowa, Conference of

Meeting: list of officers (Bull, *7*, 147)

Teachers of Psychology in Normal Schools and Colleges, Conference of
Meeting: report (BULL, 4, 335)

Teachout, Robert B.
Departure: Univ. of Oregon (SCI, 47, 559)

Tead, Ordway
Lecture: Taylor Society, managerial psychology (J APP, 9, 428)

Technical Education Board London/Asylums Committee
Scholarship: offered at Claybury Asylum (SCI, 9, 790)

Technical Education, International Congress on
Meeting: Berlin, 1938 (SCI, 87, 413)

Technical High School (Scranton, Pennsylvania)
Research: Lennon, L. J., Iowa Silent Reading Test (J APP, 27, 363-364)

Technopsychology, International Conference of
Attendance: Bingham, W. V. (BULL, 25, 198)
Attendance: Porter, J. P. (BULL, 25, 198)
Meeting: announcement (BULL, 24, 380)
Meeting: announcement, 6th (SCI, 69, 423)
Meeting: Paris, 4th (SCI, 65, 570)
Meeting: Prague, 8th (BULL, 31, 450)

Telepathy (see also Mind-reading)
Lecture: Jastrow, J. (SCI, 88, 449)
Research: Zenith Foundation, nationwide televised telepathy experiment (J APP, 21, 605)

Temperament
Lecture: Chrysostom, B. (JoP, 2, 700)
Lecture: Miller, D. S. (JoP, 2, 112)
Publication: Stewart, A. (AJP, 1, 356)

Temperature sense
Lecture: Nafe, J. P. (SCI, 87, 412)

Temple University (Philadelphia, Pennsylvania)
Appointment: Bolton, T. L. (BULL, 14, 420)
Appointment: Steele, A. G. (JoP, 11, 84)
Retirement: Bolton, T. L. (SCI, 86, 152)

Templin, Olin
Appointment: Univ. of Kansas (REV, 3, 120)

Temporal position
Lecture: Postman, L., experiment on (AJP, 57, 421-424)

Tennessee, University of (Knoxville)
Appointment: Bell, J. C. (BULL, *12*, 403)
Appointment: Dunford, R. E. (BULL, *41*, 603)
Appointnent: Frost, E. P. (JoP, *11*, 721; BULL, *11*, 443)
Appointment: Hill, D. S. (BULL, *8*, 374)
Appointment: Jost, H. (BULL, *42*, 582; SCI, *102*, 147)
Course: Bell, J. C. (BULL, *12*, 403)
Departure: Breese, B. B. (JoP, *1*, 476; SCI, *20*, 192)
Departure: Hill, D. S. (SCI, *34*, 714)
Departure: Ogden, R. M. (BULL, *11*, 352)
Departure: Rose, W. (JoP, *1*, 588)
Establishment: Institute of Aviation Psychology (J APP, *28*, 351-352)
Establishment: University Research Council (SCI, *102*, 375)
Lecture: Baldwin, J. M. (BULL, *1*, 173; JoP, *1*, 280)
Lecture: Hall, G. S. (BULL, *1*, 173; JoP, *1*, 280)
Lecture: Ogden, R. M. (BULL, *15*, 176)
Promotion: Ogden, R. M. (BULL, *7*, 148; SCI, *31*, 500; JoP, *7*, 224)
Resignation: Ogden, R. M. (JoP, *11*, 560)

Terman, Lewis Madison
Appointment: *Journal of Delinquency* (JoP, *13*, 392)
Appointment: Los Angeles State Normal School (JoP, *3*, 476; SCI, *24*, 96)
Appointment: National Research Council (J APP, *3*, 393)
Appointment: San Bernardino High School (SCI, *24*, 96)
Appointment: Stanford Academic Council (SCI, *90*, 106)
Appointment: Stanford Univ. (J APP, *6*, 301; BULL, *20*, 60; SCI, *56*, 108)
Commemorative volume on studies in personality presented at birthday dinner, 1942 (SCI, *95*, 117-118; BULL, *39*, 268)
Conference: Binet-Simon tests (BULL, *10*, 424; JoP, *10*, 560)
Course: New York Univ. (BULL, *13*, 296)
Degree: Univ. of California (BULL, *42*, 581)
Election: AAAS, president (SCI, *91*, 591)
Election: APA office (BULL, *16*, 32)
Election: Council of Thirty, American School Hygiene Assoc. (JoP, *10*, 616)
Election: International Committee on School Hygiene, member (JoP, *10*, 616)
Election: National Acad. of Sciences (BULL, *25*, 376)
Election: National Research Council, special committee (JoP, *16*, 672)
Election: Psychological Corporation, vice-president (BULL, *24*, 80; J APP, *11*, 81)
Fellowship: research on feeble-minded children (SCI, *39*, 506)
Fellowship: Stanford Univ., established (BULL, *11*, 191)
Grant: Commonwealth Fund (SCI, *60*, 588)
Leave of absence: Stanford Univ. (J APP, *20*, 166)
Lecture: intelligence (JoP, *2*, 223)
Lecture: Stanford Medical School, gifted children (SCI, *57*, 82)

Research: foster children (SCI, *60*, 588)
Research: gifted children (SCI, *56*, 510)
Research: Stanford Univ., psychical phenomena (BULL, *36*, 57)
Resignation: Stanford Univ. (SCI, *96*, 423)

Terminology
Award: essay, the confusion of psychological terms (SCI, *4*, 655)

Terminology, Committee on, APA
APA Committee on Terminology call for terms (AJP, *31*, 220)
Examines terms in sensation and cognition (JoP, *17*, 139-140)
Sends Dunlap's, K. article to APA members (BULL, *13*, 260; J APP, *13*, 260)

Terns
Research: Watson, J. B. and Lashley, K. S., Dry Tortugas (BULL, *10*, 252)

Terry, Dwight H. Lecture
Jung, C. G., Yale Univ. (SCI, *85*, 541)

Test Service Bulletin
Book abstracts, May 1939 (J APP, *23*, 420)

Tests (*see also* Intelligence tests; Mental tests)
Ability tests (J APP, *3*, 194)
Admission requirement: Princeton Univ., psychological (SCI, *56*, 42)
Appointment: Owen, R. B., Division of Psychological Tests (JoP, *15*, 168)
Lecture: Bingham, W. V., educational conference (J APP, *22*, 440)
Lecture: Conference of Experimental Psychologists, theory, value and
limitations (BULL, *10*, 211-212)
Lecture: Henmon, V. A. C., educational conference (J APP, *22*, 440)
Lecture: Intelligence, National Institute of Industrial Psychology (J APP, *23*,
744)
Lecture: Manuel, H. T., educational conference (J APP, *22*, 440)
Lecture: Starch, D., Naval Acad., psychological tests (SCI, *57*, 297)
Meeting: Educational Conference, 7th (J APP, *22*, 440)
Publication: Adams, C. R. and Lepley, W., personal audit (J APP, *25*, 360)
Publication: Dept. of Research and Test Service of the World Book Company
Report. Massachusetts Teacher Foundation (J APP, *22*, 541)
Publication: Dreese, M. and Mooney, E., interest inventory for elementary
grades (J APP, *25*, 474)
Publication: Durrell-Sullivan reading capacity and achievement tests (J APP, *21*,
719)
Publication: Dvorak, ? and Van Wagenen, M. J., diagnostic examination of silent
reading abilities (J APP, *23*, 744)
Publication: *Educational and Psychological Measurement* founded (J APP, *25*,
265)
Publication: Garth, T. A., riddles as a mental test (AJP, *47*, 342)
Publication: Iowa Silent Reading Test, new edition (J APP, *23*, 633)

Publication: Johnson, H. M., some neglected principles in aptitude-testing (AJP, 47, 159)

Publication: Kefauver-Hand Inventory (J App, 21, 130)

Publication: Michigan Vocabulary Profile Test (J App, 23, 745)

Publication: Mitchell, D., revision of bibliography of psychological tests (JoP, 16, 28)

Publication: National Committee on Teacher Examinations, objective tests (J App, 24, 98)

Publication: Otis, A. S., Normal Percentile Chart (J App, 22, 541)

Publication: Otis Quick Scoring Mental Ability Tests, Alpha, Beta, Gamma (J App, 21, 343)

Publication: Pond, F. L., inventory of reading experiences (J App, 24, 855)

Publication: Stenquist, J. L., review of mental tests (J App, 23, 311)

Publication: Sullivan, E. T., Clark, W. W. and Tiegs, E. W., California Capacity Questionnaire (J App, 25, 359)

Publication: Sullivan, E. T., Clark, W. W. and Tiegs, E. W., California Test of Mental Maturity (J App, 21, 344)

Publication: *Test Service Bulletin* (J App, 23, 420)

Publication: Thompson, J. M., business tests for high school students (J App, 21, 130)

Research: Bureau of Salesmanship Research, psychological methods (JoP, 13, 139)

Services: IBM test scoring machine, new tests announced (J App, 23, 531)

Services: Psychological Corporation, nurse testing division founded (J App, 23, 421)

Services: Psychological Corporation, test scoring machine (J App, 23, 422)

Services: Univ. of Florida, progress test program (J App, 23, 531)

Texas Agricultural and Mechanical College (College Station)

Appointment: Wilcox, G. B. (Bull, 42, 675-676)

Promotion: Varvel, W. A. (Bull, 42, 676)

Texas Christian University (Fort Worth)

Appointment: Glaze, J. A. (Bull, 25, 307)

Texas, University of (Austin)

Appointment: Baldwin, B. T. (Sci, 32, 342, 464; Bull, 7, 364)

Appointment: Bell, J. C. (JoP, 9, 364; Bull, 9, 280)

Appointment: Ellis, C. (Rev, 6, 673)

Appointment: Garth, T. R. (Bull, 17, 116)

Appointment: Hunter, W. S. (JoP, 10, 84; Bull, 10, 39; Sci, 37, 57)

Appointment: Kelley, T. L. (Bull, 11, 444)

Appointment: Perrin, F. A. C. (Bull, 14, 334; Sci, 46, 360)

Appointment: Wright, W. K. (JoP, 3, 532; Bull, 3, 319; Sci, 24, 384)

Appointment: Yarborough, J. U. (Bull, 14, 263, 334; Sci, 46, 360)

Appointment: Yoakum, C. S. (JoP, 14, 504; Bull, 14, 263; Sci, 28, 48; JoP, 5, 392; Bull, 5, 243)

Departure: Baldwin, B. T. (BULL, 9, 128; JoP, 9, 168; SCI, 35, 303)
Departure: Fite, W. (SCI, 24, 384; JoP, 3, 504, 532)
Departure: Hunter, W. S. (SCI, 44, 132)
Promotion: Brogan, A. P. (JoP, 14, 504)
Promotion: Hunter, W. S. (BULL, 11, 396)
Promotion: Mezes, S. E. (REV, 7, 531)

Texas, University of, School of Medicine (Galveston)
Promotion: Ewall, J. R. (SCI, 100, 245)
Promotion: Weisz, S. (SCI, 100, 245)

Thaxton, O. A.
Appointment: State Normal College of Pennsylvania (JoP, 1, 616)

Thelin, Ernst
Appointment: Syracuse Univ. (J APP, 16, 98; SCI, 74, 543)
Death notice (BULL, 42, 790)
Promotion: Syracuse Univ. (BULL, 29, 90)

Therapeutic Gazette
Publication: Barr, G. W., physiological effects of tea (SCI°, 16, 160)

Thesis contest
Announcement (BULL, 13, 188; JoP, 13, 308)

Thilly, Frank
Appointment: Cornell Univ. (BULL, 3, 184; JoP, 3, 308)
Appointment: Princeton Univ. (BULL, 1, 134)
Election: American Philosophical Assoc., executive committee (JoP, 7, 28)
Election: American Philosophical Assoc., officer (JoP, 9, 28)
Election: Princeton Univ., Stuart Chair in Psychology (SCI, 19, 480)
Resignation: Princeton Univ. (BULL, 3, 288)

Thomas, William D.
Death notice (SCI, 13, 877; REV, 8, 447)

Thompson, Albert Stoler
Appointment: Vanderbilt Univ. (SCI, 101, 481; BULL, 42, 486)
Departure: Univ. of Pennsylvania (BULL, 42, 486)

Thompson, Clara Mabel
Election: Assoc. for the Advancement of Psychoanalysis, vice- president (J APP, 25, 473)

Thompson, Daniel Greenleaf
Death notice (REV, 4, 567)

Thompson, Elizabeth Science Fund
Establishment (SCI°, 9, 388-389)

Grant: announcement (Sci, *15*, 276)
Grant: Girden, E., 1941 (Sci, *93*, 473)
Information (Sci°, *13*, 461)

Thompson, Helen Bradford (*see* Wooley, Helen Bradford Thompson)

Thompson, James Michael
Publication: Business tests for high school students (J App, *21*, 130)

Thompson, Lorin Andrew, Jr.
Appointment: Ohio Wesleyan Univ. (J App, *11*, 404; Sci, *77*, 304)

Thompson, Merle
Appointment: Morningside, Iowa (Bull, *14*, 366)

Thompson, William Richard
Appointment: Univ. of Florida (Bull, *42*, 331)

Thomson, David Cleghor
Appointment: Society for the Protection of Science and Learning (Sci, *88*, 544)

Thomson, Elihu
Research: physiological effects of alternate currents (Sci°, *17*, 201)

Thomson, Godfrey Hilton
Award: paper on application of Pearson's formula for psychophysics (Sci, *51*, 111; AJP, *31*, 100; JoP, *17*, 140)
Election: International Congress of Psychology, chair (J App, *24*, 245)
Election: International Congress of Psychology, secretary (J App, *23*, 530)
International Congress of Psychology postponed, 1940 (Bull, *37*, 329)

Thomson, J. Arthur
Lecture: eugenics, Galton lecture (Sci, *73*, 124)

Thomson, William
Election: Acad. of Sciences, Vienna, honorary member (Sci°, *4*, 75)

Thorndike, Edward Lee
Appointment: Columbia Univ. (Rev, *8*, 447; Rev, *6*, 344)
Appointment: Columbia Univ., Dept of Educational Research (JoP, *13*, 84)
Appointment: Harvard Univ., (Sci, *96*, 467)
Appointment: Joint Committee on Standards for Graphic Presentation (JoP, *13*, 52-53)
Appointment: National Research Council (Bull, *14*, 191; JoP, *16*, 672; JoP, *14*, 392; J App, *3*, 393)
Appointment: President's Council of Personnel Administration (Bull, *28*, 411)
Appointment: Western Reserve Univ. (Rev, *5*, 449; J App, *10*, 165)
Association with Cattell, R. B. (Bull, *35*, 333)

Award: Butler Gold Medal (BULL, 22, 504; SCI, 61, 606; JOP, 22, 392)

Degree: Athens Centenary (BULL, 34, 864; SCI, 86, 369)

Degree: Columbia Univ. (BULL, 29, 308)

Degree: Harvard Univ. (SCI, 79, 586)

Degree: Iowa State Univ. (BULL, 20, 664)

Degree: Univ. of Edinburgh (SCI, 83, 321, 367; BULL, 33, 849)

Degree: Univ. of Iowa (SCI, 57, 580)

Degree: Wesleyan Univ. (SCI, 50, 37)

Departure: Western Reserve Univ. (REV, 6, 344)

Election: AAAS, president (SCI, 80, 583)

Election: APA, officer (JOP, 9, 28; SCI, 35, 23; BULL, 9, 40)

Election: Galton Society, charter member (SCI, 47, 484)

Election: NAS (BULL, 14, 192)

Election: NYAS, exhibition chair (SCI, 11, 636)

Election: NYAS, president (SCI, 50, 588; BULL, 17, 116; BULL, 18, 111)

Honor: Alumni homecoming day (J APP, 10, 129)

Lecture: American Acad. of Arts and Sciences (SCI, 87, 232; SCI, 92, 451; SCI, 75, 632)

Lecture: carelessness (AJP, 56, 299-300)

Lecture: Cattell Jubilee (AJP, 25, 468)

Lecture: Columbia Univ. (J APP, 10, 129; SCI, 95, 190; BULL, 23, 176; SCI, 36, 784)

Lecture: Cornell Univ. (SCI, 68, 400; BULL, 26, 120; SCI, 77, 323)

Lecture: Educational Society in Baltimore, retardation (SCI, 37, 302)

Lecture: James, W. lectures, 1942 (BULL, 39, 896)

Lecture: Johns Hopkins Univ. (BULL, 10, 124; SCI, 37, 302)

Lecture: mental dynamics (AJP, 54, 132-133)

Lecture: Middletown Scientific Assoc., animal intelligence (SCI, 31, 65)

Lecture: New York State Assoc. of Consulting Psychologists (BULL, 18, 568)

Lecture: Swarthmore College (SCI, 86, 371)

Lecture: twins (JOP, 1, 224, 644)

Lecture: Union College (SCI, 36, 627; BULL, 10, 40; JOP, 10, 112)

Lecture: Univ. of Chicago (SCI, 11, 277)

Lecture: Univ. of Illinois (BULL, 7, 180; SCI, 31, 575)

Lecture: Univ. of Minnesota (SCI, 61, 113)

Lecture: Wesleyan Univ., Bennett Foundation (SCI, 71, 283)

Portrait presented: Wesleyan College (SCI, 90, 13; BULL, 36, 804)

Promotion: announcement (JOP, 1, 56)

Promotion: Columbia Univ. (SCI, 13, 440; SCI, 19, 120)

Promotion: Teacher's College (BULL, 1, 134)

Publication: Macmillan Co. (JOP, 8, 392)

Publication: note on assimilation and interference (AJP, 49, 676)

Research: education as major subject (JOP, 13, 84)

Research: semantic word count, Columbia Univ. (BULL, 36, 141)

Retirement: Columbia Univ. (SCI, 91, 381; BULL, 37, 405)

Thorndike, Robert Ladd
Leave of absence: Columbia Univ. (BULL, *40*, 152)

Thorne, Frederick Charles
Editor: *Journal of Clinical Psychology* (J APP, *28*, 531)

Thorne, Phebe Anna
Bequest: associate professorship of education and model school, Bryn Mawr College (JoP, *8*, 392)

Thornton, George Russell
Publication: note on the scoring of movement in the Rorschach test (AJP, *48*, 525)

Thorpe, Louis Peter
Appointment: Univ. of Southern California (BULL, *39*, 681)

Thought (*see also* Reasoning)
Lecture: Angell, J. R., imageless thought (SCI, *33*, 214)
Lecture: Boutroux, E., Oxford Univ., relation between thought and action (JoP, *15*, 28)
Lecture: Gildermeister, T., method (JoP, *7*, 223)
Lecture: Ogden, R. M., experiments on the thought process (JoP, *7*, 28)
Lecture: Patrick, C., creative thought (AJP, *54*, 128-131)
Lecture: selective thinking (AJP, *9*, 250)

Thouless, Robert Henry
Appointment: Univ. of Glasgow (BULL, *23*, 455; SCI, *63*, 499)
Appointment: Univ. of Manchester (BULL, *18*, 568)
Election: British Assoc. for the Advancement of Science, president (SCI, *87*, 61-62)
Lecture: points of view in psychology (SCI, *69*, 450)

Threshold
Differential limen for pitch (AJP, *50*, 450-455)

Thuma, Burton Doan
Leave of absence: Univ. of Michigan (SCI, *85*, 405)

Thurstone, Louis Leon
Appointment: Bureau of Personnel Administration (J APP, *6*, 417; SCI, *57*, 81)
Appointment: Carnegie Institute of Technology (BULL, *12*, 403; SCI, *42*, 88; JoP, *12*, 644; BULL, *14*, 263)
Appointment: Grey, C. F. Distinguished Service Professor (SCI, *87*, 387; BULL, *35*, 408)
Appointment: Trade Test Standardization Division (JoP, *15*, 336)
Appointment: Univ. of California (BULL, *28*, 79)
Appointment: Univ. of Chicago (SCI, *60*, 382; BULL, *21*, 660; BULL, *36*, 499)

Course: Univ. of Chicago (J App, 23, 311)
Departure: Univ. of Chicago (Sci, 87, 387)
Editor: *Journal of Personnel Research* (J App, 7, 371; Sci, 58, 347)
Election: American Acad. of Arts and Sciences, fellow (Bull, 34, 409)
Election: APA, president (Sci, 76, 251)
Election: National Academy of Sciences (Bull, 35, 408)
Lecture: Ohio State Educational Conference (J App, 16, 97)
Promotion: Carnegie Institute of Technology (JoP, 15, 336; JoP, 14, 616; Bull, 15, 176)
Promotion: Univ. of Chicago (Sci, 66, 168; Bull, 27, 620)
Publication: engineering aptitude test (J App, 3, 197)
Publication: psychological examinations (J App, 3, 197)

Tibbey, T. G.
Lecture: Child Study Society (JoP, 8, 644)

Ticknor and Company
Publication: the life and works of Giordano, B., English and foreign philosophical library (Sci°, 9, 190)
Publication: list, Aug., 1888 (Sci°, 12, 58)
Publication: the Nigritians by Feathermann, A. and the Melanesians by Feathermann, A. (Sci°, 9, 515)
Publication: self-consciousness of noted persons (Sci°, 8, 344)

Tiegs, Ernest Walter
Publication: California Capacity Questionnaire (J App, 25, 359)
Publication: California Test of Mental Maturity (J App, 21, 344)

Tierseele: Zeitschrift für Vergleichende Seelenkunde
Publication: begun (Bull, 10, 490)

Tigert, John James
Appointment: Army YMCA (Bull, 15, 256)
Leave of absence: Univ. of Kentucky (Sci, 47, 484; JoP, 15, 308)

Tilney, Frederick
Lecture: Assoc. for Research in Nervous and Mental Diseases (Sci, 84, 551)

Time
Publication: Boring, E. G., temporal perception and operationism (AJP, 48, 519)
Publication: Gardner, W. A., influence of the thyroid gland on the consciousness of the passage of time (AJP, 47, 698)
Research: Tresselt, M. E. errors of subjects comparing visual objects (AJP, 57, 555-558)

Times, The
Publication: American Scientists and the U.S. Strategic Air Forces in Europe (Sci, 101, 61)
Publication: Pestalozzi, J. (Sci, 9, 120)

Tinker, Miles Albert
Appointment: Univ. of Minnesota (J App, *11*, 404)
Lecture: eye-movement in reading different color combinations of print and background (AJP, *57*, 93-94)

Tippel, Max
Research: will (Sci°, *6*, 260)

Titchener, Edward Bradford
Anniversary: celebration (Sci, *45*, 567; Bull, *14*, 263-264; JoP, *14*, 420)
Appointment: APA/International Congress for Psychology (JoP, *8*, 196)
Appointment: Baird, J. W. as research assistant (Sci, *17*, 677)
Appointment: Columbia Univ. (JoP, *5*, 56; Bull, *5*, 32; Sci, *26*, 845)
Appointment: Cornell Univ. (Sci, *36*, 556; Bull, *9*, 440)
Appointment: Cornell Univ., Sage Professor (Bull, *7*, 36; JoP, *7*, 84)
Appointment: International Congress of Psychology (JoP, *2*, 56)
Award: committee for paper on Pearson's formula (JoP, *11*, 27-28)
Award: Psychophysics postponed due to war (JoP, *12*, 280; Bull, *12*, 204)
Course: Univ. of Illinois (Bull, *6*, 32)
Death notice (Bull, *24*, 571; Sci, *66*, 148; JoP, *24*, 504)
Degree: Clark Univ. (Sci, *30*, 362)
Degree: Doctor of Law conferred (JoP, *1*, 391, 448)
Editor: *American Journal of Psychology* (Rev, *2*, 641; Bull, *18*, 110)
Editor: *Festschrift* volume for Hall, G. S. (Sci, *17*, 558)
Election: International Congress of Psychology, officer (JoP, *8*, 196)
Election: International Congress of Psychology, president (Sci, *30*, 202)
Lecture: Clark Univ. (Sci, *59*, 574)
Lecture: Columbia Univ. (JoP, *8*, 112; JoP, *5*, 140; Sci, *33*, 214; Sci, *27*, 318; JoP, *1*, 280)
Lecture: Cornell Univ., mental health (Sci, *30*, 559)
Lecture: Indiana Univ. (Bull, *8*, 110; Sci, *33*, 420)
Lecture: International Congress of Arts and Sciences, St. Louis (JoP, *1*, 420)
Lecture: history of experimental psychology (Bull, *22*, 444)
Lecture: Lowell series announcement (Bull, *7*, 126, JoP, *7*, 643)
Lecture: Princeton Univ., association of ideas (Sci, *45*, 360; JoP, *14*, 364)
Lecture: Stumpf, C., systematic psychology (AJP, *32*, 156)
Lecture: Univ. of Illinois (JoP, *6*, 84; Sci, *28*, 921)
Lecture: Univ. of Iowa (Bull, *8*, 110)
Lecture: Univ. of Kansas (Bull, *8*, 110)
Lecture: Univ. of Minnesota (JoP, *8*, 168)
Lecture: visual intensity (AJP, *34*, 310)
Lecture: Wesleyan Univ. (Sci, *55*, 512; Bull, *19*, 296)
Meeting: New York State Teachers of Educational Psychology (JoP, *7*, 252)
Portrait: Cornell Univ., Laboratory of Psychology (Bull, *38*, 777)
Promotion: Cornell Univ. (Rev, *2*, 534; Sci, *2*, 15; JoP, *9*, 644)
Publication: comments on Hall's paper on early memories (AJP, *11*, 435-436)

Publication: comments on Heinrich, W. research on fluctuation of tones (AJP, *11*, 436)

Publication: correspondence to *Mind* (REV, *1*, 440)

Publication: *The Elementary Psychology of Feeling and Attention* (JoP, *5*, 252)

Publication: *Experimental Psychology, Quantitative* (JoP, *1*, 140; JoP, *2*, 504)

Publication: explanation of color-equations, *Experimental Psychology* (JoP, *2*, 55)

Publication: *A Laboratory Manual of Experimental Psychology* (REV, *6*, 344)

Publication: *Outline of Psychology* (AJP, *8*, 430; REV, *4*, 106; JoP, *1*, 140)

Publication: *Primer of Psychology* (AJP, *9*, 250)

Publication: proposes need for a new psychological journal (AJP, *11*, 279-280)

Publication: stereoscopic cards (BULL, *3*, 319; SCI, *24*, 222)

Publication: *A Text-Book of Psychology* (JoP, *6*, 420; JoP, *7*, 560)

Resignation: Editor, *American Journal of Psychology* (BULL, *23*, 112)

Translator: *Physiological Psychology* by Wundt, W. (JoP, *7*, 644; AJP, *7*, 579; SCI, *4*, 269)

Todd, John Edward

Appointment: Institute of Paper Chemistry, Appleton, Wisconsin (BULL, *39*, 681)

Todd, John Welhoff

Appointment: Indiana Univ. (BULL, *13*, 148)

Tokarskii, A. A.

Death notice (REV, *9*, 104)

Toledo University (Ohio)

Appointment: Pintner, R. (SCI, *36*, 373; BULL, *9*, 408; JoP, *9*, 588)

Tolman, Edward Chace

Election: APA, president (SCI, *84*, 307; SCI, *86*, 119)

Election: American Association of Scientific Workers, officer (SCI, *93*, 590)

Election: National Institute of Psychology (BULL, *27*, 736)

Lecture: International Congress for Unity of Sciences, motives (JoP, *33*, 392)

Meeting: Conference on Psychology of Learning, Univ. of Colorado, 1939 (BULL, *36*, 583)

Tomilin, Michael I.

Appointment: Anthropoid Experiment Station, Orange Park, Florida (J APP, *17*, 342)

Tomlinson, Brian Earle

Appointment: New York Univ. (BULL, *39*, 682)

Promotion: New York Univ. (BULL, *42*, 331)

Tones

Lecture: Bentley, M. (JoP, *2*, 223)

Lecture: Cameron, E. H. (JoP, *2*, 224)
Lecture: Seashore, C. E., quality (AJP, *55*, 123-127)

Tönnies, Ferdinand
Award: Welby Prize (AJP, *10*, 165)

Toops, Herbert Anderson
Lecture: National Vocational Guidance Assoc. (J APP, *6*, 425)
Publication: college entrance exam (BULL, *32*, 324)

Toronto, University of (Canada)
Appointment: Barber, F. L. (BULL, *3*, 35; BULL, *4*, 32)
Appointment: Dix, D. (BULL, *3*, 35)
Appointment: Hume, J. G. (SCI°, *14*, 437)
Appointment: Irving, J. A. (BULL, *42*, 485; JoP, *42*, 364)
Appointment: Jensen, M. (BULL, *4*, 32)
Appointment: Kirschmann, A. (AJP, *11*, 130; REV, *1*, 112; REV, *6*, 673)
Appointment: MacPhee, E. D. (SCI, *60*, 475)
Appointment: Robinson, T. R. (BULL, *3*, 35; BULL, *4*, 32)
Appointment: Smith, W. G. (BULL, *4*, 32; BULL, *3*, 35)
Appointment: Strong, M. K. (BULL, *3*, 35)
Grant: Baldwin, J. M. (AJP, *3*, 593)
Grant: Laura Spelman Rockefeller Fund, child study (SCI, *62*, 10)
Publication: *American Journal of Psychology* on their change in curriculum
   (SCI°, *16*, 258-259)

Torrey, Bradford
Research: bird temperaments (SCI°, *2*, 386)

Toulouse, Edouard
Editor: *Revue Scientifique* (JoP, *1*, 112)
Publication: announcement (BULL, *3*, 148)

Tower, Ralph W.
Election: NYAS, officer (JoP, *9*, 28)

Town, Clara Harrison
Announcement: opening of private practice (BULL, *11*, 396)
Appointment: Univ. of Chicago (BULL, *13*, 407)

Townley, H. C.
Appointment: Purdue Univ. (SCI, *54*, 463)

Townsend, Harvey Gates
Election: American Philosophical Assoc., president (JoP, *33*, 56)

Trabue, Marion Rex
Appointment: Univ. of Minnesota (BULL, *28*, 411)

Celebration: occupational research, 10 years (J APP, *28*, 351)
Leave of absence: Univ. of North Carolina (BULL, *28*, 411)

Trade Test Standardization Divison
Ruml, B. work (JoP, *15*, 336)

Training
Lecture: Cattell, J. McK. (JoP, *2*, 224)

Training School for Boys (Red Wing, Minnesota)
Appointment: Swedenberg, C. (BULL, *39*, 325)

Trait relationship
Publication: Anastasi, A., some ambiguous concepts in the field of mental organization (AJP, *47*, 508)

Transference
American Society for Psychical Research Committee request interested individuals (SCI°, *5*, 204)
Lecture: Fracker, G. C. (JoP, *2*, 224)
Publication: American Society for Psychical Research (SCI°, *5*, 491)

Travers, Robert Morris William
Publication: *Human Affairs: An Exposition of What Science Can do for Man* (JoP, *34*, 644)

Travis, Lee Edward
Appointment: Univ. of Iowa (BULL, *34*, 325; BULL, *24*, 312; SCI, *85*, 310)
Appointment: Univ. of Iowa, Psychopathic Hospital (SCI, *65*, 229)
Appointment: Univ. of Southern California (BULL, *35*, 577)
Appointment: U.S. Army (BULL, *39*, 681)
Fellowship: Board of National Research (BULL, *23*, 292)

Travis, Roland Charles
Appointment: Yale Univ. (SCI, *67*, 651; BULL, *25*, 568)

Traxler, Arthur Edwin
Publication: Reading speed and comprehension test (J APP, *23*, 420)

Treadway, Walter L.
Degree: Univ. of Southern California (SCI, *102*, 172)
Lecture: Acad. of Medicine, interaction between man and his environment (SCI, *84*, 530)

Trephining
Lecture: Taylor, J. W., Inca skull (SCI°, *7*, 186)

Tresselt, Margaret Elizabeth
Research: time errors in comparison of visual objects (AJP, *57*, 555-558)

Treves, Zaccaria
Death notice (BULL, *8*, 222)

Trimble, Otis Carroll
Grant: National Research Council, audition research (SCI, *80*, 585)

Trinity College (Cambridge, England)
Appointment: Macintosh, W. H. (SCI°, *3*, 111)
Appointment: MacTaggert, J. E. (REV, *5*, 109)
Donation: Cambridge Univ. for experimental psychology lab (SCI, *33*, 526; JoP, *8*, 280)

Trinity College (Dublin, Ireland)
Appointment: Macran, H. S. (SCI, *15*, 120)

Trinity College (Hartford, Connecticut)
Appointment: Urban, W. M. (SCI, *16*, 40)
Departure: Myers, E. D. (BULL, *42*, 486)
Leave of absence: Urban, W. M. (BULL, *9*, 280)

Troiano, Paolo Raffaele
Death notice (JoP, *6*, 588)

Troland, Leonard Thompson
Appointment: Harvard Univ. (SCI, *50*, 345)
Course: Yale Univ. (SCI, *45*, 63; JoP, *14*, 84)
Death notice (BULL, *29*, 460; AJP, *44*, 817)

Tropical Medicine, School of (San Juan, Puerto Rico)
Appointment: Carpenter, C. R. (SCI, *86*, 79; SCI, *92*, 307)

Trow, William Clark
Appointment: AAAP, (J APP, *25*, 265)

Trubetskoi, Sergei Nikolaevich
Discussion: of his philosophical writings *Voprosi Philosophii I Psychologii* (JoP, *13*, 503)

Trübner and Company
Publication: Clonfert, Dean of, work on the structure of language (SCI°, *5*, 40)
Publication: life and works of Giordano Bruno (SCI°, *8*, 480)

Truitt, Ralph Chess Purnell
Appointment: Mental Hygiene Society of Maryland (SCI, *66*, 34)

Truth
Lecture: Alexander, H. B. (JoP, *7*, 223)
Lecture: Boodin, J. E. (JoP, *7*, 223)

Tryon, Robert Choate
Election: Western Psychological Assoc., secretary (SCI, 79, 406)

Tsai, Loh Seng
Appointment: National Research Institute of Psychology, China (BULL, 28, 79)

Tsanoff, Radoslav Andrea
Appointment: Clark Univ. (JoP, 9, 588)

Tsukahara, Masatsugu
Lecture: sensation (JoP, 2, 112)

Tuberculosis Association, National
Election: Cullen, V. F. (SCI, 101, 635)

Tübingen, University of (Germany)
Departure: Wollenberg, R. (SCI, 24, 352)

Tucker, Willis G.
Publication: drugs (SCI°, 9, 31)

Tuckman, Jacob
Appointment: Jewish Vocational Service, Montreal (BULL, 42, 486)

Tufts College (Medford, Massachusetts)
Appointment: Carmichael, L. (SCI, 87, 184, 209, 549; BULL, 35, 259; SCI, 88, 398)
Appointment: Wellman, B. (SCI, 87, 209)
Lecture: Conant, J. B. (SCI, 88, 398)
Meeting: Eastern Massachusetts Psychologists and Psychiatrists (SCI, 90, 512)

Tufts College Medical School (Boston, Massachusetts)
Course: Dearborn, V. N. (BULL, 6, 152; SCI, 29, 335)
Course: Prince, M. (BULL, 6, 152; SCI, 29, 335)
Laboratory established (BULL, 35, 259; SCI, 87, 209)
Lecture: Carmichael, L. (SCI, 98, 260)

Tufts, James Hayden
Appointment: Illinois Committee on Social Legislation (JoP, 10, 112)
Degree: Amherst College (BULL, 1, 334)
Editor: *Psychological Bulletin* section (BULL, 5, 406; BULL, 6, 427; BULL, 7, 426)
Election: Western Philosophical Assoc. (BULL, 2, 224; JoP, 2, 308)
Lecture: Columbia Univ., thought and moral philosophy (JoP, 17, 336)
Lecture: ethics and international relations (JoP, 14, 720-721)
Lecture: Johns Hopkins Univ. (BULL, 7, 147)
Lecture: justice (JoP, 10, 252)
Promotion: Univ. of Chicago (REV, 7, 324)

Publication: letter to *JoP* editor (JoP, *10*, 615-616)
Visiting Columbia Univ. (BULL, *17*, 239)

Tuke, Daniel Hack

Death notice (SCI, *1*, 304; REV, *2*, 328)
Lecture: insanity (AJP, *1*, 361)
Memorial plans (SCI, *2*, 50; SCI, *4*, 570)
Publication: care of lunatics (AJP, *1*, 200)

Tuke, J. Barry

Candidate: Univ. of Edinburgh, parliamentary representation (SCI, *11*, 756)
Candidate: Univ. of St. Andrews, parliamentary representation (SCI, *11*, 756)

Tulane University (New Orleans, Louisiana)

Appointment: Fletcher, J. M. (BULL, *40*, 152; SCI, *96*, 492; JoP, *9*, 700)
Appointment: Hill, D. S. (SCI, *34*, 714; JoP, *8*, 588)
Appointment: Johnson, H. M. (SCI, *87*, 504)
Appointment: Odom. C. L. (BULL, *42*, 486)
Appointment: Taylor, C. (BULL, *41*, 807)
Departure: Leary, D. B. (SCI, *50*, 161)
Promotion: Landis, A. T. (BULL, *42*, 675)
Promotion: Mann, C. W. (BULL, *42*, 675)
Promotion: McClure, M. T. (JoP, *13*, 364)

Tulchin, Simon Harry

Publication: *Intelligence and Crime* (J APP, *23*, 744)

Tulsa, University of (Oklahoma)

Appointment: Small, G. D. (BULL, *42*, 583)

Turin, University of (Italy)

Publication: Institute of Experimental Psychology, Italian journal (BULL, *17*, 280)

Turnbull, George Henry

Service in the British Army (BULL, *12*, 364)

Turner, John Pickett

Appointment: College of the City of New York (JoP, *10*, 720)
Departure: Vanderbilt Univ. (JoP, *10*, 720)
Lecture: NYAS meeting, psychological analogy (JoP, *13*, 700)
Publication: index for *Journal of Mental Science* (REV, *6*, 344)

Turner, William Donald

Appointment: Institute of the Pennsylvania Hospital (SCI, *86*, 98; BULL, *34*, 635)
Fellowship: Board of National Research Fellowships (BULL, *26*, 380)
Research: sympathomimetic drugs (BULL, *34*, 636)

Tuttle, George T.
Lecture: mental illness (SCI, *34*, 914)

Twins
Lecture: Newman, H. H., Indiana Univ., heredity vs. environment (SCI, *94*, 136)
Lecture: Thorndike, E. L. (JoP, *1*, 224, 644)
Lecture: Verschuer, B. V., research (SCI, *89*, 579)
Publication: Freeman, F. N., American Educational Research Assoc., 1940 (SCI, *91*, 287)
Publication: Newman, H. H., a study of identical twins reared apart (SCI, *82*, 567)

Twitmyer, Edwin Burket
Appointment: Univ. of Pennsylvania (SCI, *46*, 612)
Death notice (BULL, *40*, 383; AJP, *56*, 451-453)
Promotion (SCI, *40*, 482)
Promotion: Univ. of Pennsylvania (BULL, *11*, 483; JoP, *11*, 588)

Twomey, David
Appointment: Boston College (SCI, *74*, 335)

Tyler, Henry Teller
Appointment: Sacramento Junior College (BULL, *39*, 895)

Tyler, John Mason
Lecture: Amherst College Science Assoc., relations of animal to human psychology (SCI°, *6*, 100)

Tyler, Leona Elizabeth
Election: Northwest College Personnel Assoc., secretary (BULL, *40*, 79)

Tylor, Edward Burnett
Death notice (BULL, *14*, 80; AJP, *28*, 313)

Tyndall, John
Publication: life sketch of Rumford (SCI°, *2*, 147)
Resignation: Royal Institution (SCI°, *9*, 363)

U

Ueno, Yōichi
Visits U. S. from Japan (J APP, 6, 82)

Uhrbrock, Richard Stephen
Appointment: Univ. of Wyoming (J APP, 11, 165)
Appointment: War Manpower Commission (SCI, 97, 158)
Leave of absence: Univ. of Wyoming (J APP, 10, 523)
Lecture: American Management Assoc., wage incentives (SCI, 81, 589)
Lecture: Downey, J. commemoration (J APP, 27, 363)

Ulrich, John Linck
Appointment: Catholic Univ. (BULL, 10, 292; SCI, 37, 906; JoP, 10, 504)
Departure: Johns Hopkins Univ. (BULL, 10, 292)

Unconscious self
Publication: Myers, G. C., *Journal of the Society for Psychical Research* (SCI*, 7, 415)

Underwood, Benton J.
Commemorative note (AJP, 22, 475)

Union College (Schenectady, New York)
Donation: Lilly, E. to Character Research Project (BULL, 41, 409-410)
Lecture: Angell, J. R. (SCI, 32, 551; JoP, 8, 28; SCI, 45, 85; BULL, 8, 32; JoP, 14, 168; BULL, 14, 80)
Lecture: McFarland, R. A., Phi Beta Kappa and Sigma Xi Chapters (SCI, 92, 553)
Lecture: Münsterberg, H. (BULL, 9, 95; JoP, 10, 168)
Lecture: Thorndike, E. L. (BULL, 10, 40; SCI, 36, 627; JoP, 10, 112)

United Nations (New York)
Appointment: Bryan, A. H., Relief and Rehabilitation Administration (SCI, *102*, 325)

United States Army (*see also listings under* Army)
Appointment: Bleckwenn, W. J., Sixth Service Command (SCI, *100*, 145)
Commission: Bernreuter, R. G., Specialists' Corps (SCI, *96*, 250)
Commission: Collier, R. M. (SCI, *97*, 199)
Commission: Haggerty, M. E. (BULL, *15*, 24)
Commission: Schachne, I., Sanitary Corps (JoP, *15*, 112)
Position: Yerkes, R. M. (JoP, *14*, 672)
Publication: memoirs of the National Acad. of Sciences, report of psychological work (J APP, *5*, 192)

United States Army Air Corps
Commission: Lepley, W. M. (SCI, *95*, 351)

United States Army Hospitals
Lecture: Kasanin, J. S., psychomatic medicine (SCI, *98*, 298)

United States Bureau of Education
Appointment: Angell, J. R. (BULL, *12*, 481)

United States Civil Service Commission
Applications accepted, occupational therapy aides and recreational aides (BULL, *38*, 126-127)
Examination: assistant physician in the Government Hospital (SCI, *10*, 383)
Position announcement: psychologist, Public Health Service (SCI, *53*, 136)
Publication: untapped resources, handicapped as governmental employees (J APP, *28*, 79)

United States Department of Agriculture
Position announcement: psychologist, Civil Service Employment (SCI, *85*, 382)

United States Employment Service
Publication: quarterly of worker-analysis activities (J APP, *27*, 363)

United States Marine Hospital
Appointment: Unsworth, H. R. (SCI, *101*, 403)

United States Naval Academy (Annapolis, Maryland)
Lecture: Starch, D., psychological tests (SCI, *57*, 297)
Lecture: Swift, E. J. (SCI, *63*, 399; SCI, *65*, 252; SCI, *53*, 89; SCI, *54*, 406; BULL, *18*, 111)

United States Naval Reserve
Commission: Britt, S. H. (SCI, *97*, 576)

Appointment: Pearson, K. (SCI°, *4*, 75)
Appointment: Penrose, L. S., Galton Chair (SCI, *101*, 170)
Appointment: Rivers, W. H. R., director of lab (AJP, *9*, 135)
Appointment: Spearman, C. (JoP, *4*, 476; BULL, *4*, 338; BULL, *25*, 376)
Course: Dixon, E. T. (AJP, *10*, 165; REV, *5*, 554)
Departure: McDougall, W. (JoP, *1*, 28)
Departure: Sully, J. (JoP, *1*, 280)
Election: Pearson, K., honorary fellow (JoP, *1*, 56)
Establishment: Dept. of Psychology (BULL, *25*, 376)
Laboratory: attempts to establish experimental psychology (REV, *4*, 452)
Laboratory: opens (REV, *4*, 567)
Lecture: Pearson, K., eugenics (SCI, *37*, 174)
Lecture: physiological psychology (REV, *1*, 214)
Lecture: Read, C., comparative psychology (SCI, *36*, 473)
Presentation: Morgan, C. L., library (BULL, *7*, 252)
Resignation: Sully, J. (SCI, *17*, 520; BULL, *1*, 174)

Unsworth, Herbert R.
Appointment: Louisiana State Univ. Medical Center (SCI, *74*, 385)
Appointment: U.S. Marine Hospital (SCI, *101*, 403)

Upper State Psychologists
Meeting: semi-annual (SCI, *66*, 351)

Upton, I. H.
Lecture: Amherst College Science Assoc., relation of the mind to the body (SCI°, *6*, 100)

Urban, Friedrich Maria
Appointment: Award Committee for Paper on Pearson's Formula (JoP, *11*, 27-28)
Promotion: Univ. of Pennsylvania (BULL, *7*, 364; JoP, *8*, 84)
Residing in Sweden (BULL, *13*, 40)
War with Austro-Hungarian Army (BULL, *11*, 352; SCI, *40*, 478; JoP, *11*, 588)

Urban, Wilbur Marshall
Appointment: Dartmouth College (BULL, *17*, 239)
Appointment: Princeton Univ. (REV, *4*, 452)
Appointment: Trinity College (SCI, *16*, 40)
Appointment: Ursinus College (REV, *5*, 677)
Appointment: Yale Univ. (JoP, *28*, 140)
Departure: Ursinus College (SCI, *16*, 40)
Editor: *Psychological Bulletin* section (BULL, *6*, 368)
Leave of absence: Trinity College (BULL, *9*, 280)
Publication (BULL, *5*, 31)
Publication: correction of article (JoP, *5*, 588)
Publication: letter to *JoP* editors (JoP, *10*, 643-644)

Ursinus College (Collegeville, Pennsylvania)
Appointment: Urban, W. M. (REV, 5, 677)
Departure: Urban, W. M. (SCI, *16*, 40)

Utah, University of (Salt Lake City)
Appointment: Peterson, J. (BULL, *8*, 373; JoP, *8*, 616)
Establishment: Child Psychiatry Program (SCI, *102*, 273)
Establishment: Dept. of Psychology (BULL, *8*, 373)
Investigation: American Assoc. of Univ. Professors (BULL, *12*, 244)
Lecture: Jensen, R. A. (SCI, *102*, 245)
Resignation: Peterson, J. (BULL, *12*, 160, 244; JoP, *12*, 476)
Resignation: Smith, F. O. (BULL, *12*, 204)

Utrecht, University of (Netherlands)
Appointment: Wernicke, K. (BULL, *1*, 174)
Promotion: Zwaardemaker, H. (AJP, *9*, 135)

Utterback, William Emil
Publication: opinion and opining (AJP, *46*, 506)

Uyeno, Yōichi (see Ueno, Y.)

Uzbek Research Institute (Samarkand)
Research: development of primitive cultures (BULL, *29*, 90)

•

V

Vailati, Giovanni
Death notice (JoP, 6, 448)

Valentine, Charles Wilfrid
Election: British Assoc., president (Sci, 71, 212)

Valentine, Willard Lee
Appointment: Northwestern Univ. (Sci, 92, 169; Bull, 37, 755)
Appointment: Ohio Wesleyan Univ. (J App, 10, 523)
Departure: Ohio State Univ. (Sci, 92, 169)
Editor: Science (Bull, 42, 791)

Valentin, Gabriel Gustav
Death notice (Sci*, 2, 28)

Van de Water, Marjorie
Publication: Psychology for the Fighting Man (J App, 27, 475)

Van Epps, Clarence
Appointment: Iowa State Univ. (Bull, 5, 379)

Van Riper, Benjamin Whitman
Appointment: Boston Univ. (JoP, 9, 168)
Appointment: State College of Pennsylvania (JoP, 12, 560)

Van Tassel, Richard J.
Death notice (Bull, 37, 827)

Van Wagenen, Marvin James
Appointment: Univ. of California (Sci, 62, 154; Bull, 22, 612)
Leave of absence: Univ. of Minnesota (Sci, 62, 154)

Van Waters, Miriam
Lecture: Child Study Assoc. of America (AJP, 9, 319)

Vance, Thomas Franklin
Appointment: Iowa College of Agriculture and Mechanic Arts (BULL, 12, 44)

Vanderbilt University (Nashville, Tennesse)
Appointment: Crawford, M. P. (SCI, 92, 31)
Appointment: Fletcher, J. M. (J APP, 10, 523)
Appointment: Munn, N. L. (SCI, 87, 342; BULL, 35, 408)
Appointment: Paschal, F. C. (SCI, 70, 191)
Appointment: Thompson, A. S. (SCI, 101, 481; BULL, 42, 486)
Departure: Lanier, L. H. (SCI, 87, 163)
Departure: Turner, J. P. (JoP, 10, 720)
Lecture: Miles, W. R., Society of Sigma Xi, aviation psychology (SCI, 99, 446)
Resignation: Paschal, F. C. (BULL, 41, 679)

Vanuxem, Louis Clark Lectures
Bronk, D. W., Princeton Univ., 1939 (SCI, 89, 314)

Vanuxem, Mary
Death notice (BULL, 42, 790)

Varvel, Walter Alphonso
Promotion: Texas Agricultural and Mechanical College (BULL, 42, 676)

Vaschide, Nicolas
Death notice (BULL, 4, 370)

Vassar College (*see also* Child Study Department of Poughkeepsie, New York)
Appointment: Blanton, S. (SCI, 64, 649)
Appointment: French, F. C. (REV, 1, 552)
Appointment: Lanier, L. H. (SCI, 87, 163; BULL, 35, 259)
Appointment: Murray, E. (BULL, 4, 370)
Appointment: Riley, I. W. (BULL, 5, 168)
Appointment: Washburn, M. F. (REV, 10, 344; SCI, 17, 440)
Conference: James', W., 100th anniversary (JoP, 38, 308)
Conference: Washburn, M. F., memorial (BULL, 37, 406)
Establishment: graduate division of conservation (BULL, 39, 132)
Establishment: Vassar Institute of Euthenics (J APP, 24, 245)
Establishment: Washburn, M. F. Fund (BULL, 39, 132)
Grant: child study (BULL, 37, 187)
Meeting: APA, Eastern Branch (SCI, 85, 331; BULL, 34, 121)
Promotion: Washburn, M. F. (BULL, 5, 348; JoP, 5, 588; SCI, 86, 490)
Promotion: Woods, E. L. (JoP, 13, 588; BULL, 13, 376)
Research: personality, Child Study Dept. (BULL, 38, 248)

Resignation: Woods, E. (JoP, *13*, 644)
Retirement: Washburn, M. F. (Sci, *87*, 163)

Vaughan, Clement Leslie
Appointment: Princeton Univ. (Bull, *4*, 336)

Vaughan, Henry F.
Election: National Sanitation Foundation (Sci, *101*, 60)

Vaughan, Wayland Farries
Lecture: Station WGY's Science Forum (Bull, *41*, 199)

Veitch, John
Death notice (Rev, *1*, 654)

Venereal disease
Research: Johns Hopkins Univ. (Sci, *50*, 110)

Veniali, Francesco
Publication: *Rivista pedagogica italiana* (Sci°, *8*, 481)

Verdin laryngograph
Research: Secor, W. B., utilizes (AJP, *11*, 435)

Vermont, University of (Burlington)
Appointment: Larrabee, H. A. (Bull, *22*, 140; Sci, *60*, 429)
Appointment: Messenger, J. F. (Sci, *29*, 656; JoP, *6*, 308; Bull, *6*, 184)
Appointment: Metcalf, J. T. (Bull, *18*, 430; Sci, *54*, 73)
Appointment: Pearson, B. (Sci, *101*, 60)
Appointment: Riker, B. L. (Bull, *42*, 582)
Appointment: Rogers, H. (Bull, *21*, 428; Sci, *59*, 552)
Appointment: Van Der Lugt, M. J. A. (Bull, *40*, 383; Sci, *97*, 199)
Death notice: Ewert, P. H. (Bull, *34*, 864)
Degree: Angell, J. R. (Bull, *12*, 280)
Departure: Squires, P. C. (Bull, *25*, 568)

Vernon, Norma Wynne
Publication: *Propaganda Analysis: An Annotated Bibliography* (J App, *24*, 656)

Verschuer, Otmar, freiherr von
Lecture: twin research from Galton, F. to the present day, Royal Society (Sci, *89*, 579)

Verworn, Max
Death notice (Bull, *19*, 63)
Departure: *Pflüger's Archiv* editorship (Bull, *17*, 200)

Veterans
Publication: Allis-Chalmers Manufacturing Co. (BULL, *42*, 487)
Publication: Univ. of Minnesota (BULL, *42*, 487)

Vienna Philosophical Society [*see also* Philosophical Society, (University of Vienna)]
Formation: help of Zimmerman, [R. ?] (SCI°, *12*, 23)

Vienna Society of Psychiatry and Neurology
Election: Jelliffe, S. E., corresponding member (SCI, *63*, 633)

Vienna, University of (Austria)
Appointment: Hillebrand, F. (REV, *2*, 534)
Appointment: Mach, E. (SCI, *1*, 363; SCI, *2*, 692; REV, *2*, 328, 534)
Course: psychology, Psychological Institute (BULL, *30*, 183; BULL, *34*, 410; J APP, *18*, 306; J APP, *20*, 274)
Establishment: philosophical society (SCI°, *12*, 23)
Position: announcement (BULL, *20*, 664)
Retirement: Krafft-Ebbing, R. v. (SCI, *15*, 320)
Retirement: Mach, E. (SCI, *14*, 302)
Tour of Psychological Institute (J APP, *17*, 97)

Villa, Guido
Appointment: *Psiche* (JOP, *9*, 56)

Vincent, George Edgar
Lecture: social psychology (SCI, *42*, 374)

Vineland Training School (New Jersey)
Anniversary: 25th (BULL, *28*, 646; SCI, *74*, 286; J APP, *15*, 25)
Appointment: Doll, E. (SCI, *36*, 47; BULL, *9*, 360; JOP, *9*, 532)
Appointment: Goddard, H. H. (SCI, *23*, 798)
Appointment: Hickson, W. J. (SCI, *36*, 113)
Appointment: Kreezer, G. (SCI, *77*, 255)
Appointment: Otis, A. S. (BULL, *14*, 366)
Departure: Doll, E. A. (BULL, *40*, 539)
Departure: Goddard, H. H. (SCI, *47*, 264)
Departure: Kreezer, G. (SCI, *87*, 482)
Establishment: Psychology Department (BULL, *3*, 216)
Psychology lab expanded (BULL, *12*, 403)

Virchow, Rudolf Ludwig Carl
Award: Helmholtz Medal, Berlin Acad. of Sciences (SCI, *9*, 300)

Virginia Academy of Science
Grant: McGinnis, J. M. (SCI, *76*, 590)
Meeting: 7th annual, Staunton Military Acad. (SCI, *69*, 571)

Virginia State Normal School (Farmville)

Appointment: Jones, E. E. (Rev, 9, 536)
Departure: Messenger, J. F. (Sci, 29, 656)

Virginia, University of (Charlottesville)

Appointment: Lefevre, A. (Bull, 2, 328)
Departure: Elder, J. H. (Sci, 95, 351)
Departure: Payne, B. (JoP, 8, 308)
Retirement: Dabis, N. K. (JoP, 3, 476)

Virginia, University of, Medical College (Richmond)

Appointment: Drewry, Jr., P. H. (Sci, 89, 313)
Promotion: Gayle, R. F. (Sci, 88, 278)

Vision

Award: Rand, M. G., Sarah Berliner Fellowship (JoP, 9, 168)
Grant: Karwoski, T. and Crook, M. N., National Research Council (Bull, 33, 578-579)
Lecture: Bartlett, F. C. (Sci, 97, 577)
Lecture: Judd, C. H. (Bull, 6, 32; Sci, 24, 792; Sci, 29, 23)
Lecture: Walters, V. W. and Gundlach, R. H., visual after- images (AJP, 43, 288)
Lecture: Woodworth, R. S. (JoP, 2, 700)
Meeting: Ohio State Univ., conference on visual problems (Sci, 94, 136)
Publication: Dennis, W., Desmonceaux's study of the newborn (AJP, 49, 677)
Publication: Pillsbury, W. B., hemeralopia, a case of night blindness (AJP, 46 655)
Publication: Rich, G. J., visual acuity (AJP, 34, 615)
Publication: *System of Diseases of the Eye* (Rev, 1, 214)
Publication: Titchener, E. B., visual intensity (AJP, 34, 310)
Publication: visual apparatus, principles of color, depth and movement (AJP, 52, 640-641)
Publication: visual intensity-discrimination, relation to phylogeny (AJP, 52, 465-467)
Research: visual acuity (AJP, 56, 603-604)
Statistics on defects (Sci°, 16, 342)
Symposium: visual fatigue, 1939 (Bull, 36, 713)
Testing: Cohn, H. (AJP, 2, 186)
Theory of size estimation, Stroobart, P. (Sci°, 5, 222)

Viteles, Morris Simon

Appointment: Personnel Research Federation (J App, 17, 212)
Election: British National Institute of Industrial Psychology (Bull, 26, 624; Sci, 69, 449)
Election: Personnel Research Council (Sci, 77, 256)
Fellowship: Social Science Research Council (Bull, 31, 380)
Meeting: Industrial Psychology, 7th International Conference (Sci, 72, 599)
Promotion (Bull, 22, 504)

Publication: information on organization of Institute of Aviation Psychology
(J App, *28*, 351-352)
Publication: *Psychological Bulletin*, military psychology (J App, *25*, 359)

Virtue
Lecture: French, F. C. (JoP, *7*, 223)

Vivisection
Petition: Society for Cruelty to Animals (Sci°, *5*, 471)
Research: Herzen, A., the senses (Sci°, *8*, 433)

Vocabulary
Lecture: Hunt, E. B., formation (AJP, *44*, 369)
Research: Psychological Corporation, survey (Bull, *28*, 645)

Vocational Adjustment Bureau
Appointment: Burr, E. (AJP, *10*, 393)

Vocational counseling
Lecture: Lehman, H. C. and Witty, P. A. (AJP, *44*, 801)

Vocational education
Publication: Federal Board of Vocational Education (Bull, *15*, 176)

Vocational guidance
Lecture: Rogers, H. A., Columbia Univ., test for (JoP, *13*, 280)
Lecture: Toops, H. A. (J App, *6*, 425)
Publication: War Service Committee of National Vocational Guidance Assoc.
(J App, *26*, 713-714)

Vocational Guidance in Music
Publication: Seashore, C. E. (J App, *1*, 299-300)

Vocational Rehabilitation, Federal Security Agencies
Publication: untapped resources (J App, *28*, 79)

Vocational Summary
Publication: Federal Board for Vocational Education (Bull, *15*, 176)

Voelker, Paul H.
Publication: Detroit General Aptitude Exam (J App, *23*, 420)

Voeltzkow, Alfred
Publication: *Nature*, crocodile habits (Sci°, *16*, 119)

Vogel, Victor H.
Appointment: Office of the Medical Division of the Office of Civilian Defense
(Sci, *96*, 11)

Volkmann, John

Appointment: Columbia Univ. (BULL, *34*, 635)

Publication: on the method of bisection and its relation to a loudness scale (AJP, *49*, 134)

Volition

Lecture: Hoernlë, R. F. A., Aristotelian Society (JoP, *10*, 196)

Voprosy philosophii i psychologii

Discussion: Trubetskoi, P. S. N. (JoP, *13*, 503)

W

Wace, Henry
Publication: opposition to Huxley's "Agnosticism" in *Popular Science Monthly* (Sci°, *13*, 299)

Wade, Bailey
Appointment: Austin College (BULL, *42*, 793)

Waggoner, Raymond W.
Appointment: Michigan State Psychopathic Hospital (Sci, *85*, 14)

Wagner, Charles
Election: American Medico-Psychological Assoc., president (Sci, *43*, 598; Sci, *37*, 936)

Wagner Institute (Philadelphia, PA)
Donation: Westbrook, R. B. (Sci, *10*, 423)
Lecture: Jennings, H. S., heredity and evolution (JoP, *11*, 221)
Lecture: Scott, W. B. (Sci, *13*, 237)

Wagner, Th.
Death notice (BULL, *10*, 424; JoP, *10*, 504)

Wagner von Jauregg, Julius, ritter
Birthday: 80th (Sci, *85*, 354)

Wagoner, Lovisa Catharine
Appointment: Univ. of Wyoming (JoP, *19*, 476)

Waismann, Friedrich
Lecture: Mind Assoc. and Aristotelian Society (JoP, *35*, 252)

Wake Forest College (Winston-Salem, North Carolina) (*see also*
Bowman Gray School of Medicine)
Appointment: Green, H. D. (Sci, *101*, 268)

Walcott, Charles Doolittle
Election: American Acad. of Arts and Sciences (Sci, *9*, 118)

Walcott, Gregory Dexter
Appointment: Government College of Tsing Hua, China (JoP, *14*, 224; Bull, *14*, 115)
Leave of absence: Hamline Univ. (Sci, *45*, 162; JoP, *14*, 224)

Walker, Francis Amasa
Lecture: American Social Science Assoc., industrial education (Sci°, *4*, 537)

Walker, Helen Mary
Publication: Pearson product moment coefficient, simplified table (J App, *22*, 218)

Walker, Jerome
Publication: primer of health lessons (Sci° *10*, 224)

Walker, John Franklin
Appointment: Univ. of Arizona (Bull, *41*, 603)

Walking
Research: Tourette, G. D. L. (Sci°, *8*, 631; Sci°, *7*, 548)

Wallace, Alfred Russel
Publication: the world of life (JoP, *7*, 644)

Wallace, William
Death notice (Sci, *5*, 340; Rev, *4*, 229)

Wallar, Gene Alan
Publication: *Occupational Orientation Inquiry* (J App, *23*, 420)

Waller, Augustus Désiré
Death notice (AJP, *33*, 450)

Wallin, John Edward Wallace
Appointment: American Assoc. of Clinical Psychologists (Sci, *48*, 598)
Appointment: Atlantic Univ. (Sci, *71*, 582)
Appointment: Baltimore Public-School Handicapped Program (Sci *70*, 63)
Appointment: Cleveland Ohio City Normal Training School (Bull, *6*, 32)
Appointment: Constitution Sesquicentennial Commission and Delaware
Tercentenary Commission Committees (Bull, *35*, 259)
Appointment: Delaware Psycho-Educational Examiners (J App, *21*, 717)
Appointment: Mellon Fellow (JoP, *9*, 672; Bull, *9*, 486)

Appointment: Ohio Bureau of Special Education (J App, 7, 370)
Appointment: Pennsylvania Normal School, East Stroudsburg (JoP, 3, 532; Sci, 24, 288, Bull, 3, 319)
Appointment: Princeton Univ. (Rev, 10, 690; Bull, 1, 414)
Appointment: Psycho-educational Clinic, Public Schools of St. Louis, MO (Sci, 11, 190-191; Sci, 39, 756)
Appointment: Psychological Research (JoP, 7, 448)
Appointment: Skillman (Bull, 7, 324)
Appointment: Univ. of Michigan (Sci, 16, 920)
Appointment: Univ. of Pittsburgh (Bull, 9, 208; Sci, 35, 416; JoP, 9, 167)
Course: Duke Univ. (Bull, 35, 259)
Election: Delaware Sesquicentennial Commission, secretary (J App, 21, 130)
Honorary Dinner: Delaware State Department of Public Instruction (Bull, 42, 406)
Lecture: Conference on Education and the Exceptional Child, Child Research Clinic of the Woods School, truancy (J App, 22, 318)
Lecture: New York Branch APA/NYAS, norms of mental development (JoP, 9, 167)
Publication. clinical psychology (J App, 10, 524)
Publication: origin of clinical section of AAAP (J App, 26, 108)

Walls, Gordon Lynn
Appointment: Univ. of Rochester (Bull, 42, 675; Sci, 102, 219)

Walton, Albert
Appointment: Stanford Univ. (J App, 14, 505)
Retirement: Pennsylvania State College (Sci, 96, 155; Bull, 39, 681)

Walton, William Edward
Appointment: Univ. of Nebraska (Sci, 91, 616; J App, 24, 518)

Wang, Ging Hsi
Appointment: Sun Yet-Sen Univ., China (Bull, 24, 380)
Spending year in U.S. (Bull, 41, 680)

War
Course: SPSSI on postwar problems (Bull, 42, 256)
Establishment: Office of Psychological Personnel (Sci, 95, 527-528)
Lecture: Bedford College, London, ethical and psychological aspects (JoP, 12, 140)
Lecture: Bingham, W. V., Canadian Psychological Assoc., psychology of war (Sci, 101, 606-607)
Lecture: Boring, E. G., psychology of perception (AJP, 55, 423-435)
Lecture: English, H. B., psychology in postwar world (Sci, 99, 405)
Lecture: Finger, F. W., Virginia Sigma Xi (Sci, 102, 420)
Lecture: Gillespie, R. D., Weir Mitchell oration, psychoneurosis in peace and war (Sci, 94, 605)
Lecture: Indiana Acad. of Science, call for papers (Bull, 40, 620)

Lecture: Mira, E., Salmon Lecture, psychiatry of war (SCI, *96*, 378)
Lecture: Murphy, G., post-war planning (J APP, *27*, 114-115)
Meeting: American Philosophical Society, symposium on psychology and education (BULL, *17*, 240)
Publication: Huntington, T. W. and Stagner, R., psychological aspects of war (BULL, *38*, 248)
Publication: National Committee for Mental Hygiene, psychosomatic medicine (SCI, *98*, 59-60)
Publication: NRC, Office of Psychological Personnel, psychology in the war (BULL, *39*, 328)
Publication: *Psychological Bulletin*, psychology of war (J APP, *26*, 391-392)
Publication: psychologists status given (BULL, *12*, 128)
Publication: *The Junior College Journal*, psychology of war (BULL, *40*, 723)
Research: Bianch's L. related problems (JoP, *13*, 448)
Research: Blum M. L., housing, survey of (BULL, *41*, 267)
Research: Mira, E. (J APP, *26*, 856-857)
Research: *Psychological Bulletin*, questionnaire (J APP, *26*, 566-570)
Research: Psychological Corporation, sentiment toward wartime advertising (J APP, *27*, 208)
Research: references, American opinions (JoP, *14*, 560)
Univ. of Pennsylvania assists postwar employment (BULL, *41*, 343)

War Conference on Industrial Health
Meeting: New York (AJP, *56*, 302)

War Department, United States
Acquisition: Battle Creek Sanitarium (SCI, *95*, 551)
Appointment: Elder, J. H. (SCI, *98*, 12; BULL, *40*, 619)
Appointment: Judd, C. H. (BULL, *40*, 231)

War Manpower Commission (*see also* Bureau of Training of)
Appointment: Charters, W. W. (SCI, *97*, 87)
Appointment: Uhrbrock, R. S. (SCI, *97*, 158)
Publication: clinical psychology not listed in field of health and welfare (J APP, *27*, 207)
Resignation: Carmichael, L., National Roster of Scientific and Specialized Personnel (SCI, *100*, 447)

War Production Board, Committee on Post-War Research
Establishment: institute to carry on work of Office of Scientific Research and Development (SCI, *100*, 246)

War Public Service Projects
Appointment: Nyswander, D. B., Federal Works Agency (BULL, *39*, 895)

War Service Committee, National Vocational Guidance Association
Publication: vocational guidance for victory (J APP, *26*, 713-714)

Warbeke, John Martyn
Leave of absence: Mount Holyoke College (JoP, *17*, 672)

Ward, Henry B.
Lecture: Illinois State Museum, psychology and its relation to conservation (Sci, *89*, 264)

Ward, James
Appointment: Cambridge Univ. (Rev, *4*, 229; AJP, *8*, 430)
Appointment: St. Andrews Univ. (Bull, *3*, 116)
Death notice (Bull, *22*, 260; Sci, *61*, 283)
Degree: Cambridge Univ. (JoP, *6*, 532)
Degree: D. Sc. *honoris causa* (JoP, *5*, 476)
Degree: Oxford Univ. (Bull, *5*, 316)
Degree: Univ. of Leipzig (JoP, *6*, 700)
Editor: *British Journal of Psychologyy* (JoP, *1*, 28)
Editor: *Journal of Psychology* (Rev, *10*, 464)
Lecture: International Congress of Arts and Sciences, St. Louis (JoP, *1*, 419)
Lecture: Princeton Univ. (JoP, *1*, 504)
Lecture: Sidgwick, H., Memorial Lecture (JoP, *9*, 700)
Lecture: Univ. of California (JoP, *1*, 280, 588; Bull, *1*, 94, 133, 452)
Lecture: Univ. of Iowa (Bull, *1*, 173)
Lecture: Univ. of St. Andrews (JoP, *5*, 196)
Lecture: U.S. (Bull, *1*, 452)
Meeting: Congress of Arts and Sciences (JoP, *1*, 280)
Portrait fund begun (Bull, *10*, 124)
Publication: psychology, *Encyclopedia Britannica* (Sci°, *7*, 304)
Publication: response to review (Rev, *3*, 243)
Represents Cambridge Univ. at Oxford celebration of Bacon (JoP, *11*, 336)
Returns to England (JoP, *1*, 616)

Warden, Carl John
Legislation: APA on precautions in animal experimentation (Sci, *77*, 189)

Wardlaw, Patterson
Election: SSPP, office (Bull, *13*, 40; JoP, *13*, 112)

Warfare of Science
Publication: White, A. D., *Popular Science Monthly* (Sci°, *13*, 299)

Warner, Francis
Publication: feelings (AJP, *1*, 200)

Warner, Mary La Vinia
Appointment: Ohio Univ. (J App, *7*, 370)

Warren, Howard Crosby
Appointment: American Assoc. of Univ. Professors (Bull, *12*, 244)

Appointment: Princeton Univ. (REV, *1*, 112; REV, *3*, 244; SCI, *3*, 284; AJP, *7*, 452)
Appointment: Society of Experimental Psychologists (SCI, *83*, 367)
Course: Princeton Univ. (AJP, *11*, 130)
Death notice: obituary by Langfeld, H. S. (AJP, *46*, 340)
Editor: *American Naturalist* (AJP, *7*, 579)
Editor: *Psychological Bulletin* (JoP, *1*, 84)
Editor: *Psychological Review* (REV, *8*, 112)
Election: AAAS, vice-president (BULL, *25*, 123)
Election: APA, council member (JoP, *8*, 55)
Election: APA, president (BULL, *10*, 40; SCI, *37*, 55)
Leave of absence: Princeton Univ. (SCI, *77*, 408)
Meeting: APA/APS (JoP, *10*, 335)
Promotion: Princeton Univ. (REV, *9*, 432; SCI, *15*, 1000)
Publication: translates Trade's *Les Lois Sociales* (REV, *6*, 119)
Resignation: *Psychological Review* (JoP, *2*, 672)
Return: Princeton Univ. (BULL, *4*, 337)

Warren, Howard Crosby Medal
Bray, C. W. (BULL, *33*, 476; SCI, *83*, 367)
Culler, E. A. (BULL, *35*, 408; SCI, *87*, 362)
Graham, C. H. (SCI, *93*, 324; J APP, *25*, 267)
Hilgard, E. R. (BULL, *37*, 405; SCI, *91*, 334)
Hull, C. L. (BULL, *42*, 406; SCI, *101*, 402)
Jacobsen, C. F. (BULL, *36*, 499)
Lashley, K. S. (BULL, *34*, 273; SCI, *85*, 354)
Skinner, B. F. (SCI, *95*, 378; BULL, *39*, 325)
Stevens, S. S. (SCI, *97*, 373)
Wever, E. G. (SCI, *83*, 367; BULL, *33*, 476)

Warren, Neil Dille
Appointment: Univ. of Southern California (BULL, *35*, 577)

Wartime Conference, National
Lecture: Carmichael, L. A. (SCI, *97*, 375)
Purpose is to use skill and talent of professionals not involved in war (SCI, *97*, 375)

Washburn College (Topeka, Kansas)
Departure: Wilm, E. C. (BULL, *9*, 408; JoP, *9*, 532)

Washburn Commemorative Volume (American Journal of Psychology)
Publication: announcement (JoP, *25*, 280; AJP, *40*, 171)

Washburn, Margaret Floy
Appointment: Cornell Univ. (SCI, *13*, 1000; REV, *7*, 428)
Appointment: Univ. of Cincinnati (REV, *9*, 431; SCI, *15*, 880)
Appointment: Vassar College (SCI, *17*, 440; REV, *10*, 344)

Appointment: Vassar College, emeritus (Sci, *86*, 490)
Appointment: Wells College (Rev, *2*, 104)
Commemorative volume of *AJP* (AJP, *40*, 171)
Death notice (Bull, *37*, 61)
Departure: Cornell Univ. (Rev, *9*, 431)
Departure: Univ. of Cincinnati (Rev, *10*, 344; Sci, *17*, 440)
Editor: *Bulletin*, section of (Bull, *10*, 332; Bull, *7*, 324; Bull, *9*, 359; Bull, *8*, 302)
Election: American Assoc. for Advancement of Science, vice- president (Bull, *23*, 112)
Election: APA, council member (JoP, *9*, 28)
Election: APA, president (AJP, *32*, 157; Sci, *53*, 18)
Election: International Congress of Psychology (Sci, *76*, 119)
Election: NAS (Bull, *28*, 410)
Election: New York State Assoc. of Consulting Psychologists (Bull, *18*, 568)
Honorary dinner by APA (Sci, *67*, 101)
Lecture: sensation (JoP, *1*, 84)
Meeting: Vassar College, memorial conference (Bull, *37*, 406)
Promotion: Vassar College (JoP, *5*, 588; Bull, *5*, 348)
Publication: *American Journal of Psychology* (AJP, *48*, 177)
Publication: Baldwin, J. M., obituary (AJP, *47*, 169)
Publication: critique of Spearman, C. (AJP, *41*, 322)
Publication: diary of Floy, Jr., M. (AJP, *56*, 301-302)
Publication: *The Animal Mind*, critique of (JoP, *5*, 587)
Research: emotional characteristics (Bull, *17*, 239)
Retirement: Vassar College (Sci, *87*, 163)

Washburn, Margaret Floy Fund
Establishment: Vassar College (Bull, *39*, 132)

Washburn, Ruth Wendell
Research: Univ. of Geneva (Bull, *34*, 499)

Washington Academy of Sciences
Lecture: Heyl, P. R., cosmic emotion (Sci, *95*, 429)
Lecture: Judd, C. H., visual perception (Sci, *24*, 792)
Lecture: Mizwa, S. P., Copernicus quadricentennial, 1943 (Sci, *98*, 361)

Washington and Lee University (Lexington, Virginia)
Appointment: Brown, W. M. (AJP, *10*, 393)
Appointment: Flick, W. A. (AJP, *10*, 393)

Washington-Baltimore Branch of the American Psychological Association
Election: officers (Bull, *35*, 188; Bull, *36*, 712; Bull, *37*, 656; Bull, *39*, 683)
Meeting (Bull, *35*, 188; Bull, *36*, 140, 304, 500, 712; Bull, *37*, 122, 405; Bull, *38*, 67, 778; Bull, *39*, 72, 683; J App, *25*, 726)

Washington College (Chesterton, Maryland)
Appointment: Freeman, F. N. (BULL, *4*, 370)

Washington, D.C. Government Hospital for the Insane
Appointment: Franz, S. I. (BULL, *7*, 75)
Departure: Sutherland, A. H. (BULL, *7*, 75)

Washington, D.C. Psychological Institute
Research: education (J APP, *19*, 106)

Washington Health and Hospital Facilities
Research: Winslow, G. E. A., survey (SCI, *101*, 428)

Washington Life Insurance Company
Publication: suicides (SCI°, *14*, 131)

Washington Philosophical Society
Lecture: Bell, A.G., fallacies concerning the deaf (SCI°, *2*, 635)
Lecture: Farquhar, E. J., dreams in their psychological relation (SCI°, *1*, 472)
Meeting (SCI°, *2*, 518, 581, 635, 698, 754; SCI°, *12*, 271)

Washington School of Psychiatry
Departure: Sullivan, H. S. (SCI, *90*, 536)

Washington State College (Pullman)
Lecture: Kirkpatrick, E. A. (JoP, *13*, 476)

Washington University (St. Louis, Missouri)
Adds faculty position in psychology and pedagogy (SCI, *17*, 920)
Appointment: Bernreuter, R. G. (J APP, *13*, 415)
Appointment: Gildea, E. F. (SCI, *96*, 511)
Appointment: Jacobsen, C. F. (BULL, *35*, 577)
Appointment: Lovejoy, A. O. (SCI, *14*, 624)
Appointment: Magdsick, W. K. (BULL, *39*, 682)
Appointment: Nafe, J. P. (SCI, *73*, 337; BULL, *28*, 324)
Appointment: Rioch, D. M. (BULL, *35*, 577)
Appointment: Swift, E. J. (SCI, *18*, 128)
Appointment: Whitehorn, J. C. (BULL, *35*, 577)
Course: Phillips, D. E. (BULL, *14*, 264)
Leave of absence: Lovejoy, A. O. (BULL, *5*, 32)
Resignation: Hawthorne, J. (BULL, *32*, 324)
Resignation: Lovejoy, A. O. (JoP, *5*, 252)
Retirement: Swift, E. J. (BULL, *28*, 324; SCI, *73*, 337)

Washington, University of (Seattle)
Appointment: Esper, E. A. (BULL, *24*, 508; SCI, *65*, 595; J APP, *11*, 405)
Appointment: Gundlack, R. (J APP, *11*, 405)
Appointment: Horton, G. P. (BULL, *32*, 324)

Appointment: Smith, S. (JoP, *8*, 616; BULL, *8*, 374; BULL, *11*, 232)
Appointment: Stevens, H. C. (BULL, *2*, 427)
Course: Starch, D. (JoP, *12*, 280)
Departure: Stevens, H. C. (JoP, *11*, 588; SCI, *40*, 408)
Presidency offered to Angell, J. R. (SCI, *40*, 743; SCI, *40*, 813)

Washingtonian Hospital (Boston, Massachusetts)

Appointment: Moore, M. (SCI, *93*, 254)
Reorganization (SCI, *93*, 254)

Wasmansdorff, E.

Publication: various forms of sorrow over loss of friends (SCI°, *6*, 407)

Waterhouse, Eric Strickland

Research: psychic phenomena (SCI, *80*, 183)

Waterman, John H.

Lecture: Child Health Program Conference (SCI, *101*, 482)

Waters, Rolland Hays

Appointment: Univ. of Arkansas (BULL, *25*, 700)
Promotion: Univ. of Arkansas (SCI, *84*, 58)
Publication: environmental change with an accompanying loss of language (AJP, *46*, 337)

Watson, Goodwin Barbour

Leave of absence: Columbia Univ. (BULL, *40*, 152)
Lecture: Child Research Clinic of the Woods School (J APP, *21*, 131, 344)
Psychological study group in Europe (J APP, *16*, 224)

Watson, John Broadus

Appointment: APA Committee on Medical Education (JoP, *9*, 28)
Appointment: Carnegie Institution of Washington (BULL, *9*, 128; SCI, *35*, 177; JoP, *9*, 112)
Appointment: Johns Hopkins Univ. (SCI, *27*, 440; JoP, *5*, 196, 392; BULL, *5*, 96; BULL, *2*, 159)
Appointment: Johns Hopkins Univ., director of psychology dept. (BULL, *13*, 260; JoP, *13*, 532)
Appointment: National Research Council (BULL, *14*, 191; JoP, *14*, 392)
Appointment: Univ. of Chicago (JoP, *1*, 336; BULL, *8*, 222)
Course: behavior psychology (BULL, *20*, 172)
Departure: Johns Hopkins Univ. (JoP, *9*, 112)
Editor: *Behavioral Monographs* (JoP, *8*, 559-560)
Editor: *Journal of Experimental Psychology* (JoP, *13*, 336; JoP, *11*, 448)
Editor: *Psychological Bulletin* (BULL, *6*, 216, 296)
Election: APA/International Congress for Psychology, executive committee (JoP, *8*, 196)
Election: APA, president (JoP, *12*, 112; SCI, *41*, 60)

Election: International Congress for Psychology, officer (JoP, *8*, 196)
Election: SSPP officer (JoP, *11*, 140)
Lecture: Clark Univ. (SCI, *59*, 574)
Lecture: Columbia Univ., animal psychology (JoP, *10*, 196; SCI, *37*, 367)
Lecture: comparative psychology (JoP, *5*, 721)
Lecture: New York Acad. of Sciences (SCI, *60*, 402)
Promotion: Thompson, J. W. Co., vice-president (SCI, *61*, 113)
Publication: correction of review (JoP, *5*, 335)
Research: Dry Tortugas to study noddy and sooty terns (BULL, *10*, 252)
Research: habits of sea gulls (BULL, *4*, 337)
Resignation: *Journal of Experimental Psychology* (SCI, *63*, 88)

Watson, Walter Samuel
Appointment: Cooper Union (SCI, *96*, 268)
Promotion: Cooper Union (BULL, *39*, 895)

Watt, Henry Jackson
Death notice (SCI, *62*, 490)
Lecture: British Psychological Society (JoP, *8*, 448)
Return: from Germany (JoP, *12*, 644; BULL, *12*, 403)

Watts, Frederick Payne
APA, Wash.-Balt. Branch, 1940 (BULL, *37*, 405)

Watts, James W.
Award: Horsley, J. Memorial Prize, psychosurgery (SCI, *96*, 36)
Publication: psychosurgery (SCI, *96*, 36)

Waugh, Karl Tinsley
Appointment: Beloit College (BULL, *6*, 427)
Election Dickinson College, president (SCI, *74*, 408)

Wayenburg, Gerard Anton Marie van
Death notice (BULL, *23*, 455)

Wayne County, Michigan (*see* Civil Service Commission of)

Wayne County Training School
Appointment: Hegge, T. G. (J APP, *14*, 304)

Wayne State University (Detroit, Michigan)
Promotion: Erickson, M. H., College of Medicine (BULL, *42*, 128)
Promotion: Pyle, W. H. (BULL, *42*, 331)

Waynesburg College (Pennsylvania)
Degree: Franz, S. I. (BULL, *12*, 244)

Weaver, Homer Ellsworth
Appointment: Univ. of Arizona (J App, *13*, 415)
Promotion: Oberlin College (BULL, *42*, 583)

Webb, Louie Winfield
Appointment: Northwestern Univ. (BULL, *14*, 116; BULL, *20*, 172)
Publication: mental alertness tests (SCI, *56*, 331)

Webber, Herbert John
Lecture: Cornell Univ., eugenics (SCI, *36*, 784)

Weber and Gauss
Monument: Göttingen (SCI, *10*, 126)

Weber, Pearl Hunter
Appointment: Illinois Woman's College (JoP, *17*, 588)

Weber-Fechner Law
Lecture: Hecht, S., Conference on Methods in Philosophy and the Sciences
(JoP, *37*, 224)

Wechsler, David
Publication: Wechsler-Bellevue Intelligence Scale (J App, *23*, 420)

Wedell, Carl Havelock
Appointment: Princeton Univ. (SCI, *87*, 411)

Weeber, Lorle Stecher (*see* Stecher, Lorle Ida)

Weidensall, Clara Jean
Conducts psychological tests at Bedford Hills Reformatory for Women, New
York (BULL, *8*, 374)

Weigle, Luther Allan
Appointment: Carleton College (JoP, *2*, 280)
Appointment: Yale Univ. (BULL, *1*, 414)
Lecture: philosophical implications in the elementary course in psychology
(JoP, *7*, 223)
Lecture: reading (JoP, *2*, 224)

Weir, Samuel
Appointment: Univ. of Cincinnati (SCI, *15*, 160)

Weisenburg, Theodore Herman
Election: Assoc. for Research in Nervous and Mental Diseases, president (SCI,
79, 9)

Weiss, Albert Paul
Appointment: Ohio State Univ. (BULL, *9*, 408; JoP, *9*, 616)

Death notice (BULL, *28*, 324; AJP, *43*, 707)
Departure: Univ. of Missouri (BULL, *9*, 408; JoP, *9*, 616)
Election: Alpha Psi Delta Psychological Fraternity, treasurer (BULL, *19*, 586)
Election: APA, council of directors (BULL, *26*, 56)
Publication: rejoinder to criticism by Gundlach, [R. H. ?] (AJP, *38*, 669)

Weiss, Edward
Appointment: National Committee for Mental Hygiene (SCI, *99*, 319, 363)

Weisz, Stephen
Promotion: Univ. of Texas, School of Medicine (SCI, *100*, 245)

Welby Prize
Announcement of (AJP, *8*, 314; REV, *3*, 705)
Award: Tönnies, F. (AJP, *10*, 165)
Deadline (AJP, *9*, 135)

Welch, William H.
Anniversary: Mental Hygiene Movement, 25th (SCI, *70*, 536)
Appointment: Johns Hopkins Univ. (SCI, *72*, 625)
Election: National Committee for Mental Hygiene (SCI, *72*, 557)

Weld, Harry Porter
Appointment: Cornell Univ. (BULL, *9*, 407; JoP, *9*, 588; SCI, *36*, 401)
Departure: Clark Univ. (BULL, *9*, 407; JoP, *9*, 588)
Election: International Congress of Psychology (SCI, *76*, 119)
Leave of absence: Cornell Univ. (BULL, *23*, 292)

Wellesley College (Massachusetts)
Appointment: Bell, J. C. (SCI, *21*, 800; JoP, *2*, 336; BULL, *2*, 426)
Appointment: Cole, L. W. (JoP, *5*, 616; BULL, *5*, 379)
Appointment: Cook, H. D. (BULL, *6*, 400)
Appointment: English, H. B. (BULL, *17*, 279)
Appointment: Gamble, E. A. (AJP, *10*, 166)
Appointment: Heidbreder, E. (BULL, *31*, 380; SCI, *80*, 31)
Appointment: Ruckmick, C. A. (BULL, *18*, 438; JoP, *18*, 392)
Appointment: Starch, D. E. (JoP, *4*, 588; BULL, *4*, 337)
Appointment: Zigler, M. J. (BULL, *21*, 428; SCI, *89*, 384; SCI, *60*, 333)
Departure: Cole, L. W. (BULL, *7*, 252)
Election: Calkins, M. W., APA president (SCI, *21*, 37; JoP, *2*, 28)
Fellowship: Cook, H. D. (BULL, *4*, 128)
Leave of absence: Gamble, E. A. (BULL, *21*, 360; SCI, *59*, 274)
Lecture: Boring, E. G. (SCI, *55*, 451)
Lecture: Gamble, E. A. (SCI, *13*, 358)
Lecture: Münsterberg, H. (JoP, *5*, 616; BULL, *5*, 379)
Promotion: Campbell, I. (BULL, *12*, 160)
Psychological lab destroyed by fire (BULL, *11*, 152)
Retirement: Calkins, M. W. (SCI, *69*, 666)

Wellman, Bertram

Appointment: Tufts College (Sci, *87*, 209; Bull, *35*, 259)

Wells College (Aurora, New York)

Appointment: Aldrich, V. C. (JoP, *41*, 532)
Appointment: Day, L. M. (Bull, *11*, 190)
Appointment: Washburn, M. F. (Rev, *2*, 104)
Appointment: Wilm, E. C. (Bull, *9*, 408; JoP, *9*, 532)

Wells, D. F.

Election: American Psychiatric Assoc., vice-president (Sci, *91*, 520)

Wells, Estelle Frances

Publication: counter reply to Newman, E. B. (AJP, *43*, 686)
Publication: rejoinder to Helson, H. (AJP, *43*, 691)

Wells, Frederic Lyman

Appointment: Boston Psychopathic Hospital (AJP, *32*, 160)
Appointment: Columbia Univ. (Bull, *7*, 426; JoP, *7*, 721; Sci, *32*, 863)
Appointment: Harvard Medical School (Sci, *53*, 363; Bull, *18*, 236)
Appointment: Harvard Univ. (Sci, *88*, 278; Bull, *35*, 796)
Appointment: McLean Hospital (JoP, *4*, 308, 420; Bull, *8*, 406; Bull, *4*, 337)
Appointment: New York State Hospital (Sci, *32*, 863)
Appointment: New York State Hopsital, Psychiatric Institute (Bull, *7*, 426; JoP, *7*, 721)
Departure: Army (Bull, *16*, 222)
Departure: Boston Psychopathic Hospital, Psychological Lab (Sci, *88*, 278)
Departure: Ward's Island (Bull, *8*, 406)
Lecture: Cattell jubilee (AJP, *25*, 468)
Lecture: Harvard Univ. (Bull, *10*, 124; JoP, *10*, 336)
Lecture: linguistics (JoP, *2*, 224, 700)
Lecture: memory examination adapted to psychotic cases (JoP, *19*, 279)
Lecture: NYAS/APA, free association (JoP, *7*, 700)
Lecture: NY Branch of APA/NYAS, medicine in psychology (JoP, *9*, 167)

Wells, George Ross

Appointment: Oberlin College (Bull, *9*, 360; JoP, *9*, 476; Sci, *36* 115)
Appointment: Ohio Wesleyan Univ. (JoP, *14*, 308; Bull, *14*, 143, 264; Bull, *15*, 24; Sci, *45*, 431)
Promotion: Oberlin College (Bull, *11*, 116, 482; Sci, *40*, 519; JoP, *11*, 196, 672)

Wembridge, Eleanor Harris Rowland (*see* Rowland, Eleanor Harris)

Wendt, George Richard

Appointment: Univ. of Pennsylvania (Sci, *85*, 560; Bull, *34*, 498)
Appointment: Univ. of Rochester (Bull, *42*, 255; Sci, *101*, 170)

Departure: Wesleyan Univ. (BULL, *42*, 255)
Lecture: science challenges society (SCI, *101*, 140)

Wenger, Marion Augustus
Appointment: Univ. of California, Los Angeles (BULL, *42*, 583)

Wenley, Robert Mark
Appointment: Baldwin Lectureship (BULL, *4*, 401)
Degree: Univ. of Glasgow (REV, *8*, 552)
Leave of absence: Univ. of Michigan (BULL, *2*, 427)
Publication: physiological psychology (JOP, *5*, 448, 560)

Werner, Heinz
Appointment: Univ. of Michigan (SCI, *78*, 359)

Wernicke, Carl
Appointment: Utrecht Univ. (BULL, *1*, 174)
Death notice (BULL, *2*, 295)

Wertham, Frederic (*see* Wertheimer, Frederick Ignace)

Wertheimer, Frederick Ignace
Appointment: Johns Hopkins Univ. (BULL, *20*, 172; SCI, *56*, 387)

Wertheimer, Max
Appointment: New School for Social Research (JOP, *31*, 532)
Course: Swarthmore College, taught by Köhler, W. (BULL, *41*, 72)
Death notice (AJP, *57*, 428-435; JOP, *40*, 616; BULL, *40*, 794)
Publication: *Social Research* translation of Gestalt theory (BULL, *41*, 268)

Wesleyan University (Middletown, Connecticut)
Appointment: Dodge, R. (REV, *5*, 449; AJP, *11*, 130)
Appointment: English, H. B. (SCI, *61*, 489; BULL, *22*, 444)
Appointment: Greene, E. B. (BULL, *22*, 672)
Appointment: Judd, C. H. (REV, *3*, 468; AJP, *7*, 579)
Appointment: Landis, C. (BULL, *23*, 412; J APP, *11*, 405; BULL, *24*, 620; J APP, *10*, 394)
Appointment: Langlie, T. A. (BULL, *24*, 620; J APP, *11*, 405)
Degree: Angell, J. R. (BULL, *21*, 240; SCI, *57*, 737)
Degree: Dodge, R. (SCI, *73*, 697)
Degree: Thorndike, E. L. (SCI, *50*, 37)
Degree: Yerkes, R. M. (BULL, *21*, 240; SCI, *57*, 737)
Departure: Dodge, R. (SCI, *36*, 591; JOP, *9*, 672; SCI, *45*, 611)
Departure: English, H. B. (J APP, *11*, 165)
Departure: Judd, C. H. (REV, *5*, 449; SCI, *7*, 713)
Departure: Landis, C. (BULL, *27*, 415; J APP, *14*, 304)
Departure: Wendt, G. R. (BULL, *42*, 255)
Expands facilities (J APP, *11*, 405; BULL, *27*, 620; SCI, *66*, 425)

Grant: Langlie, T. A., Faculty Committee on Research (Sci, *85*, 14)
Leave of absence: Armstrong, Jr., A. C. (Rev, *6*, 571; AJP, *11*, 130)
Leave of absence: Landis, C. (J App, *13*, 93)
Lecture: Thorndike, E. L., Bennett Foundation (Sci, *71*, 283)
Lecture: Titchener, E. B. (Sci, *55*, 512)
Meeting: Conference on Experimental Psychologists, 10th (Bull, *10*, 211-212; JoP, *10*, 364)
Portrait presented: Thorndike, E. L. (Bull, *36*, 804; Sci, *90*, 13)
Promotion: Dodge, R. (Sci, *15*, 720; Rev, *6*, 344)
Resignation: English, H. B. (Bull, *24*, 312)

Wesley, S. Medford
Appointment: Univ. of Southern California (Bull, *42*, 583)
Appointment: Yale Univ. (Bull, *38*, 907; Sci, *94*, 62)

Westbrook, Charles Hart
Return to U.S. (Bull, *41*, 267)

Westbrook Lectures
Jennings, H. S., Wagner Institute of Science (JoP, *14*, 224)

Westbrook, Richard B.
Donation: Wagner Institute of Science (Sci, *10*, 423)

West Chester State Normal School (Pennsylvania)
Appointment: Goddard, H. H. (Bull, *3*, 216)
Leave of absence: Baldwin, B. T. (Bull, *6*, 184)

West Virginia Academy of Science
Lecture: English, H. B., psychology in the post-war world (Sci, *99*, 405)

West Virginia State College (Institute)
Promotion: Canady, H. B. (Bull, *40*, 619)

West Virginia, University of (Morgantown)
Lecture: Dunlap, K. (Sci, *65*, 181)

West, Wilbur Dickson
Appointment: Western Michigan College of Education Camp (Bull, *42*, 331)
Departure: Wittenburg College (Bull, *42*, 331)

Western Philosophical Association
Election: officers (JoP, *2*, 280)
Election: Tufts, J. H. (Bull, *2*, 224)
Lecture: Northwestern Univ. (JoP, *10*, 224)
Lecture: Seashore, C. E., presidential (JoP, *7*, 223)
Meeting: announcement (JoP, *3*, 140; Bull, *3*, 147; JoP, *7*, 112)
Meeting: APA, Chicago (Sci, *14*, 781; Rev, *9*, 103)

Meeting: North Central Section of APA and Teachers of Psychology in Iowa (JoP, 7, 222-223)
Meeting: Univ. of Iowa (JoP, 16, 168, 251-252)
Meeting: Univ. of Michigan (JoP, 14, 196; JoP, 15, 111, 112)
Meeting: Univ. of Missouri (JoP, 1, 224)
Meeting: Univ. of Nebraska (JoP, 2, 252)
Meeting: Western Psychological Assoc. (JoP, 10, 140, 224; JoP, 9, 223-224)
Meeting: Univ. of Wisconsin (JoP, 3, 252; JoP, 17, 167)
Organization: Jan. 1, 1900 (REV, 7, 323)
Publication: report of meeting (JoP, 4, 223; JoP, 5, 168; JoP, 6, 252)

Western Psychological Association
Election: Gordon, K., president (AJP, 10, 395)
Election: McGilvary, E. B., president (JoP, 7, 308)
Election: results (SCI, 56, 221; SCI, 62, 217; SCI, 64, 39)
Meeting: AAAS (BULL, 31, 380; SCI, 79, 406)
Meeting: announcement (AJP, 57, 576-577; JoP, 3, 167; JoP, 7, 644; BULL, 32, 376)
Meeting: APA and AAAS (JoP, 8, 55)
Meeting: Bay-area Division, 1943 (AJP, 57, 96)
Meeting: postponement (SCI, 55, 616)
Meeting: Stanford Univ. (BULL, 21, 360)
Meeting: sub-regional (BULL, 40, 460)
Meeting: Univ. of California, Berkeley (AJP, 54, 607; BULL, 22, 444)
Meeting: Univ. of California, Los Angeles (AJP, 53, 616)
Meeting: Univ. of Washington, Seattle (AJP, 55, 450)
Meeting: Western Philosophical Assoc. (JoP, 10, 140, 224; JoP, 9, 223-224)
Membership list (JoP, 7, 446)

Western Reserve University (Cleveland, Ohio)
Appointment: Bach, G. R. (BULL, 42, 127)
Appointment: Chapman, J. C. (BULL, 11, 396)
Appointment: Hall, C. S. (SCI, 86, 118; BULL, 34, 326)
Appointment: Holsopple, J. Q. (JoP, 23, 420)
Appointment: Huntley, C. W., Adelbert College (SCI, 94, 512)
Appointment: Ladd, G. T. (SCI, 21, 933; JoP, 2, 364; BULL, 2, 296)
Appointment: MacDougall, R. (REV, 5, 232)
Appointment: Ohmann, O. A. (J APP, 10, 396; SCI, 94, 208)
Appointment: Otis, J. L., Personnel Research Institute (SCI, 94, 208)
Appointment: Sward, K. (J APP, 14, 505)
Appointment: Thorndike, E. L. (REV, 5, 449; J APP, 10, 165)
Course: Hertz, M., Rorschach (J APP, 25, 266)
Course: Ladd, G. T. (BULL, 5, 380)
Course: Rorschach method, 1941 (BULL, 38, 305)
Departure: Thorndike, E. L. (REV, 6, 344)
Donation: Ladd, G. T., library (BULL, 19, 350)
Establishment: Personnel Research Institute, Cleveland College (SCI, 94, 208)

Grant: Beaumont, L. D., hypertension research (SCI, 93, 37)
Laboratory: opens, psychological (SCI, 65, 614)
Lecture: Ladd, G. T., educational psychology (SCI, 28, 481)
Meeting: APA, 21st (BULL, 9, 486)
Promotion: Huntley, C. W. (BULL, 38, 777)

Western Society for Biometricians
Establishment: officers elected, 1941 (BULL, 39, 268-269)

Western Society for Psychical Research
Appointment: committees (SCI°, 6, 78)
Meeting: agenda of first (SCI°, 6, 78)

Western State Psychiatric Hospital (Pittsburgh, Pennsylvania)
Appointment: Rosenzweig, S. (BULL, 40, 618-619)
Internship: psychology available (BULL, 41, 344; BULL, 42, 192)
Name changed to Western State Psychiatric Institute and Clinic (BULL, 42, 487)

Western University (London, Ontario)
Lecture: Montague, W. P. philosophy futurists (JOP, 15, 168)

Western University (Pennsylvania)
Appointment: Huey, E. B. (BULL, 1, 452)
Establishment: psychology dept. (BULL, 1, 452; JOP, 1, 616)

Westminster College
Appointment: Whittenberg, Z. (BULL, 42, 63)

Westminster Review
Contents of July, 1888 issue (SCI°, 12, 70)

Wever, Ernest Glen
Appointment: APA, precautions in animal experiments, legislation (SCI, 77, 189)
Appointment: Princeton Univ. (J APP, 11, 405; SCI, 93, 419)
Appointment: Univ. of California (J APP, 10, 523)
Award: Warren Medal (SCI, 83, 367; BULL, 33, 476)
Grant: National Research Council (BULL, 33, 579)
Lecture: hearing theories with Bray, C. W. (AJP, 44, 192)
Promotion: Princeton Univ. (BULL, 28, 503)

Weyer, Edward Moffat
Appointment: Yale Psychological Laboratory (REV, 4, 452)

Weyl, Hermann
Lecture: Swarthmore College, Cooper, W. J. Lecturer (SCI, 77, 17)

Wheaton College (Norton, Massachusetts)
Appointment: Goldmeier, E. (BULL, 36, 711)

Wheeler, Erma Tilton
Promotion: Univ. of Pittsburgh (BULL, *42*, 581)

Wheeler, Raymond Holder
Appointment: Univ. of Kansas (BULL, *22*, 444)
Election: British Assoc. (SCI, *76*, 252)
Promotion: Univ. of Oregon (SCI, *46*, 288)
Publication: MPA, 9th annual meeting (AJP, *46*, 661)
Publication: MPA, 10th annual meeting (AJP, *47*, 518)
Return: Univ. of Oregon (SCI, *49*, 145; BULL, *16*, 222)

Wheeler, William Morton
Award: Leidy, J. Memorial (BULL, *28*, 324)

Whipple, Edwin Percy
Publication: essays (SCI°, *9*, 436)

Whipple, Guy Montrose
Appointment: Bureau of Salesmanship Research (J APP, *2*, 299; JOP, *13*, 140)
Appointment: Carnegie Institute of Tech. (BULL, *14*, 263; JOP, *15*, 335-336; JOP, *14*, 616; J APP, *2*, 196; BULL, *15*, 176)
Appointment: Cornell Univ. (AJP, *10*, 165-166)
Appointment: International Congress on School Hygiene (SCI, *37*, 625; BULL, *10*, 292)
Appointment: National Research Council (BULL, *14*, 191; J APP, *3*, 393; JOP, *14*, 392; JOP, *16*, 672)
Appointment: Univ. of Illinois (BULL, *11*, 443)
Appointment: Univ. of Michigan (BULL, *16*, 257)
Appointment: Univ. of Southern California (AJP, *10*, 396)
Course: Columbia Univ. (BULL, *8*, 146)
Death notice (AJP, *55*, 132-134)
Editor: *Educational Psychology Monograph* series (BULL, *8*, 406)
Editor: *Journal of Educational Psychology* (JOP, *6*, 700; BULL, *6*, 427)
Election: *Journal of Criminal Law and Criminology*, board (BULL, *8*, 222)
Election: New York State Teachers of Educational Psychology, chair (JOP, *7*, 252)
Grant: General Education Board (BULL, *13*, 407)
Leave of absence: Cornell Univ. (BULL, *9*, 280; JOP, *9*, 364)
Lecture: Univ. of Illinois (BULL, *9*, 360; SCI, *36*, 211)
Promotion: Cornell Univ. (BULL, *8*, 406)
Promotion: Univ. of Illinois (BULL, *12*, 440)
Research: problems of gifted children (J APP, *1*, 298-299)
Resignation: Cornell Univ. (BULL, *11*, 443)
Resignation: Univ. of Illinois (J APP, *2*, 196; BULL, *15*, 176)

White, Andrew Dickson
Publication: *Popular Science Monthly*, the warfare of science (SCI°, *13*, 299)

White, Jesse Hayes
　　Appointment: James Millikan Univ. (Sci, *72*, 87)
　　Appointment: Univ. of Pittsburgh (Sci, *28*, 483; Bull, *5*, 380)

White, Jens Gustav
　　Publication: membership limitations of counselors in Los Angeles Metropolitan
　　　　area (J App, *27*, 366)
　　Publication: personal data blank (J App, *22*, 318)

White, Martin Marshall
　　Appointment: Univ. of Kentucky (Bull, *40*, 539; Sci, *72*, 315)

White, Robert Winthrop
　　Psychological Supper Club (Bull, *37*, 656)

White, Thomas H. Fund
　　Appropriation: Western Reserve Univ. for Personnel Research Institute (Sci,
　　　　94, 208)

White, Wilbert W.
　　Publication: *The Chautauquan*, talks on memory (Sci°, *12*, 250)

White, William Alanson
　　Editor: *Bulletin of the Government Hospital for the Insane* (JoP, *6*, 446)
　　Mental Hygiene anniversary dinner (Sci, *70*, 536)

White, William Alanson Memorial Lectures
　　Sullivan, H. S., 1939, modern psychiatric conceptions (Sci, *90*, 269)

Whitehorn, John Clare
　　Appointment: Johns Hopkins Hospital, Henry Phipps Psychiatric Clinic (Sci,
　　　　93, 493; Sci, *94*, 275)
　　Appointment: Washington Univ., St. Louis (Bull, *35*, 577)
　　Departure: Washington Univ. Medical School (Sci, *94*, 275)

Whitley, Mary Theodora
　　Promotion: Columbia Univ. Teachers College (JoP, *11*, 308)

Whitley, Paul LeRoy
　　Appointment: Colgate Univ. (Sci, *66*, 151)

Whitman, C. D.
　　Appointment: Strong, R. M. research assistant (Sci, *17*, 598)

Whitman College (Walla Walla, Washington)
　　Departure: Howard, C. W. (Bull, *42*, 128)
　　Promotion: Bown, M. D. (Bull, *40*, 723)

Whitney, Arthur E.
Election: American Assoc. on Mental Deficiency, secretary-treasurer (J App, 22, 109)

Whitney, W. C. Foundation
Grant: SPSSI (Bull, 36, 499)

Whitney, William Dwight
Lecture: Sheffield Scientific School, Darwinian theory (Sci°, 1, 293)
Publication: *Encyclopedia Britannica*, philology (Sci°, 5, 162)

Whittemore, Irving Chamberlin
Appointment: Fifth Army in Italy (Bull, 41, 603)

Whitten, Benjamin Otis
Election: American Assoc. on Mental Deficiency, president (J App, 21, 241)

Whittenberg, Zelma
Appointment: Westminster College (Bull, 42, 63)

Whittier State School (California)
Publication: *Journal of Delinquency* (Bull, 13, 296)

Wichita Child Guidance Center (Kansas)
Anniversary, 10th, 1940 (Bull, 38, 126)
Appointment: Carter, Jr., J. W. (Bull, 37, 406; Bull, 38, 777)
Appointment: Hellmer, L. A. (Bull, 39, 196)
Appointment: Herndon, A. (Bull, 40, 79)
Appointment: Martin, M. F. (Bull, 42, 582)
Appointment: Pearson, F. L. (Bull, 42, 582)
Internship: Ibison, R. A. (Bull, 40, 310)
Leave of absence: Hellmer, L. A. (Bull, 40, 79)
Publication: information bulletin (Bull, 41, 410)
Retirement: Cowan, E. A. (Bull, 38, 777)

Wickham, Winfield McCoy
Psychologists Club of San Francisco, founding, president (J App, 25, 129)

Widen, Luther E.
Arctic expedition (Bull, 10, 292)

Wiesbaden
Ziehen, T., build psychological lab (JoP, 9, 140)

Wiggam, Albert Edward
Toastmaster, American Eugenics Society dinner for Holmes, S. J. (Sci, 88, 494)

Wightman, Arthur C.
Appointment: Johns Hopkins Univ. (Sci°, 14, 351)

Wilcox, George Barton
Appointment: Agricultural and Mechanical College of Texas (Bull, *42*, 675-676)

Wilcox, Warren Wesley
Publication: rejoinder to Helson, H. and Fehrer, E. V. (AJP, *44*, 578)

Wilde, Henry
Endowment: Locke, J. scholarship (AJP, *10*, 165)
Endowment: Oxford Univ. (Rev, *5*, 450)

Wilde, Norman
Appointment: Teachers College (Rev, *5*, 109)
Leave of absence: Univ. of Minnesota (JoP, *11*, 280)

Wildermuth, [?]
Research: musical sense in idiots (Sci°, *17*, 353)

Wiley, Lester E.
Grant: National Research Society (Bull, *33*, 579)

Wilhelm, Kaiser
Lecture. Columbia Univ., Krüger, F. (JoP, *9*, 224)
Lecture: Univ. of Illinois (JoP, *10*, 252)
Lecture: Univ. of Wisconsin (JoP, *10*, 252)

Wilhelm's Military Academy (Berlin)
Bust: Helmholtz, H. v., to be erected (Sci, *28*, 792)

Wilkinson, Richard
Leave of absence: Missouri State Teachers College (Bull, *40*, 459)

Will
Lecture: Hoernle, R. F. A., Aristotelian Society (JoP, *10*, 196)
Lecture: Münsterberg, H. (JoP, *1*, 168)
Research: Downey, J. E., profile (J App, *3*, 195)
Research: Tippel, M. and Rieger, C. (Sci°, *6*, 260)

Will, Frederick Ludwig
Research: theory of knowledge (JoP, *42*, 308)

Willamette University (Salem, Oregon)
Appointment: McMurtry, H. C. (Bull, *41*, 603)

William and Mary, College of (Williamsburg, Virginia)
Appointment: Coffey, A. B. (JoP, *2*, 560)

Williams and Wilkins Company (Baltimore, Maryland)
Publication: *Journal of Comparative Psychology* (JoP, *17*, 672)

Williams, A. T. P.
Lecture: National Institute of Industrial Psychology (SCI, *83* 301)

Williams College (Williamstown, Massachusetts)
Appointment: Pratt, J. B. (JOP, *14*, 392; JOP, *2*, 364; BULL, *14*, 191; SCI, *21*, 936)
Centenary celebration, Hopkins, M. inauguration (JOP, *33*, 644)
Degree: Dodge, R. (SCI, *47*, 634)

Williams, Frankwood Earl
Anniversary dinner, mental hygiene (SCI, *70*, 536)
Appointment: National Committee for Mental Hygiene (SCI, *72*, 557)
Election: National Committee for Mental Hygiene, director (SCI, *59*, 60)
Lecture: Taylor Society (JOP, *21*, 700)

Williams, Gertha
Appointment: College of the City of Detroit (J APP, *14*, 638)

Williams, J. Harold
Editor: *Journal of Delinquency* (BULL, *13*, 296; JOP, *13*, 392)

Williams, Mabel Clare
Appointment: Iowa State Univ. (BULL, *4*, 370)
Promotion: Iowa State Univ. (BULL, *7*, 324; JOP, *7*, 560)

Williams, Nesta
Appointment: Central College, Iowa (BULL, *14*, 366)

Williams, Robert Daniel
Appointment: Ohio State Univ. (BULL, *20*, 172)

Williams, Tom Alfred
Election: SSPP, member of council (JOP, *14*, 308)
Lecture: SSPP, psychoses (JOP, *7*, 28)

Williamson, Edmund Griffith
Lecture: Council of Guidance and Personnel Assoc., occupational rehabilitation
of soldiers by army (J APP, *27*, 207)
Publication: outline of graduate course for vocational counselors (J APP, *28*,
352-353)

Willoughby, Raymond Royce
Appointment: Brown Univ. (SCI, *83*, 367)
Death notice (BULL, *41*, 679)
Meeting: Psychological Supper Club (BULL, *37*, 656)
Publication: the meaning of difficulty (AJP, *48*, 167)
Publication: the term abystoma (AJP, *47*, 704)

Wilm, Emil Carl
Appointment: Wells College (BULL, *9*, 408; JOP, *9*, 532)

Course: Bryn Mawr College (BULL, *11*, 190)
Death notice (JoP, *29*, 112)
Departure: Washburn College (BULL, *9*, 408; JoP, *9*, 532)

Wilson College (Chambersburg, Pennsylvania)

Degree: Rand, G. (BULL, *40*, 619)
Promotion: Anderson, E. E. (BULL, *41*, 343)

Wilson, Edwin Bidwell

Editor: *Proceedings of the National Academy of Sciences* (BULL, *12*, 128)
Retirement: Social Science Research Council (SCI, *73*, 358)

Wilson, Milbourne Otto

Appointment: Univ. of Oklahoma (SCI, *95*, 322; BULL, *39*, 423)
Lecture: Guidance Institute of the Univ. of Oklahoma (J APP, *21*, 719)
Promotion: Univ. of Oklahoma (BULL, *24*, 380)

Wilson, Douglas James

Leave of absence: Univ. of Western Ontario (BULL, *42*, 703)

Wiltbank, Rutledge Thornton

Appointment: Univ. of Chicago (BULL, *17*, 116)

Wiltse, Sara Eliza

Research: words (AJP, *3*, 144)

Winch, William Henry

Lecture: experiments with children (JoP, *7*, 420)

Winckler, D. C.

Lecture: Medico-Psychological Assoc. of Great Britain (SCI, *58*, 439)

Wines, Frederick Howard

Editor: *International Record of Charities and Correction* (SCI°, *7*, 300)
Publication: defective, dependent, and delinquent classes (SCI°, *8*, 254-255)

Winkler, Cornelius

Birthday, 80th (SCI, *82*, 58)

Winslow, Charles Edward Amory

Award: Elizabeth Severence Prentiss Award (SCI, *102*, 642)
Lecture: Society of the Sigma Xi, Smith Chapter, science and planning in the
   post-war world (SCI, *101*, 14)
Research: Washington health and hospital facilities (SCI, *101*, 428)
Retirement: Yale Univ. (SCI, *101*, 242)

Winston Simplified Dictionary

Lewis, W. D. and Singer, E. A. (J APP, *3*, 194-195)

Winter, John
Appointment: Univ. of North Dakota (BULL, *13*, 148)

Wisconsin
Education: deaf-mutes (SCI°, *5*, 324)

Wisconsin Academy of Sciences
Meeting: Dec., 1884 (SCI°, *5*, 60-61)

Wisconsin State Normal School (Stevens Point)
Appointment: Quantz, J. O. (SCI, *14*, 744)
Appointment: Spindler, F. N. (REV, *8*, 656-657; SCI, *14*, 424)

Wisconsin, University of (Madison)
Anniversary, 50th psychology lab (BULL, *35*, 188; J APP, *22*, 106; SCI, *87*, 435)
Anniversary: 100th, James', W. (JoP, *38*, 616)
Appointment: Boswell, F. P. (SCI, *20*, 616; JoP, *1*, 644; BULL, *1*, 488)
Appointment: Cameron, N. (SCI, *91*, 593; BULL, *37*, 656)
Appointment: Cason, H. (BULL, *27*, 564)
Appointment: Dearborn, W. F. (JoP, *2*, 448)
Appointment: Farnsworth, P. R. (J APP, *22*, 106)
Appointment: Henmon, V. A. C. (BULL, *7*, 148; JoP, *7*, 224)
Appointment: Koffka, K. (J APP, *10*, 523; BULL, *23*, 456; SCI, *64*, 118; JoP, *23*, 504)
Appointment: Kuhlmann, F. (BULL, *2*, 296)
Appointment: McGilvary, E. B. (BULL, *2*, 224)
Appointment: Norton, F. P. (BULL, *1*, 488)
Appointment: Starch, D. (JoP, *5*, 644; BULL, *5*, 379)
Changes in Dept. of Philosophy (JoP, *2*, 364)
Course: Jastrow, J., mental evolution (SCI, *15*, 216)
Departure: Beier, D. C. (BULL, *42*, 791)
Departure: Coffey, A. B. (JoP, *2*, 560)
Departure: Young, K. (SCI, *91*, 138)
Degree: Dewey, J. (JoP, *1*, 391, 448)
Degree: Morgan, C. L. (JoP, *1*, 252)
Degree: Titchener, E. B. (JoP, *1*, 391, 448)
Leave of absence: Husband, R. W. (BULL, *38*, 304)
Leave of absence: Jastrow, J. (J APP, *10*, 523)
Leave of absence: Oshea, M. V. (BULL, *3*, 148)
Leave of absence: Rothney, J. W. M. (BULL, *39*, 895)
Leave of absence: Starch, D. (JoP, *16*, 644)
Lecture: Eeden, F. van, mental health (SCI, *29*, 541)
Lecture: Jastrow, J., subconsciousness (SCI, *27*, 237; SCI, *34*, 755; BULL, *9*, 359; JoP, *9*, 28; BULL, *8*, 438)
Lecture: Krüger, F. (SCI, *37*, 407; JoP, *10*, 252)
Lecture: points of view in psychology (SCI, *69*, 450)
Lecture: Wilhelm, K. (JoP, *10*, 252)

Meeting: MPA (Sci, 87, 84; Bull, 35, 188; Bull, 25, 307)
Meeting: WPA (JoP, 3, 252)
Promotion: Dockeray, F. C. (Sci, 37, 907)
Promotion: Starch, D. (Sci, 35, 984)
Resignation: Dearborn, W. F. (Sci, 29, 698)
Retirement: Jastrow, J. (Sci, 66, 148)
Return: Jastrow, J. (Rev, 6, 456)
Symposium: commemorating James', W. birth (JoP, 38, 616)
Trip: Jastrow, J. to Europe (Sci, 19, 317)

Wissler, Clark

Appointment: Columbia Univ. (Rev, 6, 673)
Appointment: New York Univ. (Rev, 9, 104)
Appointment: NRC, Division of Anthropology and Psychology (JoP, 17, 672)
Appointment: NYAS (JoP, 9, 28)
Appointment: Yale Univ. (J App, 8, 450)
Departure: Ohio State Univ. (Rev, 6, 673)
Lecture: NYAS, ergograph experiments (Sci, 15, 547)
Lecture: NYAS, the growth of boys (Sci, 15, 627)

Wistar, Issac Jones

Trip: Mediterranean and Orient (Sci, 19, 275)

Witasek, Stephan

Death notice (JoP, 12, 392; Sci, 41, 860; AJP, 26, 472; Bull, 12, 280)

Witkin, Herman Allen

Fellowship: National Research Council (Bull, 40, 539-540)

Witmer, Lightner

Anniversary: 35th, commemorative volume presentation (Sci, 75, 75)
Appointment: American Red Cross (Bull, 14, 420)
Appointment: Lehigh Univ. (Rev, 10, 690)
Course: Bryn Mawr College (Rev, 3, 356)
Election: APA (JoP, 2, 28)
Establishment: laboratory at Lehigh Univ. (JoP, 2, 364)
Honorary dinner (Sci, 65, 11)
Leave of absence: Univ. of Pennsylvania (Sci, 46, 612; Sci, 12, 735)
Lecture: gifted children (Sci, 36, 862)
Lecture: International Congress of Psychology, 6th (Sci, 30, 202)
Lecture: Principal's Conference (Sci, 39, 530)
Lecture: Sigma Xi (Sci, 41, 203)
Lecture: Univ. of Pennsylvania, Medical Dept. (JoP, 6, 168; Bull, 6, 120)
Retirement: Univ. of Pennsylvania (Bull, 34, 635)
Return: Univ. of Pennsylvania (Sci, 48, 414)

Witmer School (Devon, Pennsylvania)

(Bull, 34, 635)

Wittels, Fritz
Publication: revision of a biography on Freud (AJP, *45*, 745)

Wittenberg University (Springfield, Ohio)
Appointment: Bishop, H. G. (J App, *10*, 522; Bull, *23*, 456)
Appointment: Bishop, M. K. (J App, *10*, 522; Bull, *23*, 456)
Departure: West, W. D. (Bull, *42*, 331)
Laboratory: psychology (AJP, *40*, 171)

Witty, Paul Andrew
Lecture: vocational counseling (AJP, *44*, 801)
Publication: faculty psychology and personality traits (AJP, *46*, 500)

Wohlbrecht Foundation, The
Award: Gegenbaur, C., Univ. of Göttingen (Sci, *11*, 716-717)

Wolf, Abraham
Lecture: British Psychological Society. Aristotelian Society, Mind Assoc.,
repression (JoP, *11*, 532)

Wolf children of India (*see* Feral children)

Wolf, Irvin Simon
Anniversary: Indiana Univ. Psych. Lab, 50th (J App, *23*, 631)

Wolf, Käthe
Course: Univ. of Vienna (Bull, *34*, 410)

Wolfe, Harry Kirke
Anniversary: Univ. of Nebraska, 50th, psychology lab (Bull, *36*, 304; Sci, *89*
150)
Appointment: Univ. of Montana (Sci, *21*, 968; Bull, *2*, 296; JoP, *2*, 392)
Appointment: Univ. of Nebraska (Bull, *2*, 426; JoP, *3*, 56)
Fellowship: Nebraska, fund raising for memorial (JoP, *16*, 672)
Lecture: Alexander, H. B., remembrance sketch (JoP, *15*, 532)
Resignation: Univ. of Nebraska (Rev, *4*, 452; AJP, *9*, 135)

Wolfe, John Bascom
Appointment: Univ. of Mississippi (Bull, *33*, 578)

Wolfe, Ralph P.
Appointment: Yale Univ. (Sci, *96*, 225)

Wolffhügel, Gustav
Death notice (Sci, *9*, 301)

Wolfle, Dael Lee
Appointment: APA, executive secretary (Bull, *42*, 676)
Appointment: Univ. of Chicago (J App, *23*, 311)

Departure: Mississippi (BULL, *33*, 578)
Election: MPA, council (J APP, *25*, 266)
Lecture: Minnesota Chapter of Psi Chi (BULL, *40*, 310)
Meeting: National Research Council (BULL, *37*, 755)

Wollenberg, Robert
Appointment: Strasburg (SCI, *24*, 352)

Wolters, Albert William Phillips
Election: British Assoc., president, section J, psychology (SCI, *83*, 29)

Woman's Canadian Club
Lecture: Montague, W. P., political outlook (JoP, *15*, 168)

Women
Admittance: German universities (JoP, *5*, 504)
Award: National Assoc. of Women in Education (J APP, *28*, 80, 531)
Lecture: Wright, C. D., "condition of the working girl" (SCI°, *4*, 450)
Research: Bregman, E. (J APP, *10*, 393)

Women Psychologists, National Council of
Meeting: Columbia Univ. (BULL, *42*, 487)
Organization (BULL, *39*, 808-809)

Women's Christian Temperance Union, National
Appropriation: Iowa Child Welfare Research Station (J APP, *3*, 304-305)

Wonderlic Personnel Test
Publication: forms A and B (J APP, *27*, 207)

Wood, Casey Albert
Editor: *Carry On* (BULL, *15*, 176)

Wood, Dorothy Adkins (*see* Adkins, Dorothy)

Wood, L.
Lecture: Mass. School for Feeble-minded (BULL, *13*, 407-408)

Woodbridge, Frederick James Eugene
Appointment: Amherst College (BULL, *4*, 128)
Appointment: Berlin (JoP, *28*, 308)
Appointment: Columbia Univ. (SCI, *15*, 440; SCI, *35*, 926)
Death notice (JoP, *37*, 336)
Departure: Univ. of Minnesota (SCI, *15*, 440)
Election: American Philosophical Assoc., president (JoP, *8*, 27-28, 699; SCI, *33*, 22)
Lecture: Locke, J. (JoP, *1*, 616)
Lecture: NYAS/APA, secondary qualities (JoP, *7*, 700)

Woodbridge Memorial Lectures
Sheldon, W. H., Columbia Univ. (JoP, *40*, 168)

Woodburne, Angus Stewart
Publication: mental tests (JoP, *21*, 364)

Woodger, Joseph Henry
Lecture: International Congress for the Unity of Science (JoP, *35*, 504)

Woodman, J. Edmund
Election: NYAS, officer (JoP, *9*, 28)

Woodrow, Herbert Hollingsworth
Appointment: Barnard College, Columbia (BULL, *4*, 336; SCI, *29*, 455; JoP, *6*, 252; BULL, *6*, 152)
Appointment: Princeton Univ. (JoP, *4*, 196; BULL, *4*, 64)
Appointment: Univ. of Illinois (BULL, *25*, 444; SCI, *68*, 58)
Appointment: Univ. of Minnesota (BULL, 7, 147; JoP, 7, 223-224; BULL, *14*, 333; JoP, *14*, 644)
Election: AAAS, vice-president (BULL, *40*, 458)
Election: APA, council of directors (BULL, *26*, 56)
Election: APA, president (J APP, *24*, 855)
Lecture: APA, problem of general quantitative laws in psychology (SCI, *94*, 230)
Lecture: pitch in rhythm (JoP, *7*, 223)
Lecture: retardation (JoP, *7*, 223)

Woods, Andrew H.
Retirement: State Univ. of Iowa, College of Medicine (SCI, *94*, 297)

Woods, Elizabeth Lindley
Appointment: Child Welfare, Pasadena, California (BULL, *14*, 116; JoP, *13*, 644)
Promotion: Vassar College (BULL, *13*, 376; JoP, *13*, 588)
Resignation: Vassar College (JoP, *13*, 644)

Woods, James Haughton
Promotion: Harvard Univ. (BULL, *5*, 244)

Woods School (Langhorne, Pennsylvania) (*see also* Child Research Clinic)
Conference: Education and the Exceptional Child (J APP, *22*, 215, 317)

Woodworth, Robert Sessions
Anniversary: Columbia Univ., 50th (BULL, *39*, 326)
Appointment: Columbia Univ. (SCI, *17*, 800)
Appointment: Columbia Univ. and Bellevue Hospital and Medical College (REV, *6*, 673)
Appointment: New York State Assoc. of Consulting Psychologists (SCI, *54*, 112)
Appointment: Social Science Research Council (BULL, *28*, 255; SCI, *73*, 230)

Birthday: 70th, Columbia Univ. (Sci, *90*, 368)

Degree: Lake Erie College (Sci, *80*, 30)

Editor: *Archives of Psychology* (JoP, *3*, 644; Bull, *3*, 422)

Editor: *Bulletin*, section of (Bull, *11*, 396; Bull, *7*, 364; Bull, *13*, 407; Bull, *16*, 32, 391)

Election: APA, president (Sci, *39*, 94)

Election: Carnegie Institute, president (JoP, *1*, 721)

Election: International Congress of Arts and Sciences, secretary (JoP, *1*, 532)

Election: NYAS, officer (JoP, *9*, 28; Bull, *18*, 111, 296; Bull, *17*, 116)

Election: Social Science Research Council, member at large (JoP, *26*, 336)

Laboratories: Louisiana Purchase Exposition (JoP, *1*, 84)

Leave of absence: Columbia Univ. (JoP, *9*, 140; Bull, *9*, 95)

Lecture: American Museum of Natural History, dynamic psychology (Sci, *44*, 745)

Lecture: Cattell jubilee (AJP, *25*, 468)

Lecture: Clark Univ. (Sci, *62*, 561)

Lecture: color (JoP, *1*, 224; JoP, *2*, 112)

Lecture: Columbia Univ. (Sci, *26*, 485)

Lecture: Columbia Univ., 50th anniversary (Sci, *95*, 190)

Lecture: Connecticut College (Sci, *91*, 188)

Lecture: Connecticut Valley Assoc. of Psychologists (Bull, *37*, 257)

Lecture: Jesup lectures (JoP, *14*, 56)

Lecture: motor strength (JoP, *1*, 644)

Lecture: New York Acad. of Sciences, heredity and environment (Sci, *92*, 451)

Lecture: vision (JoP, *2*, 700)

Meeting: National Research Council, psychological factors in national morale (Bull, *37*, 829)

Membership: National Institute of Psychology (Bull, *27*, 736)

Promotion: Columbia Univ. (Sci, *29*, 455; JoP, *6*, 252; Bull, *6*, 152; Bull, *2*, 160; Sci, *21*, 480; JoP, *2*, 196)

Publication: Franz, S. I. obituary (AJP, *45*, 151)

Publication: introduction to commemorative volume presented to Terman, L. M. (Sci, *95*, 117-118)

Publication: *Psychological Issues: Selected Papers of Woodworth, R. S.* (Bull, *37*, 61)

Publication: report on Anthropology and Psychology section of NYAS (Sci, *15*, 309-310, 547, 627)

Resignation: *Psychological Bulletin* (Bull, *22*, 444)

Retirement: Columbia Univ. (Sci, *95*, 476; Bull, *39*, 423)

Woolley, Helen Bradford Thompson

Appointment: Columbia Univ. Institute of Child Welfare Research (Bull, *22*, 612; Sci, *62*, 81; J App, *9*, 319)

Appointment: Merrill-Palmer School of Detroit (J App, *9*, 203, 319)

Appointment: Univ. of Cincinnati (JoP, *7*, 644)

Election: APA, chair (Bull, *23*, 112)

Lecture: Child Study Assoc. of America (J APP, 9, 319)
Lecture: National Vocational Guidance Assoc. (J APP, 6, 425)

Worcester, Dean Amory
Appointment: Ohio Univ. (J APP, 10, 288)
Appointment: Univ. of Nebraska (SCI, 66, 78)
Appointment: Univ. of New Mexico (BULL, 11, 444; SCI, 40, 379; JOP, 11, 560)
Travel: Philippines (SCI, 9, 228)

Worcester State Hospital (Massachusetts)
Internship: available (BULL, 42, 408; SCI, 90, 204)

Words
Research: Wiltse, S. E. (AJP, 3, 144)

Workman, William Gatewood
Promotion: Emory Univ. (BULL, 40, 794)

World's Fair (New York) (see New York World's Fair)

World's Fair (St. Louis) (see Saint Louis World's Fair)

Wortis, Sam Bernard
Appointment: New York Univ., College of Medicine and Bellevue Hospital (SCI, 96, 293)

Wrenn, Charles Gilbert
Appointment: AAAP, officer (SCI, 99, 34)
Leave of absence: Univ. of Minnesota (BULL, 39, 808)

Wreschner, Arthur
Lecture: inaugural (REV, 7, 428)

Wright, Carroll Davidson
Death notice (BULL, 6, 120)
Lecture: "condition of the working girl" (SCI°, 4, 450)
Research: marriage and divorce (SCI°, 9, 411)
Research: social, sanitary and economic condition of working women (SCI°, 12, 227)

Wright, Charlotte A.
Appointment: Centenary Junior College (BULL, 41, 200)

Wright, Henry Wilkes
Lecture: dualism in psychology (AJP, 53, 121-128)

Wrightstone, Jacob Wayne
Tests of critical thinking in the social studies (J APP, 23, 421)

Wright, William Kelley
Appointment: Univ. of Texas (JoP, *3*, 532; Sci, *24*, 384; Bull, *3*, 319)
Departure: Univ. of Chicago (Sci, *24*, 384)

Wrinch, Frank Sidney
Appointment: Carnegie Institution (Sci, *17*, 558; Rev, *10*, 344)
Appointment: Princeton Univ. (Rev, *9*, 644)
Appointment: Univ. of California (Rev, *10*, 464)
Departure: Princeton Univ. (Sci, *17*, 558)

Writing
Lecture: Harris, J. H., composition (JoP, *7*, 223)
Lecture: Kline, L. W., process (JoP, *7*, 223)

Wronker, Dorothy I.
Rochester Guidance Clinic, New York, mental hygiene (Bull, *36*, 841)

Wulf, Maurice Marie Charles Joseph de
Publication: *Civilisation et Philosophie au moyen age* (JoP, *15*, 644)

Wulfeck, Wallace Howard
Appointment: Federal Advertising Agency of New York (Bull, *40*, 152; Sci, *96*, 512; J App, *26*, 857)
Appointment: Psychological Corporation (Bull, *36*, 805)
Departure: Psychological Corporation (J App, *26*, 857)
Election: Assoc. for Applied Psychology of New York, president (Sci, *100*, 27)
Meeting: psychology Corporation, APA and AAAP (J App, *25*, 600)

Wundt, Eleonore
Call for letters from Wundt, W. (Bull, *24*, 80)

Wundt, Wilhelm Max
Anniversary celebration: Leipzig (Bull, *29*, 603)
Anniversary: 50th (JoP, *2*, 721; Bull, *3*, 36; Sci, *22*, 806)
Award: Knight of the Prussian order (Bull, *9*, 208; JoP, *9*, 224; Sci, *35*, 448)
Award: renounces honors from English universities (Sci, *40*, 478; JoP, *11*, 588)
Award: Stiftung, to Univ. of Leipzig in honor of Wundt (Sci, *36*, 271)
Award: Title of Excellency and made an honorary citizen of the City of Leipzig (Sci, *30*, 402; JoP, *6*, 560; Sci, *16*, 558)
Birthday: 70th (Rev, *7*, 427; AJP, *13*, 456; Sci, *12*, 38; Rev, *9*, 643-644; Sci, *16*, 398)
Birthday: 80th (Bull, *9*, 360; AJP, *23*, 595; Sci, *36*, 271)
Birthday: centennial (Sci, *76*, 230)
Death notice (Sci, *52*, 246; AJP, *32*, 154; Bull, *17*, 351)
Degree: Univ. of Budapest (Sci, *3*, 865)
Election: Berlin Acad. of Sciences (Rev, *7*, 323)
Election: Munich Acad. of Sciences (Sci, *12*, 933)
Election: NAS, foreign assoc. (Sci, *29*, 694; JoP, *6*, 308, 504; Bull, *6*, 184)

Election: Paris Institut, Acad. of Moral and Political Sciences (REV, *3*, 355)
Election: St. Petersburg Acad. of Sciences (SCI, *17*, 276)
Equipment for Leipzig laboratory (SCI, *36*, 342)
Lecture: Columbia Univ., Hall, G. S. (JoP, *9*, 56; SCI, *35*, 101)
Lecture: Pillsbury, W. B., the Wundt centenary (AJP, *45*, 176)
Lecture: Univ. of Leipzig (JoP, *6*, 560)
Portrait of (AJP, *9*, 422)
Publication: call for letters from (BULL, *24*, 80)
Publication: *Grundriss der Psychologie* (SCI, *3*, 353)
Publication: *Lectures on Human and Animal Psychology* (SCI°, *23*, 96)
Publication: *Outline of Psychology* (AJP, *7*, 452)
Publication: translation of *Ethik* (REV, *3*, 588)
Publication: translation of *Physiologische Psychologie* (REV, *3*, 588)
Publication: translations of (AJP, *7*, 579; REV, *3*, 356; SCI, *4*, 269)

Würzburg, University of (Germany)
Appointment: Frey, M. von (AJP, *11*, 130)
Appointment: Külpe, O. (REV, *2*, 104; AJP, *7*, 152)
Appointment: Marbe, K. (JoP, *7*, 84; SCI, *17*, 320; BULL, *6*, 368)
Departure: Külpe, O. (JoP, *7*, 84)
Meeting: German Congress for Experimental Psychology (JoP, *2*, 720)

Wyatt, Frederick
Appointment: McLean Hospital (BULL, *41*, 679)

Wyatt, Horace Graham
Lecture: sex differences (AJP, *44*, 361)

Wyatt, Stanley
Appointment: Univ. of Manchester (SCI, *54*, 575)

Wyoming, University of (Laramie)
Appointment: Barnes, J. (SCI, *67*, 13)
Appointment: Barton, J. W. (BULL, *18*, 111)
Appointment: Bayley, N. (J APP, *10*, 523)
Appointment: Downey, J. E. (REV, *7*, 216, 324)
Appointment: Rahn, C. L. (BULL, *11*, 268; JoP, *11*, 721)
Appointment: Uhrbrock, R. S. (J APP, *11*, 165)
Appointment: Wagoner, L. C. (JoP, *19*, 476)
Degree: Anderson, J. E. (BULL, *39*, 682)
Leave of absence: Downey, J. E. (BULL, *19*, 410; JoP, *19*, 476; BULL, *11*, 268; JoP, *11*, 721; SCI, *56*, 73)
Leave of absence: Uhrbrock, R. S. (J APP, *10*, 523)
Seminar to honor Downey, J. E. (BULL, *40*, 540; J APP, *27*, 363; AJP, *56*, 449)

Y

Yager, Jay Lewis
Appointment: State Public Schools, Owatonna, Minnesota (BULL, 39, 325)

Yale Association of Japan
Reception: Ladd, G. T. (BULL, 3, 422; SCI, 24, 671)

Yale Corporation
Resignation: Ladd, G. T. (SCI, 20, 96; BULL, 1, 333)

Yale Laboratories of Primate Biology (see also Anthropoid Station)
Appointment: Yerkes, R. M. (SCI, 89, 266)
Grant: Rockefeller Foundation (SCI, 89, 266)
Lecture: Snyder, L. H., heredity in apes and humans (SCI, 97, 398)

Yale Laboratory of Applied Physiology
Establishment: clinic for inebriates with Connecticut Prison Assoc. (SCI, 99, 99)

Yale Medical School
Appointment: Ruggles, A. H. (SCI, 62, 396)
Establishment: Connecticut Psychopathic Hospital (SCI, 54, 246)

Yale Psychological Laboratory
Appointment: acting director (JoP, 1, 28)
Appointment: advisory committee (JoP, 1, 28)
Appointment: Matsumoto, M. (REV, 4, 452)
Appointment: Weyer, E. M. (REV, 4, 452)
Departure: Steele, W. M. (JoP, 1, 364)
Departure: Weigle, L. A. (JoP, 2, 280)
Invents device to convert electrical current voltages (SCI, 1, 724)
Publication: photographic investigation of eye movements (JoP, 1, 84)

Yale University (New Haven, Connecticut)

Appointment: Adams, D. K. (BULL, 22, 444)

Appointment: Angell, J. R. (BULL, 18, 236)

Appointment: Angier, R. P. (SCI, 50, 590; JoP, 3, 196; BULL, 35, 61; BULL, 22, 612; BULL, 17, 116; BULL, 3, 147; SCI, 86, 438; J APP, 8, 450)

Appointment: Bagby, E. (SCI, 52, 223)

Appointment: Banay, R. (SCI, 99, 99)

Appointment: Bingham, H. C. (BULL, 22, 444; SCI, 61, 388)

Appointment: Breed, F. S. (JoP, 7, 196, 252; BULL, 7, 148)

Appointment: Brown, J. S. (SCI, 94, 62; BULL, 38, 907)

Appointment: Burnham, P. S. (SCI, 96, 225)

Appointment: Cameron, E. H. (JoP, 3, 196; BULL, 3, 147; SCI, 23, 520)

Appointment: Cassirer, E. (JoP, 38, 168)

Appointment: Chapman, J. C. (SCI, 59, 398)

Appointment: DeSilva, H. R. (SCI, 88, 471)

Appointment: Dodge, R. (J APP, 8, 450)

Appointment: Doob, L. W. (SCI, 80, 137)

Appointment: Elliott, R. M. (BULL, 12, 243; JoP, 12, 504)

Appointment: French, R. L. (SCI, 94, 62; BULL, 38, 907)

Appointment: Frost, E. P. (JoP, 7, 560; BULL, 7, 220)

Appointment: Fry, C. C. (SCI, 99, 99)

Appointment: Henmon, V.A.C. (SCI, 63, 425)

Appointment: Hiscock, I. V. (SCI, 101, 242)

Appointment: Hocking, W. E. (BULL, 4, 128)

Appointment: Hovland, C. I. (SCI, 94, 62; BULL, 38, 907)

Appointment: Judd, C. H. (SCI, 18, 352, 768; JoP, 4, 252; SCI, 22, 848; SCI, 15, 360; JoP, 3, 56; BULL, 3, 56; SCI, 25, 360)

Appointment: Kurtz, A. K. (SCI, 96, 225)

Appointment: Lord, E. E. (BULL, 20, 288; SCI, 56, 602)

Appointment: Marquis, D. G. (SCI, 94, 62; BULL, 38, 907)

Appointment: Marshall, H. R. (SCI, 23, 480; JoP, 3, 196)

Appointment: McAllister, C. N. (SCI, 13, 600)

Appointment: Melton, A. W. (SCI, 80, 137)

Appointment: Miles, C. C. (SCI, 73, 491; SCI, 74, 308; BULL, 28, 412; SCI, 71, 600)

Appointment: Miles, W. R. (SCI, 73, 491; SCI, 74, 308; BULL, 28, 412; SCI, 71, 600)

Appointment: Monroe, P. (BULL, 3, 422)

Appointment: Palmer, G. H. (JoP, 3, 196)

Appointment: Riesen, A. H. (SCI, 96, 225)

Appointment: Robinson, E. S. (J APP, 10, 395; BULL, 23, 455; BULL, 24, 380; J APP, 11, 234)

Appointment: Roe, A. (SCI, 99, 99)

Appointment: Sarason, S. B. (BULL, 42, 675)

Appointment: Scofield, C. F. (BULL, 22, 444)

Appointment: Scripture, E. W. (SCI°, 19, 313)

Appointment: Spence, K. W. (SCI, 96, 268)

Meeting: APA/American Philosophical Assoc. (JoP, *11*, 56)
Meeting: Inter-American Conference of Philosophy (JoP, *40*, 280)
Meeting: International Congress of Psychology (Sci, *70*, 254)
Meeting: National Acad. of Sciences (Sci, *74*, 481)
Meeting: NYAS and New York Branch of APA (JoP, *2*, 223)
Portrait presented of Angier, R. P. (Sci, *94*, 61; Bull, *38*, 907)
Portrait: Dodge, R. (Bull, *33*, 581)
Promotion: Anderson, J. E. (Bull, *18*, 296; Sci, *53*, 456)
Promotion: Angier, R. P. (JoP, *5*, 168; Bull, *14*, 191; Bull, *5*, 96)
Promotion: Bagby, E. (Sci, *55*, 427)
Promotion: Cameron, E. H. (JoP, *7*, 196, 252; Bull, *7*, 148)
Promotion: Chapman, C. (Bull, *21*, 360)
Promotion: Duncan, G. M. (Rev, *1*, 552)
Promotion: Haggard, H. W. (Sci, *87*, 482)
Promotion: Judd, C. H. (Bull, *4*, 128)
Promotion: McAllister, C. N. (Rev, *8*, 447)
Promotion: Newhall, S. (Bull, *27*, 660)
Promotion: Riesen, A. H. (Bull, *39*, 807)
Promotion: Scripture, E. W. (Sci, *13*, 480)
Promotion: Spencer, L. (Bull, *23*, 236; Sci, *63*, 279)
Publication: child development films (J App, *18*, 722)
Research: DeSilva, H. R., automobile drivers (J App, *22*, 664; Bull, *36*, 140)
Research: Humphreys, L. G., national fellow (Sci, *90*, 391)
Resignation: Judd, C. H. (Bull, *5*, 347)
Resignation: Ladd, G. T. (Sci, *21*, 933; Bull, *2*, 296; JoP, *1*, 336, 420)
Resignation: Peter, W. W. (Sci, *101*, 504)
Resignation: Scripture, E. W. (Rev, *10*, 690; Sci, *18*, 352)
Retirement: Angell, J. R. (Sci, *85*, 195)
Retirement: Angier, R. P. (Sci, *94*, 61; Bull, *38*, 907; Sci, *93*, 276; Bull, *38*, 777)
Retirement: Winslow, C. E. A. (Sci, *101*, 242)
Return: Ladd, G. T., from Japan (Sci, *26*, 805)
Symposium: Galileo and Newton tercentenary, 1942 (JoP, *39*, 698-699)

Yale University Press
Publication: *Authority in the Modern State*, Laski (JoP, *15*, 532)

Yarborough, Joseph Ussery
Appointment: Merit Council of the Unemployment Compensation Commission of Texas (Bull, *38*, 304)
Appointment: Univ. of Texas (Sci, *46*, 360; Bull, *14*, 263, 334)
Leave of absence: Southern Methodist Univ. (Bull, *38*, 304)
Return: Southern Methodist Univ. (Bull, *40*, 539)

Yeager, Edgar L.
Anniversary: Indiana Univ. Psych. Lab, 50th commemoration (J App, *23*, 631)

Yearbook of Psychology
Publication: announcement (Bull, *40*, 620)

Yenching University (China)
Chinese Journal of Psychology founded (AJP, *49*, 142)

Yerkes Laboratories for Primate Biology (*see* Yale Laboratories of Primate Biology)

Yerkes, Robert Mearns
Appointment: *Acta Psychologica* (AJP, *48*, 174)
Appointment: Army War College (Sci, *57*, 144)
Appointment: *Journal of Comparative Neurology and Psychology* (JoP, *1*, 195)
Appointment: National Research Council (J App, *3*, 393; Bull, *14*, 191; JoP, *14*, 392)
Appointment: National Research Council, Emergency Committee in Psychology (Bull, *37*, 755)
Appointment: National Research Council for Research in Problems of Sex (Sci, *91*, 140; Bull, *40*, 231)
Appointment: Univ. of Minnesota (Bull, *14*, 191; JoP, *14*, 392; Sci, *45*, 500)
Appointment: Yale Laboratories of Primate Biology (Sci, *89*, 266)
Appointment: Yale Univ. (J App, *8*, 450)
Award: Boyleston Medical Prize (JoP, *2*, 224)
Commission: U.S. Army Sanitary Corps (Bull, *14*, 333; JoP, *14*, 672)
Degree: Wesleyan Univ. (Bull, *21*, 240; Sci, *57*, 737)
Editor: *Journal of Animal Behavior* (Bull, *17*, 435)
Editor: *Journal of Comparative Psychology* (JoP, *17*, 672)
Election: APA, council (JoP, *7*, 56)
Election: APA, president (Bull, *14*, 32)
Election: International Congress of Arts and Sciences (JoP, *1*, 532)
Election: National Research Council, Special Committee (JoP, *16*, 672)
Lecture: APA (JoP, *8*, 699-700; Sci, *34*, 680)
Lecture: behavior of higher organisms (Sci, *21*, 798)
Lecture: Brown Univ., Sigma Xi (Sci, *82*, 590)
Lecture: International Congress of Psychology (Sci, *30*, 202)
Lecture: Intersociety Constitutional Convention (J App, *27*, 365)
Lecture: Johns Hopkins Univ. Scientific Assoc., comparative psychology (Sci, *29*, 853)
Lecture: Massachussetss School for Feeble-minded (Bull, *13*, 407-408)
Lecture: National Research Council, report of the psychology committee (JoP, *16*, 307-308)
Lecture: New York Acad. of Medicine, psychological examinations of soldiers (Sci, *49*, 89)
Lecture: School of Tropical Medicine of Univ. of Puerto Rico (Sci, *87*, 136-137)

Lecture: Univ. of Minnesota, psychology methods of diagnosis (Sci, *45*, 138; JoP, *14*, 168)

Meeting: National Research Council Conference, psychological factors in national morale (Bull, *37*, 829)

Promotion: Harvard Univ. (Bull, *5*, 244; Sci, *27*, 904)

Publication: mental tests in the military (JoP, *18*, 420; JoP, *20*, 280)

Publication: methods of studying vision in animals, Watson, J. B. (JoP, *8*, 559-560)

Publication: reports appointees for psychological examining in the national army (J App, *1*, 394)

Publication: summary report from psychology committee of the National Research Council (J App, *1*, 394-395)

Research: requests for aid in problems of sex research (Sci, *89*, 126)

Return: London (Bull, *17*, 435)

Yoakum, Clarence Stone

Appointment: Carnegie Institute of Tech. (JoP, *16*, 336; J App, *3*, 290)

Appointment: Univ. of Michigan (Bull, *21*, 428)

Appointment: Univ. of Texas (Sci, *28*, 48; Bull, *14*, 263; JoP, *5*, 392; Bull, *5*, 243; JoP, *14*, 504)

Death notice (Bull, *42*, 790)

Editor: *Journal of Personnel Research* (Bull, *19*, 462)

Lecture: Taylor Society, experimental psychology in personnel problems (J App, *9*, 204)

Promotion: Carnegie Institute of Tech. (Bull, *16*, 257)

Yoder, James Willard

Election: All Saints Episcopal Cathedral (Bull, *41*, 136)

Yokum, A. Duncan

Appointment: Univ. of Pennsylvania (Sci, *24*, 448)

Youmans, Edward Livingstone memorial volume

Publication: Youmans, W. J. and E. A. (Sci°, *9*, 482)

Youmans, Eliza Ann

Publication: memorial volume of Youmans, E. L. containing manuscripts and letters (Sci°, *9*, 482)

Youmans, William Jay

Publication: memorial volume of Youmans, E. L. containing manuscripts and letters (Sci°, *9*, 482)

Young, Frederic Harold

Lecture: Peirce, C. S. (JoP, *42*, 672)

Young, George M.

Publication: his work with disabled soldiers (J App, *2*, 385-386)

Young, Herman H.
Appointment: Children's Service Bureau (J App, *3*, 289)
Appointment: Indiana Univ. (Bull, *19*, 462)
Death notice (Bull, *28*, 254; AJP, *43*, 304)

Young, Kimball
Appointment: Queens College, Flushing, N.Y. (Sci, *91*, 138)
Appointment: Univ. of Oregon (Bull, *20*, 664)
Departure: Univ. of Wisconsin (Sci, *91*, 138)
Grant: Social Science Research Council (Bull, *31*, 380)
Lecture: Child Study Assoc. of America (J App, *16*, 438)
Meeting: APA, Wash. Balt. Branch, 1940 (Bull, *37*, 405)
Publication: *German Psychological Warfare* (J App, *25*, 359)
Return: Univ. of Oregon (Sci, *57*, 556)

Young, Mary Hoover
Death notice (Bull, *31*, 79)

Young, Paul Campbell
Appointment: Louisiana Legislative Council (Bull, *41*, 199)
Promotion: Louisiana State Univ. (Bull, *41*, 72)

Young, Paul Thomas
Appointment: Univ. of Illinois (Sci, *54*, 53; Bull, *18*, 438; Bull, *19*, 63)
Grant: Committee on Scientific Research of the American Medical Assoc., appetites and food preferences in rats (Sci, *94*, 460)
Fellowship: Board of National Research Fellowships (Bull, *23*, 292)
Leave of absence: Univ. of Illinois (Bull, *23*, 412; Bull, *37*, 61)

Young, Thomas Oration
Bartlett, F. C., some current problems in visual functions and visual perception (Sci, *97*, 577)

Youtz, Richard Pardee
Appointment: Barnard College (Bull, *34*, 635)

Z

Zabriskie, Edwin G.
Election: Assoc. for Research in Nervous and Mental Diseases, president (SCI, 81, 42)

Zachry, Caroline Beaumont
Death notice (BULL, 42, 255)
Nomination: director of Bureau of Child Guidance of the New York City School System (SCI, 94, 537)

Zeitschrift für Angewandte Psychologie und Psychologische Psychologie Sammelforschung
Evolves from the *Beiträge zur Psychologie der Aussage* (AJP, 18, 529)

Zeitschrift für Hypnotismus
Renamed: *Journal for Psychology and Neurology* (REV, 10, 103)

Zeitschrift für Individual-Psychologie
Publication: begun (BULL, 11, 232)

Zeitschrift für Pädagogishe Psychologie
Publication: begun (REV, 6, 119)

Zeitschrift für Pathopsychologie
Publication: Specht, M. W. (JoP, 9, 335)

Zeitschrift für Philosophie and Philosophische Kritik
New editorial policy and content (SCI°, 6, 474)

Zeitschrift für Psychologie
Editor: Ebbinghaus, H. (BULL, 3, 116)
Editor: Schaumann, F. (JoP, 6, 700; BULL, 6, 368)
Index: psychological literature (REV, 3, 356)

Zeitschrift für Religions-Psychologie
Publication: suspended (BULL, *10*, 292; JoP, *10*, 504)

Zeitschrift für Sozialforschung
Name change: *Studies in Philosophy and the Social Sciences* (JoP, *37*, 504)

Zeller commemorative celebration
List of those attending (SCI°, *8*, 452)

Zeller, Eduard
Birthday, 89th celebration (SCI, *17*, 398)
Commemoration celebration (SCI°, *8*, 452)
Death notice (BULL, *5*, 128)
Departure: Univ. of Berlin (REV, *1*, 112)
Lecture: Hall, G. S. (SCI, *35*, 101; JoP, *9*, 56)

Zener, Karl Edward
Appointment: Princeton Univ. (J APP, *11*, 405)

Zentralblatt für Psychologie und psychologische Pädagogik
Publication: announcement (JoP, *11*, 392)
Publication: begun (BULL, *11*, 232)

Ziehen, Theodor
Appointment: Univ. of Berlin (BULL, *1*, 174; JoP, *1*, 196)
Psychological lab: Wiesbaden (JoP, *9*, 140)
Resignation: Berlin Psychiatric and Neurologic Clinic (JoP, *9*, 140; BULL, *9*, 95)

Zigler, Michael Jacob
Appointment: Ohio State Univ. (BULL, *23*, 176)
Appointment: Univ. of Southern California (BULL, *24*, 80; SCI, *65*, 180)
Appointment: Wellesley College (BULL, *21*, 428; SCI, *89*, 384; SCI, *60*, 333)

Zilsel, Edgar
Lecture: Descartes (JoP, *38*, 700)

Zimmermann, [Robert, ?]
Formation: Philosophical Society at Vienna (SCI°, *12*, 23)

Zimmermann, Emil
Appunn wire forks (JoP, *1*, 196)

Zingg, Robert Mowry
Publication: feral children (AJP, *54*, 432-435)

Zook, George Frederick
National Conference on Education Broadcasting, 2nd (BULL, *34*, 636)